FORENSIC BIOLOGY

FORENSIC BIOLOGY

Advanced Forensic Science Series

MAX M. HOUCK, PhD, FRSC
Managing Director, Forensic & Intelligence Services, LLC, St. Petersburg, FL, USA

ELSEVIER

Amsterdam • Boston • Heidelberg • London • New York • Oxford
Paris • San Diego • San Francisco • Singapore • Sydney • Tokyo
Academic Press is an imprint of Elsevier

Academic Press is an imprint of Elsevier
125 London Wall, London EC2Y 5AS, UK
525 B Street, Suite 1800, San Diego, CA 92101-4495, USA
225 Wyman Street, Waltham, MA 02451, USA
The Boulevard, Langford Lane, Kidlington, Oxford OX5 1GB, UK

First published 2016

ISBN: 978-0-12-800647-4
ISSN: 2352-6238

British Library Cataloguing in Publication Data
A catalogue record for this book is available from the British Library

Library of Congress Cataloging-in-Publication Data
A catalog record for this book is available from the Library of Congress

Publisher: Sara Tenney
Acquisitions Editor: Elizabeth Brown
Editorial Project Manager: Joslyn Chaiprasert-Paguio
Production Project Manager: Lisa Jones
Designer: Matthew Limbert

Typeset by TNQ Books and Journals
www.tnq.co.in

CONTENTS

SECTION 2 METHODS

SECTION 3 ANALYSIS

SECTION 4 INTERPRETATION

SECTION 5 PROFESSIONAL ISSUES

EDITOR: BIOGRAPHY

Max M. Houck, PhD, FRSC, is an internationally recognized forensic expert with research interests in anthropology, trace evidence, education, and the fundamentals of forensic science, both as a science and as an enterprise. He has worked in the private sector, public sector (at the regional and federal levels), and academia. Dr. Houck has published in a wide variety of areas in the field, including books, book chapters, and peer-reviewed journals. His casework includes the Branch Davidian Investigation, the September 11 attacks on the Pentagon, the D. B. Cooper case, the US Embassy bombings in Africa, and the West Memphis Three case. He served for six years as the Chair of the Forensic Science Educational Program Accreditation Commission (FEPAC). Dr. Houck is a founding coeditor of the journal *Forensic Science Policy and Management* with Dr. Jay Siegel; he has also coauthored a major textbook with Dr. Siegel, *Fundamentals of Forensic Science*. Dr. Houck lives and works in the Washington, DC, area.

LIST OF CONTRIBUTORS

CGG Aitken
The University of Edinburgh, Edinburgh, UK

RW Allen
Oklahoma State University, Tulsa, OK, USA

A Alonso
Instituto Nacional de Toxicología y Ciencias Forenses, Madrid, Spain

A Amorim
University of Porto, Porto, Portugal

J Ballantyne
University of Central Florida, Orlando, FL, USA

KN Ballantyne
Victoria Police Forensic Services Centre, Macleod, VIC, Australia

A Biedermann
The University of Lausanne, Lausanne-Dorigny, Switzerland

C Børsting
University of Copenhagen, Copenhagen, Denmark

M Breadmore
University of Tasmania, Hobart, TAS, Australia

M Brión
Xenética de enfermidades cardiovasculares e oftalmolóxicas, Instituto de Investigación Sanitaria de Santiago-CHUS, Spain

ZM Budimlija
Office of Chief Medical Examiner of the City of New York, New York, NY, USA

E Buel
State of Vermont Forensic Laboratory, Waterbury, VT, USA

E Burton
Greater Manchester Police Forensic Services Branch, Manchester, UK

JM Butler
National Institute of Standards and Technology, Gaithersburg, MD, USA

T Caragine
Office of Chief Medical Examiner of the City of New York, New York, NY, USA

A Carracedo
University of Santiago de Compostela, Santiago de Compostela, Spain

MD Coble
National Institute of Standards and Technology, Gaithersburg, MD, USA

H Miller Coyle
University of New Haven, West Haven, CT, USA

F Crispino
Université du Québec à Trois-Rivières, Trois-Rivières, QC, Canada

JM Curran
University of Auckland, Auckland, New Zealand

K Currie
Office of Chief Medical Examiner of the City of New York, New York, NY, USA

R Decorte
KU Leuven, Leuven, Belgium; University Hospitals Leuven, Leuven, Belgium

J Epstein
Widener University School of Law, Wilmington, DE, USA

KA Findley
University of Wisconsin Law School, Madison, WI, USA

WH Goodwin
University of Central Lancashire, Preston, UK

R Guijt
University of Tasmania, Hobart, TAS, Australia

L Gusmão
IPATIMUP, Porto, Portugal

C Haas
University of Zürich, Zürich, Switzerland

AJ Hansen
University of Copenhagen, Copenhagen, Denmark

E Hanson
University of Central Florida, Orlando, FL, USA

BJ Heidebrecht
Maryland State Police, Forensic Sciences Division, Pikesville, MD, USA

S Hofstadler
Ibis Biosciences Inc., Carlsbad, CA, USA

MM Houck
Forensic & Intelligence Services, LLC, St. Petersburg, FL, USA

H-M Hsieh
Central Police University, Taoyuan, Taiwan ROC

M Kayser
Erasmus MC University Medical Center, Rotterdam, The Netherlands

R Labonte
University of New Haven, West Haven, CT, USA

M Lareu
University of Santiago de Compostela, Santiago de Compostela, Spain

JC-I Lee
National Taiwan University, Taipei, Taiwan ROC; Institute of Forensic Medicine, New Taipei, Taiwan ROC

CE Lenehan
Flinders University, Adelaide, SA, Australia

JG Linville
University of Alabama at Birmingham, Birmingham, AL, USA

BR McCord
Florida International University, Miami, FL, USA

N Morling
University of Copenhagen, Copenhagen, Denmark

C O'Connor
Office of Chief Medical Examiner of the City of New York, New York, NY, USA

W Parson
Innsbruck Medical University, Innsbruck, Austria

V Pereira
IPATIMUP, Porto, Portugal

C Phillips
University of Santiago de Compostela, Galicia, Spain

K Ramsey
Greater Manchester Police Forensic Services Branch, Manchester, UK

L Roewer
Charité – Universitätsmedizin Berlin, Berlin, Germany

P Roffey
Forensic and Data Centres, Australian Federal Police, Canberra, ACT, Australia

B Saw
Australian Federal Police, Canberra, ACT, Australia

PM Schneider
University of Cologne, Cologne, Germany

N Scudder
Australian Federal Police, Canberra, ACT, Australia

A Shallan
University of Tasmania, Hobart, TAS, Australia

T Simmons
University of Central Lancashire, Preston, UK

B Sobrino
Grupo de Medicina Xenomica-USC, Instituto de Investigación Sanitaria de Santiago, Spain

M Stangegaard
University of Copenhagen, Copenhagen, Denmark

F Taroni
The University of Lausanne, Lausanne-Dorigny, Switzerland

L-C Tsai
Central Police University, Taoyuan, Taiwan ROC

RAH van Oorschot
Victoria Police Forensic Services Centre, Macleod, VIC, Australia

Ted Vosk
Criminal Defense Law Firm, Kirkland, WA, USA

SJ Walsh
Australian Federal Police, Canberra, ACT, Australia

BS Weir
University of Washington, Seattle, WA, USA

JD Wells
Florida International University, Miami, FL, USA

R Wickenheiser
Montgomery County Police Crime Laboratory, Gaithersburg, MD, USA

FOREWORD

> "The best thing for being sad," replied Merlin, beginning to puff and blow, "is to learn something. That's the only thing that never fails. You may grow old and trembling in your anatomies, you may lie awake at night listening to the disorder of your veins, you may miss your only love, you may see the world about you devastated by evil lunatics, or know your honor trampled in the sewers of baser minds. There is only one thing for it then — to learn. Learn why the world wags and what wags it. That is the only thing which the mind can never exhaust, never alienate, never be tortured by, never fear or distrust, and never dream of regretting. Learning is the only thing for you. Look what a lot of things there are to learn." — T.H. White, *The Once and Future King*

Forensic science has much to learn. The breadth of the discipline alone should render any reasonably learned person dizzy with expectations; insects, explosives, liver functions, DNA, firearms, textiles, adhesives, skeletons, and so on, the list goes on forever. That is because anything, truly *anything*, can become evidence, from a single fiber to an entire ocean liner. Forensic science does not lack for specialized knowledge (some might stay too specialized), but what it is wanting is knowledge that is comprehensive, integrated, and foundational. Introductions to forensic science abound, and many highly specialized texts are also available, but a gap exists between the two: a bridge from novice to practitioner. As the 2009 NRC report noted:

> Forensic science examiners need to understand the principles, practices, and contexts of scientific methodology, as well as the distinctive features of their specialty. Ideally, training should move beyond apprentice-like transmittal of practices to education based on scientifically valid principles. (NRC, 2009; pages 26–27).

The *Advanced Forensic Sciences Series* seeks to fill that gap. It is a unique source, combining entries from the world's leading specialists who contributed to the second edition of the award-winning *Encyclopedia of Forensic Sciences* and organizing them by topic into a series of volumes that are philosophically grounded yet professionally specialized. The series is composed of 12 volumes that cover the breadth of forensic science:

1. Professional Issues
2. Biology
3. Chemistry
4. Fingerprints
5. Firearms
6. Materials Analysis
7. Pathology

8. Anthropology
9. Engineering
10. Behavioral
11. Digital and Documents
12. Toxicology and Drugs

Each volume contains sections common to all forensic sciences, such as professionalism, ethics, health and safety, and court testimony, and sections relevant to the topics in that particular subdiscipline. Pedagogy is included, providing review questions, discussion questions, the latest references in additional readings, and key words. Thus, each volume is suitable as a technical reference, an advanced textbook, or a training adjunct.

The *Advanced Forensic Science Series* provides expert information, useful teaching tools, and a ready source for instruction, research, and practice. I hope, like learning, it is the only thing for you.

M. M. Houck, PhD, FRSC
Series Editor

Reference

National Research Council, 2009. Strengthening Forensic Science in the U.S.: A Path Forward. National Academies of Science. Washington, DC.

PREFACE

Thirty-one years ago, DNA profiling was created by Sir Alec Jeffreys and applied to forensic science. Collin Pitchfork was the first person identified using the new method and the profession of forensic science has never been the same since. Prior to this new method, fingerprinting was the primary biometric for personal identification for the last 100 years.

Based on the last census of publicly funded forensic laboratories, only 60% of forensic laboratories conduct forensic biology analyses (Durose et al., 2012). While forensic biology accounts for about one-third of the annual requests for service, about three-quarters of the total backlog in 2009 was in forensic biology. In 2004, the U.S. Department of Justice invested $1 billion to reduce the number of unprocessed convicted offender samples, which reduced the number of unprocessed samples significantly. The emphasis placed on DNA indicates its power to identify people in criminal contexts, be they victims or suspects. However, this emphasis probably came at the expense of the rest of the forensic laboratory, culminating in the critiques of traditional disciplines in the 2009 NRC report, *Strengthening Forensic Science in the US: A Path Forward*. It should be no surprise that a well-funded science is considered the "gold standard" but DNA has its weaknesses like any other science, including cognitive issues (Dror and Hampikian, 2011). A more balanced view of the role of all forensic disciplines in a case would benefit not just that case but the entire forensic industry.

DNA faces great challenges in the near future. Detection levels continue to drop, demand continues to rise, capabilities expand, and—in the face of all these—the discipline is staring down a platform change. The so-called rapid DNA systems and next generation sequencing loom over forensic laboratories, threatening massive capital costs, personnel re-training, and huge shifts in methods and procedures. The payoff is anticipated to be faster turnaround times (typically less than two hours for analysis) and increased capacity. Time will tell; change is the only constant and DNA continues to be a focal point for innovation and disruption.

This volume in the *Advanced Forensic Science Series* covers the core of forensic biology for education and training purposes. It can also act as a technical reference for those practitioners in the field. This text encapsulates the important advancements in forensic biology and represents the culmination of those tools that we successfully use today in criminal investigations and legal proceedings.

References

Durose, M., Walsh, K., Burch, A., 2012. Census of Publicly Funded Forensic Crime Laboratories, 2009. US Department of Justice, Bureau of Justice Statistics, Washington, DC.

Dror, I., Hampikian, G., 2011. Subjectivity and bias in forensic DNA mixture interpretation. Science and Justice 51 (4), 204–208.

OVERVIEW

So much of what has been published in the forensic science literature and about the profession relate to the scientific methods that are used. The notion that forensic science is "only a programmatic set of various disciplines," as Crispino and Houck put it, meaning it is little more than a toolbox filled with useful things but no real coherence or underlying philosophy, sadly persists. In that view, engineering in "only" an applied science, yet people drive over bridges, ride elevators, use electrical appliances, and fly in airplanes without a second's worry about engineering's status as science. Methods alone, however, will not build a plane or a building or a toaster. Some underlying philosophy or ethos has to exist for any science—any profession—to operate. Behind each method, regardless of the discipline, is the accumulated knowledge of successful discoveries, failed attempts, and the eventual establishment of reliable theories or even laws. Information is that which reduces uncertainty and methods are designed to be reproducible ways to reduce uncertainty. Inherent in each method, therefore, is the supporting knowledge that makes the method reliable; "the concept is synonymous with the corresponding set of operations" (Bridgman, 1928, page 14). An underlying guiding philosophy has yet to be properly articulated to frame forensic science as a peer to biology, chemistry, and the other sciences.

Methods do not a profession make, however. The scientific *discipline* of forensic science may be overflowing with methods but the *profession* is lacking in information, knowledge, and methods for operations and strategic planning to improve its products and outcomes. Analyzing evidence from a sexual assault kit is strictly biology; managing a backlog of 2000 kits with a fixed budget and 25% of the staff out on maternity leave is another. The management of forensic science has been done catch-as-catch-can for too long. Scientists tend to make bad managers for a number of reasons (Geles et al., 2000) and government is only recently seeing the benefits of evidence-based performance and accountability (Behn, 2014). Attempts have been made over the years to try to understand the scale and scope of the profession and its operations but it has been difficult. The FORESIGHT Project[1] is the most recent attempt to place the operations of the forensic laboratory on a business-like footing, using performance metrics to hold managers accountable for target goals and outcomes (Houck et al., 1999). Over 100 forensic laboratories around the world are involved in FORESIGHT, making it the dominate paradigm for strategic planning, operations, and continuous improvement.

Forensic stands at a tipping point: It has all the tools and resources to become a recognized, legitimate science whose practitioners know how to manage to greatest effect of limited resources. Whether it pulls all these together to become the discipline and profession that it could be remains to be seen. The efforts of the entirety of the forensic enterprise are necessary, for this transformation to be possible; strategic leadership will be necessary to make it happen.

[1] http://www.be.wvu.edu/forensic/foresight.htm.

Further Reading

Becker, W.S., Dale, W.M., 2003. Strategic human resource management in the forensic science laboratory. Forensic Science Communications 5 (4), 1–6.

Behn, R.D., 2014. The PerformanceStat Potential: A Leadership Strategy for Producing Results. Brookings Institution Press, Washington, D.C.

Bradford, L.W., 1980. Barriers to quality achievement in crime laboratory operations. Journal of Forensic Sciences 25, 902–907.

Bridgman, P.W., 1928. The Logic of Modern Physics. McMillan Publishers, New York, NY.

Burch, A.M., Durose, M.R., Walsh, K.A., 2012. Census of Publicly Funded Forensic Crime Laboratories, 2009. US Department of Justice, Office of Justice Programs, Bureau of Justice Statistics, Washington, DC.

Geles, C., Lindecker, G., Month, M., Roche, C., 2000. Managing Science. John Wiley & Sons, New York.

Houck, M.M., Riley, R.A., Speaker, P.J., Witt, T.S., 2009. FORESIGHT: a business approach to improving forensic science services. Forensic Science Policy and Management 1 (2), 85–95.

Koussiafes, P.M., 2004. Public forensic laboratory budget issues. Forensic Science Communications 6 (3), 1–7.

Peterson, J.L., Leggett, A.S., 2006. Evolution of forensic science: progress amid the pitfalls. Stetson Law Review 36, 621.

Tontarski Jr., R.E., Houck, M.M., Grose, W.P., Gialamas, D.M., 2012. Alternative models promote self-regulation of the forensic enterprise. Forensic Science Policy & Management 3 (3), 139–150.

Section 1. Introduction

The effect that DNA analysis, or profiling, has had on forensic science is almost incalculable. The last 30 years have been a blur of invention, application, argument, acceptance, and re-invention. DNA is readily accepted by the public and the courts now, but that was not always the case. The "DNA Wars" shoved forensic science into the spotlight only somewhat prepared for the controversies that resulted. It made forensic science better, if wary, and set the stage for many of the struggles to come, such as admissibility challenges to fingerprints, exonerations, and the wholesale quality culture that now envelopes the profession. In many ways, DNA remade forensic science without meaning to and opened up paths for the science and profession to follow that it never before considered.

Principles of Forensic Science

F Crispino, Université du Québec à Trois-Rivières, Trois-Rivières, QC, Canada
MM Houck, Forensic & Intelligence Services, LLC, St. Petersburg, FL, USA

Glossary

Abduction Syllogism in which one premise is certain whereas the other one is only probable, generally presented as the best explanation to the former. Hence, abduction is a type of reasoning in which we know the law and the effect, and we attempt to infer the cause.
Deduction Process of reasoning that moves from the general to the specific and in which a conclusion follows necessarily from the stated premises. Hence, deduction is a type of reasoning in which, knowing the cause and the law, we infer the effect.
Forensic intelligence Understanding on how traces can be collected from the scene, processed, and interpreted within a holistic intelligence-led policing strategy.
Heuristic Process of reasoning by rules that are only loosely defined, generally by trial and error.
Holistic Emphasizing the importance of the whole and the interdependence of its parts.
Induction Process of deriving general principles from particular facts or instances (i.e., of reasoning that moves from the specific to the general). Hence, induction is a type of reasoning in which, knowing the cause and the effect (or a series of causes and effects), we attempt to infer the law by which the effects follow the cause.
Linkage blindness Organizational or investigative failure to recognize a common pattern shared on different cases.
Science The intellectual and practical activity encompassing the systematic study of the structure and behavior of the physical and natural world through observation and experiment. It is also defined as a systematically organized body of knowledge on a particular subject.

Given that it identifies and collects objects at crime scenes and then treats them as evidence, forensic science could appear at first glance to be only a pragmatic set of various disciplines, with practitioners adapting and developing tools and technologies to help the triers of fact (juries or judges) interpret information gained from the people, places, and things involved in a crime. The view could be—and has been—held that forensic science has no philosophic or fundamental unity and is merely the application of knowledge generated by other sciences. Indeed, many working forensic scientists regard

 http://dx.doi.org/10.1016/B978-0-12-800647-4.00001-1

themselves mainly as chemists, biologists, scientists, or technicians and rarely as practitioners of a homogeneous body of knowledge with common fundamental principles.

Even the 2009 National Academy of Sciences, National Research Council Report failed to recognize such a concept, certainly blurred by a semantic gap in the terminology itself of field practitioners, who confuse words such as "forensic science(s)," "criminalistic(s)," "criminology," "technical police," "scientific police," and so on and generally restrict the scientific debate on analytical techniques and methods. An independent definition of forensic science, apart from its legal aspects, would support its scientific status and return the expert to his domain as scientist and interpreter of his analyses and results to assist the lay person.

What Is Forensic Science?

In its broadest sense, forensic science describes the utility of the sciences as they pertain to legal matters to include many disciplines, such as chemistry, biology, pathology, anthropology, toxicology, and engineering, among others. ("Forensic" comes from the Latin root *forum*, the central place of the city where disputes and debates were made public to be solved—hence defining the law of the city. Forensic generally means of or applied to the law.) The word "criminalistics" was adopted to describe the discipline directed toward the "recognition, identification, individualization, and evaluation of physical evidence by application of the natural sciences to law-science matters." ("Kriminalistik" was coined in the late nineteenth century by Hans Gross, a researcher in criminal law and procedure to define his methodology of classifying investigative, tactical, and evidential information to be learned by magistrates at law schools to solve crimes and help convict criminals.) In the scheme as it currently stands, criminalistics is part of forensic science; the word is a regionalism and is not universally applied as defined. Difficulties in differentiating the concepts certainly invited the definition of criminalistics as the "science of individualization," isolating this specific epistemologically problematic core from the other scientific disciplines. Individualization, the concept of determining the sole source of an item, enthroned a linear process—identification or classification on to individualization—losing sight of the holistic, variable contribution of all types of evidence. Assessing the circumstances surrounding a crime, in which the challenge is to integrate and organize the data in order to reconstruct a case or propose alternative propositions for events under examination, requires multiple types of evidence, some of which may be quite nuanced in their interpretation. This is also true in the use of so-called forensic intelligence, which feeds investigative, police, or security needs, in which one of the main reasons for failures is linkage blindness. Nevertheless, it seems that the essence of the forensic daily practice is hardly captured within the present definitions of both terms.

In the broadest sense, forensic science reconstructs past criminal events through the analysis of the physical remnants of those activities (evidence); the results of those analyses and their expert interpretation establish relationships among people, places, and objects relevant to those events. It produces these results and interpretations through logical inferences, induction, abduction, and deduction, all of which frame the hypothetico-deductive method; investigative heuristics also play a role. Translating scientific information into legal information is a particular domain of forensic science; other sciences must (or at least should) communicate their findings to the public, but forensic science is often required by law to communicate their findings to public courts. Indeed, as the Daubert hearing stated, "[s]cientific conclusions are subject to perpetual revision as law must resolve disputes finally and quickly." This doubly difficult requirement of communicating to the public and to the law necessitates that forensic scientists should be better communicators of their work and their results. Scientific inferences are not necessarily legal proofs, and the forensic scientist must recognize that legal decisions based, in part, on their scientific work may not accord with their expert knowledge. Moreover, scientists must think in probabilities to explain evidence given possible causes whereas jurists must deal in terms of belief beyond reasonable doubt. As Inman and Rudin state, "Because we [the scientists] provide results and information to parties who lack the expertise to independently understand their meaning and implications, it is up to us to furnish an accurate and complete interpretation of our results. If we do not do this, our conclusions are at best incomplete, at worst potentially misleading."

The Trace as the Basic Unit of Forensic Science

The basic unit of forensic science is the trace, the physical remnant of the past criminal activity. Traces are, by their very nature, semiotic: They represent something more than merely themselves; they are signifiers or signs for the items or events that are its source. A fiber is not the sweater it came from, a fingerprint is not the fingertip, soot in the trachea is not the victim choking from a fire, and blood droplets are not the violence against the victim, but they all point to their origin (source and activity) to a greater or lesser degree of specificity. Thus, the trace is a type of proxy data (i.e., an indicator of a related phenomenon but not the phenomenon itself). Traces come from the natural and manufactured items that surround us in our daily lives. In essence, traces are the raw material available at a crime scene that becomes forensic intelligence or knowledge. Everyday items and their traces become evidence through their involvement in criminal activities, and the activities add meaning to their existing status as goods in the world; for example, a fireplace poker is transformed into "the murder weapon" by its use as such. The meaning added should also take into account the context of the case, the circumstances under which the criminal activities occurred, and boarding the trier of fact mandate.

Traces become evidence when they are recognized, accepted as relevant (if blurred) to the past event under investigation, and collected for forensic purposes. Confusing trace, sign, and evidence can obscure the very process of trace "discovery," which lies at the root of its interpretation. Evidence begins with detection by observation, which is possible because of the available knowledge of the investigator or scientist; unrecognized traces go undiscovered and do not become evidence. When the investigator's or scientist's senses are extended through instrumental sensitivity, either at the scene or in the laboratory, the amount of potential evidence considerably increased. Microscopes, alternative light sources, instrumental sensitivity, and detection limits create increases in the number of traces that can be recognized and collected. More evidence, and more evidence types, inevitably lead to increases in the complexity not only of the search for traces but also to their interpretation. Feeding back into this system is the awareness of new (micro)traces that changed the search methods at scenes and in laboratories, with yet more evidence being potentially available.

Traces are ancillary to their originating process; they are a byproduct of the source activity, an accidental vestige of their criminal creation. To be useful in the determination of associations, traces for which the ultimate sources are unknown must be compared to samples from a known source. Comparison is the very heart of the forensic science process; the method is essentially a diagnostic one, beginning with Georges Cuvier, and it is used by many science practitioners, including medical professionals (including, interestingly, Arthur Conan Doyle, a medical doctor and author, whose Sherlock Holmes character references Cuvier's method in *The Five Orange Pips*). Questioned traces, or items, may have a provenance (a known location at the time of their discovery), but this is not their originating source; a few examples may help:

Trace (questioned)	*Source (known)*
Fiber on victim	Sweater
Gunshot residue	Ammunition discharge
Blood droplet	Body
Tool marks in door jamb	Pry bar used to open door
Shoeprint in soil	Shoe from suspect
Fingerprint on glass	Finger from suspect

The collection of properly representative known samples is crucial to accurate forensic analyses and comparisons. Known samples can be selected through a variety of legitimate schemes, including random, portion, and judgment, and they must be selected with great care. Thus, traces are accidental and known samples are intentional.

Some of the consequences of what has been discussed so far induce the capacities and limitations of a forensic investigation based on trace analysis. A micro- to nanolevel existence allows forensic scientists to plan physical and chemical characteristics in their identifications and comparisons with other similar data. This allows forensic science to be as methodologically flexible as its objects of study require. Because time is asymmetric and each criminal action is unique, the forensic investigation and analysis in any one case is wedded, to a certain degree, to that case with no ambition to issue general laws about that event ("In all instances of John Davis being physically assaulted with a baseball bat ..."). Inferences must be drawn with explicit uncertainty statements; the inferences should be revised when new data affect the traces' relevancy. Therefore, the search for traces is a recursive heuristic process taking into account the environment of the case at hand, appealing to the imagination, expertise, and competency of the investigator or scientist to propose explicative hypotheses.

Two Native Principles

With this framework, two principles can be thought of as the main native principles that philosophically support and frame forensic science. In this context, principles are understood as universal theoretical statements settled at the beginning of a deduction, which cannot be deduced from any other statement in the considered system, and give coherence to the area of study. They provide the grounds from which other truths can be derived and define a paradigm (i.e., a general epistemological viewpoint, a new concept to see the natural world) issued from an empiricist corroborated tradition and accepted by the community of practitioners in the field. Ultimately, this paradigm can even pilot the perception itself.

Although similar but nonequivalent versions are used in other disciplines, Locard's exchange principle exists as the central tenant of forensic science. The principle that bears his name was never uttered as such by Locard, but its universal statement of "every contact leaves a trace" stands as a universally accepted short-hand phrasing. Locard's principle embraces all forms of contact, from biological to chemical to physical and even digital traces, and it extends the usual perception of forensic science beyond dealing only with physical vestiges.

One of its corollaries is that trace deposition is continual and not reversible. Increases in the number of contacts, the types of evidence involved, and cross-transfers (A–B and B–A) also increase the complexity of determining the relevance of traces in short duration and temporally close actions.

Even the potentially fallacious rubric of "absence of evidence is not evidence of absence" leads to extended discussions on the very nature of proof, or provable, that aims to be definitive, notwithstanding the explanations for the practical aspects of the concept (lack of sensitivity, obscuring of the relevant traces, human weakness, actual absence, etc.). Applying Locard's principle needs to address three levels. First, the physical level, which deals with ease of transfer, retention, persistence, and affinity of materials that could better support the exchange of traces from one source to another. Second is the situational or contextual level, which is the knowledge of circumstances and environments surrounding criminal events and sets the matrix for detection, identification, and proximate significance of any evidence. Third is the intelligence level, which covers the knowledge about criminal behavior in single events or series, specific problems related to current trends in criminal behavior, and communication between relevant entities (police, scientists, attorneys, etc.); these components help the investigator in the field to focus on more meaningful traces that might otherwise go undetected.

The second, and more debated, principle is Kirk's individuality principle; again, Kirk did not state this as such beyond saying that criminalistics is the science of individualization. In its strongest form, it posits that each object in the universe can be placed demonstratively into a set with one and only one member—itself. Therefore, it asserts the universal statement, "every object in our universe is unique." Philosophers such as Wittgenstein have argued that without defined rules or limits, terms such as "the same" or "different" are essentially meaningless. There is little question that all things are unique—two identical things can still be numerically differentiated—but the core question is, "Can they be distinguished at the resolution of detection applied?" Simply saying "all things are unique" is not forensically useful. For example, each fingerprint left by the same finger is unique, but to be useful, each print must also be able to be traced back to its source finger. Therefore, uniqueness is necessary to claim individualization, but not sufficient. Thus, it is the degree of association that matters—how similar or how different these two things being compared are. Referring to Cole, "What distinguishes ... objects is not 'uniqueness'; it is their diagnosticity: our ability to assign traces of these objects to their correct source with a certain degree of specificity under certain parameters of detection and under certain rules governing such assignments," or as Osterburg stated, "to approach [individualization] as closely as the present state of science allows." Statistics are typically required to accurately communicate levels of comparison that are reproducible. In fact, Kirk noted that individualization was not absolute. ("On the witness stand, the criminalist must be willing to admit that *absolute identity is impossible to establish*. ... The inept or biased witness may readily testify to an identity, or to a type of identity, that does not actually exist. This can come about because of his confusion as to the nature of identity, his inability to evaluate the results of his observations, or because his general technical deficiencies preclude meaningful results" (Kirk, 1953, emphasis added).)

Nonnative Principles

Numerous guiding principles from other sciences apply centrally to forensic science, several of which come from geology, a cognate historical science to forensic science. That these principles come not from forensic science but from other sciences should not imply that they are somehow less important than Locard's or Kirk's notions. The first, and in many ways the most important, of the external principles is that of Uniformitarianism. The principle, proposed by James Hutton, popularized by Charles Lyell, and coined by William Whewell, states that natural phenomena do not change in scope, intensity, or effect with time. Paraphrased as "the present is the key to the past," the principle implies that a volcano that erupts today acts in the same way as volcanoes did 200 or 200 million years ago and thus allows geologists to interpret proxy data from past events through current effects. Likewise, in forensic science, bullets test fired in the laboratory today do not change in scope, intensity, or effect from bullets fired during the commission of a crime 2 days, 2 weeks, or 2 years previously. The same is true of any analysis in forensic science that requires a replication or reconstruction of processes in play during the crime's commission. Uniformitarianism offers a level of objectivity to historical sciences by generally posing hypotheses or relationships and then developing tests with respect to particular cases.

Three additional principles from geology hold as applicable to forensic science. They are as follows:

- *Superposition*: In a physical distribution, older materials are below younger materials unless a subsequent action alters this arrangement.
- *Lateral continuity*: Disassociated but similar layers can be assumed to be from the same depositional period.
- *Chronology*: It refers to the notion of absolute dates in a quantitative mode (such as "10:12 a.m." or "1670–1702") and relative dates in a relational mode (i.e., older or younger).

These three principles are attributed to Nicolaus Steno but were also formalized and applied by William Smith. A forensic example of applying the principle of superposition would be the packing of different soils in a tire tread, the most recent being the outermost. A good case of lateral continuity would be the cross-transfer of fibers in an assault given that the chances of independent transfer and persistence prior to the time of the incident would be improbable.

An example of absolute chronology in forensic science would be the simple example of a purchase receipt from a retail store with a time/date stamp on it. Examples of relative chronology abound but could range from the *terminus post quem* of a product no longer made to something hotter or colder than it should be.

See also: **Foundations:** Forensic Intelligence; History of Forensic Sciences; Overview and Meaning of Identification/ Individualization; Semiotics, Heuristics, and Inferences Used by Forensic Scientists; Statistical Interpretation of Evidence: Bayesian Analysis; The Frequentist Approach to Forensic Evidence Interpretation; **Foundations/Fundamentals:** Measurement Uncertainty; **Pattern Evidence/Fingerprints (Dactyloscopy):** Friction Ridge Print Examination – Interpretation and the Comparative Method.

Further Reading

Cole, S.A., 2009. Forensics without uniqueness, conclusions without individualization: the new epistemology of forensic identification. Law, Probability, and Risk 8, 233–255.

Crispino, F., 2006. Le principe de Locard est-il scientifique? Ou analyse de la scientificité des principes fondamentaux de la criminalistique. Editions Universitaires Européennes No. 523, Sarrebrücken, Germany. ISBN: 978-613-1-50482-2(2010).

Crispino, F., 2008. Nature and place of crime scene management within forensic sciences. Science & Justice 48 (1), 24–28.

Dulong, R., 2004. La rationalité spécifique de la police technique. Revue Internationale de Criminologie et de Police Technique et Scientifique 3 (4), 259–270.

Egger, S.A., 1984. A working definition of serial murder and the reduction of linkage blindness. Journal of Police Science and Administration 12, 348–355.

Giamalas, D.M., 2000. Criminalistics. In: Siegel, J.A., Saukko, P.J., Knupfer, G.C. (Eds.), Encyclopedia of Forensic Sciences. Academic Press, London, pp. 471–477.

Good, G. (Ed.), 1998. Sciences of the Earth, vol. 1. Garland Publishing, New York.

Houck, M.M., 2010. An Investigation into the Foundational Principles of Forensic Science (Ph.D. thesis). Curtin University of Technology, Perth.

Inman, N., Rudin, K., 2001. Principles and Practice of Criminalistics: The Profession of Forensic Science, pp. 269–270. CRC Press, Boca Raton, FL, pp. 269–270.

Kirk, P.L., 1953. Crime Investigation: Physical Evidence and the Police Laboratory. Interscience, New York, p. 10.

Kirk, P.L., 1963. The ontogeny of criminalistics. Journal of Criminal Law, Criminology, and Police Science 54, 235–238.

Kuhn, T., 1970. La structure des révolutions scientifiques. Flammarion, Paris.

Kwan, Q.Y., 1976. Inference of Identity of Source (Ph.D. thesis). Berkeley University, Berkeley.

Mann, M., 2002. The value of multiple proxies. Science 297, 1481–1482.

Masterman, M., 1970. The nature of a paradigm. In: Lakatos, I., Musgrave, A. (Eds.), Criticism and the Growth of Experimental Knowledge. Cambridge University Press, Cambridge, pp. 59–86.

Moriarty, J.C., Saks, M.J., 2006. Forensic Science: Grand Goals, Tragic Flaws, and Judicial Gatekeeping. Research Paper No. 06-19. University of Akron Legal Studies.

National Research Council Committee, 2009. Identifying the Needs of the Forensic Science Community, Strengthening Forensic Science in the United States: A Path Forward. National Academy of Sciences Report. National Academy Press, Washington, DC.

Osterburg, J.W., 1968. What problems must criminalistics solve. Journal of Criminal Law, Criminology, and Police Science 59 (3), 431.

Schuliar, Y., 2009. La coordination scientifique dans les investigations criminelles. Proposition d'organisation, aspects éthiques ou de la nécessité d'un nouveau métier (Ph.D. thesis). Université Paris Descartes, Paris; Université de Lausanne, Lausanne.

Sober, E., 2009. Absence of evidence and evidence of absence: evidential transitivity in connection with fossils, fishing, fine-tuning, and firing squads. Philosophical Studies 143, 63–90.

Stephens, C., 2011. A Bayesian approach to absent evidence reasoning. Informal Logic 31 (1), 56–65.

US Supreme Court No 92–102, 1993. W. Daubert, et al., Petitioners v Merrell Dow Pharmaceuticals, Inc. Certiorari U. S. Court Appeals Ninth Circuit. Argued 30 March 1993. Decided 28 June 1993.

Wittgenstein, L., 1922. Tractacus Logico-philosophicus. Gallimard Tel 311, Paris.

Relevant Websites

http://www.all-about-forensic-science.com—All-About-Forensic-Science.COM, Definition of forensic science.

http://www.forensic-evidence.com—Forensic-Evidence.com.

http://library.thinkquest.org—Oracle ThinkQuest—What is Forensics?.

Forensic Classification of Evidence

MM Houck, Forensic & Intelligence Services, LLC, St. Petersburg, FL, USA

Glossary

Set Any group of real or imagined objects.
Taxonomy The science of identifying and naming species with the intent of arranging them into a classification.
Taxon (pl. taxa) A group of one or more organisms grouped and ranked according to a set of qualitative and quantitative characteristics; a type of set.

Introduction

Evidence is accidental: Items are transformed into evidence by their involvement in a crime regardless of their source or mode of production. By becoming evidence, their normal meaning is enhanced and expanded. Evidence is initially categorized much as the real world (i.e., based on the taxonomy created by manufacturers). Forensic science adds to this classification to further enhance or clarify the meaning of evidence relevant to the goals and procedures of the discipline.

Methods of Classification

Set Theory

Any collection of objects, real or imagined, is a set; set theory is the branch of mathematics that studies these collections. Basic set theory involves categorization and organization of the objects, sometimes using diagrams, and involves elementary operations such as set union and set intersection. Advanced topics, including cardinality, are standard in undergraduate mathematics courses. All classification schemes are based on set theory, to a greater or lesser degree.

The notion of "set" is undefined; the objects described as constituting a set create the definition. The objects in a set are called the members or elements of that set. Objects belong to a set; sets consist of their members. The members of a set may be real or imagined; they do not need to be present to be a member of that set. Membership criteria for a set should be definite and accountable. The set, "All people in this room are over 5′5″ tall," is a well-defined, if currently unknown, set—the height of the people in the room would have to be measured to accurately populate the set. If the definition is vague then that collection may not be considered a set. For example, is "q" the same as "Q"? If the set is "The 26 letters of the English alphabet," then they are the same member; if the set is, "The 52 upper-case and lower-case letters of the English alphabet," then they are two separate members.

Sets may be finite or infinite; a set with only one member is called a single or a singleton set. Two sets are identical if and only if they have exactly the same members. The cardinality of a set is the number of members within it, written $|A|$ for set A. A set X is a subset of set Y if and only if every member of X is also a member of Y; for example, the set of all Philips head screwdrivers is a subset of the set of all screwdrivers. Forensic scientists would term this a "subclass." but that is a terminological and not a conceptual difference. Two more concepts are required for the remainder of our discussion. The union of X and Y is a set for which the members are only the members of X, Y, or both. Thus, if X were (1, 2, 3) and Y were (2, 3, 4) then the union of X and Y, written $X \cup Y$, would contain (1, 2, 3, 4). Finally, the intersection of two sets contains only the members of both X and Y. In the previous example, the intersection of X and Y would be (2, 3), written $X \cap Y$.

Taxonomy

Natural items, such as animals, plants, or minerals, often occur as evidence. These items are classified according to schemes used in other sciences such as biology, botany, or geology. It is incumbent on the forensic scientist to be knowledgeable about the classification of naturally occurring items.

In biology, taxonomy, the practice and science of classification, refers to a formalized system for ordering and grouping things, typically living things using the Linnaean method. The taxa (the units of a taxonomic system; singular "taxon") are sufficiently fixed so as to provide a structure for classifying living things. Taxa are arranged typically in a hierarchical

 http://dx.doi.org/10.1016/B978-0-12-800647-4.00002-3

structure to show their relatedness (a phylogeny). In such a hierarchical relationship, the subtype has by definition the same constraints as the supertype plus one or more additional constraints. For example, "macaque" is a subtype of "monkey," so any macaque is also a monkey, but not every monkey is a macaque, and an animal needs to satisfy more constraints to be a macaque than to be a monkey. In the Linnaean method of classification, the scientific name of each species is formed by the combination of two words, the genus name ("generic" name), which is always capitalized, and a second word identifying the species within that genus. Species names (genus species) are either italicized or underlined (for example, *Homo sapiens* [humans], *Sus scrofus* [pigs], *Canis familiaris* [domesticated dogs], and *Rattus rattus* [rats]).

The term "systematics" is sometimes used synonymously with "taxonomy" and may be confused with "scientific classification." However, taxonomy is properly the describing, identifying, classifying, and naming of organisms whereas "classification" is focused on placing organisms within groups that show their relationships to other organisms. Systematics alone deals specifically with relationships through time, requiring recognition of the fossil record when dealing with the systematics of organisms. Systematics uses taxonomy as a primary tool in understanding organisms because nothing about the organism's relationships with other living things can be understood without it first being properly studied and described in sufficient detail to identify and classify it correctly.

In geology, rocks are generally classified based on their chemical and mineral composition, the process by which they are formed, and by the texture of their particles. Rocks are classified as igneous (formed by cooled molten magma), sedimentary (formed by deposition and compaction of materials), or metamorphic (formed through intense changes in pressure and temperature). These three classes of rocks are further subdivided into many other sets; often, the categories' definitions are not rigid and the qualities of a rock may grade it from one class to another. The terminology of rocks and minerals, rather than describing a state, describes identifiable points along a gradient.

Manufacturing

Manufactured evidence is initially categorized by the in-house or market-specific system created by one or more manufacturers. Manufacturers of economic goods create their classifications through product identity or analytical methods. Set methods of production ensure a quality product fit for purpose and sale; the classification is based on the markets involved, the orientation of the company production methods, and the supply chain. Explicit rules exist on categories recognized by manufacturers and consumers as either models or brands. Materials flow downstream, from raw material sources through to a manufacturing level. Raw materials are transformed into intermediate products, which are also referred to as components or parts. These are assembled on the next level to form products. The products are shipped to distribution centers and from there on to retailers and customers.

Forensic Approaches to Classification

The supply network of raw materials, intermediate steps, production methods, intended consumer end use, and actual end use all contribute to the characteristics available for forensic taxonomic classification. Although the forensic taxonomies are unique to that discipline, they are based on the production taxonomies used in manufacturing. These characteristics form the basis for statements of significance (i.e., the relative abundance or rarity of any one particular item in a criminal context). Some objects are common but have a short-entrance horizon (e.g., iPods), but they are essentially identical at the outset; others are common with long-entrance horizons (denim blue jeans), but they have a high variance (regular, stone-washed, acid-washed, etc.). It is in the best interest of forensic scientists to understand the fundamental manufacturing processes of the items that routinely become evidence. This understanding can form the basis for statistical significance statements in courts and may provide the foundations for a more quantitative approach to testimony.

Forensic analytical methods create augmented taxonomies because the discipline uses different sets of methods and forensic scientists have different goals. Their taxonomies are based on manufactured traits, aftermarket qualities, and intended end use, but also on "as used" traits. The "as used" traits are those imparted to the item after purchase through either normal or criminal use. Forensic science has developed a set of rules through which the taxonomies are explicated. For example, forensic scientists are interested in the size, shape, and distribution of delustrants, microscopic grains of rutile titanium dioxide incorporated into a fiber to reduce its luster. The manufacturer has included delustrant in the fiber at a certain rate and percentage with no concern for shape or distribution (but size may be relevant). The forensic science taxonomy is based on manufacturing taxonomy, but it is extended by incidental characteristics that help us distinguish otherwise similar objects.

Natural, manufacturing, and forensic classifications lead to evidentiary significance because they break the world down into intelligible classes of objects related to criminal acts. Forensic science has developed an enhanced appreciation for discernment between otherwise similar objects, but it has yet to explicate these hierarchies to their benefit.

Class-Level Information

Identification is the examination of the chemical and physical properties of an object and using them to categorize it as a member of a set. What the object is made of; its color, mass, and size; and many other characteristics are used to identify an object and help refine that object's identity. Analyzing a white powder and concluding that it is cocaine is an example of identification; determining that a small translucent chip is bottle glass or yellow fibrous material and determining that they are dog hairs are also examples of identification. Most identifications are inherently hierarchical, such as classification systems themselves. In the last example, the fibrous nature of the objects restricts the following possible categories:

- Hairs,
- Animal hairs,
- Guard hairs,
- Dog hairs, and
- German shepherd hairs.

As the process of identification of evidence becomes more specific, it permits the analyst to classify the evidence into successively smaller classes of objects. It may not be necessary to classify the evidence beyond dog hairs if human hairs are being looked for. Multiple items can be classified differently depending on what questions are asked. For example, the objects in **Figure 1** could be classified into "fruit" and "nonfruit," "sports related" and "nonsports related," or "organic" and "inorganic."

Sharing a class identity may indicate two objects that come from a common source. Because forensic science reveals and describes the relationships among people, places, and things involved in criminal activities, this commonality of relationship may be critical to a successful investigation. Commonality can show interactions, limitations in points of origin, and increased significance of relationships. What is meant by a "common source" depends on the material in question, the mode of production, and the specificity of the examinations used to classify the object. For example, the "common source" for an automotive paint chip could be the following:

- The manufacturer (to distinguish it from other similar paints),
- The factory (to determine where it was made),
- The batch or lot of production (to distinguish it from other batches at the same factory),
- All of the vehicles painted with that color paint, or
- The vehicle painted with that color paint involved in the crime in question.

All of these options, and they are not exhaustive, could be the goal in an investigation of determining whether two objects had a "common source."

Uniqueness and Individualization

If an object can be classified into a set with only one member (itself), it can be said to be unique. An individualized object is associated with one, and only one, source: It is unique. Uniqueness is based on two assumptions. The first assumption is that all things are unique in space; thus, their properties are nonoverlapping. The assumption of uniqueness of space is considered axiomatic, and therefore an inherently nonprovable proposition, for numerous reasons. The population size of "all things that might be evidence" is simply too large to account. In addition, conclusive evidence is not readily available in typical forensic investigations. Because of this, as Schum notes, statistics are required.

Figure 1 A range of objects may be classified in a variety of ways, depending on the question being asked. For example, given the objects in this figure, the sets would differ if the question was "What's edible?" rather than "What is sporting equipment?".

> Such evidence, if it existed, would make necessary a particular hypothesis or possible conclusion being entertained. In lieu of such perfection, we often make use of masses of inconclusive evidence having additional properties: The evidence is incomplete on matters relevant to our conclusions, and it comes to us from sources (including our own observations) that are, for various reasons, not completely credible. Thus, inferences from such evidence can only be probabilistic in nature (Schum, 1994, p. 2).

Therefore, a statistical analysis is warranted when uncertainty, of either accounting or veracity, exists. If an absolutely certain answer to a problem could be reached, statistical methods would not be required. Most evidence exists at the class level, and although each item involved in a crime is considered unique, it still belongs to a larger class. In reality, the majority of forensic science works at a class level of resolution. Indeed, even DNA, the argued "gold standard" of forensic science, operates with classes and statistics.

It has been argued that the concept of uniqueness is necessary but not sufficient to support claims of individualization. If it is accepted that uniqueness is axiomatic, then

> what matters is whether we have the analytical tools necessary to discern the characteristics that distinguish one object from all others or, in the forensic context, distinguish traces made by each object from traces made by every other object—every object is presumably unique at the scale of manufacture. The question is whether objects are distinguishable at the scale of detection. Because all objects in the universe are in some respects "the same" and in other respects "different" from all other objects in the universe, according to Wittgenstein, what really matters is not uniqueness but rather what rules we articulate by which we will make determinations of "sameness" and "difference" (Cole, 2009, pp. 242–243).

Although things may be numerically unique at the point of production, this does not help to distinguish between otherwise similar objects at the point of detection or interpretation. This is where forensic science adds value to the investigative and legal processes.

Relationships and Context

The relationships among the people, places, and things involved in crimes are central to deciding what items to examine and how to interpret the results. For example, if

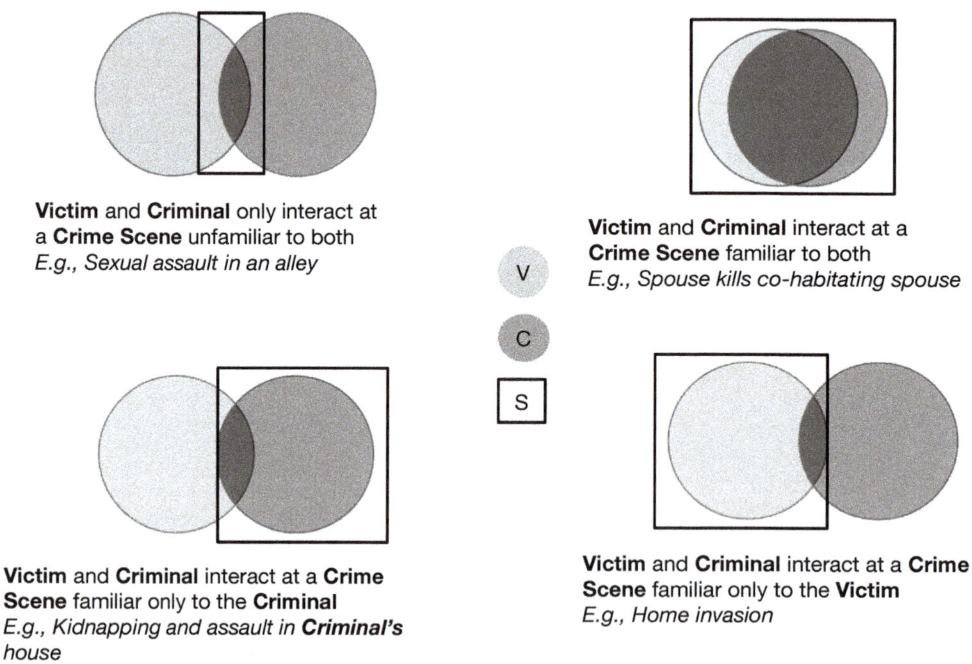

Figure 2 The relationships among suspect, victim, and scene influence what evidence is collected and what its significance is.

a sexual assault occurs and the perpetrator and victim are strangers, more evidence may be relevant than if they live together or are sexual partners. Strangers are not expected to have ever met previously; therefore, they would have not transferred evidence before the crime. People who live together would have some opportunities to transfer certain types of evidence (e.g., head hairs and carpet fibers from the living room) but not others (semen or vaginal secretions). Spouses or sexual partners, being the most intimate relationship of the three examples, would share a good deal more information (**Figure 2**).

Stranger-on-stranger crimes beg the question of coincidental associations; that is, two things that previously have never been in contact with each other have items on them that are analytically indistinguishable at a certain class level. Attorneys in cross-examination may ask, "Yes, but could not [insert evidence type here] really have come from anywhere? Are not [generic class level evidence] very common?" It has been proven for a wide variety of evidence that coincidental matches are extremely rare. The enormous variety of mass-produced goods, consumer choices, economic factors, biological and natural diversity, and other traits create a nearly infinite combination of comparable characteristics for the items involved in any one situation.

See also: **Foundations:** Evidence/Classification; Statistical Interpretation of Evidence: Bayesian Analysis; The Frequentist Approach to Forensic Evidence Interpretation.

Further Reading

Cole, S., 2009. Forensics without uniqueness, conclusion without individualization: the new epistemology of forensic identification. Law, Probability, and Risk 8 (3), 233–255.

Devlin, K., 1993. The Joy of Sets. Springer, Berlin.

Haq, T., Roche, G., Parker, B., 1978. Theoretical field concepts in forensic science. 1. Application to recognition and retrieval of physical evidence. Journal of Forensic Sciences 23 (1), 212–217.

Houck, M.M., 2006. Production taxonomies as the foundation of forensic significance. European Academy of Forensic Sciences, Helsinki, Finland.

Johnson, P., 1972. A History of Set Theory. Weber & Schmidt, New York.

Kwan, Q.Y., 1977. Inference of Identity of Source (Ph.D. thesis). University of California.

Schum, D.A., 1994. Evidential Foundations of Probabilistic Reasoning. John Wiley & Sons, New York.

Thornton, J., 1986. Ensembles of class characteristics in physical evidence examination. Journal of Forensic Sciences 31 (2), 501–503.

Underhill, P., 2000. Why We Buy: The Science of Shopping. Simon & Schuster, New York.

Interpretation/The Comparative Method

MM Houck, Forensic & Intelligence Services, LLC, St. Petersburg, FL, USA

Glossary

Alignable differences Differences that are connected to the hierarchical system of relatedness of two or more things.

Analogous trait A characteristic that is similar between two things that is not present in the last common ancestor or precedent of the group under comparison.

Analogy A cognitive process that transfers information or meaning from one subject (the analog or source) to another subject (the target).

Diagnosticity The degree to which traits classify an object.

Homologous trait A characteristic shared by a common ancestor or precedent.

Nonalignable differences Differences with no correspondence at all between the source and the target.

Introduction

Analogy, and its more specific relative comparison, is a central component of human cognition. Analogy is the process behind identification of places, objects, and people and plays a significant role in many human mental operations, such as problem-solving, decisions, perception, memory, and communication. Some researchers, including Hofstadter, have even argued that cognition is analogy. Likewise, the cognitive process of analogy and the method of comparison lie at the heart of the forensic sciences. The ability to compare is predicated on some sort of classification (more properly, a taxonomy) that results in classes, groups, or sets.

Aristotle is considered the first to approach comparison as a way to arrange the world. However, his attempt to codify the process raised an intractable problem that would only be addressed later—the classification of living things. By itself, comparison is a minimal technique, at best. A classification system—a taxonomy—is a prerequisite to a fuller comparative methodology. Comparative anatomy, one of the earliest formal applications of the method, goes beyond mere representation (mere comparison, that is) to explain the nature and properties of each animal.

The French naturalist Pierre Belon (1517–1564) compared the skeletal structures of birds to humans in his book *L'Histoire de la Nature des Oiseaux* (*History of the Nature of Birds*, 1555; **Figure 1**), and, along with the Flemish naturalist Andreas Vesalius (1514–1564), was one of the first naturalists to explicitly apply the comparative method in biology. Georges Cuvier (1769–1832) was the first to use comparative anatomy and taxonomy as a tool, not an end in itself, in his studies of animals and fossils. Cuvier was frustrated that biological phenomena could not be reconfigured into experimental conditions that would allow controlled testing, a difficulty common to many sciences (e.g., see Diamond). The intimate integration of a living organism's physiology with its anatomy created obstacles in teasing out and relating function to structure: Once an organism was dead and prepared for dissection, its function had ceased, thus confounding the relationship of form to function. Cuvier considered that careful examinations and the interrelating of structures between specimens might also prove to be useful in revealing principles of observation and comparison. Perhaps the original scientist-as-detective, Cuvier, used scattered, fractured bits of information to reconstruct the prehistory of the Earth and its animals. In a 1798 paper, Cuvier wrote on his realization of the form and function of bones as it relates to the overall identifiable anatomy of an animal, leading to the recognition of the creature from which the bone originated.

> This assertion will not seem at all astonishing if one recalls that in the living state all of the bones are assembled in a kind of framework, that the place occupied by each is easy to recognize; and that by the number and position of their articulating facets one can judge the number and direction of the bones that were attached to them. This is because the number, direction, and shape of the bones that compose each part of an animal's body are always in a necessary relation to all of the other parts, in such a way that—up to a point—one can infer the whole from any one of them and vice versa (Rudwick, 1998, p. 36).

 http://dx.doi.org/10.1016/B978-0-12-800647-4.00003-5

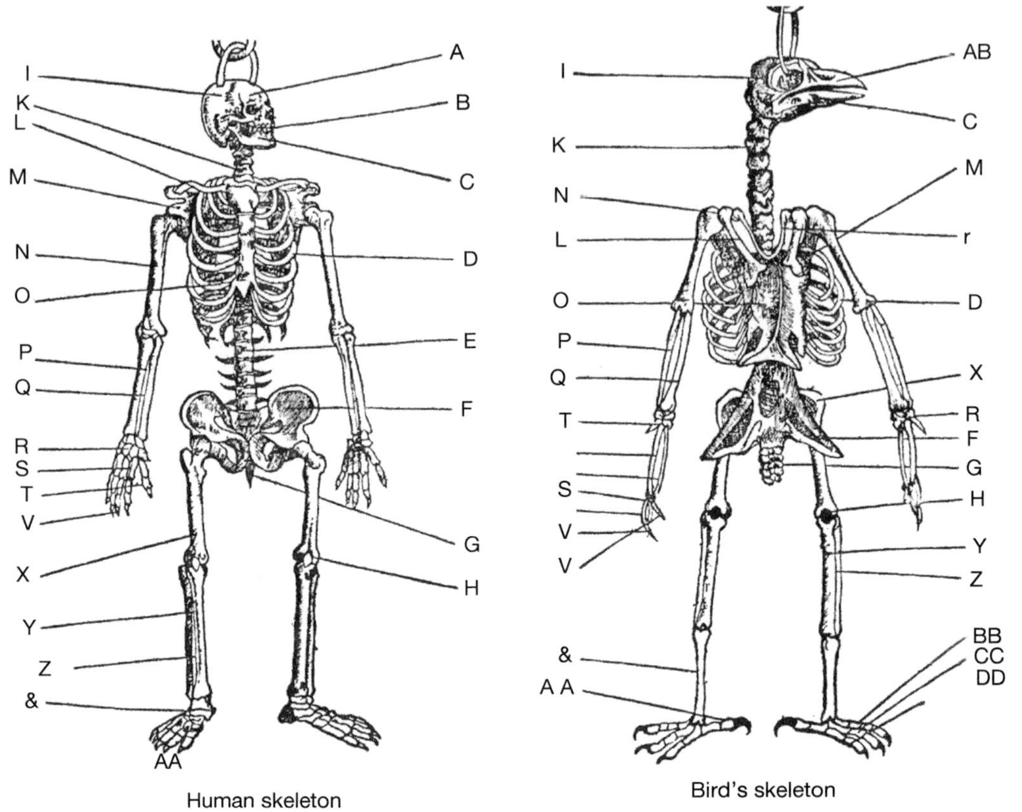

Figure 1 A drawing from Pierre Belon's 1555 book, *History of the Nature of Birds*, comparing the skeletal anatomy of birds to humans. This was one of the first books using the science of comparative anatomy. Wikimedia Commons, open source.

This has been called "Cuvier's Principle of Correlation of Parts" and is a central tenet in biology and paleontology. It is important to note that Cuvier claimed to be able to taxonomically identify an animal from a single bone, but not completely reconstruct it, as the above quote might imply. The reconstruction would only be possible with a sufficient number of bones representing the animal in question. The comparative method has been a successful cornerstone of science ever since, with new or emerging sciences, such as ecology, moving from the purely observational or descriptive approach to that of comparison through experimental or analytical methods.

A short discussion of terms in biology will help clarify concepts used in biological comparisons. The concept of homology, the same structure under every variety of form found in different animals, is the organizing foundation for comparative anatomy. Animals share homologous traits because they also share a common ancestor with the same or related trait. By contrast, analogous traits are similarities found in organisms that were not present in the last common ancestor of the group under comparison; that is, the traits evolved separately. The canonical example of the difference between homologous and analogous traits is the wings of birds and bats: They are homologous as forearms but analogous as wings—the latter structures evolved their functions separately. A homologous trait is termed a "homolog." In biology, evolution and natural selection formed the system within which these relationships developed and were maintained, homogenized, or differentiated.

In manufacturing, other external and internal constraints form the basis for homologous and analogous traits through design, function, form, and costs. Design follows from the product's intended end use, aesthetic concerns, and cost limitations. The function and form of an object tend to correlate, and variances in design cluster around necessary and sufficient criteria. For example, in **Figure 2**, although the hammer heads, opposite sides, handles, materials, weight, shape, and components all vary, they are nonetheless identifiable as hammers. If **Figure 2** were finches, as Darwin studied in the Galapagos on his historic voyage with the *Beagle*, then the base process of taxonomy would be the same but the criteria and

Figure 2 Hammers. All of the objects (a–f) are recognizable as hammers although their components vary: (a) claw hammer, (b) framing hammer, (c) geological hammer, (d) ball-peen hammer, (e) rubber mallet, and (f) upholstery hammer. Wikimedia Commons, open source.

foundations—the history and causes—would obviously vary because of the vastly different processes that produce hammers and finches.

Broadly speaking, the supply chains and distribution networks of material goods are like the phylogenetic trees based on evolutionary descent. Regardless of whether the items are biological or manufactured, the independence of traits should not be assumed. Comparative studies that do not control for historical relationships through phylogeny or supply chains may imply spurious relationships (coincidences). Forensic science is unique in its use of the comparative method to reconstruct past criminal events and sourcing of evidence, either biological or manufactured (in essence, reverse engineering to a level of distribution or manufacturing resolution).

Analogy and Comparison within a Forensic Process

Analogy is a cognitive process that transfers information or meaning from one subject (the analog or source) to another subject (the target); thus, it implies at least two things—situations or events. The source is considered to be the more complete and more complex of the two; thus, the target is less informative and incomplete in some way. The incompleteness may be due to any of several factors, alone or combined, such as damage, fracture, deterioration, or size. The elements or traits—including their relationships, such as evolutionary or supply chains—between the source and the target are mapped or aligned in a comparison. The mapping is done from what is usually the more familiar area of experience and more complete repository of information, the source, to the typically more problematic target.

Salience of the elements or traits is of prime importance. There are an innumerable number of arbitrary differences in either elements or relations that could be considered but are not useful given the question at hand ("Are both items smaller than the Empire State Building? Are they redder than a fire truck?"). Ultimately, analogy is a process to communicate that the two comparators (the source and the target) have some relationship in common despite any arbitrary differences. Some notion of possible or hypothetical connection must exist for the comparison to be made. As a forensic example, consider trace debris removed from the clothing of a suspect and the body of a victim. Although there may be no physical evidence (hairs, fibers, glass, soil, etc.) in common, the suspect's clothing and the victim's body have, at least prima facie, a common relationship (the victim is the victim and the suspect is a person of interest in the crime) until proven otherwise. Thus, common relations, not common objects, are essential to analogy and comparison.

The comparison process as a method makes several assumptions. First, the space in which the comparators are mapped is assumed to be Euclidean. Second, the method embeds the comparators in a "space of minimum dimensionality" (Tversky) based on all observed salient similarities. Each object, a, is detailed and described by a set of elements or traits, A. Any observed similarities between a and another object b, denoted as $s(a, b)$, are expressed as a function of the salient traits they are determined to have in common. The comparison and any observed familiarity can be expressed as a function of three arguments (**Figure 3**):

- $A \cap B$, the features shared by a and b;
- $A - B$, the features of a that are not shared by b; and
- $B - A$, the features of b that are not shared by a.

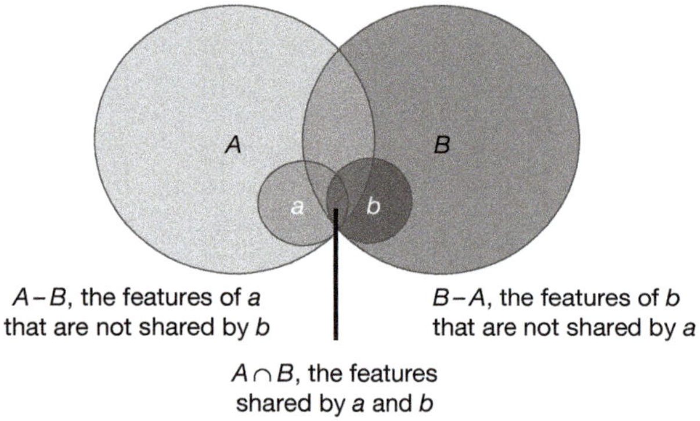

Figure 3 A comparison of observed familiarities can be expressed as a function of three arguments, which are visualized here.

Psychological studies show that people tend to pay more attention to the target (the comparator with less information) than to the source. In forensic science, this means that analysts would pay more attention to the samples from the crime scene or actors than to the known samples collected. This is true although the known has more salience because it arguably has more information and a documented provenance than the questioned sample. For example, a toy ship is quite similar to a real ship because most of the main features of the real ship are expressed in the toy (otherwise it might not be recognized as a simulacrum of its referent). However, a real ship is not as similar to the toy ship because many of the features of a real ship are not expressed in the toy (because of function, scale, or safety, among other factors). The reason for paying more attention to the target is, first and foremost, to determine if there is sufficiency of salient information in the target for the comparative process to occur (see Vanderkolk for a discussion on this).

The main determinant of feature salience for comparative purposes is the degree to which they classify an object (i.e., their diagnosticity). A feature that serves as the basis to reassign an object from one class to another class with fewer members is more salient than one that does not. Salience is hierarchical and is based on how many members of a class share that feature; thus, the goal is to place an object, by successive comparative features, into classes with increasingly fewer members. Therefore, the salience of a feature should increase inversely with the number of members of a class into which it places an object; $A \cap B$ increases and may be thought of as an expression of diagnosticity. A comparative process that does not maximize diagnosticity or exploit features that do so will have low forensic utility.

The Comparative Method within Forensic Science

The comparative method involves the aligning of the relational structures between one or more targets (items of questioned source; Qs) and one or more sources (items of known provenance or source; Ks). This alignment, to work as a method, has three constraints or requirements:

- The alignment has to be structurally consistent; that is, it has to observe a one-to-one correspondence between the comparators in an argumentative structure that is the same between the comparisons (parallel connectivity). One point of comparison can be aligned with at most one other point of comparison in the target or source. Similarly, matching relationships must have matching arguments to support them (the reason for the proposed relationship cannot be based on an unrelated argument).
- The comparison has to involve common relations but does not have to involve common object descriptions. For example, all of the evidence that came from the crime scene, need not have originated from only one source.
- Finally, comparisons are not made merely between the objects at hand but also include all of the higher order "constraining relations" that they may share (systematicity). In biology, this would relate to the evolutionary and genetic connections; for manufactured materials, this would be the design factors and the supply chain of raw materials and intermediate processes that lead to a finished consumer good. The deeper the relational history, the more higher order classes that two objects share, and the stronger the relationship they share; therefore, the greater is the chance of a shared origin. This obviates the significance of coincidental matches between otherwise similar but unrelated objects: A series of coincidences between two objects is not a salient relationship, no matter how many of them exist. Type I and type II errors stem from these coincidences.

A comparison results in a type of cross-mapping of analogous traits or phenomena that have differential relational roles in two situations (e.g., victim's clothing and crime scene). A systematic mapping between source and target is a natural method for differentiating potentially ambiguous relationships. This relates to the classification of the target and source, the identification of traits or features each has that place them in one or more sets (classes) of items. The cross-mapping is of these traits within a class. Once a source has been aligned to a target, candidate inferences, based on the source, can be projected onto the target, such as a shared source or history. For example, a handgun with blood on it can be compared to a bullet removed from a victim (through test firings of similar ammunition) and determined to have been the source (to some degree of certainty) of the bullet whereas the blood can be tested through DNA typing with the victim's known sample and be shown to have the victim as its source (again, to some degree of certainty). The fact that the victim's blood is on the handgun indicates a shared history of occurrence (lateral contemporaneity).

Comparison is selective. The requirement of systematicity is predicated on the idea that classes or sets are flexible and hierarchical. Higher order connections predict lower order relations, and commonalities that are not a part of the aligned system of relationships are considered inconsequential: A blue shoe and a blue car have little in common other than the stated color category; likewise, the fact that the source shoe and the target print might have the same kind of outsole design recedes in importance to the fact than none of the individual traits on the sole appears in the print. Differences that are connected to the hierarchical system of relatedness are called "alignable differences"; those differences with no correspondence at all between the source and the target are called "nonalignable differences." Alignable differences are more meaningful and salient than nonalignable ones because they exist within the same relationship system, making them more relevant to each other. The strange conclusion this observation leads to is that there should be more meaningful differences for comparators that are very similar (*toy train–real train*) than for ones that are less similar (*toy train–toy ship*) because the more similar comparators will have or be derived within more common systems of relationships and will have more alignable differences. As an example, consider all of the possible differences for the pair *automobile–truck* and for the pair *duck-baseball*. More alignable differences could be found for the first pair than the second: After a few differences ("You don't play sports with a duck. You don't hunt baseballs."), the list seems pointless because the two are not aligned. However, the details that could be elicited by comparing *automobile* with *truck* could go on for some time depending on the level of detail desired. Most sets of comparators in the world are dissimilar (which is why forensic comparisons tend to be stronger in exclusion than inclusion), and this "nonconsideration" heuristic makes sense given humans' cognitive load: "Intuitively, it is when a pair of items is similar that their differences are likely to be important" (Genter and Markman). Psychological experiments support this statement, and it seems to be an integral part of human cognition. Related to this idea is Wittgenstein's proposal 5.5303 in his work *Tractatus logico-philosophicus*, "Roughly speaking, to say of two things that they are identical is nonsense, and to say of one thing that it is identical with itself is to say nothing at all." This points to the need for a statistical evaluation of the strength of a comparison, either inclusive or exclusive.

See also: **Foundations:** Forensic Intelligence; Overview and Meaning of Identification/Individualization; Semiotics, Heuristics, and Inferences Used by Forensic Scientists.

Further Reading

Diamond, J., Robinson, J.A. (Eds.), 2010. Natural Experiments of History. Cambridge University Press, Cambridge, MA.

Gentner, D., Markman, A.B., 1997. Structure mapping in analogy and similarity. American Psychologist 52 (1), 45–56.

Hofstadter, D., 2001. Analogy as the core of cognition. In: Gentner, D., Holyoak, K., Kokinov, B. (Eds.), The Analogical Mind: Perspectives from Cognitive Science. MIT Press/Bradford Book, Cambridge, MA, pp. 499–538.

Markman, A.B., Gentner, D., 2000. Structure mapping in the comparison process. American Journal of Psychology 113 (4), 501–538.

Pellegrin, P., 1986. Aristotle's Classification of Living Things. University of California Press, Berkeley, CA.

Rudwick, M., 1997. Georges Cuvier, Fossil Bones, and Geological Catastrophes. University of Chicago Press, Chicago.

Tversky, A., 1977. Features of similarity. Psychological Reviews 84, 327–352.

Vanderkolk, J., 2009. Forensic Comparative Science. Academic Press, New York.

Wittgenstein, L., 1922. Tractatus Logico-philosophicus. Routledge, London, Translated by C. K. Ogden (1922), prepared with assistance from G. E. Moore, F. P. Ramsey, and Wittgenstein.

Forensic Genetics: History

A Carracedo, University of Santiago de Compostela, Santiago de Compostela, Spain

Glossary

Electrophoresis Separation of macromolecules (i.e., DNA fragments under the influence of a spatially uniform electric field).

Genetic marker Observable trait that can be used to trace the presence of genes determining (or linked with) its variable forms.

Polymorphism Simultaneous occurrence in the same locality of two or more discontinuous forms in such proportions that the rarest of them cannot be maintained just by recurrent mutation or immigration.

The Early Times

Forensic genetics can be defined as the application of genetics (in the sense of a science with the purpose of studying inherited characteristics for the analysis of inter- and intraspecific variations in populations) to the resolution of legal conflicts.

The evolution of forensic genetics has been driven by analysis of human genetic variation, beginning over a century ago with Karl Landsteiner's discovery of the human ABO blood group variants (termed polymorphisms) and his early realization that this variation was applicable in solving paternity testing cases and crimes.

During the first half of the twentieth century, different polymorphic human red cell antigens were discovered, although the application of forensic genetics to criminal casework was rather limited because of the difficulties of analyzing minute bloodstains and body fluids other than blood. In addition to the ABO system, there were about 15 other well-established blood groups with potential for forensic serology, including the MNS system, and the Kell, Duffy, Kidd, and Lutheran systems were among the most widely used in forensics.

The characterization of human variation in immunoglobulins, especially the discovery of polymorphic proteins and enzymes in serum and red blood cells, represented a significant advance in this field, particularly for paternity testing.

Since the discovery of the first serum protein polymorphism in 1956, the number of polymorphic proteins that can be analyzed by electrophoretic methods continuously increased up to the late 1970s. Haptoglobins, the group-specific component, transferrin, alpha-1-anti-trypsin, orosomucoid (some complement factors C3, C4, C6, C8, and Bf), coagulation factors (FXIII and ATIII), plasminogen, amylases (AMY1 and AMY2), and immunoglobulin markers were the most used.

The same occurred with red cell and leukocyte polymorphic enzymes, most of them discovered in the 1960s and 1970s. The more widely used were phosphoglucomutase-1, erythrocyte acid phosphatase, esterase D, adenylate kinase, glyoxalase, adenosine deaminase, glutamate-pyruvate transaminase, uridine monophosphate kinase, peptidase A, and 6-phosphogluconate dehydrogenase.

Major histocompatibility complex class I loci were introduced in 1962, 4 years after the original description by Jean Dausset of the first antigen on lymphocytes, when van Rood defined the first two alleles at what is now known as the human leukocyte antigen (HLA)-B locus.

HLAs were more polymorphic than any other genetic markers used up to that moment and represented an important improvement in paternity testing despite the fact that the methodology used (based on a microlymphocytotoxicity method first described by Terasaky in 1964) had some interpretation difficulties, partly because of the cross-reactivity of some antigens and the complexity of statistical interpretation due to linkage disequilibrium within the main HLA loci.

While studying the HLA-A and B locus antigens, it was observed that some exceptions could not be reconciled with the two-gene model, and with the use of a special technique called "capping" (antibody-mediated antigen aggregation on the cell surface), the existence of a third locus, HLA-C, was demonstrated. HLA-A, B, and C were widely used in paternity testing laboratories; at the beginning of the 1980s, some groups using monoclonal antibodies, enzyme-linked immune absorbent

 http://dx.doi.org/10.1016/B978-0-12-800647-4.00004-7

assays, and isoelectric focusing started to report some success in the analysis of HLA in fresh bloodstains.

The use of these classical genetic markers was nevertheless limited when it was necessary to analyze minimal or degraded material, which is commonly encountered in forensic cases. In addition, it was difficult to analyze biological material other than blood; therefore, the information obtained from hair, saliva, and even semen in rape cases was rather limited.

Electrophoretic techniques were preferred over immunological procedures because of the interpretation of results being more objective and because the polymorphic proteins and enzymes had low variant frequencies, making it necessary to obtain as much information as possible. For this reason, sophisticated electrophoretic methods, such as isoelectric focusing, immobilized pH gradients, or hybrid isoelectric focusing, were developed and applied. The introduction of silver-staining methodologies on polyacrylamide gels increased the sensitivity of detection and therefore the possibility of analyzing polymorphic proteins in minute bloodstains.

Despite this, the information that forensic geneticists were able to report in many cases was clearly insufficient; therefore, the discovery of hypervariable loci in minisatellites by Jeffreys et al. represented a milestone in the field and one of the most important discoveries in the history of forensic science.

DNA Typing: Minisatellites and Short Tandem Repeats

DNA typing provided evident advantages over traditional protein analysis, principally because it is more informative and can be analyzed in minute or degraded material because DNA is physically much more resistant to degradation than proteins. In addition, the same DNA genotype can be obtained from any tissue (i.e., blood, saliva, semen, hair, skin, and bones) whereas the analysis of protein markers is restricted to cells where these proteins are expressed.

Minisatellites were initially detected by hybridization of probes to Southern blots of restriction-enzyme-digested genomic DNA, and shared "core sequences" between different minisatellite loci allowed probes to be applied to simultaneously detect many independent minisatellites, yielding the hypervariable multiband patterns known as DNA fingerprints.

Multilocus probes were originally proposed for forensic genetic analysis. However, these types of probes were not very successful in the forensic field because, although highly informative, statistical problems of evaluation of the evidence in cases of band matching and standardization arose. For these reasons, multilocus probes were substituted for in the forensic field by the use of specific cloned minisatellites, "single locus probes" (SLPs), in which each revealed only a single, highly polymorphic, restriction fragment length polymorphism, thus simplifying interpretation. Typically, four SLPs were used successively to probe a Southern blot, yielding eight hypervariable fragments per individual.

It was with SLPs that the first DNA-based criminal investigation was carried out; this case culminated in the conviction of Colin Pitchfork for a double rape and homicide in Leicestershire in 1986. Very soon, DNA analysis became the standard method in forensic genetics as it was used by the majority of laboratories in the full range of applications, especially in criminal forensic casework (stain analysis and hairs) and identification.

Until the introduction of short tandem repeat (STR) analysis by polymerase chain reaction (PCR) amplification, the analysis of minisatellites with SLPs was very popular in forensic laboratories. The main advantage of SLP analysis is the enormous variability of some of the minisatellite loci and the well-documented knowledge of the mutation rate in some of them. The main disadvantages are the time needed for the analysis and the need for relatively large amounts of nondegraded DNA required for successful SLP typing. Because DNA extracted from forensic specimens is often degraded because of environmental conditions, SLP techniques have often failed to produce reliable results. The PCR has overcome these difficulties, and it has strongly enhanced the usefulness of DNA profiling techniques in forensic science.

The PCR method was devised and named by Mullis and colleagues at the Cetus Corporation in 1987, although the principle had been described in detail by Khorana et al. over a decade earlier. However, the use of PCR was limited until suitable heat-stable DNA polymerases became available from thermophilic bacteria.

Most PCR-based DNA typing systems allow alleles to be identified as discrete entities, thereby making standardization easier by avoiding most of the statistical issues that arise in matching and binning SLP bands that occupy a continuum. Additionally, apart from the increased sensitivity inherent in any PCR technique, it is more likely to be successful in analyzing old or very degraded material, mainly because of the smaller size of many of the DNA polymorphisms (SNPs and STRs), making them more amenable to analysis by PCR.

The first group of markers used after PCR amplification were HLA class II genes, especially the HLA DQA1 system analyzed with the use of sequence-specific oligonucleotide probes. Almost immediately after it was shown to be feasible to analyze DNA markers by PCR technology, kits became commercially available for several genetic loci. The AmpliType PolyMarker PCR amplification kit (Perkin–Elmer, Foster City, CA) was very popular in forensic laboratories at that time. With this kit, the loci HLA DQA1, LDLR, GYPA, HBGG, D7S8, and GC are amplified in a multiplex fashion. The last five loci listed were typed simultaneously in a single reverse dot-blot strip containing ASO probes; HLA DQA1 was typed in a separate strip.

The efforts of forensic scientists were then addressed to the amplification of fragment length polymorphisms. The minisatellite D1S80 (pMCT118) was the first one to be applied to forensic analysis, but all of these early PCR systems were superseded by STRs (alternatively termed "microsatellites"). Analysis of STRs by PCR is now the method of choice for DNA-based forensic identification.

STRs were discovered in 1989 and were applied to forensic cases at the beginning of the 1990s. The advantages of using tetra- and pentanucleotide repeat STRs (four- and five-base repeat units) over di- and trinucleotides (two- and three-base repeats) soon became apparent, and a systematic search for the most convenient STRs started. This was followed by the process of standardization of techniques and nomenclature accomplished by bodies such as Scientific Working Group on DNA Analysis Methods in the United States and European DNA Profiling Group in Europe plus the active role of the DNA Commission of the International Society for Forensic Genetics.

Another important step was the possibility of amplifying multiple STR loci in a single combined multiplex PCR reaction. When this PCR approach was coupled with direct detection of amplified products in polyacrylamide gels, STR DNA profiling became amenable to automation. Commercial STR multiplexes for manual electrophoretic systems have been available since 1993. Denaturing polyacrylamide gels were used for the separation of DNA fragments until the introduction of capillary electrophoresis that, together with the introduction of fluorescent-based dye-labeled primer technology and the use of DNA sequencers, revolutionized the field, allowing the typing of large STR multiplexes. Several commercial dye-labeled multiplexes have since become available, and all include a range of STRs plus amelogenin for sex determination. The currently used multiplexes combine 15 STRs or more. The combined discrimination power of STRs is very high, and the probabilities of two unrelated individuals matching by chance (random match probability) are lower than 10^{-15} for most of the larger STR multiplexes.

Since the mid-1990s, computer databases containing STR profiles from crime scene samples; convicted offenders; and, in some cases, persons arrested but subsequently cleared of a crime have provided law enforcement agencies with the ability to link offenders to crime scene STR profiles. Application of this technology has enabled thousands of crimes to be solved around the world. Finally, the redesign of PCR primers, which were closer to the STR repeat region, enabled the creation of "miniSTRs" in 2001 with the potential for improving analysis of degraded biological material.

Polymorphisms in Sexual Chromosomes and Mitochondrial DNA

Y-chromosome-specific polymorphisms have proved to be especially useful in forensic analysis and have been used since 1995. The applications of Y-chromosome polymorphisms include analysis of deficiency paternity testing of a male offspring (e.g., mother unavailable for testing) and different applications in criminal casework. Y polymorphisms are particularly interesting for the analysis of the male DNA fraction in stains involving male/female mixtures, the most common biological material available from the analysis of sexual crimes.

In the same way as autosomal STRs have risen in number, Y-STR marker sets have expanded and commercial multiplexes now offer an analysis of Y-STRs to create a useful haplotype. Because they are uniparental loci passed on in the parental lineage from male to male, the statistical interpretation in cases of a Y-STR match is more complicated, and appropriate corrections must be made taking into account population substructure and sampling errors. Therefore, population surveys are very important, and quality-controlled population databases have been compiled by developing a global database organized as the Y-chromosome haplotype reference database. At the same time as Y-STRs, STRs in the X-chromosome were also introduced, and these markers are of interest for some deficiency parentage testing cases.

During the time STR typing was beginning to utilize fluorescent labeling in the early to mid-1990s, mitochondrial DNA (mtDNA) was introduced for forensic applications. Analysis of the mtDNA control region, a segment of the whole mitochondrial genome, is an efficient method for the study and comparison of bones, old and degraded DNA, and, especially, the analysis of telogenic hairs. In these cases, samples of mtDNA variation can be analyzed using a variety of strategies. The combination of PCR amplification with direct DNA sequencing is usually the optimum approach for identification, and it has proved to be a reliable and reproducible method in forensic casework, used in forensic laboratories since the mid-1990s (**Figure 1**).

Single-Nucleotide Polymorphisms and the Technological Revolution

The last few years have been very exciting in the field of forensic genetics. First, a new type of marker has been introduced—single-nucleotide polymorphisms (SNPs). SNPs have a number of characteristics that make them very appropriate for forensic studies. First, they have lower mutation rates than STRs, and this is valuable for paternity testing. Second, they can be analyzed in short amplicons and, in general, short sizes are desirable because the size of the amplified product is critical for the successful amplification of degraded samples. Finally, they are very suitable for analysis using high-throughput technologies, and the use of high-density SNP microarrays has recently been successfully implemented for the identification of very distant relationship investigations in

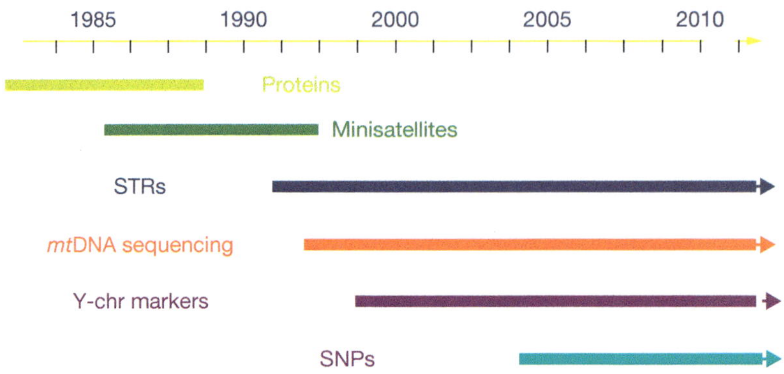

Figure 1 Genetic markers used in forensic genetics.

incomplete pedigrees. A variety of SNP panels for different forensic applications have been proposed and validated. Similarly, insertion–deletion polymorphisms, or indels, have proved to be especially valuable because they are simple, robust, and easy to analyze and interpret.

Ancestry-informative marker SNPs with marked allele frequency differences in populations have been found to be particularly useful to predict the geographic origin of individuals from biological material, and they have been successfully used in important forensic cases such as the analysis of unmatched STR profiles in the investigation of the 11-M Madrid terrorist attack. In addition, SNPs for the prediction of physical traits are being discovered and are likely to prove particularly useful to predict aspects of common phenotype variation such as eye color.

Nonhuman species in forensic genetics is an emerging field with a promising future. Forensic analysis of animal DNA has been used both when animal material (usually pet hairs) is found at crime scenes and in investigations of the illegal trade in endangered species. As with animal material, plant material can be associated with a crime scene and provide vital evidence. The same is true for analysis of bacterial strains in soil through new metagenomic approaches.

One of the most difficult problems facing the forensic biologist is the identification of body fluids. Molecular biological approaches to the identification of blood, semen, and saliva stains using analysis of specific mRNAs (which are surprisingly stable) have been described and are likely to increase in use and importance.

New-generation sequencing technologies are also going to have an impact on many of these new applications. However, despite all of these technical advances, the single most important advance in forensic genetic thinking is the realization that the scientist should address the probability of the evidence. It remains the case that statistics is still the one area of forensic genetics with more challenges in the field. Forensic genetics is nowadays a well-established discipline with a defined body of knowledge, university chairs with this denomination, scientific societies, and specific devoted journals.

See also: **Biology/DNA:** Basic Principles; History of the International Society for Forensic Genetics – ISFG; MiniSTRs; Mitochondrial DNA; Short Tandem Repeats; Single-Nucleotide Polymorphisms; X-Chromosome Markers.

Further Reading

Bogusz, M.J., 2008. Handbook of Analytical Separations. Forensic Science, vol. 2. Elsevier, Academic Press, Amsterdam.
Butler, J.M., 2010. Fundamentals of Forensic DNA Typing (Chapter 3). Elsevier Academic Press, New York.
Butler, J.M., 2012. Advanced Topics in Forensic DNA Typing: Methodology. Elsevier Academic Press, New York.
Editorial, 2007. Launching forensic science international daughter journal in 2007 forensic science international: genetics. Forensic Science International Genetics 1, 1–2.
Jeffreys, A.J., Wilson, V., Thein, S.L., 1985. Hypervariable minisatellite regions in human DNA. Nature 314, 67–73.
Jobling, M.A., Gill, P., 2004. Encoded evidence: DNA in forensic analysis. Nature Reviews Genetics 5 (10), 739–751.
Kayser, M., de Knijff, P., 2011. Improving human forensics through advances in genetics, genomics and molecular biology. Nature Reviews Genetics 12 (3), 179–192.
Weber, J.L., May, P.E., 1989. Abundant class of human DNA polymorphisms which can be typed using the polymerase chain reaction. American Journal of Human Genetics 44, 388–396.

Relevant Websites

http://www.cstl.nist.gov/strbase/.
http://www.isfg.org/.

Basic Principles

A Amorim, University of Porto, Porto, Portugal

Glossary

Allele Each of the alternative forms of materializing the genetic information at a locus.

Codominance The relationship between alleles (symbolized by A1 and A2) that phenotypically allows the distinction between all genotypes involving any pairwise combination of them.

Dominance An allele (symbolized as A) is said to be dominant relative to another one (recessive, symbolized by a) if those that are homozygous (AA) are phenotypically indistinguishable from those that are heterozygous (Aa).

Gene Synonym of locus or allele, depending on context.

Genetic marker Observable trait that can be used to trace the presence of genes determining (or linked with) its variable forms.

Genotype Each of the classes into which the individuals of a population can be grouped according to the allelic state of the locus under study. For example, in homozygosity, the locus is occupied by a pair of identical alleles, whereas in heterozygosity, two different alleles occupy the same locus.

Hardy–Weinberg principle The generalization of Mendelian theory to the population level. Assuming panmixia (random matings, infinite population size) and absence of mutation, selection, and migration, the following relation between allelic and genotype frequencies is expected:

$$\left(\sum \text{gene frequencies}\right)^2 = \sum \text{genotype frequencies}.$$

For instance, if p and q stand for the allele frequencies (A and a) at a locus; then

	A p	a q
A p	AA p^2	Aa pq
a q	Aa qp	aa q^2

Heterozygosity See *Genotype.*

Homozygosity See *Genotype.*

***Locus* (plural: *loci*)** Level of genetic information corresponding to a Mendelian characteristic.

Mendelian characteristic Observation unit that presents a discontinuous distribution (the individuals appear grouped into classes) in the population under study and for which a simple mode of transmission can be established.

Mendelian chessboard Algorithm used to facilitate the prediction, in probability, of the genetic structures of the offspring, knowing the genotypes of the parents. For example, to predict the genetic structure of the offspring from the Aa × Aa mating type

		Types of gametes	
		A ½	a ½
Types of gametes	A ½	AA ¼	Aa ¼
	a ½	aA ¼	aa ¼

Expected genotype proportions 1/4 AA; 1/2 Aa; 1/4 aa (or 1:2:1).

Expected phenotype proportions 3/4 A; 1/4 a (or 3:1).

***Mendelian theory of heredity* (applied to the study of the homogametic transmission of one characteristic)** For each Mendelian characteristic, two alleles exist per locus per individual (one of maternal origin, another paternal); in each gamete, only one is present, the choice being random (i.e., for a heterozygous individual, the probability of each type of gamete is 1/2).

Phenotype Each of the classes into which the individuals of a population can be grouped according to a Mendelian characteristic.

Recessivity See *Dominance.*

 http://dx.doi.org/10.1016/B978-0-12-800647-4.00005-9

Definition

According to the official journal (*Forensic Science International: Genetics*) of one of the leading international scientific societies devoted to this field, forensic genetics can be defined as "The application of genetics to human and nonhuman material (in the sense of a science with the purpose of studying inherited characteristics for the analysis of inter- and intraspecific variations in populations) for the resolution of legal conflicts." Many other sciences have been applied to forensics, but forensic genetics possesses a profoundly different epistemological status among all other sister disciplines. Indeed, traditional forensic sciences rely upon a central assumption—the principle of discernible uniqueness. Under this principle, if two marks are indistinguishable, they must have been produced by the same agent. Conversely, markings produced by different agents should be observably different; therefore, when a pair of markings is not observably different, the conclusion is that they were made by the same agent. Genetics proceeds in the opposite way; it does not rely on the uniqueness assumption and, in contrast, it deals with *types* of observations that are not individually unique. In fact, they are indistinguishable among all members of the same observational class.

The full comprehension of these differences requires a brief overview of the genetic theory, which will be the next section's theme, but it is possible to entertain a brief comparative analysis of the two contrasting approaches. In classical fingerprints (or bullets, photos, etc.), expert comparisons use a wide range of techniques, and a set of measurements is obtained. These data, along with visual inspection and qualitative evaluations, are contrasted and the expert, on the basis of previous experience, delivers an opinion (seldom quantified) on the questioned identity of the marks and, according to the uniqueness principle, on the corresponding author or producer. It is not infrequent to register opposite expert opinions upon the same evidence and a high level of error rates that are not significantly different from those observed among untrained eyewitnesses' testimonies. Conversely, *forensic genetics* does not *seek individually distinctive features* in a genetic profile. Significantly, the genetic expert performs typings on the biological samples to be compared. In other words, each of the analyses assigns the sample (and its donor) to a group (not formally different from the classical ABO blood groups).

Genetic Theory and Probabilities

The foundations of the genetic theory were laid almost 150 years ago by Gregor Mendel. The field of application is limited to characteristics, or observation units (from classical traits such as color or form to the outputs of technologically sophisticated methods such as electrophoresis or mass spectrometry), for which the population under study shows discontinuous variation (i.e., the individuals appear as grouped into discrete classes, called *phenotypes*). The theory assumes that for each of these characteristics, a pair of genetic information units exists in each individual (*genotype*), but only one is transmitted to each offspring at a time with equal probability (1/2). Therefore, for nonhermaphroditic sexually reproducing populations, each member inherits one of these genetic factors (*alleles*) paternally and the other one maternally; in the case when both alleles are of the same type, the individual is said to be a *homozygote*, and the individual is said to be a *heterozygote* when the alleles are distinct. The theory further assumes that for each of the observable units (or Mendelian characteristics), there is a genetic determination instance (a genetic *locus*; plural: loci) where the alleles take place and that the transmission of information belonging to different loci and governing, therefore, distinct characteristics is independent. It is now known that for some characteristics, the mode of transmission is more simple and that not every pair of loci is transmitted independently, but the hereditary rules outlined above apply to the vast majority of cases.

These rules allow us to predict the possible genotypes and their probabilities in the offspring knowing the parents' genotypes or to infer parents' genotypes given the offspring distributions. These predictions or inferences are not limited to cases in which information on relatives is available. In fact, soon after the "rediscovery" of Mendel's work, a generalization of the theory from the familial to the population level was undertaken embodied in what is now known as the *Hardy–Weinberg principle*. This formalism states that if an ideal infinite population with random mating is assumed, and in the absence of mutation, selection, and migration, then the squared summation of the allele frequencies equals the genotype distribution. That is, if at a certain locus, the frequencies of alleles A1 and A2 are f1 and f2, respectively, then the expected frequency of the heterozygote A1A2 will be $f1 \times f2 + f2 \times f1 = 2f1f2$ (note that "A1A2" and "A2A1" are indistinguishable and are collectively represented by convention simply as A1A2); conversely, if the frequency of the homozygote for A1 is f1, then the allele frequency would be the square root of this frequency (because the expected frequency of this genotype is $f1 \times f1$).

To apply this theoretical framework to judicial matters, it must be clear that "forensics" implies conflict, a difference of opinion, which formally translates into the existence of (at least) two alternative explanations for the same fact. In the simplest situation, the evidence is explained to the court as (1) being caused by the suspect (the prosecution hypothesis) or, alternatively, (2) resulting from the action of someone else (according to the defense).

Therefore, to understand how genetic expertise can provide means to differently evaluate the evidence under these hypotheses, a brief digression into the mathematics and statistics involved is required. The first essential concept to be defined is probability itself. The probability of a specific event is the frequency of that event, or, in more formal terms, the probability of an event is the ratio of the number of cases favorable to it to the number of all cases possible. It is a convenient way to quantitatively summarize our previous experience on a specific case and allows us to forecast the likelihood of its future occurrence. However, this is not the issue at stake when we move to the forensic scenario—the event *has occurred* (both litigants agree upon that), but there is a disagreement on the causes behind it, meaning that the same event can have different probabilities according to its causation.

Let us suppose that a biological sample (a hair, organic fluid, etc.) not belonging to the victim is found at a homicide scene. When typed for a specific locus, it shows the genotype "19" as well as the suspect (provider of a "reference sample"). If the allele 19 frequency in the population is 1/100, then the probability of finding such a genotype by chance is thus 1/10,000. Therefore, under the prosecutor's hypothesis (the crime scene sample was left by the suspect), the probability of this type of observations (P|H1) is 1/10,000. While assuming the defense explanation (the crime scene sample was left by someone else), the probability of the same observations (P|H2) would be 1/10,000 × 1/10,000. In conclusion, the likelihood ratio takes the value of 10,000 (to 1), which means that the occurrence of such an event is 10,000 times more likely if both samples have originated from the same individual than resulting from two distinct persons (again provided that the suspect does not have an identical twin). Note that this likelihood ratio is often referred as the "probability of identity," although it is not a probability in the strict sense.

Genetic Information and DNA

Forensic genetics was developed well before the establishment of both the chemical basis and the structure of the genetic material, and direct analysis of DNA for forensic purposes had still to wait for many technological advances. Before this revolution, loci were just abstract entities, and the molecular bases of the observable differences were not ascertained. Genotypes were inferred from phenotypes in controlled experimental conditions (in humans, passive experiments in which the transmission rules were assessed in bona fide families), defining genetic markers, such as the first one used in forensics, the ABO system of blood groups. Although the typings were robust and reliable, these indirect genetic analyses had many limitations and disadvantages. On the one hand, the number of genetic polymorphisms amenable to forensic applications was very limited and, consequently, their informative power; moreover, they could provide ethically sensible data, such as those related to individual health status. The ability to directly assess DNA individual differences in genomic regions devoid of coding capacity (i.e., without expression in terms of visible or clinically relevant characteristics) removed such difficulties and limitations.

DNA analysis confirmed that genetic information is digital, directly resulting from the chemical nature of its repository and composed by a variable sequence of units that are symbolized by A, T, G, and C. This implies that at a particular location of the genetic sequence, an individual is defined by a pair of occupation states out of a very finite set of possible choices. In the simplest case, he/she would be either A/A, A/T, A/G, and so forth, each of these pairs defining his/her genotype. To achieve a satisfactory probability of distinguishing any pair of individuals, we must analyze a good number of positions in the genetic material (to generate a profile) for which of them the population diversity has been previously found to be reasonably high. The validated routine forensic genetic analyses currently in use is a preparative technique (PCR, polymerase chain reaction) that specifically detects (and amplifies) short regions of DNA from our genome. The regions currently used have been selected according to two criteria: (1) to correspond to noncoding tracts (i.e., there is, to our knowledge, no information contained there and so no physical or psychological characteristics of the individual can be inferred from its analysis) and (2) to be highly polymorphic (i.e., the DNA sequence is quite variable).

In conclusion, although proceeding conceptually and methodologically in an opposed way to the uniqueness principle common to other forensic sciences, in modern forensic genetics, the typing of a modest number of these markers in an individual results in a genotype constellation that turns out to be, in practical terms, almost unique (provided no identical twins are involved); that is, the chance of finding two random individuals with the same profile with a standard battery is less than 1 in 1 trillion.

See also: **Biology/DNA:** Bayesian Networks; DNA – Statistical Probability; Databases; Forensic Genetics: History; History of the International Society for Forensic Genetics – ISFG; Parentage Testing and Kinship Analysis; Significance.

Further Reading

Anonymous, 2007. Launching forensic science international daughter journal in 2007: forensic science international: genetics. Forensic Science International: Genetics 1, 1–2.

Butler, J.M., 2005. Forensic DNA Typing: Biology, Technology, and Genetics of STR Markers. Elsevier, New York.

Jobling, M.A., Gill, P., 2004. Encoded evidence: DNA in forensic analysis. Nature Reviews Genetics 5 (10), 739–751.

Saks, M.J., Koehler, J.J., 2005. The coming paradigm shift in forensic identification science. Science 309 (5736), 892–895.

Relevant Websites

http://www.aafs.org—American Academy of Forensic Sciences.
http://www.cstl.nist.gov—Short Tandem Repeat DNA Internet DataBase.
http://dna-view.com—Forensic Mathematics.
http://www.isfg.org—International Society for Forensic Genetics.
http://www.mendelweb.org—MendelWeb.

Overview

JD Wells, Florida International University, Miami, FL, USA
JG Linville, University of Alabama at Birmingham, Birmingham, AL, USA

Glossary

Allele One of the variant forms of a single genetic locus.
D-loop An approximately 1000 base gene-free section of the vertebrate animal mitochondrial DNA molecule. The name is an abbreviation of "displacement loop," so-called because the two DNA strands in this region are often displaced from each other to form a loop structure.
DNA capillary electrophoresis A process by which DNA molecules are separated by size as they move through a polymer-filled glass capillary tube. For a typical forensic DNA analysis, the DNA has been fluorescently labeled for detection by a camera at the far end of the capillary. Molecules of equal length register as a colored peak on the resulting data file.
Electropherogram The graphics file that is the end product of most forensic DNA analyses. See DNA capillary electrophoresis.
Genetic locus (pl. loci) The DNA at a particular physical location on a chromosome.
Haplotype A haploid genotype.
Heterozygous A condition in a diploid organism in which two different alleles occur for a given locus.
Homozygous A condition in a diploid organism in which identical alleles occur for a given locus.
Phenotype An organism's physical and physiological characteristics.
Power of discrimination The probability that an identification test will distinguish between two randomly selected individuals.

Deoxyribonucleic Acid

Overview

The basic technology

We present here a brief introduction. More detailed descriptions of forensic deoxyribonucleic acid (DNA) technology can be found in the other DNA chapters of this volume.

Standard forensic DNA techniques utilize the polymerase chain reaction (PCR). PCR is an in vitro method for making a tremendous number of copies of a selected genetic locus. The process is also commonly called DNA amplification. PCR permits the analysis of a minute starting amount of sample DNA and produces the extremely concentrated DNA solution required for later steps in the genotyping protocol.

PCR can only take place if short synthetic DNA molecules, called primers, complement (i.e., match according to the base pairing rules of double-stranded DNA) the sample DNA on either side of the target locus. The DNA sequence of the PCR primers, therefore, determines the specificity of the test, that is, the locus that will be genotyped and the species on which the test will work. A multiplex PCR simultaneously amplifies more than one locus, and the greater the number of loci, the more discriminating the test.

A highly polymorphic locus is one with a large number of alleles. The loci used in forensic DNA analysis can be classified as those in which the alleles differ in length or those that differ in the sequence of bases. In fact, two alleles that vary in length must also vary in sequence, but these categories are useful because they correspond to differences in the technology of measuring and reporting a DNA fragment's length compared to measuring and reporting its sequence. The data produced are in the form of a graphics file electropherogram (**Figures 1–3**). The set of alleles observed for an individual is that individual's genotype, often referred to in the forensic science world as a DNA profile or DNA type.

Almost all human identity and paternity test DNA profiles consist of a set of short tandem repeat (STR) loci. STR alleles show length variation, and these loci are located on chromosomes within the cell nucleus. A smaller number of tests are based on the sequence of the mitochondrial DNA D-loop.

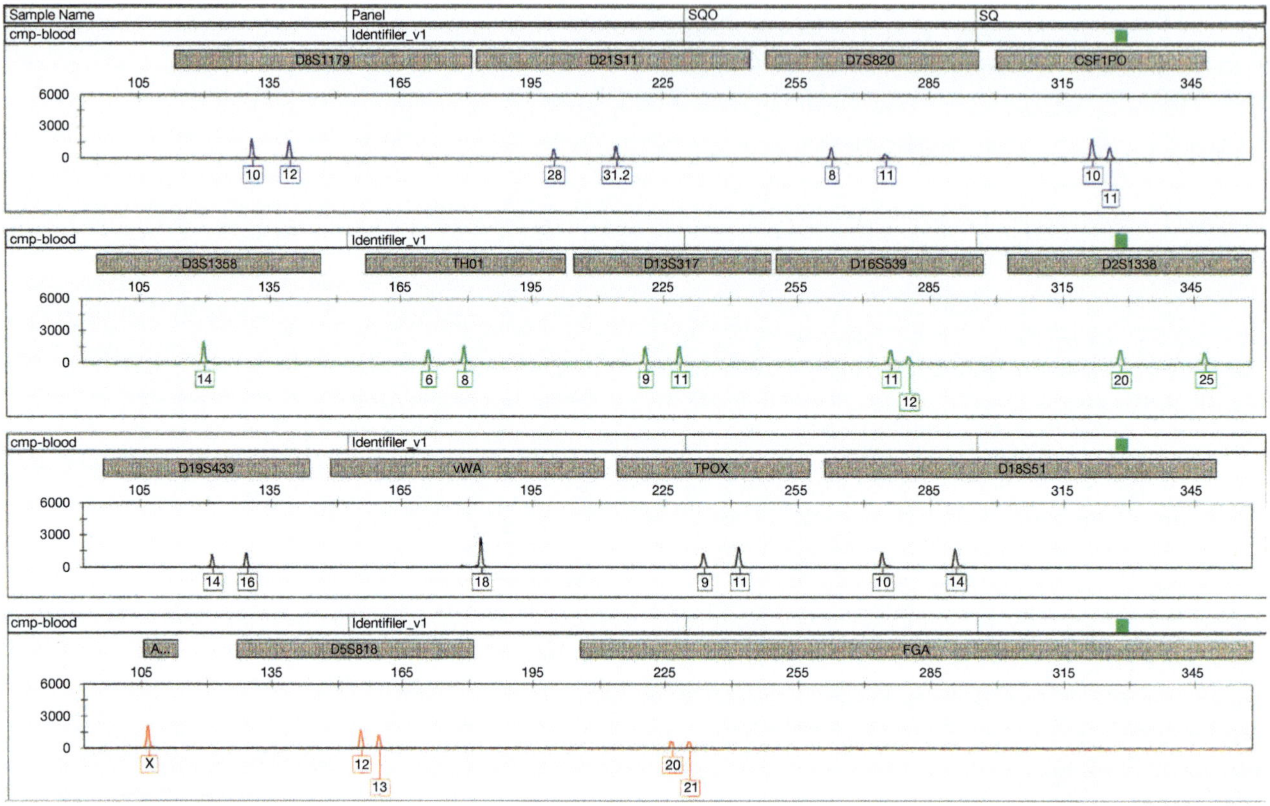

Figure 1 The typical data file produced by human short tandem repeat (STR) analysis. This particular polymerase chain reaction multiplex includes 15 STR loci plus a locus for sex determination. Each peak represents an STR allele and was produced by the fluorescent signal of a population of DNA molecules of the same length. The DNA molecules were separated by size during electrophoresis with shorter molecules shown here on the left and larger molecules on the right.

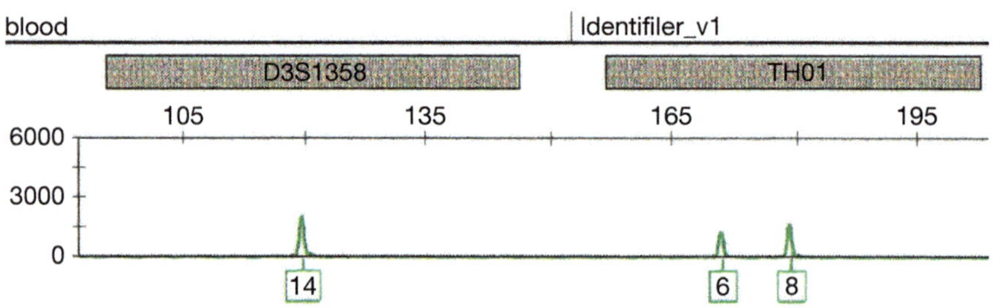

Figure 2 An expanded section of **Figure 1** showing the alleles at two loci. This profile is homozygous at locus D3S1358, as indicated by the single peak, and heterozygous at TH01. Peak labels identify the individual alleles, named according to the number of times a particular sequence is repeated within the molecule.

Fundamental to the interpretation of a forensic DNA test is an estimate of the proportion of the population likely to have a particular profile. This provides, among other things, the random match probability (RMP) or the chance that an unrelated person selected at random would show the same genotype as the suspect. (Although the forensic DNA literature often refers to "related" and "unrelated" humans, in fact the distinction is between close relatives and all others. All humans are genealogically related.) The vanishingly small RMP typically reported for an STR profile match does not reflect any direct survey of that genotype's proportion in the population. Such a survey would probably be impossible to perform.

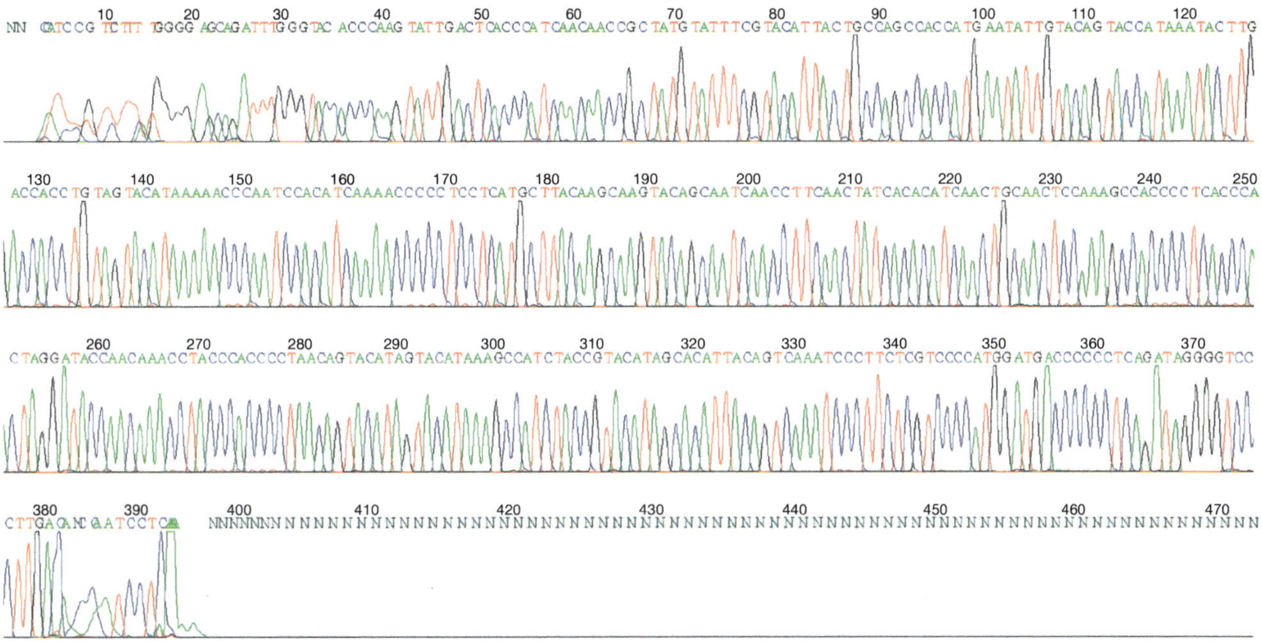

Figure 3 The typical electropherogram produced by mitochondrial DNA sequence analysis.

Instead, the calculation relies on the fact that the alleles usually fit a model of statistical independence; the presence of one allele in no way predicts the presence of the other alleles in the profile. Statistical independence allows one to use the product rule, a fundamental law of probability, plus some basic population genetic models, to multiply the individual allele proportions (variables that can much more easily be empirically measured) and thereby calculate the proportion of the population expected to have a never-before-observed STR profile.

The proper interpretation of a forensic DNA analysis can seem counterintuitive. Judges and juries want to know if the DNA test proves guilt or innocence. They expect the expert to tell them if a particular item of biological evidence came from the suspect. Statisticians almost universally agree that a forensic DNA analyst should not interpret the test in either manner. One common recommendation is to present the test results in the form of a likelihood ratio (LR), a mathematical term by which the probability of the test results given a scenario advocated by the prosecution is compared to the probability of the test results given a scenario advocated by the defense. $LR > 1$ favors the prosecutor's case, but it is not by itself a measure of guilt.

Put in everyday words, interpretation of a *simple* forensic DNA analysis might be as follows. The genetic evidence is that STR profiles of semen from a rape kit and blood drawn from a suspect match. The prosecution claim is that the suspect is the source of the semen sample. The defense claim is that an unknown man with the same STR profile as the defendant is the source of the semen sample. The numerator of the LR is 1. This is the probability that the semen and suspect profile would match if he were the source. The denominator is the RMP, for example, 10^{-17}. In words, the resulting huge LR can be translated as "either the suspect left the semen sample or something extremely unusual happened." However, determining guilt or innocence may depend on other factors. There may be reason to think that the suspect and victim had consensual sex. It may be that despite the minute RMP, the suspect has an ironclad alibi, and a random match is a more reasonable explanation. During an era of less discriminating tests (only 6 markers tested instead of the 13 or more commonly examined today), two men were found to have the same STR profile with an RMP of $\sim 1/30$ million.

The conservative nature of forensic DNA typing

Despite the fast pace of technological innovation in molecular biology, the adoption of new methods of forensic DNA human identity testing is constrained by several factors. Probably most important is the inconvenience and expense required to change the core set of genetic loci used by laboratories. Were this change to happen, newly generated genotypes could not be compared to previous results, including the earlier casework and the existing convicted offender databases. Probably less important, but still relevant, is the fact that an analyst who performs or commissions a well-established procedure can rely on precedent when it is time to argue admissibility in court.

As of this writing, the genotyping technology that is the most attractive alternative to STRs for forensic purposes is single nucleotide polymorphism (SNP) analysis. A potential relative advantage of SNPs is that they can be typed from samples that are too degraded for recovering an STR profile. Although an individual SNP is usually biallelic, that is, it has only two alleles compared to ~10–40 for a typical STR, it is possible to simultaneously analyze so many SNP loci that the test is as discriminating as a standard STR multiplex reaction. It is unlikely, though, that SNPs will replace STRs anytime soon. In addition to the problem of generating new population databases, a biallelic locus makes it extremely difficult to interpret a mixture of two or more individuals.

Innovation in forensic DNA analysis

The practical concerns listed above have not halted forensic genotyping innovation. Recent and likely future changes in technology and procedure include the following.

Improved methods for generating a standard profile

Recent progress has been particularly strong in the development of new ways to produce standard profiles. Mini-STRs are recently developed PCR methods for the core loci. Because the amplified regions are shorter than the DNA fragments produced by most human identity testing kits, mini-STRs recover a genotype from a sample too degraded for conventional methods. Standard STR profiles have also been generated using instruments quite different from the common capillary electrophoresis (CE) platform. This includes CE performed in miniature on a silicon chip or much faster STR sizing using mass spectrometry.

New tests for eliminating a suspect

Although, for the reasons given above, new loci are less valuable than a conventional STR genotype for interpreting a match between samples, these concerns do not prevent the use of a novel locus for excluding a suspect as the source of a sample. The latest commercial human identity testing kits include additional STR loci for this purpose.

Increased automation

Forensic DNA laboratories face a large sample backlog, and the volume of items submitted for DNA testing will continue to increase. Governments steadily expand the list of offenses for which arrestees are profiled and for which convicted offenders are entered in the database. Investigators submit an expanding selection of sample types and seek DNA results from a broader range of crimes. Automation of routine procedures offers the promise of allowing laboratories to process more samples at a lower cost, as well as avoiding the human errors that may occur more frequently when processing samples manually.

Liquid handling robots can perform almost all DNA "wet lab" procedures. Robots are able to complete these highly repetitive steps that would otherwise require the time of a DNA analyst. Robots are also less likely to make pipetting errors that could result in failed samples and false exclusions or false inclusions due to accidental sample switches.

In addition to the automation of laboratory procedures, software can interpret an STR electropherogram with little or no human involvement. Currently, it is typical for a human to review the profile alleles generated by analytical software and to manually adjust the interpretation according to any perceived problem. Often the software will have flagged any ambiguity. Expert system versions of analytical software can be trained to mimic the decisions made by a human when resolving these ambiguities, thereby allowing a lab to increase workflow without increasing the number of analysts.

Laboratories have already begun to automate the analysis, particularly for individual steps in the processing of routine samples such as convicted offender tissue stored on a paper punch. The future of forensic DNA analysis promises to include more automation. It is likely that robots will perform multiple steps without human intervention, further reducing costs and the risk of mishandling samples. Although not in frequent use, all-in-one DNA chip technologies offer a method for combining all steps to produce an STR profile that is compatible with current databases.

Expanding the scope of analysis beyond individual identification

Familial searches

While a traditional search of a convicted offender database only looks for exact matches of alleles at all loci, a close partial match could correspond to a close relative. Investigators have used this information to investigate siblings, parents, and offspring of the convicted offenders on the generated list. For male offenders, the list could be narrowed by additional analysis of Y-STRs from both the evidence and convicted offender's DNA sample. A matching Y-STR profile would suggest a paternal link between the unknown person and convicted offender and would help to eliminate spurious partial matches at other loci. The results of this familial search, coupled with more traditional investigative techniques, could justify collecting a sample from the relative in question and determining whether his or her profile matches that of the unknown sample.

Determining an individual's phenotype or ethnicity

For years, forensic DNA analysis has distinguished male from female. Other information about a person's appearance can be inferred by analyzing DNA polymorphisms in genes that have an effect on features such as eye color, hair color, and skin pigmentation. Certain haplotypes of the OCA2 and HERC2 genes have been associated with either light or dark eye color, already resulting in the development of a multiplex genotyping assay for predicting eye color. Polymorphisms in several pigmentation genes are known to control hair and skin color, and one can easily envision the future development of assays to predict these and other traits.

Even loci with no known effect on phenotype, such as the standard forensic STRs, reflect the historical genetic isolation between geographic human populations. Allele proportions vary between human races and ethnic groups, and a profile composed of a large number of loci can predict a person's self-identified race with a high degree of accuracy.

Both familial searches and DNA phenotyping raise concerns about privacy and civil rights. In familial searches, an unknown profile is compared to a database of millions of individuals. Although a familial search could help to identify relatives of the unknown contributor, unrelated individuals will also be included in the search results. There is a question of whether these search results would warrant further investigation of any of the convicted offenders' relatives given the knowledge that the results would include many coincidental matches to convicted offenders whose relatives had no involvement with the crime in question. When using DNA phenotyping, a similar problem would occur, as traits such as eye color and skin pigmentation are certainly not specific to an individual. The information might unfairly be used by investigators to pursue an individual who fits the vague profile generated from the phenotyping, but who is not the evidence donor. Also, until the limits of DNA phenotyping are fully understood, investigators may exclude the actual contributor if the phenotype profile is incorrect.

Some limitations of current forensic DNA methods

The scientific and legal communities, and the general public as well, now treat the performance of DNA profiling as the standard by which many other forensic science techniques should be judged. This status reflects a genetic profile's inherent power of discrimination and also the fact that certain conclusions, such as tracing semen from a rape victim to a suspect who has no other association with the victim, are particularly incriminating. The basic scientific principles and technology of DNA profiling are common to a broad selection of nonforensic scientific fields. This subjects forensic DNA analysis to much more outside expert scrutiny than is applied to analytical techniques that exist only to serve the legal system. This scrutiny was both intense and highly critical during the late 1980s and early 1990s. Because the technology was so new, forensic scientists could respond to early critiques without worrying about potentially triggering the reexamination of a large number of settled court cases (a concern that hinders the reform of analytical methods with a longer history). As a result, forensic DNA analysis is governed by more modern and sophisticated professional standards than many other areas of forensic science.

One should realize, however, that DNA profiling is not 100% free of unavoidable errors, subjective conclusions, or debate concerning proper statistical interpretation of the results. Even if all evidence handling and laboratory procedures are properly done, it is still possible to generate an erroneous genotype. Fortunately, there is good reason for believing that the risk of a false-positive match between two individual profiles, such as might incriminate an innocent person, is extremely low. For example, if the risk of a false inclusion were not extremely low then there should be an example of a database "cold hit" that matched someone who either was deceased when the crime was committed or had an airtight alibi. This has never been reported for a full DNA profile using current tests, although as described above it did occur using earlier, less discriminating, technology.

Individual variation in PCR primer site sequences results in a failure to amplify an allele in about 1/100–1/4000 individuals depending on the target locus. Such an individual could falsely appear to be homozygous at that locus. This error can be corrected by simply reanalyzing the sample using a different set of primers, but of course for this to happen the analyst must have reason to doubt the original result. One potential clue is allele peak height on the electropherogram. A homozygous peak is usually higher than a heterozygous peak.

The issue of stochastic effects, such as STR "dropin," the amplification of a false allele and "dropout," the failure to amplify a true allele, has recently been revived as investigators sought to expand the range of biological evidence to include ever smaller amounts of starting material. Amplification artifacts cause more uncertainty when analyzing an amount of DNA below the recommended threshold for a standard STR amplification protocol. This is in addition to the fact that the smaller the amount of sample DNA, the more susceptible the analysis is to environmental DNA contamination. Many investigators wish to utilize trace amounts of DNA, such as might be deposited when someone briefly touches an object. These samples, sometimes referred to as low copy number, can often yield an STR profile, especially if additional PCR program cycles are used. Considerable research has gone into developing more sensitive forensic DNA methods, that is, those that will perform well with even smaller amounts of sample DNA, but at present, there is no scientific consensus on how an analyst should proceed when stochastic amplification effects are likely to impact the profile.

Allelic dropout is also a characteristic of degraded DNA, even if the total quantity is not low. This effect is predictable in that it is the larger alleles, that is, those to the right in a typical electropherogram, that are most reduced in peak height. Therefore, a pattern of unusual decrease in peak heights with increasing allele size will alert the analyst that the DNA template is degraded. When an entire locus is not represented in the profile, it is apparent that allelic dropout has occurred. A more ambiguous situation is presented when a locus from a degraded profile has a single allele of reduced height. The source individual might be homozygous for that allele, or heterozygous with one allele missing. "Locus dropout," of course, results in a partial profile. Fewer loci mean a less discriminating test.

Perhaps, the most difficult interpretation issues commonly encountered during STR casework involve a mixture. An item of biological evidence, such as a bloodstain, may have come from more than one individual. Rarely do two people contribute the same amount of DNA to the sample, so most often there will be minor and major contributors, as indicated by greater-than-usual variation in allele peak height on the electropherogram. Inferring individual genotypes within the mixture is sometimes possible, particularly if one or more of the contributors are known. A common example of this is a stain that includes the victim's (known) genotype, and the interpretation may be almost as straightforward as with an unmixed sample. If the mixture is assumed to include only the perpetrator and the victim, yet the profile includes an allele not found in either the victim or suspect, then the suspect will be excluded.

Unfortunately, interpretation of a mixture is often not straightforward. Factors such as shared alleles, a large number of contributors, and a minor contribution low enough to be in the realm of stochastic effects can make the interpretation both very complicated and subjective. In several surveys, experienced forensic DNA analysts showed the same mixed profile reached different conclusions about whether a suspect should be excluded as a contributor.

Mitochondrial DNA often displays a special kind of mixture, that of more than one haplotype, within the same individual. As a result, it is not unusual for two tissue samples from the same individual to not match according to forensic mitochondrial DNA (mtDNA) analysis. This condition, called heteroplasmy, can take the form of >1 haplotype found in one item, for example, a single tooth or in separate samples, for example, blood and a hair from the same person. Because of this phenomenon, as well as statistical issues discussed below, forensic scientists are much more cautious when interpreting an mtDNA haplotype compared to an STR profile. Heteroplasmy does not occur randomly within the human D-loop. There are known point mutation "hotspots" and likely insertion/deletion homomeric stretches (e.g., several cytosine bases in a row). An analyst may be less inclined to exclude if the known and questioned samples differ only at one of these sites.

Experts continue to debate the finer points of how forensic DNA results should be statistically interpreted, and clearly there is some room for improvement. For example, peak height, which provides some indication of the alleles from a single contributor of a mixture, could be incorporated in a LR calculation, but this is seldom practiced. Standards of paternity testing allow for germ line mutation by failing to exclude when a child lacks any of the alleged father's alleles at a single locus. The assumption is that the child could have inherited an allele altered by mutation from the one found in the alleged father. However, this treats all possible mutations as being equally likely, and this is not biologically realistic. No distinction is made between a child with an allele very unlikely to be produced by the hypothesized paternal mutation and a child with the allele most likely to result from the hypothesized mutation.

The greatest practical statistical concern, though, is perhaps the lack of an agreed upon way to estimate the rarity of some mtDNA and Y chromosome genotypes. These are single, haploid loci in that they do not undergo recombination. An analyst may characterize >1 location on either molecule, but these separate "loci" are not statistically independent, and together they constitute a single allele. For those haplotypes that have been observed in >1 individual, the observed proportion in the database may be a good estimate of the true proportion. However, most such haplotypes generated from casework have never been seen elsewhere, and there is no general agreement on how to estimate the RMP.

Nonhuman DNA analysis

Although the great majority of forensic DNA tests are performed on human tissue, forensic analysis of nonhuman DNA has become routine and can be of crucial importance to an investigation. In most cases, nonhuman biological evidence is processed in a laboratory that does not do human tissue casework. The following is a brief description of some of these applications.

Domestic animal identity and paternity testing

There are STR and mtDNA profiling protocols for several pet and livestock species that are almost identical to those applied to humans. The potential criminal investigation applications are similar as well. For example, identifying the individual source of cat hair on a suspect's clothes could place him at the crime scene. Domestic animal paternity testing is more likely to serve a commercial purpose, such as to verify a valuable pedigree.

Identification of a bioterror agent

Investigating or counteracting an effort to cause terror using a highly infectious pathogen must involve identifying the pathogen species. Knowing the species, or in some cases the strain or isolate, determines whether or not there is a real danger, and also the medical procedures needed to protect emergency workers and the population at large. Obviously, time may be of the essence is such a scenario, and PCR-based genotyping is faster than traditional laboratory culture methods for identifying a microbial pathogen. Finding the perpetrator may require that investigators narrow the search to an individual laboratory strain to which a suspect had access. Many of the human pathogens that are the best candidates for "weaponization" show very little intraspecific variation. Therefore, an extremely discriminating genetic test may be needed to distinguish between laboratory cultures.

A long list of molecular genotyping methods has been developed for these purposes, but they will not be reviewed here. Techniques currently in use include real-time PCR for species determination and multilocus variable number of tandem repeat analysis for distinguishing strains within species.

Enforcement of hunting and conservation laws

The illegal trade in protected species often involves processed products, such as powdered tiger bone added to a traditional medicine preparation, which therefore cannot be recognized by their appearance. The most common DNA-based method of animal species identification is based on protein-coding mtDNA sequence data. For vertebrates, this is usually the gene for cytochrome *b* (Cyt *b*), and less often the noncoding D-loop. For invertebrates, this is usually cytochrome *c* oxidase subunit one (COI) and/or subunit two (COII). Many scientists have recently advocated the use of one segment of COI as a standard "DNA barcode" for animal species identification. MtDNA is less useful for distinguishing plant species, the identification of which depends on a variety of other loci.

Some species may be legally harvested but only under certain conditions such as a particular time of year or from a particular population. If geographic populations of a single species differ in allele proportions, then the source of an individual can be inferred by calculating the probability of observing the questioned individual's genotype in each population. The individual is then "assigned" to the population for which that probability is sufficiently higher than for other populations. Finally, as described above for domestic animals, the illegal harvest of a wild individual may be investigated using an identity test. In this manner, butchered meat at a suspect's home, possibly taken in a legal manner, can be linked to tissue, such as a bloodstain, at the scene of an illegal hunt.

Fraud concerning high-value foods

Deceptive practices abound in the sale of expensive food items. This includes mislabeled caviar, much of the fish served in upscale restaurants, processed foods that do not fit the product definition (e.g., "Mozzarella di Bufala" made from cow rather than buffalo milk), the adulteration of Basmati rice with grains of a less desirable variety, and so on. The list is endless.

The genetic species determination test for a given type of food varies depending on the taxonomic category, but many of the procedures listed in the preceding paragraphs may be employed.

Insects used in a death investigation

Insects that feed on a corpse can aid death investigators, in most cases by providing clues concerning the time of death. The immature life stages typically collected from the death scene have few anatomical characters useful for the identification. DNA-based identification of forensic insects most often uses COI + II sequence data.

See also: **Biology/DNA:** Basic Principles; DNA—Statistical Probability; Introduction to Nonhuman DNA Typing; Low-Template DNA Testing; MiniSTRs; Mixture Interpretation (Interpretation of Mixed DNA Profiles with STRs Only); Short Tandem Repeats; Single-Nucleotide Polymorphisms; **Methods:** Capillary Electrophoresis in Forensic Biology.

Further Reading

Budowle, B., Allard, M.W., Wilson, M.R., Chakraborty, R., 2003. Forensic mitochondrial DNA: applications, debates, and foundations. Annual Review of Genomics and Human Genetics 4, 119–141.

Budowle, B., Chakraborty, R., Van Daal, A., 2010. Author's response. Journal of Forensic Sciences 55, 269–272.

Budowle, B., Onorato, A.J., Callaghan, T.F., et al., 2009. Mixture interpretation: defining the relevant features for guidelines for the assessment of mixed DNA profiles in forensic casework. Journal of Forensic Sciences 54, 810–821.

Evett, I.W., Weir, B.S., 1998. Interpreting DNA Evidence: Statistical Genetics for Forensic Scientists. Sinauer, MA.

Gershaw, C.J., Schweighardt, A.J., Rourke, L.C., Wallace, M.M., 2011. Forensic utilization of familial searches in DNA databases. Forensic Science International Genetics 5, 16–20.

Gill, P., Buckleton, J., 2010. Commentary on: Budowle B, Onorato AJ, Callaghan TF, Della Manna A, Gross AM, Guerrieri RA, Luttman JC, McClure DL (2009) mixture interpretation: defining the relevant features for guidelines for the assessment of mixed DNA profiles in forensic casework. Journal of Forensic Sciences 54 (4), 810–821. Journal of Forensic Sciences 55, 265–268.

Gill, P., Werret, D.J., Budowle, B., Guerrieri, R., 2004. An assessment of whether SNPs will replace STRs in national DNA databases—joint considerations of the DNA working group of the European Network of Forensic Science Institutes (ENFSI) and the Scientific Working Group on DNA Analysis Methods (SWGDAM). Science and Justice 44, 51–53.

Higuchi, R., von Beroldingen, C.H., Sensabaugh, G.F., Erlich, H.A., 1988. DNA typing from single hairs. Nature 332, 543–546.

Mafra, I., Ferreira, I.M.P.L.V.O., Oliveira, M.B.P.P., 2008. Food authentication by PCR-based methods. European Food Research and Technology 227, 649–665.

McCord, B., 2003. Troubleshooting capillary electrophoresis systems. Profiles in DNA 6, 10–12.

Menotti-Raymond, M.A., David, V.A., O'Brien, S.J., 1997. Pet cat hair implicates murder suspect. Nature 386, 774.

National Research Council Committee on DNA Forensic Science, 1996. The Evaluation of Forensic DNA Evidence. National Academy Press, Washington, DC.

Palumbi, S.R., Cipriano, F., 1998. Species identification using genetic tools: the value of nuclear and mitochondrial gene sequences in whale conservation. Journal of Heredity 89, 459–464.

Phillips, C., Prieto, L., Fondevila, M., et al., 2009. Ancestry analysis in the 11-M Madrid bomb attack investigation. PLoS One 4, e6583.

Roby, R.K., 2008. Expert systems help labs process DNA samples. National Institute of Justice Journal 260, 16–19.

Valenzuela, R.K., Henderson, M.S., Walsh, M.H., et al., 2010. Predicting phenotype from genotype: Normal pigmentation. Journal of Forensic Sciences 55, 315–322.

Relevant Websites

http://www.dnalc.org—Cold Spring Harbor DNA Learning Center.
http://dna-view.com—Forensic Mathematics.
http://www.innocenceproject.org—Innocence Project.
http://www.isfg.org—International Society for Forensic Genetics.
http://www.mitomap.org—MITOMAP. A Human Mitochondrial Genome Database.
http://www.cstl.nist.gov—STRbase. A Comprehensive Source of Information on Forensic DNA Analysis.
http://www.lab.fws.gov—U.S. Fish & Wildlife Service Forensics Laboratory.

Key Terms

Analogy, Artifacts, Automation, Bioterrorism, Classification, Comparison, Conditional probability, Conservation, Controversy, Crime, Defense, DNA, DNA polymorphisms, Epistemology, Evidence, Expected frequency, Familial search, Food fraud, Forensic, Forensic genetics, Genetic markers, Genotype, History, Hypotheses' relative likelihood, Innovation, Kirk, Limitations, Locard, Method, Nonhuman, Paradigm, Phenotype, Phenotyping, Polymorphism, Population genetics, Prosecution, Science, Set, Short tandem repeat, Stochastic effects, Taxon, Taxonomy.

Review Questions

1. If the "basic unit of forensic science is the trace," how does DNA fit within this conceptual framework? What would it be a "physical remnant" of?
2. What are the three levels that Locard's principle needs to address?
3. Besides Locard's principle, what else do Crispino and Houck consider to be a "native" forensic principle?
4. What are the non-native principles that forensic sciences uses? Give an example of each one in action.
5. What is the difference between uniqueness and individualization?
6. When was DNA profiling first described and by who?
7. Name four blood typing systems that were used early in forensic biology.
8. Why were human leukocyte antigens (HLAs) a significant improvement? What were some issues with the method?
9. What kept the polymerase chain reaction (PCR) from early adoption in forensic biology methods?
10. When were short tandem repeats (STRs) discovered? When were they used in forensic biology?
11. What's the benefit of miniSTRs?
12. Why are single-nucleotide polymorphisms (SNPs) useful for forensic biology?
13. What is the difference between probability in general and probability as used in forensic genetics?
14. Amorim describes DNA as being "digital." What does that mean?
15. What are the criteria for choosing the regions of the human genome used in forensic genetics?
16. What is the difference between genotype and phenotype? Which is more important in forensic biology? Forensic genetics?
17. Do you agree with Amorim's statement that, "forensic genetics does not seek individually distinctive features in a genetic profile?" Why or why not?
18. What are the assumptions associated with the Hardy–Weinberg principle?
19. Write out a timeline of milestones in forensic biology, from its inception to the latest development.
20. What are the roles of the Y- and X-STRs in paternity testing?

Discussion Questions

1. The concepts of class and individualizing evidence are central to forensic science. If, as Amorim says, "forensic genetics deals with *types* of observations (phenotypes), so that all individuals classified in the same group are considered identical; individualization is indeed never reached in formal terms, but only in a probabilistic fashion," then how is forensic DNA analysis not class-level evidence?
2. Mock jurors in a study published in *Psychological Science* (Koehler, 2004) reported being more impressed by an association with the probability 0.1 in 100 than with 1 in 1000, although they are mathematically identical. This is only one of many studies indicating that nonscientists do not understand statistics. Given this, how well do forensic biologists explain their results, especially those beyond the perception of most individuals (e.g., 1 in 1 trillion)? How could this be improved? What are the dangers in reporting and testifying?

3. The cost for sequencing an entire human genome dropped below $1000 (U.S.) in 2014; the cost per sample for conventional forensic DNA analysis in the same year was $481. What are the implications for forensic biology as technology speeds up, gets cheaper, and provides more information than ever before?
4. Crispino and Houck note that "[e]vidence begins with detection by observation, which is possible because of the available knowledge of the investigator or the scientist; unrecognized traces go undiscovered and do not become evidence." Because DNA evidence can be invisible to the unaided eye, what are the implications for biological evidence and "undiscovered traces"? How do forensic scientists ensure the discovery of all relevant biological traces?
5. Kirk is quoted as saying, "On the witness stand, the criminalist must be willing to admit that *absolute identity is impossible to establish.* ... The inept or biased witness may readily testify to an identity, or to a type of identity, that does not actually exist." What are the implications for the interpretation of forensic evidence if absolute identity if impossible to establish? If forensic scientists cannot speak of absolute identity, then what can they use?

Additional Readings

Koehler, J., 2004. Thinking about low-probability events: an exemplar-cuing theory. Psychological Science 15 (8), 540–546.

Le Roux, D., Root, B.E., Reedy, C.R., Hickey, J.A., Scott, O.N., Bienvenue, J.M., de Mazancourt, P., 2014. DNA analysis using an integrated microchip for multiplex PCR amplification and electrophoresis for reference samples. Analytical Chemistry 86 (16), 8192–8199.

Wells, J.D., Stevens, J.R., 2008. Application of DNA-based methods in forensic entomology. Annual Review of Entomology 53, 103–120.

Section 2. Methods

Is DNA analysis biology or chemistry? "Sacrilege," a biologist might cry, but the truth remains that modern DNA profiling is essentially chromatography of a single, specific biological molecule. What happens after the separation becomes applied biology, working with molecular methods, with population genetics and statistics taking the final bow. Where, then, is the biology in all of this? Forensic DNA scientists must fight to keep the biology—the fundamental science—in mind as they become increasingly abstracted from the form of the evidence, be it blood, semen, or tissue.

Capillary Electrophoresis: Basic Principles

A Shallan, R Guijt, and M Breadmore, University of Tasmania, Hobart, TAS, Australia

Abbreviations

BGE Background electrolyte
C Concentration of the component in the sample solution
CE Capillary electrophoresis
CSE Capillary sieving electrophoresis
D_m Diffusion coefficient of the analyte
DNA Deoxyribonucleic acid
E Applied electric field
ε Dielectric constant of the medium
ECD Electrochemical detection
EKC Electrokinetic chromatography
EOF Electroosmotic flow
GC Gas chromatography
HPLC High-performance liquid chromatography
H_{th} Height equivalent to the theoretical plates
IEF Isoelectric focusing
ITP Isotachophoresis
L_d Capillary length from injection to detector
L_{tot} Total capillary length
μ_{app} Apparent mobility
μ_{EOF} Electroosmotic mobility
μ_{ep} Electrophoretic mobility
MS Mass spectrometry
m/z Mass-to-charge ratio
N Number of theoretical plates
Δp Pressure difference
pI Isoelectric point
Q Injection quantity
q Charge
r_i Radius of the ion
r_d Capillary inner diameter
η Solution viscosity
SDS Sodium dodecyl sulfate
SiO^- Silanoate group
SiOH Silanol group
t Migration time
t_{inj} Injection time
UV Ultraviolet
V Applied voltage
v_i Velocity of an ion
v_{inj} Injection volume
$w_{1/2}$ Temporal peak width at half-height
ζ Zeta potential
ZE Zone electrophoresis

Glossary

Capillary electrophoresis Electrophoresis in a circular tube with an internal diameter less than 100 μm.

Electroosmotic flow (EOF) Flow of solvent through movement of ions held near a charged surface in an electric field.

Electrophoresis Movement of ions in an electric field.
Electrophoretic mobility Constant that defines the speed and direction of movement of ion.
Joule heating Heat generated from movement of ions in an electric field during electrophoresis.
Microchip electrophoresis Electrophoresis in a micrometer channel sealed in a flat planar substrate.

Introduction

Capillary electrophoresis (CE) is one of the most powerful liquid-phase separation techniques. Evolving about 30 years ago out of the traditional electrophoretic techniques, such as slab gel electrophoresis, it became a rapid alternative to high-performance liquid chromatography (HPLC) and gas chromatography (GC). The reasons for this were many and varied: high speed, high efficiency, different selectivity, and the ability to sample small volumes. There was much hype and promise, and although it has not replaced HPLC and GC as was touted in the early days, it is nevertheless the method of choice in several key areas that are of particular relevance to forensic science that are discussed in the following chapter.

At its most basic level, electrophoresis is the movement of ionic species in conductive media under an applied electric field. Although much of the fundamental understanding of electrophoresis comes from around the 1900s with the pioneering work of Kohlraulsch, the first demonstration of electrophoresis as a separation technique dates back to the 1930s with the elegant moving boundary experiments of Tiselius on the separation of human serum. The separation was performed in a glass U-tube, with an internal rectangular cross-section of 3 × 25 mm. However, the large scale of the tube led to excessive heat production, which resulted in poor resolution. To counteract this, a solid support, such as paper, starch gel, agarose, cellulose acetate, and polyacrylamide gel, was used, and of course, spawned the development of sodium dodecyl sulfate (SDS)–polyacrylamide gel electrophoresis. When combined with isoelectric focusing (IEF), this created a two-dimensional system that has been the cornerstone of proteimic studies (the separation and differential expression of proteins within a sample) for the last 3 decades. In the late 1970s, a different approach to overcoming the heat issue was presented in Europe by Hjerten, in which narrow diameter tubes were used. Independently in North America, Jorgenson and Lukacs did the same thing, although on a much smaller scale using micron-sized fused silica capillaries developed for capillary GC, and it is this format that is implemented around the world today and is most well known for being the platform for sequencing DNA. The most recent significant advancement in the field of electrophoresis has been its implementation in planar microchips in the early 1990s. This has taken separations that used to require hours in gels, to tens of minutes in capillaries, to tens of seconds in microchips. Many of the concepts discussed here for capillaries are equally applicable to microchips (**Table 1**).

For more complete details of the history of electrophoresis, the reader is referred to the texts listed in the *Further Reading*.

Fundamentals of CE

As mentioned above, the basic premise of an electrophoretic separation is that different charged species will move at a different velocity and can thus be separated. Although correct on a conceptual level, the truth is that it is far more complex, because there exists a complex interplay between the analyte ions, the capillary surface, and additives placed in the electrolyte.

Electrophoretic Mobilities

The electrophoretic mobility of an ion (μ_{ep}) can be described in terms of physical parameters when the electrical force is equal to frictional force:

$$\mu_{ep} = \frac{q}{6\pi\eta r_i} \qquad [1]$$

where q is the charge, η is the viscosity, and r_i is the radius of the ion. From this equation comes the notion that the speed at

Table 1 Milestones in capillary electrophoresis development

Year	*Achievement*
1937	Moving boundary electrophoresis; Tiselius
1952	Paper electrophoresis; Consden
1955	Starch gel electrophoresis; Oliver Smithies
1961	Isoelectric focusing; Svensson
1970	Capillary isotachophoresis; Everaerts
1979	Defining CE experiments; Mikkers
1981	Capillary electrophoresis; Jörgenson and Lukacs
1984	Micellar electrokinetic chromatography; Terabe
1985	Capillary isoelectric focusing; Hjertén
1992	Microchip electrophoresis, Manz

which an ion moves is related to its charge-to-size ratio (q:r_i). Practically, it is more useful to consider this as the charge-to-shape ratio because it is the shape created by the solvated ions that really governs the frictional force and influences the mobility. It should also be obvious from this equation that the sign of the charge (i.e., whether the ion is an anion or a cation) will influence the direction in which the ion moves; thus, anions and cations will move in different directions. Their simultaneous separation would be nontrivial if it were not for the very important and crucial phenomena of electroosmosis.

Electroosmosis and the Electroosmotic Flow

Electroosmosis is observed when an electric field is applied to a conductive solution in a capillary that has fixed charges on its interior wall. In a fused silica capillary, which is the most commonly used in CE, the inner surface contains ionizable silanol groups (SiOH) that have pk_a values from 4 to 6. At pH values greater than 4, silanol groups ionize, giving the anionic form, silanoate (SiO^-); thus, the surface has a negative charge. This attracts positively charged cations from the bulk solution forming a double layer with positive charge density that decreases exponentially as the distance from the wall increases. A potential difference very close to the wall will be created and this is called the zeta potential. As shown in **Figure 1**, the innermost layer close to the capillary surface is essentially static and is termed the *inner Helmholtz* or *stern layer* and the second layer is more diffuse and is termed the *outer Helmholtz plane*. Upon application of an electric field, cations in the second more diffuse layer migrate in the direction of the cathode; in doing so, they drag associated solvent molecules along with them thus giving rise to the electroosmotic flow (EOF). The force propelling the liquid originates at the charged surface, and this causes the flow to move in a "plug"-like fashion in contrast to the parabolic profile observed when pressure is used to pump liquid (**Figure 2**). It is this difference in flow profile that is one of the main reasons for the high efficiencies that can be obtained by electrophoresis.

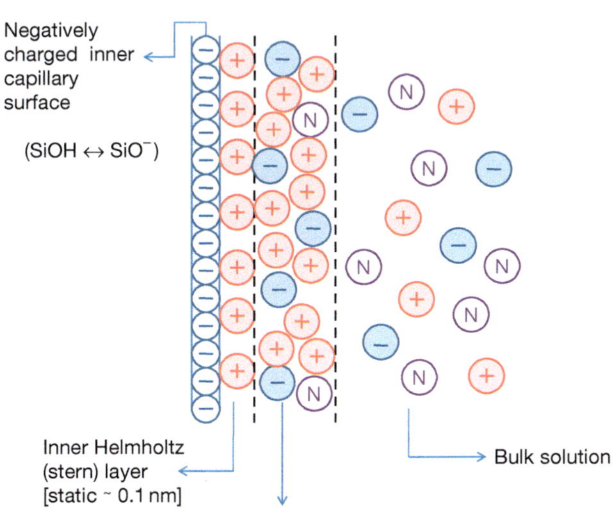

Figure 1 Electric double layer in fused silica capillaries.

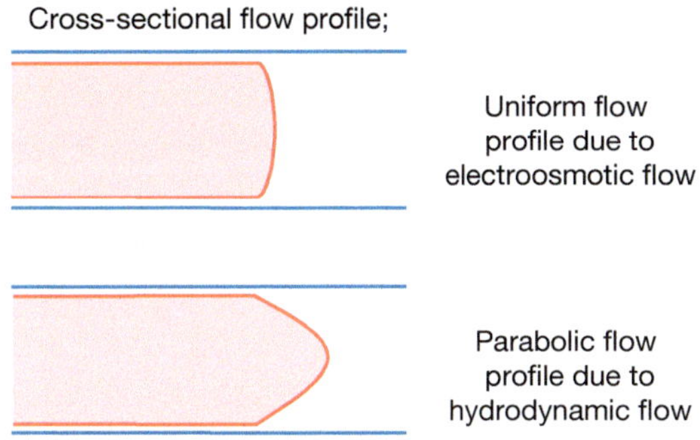

Figure 2 Uniform flow profile in capillary electrophoresis.

One of the most important implications of having EOF is that it will physically move the liquid through the capillary, and the electrophoretic separation is superimposed on top of this flow. This EOF or bulk flow acts as a pumping mechanism to propel all molecules (cationic, neutral, and anionic) toward the detector with separation ultimately being determined by differences in electrophoretic migration of the individual analyte. The net apparent mobility (μ_{app}) is the vector sum of the μ_{EOF} and μ_{ep}:

$$\mu_{app} = \mu_{ep} + \mu_{EOF} \qquad [2]$$

As shown in **Figure 3**, in a fused silica capillary with the EOF directed toward the cathode, cations will reach the detector fastest in the order of decreasing μ_{ep} because their μ_{ep} is in the same direction because the μ_{EOF} are acting in the same direction. Next will be neutral molecules, which will migrate as a single unresolved peak with the EOF. After the EOF, the anions will emerge in the order of increasing μ_{ep} because their mobility is in the opposite direction to the EOF. It is important to note that anions with a mobility μ_{ep} greater than μ_{EOF} will never reach the detector and will migrate out through the inlet of the capillary.

The velocity of an ion (v_i) can be given by

$$v_i = \mu_{app}E = (\mu_{ep} + \mu_{EOF})E \qquad [3]$$

where E is the applied electric field (in V m^{-1}) and is simply a function of the applied voltage (in V) and the total capillary length (L_{tot}, in m):

$$E = \frac{V}{L_{tot}} \qquad [4]$$

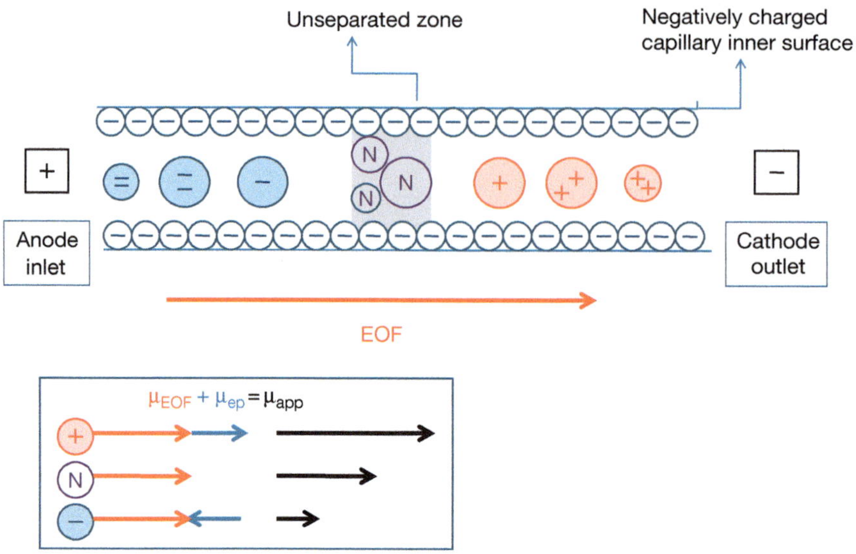

Figure 3 Migration of solutes in capillary electrophoresis.

Calculation of μ_{app} can be achieved directly from the electropherogram from

$$\mu_{\mathrm{app}} = \frac{L_{\mathrm{d}}L_{\mathrm{t}}}{tV} \qquad [5]$$

where L_{d} is the length of the capillary to the detector (in m) and t is the migration time of the analyte (in s).

Similar to the equation for the μ_{ep}, the μ_{EOF} is given by

$$\mu_{\mathrm{EOF}} = \frac{\varepsilon\zeta}{\eta} \qquad [6]$$

where ε is dielectric constant of the medium, ζ is zeta potential, and η is the solution viscosity. It follows from this equation that the magnitude and direction of the EOF will be proportional to the zeta potential. The zeta potential is largely dependent on the electrostatic nature of the surface, and this is an important factor to consider when performing electrophoretic separations in microchips, which are now more commonly made in plastic via mass replication techniques. What is less obvious from Eqn [4] is that it can also be affected by several factors, such as pH, ionic strength, temperature, the electric field, and the presence of some additives. For example, with increased ionic strength there is more double-layer compression and hence a decreased zeta potential; therefore, a reduced EOF is obtained. Using Eqn [3] and using the migration time of a neutral marker, such as acetone, thiourea, and pure water, it is possible to calculate μ_{EOF}. It is then simple to calculate the value of μ_{ep} for each ion using Eqn [2]. Values of electrophoretic mobility are now frequently tabulated, with the most easily accessible values obtained from the electronic database of the simulation software Peakmaster or Simul.

EOF Control

Although the EOF can be beneficial for performing some separations, good control of the EOF is required to achieve the best results. The quickest and most efficient separations are usually obtained in a co-EOF mode in which the EOF is in the direction of the ion mobility of interest whereas the best resolution is obtained in a counter-EOF mode in which the EOF is in opposite direction to the mobility of the ions. In addition, electrophoretic separation modes such as IEF and capillary sieving electrophoresis (CSE) often require reduction of EOF.

Controlling the magnitude of the EOF in a fused silica capillary can be achieved by simply varying the pH. At low pH, the silanol groups are protonated and there is very little EOF. At a pH greater than 8, these same groups are completely ionized, giving rise to a strong EOF toward the cathode. More stable and repeatable EOF is most easily achieved through capillary wall modifications, either permanent or dynamic. Permanent wall modification through covalent attachment is achieved through silylation followed by deactivation with a suitable functional group, polyacrylamide, polyethylene glycol, or polysaccharides, and a number of these are commercially available. An even simpler approach relies on dynamic modification of the surface by addition of an appropriate modifier to the background electrolyte (BGE). The modifier interacts with the capillary wall and in this way affects the EOF. Addition of anionic (or cationic) surfactants may increase (or decrease) the EOF. Also, neutral hydrophilic polymers that adsorb to the capillary wall through hydrophobic interactions will decrease EOF by shielding surface charge and increasing viscosity. The downside of using a dynamic coating is that there is potential interaction

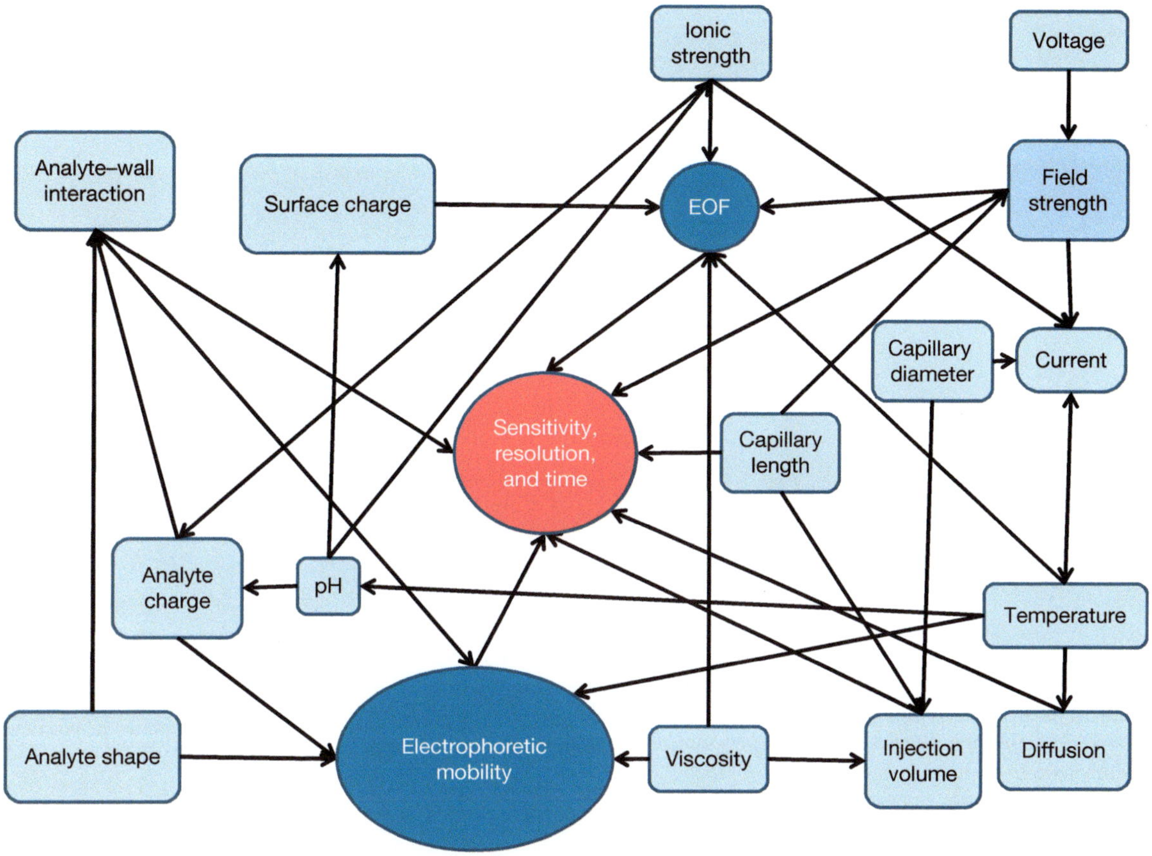

Figure 4 Factors affecting separation in capillary electrophoresis.

with the analytes, which may be undesirable in some instances. To overcome this, there has been considerable research over the past decade on the formation of semipermanent capillary coatings created through the use of double-tailed surfactants or through the use of multiple layers of alternating charged polyelectrolytes. These are attractive because the capillary may need to be recoated between separations, or only once a day, and they ensure that the same exposed surface is obtained irrespective of the material, allowing the same surface chemistry to be used in plastic and glass microchips and improving intercapillary and interchip repeatability.

Background Electrolytes

The composition of the electrolytes inside of the capillary is typically what defines the mode of separation that occurs and the order in which peaks move past the detector. The solution chemistry requirements for the mode of separation are discussed in more detail below, but within each separation mode, variation of the composition will change the selectivity. For example, taking zone electrophoresis (ZE), the exact composition of the electrolyte will influence the sensitivity, resolution, and separation time, as depicted in **Figure 4**. For example, changing the pH of the electrolyte will change the net charge of weak acids and bases, which will affect the μ_{ep}, leading to a change in resolution and separation time. pH may also change the surface charge and zeta potential of the capillary, thus changing the EOF, which will also affect the same criteria. Changing the pH of the electrolyte will also change the ionic strength, which will affect both μ_{ep} and EOF, thus also influencing the separation. Similarly, adding an organic solvent such as methanol will change the solvation of the ions and the viscosity of the electrolyte, which will again influence mobility and EOF.

The complexity of electrophoresis can often be daunting to the electrophoresis newcomer, but there are a number of general principles and conditions that can be used to rapidly identify the feasibility of a specific separation, which can then be further refined as necessary. Phosphate buffers at pH 2 and 7, and borate at pH 9, at a concentration of 10–50 mM are suitable electrolytes to start with because they provide a reasonable ionic strength and have excellent transmission

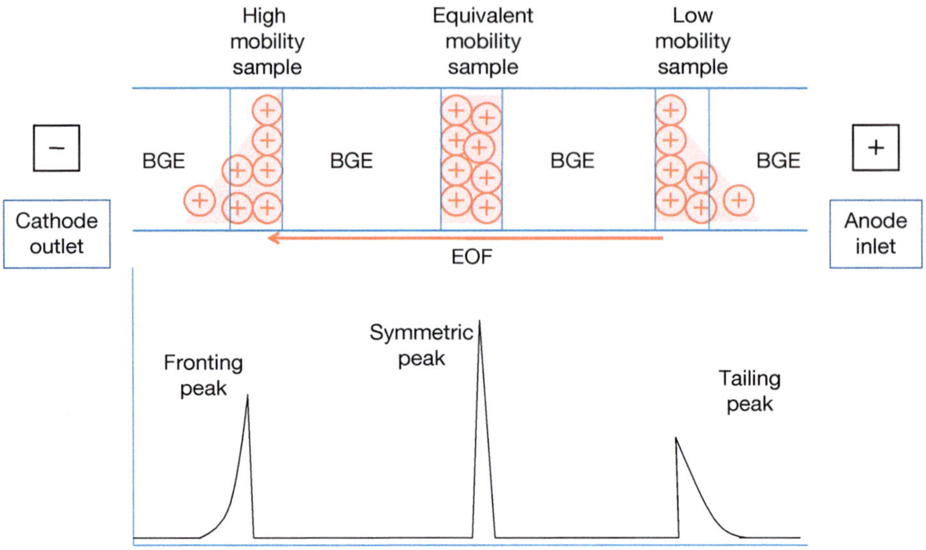

Figure 5 Peak distortions due to differences in mobilities between sample and background electrolyte.

properties for ultraviolet (UV)–visible (vis) detection. For mass spectrometry (MS) detection, 1 M formic acid and acetic acid provide low pH options, whereas at high pH, 10–100 mM ammonium acetate/formate is the most popular option, and conductivity detection typically uses 20–50 mM histadine-(2-[N-Morpholino] ethanesulfonic acid). It can also be simpler when starting to perform separations in a co-EOF manner or in a suppressed EOF environment. Unmodified fused silica capillaries are good for cations and for anions at low pH in which the EOF is suppressed. If a high pH is required for anion separations, then reversing the EOF is easily done by incorporating a cationic surfactant (such as cetyl trimethylammonium bromide) into the electrolyte or by coating the capillary as discussed above. If the analytes are neutral, then a suitable additive such as SDS must be added to perform an electrokinetic chromatography (EKC) separation.

Once conditions for a basic separation have been established, there are then a myriad of electrolyte additives that can be used to enhance the separation in one way or another. This may be simply changing the type of salts used in the electrolyte (through for example, differences in ion-association interaction), changing the solvent (organic solvents and mixed solvents can provide uniquely different selectivity), the addition of additives to alter charge or size through secondary equilibria, and various combinations of these. It is this ability to vary the position of a peak within a separation and to adjust the conditions to manipulate the system to achieve the desired outcome that is one of the reasons that electrophoresis is such a powerful separation technique. The other is the high efficiency.

Maximizing Efficiency

It is misleading to discuss theoretical plates in electrophoresis; nevertheless, it is a convenient concept to describe analyte peak shape and for comparison with other separation techniques. Efficiency is described by the number of theoretical plates (N) and is related to the height equivalent to the theoretical plates (H_{th}) by

$$N = \frac{L_d}{H_{th}} \qquad [7]$$

where L_d is the effective length of the capillary. The theoretical plate number can be determined directly from an electropherogram by

$$N = 5.54\left(\frac{t}{w_{1/2}}\right)^2 = \mu_{app} \times \frac{V}{2D_m} \qquad [8]$$

where t is the migration time, $w_{½}$ is the temporal peak width at half-height, and D_m is the diffusion coefficient of the analyte.

CE has much higher efficiencies than can be achieved by HPLC, with typical plate numbers from 100,000 to 500,000 plates per meter. This is primarily because CE does not have many of the sources of inefficiency that HPLC does and because of the flat plug-like profile of the EOF. Ideally in CE, the zone dispersion is only due to longitudinal diffusion. In reality, inherent in all electrophoretic separations is electromigration dispersion. This arises when there is a difference in electrophoretic mobility of the analyte and the electrolyte co-ion (**Figure 5**). If the analyte ion has a higher μ_{ep} than that of the electrolyte co-ion, then the peak will be fronting; if the μ_{ep} are equal, then the peak will be symmetrical; and if the analyte has a lower μ_{ep}, then the peak will be tailed. Electromigration dispersion can be decreased by matching the mobilities of the buffer constituent to the sample mobility or by maintaining a running buffer concentration approximately two orders of magnitude higher than that of the sample.

During any electrophoretic separation heat will be generated. The temperature increase depends on the power and is determined by the capillary dimensions, the conductivity of the buffer, and the applied voltage. If the heat is not dissipated efficiently, then temperature gradients can develop across the capillary with ions in the center of the capillary having a higher μ_{ep} than those at the capillary wall and band broadening will be observed. This can be a significant issue when performing separations in plastic microchips that have a lower thermal conductivity than glass and cannot dissipate the heat as effectively. There are several methods that indicate excessive heat generation and possible temperature gradients. These phenomena may be indicated if efficiency is reduced as the voltage is increased. In addition, a disproportionate increase in current with voltage, Ohm's law, indicates temperature gradients. Measures to control Joule heating may include reducing the capillary inner diameter, active temperature control, or the use of low-mobility buffers, which contain large, minimally charged ions, such as Tris, borate, and histidine.

One other major source of band broadening in CE is that of wall interaction. Depending on the extent of interaction, peak tailing and even total adsorption of the solute can occur. The primary causes of adsorption to the fused silica walls are electrostatic interactions between charged analytes and the charged wall and hydrophobic interactions. Significant adsorptive effects have been observed, especially for large peptides and proteins, and it is imperative to minimize these to obtain highly efficient separations. The use of zwitterionic buffer systems and pH and ionic strength extremes can be useful for overcoming these issues, but the most prominent approach is to modify the capillary wall to limit solute adsorption.

Modes of Separation in Electrophoresis

One of the highly attractive features of electrophoresis is the ability to perform a number of different types of separations through simple variation of the capillary and electrolyte chemistry. These can be classified into several separation modes, each possessing its characteristic separation mechanism. These can be implemented in both capillaries (abbreviated with a c at the front) and microchips (abbreviated with an m at the front) with the same level of ease.

Zone Electrophoresis

ZE is the most widely used mode. It is fundamentally the simplest form of CE, mainly because the capillary is only filled with buffer. Separation occurs because solutes migrate in discrete zones and at different velocities and are separated solely based on differences is μ_{ep}. Both anionic and cationic solutes can be separated simultaneously by ZE due to EOF (**Figure 3**). However, some analytes cannot be separated by this classical version of electrophoresis because they are neutral or they may not differ significantly in electrophoretic mobility.

Electrophoretic Chromatography

To allow the separation of neutral compounds, an additive is added to the electrolyte, which forms a dispersed phase moving at a different velocity with which the analytes interact. To achieve separation, either the analytes or this secondary phase should be charged. One of the main attractions of EKC is the simplicity with which the system can be varied. The nature of the additive governs the type of interaction whereas the concentration controls the capacity, thereby providing considerable scope for optimization. This has several advantages over chromatography, including that neutral species migrate between the EOF and the additive, thus there is no infinite migration time, and the entire contents of the capillary can be removed after each separation rather than waiting for the last peak to emerge from the column as is required for HPLC. Although initially developed to allow neutral analytes to be separated by electrophoresis, it can also be used to improve the resolution of charged analytes.

Micellar EKC was first used to demonstrate the separation of neutral compounds by CE in which the secondary phase is a micelle dispersed in the BGE. A potential problem with the use of ionic surfactants, especially at high concentrations, is the increase in current. Even with narrow bore capillaries (25–50 μm), the use of extremely high electric fields is often avoided and efficient capillary thermostating is necessary. In microemulsion EKC, a microemulsion droplet is used as the dispersed phase. Microemulsion droplets, either oil-in-water or water-in-oil, are thermodynamically stable transparent nanodroplets stabilized by surfactants and cosurfactants. The microemulsion droplets are more flexible and can swell better than micelles, providing a wider separation window and a higher resolution. However, preparation of the microemulsion can be complicated and time-consuming, and not all microemulsions have suitable stability.

Chiral EKC allows the separation of enantiomers by using a chiral selector as an additive. Charged and neutral cyclodextrins, macrocyclic antibiotics, crown ethers, chiral metal complexes, and chiral surfactants have all been used to form dynamic diastereomeric complexes that can be separated. This is a particularly powerful application of CE because the type and concentration of chiral selector can be easily changed to optimize the separation of a specific enantiomeric pair at much lower cost than can be achieved by HPLC and GC. The ability to separate enantiomers is of particular importance in some forensic applications in which one enantiomer is legally allowed whereas the other is not. Examples include the isomers of 3-methoxy-*N*-methylmorphinan, propoxyphene, norpseudoephedrine, and cocaine as well as compounds in which there is a more significant physicoactive response from one isomer over the other (e.g., with amphetamines). These types of applications (and others) are discussed in more detail elsewhere in the encyclopedia.

Sieving Electrophoresis

Sieving electrophoresis involves the addition of a sieving medium to the BGE. The separation is based on differences in size and shape of the charged analytes and is particularly useful for the separation of large biological molecules such as proteins and DNA. Most commonly used today are solutions of water-soluble polymers (e.g., linear polyacrylamide) that form an entangled network through which the analytes migrate. These have a low viscosity and can be replaced between each separation, thus providing improved repeatability and performance. They also overcame many of the issues with capillary gel electrophoresis in which the capillary is filled with a cross-linked gel (such as an acrylamide gel). CSE was the basis of a generation of DNA sequencing instrumentation and can be performed on commercial instrumentation featuring 96 individual capillaries for high-throughput sequencing and is most commonly used within the forensic community for DNA profiling based on the CSE separation of polymerase chain reaction-amplified short tandem repeats.

Electrochromatography

Electrochromatography, as the name implies, is a combination of CE and HPLC in which there is a heterogeneous phase inside of the capillary. This can be achieved through a capillary, filled, packed, or coated with a stationary phase, and the migration is determined by a combination of electrophoretic migration and chromatographic retention. There are many practical difficulties in performing capillary electrochromatography, but it is attractive when using MS detection because many EKC methods are not compatible with this method of detection.

Isoelectric Focusing

IEF is an electrophoretic technique for the separation of amphoteric analytes according to their isoelectric point (pI) by the application of an electric field along a pH gradient formed in a capillary. In contrast to most modes of electrophoresis, the whole capillary is filled with a mixture of sample and ampholyte mixture and each analyte is focused at its pI. It is a high-resolution technique and can be used to separate proteins that differ by 0.005 pI units and less. The protein zones remain narrow because a protein that enters a zone of different pH will become charged and migrate back.

Isotachophoresis

Isotachophoresis (ITP) involves the injection of the sample between a leading electrolyte and terminating electrolyte. When the voltage is applied, the analytes that have a μ_{ep} bracketed by the leader and terminator form zones in order of decreasing mobility with the length of the zone proportional to the concentration of that analyte. ITP is particularly powerful for trace analysis because low-abundant components have their concentration adjusted up to the steady-state ITP plateau concentration defined by the composition of the leading electrolyte.

Instrumentation and Sample Handling

All of the above -mentioned modes of electrophoresis can be performed in essentially the same instrumentation in capillaries and microchips, but there are some differences in hardware between the two platforms. A schematic for CE is shown in **Figure 6**. The closed circuit is composed of a high-voltage power supply (5–30 kV), two electrodes, two buffer reservoirs, and the separation capillary (typically 25–75 μm inner diameter). Sample is introduced into the capillary from one end by pressure, vacuum, or by voltage. A detector is used to monitor the separated analytes through a window made on the capillary wall.

The capillary column is a key element of the CE separation. Fused silica is by far the most frequently used material, although columns made of Teflon and other plastic materials can also be used. The widespread use of fused silica is due to its intrinsic properties, which include good optical transparency, making absorbance detection easily feasible over a wide range of UV–vis wavelengths. Fused silica is also easy to manufacture into capillaries with diameters of a few micrometers.

Sample can be introduced into the capillary in two common ways in CE. In hydrodynamic injection, a pressure difference between the inlet and outlet is applied to move the sample into the capillary. The injection volume (v_{inj}) can be calculated by the following equation:

$$v_{inj} = \frac{\Delta p \pi r_d^4 t_{inj}}{8 \eta L_{tot}} \quad [9]$$

where Δp is the pressure difference, r_d is the capillary inner diameter, t_{inj} is the injection time, and η is the viscosity of the buffer. With hydrodynamic injection, the quantity of the sample loaded is nearly independent of the sample matrix.

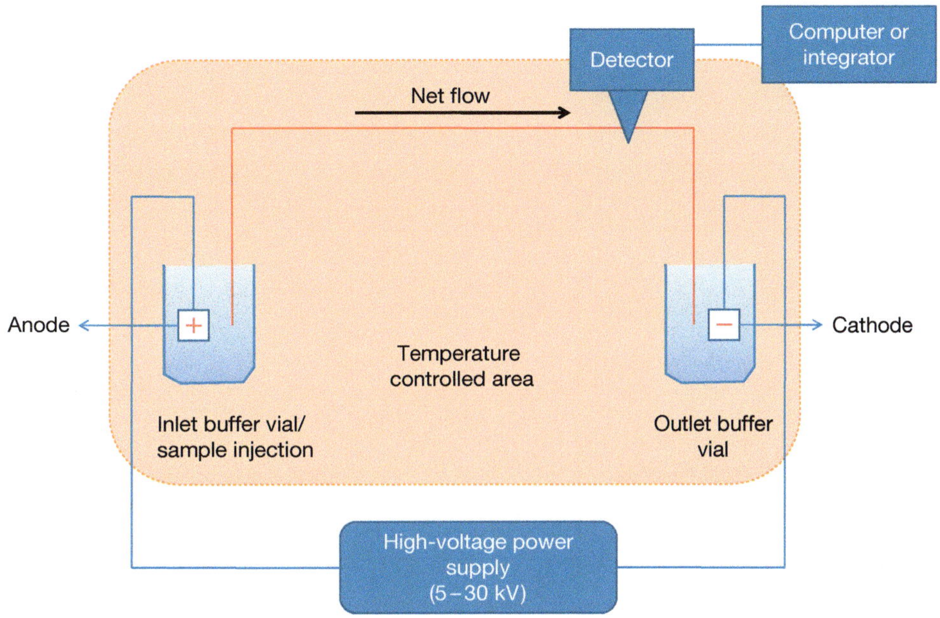

Figure 6 Basic capillary electrophoresis instrumentation.

In electrokinetic injection, a voltage is applied across the capillary and solutes enter the capillary because of μ_{ep} and μ_{EOF}. The injection quantity (Q) of a component can be given by

$$Q = \frac{(\mu_{ep} + \mu_{eo})\pi r_d^2 V t_{inj} c}{L_{tot}} \quad [10]$$

where c is the concentration of the component in the sample solution. Variations in conductivity, which can be due to matrix effects such as a large quantity of an undetected ion such as sodium or chloride, result in differences in voltage drop across the sample and hence the quantity loaded. Because of these phenomena, electrokinetic injection is generally not as reproducible as its hydrodynamic counterpart, but this can be easily corrected for with the use of an internal standard.

Instrumentation for microelectrophoresis is slightly different (**Figure 7**). The power supply is typically smaller, from 3 to 10 kV; there are four reservoirs on the microchip, three of which house buffer with sample in the other. Injection is performed at the intersection of two microchannels interconnected in a "cross"; thus far, fluorescence detection is the most common form of detection. The chip material has significant implications on the separation and can be either glass or plastic, with the latter preferred because of the ability to produce them quickly and cheaply in commercially viable quantities.

Sample Concentration

One of the major limitations of electrophoresis is its high limits of detection. This arises from the small dimensions of the capillary and microchip, which limit the volume of the sample that can be injected and the optical path length when spectrophotometric detection is used. In general, the injected sample plug is usually 1% of the total separation length to maintain high efficiency. This translates to injection volumes of approximately 0.5–50 nL. It is possible to inject more than this, but the analytes must be concentrated or stacked to preserve separation efficiency and avoid overloading. A number of online approaches have been developed to address this issue and are based on either chromatography through integration with solid-phase and liquid-phase extraction or electrophoresis through changes in analyte velocity. Electrophoretic methods are far simpler to implement than those based on chromatography, and a number of powerful methods have been developed, which are collectively known as *stacking*. Field-amplified sample stacking is the simplest method for online preconcentration because it is induced by injecting the sample dissolved in sample that has conductivity at least 10 times lower than that of the BGE. This causes a higher electric field strength to fall over the sample and the ions migrating through a low-conductivity solution into a high-conductivity BGE slow down at the boundary of the two solutions and "stack" into a narrow zone. There are a large number of variants based on large volumes and exploitation of ITP and IEF phenomena. These approaches can all improve detection limits by 100–1000. An alternative approach developed for EKC, called *sweeping*, relies on the accumulation of the analytes by the additive as it moves through the sample. This has been shown to be suitable for both charged and neutral solutes and can

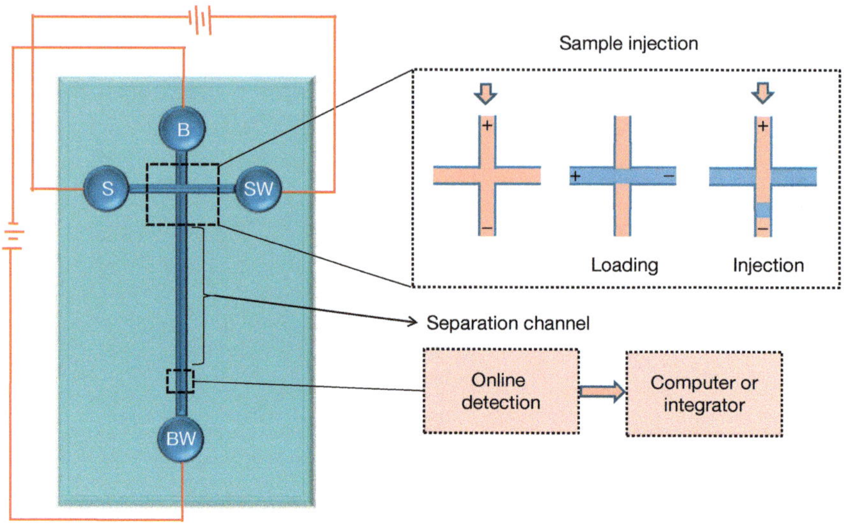

Figure 7 Schematic diagram of capillary electrophoresis microchip and sample injection: buffer inlet (B), buffer waste (BW), sample inlet (S), and sample waste (SW).

improve detection limits by 100–1000. When these strategies are used with electrokinetic injection, then it is possible to improve detection limits by 1,000,000-fold.

Detection Methods

There are several detection methods available, with the most common compared in **Table 2**. These can be either performed on-capillary or end-capillary. On-capillary (and on-chip) detection involves detection of the analytes as they migrate through the capillary/microchannel, and it is typically performed with either spectrophotometry or contactless conductivity detection. End-capillary detection is performed on the effluent of the capillary, which is focused or collected into the detector and is required for some forms of detection, such as MS. On-capillary detection such as this reduces the peak distortion and loss of resolution that can be observed in end-capillary methods.

Spectrophotometric methods

Spectrophotometric detection is achieved by monitoring the change in light induced by the target analytes as they migrate through a detector. However, when performed on-capillary, sensitivity is limited by the small capillary internal diameter, which defines the path length. UV–vis absorption is the most widely used detection method in capillaries because it is cheap and has wide applicability, and most commercial instruments now come equipped with diode array detectors, which allow for monitoring at multiple wavelengths and the collection of full spectra. It is not widespread in microchips, primarily because of the significant UV absorbance of many microchip materials and the difficulty in obtaining long path lengths.

The problem of low sensitivity can be partially solved through the use of laser-induced fluorescence. Detection limits as low as 10^{-14} to 10^{-18} mol have been reported; however, the major drawback is that most analytes do not fluoresce well and must be derivatized with fluorescent reagents first to improve sensitivity. This has been most widely implemented in microchips.

Mass spectrophotometric detection

MS detection is the most powerful detection technique and is becoming increasingly important in forensics for the absolute identification of components and its ability to differentiate overlapping peaks with distinct mass-to-charge ratio (m/z). It can be interfaced off-line with matrix-assisted laser desorption/ionization; however, it is far more common to interface online with electrospray ionization. Interfacing CE to MS is much more difficult than liquid chromatography because of the smaller volume of effluent and the need to maintain a stable electric circuit for electrophoresis, and highly sensitive and robust interfaces are required before this detection technique will become widespread. Microchips can be interfaced directly to the MS, but there are even more significant issues than with capillaries.

Electrochemical detection

Electrochemical detection (ECD) can be carried out in either on-capillary or end-capillary. It can be classified into amperometry, conductimetry, and potentiometry according to operation principles. Amperometry is the most sensitive, but it is

Table 2 Common detection methods for capillary and microchip electrophoresis

Method	*Mass detection limit (mol)*	*Concentration detection limit (M)*[a]	*Advantages/disadvantages*
Ultraviolet–visible absorption	10^{-13} to 10^{-15}	10^{-5} to 10^{-8}	• Universal • Diode array offers spectral information • Not common in microchips
Laser-induced fluorescence	10^{-18} to 10^{-20}	10^{-14} to 10^{-16}	• Extremely sensitive • Usually requires sample derivatization • Expensive
Amperometry	10^{-18} to 10^{-19}	10^{-10} to 10^{-11}	• Sensitive • Selective but useful only for electroactive analyses • Requires special electronics and integrated detection electrodes
Conductivity	10^{-15} to 10^{-16}	10^{-7} to 10^{-8}	• Universal • Simple when implemented in contactless mode
Mass spectrometry	10^{-16} to 10^{-17}	10^{-8} to 10^{-9}	• Sensitive and offers structural information • Interface to Mass spectrometry nontrivial
Indirect ultraviolet, fluorescence, amperometry	10–100 times less than direct method	—	• Universal • Lower sensitivity than direct methods

Source: Ewing AG, Wallingford RA, and Olefirowicz TM (1989) Capillary electrophoresis. *Analytical Chemistry* 61: 292–303A.

only responsive to electroactive analytes. For conductivity detection, a major consideration is selection of the appropriate BGE to maintain conductivity differences between the BGE and the analytes. At the same time, mobility differences between the analyte ions and co-ions in the BGE should be minimal to obtain symmetric peaks. The development of noncontact contactless conductivity detection has seen recent growth in this form of detection. It is interesting to note that because of the ability to easily integrate electrodes in microchips, ECD is actually easier to implement in microchips than in capillaries.

Future Directions

Electrophoresis in the capillary format is nearly 30 years old, whereas in microchips it is nearly 20 years old. However, there are still a number of issues that have yet to be resolved. There is no doubt that there will be a continued drive toward the microchip platform, particularly through the integration of sampling handling to make a so-called *micro-Total Analysis System*. Many of these have already begun to appear with the biggest market being that in the field of DNA analysis, and there are already numerous microchip systems describing the integration of extraction, amplification, and separation in a single microchip. However, these devices are highly complex and far from routine use, and considerable development needs to occur before these will become widespread. It is also necessary to note that many of the issues that have limited the applicability of CE, such as sensitivity and repeatability, are even more problematic in microchips, and these have yet to be resolved. Finally, interfacing both capillaries and microchips with MS does need to have a robust, sensitive, and reliable solution, and although there has been significant development in this area, there is still as yet no commercially reliable interface that can match the sensitivity and performance achieved with liquid chromatography-MS.

See also: **.Biology/DNA:** Short Tandem Repeats; **Biology/DNA/Methods/Analytical Techniques:** Capillary Electrophoresis in Forensic Genetics; **Methods:** Capillary Electrophoresis in Forensic Biology; Capillary Electrophoresis in Forensic Chemistry.

Further Reading

Breadmore, M.C., 2007. Recent advances in enhancing the sensitivity of electrophoresis and electrochromatography in capillaries and microchips. Electrophoresis 28 (1–2), 254–281.

Consden, R., Stanier, W.M., 1952. Ionophoresis of sugars on paper and some applications to the analysis of protein polysaccharide complexes. Nature 169, 783–785.

Cruces-Blanco, C., Garciá-Campaña, A.M., 2011. Capillary electrophoresis for the analysis of drugs of abuse in biological specimens of forensic interest. Trends in Analytical Chemistry. http://dx.doi.org/10.1016/j.trac.2011.06.019.

Everaerts, F.M., Verheggen, ThP.E.M., 1970. Isotachophoresis. Electrophoretic analysis in capillaries. Journal of Chromatography 53 (2), 315–328.

Ewing, A.G., Wallingford, R.A., Olefirowicz, T.M., 1989. Capillary electrophoresis. Analytical Chemistry 61, 292A–303A.

Harrison, D.J., Manz, A., Fan, Z., Lüdi, H., Widmer, H.M., 1992. Capillary electrophoresis and sample injection systems integrated on a planar glass chip. Analytical Chemistry 64 (17), 1926–1932.

Hjertén, S., Zhu, M-d, 1985. Adaptation of the equipment for high-performance electrophoresis to isoelectric focusing. Journal of Chromatography 346, 265–270.

Issaq, H.J., 2002. Thirty-five years of capillary electrophoresis: advances and perspectives. Journal of Liquid Chromatography and Related Technologies 25 (8), 1153–1170.

Jorgenson, J.W., Lukacs, K.D., 1981. Zone electrophoresis in open-tubular glass capillaries. Analytical Chemistry 53 (8), 1298–1302.

Klampfl, C.W., 2009. CE with MS detection: a rapidly developing hyphenated technique. Electrophoresis 30 (supplement 1), S83–S91.

Landers, J.P. (Ed.), 2008. Handbook of Capillary and Microchip Electrophoresis and Associated Microtechniques. CRC Press, Boca Raton, FL.

Lucy, C.A., MacDonald, A.M., Gulcev, M.D., 2008. Non-covalent capillary coatings for protein separations in capillary electrophoresis. Journal of Chromatography A 1184 (1–2), 81–105.

Mikkers, F.E.P., Everaets, F.M., Verheggen, T.P.E.M., 1979. High performance zone electrophoresis. Journal of Chromatography 169, 11–20.

Righetti, P.G., 2005. Review. Electrophoresis: the march of pennies, the march of dimes. Journal of Chromatography A 1079, 24–40.

Smithies, O., 1955. Zone electrophoresis in starch gels: group variations in the serum proteins of normal human adults. Biochemical Journal 61 (4), 629–641.

Svensson, H., 1961. Isoelectric fractionation, analysis, and characterization of ampholytes in natural pH gradients I. The differential equation of solute concentrations at a steady state and its solution for simple cases. Acta Chemica Scandanavia 15, 325–341.

Terabe, S., Otsuka, K., Ichikawa, K., Tsuchiya, A., Ando, T., 1984. Electrokinetic separations with micellar solutions and open-tubular capillaries. Analytical Chemistry 56 (1), 111–113.

Tiselius, A., 1937. A new apparatus for electrophoretic analysis of colloidal mixtures. Transactions of the Faraday Society 33, 524–531.

Zaugg, S., Thormann, W., 2000. Enantioselective determination of drugs in body fluids by capillary electrophoresis. Journal of Chromatography A 875, 27–41.

Relevant Websites

http://www.chromedia.org/—Chomedia.

http://web.natur.cuni.cz/gas/—Peakmaster and Simul: Electrophoresis Simulation Software.

Capillary Electrophoresis in Forensic Biology

RAH van Oorschot and KN Ballantyne, Victoria Police Forensic Services Centre, Macleod, VIC, Australia

This article is a revision of the previous edition article by B.R. McCord & E. Buel, volume 1, pp. 127–135, © 2000, Elsevier Ltd.

Glossary

Allele Any of the forms of the same gene that occur at the same locus on a homologous chromosome but differ in base sequence.

Amplicon A small sequence of DNA that has been amplified by PCR.

Autosomal STR Any STR located on the autosomal chromosomes (i.e., nonsex chromosomes).

Deoxynucleotide triphosphate (dNTP) A monomer, or single unit, of DNA or deoxyribonucleic acid.

Loci (singular locus) The specific position, in all homologous chromosomes, of a particular gene or one of its alleles.

Multiplexes The simultaneous amplification of two or more DNA targets in a single PCR reaction.

Polymerase chain reaction (PCR) A method whereby a specific sequence of nucleotides within a double-stranded DNA is amplified.

Polymorphism The regular and simultaneous existence in the same population of two or more alleles, at a frequency existing in more than 1% of the population, which cannot be due to recurrent mutations.

Primer Short, synthetic fragments of single-stranded DNA that are complementary to DNA sequences that flank the target region to be amplified by PCR.

Short tandem repeat or microsatellite (STR) A DNA sequence from two to six nucleotides, which is tandemly repeated from 5 to 5000 times.

Single-nucleotide polymorphism (SNP) A single nucleotide position in a genome sequence at which alternative alleles are present at an appreciable frequency within a population.

Introduction

This article aims to highlight the changes in the methodology and use of capillary electrophoresis (CE) by forensic biologists since the publication on the same subject by McCord and Buel in the first edition of the Encyclopedia of Forensic Sciences over 10 years ago. The main focus will be on the current status of CE applications by forensic biologists, summarizing the main processes and factors involved in performing CE for a range of marker systems. This article will conclude with a brief consideration of what the near future may hold for CE in forensic biology.

CE Methodology

Since its development in the 1980s, CE has become widely used throughout molecular biology to separate and detect ionic molecules based on their size and charge. Compared to other methods of detecting genetic variability (such as mass spectrometry (MS), high-performance liquid chromatography (HPLC), and probe-based hybridization), CE offers reproducible results with high sensitivity, resolution, and precision, with the additional advantage of being fully automatable for high-throughput sample analysis, and being relatively low cost. Although forensic laboratories had previously used autoradiography, slab-gel electrophoresis (such as the Hitachi FMBIO Scanners or ABI 377), or UV-based CE (with the Beckman P/ACE instruments), the vast majority have now moved to multicolor laser-based detection with the Applied Biosystems ABI Prism 310, 3100/3130xL, or the newer 3500xL Genetic Analyzers. The increased flexibility and throughput has enabled laboratories worldwide to accommodate the ever-increasing numbers of samples submitted for forensic profiling, as well as expand the numbers and types of markers analyzed.

The basic components of a CE system are similar regardless of the type or model employed. These include a variable high voltage power supply (0–30 kV), a fused silica (SiO_2) capillary, with a 330-μm external diameter and an internal diameter of 25–75 μm, two buffer reservoirs, two electrodes, and an

 http://dx.doi.org/10.1016/B978-0-12-800647-4.00008-4

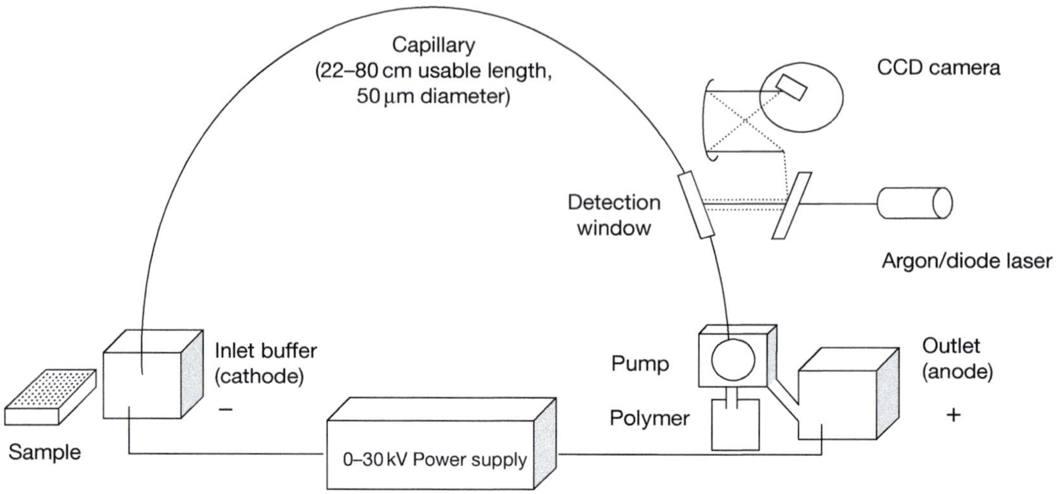

Figure 1 Schematic illustration of capillary electrophoresis systems used for DNA analysis.

on-capillary detector (**Figure 1**). Although there are multiple techniques and chemistries for each stage of the CE process, only those most commonly employed in forensic laboratories will be described in detail below. These can be separated into three broad stages: injection, separation, and detection.

Injection

One of the main advantages of CE is its ability to inject extremely small volumes of sample. All CE systems currently in use employ an electrokinetic injection system to introduce the molecules to the capillary for separation. An electric voltage is applied to the end of the capillary while it is immersed in the deoxyribonucleic acid (DNA) sample. The negative charge of the DNA, combined with the flow of current from the applied voltage, draws the DNA into the capillary. The amount introduced is dependent on the mobility and concentration of the DNA, the injection time, the voltage applied, and the ionic strength of the sample in comparison to the buffer used for electrophoresis. Altering any of these factors will alter the amount of DNA introduced to the capillary. It should be noted that the presence of competing negatively charged ions, such as chloride ions from the polymerase chain reaction (PCR), will alter the sample conductivity, and thus the injection properties. As these ions are smaller than the DNA molecules to be analyzed, they will be introduced preferentially. Purifying the PCR product with silica spin columns or dialysis effectively reduces the concentrations of competing ions, unincorporated primers, and deoxynucleotide triphosphates (dNTPs), ensuring maximal injection of the target DNA. The dilution of the PCR reaction in high-quality formamide can aid in reducing the concentration of competing ions and also denatures the DNA to ensure reproducible migration times. Purification and the use of formamide also increase the amount of sample injected by facilitating the stacking of the molecules, resulting in a sharper injection zone (**Figure 2**). When the ionic strength of the sample is lower than that of the buffer within the capillary, the strength of the electric field created by applied voltage is maximized at the interface of the sample and buffer. This field effectively mobilizes the DNA, forcing them to move rapidly toward the capillary and form a narrow "stack" at the interface. Stacking results in rapid, efficient separation and minimizes the diffusion of the migrating sample producing a sharper band. However, the differing mobility of each type of molecule during electrokinetic injections and stacking means that the process is qualitative only—the concentrations of molecules injected can differ greatly from those in the original sample.

Although not employed on CE instruments currently in use in forensics, hydrodynamic injection is another method available. The application of a pressure difference between the two ends of the capillary results in DNA being introduced in amounts relative to the injection time, the pressure difference, the sample viscosity, and the inner diameter of the capillary. As this method does not rely on sample conductivity, ions present in the sample do not affect the injection process, resulting in a more reproducible, and thus quantitative, method. However, the wider injection bands given with hydrodynamic injections give poor resolution, preventing accurate sizing of products.

Separation

The efficient separation of analytes is not only controlled by the matrix in which separation is achieved but also the type of

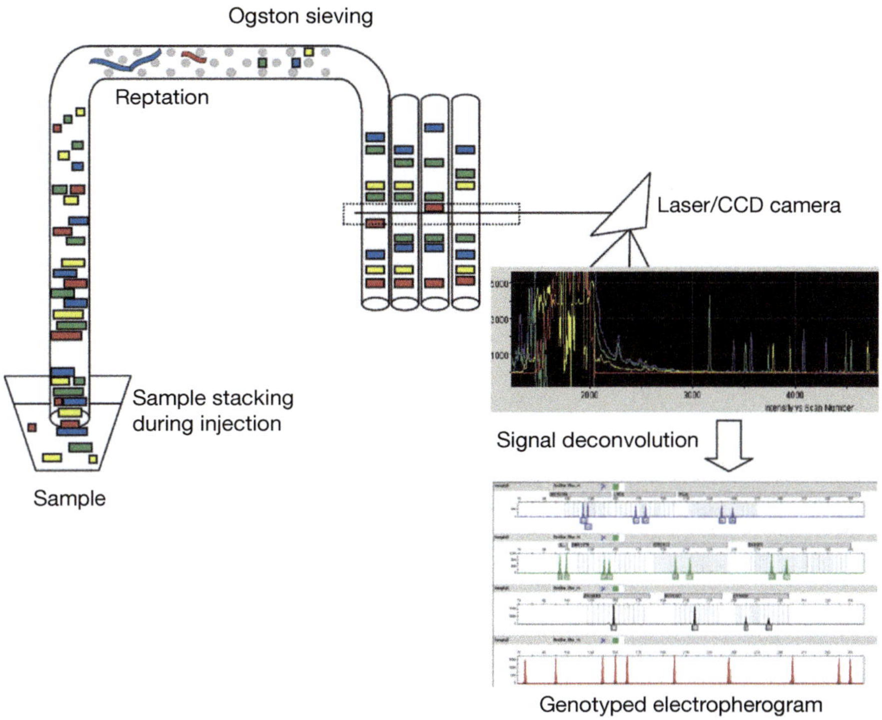

Figure 2 Schematic illustration of the CE process. Electrokinetic injection introduces the DNA to the capillary via sample stacking. During migration through the capillary, separation is achieved via Ogston sieving for small molecules, and reptation for the large molecules. Detection of the fluorescent dyes is performed by an argon/diode laser, with the raw signal deconvoluted relative to prior spectral calibrations to produce the separated fluorescent signals for each dye.

capillary employed, the electrophoresis buffer, and the strength of electric field applied during the process.

Modern CE instruments utilize entangled polymers to ensure maximal separation, giving superior results to the previously used cross-linked polyacrylamide and agarose gels. Entangled polymers, such as the polydimethylacrylamide POP-4, -6, and -7 from Applied Biosystems, act as molecular sieves that retard large molecules as they pass through the pores formed by the polymer. DNA molecules smaller than the pores can migrate rapidly by Ogston sieving, with the rate of movement proportional to their ability to find and pass through pores. Molecules larger than the pore size move through the polymer by reptation—elongated DNA molecules that "snake" through the pores, in a considerably slower process. While POP-4 is suitable for short tandem repeat (STR) and single-nucleotide polymorphism (SNP) typing, the higher polymer concentrations in POP-6 and POP-7 provide greater resolution for DNA sequencing.

Capillaries used in Applied Biosystems' CE instruments are composed of uncoated silica, with a length of 36 cm most commonly used for STR and SNP analysis. While the lack of coating aids in detection, it can result in electroosmotic flow (EOF) during electrophoresis. Charged silanol groups on the interior of the capillary can force the solution to flow toward the negative electrode, impeding the separation of DNA. The induction of EOF is suppressed when using POP polymers, as they mask the charged sites on the capillary walls and provide a viscous layer to resist the flow. Over time, however, contaminants can build up on capillary walls, creating a double charge layer and inducing EOF. For this reason, uncoated capillary arrays are useable for limited numbers of injections before reproducibility when migration times declines.

Detection

Fluorescence-based detection is now the most commonly used method within forensic laboratories. As multicolor detection has been developed (from 4 to 5 with the ABI 310 and 3100 series, to 6 with the ABI 3500 series), highly multiplexed assays have become possible. By attaching a fluorescent dye label to the 5′ end of one in the PCR primer pair for each locus, laser detection can be utilized, and with multiple dyes, loci with overlapping allele size ranges can be analyzed simultaneously. Combinations of rhodamine and fluorescein dyes, designed to absorb light at a single wavelength but emit at different wavelengths, are typically used. Newer fluorescent dyes (such as 6-FAM and VIC) have increased levels of fluorescence compared to the older 5-FAM and JOE, and as such have aided in increasing the sensitivity of current STR amplification kits.

Older CE machines (ABI 310 and 3100 series) use an argon ion laser to excite the fluorophore at 488 and 514 nm, while the newer 3500 series of CE instruments utilize a solid-state diode laser exciting at 505 nm. The diodes are considerably more efficient than the older argon lasers, with a smaller size and power consumption, and greatly increased longevity. Following excitation, the emission spectra of each dye is detected with a charge-coupled detector (CCD) camera as it migrates past the capillary detection window. The signal must then be deconvoluted by comparison to a reference spectral matrix to separate the individual spectra of each dye (due to overlapping excitation/emission spectra between the fluorophores), to place the signal into the appropriate color. The level of fluorescence detected is proportional to the number of dye molecules present, and thus the relative concentrations of each product can be determined. To size the molecules, an internal standard of known size fragments, labeled with a dye different from those of the unknown fragments, that span the anticipated size range of the unknown fragments, must be included and run simultaneously with the sample. Allelic ladders, composed of multiple fluorescently labeled PCR products of known alleles for each locus within the multiplex, can aid in accurate allele designation, although they are not strictly necessary due to the reproducible migration of DNA fragments within modern CE systems.

Interpretation of Electropherograms

With any fluorescence-based measurement, there is a certain level of background noise present that must be accounted for when interpreting the signal. The level may differ between instruments, due to slight differences in CCD cameras and laser effectiveness and alignment. It may also change within the same instrument over time, due to the buildup of contaminants within the capillaries, pump, and capillary detection window. In addition to changing the level of the baseline, these factors may also interfere with the detection of the fluorescent signal, reducing the efficiency of detecting the target. Due to these variations, it is customary to impose two thresholds on the interpretation of signals: analytical and stochastic. The analytical threshold is the average fluorescent signal (converted to peak height) from nonallelic peaks, plus three (or more conservatively 10) standard deviations. This ensures that minor noise peaks are not called as genuine signals during genotyping. The stochastic threshold represents the level below which signals cannot be used to determine the true genotype present, for example, designating a locus as homozygous or heterozygous. Although the peak heights are a reflection of the amount of DNA template added to the PCR, at lower levels of template the amount of product may be insufficient to create equal amplification between and within loci. Thus, the stochastic threshold is used to ensure that these biases do not result in incorrect genotyping in the presence of allele dropout or overamplification. Dilution series of representative samples may be used to set the stochastic threshold, with the limit being set at the peak height at which a heterozygote can be reliably detected without one of the alleles falling below the analytical threshold. In addition, sizing precision cutoffs may be required to monitor differences in migration times between runs and instruments. Although identical alleles will generally have sizes within 0.15 bp of each other, variations in temperature, formamide, or instrument cleanliness can cause increased variation in migration times. Imposing a sizing precision cutoff around allelic genotyping size ranges can aid in detecting samples that have been affected by these factors during electrophoresis.

Recent Developments in CE

In addition to the development of improved polymers for separation, the increased dye fluorescence, and the inclusion of diode lasers mentioned above, there have been other key improvements in CE in recent years. High-throughput instruments are now available, with 4–96 capillary formats. This represents a significant increase from the original single-capillary ABI 310, enabling forensic laboratories to process samples substantially faster. The time required for fragment analysis has also decreased, from 45 min per injection with the 3100 to 35 min on the 3500. All these advances have enabled the total analysis time to decrease from 48 h for 96 samples with the ABI 310 to 2.5 h for 96 samples on a 24-capillary 3500xL, to only 35 min with a 96-capillary 3730xL.

The 3500 series has also introduced a new feature to CE, providing the ability to normalize fluorescent signals between samples, injections, or even instruments. This allows the elimination of natural variations that occur between runs in injection or detection efficiency, or to minimize variations in peak heights caused by pipetting errors within individual samples. However, as normalization alters peak heights by up to threefold, low-level mixtures may artificially appear to be single source, or artifact peaks may appear above the analytical threshold defined during validation studies. As such, there are some concerns about the appropriateness of normalization (as it is currently done) for casework samples, and the impact this may have on interpretation.

CE Typing Methodologies Used by Forensic Biologists

STR Typing

The primary use of CE by a forensic biologist is for the typing of STRs from biological samples to generate a profile from highly polymorphic genetic markers, which differ between individuals. Such profiles can be generated from almost any biological fluid or tissue. They are mainly generated from: crime scene samples, such as dried stains of blood, semen, or saliva, skin deposits (touched objects), and hair roots collected from a wide array of exhibit types; known person and convicted offender samples such as mouth swabs; or disaster victim and missing person identification related samples that could include any of the above as well as tissue or bone samples. The ability to individualize samples is determined by the level of polymorphism of individual STR loci and the number that are used to generate a profile. The forensic community has judiciously selected a small set of STRs that are to be used to create profiles. This allows comparison of generated profiles among samples from the same case, different cases, laboratories, jurisdictions, countries, and over time. Twelve years ago, forensic biologists started to implement methodologies whereby multiple loci could be amplified and typed simultaneously, saving precious samples and providing labor efficiency gains. The early multiplexes amplified three or four loci that had an average combined match probability in the realm of ~1 in 1000 to ~1 in 10,000. However, multiplexes have now been expanded to contain 9–21 STRs, greatly increasing the discrimination power (with combined match probabilities in the realm of 1×10^{-11} to 1×10^{-27}). Most of the individualization kits in current use also include a sex marker, amelogenin, located on the X- and Y-chromosomes (different lengths on each) to assist in determining if the sample originates from a male or a female.

The use of PCR to amplify STRs has significantly improved the ability to generate profiles from smaller quantities and poorer quality DNA compared to previous methodologies. While this methodology also has its limits, these too are being extended. The ability to generate profiles from trace samples has improved through the optimization of kit buffers, improved primer design, and the use of increased number of amplification cycles. To increase profiling success rates from highly degraded samples (these may be encountered when dealing with very old samples, and samples exposed to extreme conditions such as fire, water, or burial) kits have been designed to incorporate reengineered primers that bind closer to the relevant core repeat unit sequences, thus generating a shorter amplicon. These shorter amplicons still include all the repeat units allowing the allele to be identified (i.e., concordance with typings for the same loci using different primers).

To enable the incorporation of so many loci, often with similar sizes, within a single assay has required considerable research and development into multiplex design and optimization. Combining up to 34 primers within a single reaction requires extremely precise design to avoid spurious interactions occurring between pairs of primers, or between primers and nontarget sections of the genome. The use of smaller amplicons also complicates design, as there is less choice for primer sequences. This inevitably leads to some compromise in the placement of primers, with some primers displaying lower amplification efficiencies than others. This can be rectified by careful selection of fluorescent dyes for each primer pair, in addition to altering relative primer concentrations. As the common dyes differ considerably in fluorescence intensity, STRs that amplify poorly can still be reliably detected by using the most sensitive dye, while those STRs that display increased amplification relative to the others can be balanced by using a dye with lower fluorescence. In this way, the signal received during CE is approximately equal between all loci and dyes.

While highly discriminating, there are specific situations where the use of autosomal STRs is not effective in individualizing the person of interest. This includes situations where the target DNA is a very minor component within a mixture of multiple DNA sources that cannot, or has not, been differentially extracted. This type of situation occurs frequently when dealing with sexual offense–related samples. In such circumstances, the use of Y-chromosome STRs can be of assistance in identifying males. Commercial Y-STR multiplexes with 9–23 Y-STRs are available, but as the majority of the Y-chromosome is inherited as a block through the male lineage, only the frequency of the genetic profile in the population can be used as a statistic and is thus not as powerful as the autosomal-derived STR profiles. As individual Y-STRs are (usually) homozygous, their analysis is simplified compared to autosomal STRs, without the possibility of false homozygous genotypes being reported.

For kinship analysis, X-chromosome STRs can be used to examine relationships, particularly in deficiency cases. For example, in a father/daughter paternity case without any maternal relations available, X-STR analysis can be considerably more instructive than autosomal STRs. To date, 53 X-STRs spread across the chromosome in four linkage groups have been described for forensic use.

All of the different STR systems are commonly analyzed with similar CE methods, with a 36-cm capillary and POP-4 polymer to provide single-base resolution between alleles. Commercial STR multiplex kits generally produce extremely reproducible results, with migration times (and therefore derived sizes) similar between samples, injections, and instruments. However, instrument artifacts may interfere with genotyping STR alleles if run conditions are nonoptimal. Transitory increases in voltage during the electrophoresis stage, bubbles in the capillary, or crystallized polymer can result in spikes appearing in the electropherogram. These are non-reproducible between runs and generally can be recognized by the sharp narrow peak morphology. Dye blobs, created from unbound fluorescent dye molecules, may be present in all samples amplified with the same primer stock if primer purification during synthesis was incomplete. Each dye has a reproducible migration and can thus be identified by its presence in all amplified samples, including negative controls.

Mitochondria Typing for Individualization

In extremely degraded samples, where the nuclear DNA is unable to provide a profile, mitochondrial DNA (mtDNA) profiles can be generated as an alternative. The mtDNA has a structure that is more robust than nuclear DNA, and as it has tens or hundreds of copies per cell, the target sequence is present in far higher quantities than nuclear DNA. To obtain a mtDNA profile, forensic biologists sequence the 342 bp Hypervariable I and/or 268 bp Hypervariable II regions or alternatively just type for SNPs at specific sites within these regions. The generated profiles, however, have very poor discrimination potential relative to what STRs can provide. As they are inherited via maternal lineages, these profiles have limitations in that they are unable to distinguish among maternal relatives. Mitochondrial DNA profiling is more widely used in paternity testing, disaster victim identification, or historical reconstructions. For sequencing, the use of POP-6 or POP-7 polymers for CE is recommended, as this will provide considerably enhanced base resolution. Depending on the size of the amplicons, the capillary used may also need to be lengthened, to 50 or 80 cm, to ensure that the complete sequence is obtained. Purification of the sequencing product prior to CE analysis is critical for successful analysis, as unincorporated fluorescent dideoxynucleotides will severely impact on the quality of the sequencing trace.

SNP Typing for Individualization

SNPs have been identified and advocated as a replacement for STRs for individualization purposes, partly because they should allow useful profiles to be obtained from highly degraded samples. However, for various reasons these are not in regular use by forensic biologists. These include: the need to multiplex many more loci to gain the same discrimination potential as STRs, which is methodologically challenging; the need for consistency in profiling systems, as moving to a new profiling system would require retesting all existing samples with the new system (which in many instances would not be possible due to the unavailability of the sample), or testing all new samples with both systems at great expense; and finally, the improvements in the engineering of the core STR systems and typing methodologies have increased the ability to generate STR profiles from highly degraded and trace samples, so the gains made by moving to SNPs would be minimal. The currently used STR systems serve the forensic biologists well.

SNPs do however provide a useful tool to forensic biologist for other purposes. STRs do not provide any phenotypic information about the individual that may be of assistance to criminal investigations. Specific SNPs can be typed that help identify features of an individual that could be highly useful to investigating officers for identifying potential suspects or reducing the number of individuals within a suspect pool. These include SNPs that can help determine biogeographical ancestry and those that can help reveal externally visible traits.

SNP Typing for Biological Ancestry and Physical Identification Typing

Unlike SNPs used for individualization, which vary randomly between individuals, ancestry-informative SNPs have clearly defined distributions across human populations. Due to their evolutionary history and mode of inheritance, particular Y-chromosome and mtDNA SNPs can clearly reveal the continental and population origins of an individual. These markers have been extensively utilized to aid our understanding of human migration and evolution. While highly informative, reliance on just Y-chromosome and mtDNA SNPs can be limited depending on the sex of the individual, or if the individual has an admixed biological ancestry. Whole genome SNP analysis, covering hundreds of thousands of SNPs, is revealing many population-specific autosomal SNPs that could be used to create panels to identify the biological ancestry of the sample donor. These types of markers to assist investigators has been demonstrated to be useful but has not yet been adopted as a routinely used tool by the wider community of forensic practitioners. Further investigations of relevant markers for relevant populations, development and validation of optimized kits, and demonstrated successes of their utilization should see these types of markers/kits being employed more in the future.

While still in its infancy, SNPs strongly associated with genetically controlled physical features of relevance to forensic investigators are beginning to be discovered. This is being greatly assisted by the increased knowledge of the genetics underpinning particular traits and the availability of whole genome SNP data of individuals with different physical traits. SNPs associated with particular hair colors have been available for some time and have been utilized in forensic casework. SNPs strongly associated with specific iris colors have also been identified and are starting to become available for forensic investigation applications. Markers for other physical features are being sought, but extensive further investigations are required before suitable markers are found, accurate and robust typing systems developed, and these then routinely utilized by forensic practitioners.

Genotyping SNPs with CE, although similar to STR genotyping, has its own specific methodological challenges that must be considered. The single base extension method of SNP genotyping has the distinct advantage that amplicons can be extremely small. However, it is inadvisable to reduce the extension primer below around 20 bases in size, as migration times and sizing can be inexact at this low size. In addition, incomplete purification can leave large dye blobs that can obscure allelic peaks at these low sizes. Although many laboratories use POP-4 successfully for SNP genotyping, POP-6 or POP-7 can provide sharper resolution, allowing for smaller size differences between loci during the multiplex design.

Other Uses

Other uses for CE are emerging including the detection of specific mRNA fragments to help identify the biological fluid or tissue origin of a forensic sample. While not yet in common use, this has the potential to replace a variety of existing chemical and immunological tests with a single efficient, highly specific, and highly sensitive methodology. This methodology also has the capacity to expand the types of biological fluids and tissues that could be readily identified, thus enhancing the forensic biologist's tool kit to assist criminal investigations. For forensic usage, many assays have been developed to use CE analysis, rather than the more common quantitative real-time PCR (qPCR) methods. Although this reduces the ability to accurately quantitate the amount of the specific mRNA transcript present, there are benefits to CE processing. As the number of dyes available, and simultaneous detection of these, is greater in CE, large multiplexes with many mRNA targets can be created and analyzed in a single assay, whereas qPCR is limited to two or three transcripts per assay. This not only limits sample consumption but also allows greater throughput. The analysis of mRNA with CE utilizes the same fragment analysis protocols as STR typing, allowing the use of common electrophoresis and genotyping methods.

The Future of CE in Forensic Biology

As the number and types of markers analyzed grows within forensic biology, so too will the need for sensitive, reliable, and rapid detection techniques. Although CE is firmly entrenched as the method of choice for all current analyses, there are many new possibilities on the horizon. Microchip CE is certainly a leading possibility to allow rapid genotyping at crime scenes in the future. In current models of these devices, 7- to 16-cm channels are etched in glass wafers, allowing PCR products to be separated within a linear polyacrylamide matrix. Separation can be completed in only 30 min, with single-base resolution achievable from the commercial STR kits. The addition of biotin labels to PCR primers additionally allows on-chip PCR product purification, saving time and preventing ionic interference. The recent development of microfabricated devices for DNA purification, PCR amplification, and CE has enabled the production of portable microchip analyzers capable of real-time DNA analysis for use at crime scenes. However, these tools have not yet been adopted by the community, possibly due to decreased sensitivity and reliability compared to conventional analyzes.

Mass spectrometry offers an alternative to CE, separating amplicons in only seconds, with extremely reproducible sizing of STR alleles. In addition, time-of-flight MS can provide information on internal sequence variations, increasing discrimination power by 20–30%. Although undoubtedly useful, the dominance of CE within forensic biology and the high cost of MS instruments have limited the adoption of MS for genotyping purposes. However, as the use of SNPs increases in forensic biology, it is possible that high-throughput, MS-based SNP genotyping methods such as Sequenom MASSArray will become more widely used. Unlike the current SNaPshot methods where a maximum of 20–25 SNPs can be multiplexed, Sequenom can readily cater to 40–50 SNPs per assay. At present, a minimum of 5 ng of DNA is required per assay when typing for SNPs using MS-base SNP genotyping methods, which diminishes its use for many forensic type samples, although the sensitivity may increase as the technology develops. Although an extremely useful tool for efficient SNP genotyping, it cannot be used for STR genotyping and as such is not likely to be exclusively used as CE has been.

Similarly, next-generation sequencing techniques have the potential to provide sequence variant information and increased accuracy in mixture genotyping. By sequencing each molecule within a sample for each marker of interest, the relative contributions of each individual within a mixture can be determined, allowing alleles to be more accurately assigned to a single contributor. However, at present these methods do not display the level of accuracy needed for forensic usage and, additionally, require large quantities of DNA.

Conclusion

CE has become the predominant method of analysis within forensic biology, for several key reasons. The high level of resolution provided by entangled polymers provides sufficient resolution to genotype STRs and SNPs with high accuracy, while multicolor fluorescence detection permits highly multiplexed assays to be used. The introduction of high-throughput systems with multiple capillaries and rapid analysis times allows laboratories to keep pace with ever-increasing sample numbers, with automated systems decreasing analysts' input. Future developments are likely to allow greater flexibility and ease of use, as increasingly accurate portable CE systems are produced.

See also: **Biology/DNA:** Ancestry Informative Markers; Basic Principles; Forensic DNA Phenotyping: DNA Testing for Externally Visible Characteristics; Future Analytical Techniques: DNA Mass Spectrometry; Low-Template DNA Testing; MiniSTRs; Mitochondrial DNA; Mixture Interpretation (Interpretation of Mixed DNA Profiles with STRs Only); Short Tandem Repeats; Single-Nucleotide Polymorphisms; X-Chromosome Markers; **Biology/DNA/Methods/Analytical Techniques:** Capillary Electrophoresis in Forensic Genetics; **Biology/DNA/RNA:** mRNA and MicroRNA for Body Fluid Identification; **Methods:** Capillary Electrophoresis: Basic Principles; Capillary Electrophoresis in Forensic Chemistry.

Further Reading

Bandelt, H.J., Salas, A., 2012. Current next generation sequencing technology may not meet forensic standards. Forensic Science International: Genetics 6, 143–145.

Butler, J.M., 2006. Genetics and genomics of core short tandem repeat loci used in human identity testing. Journal of Forensic Sciences 51, 253–265.

Butler, J.M., 2010. Fundamentals of Forensic DNA Typing. Elsevier Academic Press, San Diego, USA.

Butler, J.M., Buel, E., Crivellente, F., McCord, B.R., 2004. Forensic DNA typing by capillary electrophoresis using the ABI Prism 310 and 3100 genetic analyzers for STR analysis. Electrophoresis 25, 1397–1412.

Frudakis, T.N., 2008. Molecular Photofitting, Predicting Ancestry and Phenotype Using DNA. Academic Press, London.

Gilder, J.R., Doom, T.E., Inman, K., Crim, M., Krane, D.E., 2007. Run-specific limits of detection and quantitation for STR-based DNA testing. Journal of Forensic Sciences 52, 97–101.

Gill, P., 2002. Role of short tandem repeat DNA in forensic casework in the UK – past, present and future perspectives. Biotechniques 32, 366–385.

Kayser, M., 2007. Uni-parental markers in human identity testing including forensic DNA analysis. Biotechniques 43, Sxv–Sxxi.

Kayser, M., de Knijff, P., 2011. Improving human forensics through advances in genetics, genomics and molecular biology. Nature Reviews Genetics 12, 179–192.

Kidd, J.R., Friedlaender, F.R., Speed, W.C., Pakstis, A.J., De La Vega, F.M., Kidd, K.K., 2011. Analyses of a set of 128 ancestry informative single-nuleotide polymorphisms in a global set of 119 population samples. Investigative Genetics 2, 1.

Lao, O., van Duijn, K., Kersbergen, P., de Knijff, P., Kayser, M., 2006. Proportioning whole-genome single-nucleotide-polymorphism diversity for the identification of geographic population structure and genetic ancestry. American Journal of Human Genetics 78, 680–690.

Liu, P., Yeung, S.H.I., Crenshaw, K.A., Crouse, C.A., Scherer, J.R., Mathies, R.A., 2008. Real-time forensic DNA analysis at a crime scene using a portable microchip analyser. Forensic Sciences International Genetics 2, 301–309.

McCord, B.R., Buel, E., 2000. Capillary electrophoresis in forensic biology. In: Siegel, J.A., Saukko, P.J., Knupfer, G.C. (Eds.), Encyclopedia of Forensic Sciences, first ed. Academic Press, London, pp. 127–135.

Moreno, L.I., McCord, B., 2007. Separation of DNA for forensic applications using capillary electrophoresis. In: Lander, J.P. (Ed.), Handbook of Capillary and Microchip Electrophoresis and Associated Microtechniques, third ed. CRC Press, Boca Raton, USA, pp. 733–756.

Oberacher, H., Parson, W., 2007. Forensic DNA fingerprinting by liquid chromatography–electrospray ionization mass spectrometry. Biotechniques 43, Svii–Sxiii.

Phillips, C., Prieto, L., Fondevila, M., 2009. Ancestry analysis in the 11-M Madrid bomb attack investigation. PLoS One 4, e6583.

Van Oorschot, R.A.H., Ballantyne, K.N., Mitchell, R.J., 2010. Forensic trace DNA: a review. Investigative Genetics 1, 14.

Walsh, S., Lindenbergh, A., Zuniga, S.B., et al., 2011. Developmental validation of the IrisPlex system: determination of blue and brown iris colour for forensic intelligence. Forensic Sciences International Genetics 5, 464–471.

Westen, A.A., Nagel, J.H., Benschop, C.C., Weiler, N.E., de Jong, B.J., Sijen, T., 2009. Higher capillary electrophoresis injection settings as an efficient approach to increase the sensitivity of STR typing. Journal of Forensic Sciences 54, 591–598.

Yeung, S.H.I., Greenspoon, S.A., McGuckian, A., et al., 2006. Rapid and high-throughput forensic short tandem repeat typing using a 96-lane micro-fabricated capillary array electrophoresis microdevice. Journal of Forensic Sciences 51, 740–747.

Relevant Websites

http://www.appliedbiosystems.com—Applied Biosystems.
http://www.cstl.nist.gov/strbase—STRBase.
http://empop.org—Mitochondrial DNA Database (EMPOP).
http://www.promega.com—Promega.
http://www.yhrd.org—Y-chromosome Database (YHRD).

Capillary Electrophoresis in Forensic Genetics

BR McCord, Florida International University, Miami, FL, USA
E Buel, State of Vermont Forensic Laboratory, Waterbury, VT, USA

Glossary

Adenylation Tendency of the polymerase to add an additional base (often adenosine) to the terminal end of the amplified fragment.

Capillary gel electrophoresis An analytical procedure in which DNA samples are separated by size based on their ability to migrate through an entangled polymer sieving matrix.

CODIS A database of DNA profiles collected from crime scenes, convicted offenders, and missing persons.

Electroosmotic flow Bulk flow created in a capillary due to the effects of wall charges in the presence of high electric fields. The effect can create reproducibility problems if the entangled polymer matrix improperly coats the capillary wall.

Microfluidic electrophoresis The performance of electrophoresis in small channels etched into plastic and glass plates.

PCR Polymerase chain reaction—an enzymatic technique used to amplify DNA fragments.

STR Short tandem repeat—a sequence of four or five DNA bases repeated for multiple times at a particular genetic locus. The number of repeated sequences can vary between individuals.

Stutter The tendency of STR amplifications to produce a smaller peak one repeat unit shorter than the main product due to slippage during amplification.

Introduction

Development of methods for amplification and detection of DNA fragments using polymerase chain reaction (PCR) has resulted in rapid and dramatic advances in forensic DNA typing. Using the PCR, it is possible to easily produce analytically significant amounts of a specified DNA product from trace quantities of DNA. In its forensic application, the PCR is used to demarcate and amplify known polymorphic sites on a distinct chromosome and produce discrete and easily characterized fragments of DNA. At present, the most widely utilized method for genetic analysis involves the simultaneous determination of a set of 13 or more short tandem repeats (STRs). Forensic STR loci consist of a repetitive motif of four to five bases, with the number of repeats varying from one individual to other.

Introduction of PCR-based forensic assays has also resulted in a need for efficient and automated procedures for analysis of the reaction products. This requirement has been the driving force behind the development of capillary electrophoresis (CE) methods for DNA analysis. In CE, DNA separations are performed in thin, 50-μm, fused silica capillaries filled with a sieving buffer. These capillaries have excellent capabilities to dissipate heat, permitting much higher electric field strengths to be used than slab gel electrophoresis. As a result, separations in capillaries are rapid and efficient. Additionally, the capillaries can be easily refilled and manipulated for efficient and automated injections. Detection occurs via fluorescence through a window etched in the capillary. Both single-capillary and capillary-array instruments are available with array systems capable of running 16 or more samples simultaneously for increased throughput.

The most common forensic markers used in forensic genetics are STRs. STRs are tandemly repeated nucleotide sequences of two to six base pairs in length. The number of repeated sequences varies between individuals and results in a high degree of length polymorphism. STRs are abundant throughout the human genome, occurring at an average rate of every 6–10 kb. Tetrameric and pentameric repeats are most commonly used in forensic analysis. These loci tend to produce less stutter than the di- or trimeric repeats, and much work has been done to validate their use in forensic casework. A core set of 13 loci has been established by the Federal Bureau of Investigation for use in the Combined DNA Index System

 http://dx.doi.org/10.1016/B978-0-12-800647-4.00009-6

Table 1 Thirteen STR loci approved for use with CODIS[a]

STR locus	*Chromosome*	*Repeat motif*	*Number of repeats*[b]
FGA	4	CTTT[c]	18–30
VWA	12	TCTA	11–22
D3S1358	3	TCTA	11–20
D21S11	21	TCTA	25–36
D8S1179	8	TATC	8–19
D7S820	7	GATA	6–15
D13S317	13	TATC	8–15
D5S818	5	AGAT	7–16
D16S539	16	GATA	5–15
CSF1PO	5	AGAT	6–15
TPOX	2	AATG	6–13
THO1	11	TCAT	3–11
Amelogenin[d]	X,Y		

[a]Data obtained from STR base, published by NIST, http://ibm4.carb.nist.gov:8800/dna/home.htm and from the Profiler and Profiler + users manuals, Perkin-Elmer, Foster City, CA.
[b]The range of repeats is approximate as new alleles are constantly being discovered.
[c]FGA as well as other loci in this list have complex patterns of repeats. The most common is given.
[d]Amelogenin is a sex-linked marker, which contains a six-base deletion in the X chromosome.

(CODIS) (**Table 1**). An additional set of STRs present on the Y chromosome has also been developed. These markers are particularly useful in resolving mixtures of male and female DNA, as these loci are not present in female cells. CE systems are ideal for separation of STRs because of the ready availability of information on size and intensity of each individual locus.

When used with STR analysis, CE systems require specialized techniques. The high ionic strength of the PCR mixture inhibits CE injection methods requiring sample dilution with formamide or deionized water, and separations must be performed using highly viscous entangled polymer buffers for optimum resolution. Detection of STRs is carried out by measuring the fluorescence of dye-labeled primers that have been incorporated into each DNA strand during the amplification process. A single laser is used to detect as many as five different dye labels. Lastly, the serial nature of CE separations requires internal and external standardization to achieve highly precise measurements. CE separations are best described by dividing the process into three main steps: separation, injection, and detection.

Theory of CE

Separation

DNA fragments are difficult to separate under normal CE conditions due to their virtually constant charge-to-mass ratio. Therefore, analyses are performed using a replaceable sieving matrix, consisting of a water-soluble polymer dissolved in a suitable buffer. Such solutions are referred to as entangled polymer buffers, and the DNA sieved is based on its ability to fit within pores created within the polymer matrix. The fact that these polymer matrices are not rigid makes them different from rigid agarose or polyacrylamide gels traditionally used in DNA analysis. The advantage of using an entangled polymer buffer is that fresh polymer solution can be pumped into the capillary at the conclusion of each analysis, cleaning the capillary and limiting problems with carryover. Experiments carried out using a variety of entangled polymer buffers have shown that with careful optimization of molecular weight and concentration, high-resolution DNA separations can be produced.

Several different mechanisms have been postulated to describe the separation of DNA in physical gels. These include transient entanglement coupling, Ogston sieving, and reptation. At low concentrations of polymer, separation takes place by means of a frictional interaction between the DNA and the polymer strands. This mechanism is known as transient entanglement coupling. At higher concentrations of polymer, individual polymer molecule strands begin to interact, producing a mesh. The polymer concentration at which this occurs is known as the entanglement threshold. Above the entanglement threshold, DNA fragments separated by sieving through transient pores created in the polymer mesh (**Figure 1**). Fragments, which are larger than the average pore size, reptate or move in a snake-like manner through the mesh. The key to producing an acceptable separation is to specify a polymer concentration at which the size of these virtual pores approximates the radius of gyration of the DNA fragment (average size of a DNA fragment in solution).

There are a number of key parameters involved in the development of a reliable separation of DNA using entangled polymers. In addition to concentration, the polymer length

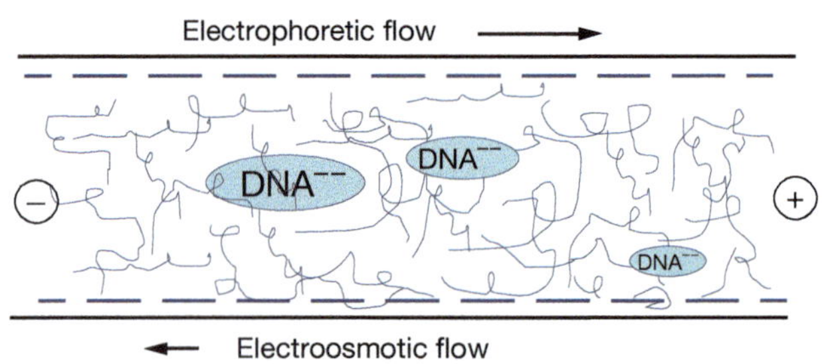

Figure 1 DNA is sieved through transient pores created in the polymer mesh. Smaller fragments are less impeded by the mesh and elute first. Movement of DNA strands occurs due to counteracting forces. The electric field results in migration of negatively charged DNA, whereas electroosmotic forces created by wall potentials produce a bulk flow in the opposite direction. Polymers like POP_4 (4% polydimethylacrylamide) reduce electroosmosis by coating capillary walls producing a more reproducible separation.

must be kept to a minimum to reduce viscosity and permit refilling of the capillary. Other important characteristics of entangled polymers include the relative stiffness and polydispersity of the polymer and its ability to coat the capillary walls. Uncoated silica capillaries have significant wall charge at the pH used to separate DNA. These charges can induce a bulk flow in the capillary walls when the electric fields are high. This effect is known as the electroosmotic flow (EOF) and can result in irreproducible changes in DNA migration from run to run. EOF is minimized by using polymers such as polydimethyl acrylamide (POP), which coat capillary walls and neutralize wall charge effects. Furthermore, internal dye-labeled ladder standards are added to help compensate for any mobility shifts during the run.

Another important issue in DNA separation is the flexibility of the molecule, which can be characterized by a parameter known as the persistence length. Single-stranded DNA (ssDNA) is far more flexible (shorter persistence length) and produces superior separations when compared to double-stranded DNA (dsDNA), which is quite stiff and interacts poorly with the polymer matrix. As a result, it is very important to denature the DNA and maintain it in its single-stranded state throughout the separation. To do this, the DNA is denatured in formamide before injection, and separations are carried out at elevated temperatures and with high concentrations of denaturants, such as urea and pyrrolidinone, to maintain this denatured state. Generally speaking, dsDNA migrates faster and at lower resolution in standard CE systems. Its appearance can sometimes be observed in improperly denatured samples.

Injection and Sample Preparation

In order to inject a DNA sample, each individual capillary is dipped into a sample vial containing a mixture of PCR products and formamide. A positive voltage is then applied to the capillary to move the negatively charged DNA into the capillary orifice. This type of injection is known as an electrokinetic injection, and typically voltages of 3–15 kV are applied over a period of 3–10 s depending on type of instrument and number of capillaries used. The quantity of DNA onto the capillary by this technique can be described by the following formula:

$$Q_{\mathrm{DNA}} = \pi r^2 [\mathrm{DNA}] Et(\mu_{\mathrm{ep}} + \mu_{\mathrm{eor}})$$

where E is the field strength, t is the time, r is the capillary radius, μ_{ep} is the electrophoretic flow, and μ_{eof} is the EOF. From this equation, it is easy to see that longer injections at higher field strengths will inject larger quantities of DNA. However, it should be noted that other ions present in the sample matrix will compete with DNA for injection. Thus, the quantity of DNA injected is also a function of the ionic strength of the solution, as well as the mobility of other negative ions that might be injected instead of DNA. In addition, longer injections can induce band broadening with an overall loss of resolution.

In general, electrokinetic injections produce narrow injection zones but are highly sensitive to the sample matrix. The injection of PCR products can produce such problems because of the high ionic strength of the sample matrix (>50 mM Cl^-). To overcome this problem, PCR samples are typically diluted in deionized formamide. This process serves two purposes—it reduces ionic strength and dentures the DNA, permitting efficient and selective injections.

This dilution step increases the quantity of DNA injected through a process known as stacking. Also called field amplified injection, stacking occurs when the ionic strength of the sample zone is lower than that of the buffer. Since the current through the system is constant, the lack of charge carriers in the sample zone produces a strong electric field that ends abruptly at the interface between the low-ionic strength sample zone and the higher-ionic strength buffer in the capillary (**Figure 2**). DNA molecules stack and focus at this interface. Stacking allows a large sample zone to be loaded onto the capillary with a minimum of band broadening, increasing both the sensitivity and the efficiency of the injection.

Sample Injection

Interestingly, it is possible to further enhance DNA signal intensity by dialyzing the PCR product with spin filtration- or float membrane-based methods. These techniques are known as post-PCR purification methods and are utilized to accentuate the stacking process and can greatly improve sensitivity. Laboratories performing such processes must carefully validate these procedures as they can produce variable results when

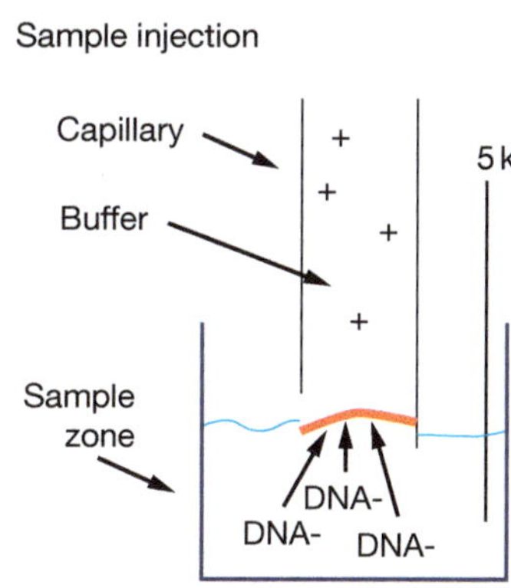

Figure 2 DNA is injected using an applied voltage. Because electric field is inversely proportional to ionic strength, DNA and other negatively charged ions move rapidly to the interface between the low conductivity sample zone and buffer. This process is known as stacking.

used with low levels of DNA template. In such cases, replicate analysis and careful attention to contamination controls are necessary.

Detection and Data Analysis

Fluorescence detection of DNA by CE methods is achieved by derivatizing the DNA using dyes to produce fluorescent adducts. The dye molecules are covalently bound to the DNA fragments during the PCR process. To do this, a dye molecule is added to the 5′ end of one member of each primer pair. Upon completion of the PCR, the targeted DNA molecules are labeled with a fluorophore. By using a variety of different dyes in a single multiplexed reaction, individual loci can be isolated, amplified, and labeled with specific dyes. The dyes used in these reactions absorb at similar wavelengths but emit at different wavelengths. Thus, a single laser can be used to excite four or more dyes.

A multichannel analyzer is then used to identify the specific PCR product by means of the wavelength of emission of the bound dye and the length of the fragment. To minimize interference with other dye-labeled products, the internal sizing standard is labeled with a different fluorescence dye than that of the product. Modern CE systems with five dye capability permit detection of labeled STRs in four fluorescent channels, while the fifth channel is reserved for the internal standard. For such systems, specific algorithms have been developed to deconvolute the fluorescence signals and avoid interference from overlapping dyes.

Sample Preparation

Purified template DNA can be amplified to yield products from a single STR locus, or multiple primers can be added to simultaneously amplify multiple STR loci. PCR cocktails are commercially available for multiplex PCRs that include primers for as many as 15 different loci. The products of these reactions are labeled and simultaneously amplified with as many as four different fluorescent dyes. The PCR products are then prepared for CE injection by mixing approximately 1 μl of PCR product with 24 μl of deionized formamide. In addition, a red or orange dye-labeled internal standard is used to permit allele sizing.

Care must be taken when using formamide as an injection solvent because the products of its decomposition are ionic and can inhibit the injection process. For this reason, the conductivity of the formamide should be tested, and control samples should be run before routine analysis. To yield denatured fragments ready for electrophoresis, the prepared sample solution is typically heated at 95°C and then snap cooled in an ice bath. Because formamide is such a strong denaturant and can denature properly prepared DNA samples without heating, this heating and cooling step is skipped in many laboratories. Deionized water can be substituted for formamide, but in this case, snap cooling is absolutely necessary as long-term DNA stability is compromised in deionized water.

Because the quantity of DNA injected is dependent on the ionic strength of the sample solution, it is also possible to greatly enhance DNA injection using what are known as post-PCR cleanup procedures. Such procedures should be used with caution as low conductance solutions can be prone to carryover effects and may also result in detection of stochastic amplification. Proper validation of such procedures is important, and consistency can be maintained through good quantification controls and regulation of sample ionic strength.

Analytical Separation

Electrokinetic injection is routinely employed to apply samples onto the capillary column. Injection time may be varied within certain ranges to affect the amount of sample applied to the column without adversely affecting resolution. Varying the injection time from 1 to 10 s has been shown to increase sample input while maintaining the resolution of the system. A particular advantage of CE is the ability to quickly reanalyze more dilute samples by simply increasing the injection time. As a result, many laboratories will validate two different injection times, one shorter and the other longer.

The separation media employed for analysis include poly-dimethyl acrylamide, urea, pyrrolidine, and EDTA in a TAPS buffer at pH 8.0. The polymer provides the separation, the TAPS buffer maintains the ionic strength and pH, the urea and pyrrolidine keep the DNA denatured, and the EDTA sequesters metals that can affect DNA resolution. Most forensic laboratories have opted to purchase prepared polymer solutions for reasons of quality control and simplicity of use. Varying the polymer concentration, through the purchase of the appropriate separation media or by preparation, allows the user to fine-tune resolution.

The STRs under current use contain alleles that generally differ by two, four, or five base repeat units, however, variants that contain deletions of a single base can occur in these systems. As a result, it is important to design separation systems that can also resolve variant alleles. In situations where increased resolution of alleles is necessary, column length or polymer concentration can be increased. However, both of these procedures can increase migration times, a concern for laboratories with large numbers of samples. Monitoring the resolution of a system allows the analyst to recognize degradation in column performance or inappropriate sample preparation. As the column ages through continued use or inadequate maintenance, sample resolution may deteriorate. Samples prepared in formamide that has not been sufficiently deionized will also show poor resolution.

Resolution between two peaks can be calculated using the standard equation:

$$R = \frac{2(t_2 - t_1)}{w_1 + w_2}$$

where t is the migration time of the peak and w is the peak width. Since the peak at baseline is difficult to determine, the shape of the CE peak can be assumed to be Gaussian with a width of 4σ, and the previous equation can be converted to:

$$R = \frac{1.18(t_2 - t_1)}{w_{h1} + w_{h2}}$$

where w_h is the peak width at half height. System resolution can also be quickly evaluated using a mixture containing STR alleles that vary by one base. The STR system THO 1 has a variant (allele 9.3) that is one base less than expected. This allele can be mixed in equal proportions with the nonvariant allele 10. After this mixture is run on the capillary, the evaluation of the relative height of the peaks versus the valley point between them yields a ratio that can be monitored to obtain the relative resolution of the system.

Genotyping

Multiple STR loci are determined during a single analysis by adjusting the fragment length of each PCR product and by labeling sets of different primers with dyes that fluoresce at differing wavelengths. Primers are carefully designed to produce DNA with allele sizes that do not overlap. This permits the analysis of three to four STR loci, which are labeled with the same color. **Figure 3** illustrates this procedure by showing the result of the amplification of a male DNA sample using the Profiler Plus STR kit (Life Technologies™). Each lane in the electropherogram consists of three STR loci labeled with a different dye. In addition, a sex marker, amelogenin, is shown in the green lane. Numbers under the individual peaks indicate the allele number and its relative intensity. STR loci are identified by their size and their dye label. The task of separating and identifying the alleles is performed using CE instruments equipped with detector arrays capable of analyzing all dyes simultaneously.

The peaks resulting from this analysis can be genotyped through the use of software supplied by the instrument manufacturer. Typically, electrophoresis is conducted by combining amplified products with an internal size standard

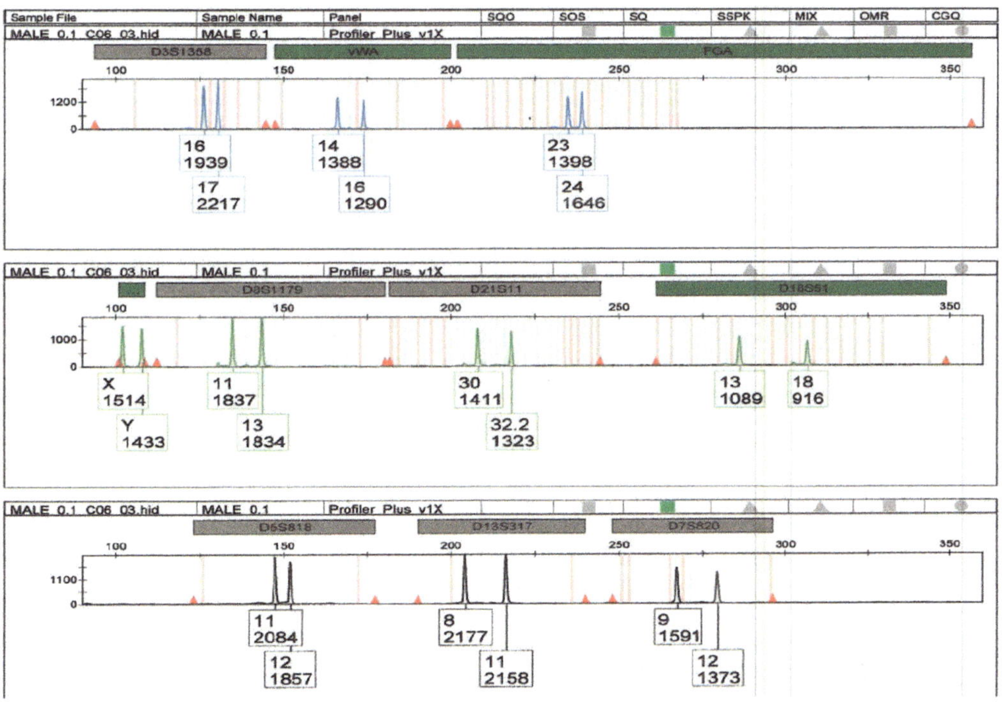

Figure 3 An analysis of a male sample amplified using the Profiler plus multiplex amplification kit. The results have been split into three panels to aid in analysis. Each gray panel indicates a different STR locus and is identified above the panel. The dark gray zones within the lighter gray indicate potential locations of alleles for each locus. A sex typing locus (amelogenin) produces a six-base deletion in the X chromosome.

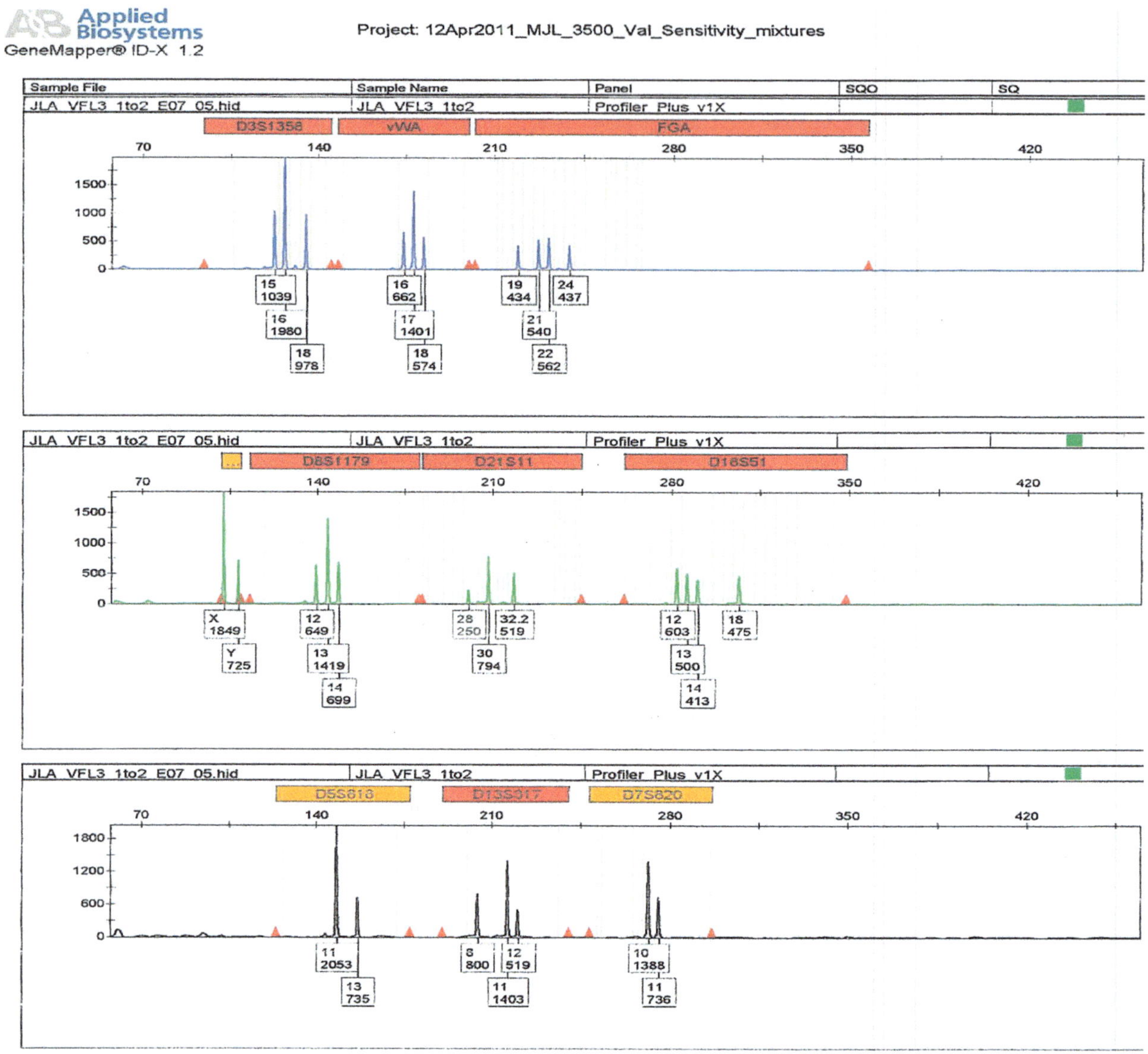

Figure 4 The analysis of a 1:1 mixture of male and female DNA using the Profiler plus STR kit. Peak ratios at each locus vary depending on the number of shared alleles.

that is labeled with a fluorescent dye that is different from those used to tag the STR loci.

During each analysis a sizing ladder (not shown in **Figure 3**) is added to provide an internal reference to standardize the electrophoretic run and permit the calculation of the base sizes of the detected peaks. The calculated sizes can be compared to those sizes obtained from a previously run allelic ladder, a control sample containing a mixture of all possible alleles. Once allele sizes are determined, a table is prepared of all detected alleles at each locus in a sample. If the sample is from a single source, the frequency of the genotype in a given population can then be calculated by multiplying together the component frequencies calculated for each locus. The resultant frequencies can be quite small. For example, the power of discrimination for the Profiler Plus STR kit is approximately 1 in 10^{11}.

Mixture Analysis

Mixtures (samples that contain DNA from more than one individual) must be anticipated in the analysis of forensic specimens. These specimens may be a composite of body fluids from different individuals and will produce complex DNA profiles. To complicate the analysis of mixtures, STR patterns from one individual may contain imbalanced peaks and PCR artifacts known as stutter. Stutter peaks are amplified products resulting from the "slippage" of DNA polymerase during amplification where the enzyme and growing DNA chain are out of alignment with the target DNA. The resulting fragment is usually four bases less than the true allelic peak, although weaker signals consisting of sets of peaks four bases apart may also be seen. Some loci have yielded stutter peaks of >10% of the height of the true peak. In the interpretation of mixtures, the possibility of stutter peaks must be taken into account, and interpretations should be adjusted based on the amount of stutter observed at a particular locus. Typically, a mixture is suspected when peak heights rise above typical stutter values for a particular locus. Another problem in the interpretation of mixtures is that peaks obtained from a heterozygous locus may vary by as much as 30%. Deviations of this size, although uncommon, must be considered in the evaluation of mixtures. Differences in the expected peak ratio in a sample that presents a heterozygous pattern can indicate a mixed sample whose alleles have coelectrophoresed. Fortunately, when multiple allelic systems are evaluated, other loci may show three or four peaks, establishing the specimen as a mixture, and can be used to determine if the altered ratio could be due to an overlapping allele. **Figure 4** illustrates the analysis of a sample of mixed DNA.

The balance observed between loci is an additional consideration in the assessment of mixtures. Although commercially available STR amplification kits attempt to achieve a balance across all loci, the efficiency of amplification of larger loci can decrease, particularly in situations where degraded DNA is present. Under such circumstances, shorter PCR products will predominate as few of the longer fragments of template have survived. In some situations, minor peaks can disappear later in the electropherogram because of poor amplification or degradation.

Occasionally, nonallelic peaks also cause problems in the interpretation of a mixed sample. These peaks may be the result of unbound dye, electrical interference, or other sample artifacts. There are also PCR artifacts such as adenylation, which produce peaks one base less than the true allelic peak. In most STR systems, the amplification process promotes the non-template addition of a nucleotide (usually an A) to the end of the PCR product. This yields an amplicon that has been increased in size by one base. Under some conditions, such as excessive amount of template DNA or Taq inhibitors, the complete conversion of all the products to the $n + 1$ state may not occur. Often this condition can be rectified by increasing the extension time for the amplification. Finally, mutations or rare genetic events may give rise to unusual profiles that can be mistaken as a mixture. In addition, mutations at primer sites may lead to genotyping variations at particular loci, due to differences in the location of primer annealing sites used by various manufacturers of STR amplification kits.

Analysis of Mitochondrial DNA

There are circumstances in forensic analysis in which there is insufficient nuclear DNA to perform PCR. These cases involve samples such as shed hairs or those that are highly degraded. In these circumstances, there may still be enough mitochondrial DNA (mtDNA) to permit PCR amplification. The DNA present in mitochondria is approximately 16,000 bases long and contains a section known as the control region, which contains a number of polymorphic sites that are usually point mutations. In this procedure, certain hypervariable segments of the control region are PCR amplified and sequenced. These sequences are then compared to a known standard in order to identify polymorphic sites. CE is used in this process both to determine if the amplified product is present in sufficient quantity and in the subsequent sequencing. The quantification step is carried out before the sequencing step. A small portion of the amplified product is analyzed in its native state using a short 27-cm capillary at 15,000 V or a short channel etched in a microfluidic CE chip. In the analysis, an intercalating dye is added to the amplified sample to provide a fluorescent product. Total analysis time is below 4 min. The peak intensity of the amplified DNA is compared to an internal standard to determine the quantity of amplified material.

Figure 5 illustrates this separation. The electropherogram is checked to determine if any contaminants, such as primers or extraneous amplified product, are present in the sample. These materials can interfere with the sequencing reactions and reduce the quality of the result. The results of this analysis are used to adjust the amount of template used for the sequencing reaction. The products are then analyzed on CE-based sequencers using the same separation principles detailed above.

Future Applications

Presently, a number of researchers are developing smaller, more compact systems based on microchip technology. By using photolithography, multiple channels can be etched into silicon wafers and the entire capillary array can be placed on a glass or plastic chip. Tightly focused sample injections on a microchip permit fast electrophoretic separations using relatively short channels. A further advantage of this technique is that sample preparation and detection apparatus can be built into the chip design. Thus, the entire process from DNA extraction to PCR to separation to detection can be integrated into a single device. **Figure 6** shows an example of an integrated microfluidic device in which laboratory procedures such as extraction, amplification, separation, and detection are all combined.

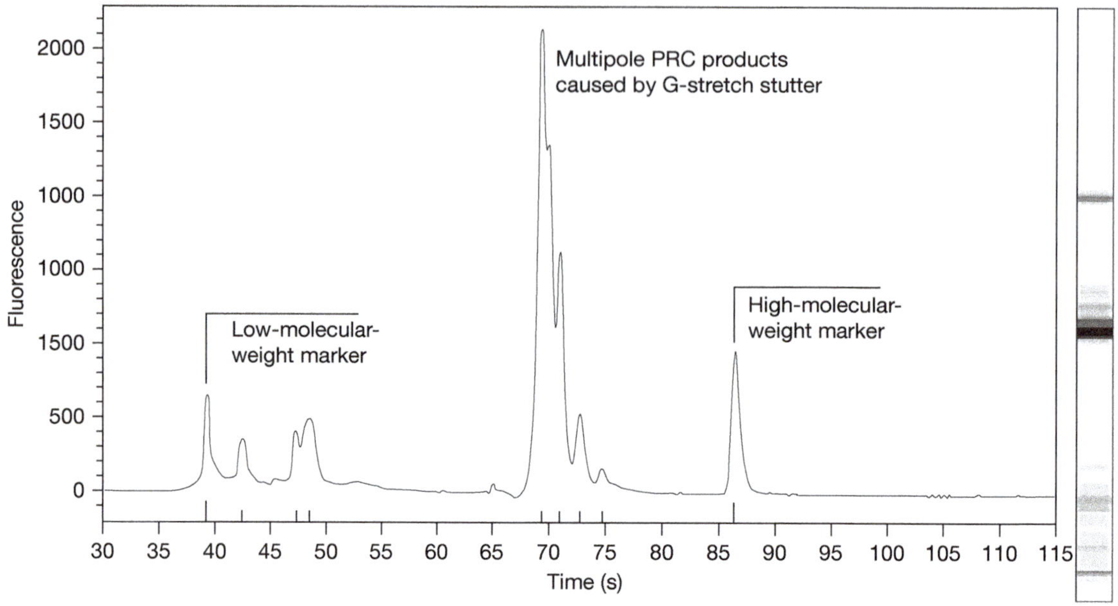

Figure 5 The analysis and quantitation of mitochondrial DNA in under 100 s using an Agilent 2100 Bioanalyzer. The quantity of DNA produced is determined with reference to the internal standard. The presence of additional peaks around the main peak indicates the presence of multiple PCR products caused by G stretch stutter and indicates reamplification of this particular sample may be necessary to produce an accurate sequence. Copyright by Agilent Technologies—Reproduced with Permission.

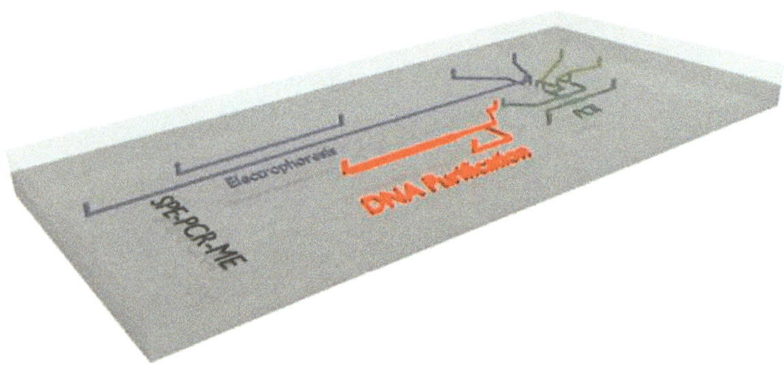

Figure 6 Microfluidic DNA analyzer: This system, currently under development by James Landers at the University of Virginia, combines DNA extraction, PCR amplification, STR separation, and fluorescent detection in a single integrated device.

Conclusions

CE is a technique that provides the DNA analyst with much flexibility. CE systems utilize replaceable physical gels, which are pumped into the capillary at the beginning of each analysis. DNA quantitation, genotyping, and sequencing are all possible using this technique. Sample injection, separation, and analysis are easily automated. Multichannel fluorescence detection permits multiplex PCRs to be simultaneously analyzed, greatly conserving precious forensic samples. Capillary array systems further increase throughput. The resulting data can be analyzed to detect the presence of mixtures, processed, and stored in a database known as CODIS. Present systems under development will utilize microfluidic chips in which integration of the entire process of DNA analysis from extraction to analysis is possible.

See also: **Biology/DNA:** DNA Databases; DNA Extraction and Quantification; Introduction to Nonhuman DNA Typing; Low-Template DNA Testing; MiniSTRs; Mitochondrial DNA; Mixture Interpretation (Interpretation of Mixed DNA Profiles with STRs Only); Short Tandem Repeats; Single-Nucleotide Polymorphisms; **Biology/DNA/Botany:** Cannabis DNA Typing Methods; **Biology/DNA/Wildlife:** DNA and Endangered Species; **Methods:** Capillary Electrophoresis: Basic Principles; Capillary Electrophoresis in Forensic Biology; Capillary Electrophoresis in Forensic Chemistry; Field-Deployable Devices.

Further Reading

Buel, E., Schwartz, M.B., LaFountain, M.J., 1998. Capillary electrophoresis STR analysis: comparison to gel-based systems. Journal of Forensic Science 43, 164–170.

Butler, J., Buel, E., Crivelente, F., McCord, B., 2004. Forensic DNA typing by capillary electrophoresis. Electrophoresis 25 (10–11), 1397–1412.

Easley, C.J., Karlinsey, J.M., Bienvenue, J.M., et al., 2006. Totally-integrated genetic analysis in an electrophoretic microchip with sample in-answer out capability. Proceedings of the National Academy of Science 103 (51), 19272–19277.

Heller, C. (Ed.), 1997. Analysis of Nucleic Acids by Capillary Electrophoresis. Friede Vieweg, Wiesbaden.

Jensen, M., 2004. Use of the Agilent 2100 Bioanalyzer and the DNA 500 Labchip in the Analysis of PCR Amplified Mitochondrial DNA. Application Note. http://www.chem.agilent.com/Library/applications/5989-0985EN.pdf.

Lazaruk, K., Walsh, P.S., Oaks, F., et al., 1998. Genotyping of forensic short tandem repeat (STR) systems based on sizing precision in a capillary electrophoresis instrument. Electrophoresis 19, 86–93.

Moreno, L., McCord, B., 2008. Separation of DNA for forensic applications. In: Landers, J. (Ed.), Handbook of Capillary Electrophoresis. CRC Press, Boca Raton, FL, pp. 761–784.

Rodriguez, I., Lesaicherre, M., Tie, Y., et al., 2003. Practical integration of polymerase chain reaction amplification and electrophoretic analysis in microfluidic devices for genetic analysis. Electrophoresis 24, 172–178.

Wallin, J.M., Buoncristiani, M.R., Lazaruk, K., Fildes, N., Holt, C.L., Walsh, P.S., 1998. TWGDAM validation of the AmpFlSTR blue PCR amplification kit for forensic casework analysis. Journal of Forensic Science 43, 854–870.

Woolley, A.T., Hadley, D., Landre, P., deMello, A.J., Mathies, R.A., Northrup, M.A., 1996. Functional integration of PCR amplification and capillary electrophoresis in a microfabricated DNA analysis device. Analytical Chemistry 68, 4081–4086.

Chromatography: Basic Principles

CE Lenehan, Flinders University, Adelaide, SA, Australia

Abbreviations

GC Gas chromatography
HPLC High-performance liquid chromatography
SEC Size-exclusion chromatography
TLC Thin-layer chromatography

Glossary

Analytes The analytes are the substances of interest that are being separated from the sample matrix by chromatography.
Chromatogram A chromatogram is a plot showing detector signal versus time; peaks are usually observed on the chromatogram when an analyte is emerging from the column.
Chromatograph A chromatograph is the instrument used to perform a chromatographic separation.
Eluate The eluate is the mobile phase leaving the column; it is usually monitored by some form of detection system.
Eluent The eluent is the solvent carrying the analyte through the stationary phase.

Introduction

In the majority of cases, samples encountered in the forensic science laboratory comprise a complex mixture of substances. Often, the forensic scientist is interested in looking at one or a number of these components (e.g., the level of a drug in a blood sample); however, there are very few analytical methods that are selective for a single chemical species. In reality, most compounds need to be relatively pure in order to identify them. Consequently, the analyte of interest must be separated from other compounds in the sample matrix in order to allow its identification and quantification. Chromatography is a powerful and versatile technique that is routinely used by forensic scientists for this purpose.

All chromatographic separations are based on the distribution of the sample components between two phases: the stationary phase and the mobile phase. The sample is dissolved in the mobile phase (which may be a liquid, solid, or supercritical fluid) and forced through an immiscible stationary phase. The stationary phase is generally solid particles or a viscous liquid fixed to the surface of a column or solid particles. On traveling through the stationary phase, molecules within the sample distribute themselves differently between the two phases. Molecules with a strong affinity for the stationary phase move slowly through the system. Conversely, molecules with a weak affinity for the stationary phase migrate very quickly through the system. This difference in migration rates allows the components to separate into discrete bands that can then be analyzed. A generalized schematic diagram showing a chromatographic separation is shown in **Figure 1**.

Classification of Chromatographic Techniques

There are many different ways in which chromatographic separations can be performed. Consequently, chromatographic methods are often classified into subcategories. First, the physical setup of the stationary phase can be either planar or column based. In planar chromatography, the stationary phase is fixed onto a flat surface. Thin-layer chromatography is a good example of planar chromatography. Alternatively, column chromatography uses a column to house the stationary phase. Most chromatographic separations used in the forensic

 http://dx.doi.org/10.1016/B978-0-12-800647-4.00010-2

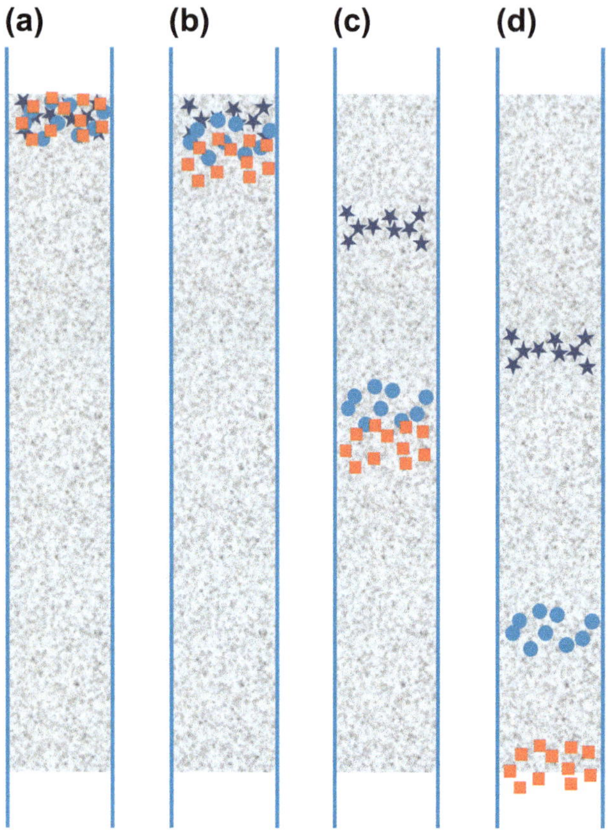

Figure 1 A diagram showing the principle of chromatographic separations. (a) A small volume of sample is placed at the top of the column that is filled with stationary phase and solvent. (b–d) Mobile phase is added to the top and allowed to slowly elute through the column, individual molecules interact with the stationary phase to different degrees, and thus take differing times to move through the column.

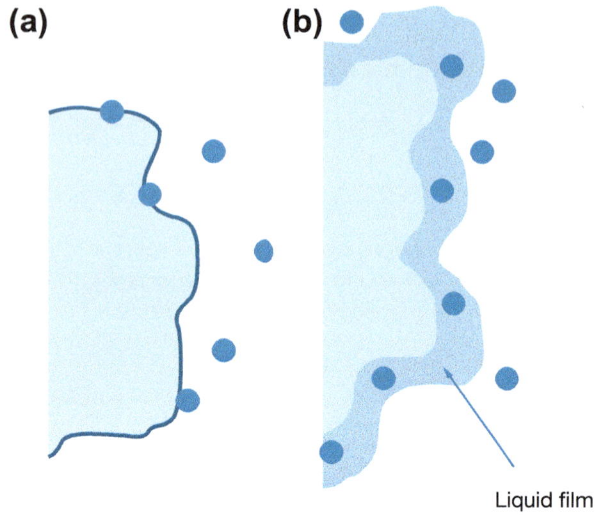

Figure 2 Schematic diagram showing the interaction of analyte molecules with the stationary phase (shown as a cross-section). (a) An adsorption mechanism—analyte molecules are adsorbed directly to the stationary-phase surface. (b) A partition mechanism—analyte molecules are dissolved in a viscous liquid stationary phase bonded to the surface of a particle.

laboratory use some form of column chromatography. Second, the chromatographic technique is often classified according to the physical state of mobile phase (gas, liquid, or supercritical fluid) employed as the eluent. Gas chromatography (GC) and high-performance liquid chromatography (HPLC) are commonly employed in the forensic laboratory, whereas supercritical fluid chromatography is less commonly found. In recent times, ultra-high-performance liquid chromatography (UHPLC) has emerged as a more powerful separation technique than HPLC, offering reduced run times and increased separation power. UHPLC is increasingly being used in the forensic context.

Chromatographic techniques can be further subclassified upon the basis of the separation mechanism involved: adsorption, partition, ion exchange, size exclusion, and affinity. Liquid chromatography (LC) often employs separations based on an adsorption mechanism. In this case, molecules or ions adhere (adsorb) to the surface of the stationary phase (the adsorbent) via weak intermolecular forces. In general, the "like dissolves like" principle can be applied. A nonpolar molecule will adsorb to a nonpolar stationary phase but will have little affinity for a polar stationary phase. Similarly, a polar molecule will adsorb to a polar surface but will be only weakly attracted to a nonpolar surface. Alternatively, most GC separations are based on a partition mechanism, whereby the molecules partition between two immiscible fluid phases. In GC, the stationary phase is most commonly a viscous liquid bonded to the interior of an open tubular column. The molecules being separated move in and out of this liquid in a mechanism analogous to a liquid–liquid extraction. A general schematic diagram showing adsorption and partition mechanisms is shown in **Figure 2**.

Ion-exchange chromatography (often referred to as ion chromatography) allows the separation of ionic molecules based on their charge. The surface of the stationary phase has ionic functional groups that bind to analyte molecules based on coulombic (ionic) interactions. This type of chromatography is generally further subdivided into two groups: cation exchange and anion exchange. Cation exchange chromatography retains cations due to the negatively charged functional groups on the surface of the stationary phase. These can then be eluted from the stationary phase by introducing a competing cation such as H^+ to force the molecules back off the surface and into the mobile phase (thus exchanging places at the surface). Anion exchange chromatography retains anions as a result of positively charged functional groups on the stationary-phase surface. In this case, the ions are eluted from the column by introducing a competing anion into the mobile phase, for example, hydroxide, which will exchange places with the bound anion. Generalized reaction schemes for the separation of ions by cation and anion exchange are shown below. In general, the higher the charge of the ion the greater the affinity for the charged stationary phase, and the more slowly it will move through the system.

$$R^+ - X^- + Y^+ - A^- \underset{\text{Anion-exchange mechanism}}{\rightleftharpoons} R^+ - A^- + Y^+ - X^-$$

$$R^- - Z^- + B^- - C^+ \underset{\text{Cation-exchange mechanism}}{\rightleftharpoons} R - C^+ + B^- - Z^+$$

Size-exclusion chromatography is also known as gel permeation chromatography. As the name indicates, in this form of chromatography, molecules are separated based on their molecular size. Molecules move through a porous stationary phase. Small molecules can move into the pores and become trapped, effectively removed from the bulk flow of the mobile phase. Larger molecules are unable to move into the pores, are washed around the stationary phase, and elute quickly. The average residence time in the pores depends on the pore size of the stationary phase and the effective size of the analyte molecules (**Figure 3**).

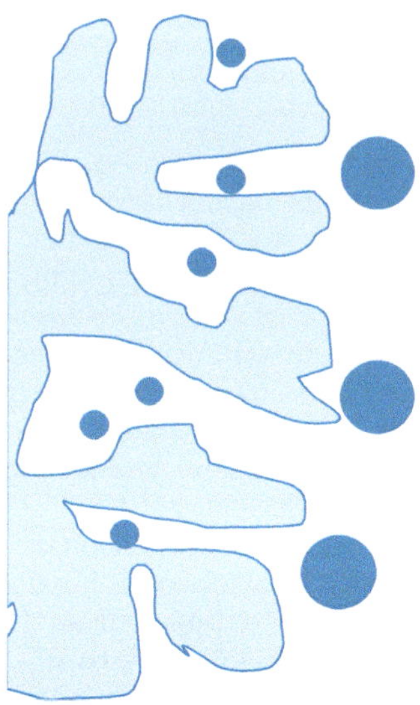

Figure 3 Schematic diagram showing the interaction of analyte molecules with a porous stationary phase. As can be seen, small molecules move into the pores and are retained, whereas larger molecules are washed through.

LC methods are often subdivided into two further categories, those of normal-phase and reversed-phase chromatography. In normal-phase LC, the stationary phase is generally a polar solid such as silica or alumina, and the mobile phase is nonpolar. Historically, LC separations were generally performed using "normal-phase" strategies. In the 1970s, nonpolar stationary phases were introduced for use with polar mobile phases such as water and methanol. These were termed reversed-phase systems. Reversed-phase systems based on an octadecyl carbon chain (C18) bonded to the surface of the stationary phase are the most commonly employed LC strategy in forensic laboratories.

As stated earlier, chromatographic separations are generally performed in some type of column setup. Column chromatography can be further subdivided into two types based on the type of column used: packed column chromatography and open tubular capillary column chromatography. Packed columns are filled with small particles that either serve as the stationary phase (adsorption chromatography) or serve as the support for a nonvolatile liquid coating that acts as the stationary phase (partition chromatography). A variety of stationary phases is available. Packed columns are commonly used in LC. The use of packed columns in GC is relatively rare; however, they can be employed when increased sample capacity is required. Open tubular capillary chromatography is generally employed in GC and less commonly in LC. There are three types of open tubular columns. In wall-coated open tubular columns, the capillary wall serves as a support for a liquid film coating, which acts as the stationary phase (partition chromatography). Support-coated open tubular columns contain solid microparticles that are coated with stationary phase fixed to the walls of the capillary (partition chromatograph). Finally, adsorption chromatography can be achieved using porous-layer open tubular columns, which have solid microparticles attached to the wall.

Chromatographic Distribution Equilibria

The effectiveness of a chromatographic separation depends in part on the distribution of the sample components between the stationary phase and the mobile phase. This distribution equilibria can generally be described as the transfer of the analyte (S) between the two phases. Therefore, we can write,

$$S_{(\text{mobile})} \rightleftharpoons S_{(\text{stationary})}$$

As with all equilibrium reactions, this reaction can be described by an equilibrium constant. In this case, it is known as the distribution constant (K_C):

$$K_C = \frac{[S]_{\text{stationary}}}{[S]_{\text{mobile}}}$$

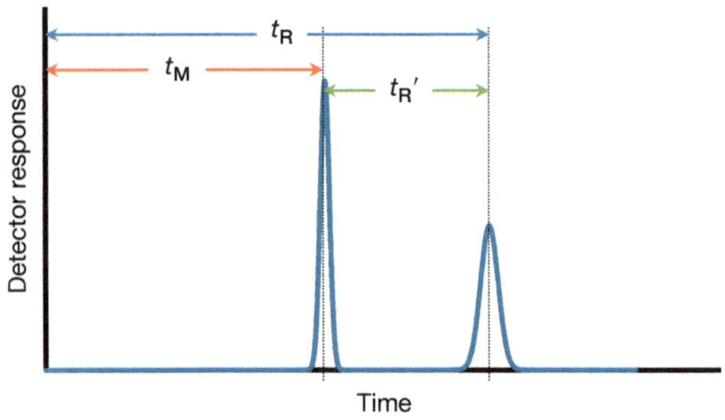

Figure 4 Example chromatogram showing the separation of two compounds. The first compound is unretained by the column and elutes at t_M; the second compound is retained from the column eluting later at t_R.

The magnitude of the distribution constant is governed by the temperature, the type of compound, as well as the chemical composition of the stationary and mobile phases. Should these be kept constant, the separation will be able to be reliably reproduced. Analytes with a large K_C will be more strongly retained by the stationary phase and thus take longer to elute from the column. If, under certain conditions, two analytes had the same K_C, they would not be separable, and a different set of chromatographic conditions would need to be used. By appropriate choice of the stationary- and mobile-phase compositions, the distribution constants could be adjusted to allow their separation. In an ideal case, the K_C values for each analyte would be considerably different and all compounds within the mixture would be well separated.

Although the distribution constant is fundamental to chromatographic separations, it is not readily measured. Alternatively, analytes are usually monitored (using some type of detector) as they are eluted from a chromatography column. The result is a plot showing detector signal versus time, known as a chromatogram. **Figure 4** shows a typical chromatogram showing the chromatographic separation of two compounds. In this case, an unretained compound elutes first, followed by a compound that has been retained by the column.

As illustrated in **Figure 4**, the retention time (t_R) for each analyte is the time taken from injection of the sample mixture onto the column until the component reaches the detector. In many cases, a sample may contain species that are not retained by the stationary phase. These unretained compounds travel through the stationary phase in the minimum time possible. The time taken for an unretained peak to reach the detector is known as the void time (t_M). The void time provides a measure of the amount of time an analyte will spend moving in the mobile phase. The adjusted retention time is a measure of the time the analyte spends in/on the stationary phase. This can be measured by subtracting the void time (t_M) from the observed (t_R) as shown below:

$$t'_R = t_R - t_M$$

The retention factor, k, is the ratio of the adjusted retention time (t'_R) to the void time (t_M) and is often used to compare the migration rates of analytes. That is because, for a fixed set of chromatographic conditions (stationary phase, mobile phase, and analyte), the value for k will be the same, regardless of flow rate:

$$k = \frac{t'_R}{t_M}$$

The retention factor can be related to the distribution coefficient (K_C) as it is effectively a measure of the time the analyte spends in each phase:

$$k = \frac{t'_R}{t_M} = \frac{\text{time spent in stationary phase}}{\text{time spent in mobile phase}} = \frac{[S]_{\text{stationary}}}{[S]_{\text{mobile}}}$$

The separation factor, α, is a measure of the relative retention of two components and can be defined as the ratio of their two adjusted retention times:

$$\alpha = \frac{t'_{R_2}}{t'_{R_1}}$$

where $t'_{R2} > t'_{R1}$. Accordingly, the value for α is always >1. In general, the greater the relative retention, the greater the separation between the components. Similarly to k, α is proportional to the ratio of the two analytes' distribution coefficients.

Band Broadening in Chromatography

The efficiency of a chromatographic separation depends on two factors: (1) the difference in distribution coefficients as described earlier and (2) the broadness of the band of eluting analyte molecules. Band broadening results as analyte molecules traveling through the stationary phase tend to diffuse into a Gaussian-shaped band. Band broadening occurs to some extent in all chromatographic systems. In general, the wider the bands, the poorer the separation. Additionally, the longer the molecule spends on the stationary phase, the broader the band becomes. This results in a broader peak on the chromatogram, and thus poorer separation efficiency.

The resolution, R_s, tells us how far apart two analyte peaks are relative to their widths and is defined as:

$$R_s = \frac{2(t_{R_2} - t_{R_1})}{W_{b1} + W_{b2}} = \frac{0.589(t_{R_2} - t_{R_1})}{W_{1/2}\ \text{average}}$$

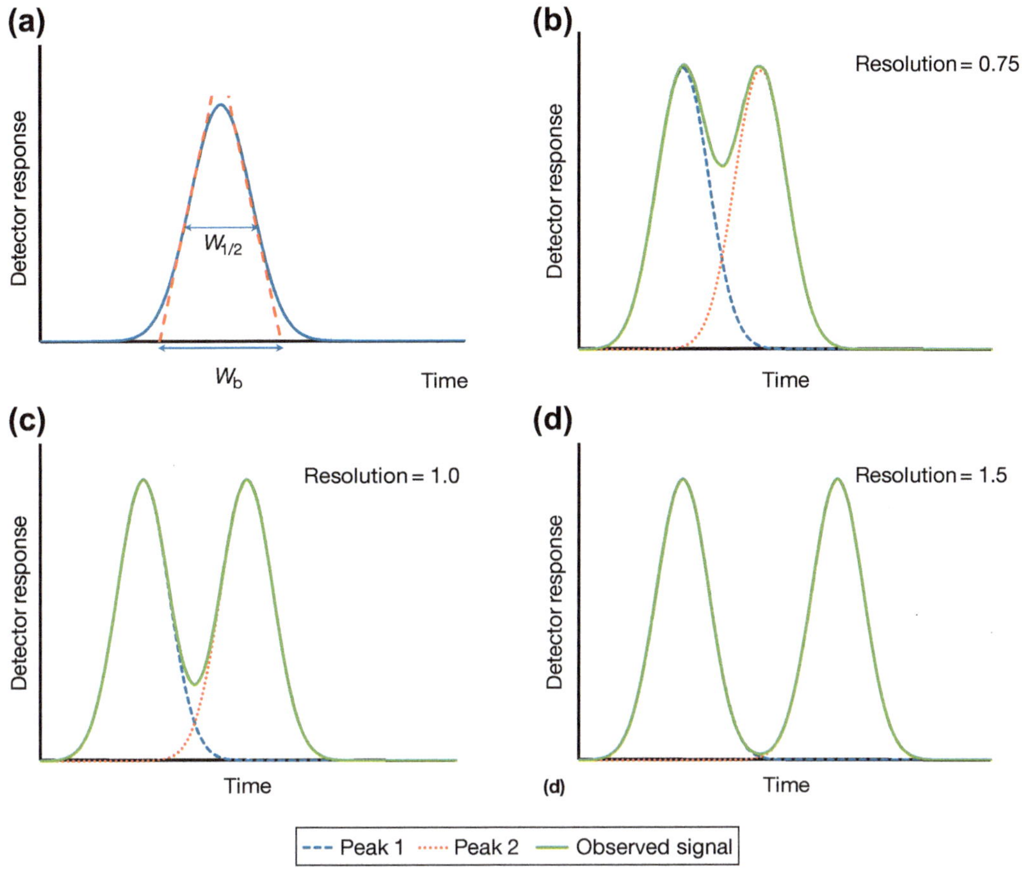

Figure 5 (a) Ideal Gaussian peak showing how W_b and $W_{1/2}$ are measured and (b–d) plots showing the effect of resolution of two individual peaks on the observed chromatogram. The solid line represents the observed signal, with the dashed lines representing the individual peaks.

where W_b is the peak width at baseline and $W_{1/2 \text{ average}}$ is the average peak width at half height, as shown on the idealized Gaussian peak in **Figure 5**. As shown below, separations where R_s values are <1.5 exhibit some overlap between the peaks. For quantitative analysis, a resolution of >1.5 is ideal.

Band broadening within the chromatographic system results from three different broadening processes: eddy diffusion (A), longitudinal diffusion (B), and interphase

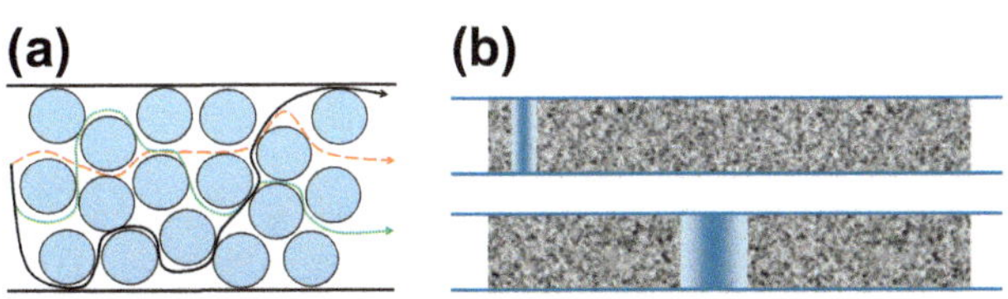

Figure 6 Schematic diagram showing modes of broadening in chromatography. (a) Multiple pathways traveled by the analyte through a packed column (eddy diffusion) and (b) longitudinal diffusion.

mass transfer (C). These processes are discussed separately, below.

A molecule (or ion) can travel throughout a packed stationary phase via a multitude of different pathways. As shown in **Figure 6(a)**, the length of these pathways can differ significantly. As a result, analyte molecules may reach the detector over a time interval, leading to a broad peak. This broadening effect is termed eddy diffusion and is independent of mobile-phase velocity. Eddy diffusion (A) is related to average particle diameter (d_p) and packing geometry (λ) by

$$A = 2\lambda d_p$$

Eddy diffusion is minimized by using small uniform stationary-phase particles and tighter packing. Typical values are around 1.0 for a well-packed column.

Figure 6(b) illustrates the longitudinal diffusion of analyte molecules. Longitudinal diffusion describes the spread of analyte molecules or ions through random motion from regions of higher concentration to regions of lower concentration. Longitudinal diffusion (B) is related to the diffusion coefficient of the analyte in a given medium (D_M), an obstruction factor resulting from the packing (γ):

$$B = 2\gamma D_M$$

D_M is a function of both the analyte and the mobile phase, and γ is a constant that depends on the quality of the stationary-phase packing. Consequently, the magnitude of B can only be changed by varying the type, pressure, and/or flow rate of the mobile phase. Longitudinal diffusion is particularly important in GC and can be reduced by using high flow rates and/or denser gases. In LC, longitudinal diffusion is generally relatively small.

Broadening due to interphase mass transfer (C) results from the finite time taken for a molecule to equilibrate as it moves between the two phases. For packed columns, interphase mass transfer is dependent on the diffusion coefficient (D_M) and the particle diameter (d_p) and is approximated by

$$C = \frac{1}{6}\frac{d_p^2}{D_M}$$

Interphase mass transfer is minimized by reducing the mobile-phase flow rate in order to allow the analyte molecules more time to equilibrate between the two phases. It is also minimized by using small particles, thin films of stationary phase, higher temperatures, and low-viscosity mobile phases. As a general rule, broadening in packed chromatography columns is most strongly influenced by the diameter of the stationary-phase particles. In contrast, the broadening in open tubular columns is influenced by column diameter, with reduced diameter resulting in decreased broadening.

These terms can be combined to determine column efficiency as defined by the height of a theoretical plate (H) and the linear mobile-phase velocity (u). This equation is known as the van Deemter equation and is generally applied in GC. Ideally, the value for H should be minimized to reduce band broadening and thus improve peak separation.

$$H = A + \frac{B}{u} + Cu$$

A representative van Deemter plot showing linear velocity versus H is shown in **Figure 7** below. As can be seen, the flow rate has significant impact on the overall efficiency of the chromatographic separation.

The term *theoretical plate* is derived from distillation theory; in chromatography, the theoretical plate can be thought of as representing a single equilibrium step. The more theoretical plates (N) on a separation, the higher the efficiency of the separation. The number of theoretical plates is related to H and column length (L) via the following:

$$N = \frac{L}{H}$$

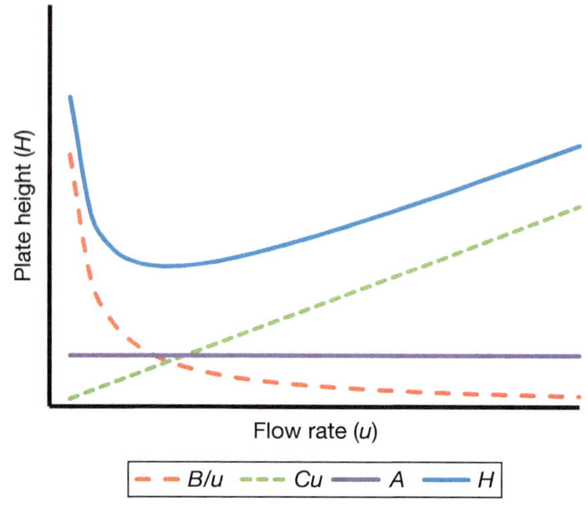

Figure 7 Exemplar van Deemter plot showing effect of flow rate on efficiency as measured by the height equivalent to a theoretical plate (H). Dotted lines show the contribution from the individual diffusion mechanisms.

N can be directly obtained from a chromatogram, the retention time of standard, and the peak width:

$$N = 16\left(\frac{t_R}{W}\right)^2 = \frac{5.545t_R^2}{W_{1/2}}$$

Additional Comments on Band Broadening

When open tubular columns are used in GC, the effect of eddy diffusion is removed due to the absence of packing materials, and the modified Golay equation applies:

$$H = \frac{B}{u} + Cu$$

In HPLC, an additional mass-transfer term needs to be incorporated to account for different mass transfer in each phase as described by the Huber equation, where C_s and C_m are the stationary-phase and mobile-mass-transfer terms, respectively:

$$H = A + \frac{B}{u} + C_s u + C_m u$$

In general, the eddy diffusion term and longitudinal diffusion term are very small when compared to the mass-transfer terms in HPLC; thus a reduced form of this equation is usually used:

$$H = C_s u + C_m u$$

Optimization of Chromatographic Performance

Chromatographic performance is optimized by varying experimental conditions until the components of a mixture are well separated. Consideration is often taken to the time frame of the separation. Optimization experiments are generally aimed at (1) adjusting the distribution equilibria of the analytes (thus changing the migration rates) or (2) reducing band broadening. Adjustments to the distribution equilibria can be achieved by changing the chemical composition of the mobile or stationary phase and adjusting the temperature. As described earlier, band broadening can be reduced by judicious choice of flow rate, minimizing particle or column diameter, and reducing film thickness.

See also: **Methods:** Gas Chromatography; Liquid and Thin-layer Chromatography; Liquid Chromatography–Mass Spectrometry.

Further Reading

Bayne, S., Carlin, M., 2010. Forensic Applications of High Performance Liquid Chromatography. CRC Press, Boca Raton.

McNair, H.M., Miller, J.M., 2009. Basic Gas Chromatography, second ed. John Wiley & Sons, Inc, Hoboken, NJ.

Miller, J.M., 2005. Chromatography Concepts and Contrasts, second ed. John Wiley & Sons, Inc, Hoboken, NJ.

Pollettini, A., 2011. HPLC in the forensic sciences. In: Corradini, D. (Ed.), Handbook of HPLCChromatographic Science Series, second ed., vol. 101. CRC Press, Boca Raton, FL, pp. 661–682.

Robards, K., Haddad, P.R., Jackson, P.E., 1994. Principles and Practice of Modern Chromatographic Methods, third ed. Academic Press, Elsevier Science Limited, London.

Snyder, L.R., Kirkland, J.J., Dolan, J.W., 2010. Introduction to Modern Liquid Chromatography, third ed. John Wiley & Sons, Inc, Hoboken, NJ.

Relevant Websites

http://www.chromatography-online.org—Chromatography Online.

http://www.chromedia.org—Chromedia.

mRNA and MicroRNA for Body Fluid Identification

C Haas, University of Zürich, Zürich, Switzerland
E Hanson and J Ballantyne, University of Central Florida, Orlando, FL, USA

Glossary

Ct value Cycle number at which the fluorescence signal generated by the amplification of a gene passes a preset threshold (point at which fluorescent signal is distinguishable from baseline).

Delta Ct (dCt) method The dCt is obtained by subtracting the average body fluid gene Ct from the average housekeeping gene Ct. A positive dCt value indicates that a body fluid gene is present in higher abundance than the housekeeping gene, whereas a negative dCt value indicates that a body fluid gene is present in lower abundance than the housekeeping gene.

Microarray analysis Hybridization of a nucleic acid sample to a very large set of oligonucleotide probes, which are attached to a solid support (usually a glass slide or silicon thin-film cell), to determine the sequence or to detect variations in a gene sequence or expression or for gene mapping.

Minor groove binder (MGB) probes Hybridized to internal regions of qPCR products during the annealing stage, MGB probes incorporate a 5′ reporter dye and a 3′ nonfluorescent quencher. Following hybridization to their complementary DNA template, they are degraded by the 5′–3′ exonuclease activity of the Taq polymerase during extension, releasing the fluorescence of the reporter dye.

Pseudogenes Nonfunctional homologs of known genes that have lost their protein-coding ability. So-called processed pseudogenes are retrotransposed from mRNA and incorporated into the chromosome; they do not have introns or promoters.

Real-time PCR (qPCR) Monitors the accumulation of PCR product (changes in fluorescent signal) formation during amplification using either a fluorescently labeled probe (specific sequence within the target region; e.g., MGB probe) or an intercalating dye specific for DNA (e.g., SYBR green).

Introduction

The presence of body fluids can indicate the location of potential sources of DNA that, once recovered, may be used to identify the donor of the stain. While the most common body fluids found at crime scenes are blood, saliva, and semen, other fluids such as vaginal secretions, menstrual blood, urine, and sweat can be encountered. Conventional methods for body fluid stain analysis involve the use of enzymatic or immunological tests (**Table 1**). Due to limited specificity (i.e., cross-reactivity with other species or tissues), many of these tests are presumptive in nature. Furthermore, no routinely used tests are available for the identification of vaginal secretions, menstrual blood, and sweat.

Identification of the tissue source of a biological stain can be crucial to the investigation and prosecution of a case. An example demonstrating the importance of identifying the body fluid could be that DNA from a sexual assault victim is found in a suspect's vehicle and the suspect claims it was present due to casual contact since the victim had ridden in his car numerous times. However, the significance of this evidence would increase if the source of the DNA could be shown instead to originate from the victim's vaginal secretions, a circumstance which would be more difficult to attribute to casual contact as opposed to a sexual assault. To provide operational forensic laboratories with improved methodologies for body fluid identification, attempts to utilize molecular-based identification techniques are being developed. Messenger RNA (mRNA) and microRNA (miRNA) profiling are promising new methods for the identification of body fluids in biological stains. These are considered as confirmatory tests that conclusively identify a body fluid.

mRNA profiling is based on the premise that each single tissue type is comprised of cells that have a unique transcriptome or gene expression (i.e., mRNA) profile. A number of markers have been identified for the forensically most relevant body fluids, that is, blood, saliva, semen, vaginal secretions, menstrual blood, and sweat. mRNA is notorious for its rapid postmortem and in vitro decay, due to ubiquitously present RNases. This was expected to be especially problematic as biological stains from casework are often challenged by moisture, UV light, temperature, and suboptimal environmental

 http://dx.doi.org/10.1016/B978-0-12-800647-4.00011-4

Table 1 Summary of conventional enzymatic and immunological methods for body fluid analysis

Classification	*Protein*	*Method*
Blood		
Chemiluminescent	Heme	Luminol, fluorescein, Bluestar
Chemical	Heme	Benzidine, Kastle–Meyer, O-toludine, tetramethylbenzidine/hemastix, leucomalachite green
Crystal test	Heme	Teichman, Takayama
Immunological	Hemoglobin	HemeSelect, ABAcard, HemaTrace, Hexagon OBTI, RSID-blood
Saliva		
Chemical	α-Amylase	Starch–iodine, Phadebas, Amylose azure, Rapignost-Amylase, SALIgAE
Immunological	α-Amylase	RSID-saliva
Semen		
Chemical	Acid phosphatase	Alpha-naphthyl phosphate/Brentamine Fast Blue, beta-naphthol/Fast garnet B, alpha-naphthol/Fast Red AL
Crystal tests	Choline, spermine	Florence, Barberio, Puanen's tests
Microscopic		Christmas tree, haematoxylin/eosin, Baecchi's method, Papanicolaou's staining
Immunological	Prostate-specific antigen	Biosign, ABAcard, Chembio, Medpro, Onco-screen, PSA-check-1, Seratec PSA Semiquant
	Semenogelin	RSID-semen, Nanotrap Sg
Urine		
Chemical	Urea	Nessler's reagent, *p*-dimethylaminocinnamaldehyde, urease/bromthymol blue
	Creatinine	Jaffe test, Salkowski test
Immunological	Tamm–Horsfall glycoprotein	RSID-urine

Source: Adapted from Virkler, K., Lednev, I.K., 2009. Analysis of body fluids for forensic purposes: from laboratory testing to non-destructive rapid confirmatory identification at a crime scene. Forensic Science International 188, 1–17.

pH, thus potentially resulting in mRNA of insufficient quality for analysis. Quite unexpectedly, however, a high stability of mRNA in dried stains, even from old and compromised samples, has been reported.

Recently, there has been an explosion of interest in a class of small noncoding RNAs, miRNAs, whose regulatory functions in various developmental and biological processes have been identified. Numerous studies have indicated that miRNAs are also expressed in a tissue-specific manner and therefore may be used to identify body fluids. Due to their small size (~18–24 bases in length), miRNAs may be more stable than mRNAs and therefore more suitable for use with degraded and environmentally compromised samples frequently encountered in forensic casework.

Messenger RNA

mRNA is a single-stranded nucleic acid, consisting of four kinds of nucleotides: uracil, guanine, adenine, and cytosine. mRNA is transcribed from a DNA template and carries coding information to the ribosomes, where it is translated into a protein (**Figure 1**).

During transcription, RNA polymerase II makes a complementary copy of a gene from DNA to pre-mRNA. Eukaryotic pre-mRNA undergoes extensive processing: 5′ cap addition, splicing, editing, and polyadenylation. The 5′ cap is critical for recognition by the ribosome and protection from RNases. During splicing, certain stretches of noncoding sequences (introns) are removed. Pre-mRNA can sometimes be spliced in several different ways; as a result, a single gene can encode multiple proteins (alternative splicing). In some instances, an mRNA is edited by changing its nucleotide composition. The poly(A) tail at the 3′ end helps to protect mRNA from degradation by exonucleases. Polyadenylation is also important for transcription termination, export of the mRNA from the nucleus, and translation.

The mature mRNA is exported from the nucleus to the cytoplasm, where it is translated into protein by the ribosome. During translation, the sequence of nucleotides in the mRNA molecule is read in sets of three nucleotides (called codons), each of which codes for a specific amino acid. The resulting polypeptide will later fold into an active protein. mRNA is degraded by several decay pathways. The limited lifetime of mRNA enables a cell to alter protein synthesis rapidly in response to its changing needs.

Detection Technology

mRNA profiling includes three main steps: RNA extraction, reverse transcription (RT), and amplification/detection. Total RNA and DNA can be coextracted from the same stain, either manually or with an extraction kit. The RNA extract should be cleaned from residual DNA using a DNase treatment. It is beneficial to quantify the RNA and put a defined amount into the RT reaction to avoid false positive and negative signals.

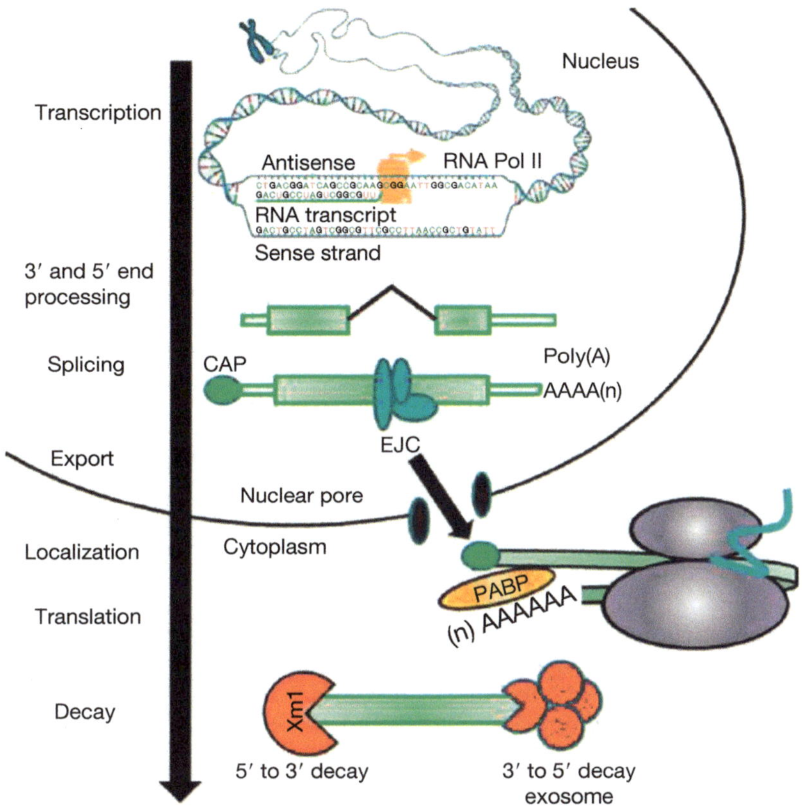

Figure 1 The life cycle of messenger RNA (mRNA) in eukaryotic cells: In the nucleus, RNA polymerase II transcribes a chromosomal gene sequence to pre-mRNA. mRNA processing includes 5′ cap addition, intron splicing, editing, and addition of the poly(A) tail. The mature mRNA is then transported to the cytoplasm involving the exon junction complex (EJC). The poly(A) tail of the mRNA interacts with poly(A)-binding protein (PABP), resulting in mRNA circularization and translation initiation. The small ribosomal subunit scans the mRNA until an appropriate start codon has been reached. Once the ribosomal preinitiation complex is formed, the large ribosomal subunit joins and translation begins. mRNA is degraded by several decay pathways. Adapted from Brooks, S.A., 2010. Functional interactions between mRNA turnover and surveillance and the ubiquitin proteasome system. Wiley Interdisciplinary Reviews: RNA 1, 240–252, copyright 2010, with permission from John Wiley & Sons Ltd.

In the RT reaction, mRNA is reverse-transcribed into complementary DNA (cDNA) using random primers. cDNA is then amplified with fluorescence-labeled, tissue-specific primers (end-point polymerase chain reaction—PCR) and amplicons are separated and detected with capillary electrophoresis. Alternatively, cDNA may be analyzed using real-time quantitative PCR (qPCR) with tissue-specific primers and a minor groove binder (MGB) probe. qPCR assays include a housekeeping gene to normalize the expression of the tissue-specific genes. mRNA markers can be combined in multiplexes, for end-point PCR as well as qPCR, which amplify several markers for one or several body fluids in a single PCR. Coextracted DNA can be analyzed according to standard short tandem repeat (STR) protocols (see Chapters 40 and 50).

Tissue-Specific mRNA Markers

A number of mRNA markers have been identified for the forensically most relevant body fluids, that is, blood, saliva, semen, vaginal secretions, menstrual blood, and sweat. **Table 2** lists a selection of commonly used markers that have been reported as fluid-specific and, in addition, some mRNA markers that have not yet been extensively tested or shown to cross-react with other body fluids. Approaches to find tissue-specific markers include searches for tissue-specific proteins or bacteria in the literature or online expression databases (e.g., BioGPS), whole-genome expression analysis, or whole-transcriptome shotgun sequencing. Primers are designed to overlap exon–exon junctions or span an intron to ensure

Table 2 Genes that have been reported to be expressed in a tissue-specific manner or body fluid-specific bacteria

Gene	*Function/localization of protein*
Blood	
Hemoglobin α (HBA), hemoglobin β (HBB)	Alpha- and beta-subunit of hemoglobin A
Aminolevulinate synthase 2 (ALAS2)	Erythroid-specific mitochondrial enzyme that catalyzes the first step in the heme biosynthetic pathway
CD3 gamma molecule (CD3G)	Part of the T cell receptor-CD3 complex, which plays an important role in coupling antigen recognition to several intracellular signal-transduction pathways
Ankyrin 1 (ANK1)	Erythrocyte membrane protein, which provides the primary linkage between the membrane skeleton and the plasma membrane
Porpho-bilinogen deaminase (PBGD), erythroid form	Third enzyme of the heme biosynthetic pathway
β-spectrin (SPTB)	Erythrocyte membrane protein
Glycophorin A (Glyco A)[a]	Glycophorin A is a major sialoglycoprotein of the human erythrocyte membrane and carries the M or N group antigen
Saliva	
Histatin 3 (HTN3)	Part of the nonimmune host defense system in the oral cavity
Statherin (STATH)	Salivary protein that binds hydroxyapatite and acts as an inhibitor of precipitation of calcium phosphate salts in the oral cavity
Mucin 7 (MUC7)	Small salivary mucin, which is thought to play a role in facilitating the clearance of bacteria in the oral cavity and to aid in mastication, speech, and swallowing
Semen	
Protamine 1 and 2 (PRM1, PRM2)	During spermatogenesis, histones are replaced by protamines, which are essential for the highly condensed chromatin structure in the sperm nucleus
Transglutaminase 4 (TGM4)	The transglutaminase family catalyzes the irreversible cross-linking of peptide-bound glutamine residues either with peptide-bound lysines or with primary amines; TGM4 is specific to the prostate
Prostate-specific antigen, kallikrein 3 (PSA)	Serine protease, found in seminal fluid, prostatic fluid, male serum, and male and female urine
Semenogelin 1 (SEMG1)	Protein originating in the seminal vesicles
Vaginal secretions	
Mucin 4 (MUC4)[b]	Mucins protect the surfaces of the reproductive tract epithelium from pathogen penetrance and modulate sperm entry into the uterus
Human beta-defensin 1 (HBD1)[b]	Antimicrobial peptide of urogenital tissues
Lactobacillus crispatus[a], *Lactobacillus gasseri*[a]	Lactobacilli are specific to the vagina
Menstrual blood	
Matrix metalloproteinases 7, 10, 11 (MMP7, MMP10, MMP11)	Endopeptidases involved in the breakdown of extracellular matrix components
Sweat	
Dermcidin (DCD)[a]	Antibiotic peptide, secreted by sweat glands

[a]Indicates markers from single studies that have not yet been extensively tested.
[b]Indicates markers that have been shown to cross-react with other body fluids.

that the obtained products are not due to the presence of contaminating DNA. The tissue-specific genes should not possess pseudogenes (nonfunctional homologs of the genes) because processed pseudogenes cannot be distinguished from cDNA by mRNA profiling.

Results and Interpretation

The evaluation of mRNA markers for forensic use includes testing their sensitivity and specificity, as well as performance with casework samples. The abovementioned blood, saliva, and semen markers show a high degree of specificity and no relevant cross-reaction with other human tissues/body fluids or with other species. It has been demonstrated that the corresponding mRNA markers can be detected in samples as small as 0.001 μl blood, 0.05 μl saliva, and 0.01 μl semen. The analysis of sperm and seminal plasma markers allows for the differentiation between samples from aspermic (absence of sperm in semen) men and normospermic men (with normal sperm production). The vaginal markers mucin 4 (MUC4) and human beta-defensin 1 (HBD1) cross-react with buccal cells (i.e., saliva) and are therefore only of limited use in forensic casework. The matrix metalloproteinases (MMP) markers confirm the presence of menstrual blood, but a minor expression is also found in vaginal cells. This complicates the interpretation of a positive MMP result, but could be overcome by comparing the result to a housekeeping gene and/or the vaginal secretion markers HBD1 and MUC4, which are expressed quite constantly and strongly during the whole menstrual cycle. The blood markers are rather weak in menstrual blood samples, because whole blood accounts for only 30–50% of the total flow in most women. Additional mRNA markers have been suggested for the identification of vaginal secretion, menstrual blood, and sweat, but have not yet been extensively tested for forensic use. To date, no mRNA markers for the identification of urine are available, probably due to the limited number of cells and/or low mRNA expression in dried urine stains.

False positive and negative signals can be caused by the fact that expression of tissue-specific transcripts is indeed abundant in the respective body fluid, but not necessarily absent in others. Therefore, a defined amount of RNA should be used in the RT reaction for standardization. To date, no robust human-specific RNA quantification system is available. Fluorescence-based RNA quantification methods are sensitive and convenient, but might have limited casework utility because they are not human-specific. Thus, bacterial RNA, which is found in abundance in buccal or vaginal swabs, will result in an underestimation of the amount of human RNA in these sample types.

A positive control consisting of a marker expressed in all tissue types would confirm a successful analysis. However, no housekeeping gene has been described that is suitable for the detection of all tested body fluids. Saliva and semen, for example, show very little or no expression of common housekeeping genes (glyceraldehyde 3-phosphate dehydrogenase, 18S ribosomal RNA, transcription elongation factor 1α, ubiquitin-conjugating enzyme), presumably because of limited cell metabolism in spermatozoids and the desquamated cells of the cheek mucosa. In addition, housekeeping genes are likely to have pseudogenes. Coextracted DNA might serve as a positive control for the presence of human cells. A concurrent negative RNA result would suggest that none of the analyzed human body fluids is present or that the mRNA is degraded and no result can be obtained. In the case of degradation, housekeeping genes would also be affected.

Several negative controls can be included during mRNA analysis to identify possible contamination: extraction blank (no sample added to lysis and purification reaction); RT blank (water in place of RNA added to RT reaction); RT minus (no reverse transcriptase added to RT reaction), to identify possibly contaminating DNA (frequently a larger size than the expected RNA product) or the presence of pseudogenes (same size as RNA product); and amplification blank (water in place of cDNA added to PCR reaction).

Since casework material is often limited, an important advantage of body fluid identification by mRNA profiling is the possibility of simultaneously isolating RNA and DNA from the same stain and the ability to multiplex numerous mRNA markers for the identification of one or several body fluids. The quantity and quality of coextracted DNA is also sufficient for casework and environmentally exposed samples, even though the yield might be lower compared to non-coextraction methods. The mRNA/DNA coextraction strategy is a reliable, confirmatory, and time-saving option for the identification of body fluids in forensic casework that requires less sample consumption and is also compatible with the current DNA analysis methodology.

MicroRNA

miRNAs are a class of small noncoding RNAs, 18–24 nucleotides in length, which regulate many cellular processes at the post-transcriptional level. They bind to complementary sequences on target mRNA transcripts, usually resulting in translational repression and gene silencing (**Figure 2**). The human genome encodes over 1000 miRNAs.

Most miRNA genes are found in intergenic regions or introns and are transcribed by RNA polymerases to primary miRNA (pri-miRNA). Pri-miRNAs are processed by the enzyme "Drosha," resulting in long hairpin-containing precursor miRNA (pre-miRNA). "Exportin-5" transports pre-miRNA from the nucleus to the cytoplasm. An RNase called "Dicer" cleaves the pre-miRNA and produces double-stranded mature miRNA. Argonaute protein (Ago2) and Dicer together form the ribonucleoprotein RNA-induced silencing complex (RISC). One strand of the mature miRNA is incorporated in the RISC and guides the complex to its RNA target by interacting with the three prime untranslated regions (3′ UTR) of the mRNA. miRNA-mediated gene regulation depends on the complementarity between miRNA and target mRNA: If there is perfect complementarity, Ago2 can cleave the mRNA and lead to direct mRNA degradation; if there is only partial complementarity, the silencing is achieved by preventing translation. This mechanism implies that any given miRNA can bind to a broad spectrum of different mRNAs and any given mRNA can be bound by several miRNAs, thereby expanding miRNA regulatory potential. In addition, miRNA regulation can fine-tune and optimize protein levels using a "rheostat"-like mechanism.

Detection Technology

The analysis steps of miRNA profiling are similar to those of mRNA profiling: RNA extraction, miRNA-specific RT, and amplification/detection. Total RNA is extracted, DNase-treated, and quantified in exactly the same way as described for mRNA. The short length of mature miRNAs (~22 nucleotides) prohibits the conventional design of a random-primed RT step followed by a specific qPCR assay. Two different approaches can be used for RT of miRNAs. The first involves the use of miRNA-specific stem-loop primers. Alternatively, miRNAs are simultaneously polyadenylated and all RNAs (miRNA, mRNA, and other small RNAs) are reverse-transcribed using both random and oligo-dT primers. cDNA is analyzed with qPCR

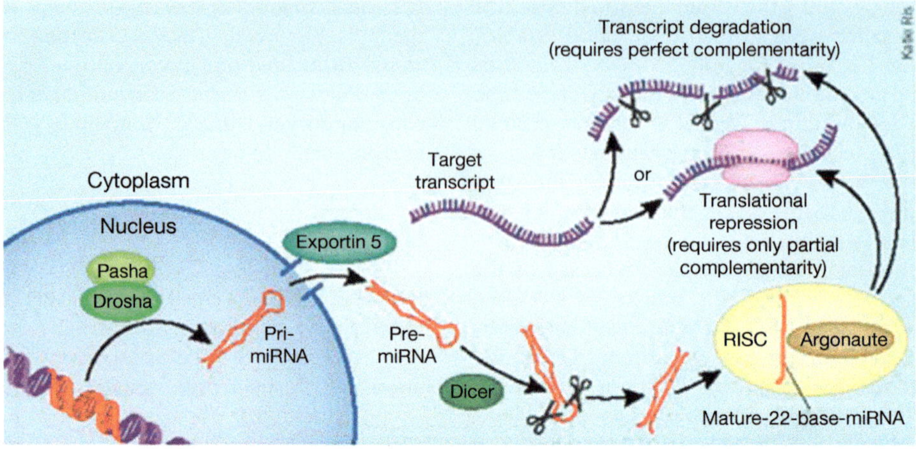

Figure 2 The life cycle of microRNA (miRNA) in eukaryotic cells: A primary miRNA (pri-miRNA) transcript is encoded in the cell's DNA and transcribed in the nucleus, processed by the enzyme Drosha, and exported into the cytoplasm where it is further processed by Dicer. After strand separation, the mature miRNA represses protein production either by blocking translation or causing mRNA degradation. Reprinted from Mack, G.S., 2007. MicroRNA gets down to business. Nature Biotechnology 25, 631–638, copyright 2007, with permission from Macmillan Publishers Ltd.

using miRNA-specific primers and an MGB probe or SYBR green for detection. Currently, one or several small RNAs are used for normalization of miRNA abundances across tissues, employing the delta Ct method. miRNA markers and reference genes (small RNAs used for normalization) can also be included in a multiplex system for simultaneous amplification and detection, the only restriction being the limited number of dyes available for qPCR assays.

Tissue-Specific miRNA Markers

Over 16,000 miRNAs, across 153 species, have been entered into the miRBase, a searchable database of miRNA sequences and annotations, with hairpin and mature sequences available. Through studies of these miRNAs, the biomedical research community has suggested that the miRNome may be a more precise representation of a cell type and condition than the transcriptome. Numerous miRNAs have been reported to be tissue-specific and could be used to identify the body fluid origin of forensic biological stains. Human miRNA markers were screened in forensically relevant body fluids (blood, semen, saliva, vaginal secretion, menstrual blood) by two different research groups using different approaches, resulting in differing body fluid-specific miRNA markers (**Table 3**). One approach surveyed the expression of 452 miRNAs in several body fluids through qPCR. The other approach detected the expression levels of 718 miRNAs in several body fluids on a microarray and validated potential candidates through qPCR.

Results and Interpretation

The evaluation of miRNA markers for forensic use is based on a few publications. Hanson et al. propose a panel of differentially expressed miRNAs that are characteristic of an individual body fluid. None of the selected miRNAs is truly body fluid-specific in the sense that it is expressed uniquely in one tissue and not in any other. Expression levels of miRNA pairs are displayed in 2D scatter plots, and distinct clustering of each body fluid can be observed, separating the body fluid of interest from the others. Twenty-one human tissues also exhibited

Table 3 Human miRNAs that have been reported to be expressed in a tissue-specific manner

Blood	*Saliva*	*Semen*	*Vaginal secretion*	*Menstrual blood*	*Reference genes*
hsa-miR-451	hsa-miR-658	hsa-miR-135b	hsa-miR-124a	hsa-miR-412	RNU6b
hsa-miR-16	hsa-miR-205	hsa-miR-10b	hsa-miR-372	hsa-miR-451	RNU24
hsa-miR-144		hsa-miR-135a			RNU44
hsa-miR-185		hsa-miR-891a			RNU48

differing expression profiles. Zubakov et al. present two miRNA markers each for the identification of blood and semen. These miRNA markers are not prone to degradation in samples stored for 1 year. A high sensitivity of the qPCR assay has been shown in that miRNAs could be detected from as little as 0.1 pg total RNA. Notably, the sets of miRNAs proposed by Hanson et al. and Zubakov et al. are completely exclusive and nonoverlapping. While the specificity of the Hanson et al. blood and semen miRNA candidates was confirmed, the specificity for the Hanson et al. saliva, vaginal secretions, and menstrual blood miRNA candidates could not be reproduced by Zubakov et al. However, Zubakov et al. also reported discrepancies between the microarray data and subsequent specificity confirmation testing for numerous miRNA candidates. These discrepancies may, in part, be due to the differing technologies used to detect and analyze miRNA expression. Therefore, additional work will be necessary to determine the most suitable candidates and analytical methodologies.

In addition to an evaluation of analytical methods and platforms, further studies are necessary to evaluate miRNA profiling with forensic samples. A proposed advantage of miRNAs is the suitability for use with challenging samples, such as environmentally exposed and heavily degraded biological stains. However, extensive evaluations of such samples will be necessary before definitive conclusions can be made. Additionally, direct comparison studies examining the stability and sensitivity of miRNA and mRNA markers in these challenging samples will need to be performed to determine which RNA biomarker may be most suitable for use in forensic casework. It will also be necessary to examine potential expression effects caused by diseased or nonhealthy tissue or fluids because of the potential role of miRNAs in various disorders or cancers. Furthermore, the species specificity of the identified candidates will need to be demonstrated when possible.

Despite the need for additional work, these initial studies indicate that miRNA profiling may play a role in the identification of forensically relevant biological fluids. As new miRNAs are identified, novel body fluid-specific candidates may be found. Some miRNA analytical methods allow for the simultaneous evaluation of mRNA and miRNA and, therefore, a combination of both RNA biomarkers may provide additional and necessary specificity for the identification of all forensically relevant biological fluids and tissues.

Other Applications of RNA in Forensic Science

In forensic casework analysis, it has become necessary to obtain genetic (i.e., STR) profiles from increasingly smaller amounts of biological material left behind by persons involved in criminal offenses. The ability to obtain profiles from trace biological evidence is routinely demonstrated with so-called touch DNA evidence, generally perceived to be the result of DNA obtained from shed skin cells transferred from donor to an object or person during physical contact. Several studies clearly demonstrate the ability to obtain genetic profiles from trace biological evidence but they, out of necessity, bypass the critical identification of the source of the biological material. mRNA profiling may also be applied to the identification of skin cells and some promising candidates have already been described.

Other forensic applications using RNA are also being explored, such as using RNA degradation as a parameter for the determination of the postmortem interval and the age of biological stains (time since deposition). Good correlations have been demonstrated under controlled circumstances, but in forensic settings, unfortunately, conditions are not predictable. Additionally, it has been demonstrated that it is possible to identify age-specific expression patterns allowing for a possible determination of the biological age of a bloodstain donor. The age of external and internal wounds is another important question in forensic pathology, which could be answered by measuring mRNAs coding for proteins involved in the cell reaction to injury. Some suitable markers have already been evaluated. Another area of interest is the cause and mechanism of death. mRNA profiling could offer insight into the pathological mechanisms leading to death by disclosing the functional and morphological changes of cells immediately preceding death. Postmortem tissue undergoes immediate changes, a fact which has to be considered when studying premortem gene expression. This is a complex field, currently at its very beginning.

See also: **Biology/DNA:** Basic Principles; DNA Extraction and Quantification; Short Tandem Repeats; **Biology/DNA/Methods/Analytical Techniques:** Capillary Electrophoresis in Forensic Genetics; **Methods:** Capillary Electrophoresis: Basic Principles; Capillary Electrophoresis in Forensic Biology.

Further Reading

Ballantyne, J., 2000. Serology overview. In: Siegel, J.A., Saukko, P.J., Knupfer, G.C. (Eds.), Encyclopedia of Forensic Sciences. Academic Press, London, pp. 1322–1331.

Bauer, M., 2007. RNA in forensic science. Forensic Science International: Genetics 1, 69–74.

Courts, C., Madea, B., 2010. Micro-RNA – a potential for forensic science? Forensic Science International 203, 106–111.

Fleming, R.I., Harbison, S., 2010. The use of bacteria for the identification of vaginal secretions. Forensic Science International: Genetics 4, 311–315.

Haas, C., Hanson, E., Anjos, M.J., et al., 2012. RNA/DNA co-analysis from blood stains – results of a second collaborative EDNAP exercise. Forensic Science International: Genetics 6 (1), 70–80. http://dx.doi.org/10.1016/j.fsigen.2011.02.004.

Haas, C., Hanson, E.K., Ballantyne, J., 2011. Capillary electrophoresis of a multiplex reverse transcription–polymerase chain reaction to target messenger RNA markers for body fluid identification. In: Alonso, A. (Ed.), DNA Electrophoresis Protocols for Forensic Genetics. Humana Press, New York.

Haas, C., Klesser, B., Maake, C., Bär, W., Kratzer, A., 2009. mRNA profiling for body fluid identification by reverse transcription endpoint PCR and realtime PCR. Forensic Science International: Genetics 3, 80–88.

Hanson, E.K., Ballantyne, J., 2010. RNA profiling for the identification of the tissue origin of dried stains in forensic biology. Forensic Science Review 22, 145–158.

Hanson, E.K., Lubenow, H., Ballantyne, J., 2009. Identification of forensically relevant body fluids using a panel of differentially expressed microRNAs. Analytical Biochemistry 387, 303–314.

Juusola, J., Ballantyne, J., 2005. Multiplex mRNA profiling for the identification of body fluids. Forensic Science International 152, 1–12.

Landgraf, P., Rusu, M., Sheridan, R., et al., 2007. A mammalian microRNA expression atlas based on small RNA library sequencing. Cell 129, 1401–1414.

Sakurada, K., Akutsu, T., Fukushima, H., Watanabe, K., Yoshino, M., 2010. Detection of dermcidin for sweat identification by realtime RT-PCR and ELISA. Forensic Science International 194, 80–84.

Vennemann, M., Koppelkamm, A., 2010. mRNA profiling in forensic genetics I: possibilities and limitations. Forensic Science International 203, 71–75.

Virkler, K., Lednev, I.K., 2009. Analysis of body fluids for forensic purposes: from laboratory testing to non-destructive rapid confirmatory identification at a crime scene. Forensic Science International 188, 1–17.

Zubakov, D., Boersma, A.W., Choi, Y., et al., 2010. MicroRNA markers for forensic body fluid identification obtained from microarray screening and quantitative RT-PCR confirmation. International Journal of Legal Medicine 124, 217–226.

Relevant Websites

www.biogps.gnf.org – BioGPS.
www.mirbase.org – microRNA Database.

Key Terms

Adenylation, Basic principles, Blood, Body fluid identification, Capillary electrophoresis, Capillary gel electrophoresis, Chromatography, CODIS, Confirmatory test, DNA, DNA sequencing, DNA typing, Electrokinetic chromatography, Electrokinetic injection, Electroosmosis, Entangled polymer, Explosives, Fluorescence, Fluorescent dye, Forensic science, Gel electrophoresis, Illicit drugs, Isotachophoresis, Menstrual blood, Messenger RNA (mRNA), Microfabricated device, Microfluidic chip, MicroRNA (miRNA), mtDNA, Multiplex, PCR, Polymer, Presumptive test, Saliva, Semen, Separation, Short tandem repeat, Sieving electrophoresis, Single-nucleotide polymorphism, Skin, Stacking, Stutter, STR, STR separation, Sweat, Urine, Vaginal secretion, Zone electrophoresis.

Review Questions

1. What role does electroosmotic flow play in chromatographic separation, that is, resolution? What factors affect electroosmotic flow, and how does this relate to separation?
2. How does CE used in chemistry differ from its application in biology? What aspects are the same?
3. What factors determine the distribution constant, K_c? Describe the relationship between K_c, retention time (t_R), and void time (t_M).
4. What is a fluorophore?
5. What is the stochastic threshold? Why is it important in forensic biology?
6. What important issues are there in using CE on DNA, specific to that polymer?
7. Does introducing more DNA into the CE necessarily improve the results? Why or why not?
8. What are some of the concerns with using formamide?
9. What is the relationship between injection time and resolution?
10. How are STR loci identified?
11. What is stutter? How does it originate?
12. What is a mixture? What is the relationship between stutter and mixtures?
13. How might minor peaks disappear in the electropherogram?
14. PCR-based forensic assays revolutionized DNA analysis; what were the implications for this technology given the demands of forensic biology casework?
15. What does Combined DNA Index System (CODIS) stand for?
16. How many loci are approved for CODIS?
17. Why are DNA fragments difficult to separate under normal CE conditions? How is this difficulty overcome?
18. What is transient entanglement coupling?
19. What is denaturing?
20. When would mitochondrial DNA be used?

Discussion Questions

1. Current methods in forensic DNA are based on chemical separation of the biological molecules, which is chromatography, instrumentation used in most chemistry laboratories to separate a wide variety of molecules. Portions of the DNA molecule have dyes bound to them during analysis for detection via fluorescence, a chemical response. Therefore, is DNA analysis chemistry or biology?
2. Up to the point where the allele frequencies are used to calculate random match probabilities, DNA is still class-level data. What about DNA allows it to move to a statistical level?
3. Why are only 13 loci allowed in CODIS?
4. Assume that at some point in the future, whole human genome sequencing is as cheap as current methods. Beyond cost, what are the implications to moving to this new platform? What are the productivity and ethical issues surrounding using a person's entire genome?
5. What do you think was the turning point in forensic DNA analysis? What was the most important advance or innovation?

Additional Readings

Dror, I.E., Hampikian, G., 2011. Subjectivity and bias in forensic DNA mixture interpretation. Science and Justice 51, 204–208.
Kelly, H., Bright, J.-A., Buckleton, J.S., Curran, J.M., 2014. A comparison of statistical models for the analysis of complex forensic DNA profiles. Science & Justice 54, 66–70.

Section 3. Analysis

It seems as if a new way of analyzing DNA appears every few years; this is especially true now with the advent of so-called rapid DNA (Asplen, 2011) promising three to seven samples completed in less than two hours. If this technology sounds disruptive, consider the advances outlined in this section and how they changed the status quo of forensic DNA analysis in their day. Forensic science and innovation do not always go hand in hand. It takes time to ensure accuracy and validity, to have investigators buy into a new procedure, and ultimately to have the courts accept it as solid science. Think how difficult it is to change a simple habit in a daily routine; standard operating procedures are *legislated habits* embedded in a system of other legislated habits (the rest of the laboratory), making them that much harder to change. Analysis lies at the core of what forensic scientists do with biological samples, and given the intense focus on forensic DNA, many more changes are likely to come sooner than later.

Asplen, C. 2011. Rapid DNA Analysis is Coming—Rapidly. *Forensic Magazine*, December 14, online at: http://www.forensicmag.com/articles/2011/12/rapid-dna-analysis-coming%E2%80%94rapidly

DNA Extraction and Quantification

A Alonso, Instituto Nacional de Toxicología y Ciencias Forenses, Madrid, Spain

DNA Extraction

The process of isolating purified nuclear and/or mitochondrial DNA from both forensic specimens (blood, semen or saliva stains, hairs, muscle, bones, teeth, etc.) and reference samples (buccal swabs, blood spots on Fast Technology for Analysis of nucleic acids (FTA), or liquid blood) is a crucial step to DNA profiling. Advances in forensic DNA extraction systems have been aimed at increasing the efficiency in the amount of purified DNA recovered (free from polymerase chain reaction (PCR) inhibitors) and automating the process for high-throughput analysis while maintaining a high integrity of the DNA molecule.

Currently, the validated methods for DNA extraction most widely used in forensic laboratories can be classified into three groups on the basis of their purification strategies: organic (phenol–chloroform) extraction, solid-phase DNA extraction methods (silica based), and ionic chelating resins (Chelex). Specific procedures using some of these basic DNA isolation principles (or a combination of them) have been developed depending on the type of sample source. These include the differential lysis procedure for the selective extraction of sperm cells, special procedures for bone and teeth DNA extraction, the procedure for DNA purification on reference biological samples spotted on FTA paper, or previous selection of specific cell types by laser-capture microdissection coupled with DNA extraction.

Automated DNA extraction procedures with different robotic platforms have also been implemented in forensic labs for high-throughput sample preparation, avoiding manual errors while improving sample tracking and reproducibility. Quality standards for DNA extraction in forensic labs include preventive measures against DNA contamination as well as the use of appropriate positive and negative controls for monitorization (**Figure 1**).

Organic (Phenol–Chloroform) Extraction

Organic extraction has been one of the DNA extraction methods most used in the forensic field. The first step of any DNA extraction assay is the breakdown of cell membranes and proteolytic digestion in the presence of sodium dodecylsulfate (SDS) and proteinase K. DNA is first purified by mixing thoroughly the cell lysate with a phenol–chloroform solution followed by centrifugation in order to separate the organic phase, where proteins become trapped, from the supernatant aqueous phase, where DNA remains. DNA in the aqueous phase is

 http://dx.doi.org/10.1016/B978-0-12-800647-4.00012-6

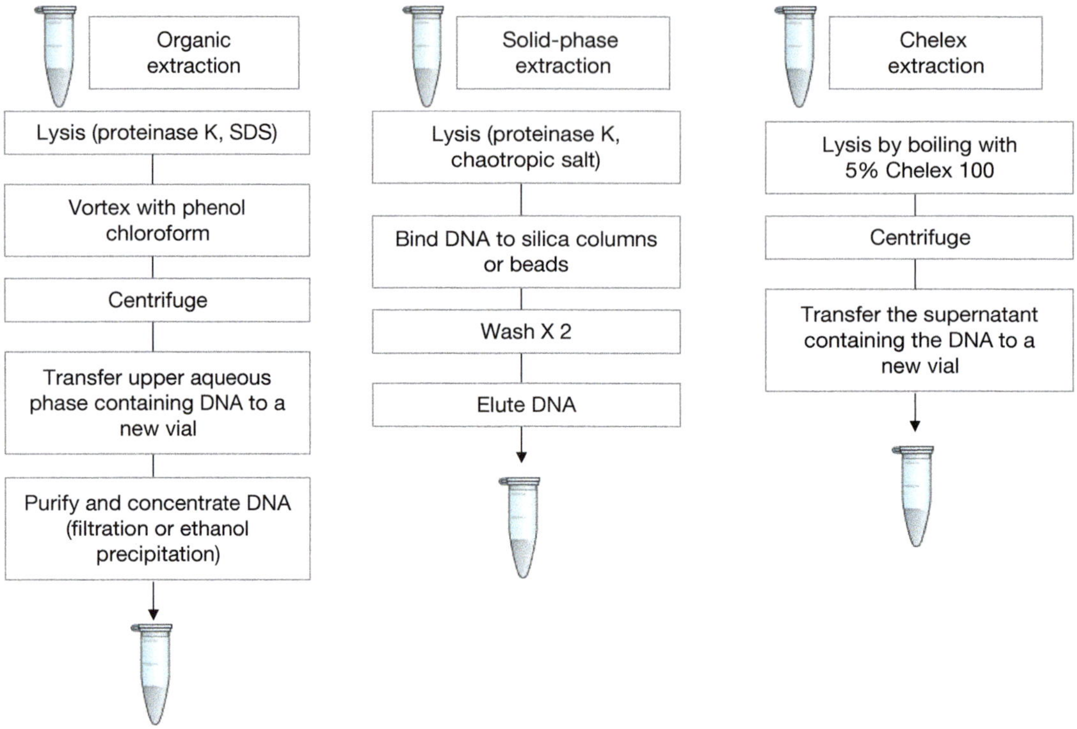

Figure 1 Flowchart of most common forensic DNA extraction methods.

further purified by precipitation with ethanol and finally resuspended in a low-salt buffer.

For maximal DNA recovery and purity, the organic method protocol developed in many forensic labs involves a filtration purification step of the aqueous phase (instead of ethanol precipitation) using Centricon, Microcon, or, more recently, Amicon filter devices for DNA washing and concentration by centrifugation through membranes with different pore sizes (30–100 kDa) (Millipore, Billerica, MA). Although this method is very efficient for the recovery of double-stranded high-molecular-weight DNA free from PCR inhibitors, it is time consuming, requires multiple tube transfers, and is difficult to automate.

Solid-phase DNA Extraction Methods

This extraction method is based on the ability of DNA to bind to silica in the presence of chaotropic salts such as guanidinium thiocyanate, sodium iodide, and guanidinium hydrochloride. Typically, cells are first lysed with proteinase K to release the DNA, and then a binding buffer containing a chaotropic salt is added to prepare DNA for adsorption to the silica at pH < 7.5. Once DNA binds to silica, unwanted impurities can be rinsed away after subsequent washing steps, DNA may be eluted under alkaline conditions and low salt concentrations.

The silica method can be carried out in two different formats: silica columns and silica-coated paramagnetic beads. In the first case, after DNA binding in the column, washing of impurities and DNA elution are made by centrifugation. In the magnetic beads procedure, washing steps and DNA elution are facilitated simply by applying a magnetic force without the need of centrifugation devices.

Magnetic bead-based purification is currently one of the procedures best suited for DNA isolation in the forensic field as it enables rapid DNA purification with very efficient removal of PCR inhibitors, and it is suitable for high-throughput extraction using robotic platforms.

Chelating Resins (Chelex)

A rapid and inexpensive procedure for DNA extraction that has become popular in the forensic field is the use of chelating resins, such as Chelex 100 (Bio-Rad Laboratories, CA). These resins can bind divalent ions such as Ca^{2+} and Mg^{2+}, deactivating unwanted nucleases and, therefore, protecting DNA molecules from cleavage. In most protocols, forensic samples are added to a 5% Chelex suspension, boiled for several minutes, and then centrifuged to remove the resin, leaving DNA in the supernatant.

Unfortunately, the boiling procedure of chelating resins denatures DNA and yields single-stranded DNA that can be analyzed only by PCR-based methods. On the other hand, the DNA purity is not as good as that obtained with the organic extraction or the solid-phase procedures.

DNA from FTA Spots

FTA® is an acronym for fast technology for analysis of nucleic acids. It consists of a cellulose-based matrix treated with a weak base, a chelating agent, an anionic surfactant or detergent, and a uric acid (or a urate salt). Biological samples, such as blood or saliva, can be applied to FTA cards whose chemicals lyse cells, and the released DNA remains immobilized. This system provides DNA preservation, avoiding nuclease damage and microbial development, allowing long-term storage at ambient temperature under dry conditions. FTA is currently widely implemented by several forensic laboratories for DNA collection of reference saliva or blood samples.

There are two main strategies for DNA extraction from FTA paper. One is to wash out proteins and cellular debris from the FTA spot, keeping the DNA bound to the FTA, and then use a clean paper punch to perform the PCR analysis. Alternatively, DNA can be eluted from FTA by a Chelex extraction or other procedures using the eluted DNA for further analysis.

The main advantages of FTA are the feasibility of automation and its long-term preservation due to its storage capabilities under ambient temperature.

Differential Lysis

A specific protocol for the selective separation of epithelial cell DNA from sperm DNA in sexual assault cases was developed in 1985 by Peter Gill. The procedure is a modified version of the organic extraction method based on the resistance of sperm nuclei to be lysed in the absence of a reducing agent such as dithiothreitol (DTT). The protocol involves a first lysis step in the presence of SDS and proteinase K aimed to release the female epithelial cells DNA in the supernatant. The washed pellet of sperm cells is subsequently lysed by treatment with SDS, proteinase K, and DTT, and the sperm DNA is recovered from the supernatant of this second lysis fraction. The success of this method to separate sperm DNA from vaginal cell DNA depends on the relative number of each cell type and the conditions of preservation of the forensic evidence. Failure to separate the male and female fractions by this procedure results in a mixed DNA profile.

DNA Extraction from Bones and Teeth

Several specific protocols have been described for DNA extraction from bones and teeth. All of them entail two primary steps: (1) previous preparation of compact bone tissue or teeth dentine powder by pulverization in liquid nitrogen using a freezer mill and (2) the use of high concentrations of ethylenediaminetetraacetic acid (EDTA) to demineralize the hydroxyapatite matrix making osteocytes or odontocytes accessible to lysis. Early forensic protocols performed demineralization of bone samples by extensive EDTA washes before the lysis step with the subsequent loss of cellular material during different washing steps and high risk of sample contamination. More recently, a number of protocols have been developed for complete demineralization during the lysis step (using a lysis buffer containing 0.5 M EDTA), resulting in full physical dissolution of the bone sample and maximal recovery of DNA. Bone or teeth powder lysates are then submitted to organic extraction followed by Amicon filtration or purified by silica solid-phase procedures.

Laser Capture Microdissection

Laser capture microdissection (LCM) is a technique that allows selecting and collecting specific cell types. It is of particular interest in the forensic field for specific sperm cell separation from mixtures of biological fluids in sexual assault cases. It combines existing light microscopic instrumentation with laser beam technology. There are two general methods of LCM: ultraviolet (UV) cutting systems and infrared (IR) capture systems. While in the IR system, after visualization of the cells of interest via microscopy, they are isolated by transfer of laser energy to a thermolabile polymer with formation of a polymer-cell composite. In the UV system, cells can be selectively captured by photovolatilization of cells surrounding the target cells. In both methods, captured sperm cells are transferred to a vial for DNA extraction. The LCM technique is used particularly in unbalanced mixtures in which very low levels of sperm cells are mixed with a high content of epithelial cells of the victim. As the number of captured cells is usually very small, the DNA extraction process is usually done by cell lysis in a small volume in the presence of proteinase K and a nonionic detergent such as Tween 20. Subsequent inactivation of the proteinase by a heat shock in the same vial of capture is carried out to finally obtain the DNA for downstream PCR analysis, minimizing the possibility of contamination and preventing the loss of DNA that could occur during the procedures for DNA purification.

Automation of DNA Extraction

Development of robotic platforms for the extraction of DNA has been fundamental in ensuring a high-throughput processing of both reference samples and forensic evidences as well as guaranteeing reproducibility and sample tracking. Automation has been implemented in many forensic labs dealing with DNA profiling from large batches of reference samples for inclusion in national DNA databases. Automation has also become of great interest in disaster victim identification cases, enabling laboratories to speed up the process of DNA identification of missing persons.

Most of the DNA extraction robots are based on solid-phase procedures with paramagnetic beads. There are several robotic stations for both small-scale and high-throughput processing as well as validated specific protocols for automated extraction of reference samples (blood, saliva, and FTA) and forensic samples (semen stains, blood, saliva, hair, bones, etc.). EZ1 (Qiagen), Maxwell 16 (Promega), and Automated Express (Life Science) are examples of small-scale platforms for automated DNA extraction of 6–16 samples simultaneously using paramagnetic beads, which have been validated for forensic samples. The Tecan Freedom EVO automated liquid-handling workstation and the Beckman 2000 robot workstation are high-throughput platforms that can handle up to 96 samples at a time and are also validated for forensic analysis.

Microfluidic DNA Extraction Devices

The development of miniaturized devices for DNA preparation, manipulation, and analysis at the micron (microtechnology) or submicron level (nanotechnology) has become one of the most active research areas in molecular biology. They offer several advantages over conventional techniques that include reduced sample and reagent consumption, high-throughput and high-speed analysis, and easy automation and integration of different molecular analysis in a single biochip. In addition, microfabrication enables labs to increase the detection limit with the potential to manipulate DNA at the level of individual molecules with very important implications for the analysis of traditional challenges (DNA mixtures, low copy number, etc.) in forensic genetics. With respect to this technology, silica solid-phase microchips have been developed for DNA extraction from forensic samples as well as some prototype microdevices for the differential lysis procedure.

DNA Quantification

Quantification of human nuclear DNA from forensic samples is a recommended procedure (FBI Quality Assurance Standard 9.4) for a reliable DNA profiling based on multiplex PCR amplification and capillary electrophoresis detection of short tandem repeat (STR) markers. The first purpose of nuclear DNA quantification is to adjust the DNA input (around 0.5–1 ng of DNA template) in subsequent multiplex PCR–STRs assays for optimal performance. On the one hand, an adequate amount of DNA determination prevents PCR failures that are due to the absence of DNA or avoids STR–PCR artifacts, such as random allele dropout, produced by stochastic amplification effects from low-template DNA (LT-DNA) samples (under 100 pg of DNA). On the other hand, it prevents off-scale over-amplification artifacts (including $n - 1$ peaks, increased stutter bands, and pull up) associated with an excess of DNA input in the PCR. In addition, an accurate DNA quantification helps to prevent the unnecessary waste of DNA, especially important when analyzing LT-DNA samples.

Until recently, forensic laboratories have been using the slot-blot hybridization approach to target the D17Z1 locus, a highly repetitive alphoid primate-specific sequence, for DNA quantification in forensic casework. However, this methodology, with a detection limit above the limit of the STR profiling approaches, was often not sensitive enough to detect low-copy number forensic DNA samples. Moreover, the method is labor intensive, time consuming, and poorly suited to high-throughput sample flow.

Several studies have demonstrated the usefulness of real-time PCR using Taqman probes or SYBR Green chemistry for sensitive, specific, and high-throughput DNA quantification assays using autosomal, X and Y chromosomes, and mitochondrial DNA targets.

The development of commercially available real-time PCR human DNA quantification kits has also contributed to a worldwide use of real-time PCR in forensic genetics. Current DNA quantification kits are mainly based on three real-time PCR chemistries: the 5′ nuclease activity assay using Taqman probes (Quantifiler Duo, Applied Biosystems); the Plexor chemistry using fluorescently labeled, iso-dC-containing primers (Plexor® HY System, Promega Corporation); or the use of Scorpion primers (Quantiplex Kit, Qiagen). Despite quantitation of total human DNA, these validated DNA assays offer qualitative data of great interest for forensic genetic typing: quantification of the presence of PCR inhibitors in the DNA extract, sex determination, and quantitative estimation of the proportion of the male component in mixtures of male and female biological fluids.

Current Real-time PCR Chemistries for Human DNA Quantification

There are three commercially available fluorogenic chemistries to monitor the real-time progress of the PCR for the purpose of human DNA quantification that are validated for forensic samples: (1) by measuring the 5′ nuclease activity of the Taq DNA polymerase to cleave a target-specific fluorogenic probe (a TaqMan probe: an oligonucleotide, complementary to a segment of the template DNA, with both a reporter and a quencher dye attached, which only emits its characteristic fluorescence after cleavage); (2) by measuring the decrease of fluorescence using one primer synthesized with an iso-dC residue as the 5′-terminal nucleotide linked to a fluorescent label and using dabcyl-iso-dGTP in the nucleotide mix (which pairs specifically with iso-dC) that quenches the signal of the fluorescent label primer when incorporated in the amplicons during the PCR; and (3) using scorpion primers that are bifunctional molecules containing a PCR primer covalently linked to a probe, which incorporates a fluorophore, and a quencher, which inhibits fluorescence. During PCR, when the probe binds to the PCR products, the fluorophore and quencher become separated, leading to an increase in fluorescence.

The application of double-stranded DNA-binding dye chemistry, such as SYBR Green, to DNA quantification from forensic samples has also been described. One drawback of SYBR Green-based detection is that nonspecific amplifications (primer–dimer, nonhuman products, etc.) cannot be distinguished from specific amplifications. On the other hand, the amplicon/dye ratio varies with amplicon length. Furthermore, SYBR Green can only be used in singleplex PCRs.

Real-time analysis of the fluorescence levels (increase or decrease depending on the chemistries) at each cycle of the PCR (amplification plot) allows obtaining a complete picture of the whole amplification process for each sample. In the initial cycles of PCR, a baseline is observed without any significant change in fluorescence signal. An increase in fluorescence above the baseline (or a decrease in fluorescence in the case of Plexor HY System) indicates the detection of accumulated PCR product. The higher the initial input of the target genomic DNA, the sooner a significant increase (or decrease for Plexor HY System) in fluorescence is observed. The cycle at which fluorescence reaches an arbitrary threshold level during the exponential phase of the PCR is named Ct (threshold cycle). A standard curve can be generated by plotting the log of the starting DNA template amount of a set of previously quantified DNA standards against their Ct values. Therefore, an accurate estimation of the starting DNA amount from unknown samples is accomplished by comparison of the measured Ct values with the Ct values of the standard curve.

Real-time PCR Nuclear DNA Quantification Assays

Two validated real-time PCR kits for human nuclear DNA quantification are currently used in forensic DNA labs. Both kits allow simultaneous detection of one autosomal (single or multicopy) target (for total human DNA quantitation), a target of chromosome Y (for male human DNA quantitation), and one internal PCR control (IPC; to evaluate PCR inhibition) using Taqman (Quantifiler Duo) or Plexor Chemistry (Promega). More recently, a new kit based on Scorpion primers chemistry (Qiagen) has been validated in the forensic field targeting an autosomal multicopy marker and also including one IPC. **Table 1** shows the different targets included in these validated real-time PCR kits.

Many other designs based on real-time PCR (mostly based on TaqMan chemistry) have been developed and validated in the forensic field to target single-copy autosomal markers, Alu repetitive elements, or X and Y chromosome-specific regions. The National Institute of Standards and Technology has developed a human DNA quantification standard (SRM 2372) intended for forensic applications that consists of three well-characterized human genomic DNA materials. The use of the same certified standard for human DNA quantification is expected to improve reproducibility across different laboratories and among different real-time PCR assays.

Real-time PCR Mitochondrial DNA Quantification

The use of a Taqman real-time PCR assay for quantification of mitochondrial human DNA (mtDNA) from forensic specimens was first described by Andréasson et al. in 2002 by targeting a 142 bp region spanning over the genes for tRNA lysine and ATP synthase 8 that can be amplified in a single PCR reaction or in combination with a nuclear DNA target. The specific quantification of human mtDNA by a Taqman real-time PCR assay of two different mtDNA fragment sizes (113 and 287 bp) within the hypervariable region I (HV1) of the mtDNA control region has also been described as a useful

Table 1 Targets included in real-time PCR forensic kits for nuclear human DNA quantification

Real-time PCR kit	*Human DNA target*	*Male DNA target*	*Internal PCR control*
Quantifiler Duo	RPPH1 (Ribonuclease PRNA component H1) 140 bp	SRY (Sex-determining region Y) 130 bp	Artificial template 130 bp
Plexor HY system	RNU2 locus (Human U2 small nuclear RNA) 99 bp	TSPY gene (Testis-specific protein Y encoded) 133 bp	Artificial template 150 bp
Quantiplex	Proprietary region present on several autosomes of the human genome 146 bp		Artificial template 200 bp

Note: Quantifiler Duo and Plexor HY System allow simultaneous quantitative analysis of human and male DNA, while Quantiplex only permits detection of a human multicopy DNA target. Three kits include an internal PCR control to monitor PCR inhibition. The size of each amplicon is shown in base pairs (bp).

tool to evaluate the mtDNA preservation state (degradation) from ancient bone samples. A 69 bp fragment of the mtDNA NADH dehydrogenase subunit 1 (ND1) locus has also been used as a target for mtDNA quantitation in forensic specimens using a TaqMan duplex real-time PCR assay that allows simultaneous quantification of human nuclear DNA. Another mtDNA target used in forensics by a TaqMan-MGB assay is a 79-bp fragment of a conserved region of the human mtDNA, which is coamplified with an autosomal and a Y-chromosome target. Recently, it has been described as a novel forensic utility of quantitative real-time PCR using TaqMan-MGB probes, targeting the highly variable mitochondrial single nucleotide polymorphism16519T/C to investigate heteroplasmic mixtures with an accurate quantification of the minor allele down to 9%.

At this time, there is no commercially available real-time PCR assay for quantification of mtDNA nor has there been developed a standard for mtDNA quantification in forensic materials. These seem to be some of the reasons why mtDNA quantitation is much less widespread in forensic casework.

Acknowledgment

The author especially thanks Coro Fernández for proofreading the manuscript and for her comments that have substantially improved the content of this article.

See also: **Biology/DNA:** Accreditation in Forensic DNA Analysis; Disaster Victim Identification; DNA Databases; Low-template DNA Testing; Mixture Interpretation (Interpretation of Mixed DNA Profiles with STRs Only); Short Tandem Repeats.

Further Reading

Alonso, A., García, O., 2007. Real-time quantitative PCR in forensic science. In: Rapley, R., Whitehouse, D. (Eds.), Molecular Forensics. John Wiley & Sons Inc., New York, pp. 59–71.

Alonso, A., Martín, P., 2005. A real-time PCR protocol to determine the number of amelogenin (X-Y) gene copies from forensic DNA samples. In: Carracedo, A. (Ed.), 2005. Forensic DNA Typing Protocols Methods Mol Biol 297, pp. 31–44.

Alonso, A., Martin, P., Albarrán, C., et al., 2004. Real-time PCR designs to estimate nuclear and mitochondrial DNA copy number in forensic and ancient DNA studies. Forensic Science International 139, 141–149.

Andreasson, H., Gyllensten, U., Allen, M., 2002. Real-time DNA quantification of nuclear and mitochondrial DNA in forensic analysis. BioTechniques 33, 402–411.

Anslinger, K., Bayer, B., Mack, B., Eisenmenger, W., 2007. Sex-specific fluorescent labelling of cells for laser microdissection and DNA profiling. International Journal of Legal Medicine 121, 54–56.

Barbisin, M., Fang, R., O'Shea, C.E., Calandro, L.M., Furtado, M.R., Shewale, J.G., 2009. Developmental validation of the Quantifiler Duo DNA Quantification kit for simultaneous quantification of total human and human male DNA and detection of PCR inhibitors in biological samples. Journal of Forensic Sciences 54, 305–319.

Bienvenue, J.M., Duncalf, N., Marchiarullo, D., Ferrance, J.P., Landers, J.P., 2006. Microchip-based cell lysis and DNA extraction from sperm cells for application to forensic analysis. Journal of Forensic Sciences 51, 266–273.

Bienvenue, J.M., Legendre, L.A., Ferrance, J.P., Landers, J.P., 2010. An integrated microfluidic device for DNA purification and PCR amplification of STR fragments. Forensic Science International Genetics 4, 178–186.

Butler, J.M., 2009a. DNA extraction. In: Butler, J.M. (Ed.), Fundamentals of Forensic DNA Typing. Academic Press, Amsterdam, pp. 99–110.

Butler, J.M., 2009b. DNA quantification. In: Butler, J.M. (Ed.), Fundamentals of Forensic DNA Typing. Academic Press, Amsterdam, pp. 111–124.

Gill, P., et al., 1985. Forensic applications of DNA fingerprints. Nature 318, 577–579.

Hochmeister, M.N., Budowle, B., Borer, U.V., Eggmann, U., Comey, C.T., Dirnhofer, R., 1991. Typing of deoxyribonucleic acid (DNA) extracted from compact bone from human remains. Journal of Forensic Sciences 36, 1649–1661.

Horsman, K.M., Bienvenue, J.M., Blasier, K.R., Landers, J.P., 2007. Forensic DNA analysis on microfluidic devices: a review. Journal of Forensic Sciences 52, 784–799.

Kline, M.C., Duewer, D.L., Travis, J.C., et al., 2009. Production and certification of NIST standard reference material 2372 human DNA quantitation standard. Analytical and Bioanalytical Chemistry 394, 1183–1192.

Loreille, O.M., Diegoli, T.M., Irwin, J.A., Coble, M.D., Parsons, T.J., 2007. High efficiency DNA extraction from bone by total demineralization. Forensic Science International Genetics 1, 191–195.

Murray, C., McAlister, C., Elliott, K., 2007. Identification and isolation of male cells using fluorescence in situ hybridisation and laser microdissection, for use in the investigation of sexual assault. Forensic Science International Genetics 1, 247–252.

Nagy, M., 2007. Automated DNA extraction techniques for forensic analysis. In: Rapley, R., Whitehouse, D. (Eds.), Molecular Forensics. John Wiley & Sons Inc., New York, pp. 37–58.

Nicklas, J.A., Buel, E., 2003. Development of an Alu-based, real-time PCR method for quantitation of human DNA in forensic samples. Journal of Forensic Sciences 48, 936–944.

Swango, K.L., Hudlow, W.R., Timken, M.D., Buoncristiani, M.R., 2007. Developmental validation of a multiplex qPCR assay for assessing the quantity and quality of nuclear DNA in forensic samples. Forensic Science International 170, 35–45.

Timken, M.D., Swango, K.L., Orrego, C., Buoncristiani, M.R., 2005. A duplex real-time qPCR assay for the quantification of human nuclear and mitochondrial DNA in forensic samples: implications for quantifying DNA in degraded samples. Journal of Forensic Sciences 50, 1044–1060.

Vandewoestyne, M., Deforce, D., 2010. Laser capture microdissection in forensic research: a review. International Journal of Legal Medicine 124, 513–521.

Walker, J.A., Hedges, D.J., Perodeau, B.P., et al., 2005. Multiplex polymerase chain reaction for simultaneous quantitation of human nuclear, mitochondrial, and male Y-chromosome DNA: application in human identification. Analytical Biochemistry 337, 89–97.

Relevant Websites

http://www.cstl.nist.gov—DNA Quantitation Efforts by the NIST Forensics/Human Identity Project Team.

http://www.dna.gov—DNA Initiative. (Human DNA Quantitation).

http://www.dna.gov/training—DNA Initiative. DNA extraction and quantification.

Marketing http://marketing.appliedbiosystems.com—Applied Biosystems Prepfiler system.

http://marketing.appliedbiosystems.com—QuantifilerDuo.

System https://www.promega.com—Plexor HY system.

http://www.promega.com—Promega DNA IQ system.

http://www.qiagen.com—Qiagen DNA Extraction methods in forensic.

http://www.qiagen.com—Quantiplex.

Short Tandem Repeats

M Lareu, University of Santiago de Compostela, Santiago de Compostela, Spain

Glossary

Amplicon Polymerase chain reaction (PCR)-amplified DNA segment.

Autosomes/autosomal The chromosome component not related to sex determination (complementary to the X and Y).

Capillary electrophoresis Separation of DNA fragments based on their size and by electroinjection into a capillary with a transparent window at a fixed distance from the injection position, where excitation by a laser allows four to six color signals to be read by a charge-coupled device camera at timed intervals.

CCD Charge-coupled device.

Di-, tri-, tetra-, and pentanucleotide repeats Short tandem repeat (STR) units comprising 2, 3, 4, and 5 base pair repeated DNA segments (alternatively termed units or motifs).

DNA sequencing Analysis of the base sequence of an amplified segment of DNA.

Multiplex A PCR amplification combining multiple DNA sites, i.e., markers, per reaction.

PCR and Cyclers Polymerase chain reaction, amplification of targeted DNA segments using site-specific primers, and heat-stable DNA polymerase. The PCR depends on cycled heating–cooling steps controlled by automated temperature cyclers.

The Genetics of Short Tandem Repeats. Short Tandem Repeats as a Class of Satellite DNA and the Genomic Characteristics of the Core Forensic Markers. Early Consensus on Ideal Forensic Short Tandem Repeats

A short tandem repeat (STR) consists of an array of tandemly reiterated, normally identical, multibase motifs (often termed repeat units or simply repeats) that vary in number. They belong to the common genomic element of repeat sequence or repetitive DNA, which ranges from small, single-site tandem repeat loci to much larger recurrent elements at multiple, genome-dispersed locations, such as SINES, LINES, and transposons. Tandemly repeated sequence is often termed satellite DNA because of atypical base composition changing DNA buoyancy in density gradient separations, giving three low-density satellite bands. The bulk of satellite DNA comprises repeats with numerous, long motifs creating segments up to 5 mb long, but two other types are much shorter: minisatellites have tandem repeats above 10 base pairs (bp) and reach 0.5–30 kb in length, and microsatellites–STRs have 2–10 bp repeats in very short arrays typically 20–100 bp long. The relatively short length of STRs is critical because it makes them the most amenable to amplification by polymerase chain reaction (PCR) and therefore ideal to forensic markers. In contrast, minisatellites include DNA polymorphisms originally used in pioneering genetic fingerprinting techniques, but are too long to be amplified, and therefore show markedly less forensic sensitivity.

Human STRs occur approximately once every 2 kb with the most frequent type composed of 2 bp, dinucleotide repeats. Dinucleotide STRs are widely used as linkage markers with chromosome-centered kits available, so have found their way into occasional relationship testing use. However, excessive PCR stutter with dinucleotide repeats (see the section "Irregularities Seen in Routine STR Profiling. Nonstandard Alleles, Complex Forensic STR Profiles, and the Importance of Detection Thresholds") means all forensic STRs comprise 3, 4, or 5 bp repeat motifs with most tetranucleotides (4 bp). **Figure 1** summarizes the structure of TH01, a typical tetranucleotide forensic STR; genomic positions of 23 core and 15 supplementary STRs; and the proportion in humans of each repeat type. With ~200,000 potentially suitable tetranucleotide STRs, it is necessary to review how the current set of 23–38 was selected. First, the chromosome distribution of forensic STRs in **Figure 1** highlights the need for fully segregating positions across the genome and for same-chromosome (syntenic) pairs at well-separated sites. This characteristic was among the features considered ideal when originally choosing forensic STRs. Second, it was desirable to choose loci with high levels of variability but which had manageable repeat numbers giving short enough amplified fragments for robust

 http://dx.doi.org/10.1016/B978-0-12-800647-4.00013-8

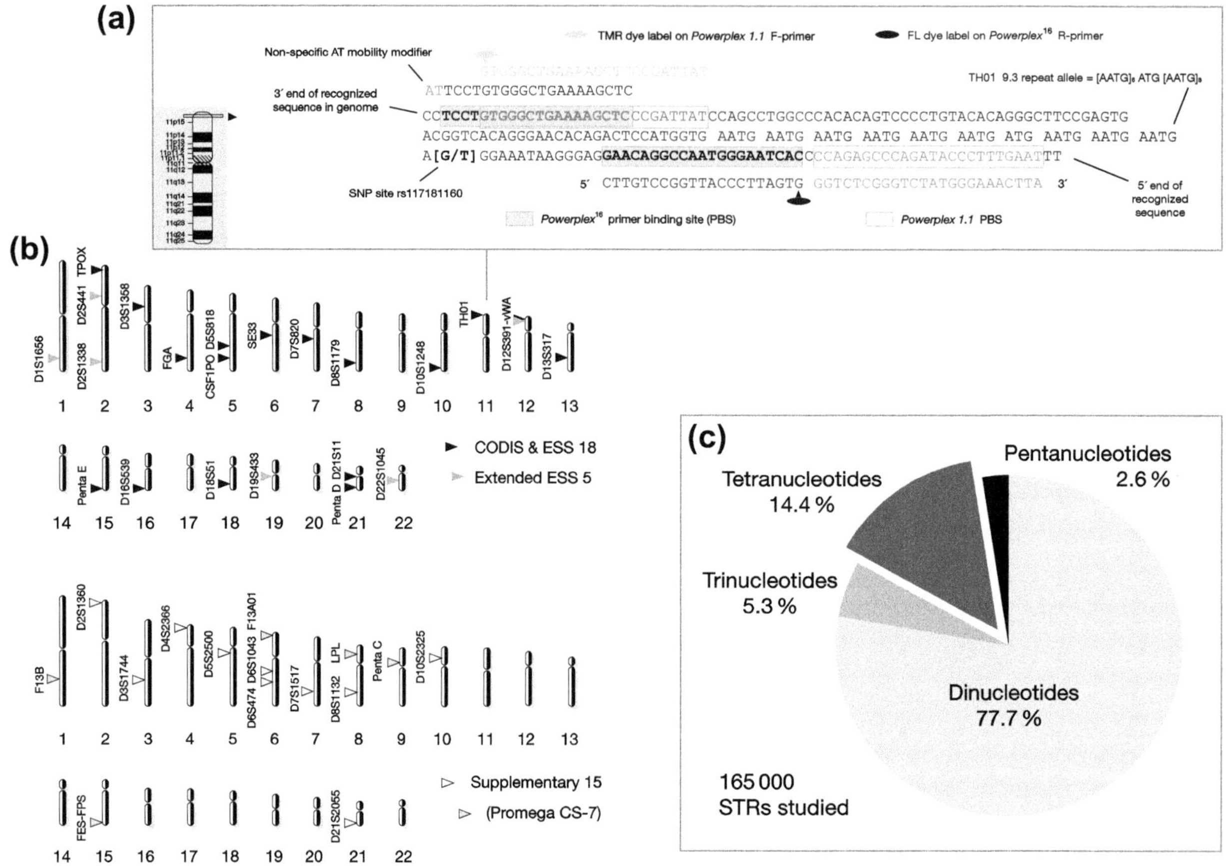

Figure 1 (a) Principal genomic features of a simple forensic short tandem repeat (STR): TH01. (b) Chromosome distribution of 23 core forensic identification STRs, upper panel, and 7 + 8 supplementary STRs (Promega CS-7 and Qiagen Investigator HD, respectively) lower panel. (c) Ratio of repeat unit nucleotide numbers in the largest survey of human autosomes.

and readily multiplexed PCR. STRs must ideally give comparable performance between shortest and longest repeats and be easily accommodated in limited electrophoresis-sized windows. Third, a feature of STRs quickly seen as important was repeat sequence complexity. Early trials of STRs TH01 and SE33 in 15 laboratories demonstrated that simple STRs (e.g., TH01) with limited repeat numbers were much more reliably typed than complex loci typified by SE33 with numerous repeats comprising 2, 3, and 4 bp repeat motifs. The fact that complex repeat STRs tend to be more polymorphic required a balance to be struck between variability and repeat complexity, leading to choice of much less polymorphic TPOX and CSF1PO STRs, while SE33 has only recently undergone increasing readoption with an obvious value as the most discriminatory forensic STR. This partly reflects more precise electrophoretic resolution with modern capillary-based instruments where single base differences are more precisely measured than before. It is arguably the case that balancing complexity and variability had previously constrained marker choice, but as the current core 23 STRs are informative enough for nearly all forensic tasks, this did not become a major restriction. **Figure 2** gives a 1985–2010 timeline showing STRs introduced in gradually expanded sets. As the literature has lacked a clearly outlined STR set overview to date, **Figure 3** summarizes the relationship between all current forensic STRs, their kits, and the United States versus European minimum or extended sets.

Lastly, it is important to note that STRs are common in all eukaryotic species and share the key characteristics of being abundant, short in length, and highly polymorphic, so they provide an ideal means to identify, establish kinship relationships, and infer population affinities in most animals, indeed in plants, as well as humans. Animal forensics such as pet-hair analysis therefore uses identical approaches (and shares the same interpretative problems) to those outlined below for human STRs.

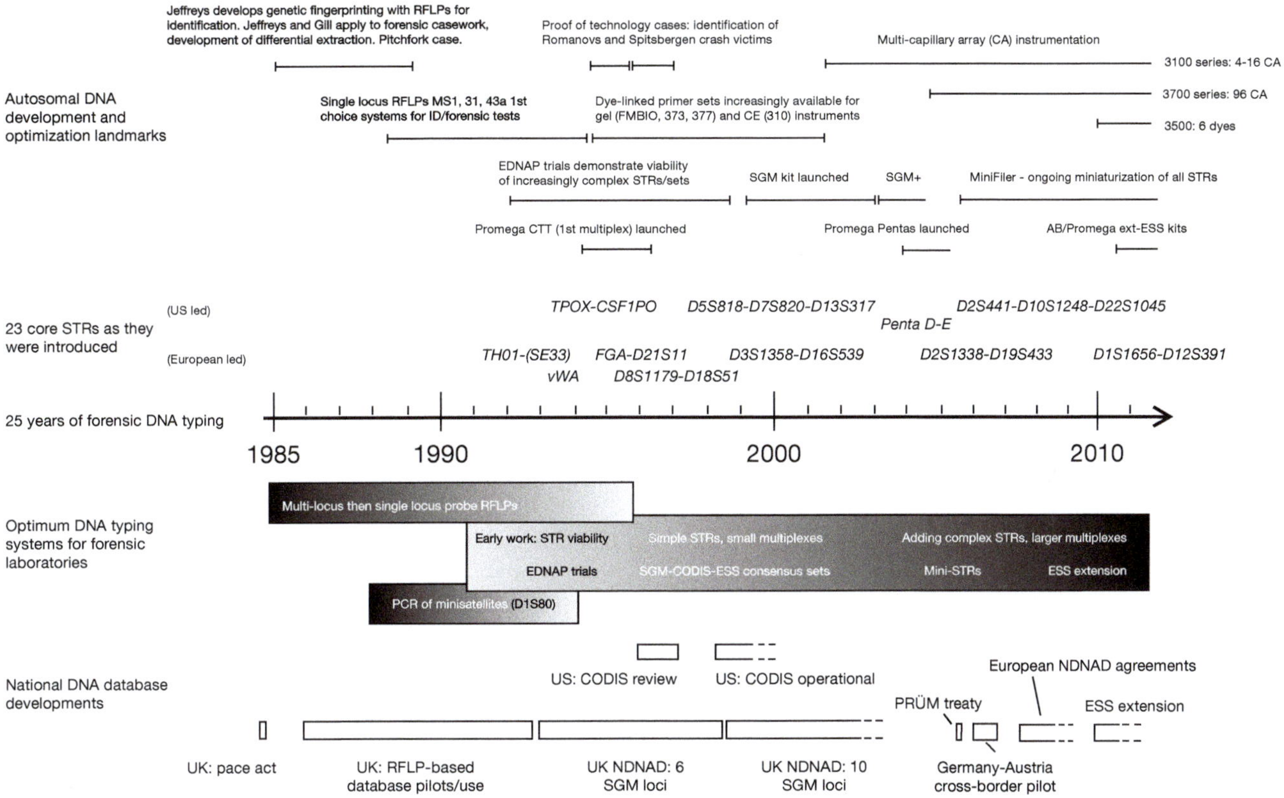

Figure 2 Time line of development of landmark DNA analysis approaches, introduction of core identification short tandem repeats (STRs), forensic typing systems, and DNA database developments.

The Principles of Forensic Dye-labeled STR Typing: PCR Amplification, the DNA Profile, and the Match Probability

The STR typing system using dye-labeled PCR primers has stayed largely unchanged for at least 15 of the 20-year history of forensic STR analysis shown in **Figure 2**. This is because the combination of capillary electrophoresis (CE) detection of dye-labeled fragments following PCR amplification of STR sequences creates a typing system that is extremely sensitive, easily multiplexed, readily applied to poor or scant forensic sources of DNA using well-validated chemistry/instrumentation, and provides a direct relationship between the signal strength and the amount of DNA molecules put into the amplification. This latter characteristic is crucial to detecting low levels of DNA in both single-source evidential material and in detecting mixtures, so that necessary adjustments can be made to pursue further amplifications, or in mixtures, to the profile interpretation framework so allelic components of individual contributors can be identified. In the early stages of STR typing development, the main limiting factors were perceived to be level of multiplexing possible in single-tube reactions, electrophoretic resolution of single-base allele differences, actual size ranges of amplified fragments, and instrument sensitivity/signal quality. In this section, the typing process is outlined, and the efforts to overcome these original limitations are detailed. The section titled "Irregularities Seen in Routine STR Profiling, Nonstandard Alleles, Complex Forensic STR Profiles, and the Importance of Detection Thresholds" reviews common irregular patterns (not strictly problems) encountered in forensic STR typing.

PCR amplification was the single-most important step forward in forensic DNA analysis, leading to greatly improved sensitivity for STR typing compared to the original genetic fingerprinting techniques and therefore considerably widening the scope of biological contact traces amenable to analysis. Primer sequences recognize a unique genome sequence to focus on this target STR segment alone. Amplified fragments or amplicons, therefore, comprise a DNA segment containing the unique primer sequence (one strand dye labeled), the repeat region of variable length, and the intermediate sequences between primer and repeats. Largely due to their short size and

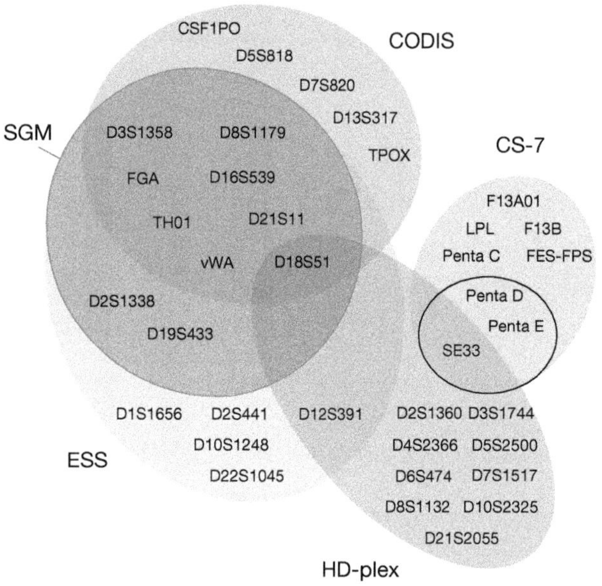

Figure 3 Overlapping and multiplex-specific short tandem repeat (STR) marker sets, core systems grouped leftmost (plus SE33, Penta D/E), and new supplementary STR multiplexes rightmost. Bold SGM/ESS/CODIS STRs are the original ESS set of seven loci and the lower five STRs in the ESS group are the extended ESS set. All national DNA database (NDNAD) regimes use sets of the 20 STRs shown on the left with the exception of the German NDNAD that includes SE33.

the relative uniformity of chosen loci, STRs have proved to be extremely robust components of PCR multiplexes. Multiplexing requires comparable reaction dynamics per primer pair—notably the Tm or optimum temperature that primers can bind specifically to their recognition sequences. Similarly, the small size differences between shortest and longest repeat alleles provide more balanced rates of amplification across all size ranges. Lastly, PCR cyclers developed in the mid-1990s using more precise Peltier temperature control have provided greatly improved reliability and more consistent performance—both between cyclers and within their temperature transfer plates. This led to much more predictable amplification when applying suitably prepared commercial PCR kits of optimum primer sets, high-performance DNA polymerase, buffer, and reaction components. Early consensus on best-performing, forensically ideal STRs also helped to accelerate production of well-balanced multiplex kits. However, possibly of more benefit to forensic STR analysis was the accompanying improvement in the instruments available to detect and size the amplified STR fragments.

Early in the development of forensic STR typing, instruments created for automated DNA sequencing were adapted to analyze STR amplicons. They used sequencing dyes and instrumentation meant for the four colors, each originally dedicated to one base terminator, available for PCR fragment analysis—three for amplicon labeling and one (red) for a standardized size ladder. Use of dedicated size standards focused on short base pair ranges allowed accurate size estimation from a mobility reference curve. This is made for size standards co-run in each capillary and minimizes the effects of mobility variation between samples. The blue, green, and yellow dyes are readily attached to the end of one PCR primer without interfering with amplification efficiency. Therefore, it was a straightforward step to extend multiplexing up to four STRs per dye label by combining markers with nonoverlapping amplicon size ranges. A dual fragment X–Y gender marker based on a 6 bp sequence deletion in the X chromosome amelogenin gene is included in all kits. Depending on total repeats, three to four STRs can be divided across a size window of ~100–400 bp. However, this represents the original strategy of arranging actual amplicon sizes to span the window. More recently, mass modification using "drag-chute" elements within the primers or nonspecific sequence tails (**Figure 1** shows a 2 bp primer tail for TH01) allows more precise size range adjustment, so that amplicons can be miniaturized yet still occupy upper size ranges, while potentially extra STRs can be accommodated. Furthermore, the number of dyes available has risen to five, further extending the multiplex ceiling by ~20% more STRs with an orange dye now used for sizing.

The resulting DNA profiles consist of multiple peaks corresponding to dye-labeled amplicons passing a laser and charge-coupled device (CCD) camera at the read window at recorded time intervals. While profiles can be individually reviewed by STR and by dye, most are automatically analyzed by analysis software that recognizes peaks in prescribed positions for each allele derived from a concurrently run reference ladder of the common repeat variants. These positions vary minimally between capillaries but more between runs and instruments—a rule of thumb being ±0.5 bp, but most procedures can adequately use one or two allele reference ladders per run of up to 96 samples. Rare alleles comprising unusual repeat numbers or intermediate repeat structures (such as 1, 2, and 3 bp repeat motifs among regular tetranucleotide alleles) are not usually included in allele ladders, but rare alleles generally migrate to positions that can be correctly aligned and named. Excessive sequence variation among the repeat region motifs can lead to irregular mobility so that same-size fragments with very different underlying sequences migrate differently. This characteristic represents a potential drawback for SE33, but all other forensic STRs have more regular motif structures and, therefore, show almost entirely predictable mobilities.

As STR typing is a single reaction in one tube, it provides major benefits compared to other forms of forensic analysis.

First, the dye-labeled amplicons generate peak heights and their ratios in direct proportion to the input DNA, giving a system for inference of likely preamplified DNA levels and making mixture interpretation of simple two-donor multiple-peak profiles a viable option. Second, minimal tube transfers are involved in the protocol: sample to extraction tube, extract to PCR tube, and amplicon to CE sample plates—so STR analysis has relatively low sample switch rates compared to other forensic protocols. Lastly, the system has considerable potential to be streamlined and quickened. As a result, there is an interest in utilizing faster acting polymerases, shorter cycles, and direct DNA input (i.e., lysing cells in the PCR tube).

The statistical analysis of profiles is the last of the major features of STR analysis that provided a quantum shift in ease of use and quality of data compared to previous forms of DNA profiling. STRs brought limited size-range discrete alleles, eliminating the complexities of reporting continuous patterns of DNA mobility where the much longer alleles of DNA fingerprint microsatellites required placement in broad, loosely defined, continuous mobility windows. In effect, STRs have mobility variation windows less than 1 bp, so each allele can be precisely differentiated. This provides a simple system to construct a profile frequency because the population allele frequency estimation on which it is based is accurate and much more representative of the true patterns of variability than before. As the composite STRs in a profile have been chosen to be independently segregating, and extensive testing continues to suggest they are neutral loci (not subject to changes in allele frequencies within a population due to selection), their allele frequencies can be combined to provide an unbiased single likelihood of the profile in the population. **Figure 4** shows an example profile with composite locus frequencies combined to form a final profile frequency. This value can be used to report a random match probability (RMP; one over the profile frequency) representing the chance of an identical profile in unrelated individuals from the same population. The issue of which populations to use is still sometimes contested, but the ease with which a range of population data can be accessed by a laboratory to prepare different likelihoods helps address arguments that hindered proper assessment of STR statistics in early court cases. Further population statistical refinements have been added, notably use of theta adjustments for population stratification. A common initial courtroom challenge to STR population data was the problem that allele frequency estimates based on broad population group estimates might be unrepresentative of smaller, often isolated, subpopulations from which a defendant may originate. Therefore, without suitable adjustment, allele frequencies tend to underestimate those of subpopulations and the rarity of the profile is artificially exaggerated. A theta value of 0.01–0.02 is now commonly applied to compensate for the potential of allele frequency underestimation in subpopulations.

Irregularities Seen in Routine STR Profiling. Nonstandard Alleles, Complex Forensic STR Profiles, and the Importance of Detection Thresholds

Irregularities encountered with routine profiling of normal forensic DNA can be divided into two types: arising from the genetics of the STR and caused by the PCR or CE detection process. The observation of complex STR profiles is a different phenomenon and concerns the difficulties of interpreting profile patterns seen when amplifying low-level DNA (herein LCN) or mixed source DNA from different donors. Genetic irregularities are rare and largely manageable since invariably only one composite STR is affected. Particular features of the signal peaks in a profile arising from PCR or CE are also manageable but can often be overlooked by laboratories if insufficient attention is paid to establishing laboratory-specific detection thresholds from experimental and routine profile data. This has a direct bearing on the interpretative framework used to analyze LCN DNA or mixed profiles because appropriate detection thresholds are needed to properly define the limits of allele detection possible from such complex profiles. Progressive improvements in both sensitivity of CE instruments and PCR performance from reformulated kits means complex profiles are seen more often in routine criminal casework as LCN DNA is now amplified to detectable levels much more frequently.

Genetic-based STR irregularities include repeat slippage mutations, genomic null alleles (that may be kit specific), triallelic patterns, sequence-based mobility shifts, and off-ladder alleles including intermediate repeats and interlocus alleles. STR repeat slippage mutations are created when DNA is copied and a repeat is lost or gained due to the cell's polymerase slipping when aligning copied strands in meiosis (uncommon or undetected in mitosis). Mutation is therefore largely confined to the germ line, that is, occurring in gametogenesis and detected comparing related individuals. Slippage, therefore, affects interpretation of relationship testing results but is notably much more common in STRs than other variant loci, for example, single nucleotide polymorphisms (SNPs). Slippage typically occurs in single STRs at variance with the other results but can occur in multiple loci—particularly when combining STRs with higher mutation rates such as SE33. This becomes a significant problem when only a deficient pedigree is available to test and a wrongly named first-degree relative of the true father (e.g., brother) shows few STR exclusions. This represents a principal application for the supplementary STRs shown in **Figure 3**. In criminal STR profiling, null and nonstandard alleles are the main genetic irregularities, consequently *STRbase* includes reference libraries collating variant alleles, triallelic patterns, and null alleles listed by typing kits compared. In terms of routine typing, the main issues with variant allele definition are length estimation compared to reference ladders and assignment of a suitable allele frequency.

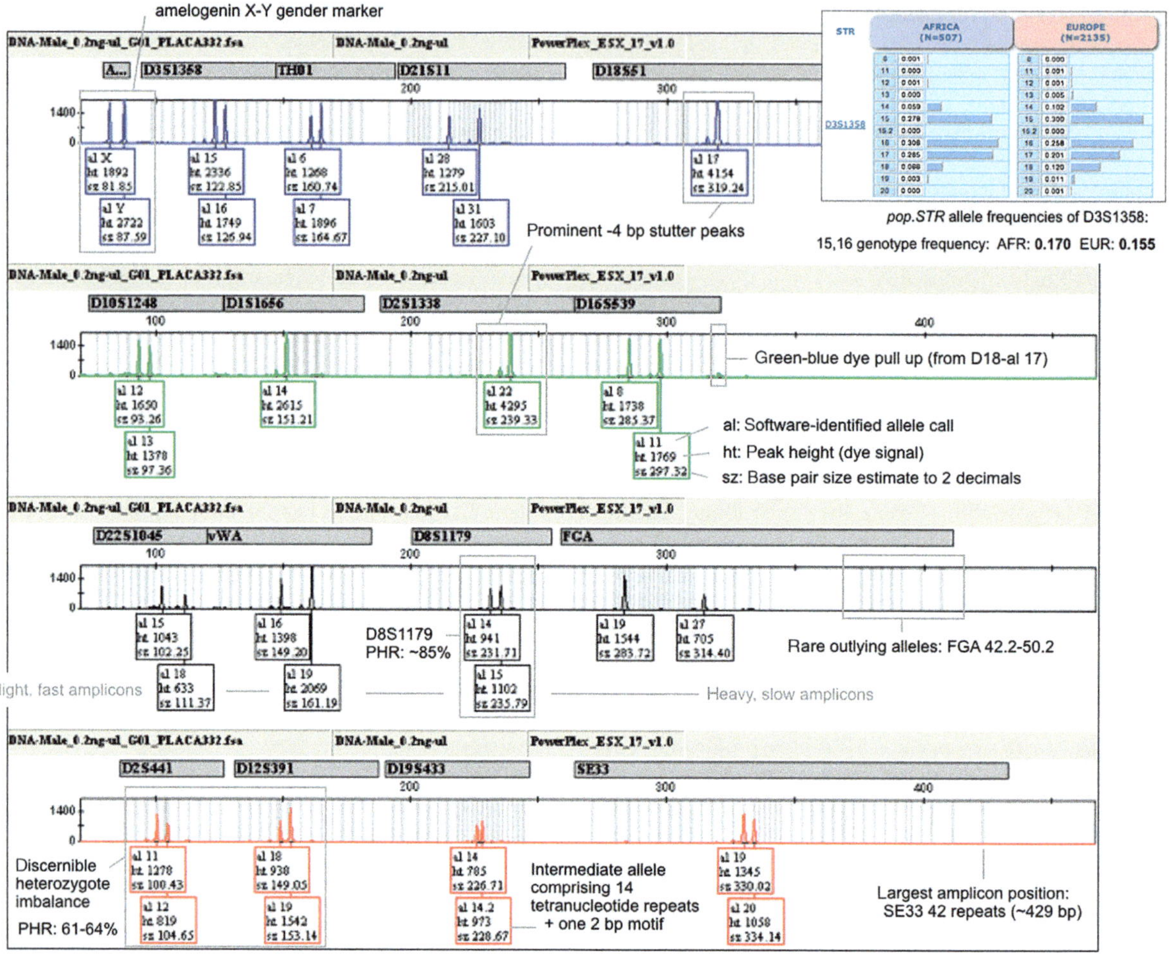

		AFR	EUR			AFR	EUR			AFR	EUR			AFR	EUR
D3S1358	15–16	0.17	0.155	D10S1248	12–13	0.058	0.002	D22S1045	15–18	0.004	0.006	D2S441	11-12	0.091	0.06
TH01	6–7	0.185	0.108	D1S1656	14	0.051	0.018	vWA	16–19	0.069	0.038	D12S391	18-19	0.087	0.06
D21S11	28–31	0.015	0.023	D2S1338	22	0.019	0.004	D8S1179	14–15	0.154	0.104	D19S433	14-14.2	0.035	0.027
D18S51	17	0.031	0.017	D16S539	8–11	0.026	0.01	FGA	19–27	0.001	0.002	SE33	19-20	0.028	0.01

Profile frequency (RMPs) from cumulative genotype frequencies: **AFR 7.05×10^{-24}** / **EUR 4.34×10^{-28}**

Figure 4 Characteristics of a typical 16-short tandem repeat (STR) multiplex profile generated by the Promega ESX-17 kit. The labeled gray bars above each peak set denote the size windows of the majority of recorded alleles in that STR represented in the reference allelic ladder. The inset graphic top right shows a *pop.STR* population frequency output example for D3S1358 and the lower table the component genotype frequencies for all 16 STRs in two population groups. The cumulative product of the individual genotype frequencies: the profile frequency and random match probability (RMP) are calculated for each population.

Figure 5 shows two examples for nonstandard STR alleles, an off-ladder allele and a mobility-shift variant, illustrating single base-pair resolution generally provides a robust system for recognizing rare variants. The allele can often be verified by coelectrophoresis with a reference spike, for example, combining a common TH01 9.3 with a rare 10 allele (particularly when paired with an inconveniently distant heterozygote allele such as a 6). In research terms, the U.S. National Institute of Standards and Technology (NIST), the host organization of *STRbase*, endeavors to sequence a proportion of variants reported to their Web site. Interlocus alleles falling between reference ladder spans can be difficult to assign to a particular STR if both are homozygous, but one simple approach is to review allele frequencies of each homozygote to deduce which is more likely, then pair the variant accordingly. Null alleles occur when a primer-binding sequence harbors a deletion or an SNP close to the 3′ end and would be undetectable if all kits used identical primers. In this case, a heterozygote with a null

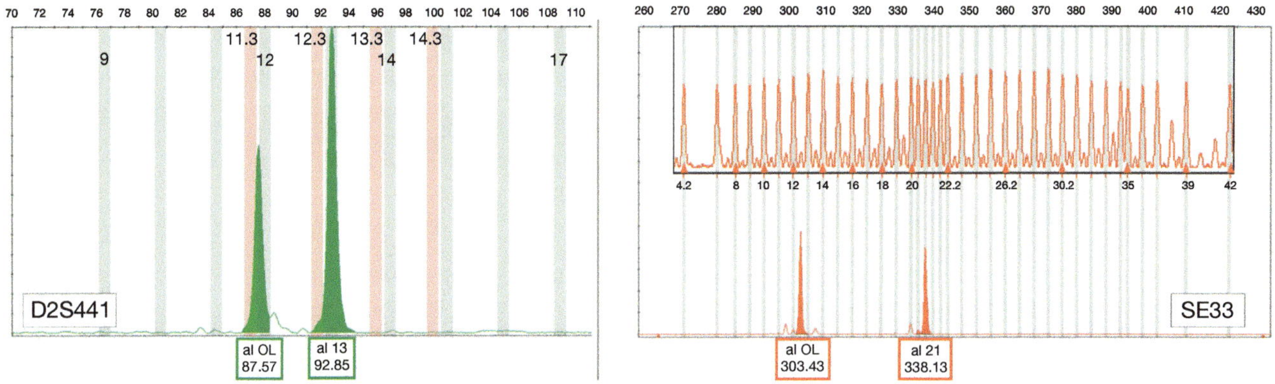

Figure 5 Two examples of nonstandard short tandem repeat (STR) alleles. D2S441 peaks indicate an unequivocal 13 allele and a peak falling between the expected 11.3 and 12 repeat allele size windows possibly due to sequence variation causing mobility shift. SE33 peaks have the allelic ladder superimposed above. The off-ladder (marked OL) peak indicates a likely 12.2 allele but with a size estimate closely matching an inferred position (closest ladder alleles = 12 and 13, 301.29 and 305.5 bp, respectively).

variant on one chromosome would show an apparent homozygous allele for the other albeit commonly at detectably lower signal heights. However, forensic STR kits from different manufacturers use multiple primer designs; hence, deletions or SNPs in primer-specific locations show nulls as a homozygote (or more rarely imbalanced heterozygote peaks) not seen in the alternative primers, so these are often termed kit discordancies. Note that deletions may occur in intermediate sequences (between primer and repeats) specific to a primer set as well as in primer-binding sites. Kit discordancies have obvious consequences for database searches of profiles typed with an alternative primer set to the database entries. At the moment, there are increasing efforts to manage the scrutiny of discordancies by parallel typing of large cohorts of population samples since nearly all deletions and SNPs are rare. Manufacturers can also address many of the more common discordancies by incorporating redundant primers (multiple recognition sequences) binding to the variant sequence and recovering the repeat allele on that chromosome. Mobility shift due to sequence variation is an ongoing problem in complex STRs, but the successful inclusion of SE33 in the German NDNAD suggests that laboratories can readily cope with sequence microvariation.

PCR and CE factors can create profile irregularities, but a well-optimized STR protocol should produce clean profiles, while a properly established dye wavelength matrix will eliminate the main problems of signal linearity limits (signal overload) and signal pull up from cross-dye detection interference. In nearly all cases, complex profiles are a consequence of the nature of the input DNA. They present considerable interpretative challenges and are covered in depth in other articles regarding LCN and mixtures. An important point is that complex profiles inevitably lead to differences in interpretation among experts and, therefore, disagreement between prosecution and defense specialists in court. As a very generalized summary, LCN profiles can have signals close to or below levels normally classified as noise and tend to show allele and locus dropout (loss of matched peaks) and/or allele drop-in (spontaneous appearance of random, unmatched alleles). Mixed profiles reveal themselves as more than two alleles in a proportion of STRs and detectable peak imbalances. Therefore, establishing certain detection thresholds is an essential preparation for differentiating artifact signal from allele detection signal in complex profiles. The key thresholds are stutter, peak height ratio (PHR), analytical threshold (AT), and stochastic threshold (ST). Thresholds should be properly gauged by all STR typing laboratories for their input DNA, PCR regimes, kits, and CE instrumentation. At the time of writing, consensus has been reached about how to instigate this process, and comprehensive guidelines are now in place for this critical aspect of STR analysis.

Stutter is a PCR artifact caused by polymerase slippage during PCR creating a detectable peak −4 bp shorter/faster than the allele peak, generally 5–15% of allele peak heights. A much weaker +4 bp following peak can also occur. PHR measures the normal heterozygote peak-pair ratio limits based on screening of signal balance in a broad range of normal crime case profiles. AT sets a minimum peak height below which an allele assignment becomes unreliable since it is imbedded in background noise signals. Despite being easy to establish with negative controls or nonpeak area measurements, most laboratories use a default 50 relative fluorescent units. However, increased PCR success with LCN DNA leads to fewer negative profiles and more showing peaks at or below the AT. Therefore, proper AT preparation increases the reliability of assigning alleles from LCN signals. Likewise, LCN PCR is highly prone to stochastic effects where one strand amplifies preferentially at random and heterozygotes consequently show marked imbalance and can only be reliably recognized with reference to the laboratories' routine PHR range. Extreme heterozygote imbalance is manifested as one allele failing to amplify completely despite signal from the other and requires establishing the ST. ST measures the highest surviving peak height seen when dropout is known to occur based on experimentally reproduced LCN analyses, such as dilution series. ST records a limited range of maximum homozygote peak heights seen when the paired alleles drop out. Therefore, a thorough knowledge of ST and PHR values is a key to differentiating LCN stochastic effects from normal heterozygote peak ratio imbalance. Stutter and PHR are clearly the key factors in mixture interpretation, and luckily both are easily established from any previously recorded CE data.

For mixture interpretation, laboratories can establish their own mixture ratio limit—predetermined major/minor peak ratios that are considered sufficiently differentiated to allow assignment of alleles to different contributors. Simple ranges of control DNA artificial mixtures provide an adequate means to begin introducing mixture detection limits. A simple mixture rule of thumb divides a profile into three zones: the 5–10% of observed highest peak of the stutter zone; the 10–70% mixture zone (i.e., peaks outside of PHR values); and the signal zone >70% of the highest heterozygote peak. A debatable issue in establishing minimum levels of stutter and PHR is whether these are recorded for whole profiles, per STR, or per allele. For example, stutter levels for TH01 9.3 alleles are much lower than the other alleles, and different STRs show varying stutter and heterozygote ratios. A final cautionary note is that thresholds are not set in stone but require constant maintenance based on evolving cycling conditions, kit formulations, and instrument performance, creating an almost continuous validation process for laboratories tackling LCN analysis and mixture interpretation.

New Developments in STR Typing

Space does not allow thorough coverage of latest developments in STR typing, but it is important to be aware of areas that merit further development. These include rapid PCR, portable STR analysis, ancestry inference, and mass spectrometric STR typing permitting detection of repeat region sequence variation. Rapid PCR potentially allows amplification reactions shortened from 3 h to ~40 min. Proof-of-principle studies indicate using more rapidly activated polymerases and three- to sixfold reductions in cycling times works well. The prospects for mobile, real-time STR typing technologies for rapid screening at the scene of a crime or point of arrest are also promising. A study of the viability of a system known as melting curve detection using multiple allele fluorescent probes showed that STRs D18S51, TH01, and D8S1179 could be typed with this potentially portable system, although discrimination is compromised by use of just three STRs. The potential for ancestry inference from STR data, use of mass spectrometry to type STRs, and detect sequence changes within repeat motifs are covered in other articles in this book.

Beyond the Core Loci: New STRs

Figure 6 reflects how the numbers of STRs routinely used may soon be dictated by new operational needs such as familial searching and improving relationship testing statistics in identification of missing persons—when pedigrees are incomplete or bridge several generations. This raises the issue of whether additional STRs should now be assessed or be available to the DNA laboratory when more discriminatory information is required in certain scenarios. It is important to note that the supplementary STRs detailed here offer considerable scope for exploiting the sixth dye potentially available in Applied Biosystems 3500 CE instruments.

An extra 14 STRs have recently been released in two kits: Promega CS-7 7-plex (five novel STRs including Penta C) and Qiagen Investigator HDplex 12-plex (nine novel). Additionally, a first population-tailored STR, D6S1043, is a part of the SinoFiler™ kit (Applied Biosystems) available to East Asian laboratories. The genomic positions of these extra STRs shown

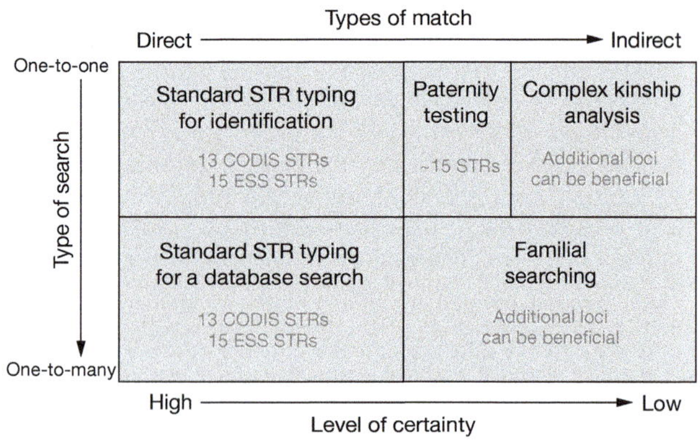

Figure 6 The balance between forensic operational needs, levels of certainty, and numbers of short tandem repeats (STRs) typed in routine or supplemented analyses. Reproduced with the kind permission of Kristen O'Connor from O'Connor KL, Butts E, Hill CR, Butler JM, and Vallone PM (2010) Evaluating the effect of additional loci on likelihood ratio values for complex kinship analysis. In: *Proceedings of the 21st International Symposium on Human Identification.* San Antonio, TX, October 10–14.

in **Figure 1** indicate some close proximities for certain syntenic pairs, but a detailed genetic map of 39 forensic STRs is now available to help address linkage issues. It should be noted that adding more STRs does not always solve the problem of ambiguous relationship likelihoods in complex pedigrees. Furthermore, allowance must be made for the degree of linkage between established and novel STRs when occasionally expanding STR typing for the analysis of close relatives.

Lastly, NIST has developed a 26-component mini-STR set, designed from the start to be typed from very short amplicons and easily accommodated into relatively narrow-sized windows. Three STRs have since been incorporated in the extended ESS set, while one component shows inconsistencies, providing 22 STRs that are potentially highly sensitive for analyzing degraded DNA.

See also: **Biology/DNA:** Accreditation in Forensic DNA Analysis; Ancestry Informative Markers; DNA Extraction and Quantification; Future Analytical Techniques: DNA Mass Spectrometry; Low-template DNA Testing; MiniSTRs; Mixture Interpretation (Interpretation of Mixed DNA Profiles with STRs Only); Single-nucleotide Polymorphisms; X-Chromosome Markers.

Further Reading

Brown, T.A., 2002. Genomes, vol. 2. Wiley-Liss, Oxford. Available online at NCBI Bookshelf. http://www.ncbi.nlm.gov/books/NBK21128/.

Butler, J.M., 2009. Fundamentals of Forensic DNA Typing. Academic Press, San Diego, CA.

Butler, J.M., 2011. Advanced Topics in Forensic DNA Typing: Methodology. Academic Press, San Diego, CA.

Butler, J.M., 2012. Advanced Topics in Forensic DNA Typing: Interpretation.

Goldstein, D.B., Schlotterer, C., 1999. Microsatellites, Evolution and Applications. Oxford University Press, Oxford.

Relevant Websites

http://alfred.med.yale.edu/, http://spsmart.cesga.es/popstr.php, http://strbase.org/—Allele frequency databases. ALFRED and pop.STR (global coverage of most STRs), STR-base (European coverage of SGM+ STRs), respectively.

http://www.cstl.nist.gov/strbase/—STRbase. Comprehensive and constantly updated Web resource for forensic DNA analysis topics.

http://www.fbi.gov/about-us/lab/codis/swgdam-interpretation-guidelines—Profile interpretation and detection thresholds. Despite ongoing debate, a suitable starting point is the SWGDAM online guideline documents.

http://www.promega.com/geneticidtools/powerstats/—Statistical analysis of population data. Promega Powerstats, an Excel template for allele frequency and discrimination power calculations from user's in-house genotype data.

http://www.promega.com/resources/articles/profiles-in-dna/—Promega Profiles in DNA series: Succinct but highly informative online articles with strong emphasis on forensic STR analysis.

Single-Nucleotide Polymorphisms

C Børsting and N Morling, University of Copenhagen, Copenhagen, Denmark

Abbreviations

bp Base pairs
CE Capillary electrophoresis
CODIS Combined DNA index system
PCR Polymerase chain reaction
SBE Single-base extension
SNP Single-nucleotide polymorphism
STR Short tandem repeat

Glossary

Electrophoresis A method for separation of molecules based on their size and electrical charge.
Hardy–Weinberg equilibrium A locus is in Hardy–Weinberg equilibrium when allele and genotype frequencies in a population remain constant from generation to generation.
Heterozygosity The fraction of individuals in a population that is heterozygous for a particular locus.
Match probability The probability that two unrelated individuals have the same genotype.
Multiplex PCR/SBE Standard PCR or SBE reactions involving multiple targets.
Nucleosome A DNA–protein complex that forms the basic unit of DNA packaging.
Polymerase chain reaction A method for generating millions of copies of specifically selected DNA sequences from just a few copies of DNA.
Single-base extension A method for determining the identity of a single nucleotide at a specific position in a DNA sequence. The method is also known as minisequencing.

Introduction

Single-nucleotide polymorphisms (SNPs) are base pair (bp) variations at specific locations in the genome. As per definition, a genetic variation at a single bp locus is not considered to be an SNP unless at least two alleles have frequencies of more than 1% in a large population of unrelated individuals. The haploid human genome consists of approximately 3 billion bp. The number of SNPs is estimated to be 10–11 million, which gives an average of one SNP per 275 bp. The vast majority of SNPs have only two alleles, because the mutation rate at a particular bp position is extremely low and it is highly unlikely that two point mutations happen at the same position over time. For this reason, SNPs have been used extensively to map the history of populations by identifying the distribution of SNP alleles among existing and past populations. SNP markers are also the best choice for construction of a dense set of polymorphic markers that can be used for studying the association between the markers and a particular trait or disease.

SNPs have many potential uses in forensic genetic investigations, including estimation of ethnicity, human traits, or diseases. These issues are addressed in other articles of this book. Here, the use of SNPs for human identification is discussed.

SNPs versus Short Tandem Repeats

Short tandem repeats (STRs) have been the preferred markers for forensic genetic investigations since the 1990s, and today, standardized commercial kits with STRs are used by forensic laboratories across the globe. The advantages and disadvantages of STRs and SNPs are compared in the following discussion.

 http://dx.doi.org/10.1016/B978-0-12-800647-4.00014-X

Power of Discrimination

One SNP locus is less informative than one STR locus because SNP loci have only two possible alleles and the STR loci typically used in forensic genetics have 8–15 different alleles. The match probability P for n SNP loci can be approximated as a simple function of n and the frequency of the least common allele, ρ, by assuming that all SNPs are in Hardy–Weinberg equilibrium and that ρ is constant for all loci:

$$P = \left(\rho^2\right)^n + (2\rho(1-\rho))^n + \left((1-\rho)^2\right)^n$$

The match probability has the highest value for $\rho = 0.5$ but does not change very much when ρ is 0.3–0.5. If ρ is between 0.2 and 0.5, 50 SNPs give a combined match probability equivalent to that of 12 STRs. Thus, panels of SNPs that can match the commonly used STR panels, for example, the 13 combined DNA index system (CODIS) loci or the 12 European standard set loci, should include at least 50 SNPs with a minimum heterozygosity of 0.32 ($\rho = 0.2$) and a preferable heterozygosity of 0.42 ($\rho = 0.3$) or higher.

Mutation Rates

Mutations pose a major problem in relationship testing. A mutation may result in a genetic inconsistency between the child and a parent, and even though the parent matches the child at all other investigated loci, the conclusion will be ambiguous and the results may speak in favor of two or more likely scenarios. Relatives share a high number of alleles, and only a few genetic inconsistencies are expected between a child and, for example, an uncle or a grandfather. Therefore, genetic inconsistencies between a child and an alleged parent could be due to mutations, and the alleged parent could be the true parent, or the results could indicate that the alleged parent was a close relative of the true parent.

The mutation rates of the commonly used STRs are typically 0.001–0.003, whereas the mutation rates of SNPs are estimated to be 0.00000001. Mutations are present in one of the 13 CODIS loci in approximately 3% of all mother–child–father trios. In contrast, mutations will be extremely rare if SNPs are investigated.

Amplicon Lengths

When a cell dies and the content is spilled into the surroundings, DNA is quickly degraded into smaller pieces. The rate of the degradation process varies depending on temperature, humidity, pH, light, presence of microorganisms, and other environmental factors. It is generally believed that the DNA in nucleosome complexes are better protected from degradation and a distinct pattern of nucleosome-sized fragments are observed as the degradation progresses. The length of DNA in the nucleosome core is 146 bp, and it is difficult to amplify longer fragments by conventional polymerase chain reaction (PCR) in highly degraded DNA.

The length of the PCR product with an SNP locus needs only to be the length of the PCR primers plus 1 bp (the SNP position). PCR primers are usually 15- to 18-bp long, and thus, a PCR product containing an SNP locus may be shorter than 40 bp. In contrast, the commonly used STR alleles have up to 40 tandem repeat units, each with a size of 4 bp, and consequently, PCR products containing an STR locus can measure 200 bp or longer. Furthermore, STRs are usually detected by electrophoresis, and in order to separate and identify all the loci in one experiment, the longest PCR products in the commercial multiplexes should be as long as 400–450 bp. Consequently, partial STR profiles are frequently observed when the DNA is highly degraded, whereas SNP typing of the same material results in complete profiles (see **Figure 1** for example).

In mass disasters such as the World Trade Center terrorist attack in 2001 or the South Asian tsunami in 2004, the victims may be impossible to identify by visual inspection because the remains are highly fragmented, decomposed, or burned. Recovered DNA may be highly degraded, and if reference materials from the missing persons are not available, the victims must be identified via reference samples from close relatives. The low mutation rate of SNPs and the possibility of typing highly degraded DNA make SNPs very useful in mass disaster investigations. SNPs were used for human identification at the World Trade Center attack, but the SNP assay was still in a test phase and the results were predictably poor. Only assays that are properly validated and preferentially used routinely by the investigating laboratories should be used in the chaotic and stressful environment of a mass disaster.

PCR Artifacts

PCR artifacts known as stutters are generated during the PCR amplification of tandem repeats. Stutters formed by amplification of the STRs commonly used in forensic genetics are usually one repeat shorter than the target sequence, but stutters of other lengths are sometimes observed. It has been proposed that stutters are formed when unfinished extension products dehybridize from the target DNA during elongation and subsequently anneal to the STR sequence in another position (known as slipped-strand mispairing). Usually, the stutter peak is much lower (<10%) than the peak originating from the parent allele in the electropherogram. However, if the number of initial target DNA molecules is low and the stutter is formed during the first critical cycles of the PCR, there is a risk that the stutter peak may be as high as the parent peak and it may be misinterpreted as a true allele and assigned to the sample. Furthermore, unfinished extension products will be formed in higher numbers when PCR is performed on highly degraded DNA, because PCR primers will anneal to strands where the target sequences are interrupted. Stutters are also a major problem in the analysis of mixtures, because it can be difficult to conclude whether a small peak in

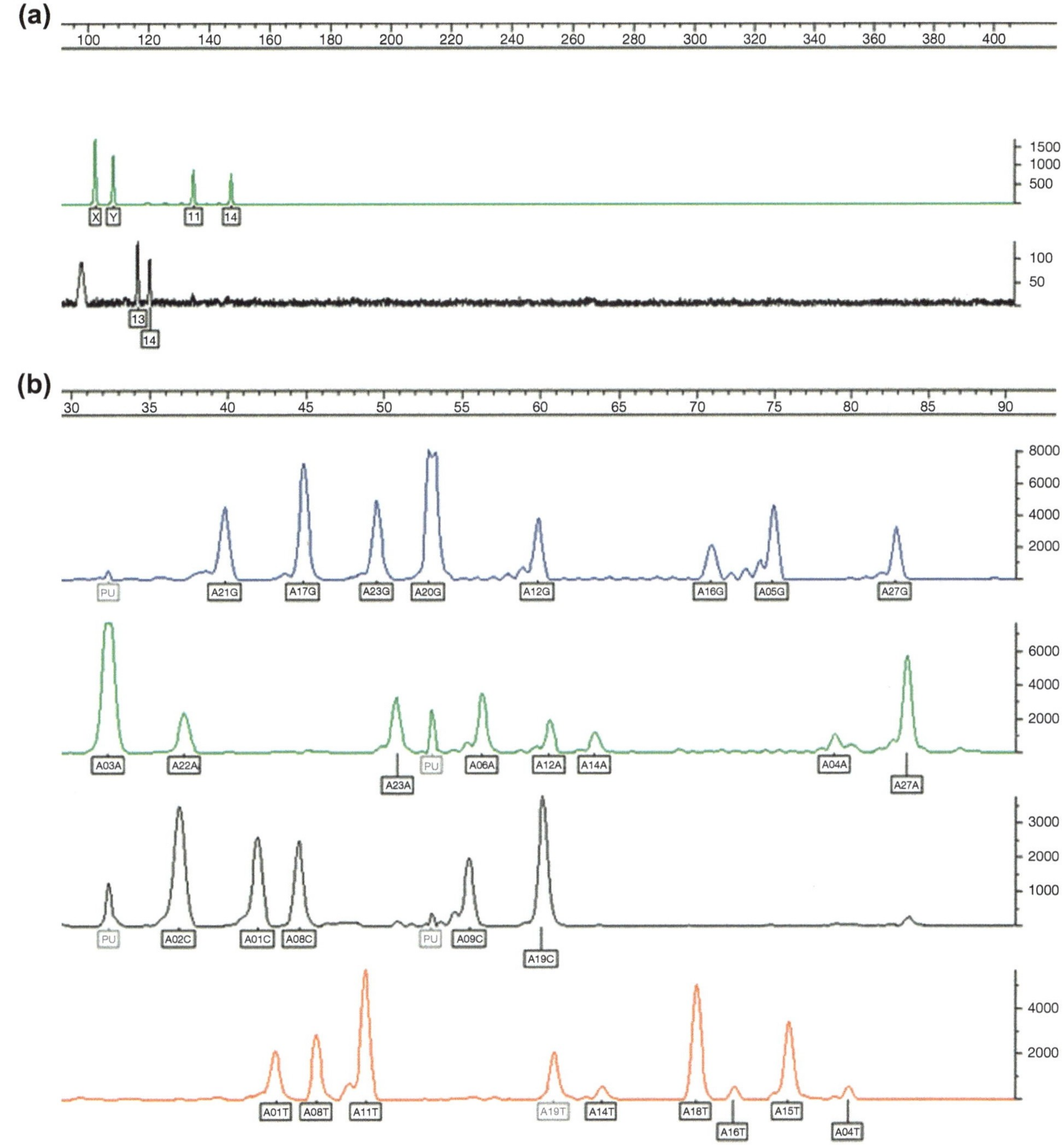

Figure 1 DNA was extracted from a bone sample. The sample was typed with (a) the AmpF*l*STR® SEfiler Plus™ PCR amplification kit (Applied Biosystems) and (b) the SNP*for*ID multiplex. Approximately 250 pg DNA was used for the PCRs. Amelogenin and two STR loci (D8S1179 and D19S433) were typed with the STR kit. Allele calls are shown in boxes. No fragment with a 6-FAM™ (blue) or PET® (red) dye was detected. The match probability based on the STR results was 8.1×10^{-3}. A total of 49 SNPs were typed with the SNP*for*ID multiplex. The results from 21 of the 49 SNPs are shown. Allele calls are shown in boxes, for example, "A21G," which is the G allele of SNP number A21 (rs722098). "PU" is a pull up. The match probability based on the SNP results was 1.2×10^{-21}.

a stutter position is in fact a stutter or an amplification product from another individual that contributed less to the mixture.

Stutters are not formed in the amplification of SNP loci. Even if unfinished extension products are formed by slippage or because the target DNA is highly degraded, the unfinished extension products can only anneal to one unique position and they will simply function as a primer in the next PCR cycle.

Databasing

National and international databases contain millions of STR profiles from known criminal offenders, victims, and trace samples collected from crime scenes over a period of more than two decades. It would be an overwhelming task to type all these samples again to create a similar SNP database, and in some cases, it will be impossible because the samples have been used up or discarded and cannot be replaced. Therefore, STRs will most likely remain the preferred markers in crime casework, and SNPs may be used only as a supplementary tool in future crime investigations. In relationship casework, the profiles are not stored for future use, and it may become more common to use SNPs instead of STRs, especially because of the low mutation rate of SNPs (see Mutation Rates).

Mixtures

SNP loci are not very informative when the sample contains DNA from more than one person, which is something frequently observed in trace samples from crime scenes. If both SNP alleles are detected in the mixture, there is no discriminatory power at that locus, and any individual may have contributed to the mixture. The SNPs for forensic panels are selected because they are highly polymorphic, and, therefore, there is a high probability that both alleles will be detected in mixtures of two or more individuals. If one of the individuals who contributed to the mixture is homozygous at a particular locus, there is $\rho^2 + 2\rho\ (1 - \rho)$ percentage chance (75%, if $\rho = 0.5$) that another individual in the mixture has the other allele. With STRs, it is possible to estimate the number of contributors in the mixture from the number of detected alleles, and sometimes it is even possible to estimate the STR profiles of the minor and major contributors based on the amplification strength of the alleles. None of this is possible with SNP loci.

SNP Typing Methods

The increasing interest in SNPs shown by many different scientific disciplines during the last 20 years has resulted in the continuous development of SNP typing platforms. In general, these platforms employ one of the four common technologies: hybridization, primer extension, ligation, or invasive cleavage. Some platforms are high-throughput platforms that can type thousands of SNPs from a few individuals or a few SNPs from thousands of individuals at the same time and at a low cost. Within the forensic community, there has been a great interest in these technologies because many forensic laboratories have experienced a large increase in samples that need to be processed, and, at the same time, there has been an increased demand for faster and cheaper investigations. Unfortunately, the high-throughput SNP platforms have not been developed specifically for forensic purposes. Typically, these platforms use 10–200 ng of DNA per sample per experiment, which is an acceptable amount if the sample is taken in the form of, for example, blood or a buccal swab from an individual. However, it is a lot more DNA than typically recovered from trace samples at crime scenes. In forensic genetics, high sensitivity is pivotal and investigations must be successfully completed from very small amounts of DNA (typically 100–500 pg). Therefore, the attempts to implement high-throughput SNP platforms for routine forensic genetic investigations have so far been unsuccessful. Instead, the SNP typing assays developed for forensic genetics are based on the low-throughput PCR–SBE–CE protocol described below. This method is highly accurate and sensitive, and it can be performed with the same instruments used for standard STR analyses.

SNP Typing by PCR–SBE–CE

SNP typing assays developed for forensic genetic purposes usually involve an initial multiplex PCR followed by a multiplex single-base extension (SBE) reaction and detection of the SBE products by capillary electrophoresis (CE). A multiplex PCR is a standard PCR except that multiple fragments are amplified simultaneously. This reduces the time and cost of the assay, and importantly, it reduces the amount of sample material that is required. Multiplexing of up to five fragments is usually feasible without difficulty. However, as the number of desired products increases, there is an increased risk of formation of primer dimers and unwanted amplification products. Furthermore, it becomes increasingly difficult to ensure that all fragments are amplified equally efficiently and extensive optimization of large multiplexes is usually required.

The SBE reaction is performed as consecutive cycles of denaturation of the PCR products, annealing of the SBE primers to the PCR products, and SBE (**Figure 2**). The SBE primer anneals to the single-stranded PCR product immediately upstream of the SNP position, and the DNA polymerase adds a fluorescently labeled dideoxyribonucleotide, complementary to the nucleotide in the SNP position, to the SBE primer. SBE reactions can be multiplexed, and many SBE products can be analyzed simultaneously by electrophoresis (see **Figure 1** for example). In the electropherogram, the length of the SBE primer identifies the SNP locus, and the color of the fluorescent label identifies the SNP allele.

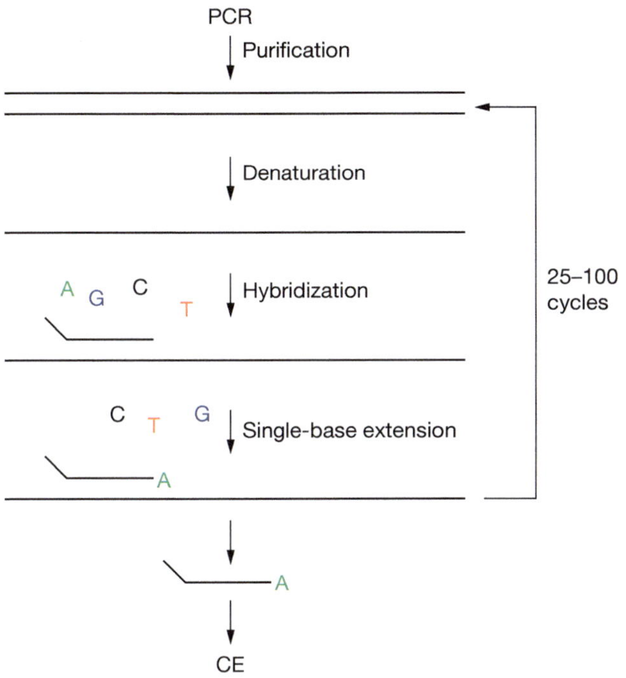

Figure 2 Diagram of the PCR–SBE–CE protocol. Fluorescently labeled ddNTPs are shown as bold letters (A, C, G, and T). The colors of the letters correspond to the dye windows in the electropherogram (see **Figure 1**).

For heterozygous individuals, the SBE primers are labeled with two different dyes, and, consequently, the extended SBE primers are detected at different wavelengths and appear in different dye windows of the electropherogram. This is exemplified in **Figure 1**, where the G and A alleles of the SNP locus named A23 (rs826472) appear in the blue and the green dye windows, respectively. The signal strengths of the two alleles are not necessarily equal because the strengths of the fluorophore emissions vary between the fluorophores.

By defining locus-specific rules for data analysis based on the peak height or the peak area, it is possible to introduce a quality gage on each allele call. The relative signal strengths of the two alleles at a locus are reproducible from experiment to experiment and from sample to sample. Usually, the acceptable peak height ratio of a heterozygous allele call may be defined as $m \pm 40\%$, where m is the mean of observed ratios in approximately 100 unrelated heterozygous individuals. Similarly, the signal-to-noise ratio of homozygous allele calls can be clearly defined. The ratio depends on the fluorophore, but usually a signal-to-noise ratio of 5–20 to 1 is adequate. The rules for data analysis ensure consistency in the data analysis, and they simplify training of new analysts. Furthermore, they are important for the evaluation of the sample itself. With STRs, it is usually easy to detect mixtures, simply because more than two alleles will be observed at several loci. With biallelic SNPs, it is not possible to detect more than two alleles, and it is not immediately evident whether the typing results originate from one or more individuals. The only method for determining whether the sample is contaminated or contains DNA from more than one individual is to look at the signal strengths. An individual may have an unusual peak height ratio at a given locus because the signal from one allele is weak. This is typically caused by a mutation in one of the PCR or SBE primer binding sites. However, if the peak height ratio is suspicious at several loci, it is a strong indication that the sample contains DNA from more than one individual. Applying rules for data analysis makes it possible to readily identify mixtures even in 20:1 ratio.

Currently, there is no software that supports locus-specific rules for data analysis or even comparison of results in different dye windows. Instead, it is necessary to export the data from the analysis programmed and perform the quality gaging in a spreadsheet. Suspicious allele calls can be identified and the electropherogram subsequently reanalyzed with the purpose of deciding whether the suspicious allele calls should be rejected or accepted.

SNP Typing Assays for Human Identification

In the last decade, several SNP typing assays have been proposed for human identification purposes. Two of these assays, the SNP*for*ID assay and the assay based on the individual identification SNPs (IISNPs), have the necessary discriminatory power to function as an alternative or supplement to the standard STR investigations performed in modern forensic genetic laboratories. The histories of the two assays are briefly described below.

The SNP*for*ID Assay

In 2002, five European forensic laboratories formed the SNP*for*ID consortium with support from the European Community. The purpose was to investigate the use of SNPs in forensic genetics. Several assays were developed via this initiative including SNP assays for prediction of ethnic origin (autosomal SNPs) and of paternal (Y chromosome SNPs) and maternal lineages (mitochondrial SNPs). However, the main objective of the consortium was to develop an SNP typing assay with at least 50 SNPs for identification of human individuals. Criteria were defined for the selection of the SNP*for*ID SNPs to ensure (1) that the SNPs were highly polymorphic in most human populations (heterozygosity >0.32), (2) that the SNPs were not in linkage disequilibrium, (3) that the SNPs were unlikely to be associated with cellular functions or with STR loci commonly used in forensic genetic investigations, and (4) that all the SNPs could be amplified by PCR in one reaction. A final panel of 52 SNPs was selected. Typing data from populations on all six continents have confirmed that the SNPs are polymorphic in all populations, and no evidence of linkage disequilibrium between any of the selected SNPs has been found. The match probabilities calculated from these populations ranged from 10^{-16} to 10^{-21}.

A multiplex PCR was developed that allowed the amplification of all 52 SNPs in one PCR. This ensured that the sensitivity of the assay was very high, and it was demonstrated that all SNPs could be typed in a single reaction using less than 100 pg of DNA, which is the amount of DNA found in 15 human diploid cells. The amplicon lengths ranged from 59 to 115 bp, and 38 of the amplicons were shorter than 100 bp. It was demonstrated in a number of different studies of highly degraded DNA that the SNP*for*ID assay was superior to the commercial STR kits. **Figure 1** shows an example of a highly degraded bone sample typed with an STR kit and the SNP*for*ID assay. A positive identification of the individual was not possible with the STR kit because fragments longer than 150 bps were not amplified. In contrast, the calculated match probability based on the SNP*for*ID assay provided convincing evidence of identification.

The SNP*for*ID assay was tested in interlaboratory exercises within the SNP*for*ID consortium and the European DNA Profiling Group. Overall, it seemed relatively easy to introduce the assay in forensic genetic laboratories. However, it was also clear that the best-performing laboratories were those with previous experience with the PCR–SBE–CE method and that extensive training in the analysis of the SNP typing results was required. The SNP*for*ID assay has been implemented in a few forensic genetic laboratories mainly as a supplementary tool in relationship casework. The usefulness of the SNP*for*ID assay has been demonstrated both in typical relationship cases and in cases involving identification of human remains.

Individual Identification SNPs

A group of population geneticists from Yale University in New Haven, Connecticut (USA) have worked to identify the best possible selection criteria for a panel of IISNPs. Four criteria were defined: (1) high heterozygosity (global average >0.4), (2) low allele frequency variability between populations (global $F_{st} < 0.06$), (3) average match probability comparable to the standard CODIS STR panel, and (4) the SNPs should be essentially unlinked. A total of 92 IISNPs were selected based on the first two criteria, and a subset of 45 SNPs fulfilled all criteria. SNP typing data from 2300 individuals in 44 different populations were generated by singleplex PCR analyses and used to validate the SNP panel. Match probabilities calculated from the 45 unlinked SNPs ranged from 10^{-15} to 10^{-18}.

Recently, 41 of the unlinked IISNPs and three of the other IISNPs were multiplexed by a group from Hebei University in China. The multiplex was highly sensitive and the 44 SNPs could be amplified in one PCR reaction using only 125 pg of DNA. The amplicon lengths ranged from 69 to 125 bp, and 17 of the amplicons were shorter than 100 bp. The performance of the assay was tested on degraded samples, and it was demonstrated that more information could be obtained with the SNP typing assay than with one of the commonly used STR kits.

So far, there is only one report on a multiplexed assay with IISNPs, but it is likely that this assay may be tested by other forensic laboratories or that other combinations of IISNPs are put together in other multiplexes in the future.

See also: **Biology/DNA:** Ancestry Informative Markers; Disaster Victim Identification; Forensic DNA Phenotyping: DNA Testing for Externally Visible Characteristics; Mitochondrial DNA.

Further Reading

Børsting, C., Morling, N., 2011. Mutations and/or relatives? Six case work examples where 49 autosomal SNPs were used as supplementary markers. Forensic Science International: Genetics 5, 236–241.

Børsting, C., Sanchez, J.J., Hansen, H.E., et al., 2008. Performance of the SNP*for*ID 52 SNP-plex assay in paternity testing. Forensic Science International: Genetics 2, 292–300.

Børsting, C., Rockenbauer, E., Morling, N., 2009. Validation of a single nucleotide polymorphism (SNP) typing assay with 49 SNPs for forensic genetic testing in a laboratory accredited according to the ISO 17025 standard. Forensic Science International: Genetics 4, 34–42.

Gill, P., 2001. An assessment of the utility of single nucleotide polymorphisms (SNPs) for forensic purposes. International Journal of Legal Medicine 114, 204–210.

Krawczak, M., 1999. Informativity assessment for biallelic single nucleotide polymorphisms. Electrophoresis 20, 1676–1681.

Lou, C., Cong, B., Li, S., et al., 2011. A SNaPshot assay for genotyping 44 individual identification single nucleotide polymorphisms. Electrophoresis 32, 368–378.

Pakstis, A.J., Speed, W.C., Fang, R., et al., 2010. SNPs for a universal individual identification panel. Human Genetics 127, 315–324.

Phillips, C., Fondevila, M., García-Magarinos, M., et al., 2008. Resolving relationship tests that show ambiguous STR results using autosomal SNPs as supplementary markers. Forensic Science International: Genetics 2, 198–204.

Sanchez, J.J., Børsting, C., Morling, N., 2005. Typing of Y chromosome SNPs with multiplex PCR methods . In: Carracedo, A. (Ed.), Forensic DNA Typing Protocols. Methods in Molecular Biology, vol. 297. Humana Press, Totowa, USA, pp. 209–228.

Sanchez, J.J., Phillips, C., Børsting, C., et al., 2006. A multiplex assay with 52 single nucleotide polymorphisms for human identification. Electrophoresis 27, 1713–1724.

Sobrino, B., Brion, M., Carracedo, A., 2005. SNPs in forensic genetics: a review on SNP typing technologies. Forensic Science International 154, 181–194.

Relevant Websites

http://www.gwascentral.org—GWAS central.
http://hapmap.ncbi.nlm.nih.gov—International HapMap project.
http://www.ncbi.nlm.nih.gov—National Center for Biotechnology Information.
http://www.genome.gov—National Human Genome Research Institute.
http://www.cstl.nist.gov—Short Tandem Repeat DNA Internet database.
http://www.snpforid.org—SNPforID project.
http://alfred.med.yale.edu—The allele frequency database.

MiniSTRs

MD Coble, National Institute of Standards and Technology, Gaithersburg, MD, USA

Introduction

The forensic DNA community's movement away from single-locus variable number tandem repeat (VNTR) markers analyzed with restriction fragment length polymorphism (RFLP) enzymes to short tandem repeat (STR) markers was an important decision for forensic DNA testing. Polymerase chain reaction (PCR) amplification of fluorescently labeled DNA primers of STR loci increased sensitivity of the reaction and allowed for testing of lower DNA quantity samples (from micrograms to hundreds of picograms). The introduction of capillary electrophoresis (CE) was also an important technological advance that increased the speed of testing from weeks with VNTR–RFLP markers to hours with STR markers and helped to automate the process by eliminating laborious processes such as gel pouring and manual loading of samples.

The general structure of STR markers is presented in **Figure 1(a)**. The tandem-repeating units of most forensic STR markers are comprised of a sequence motif of four (tetra) nucleotide bases (e.g., GATA). The number of tandem repeats at any marker can vary widely in the population. In **Figure 1(a)**, the STR marker on this chromosome has 10 tetranucleotide repeats for a total of 40 base pairs (bps). At specific locations upstream and downstream of the tandem repeats are regions where the fluorescently labeled PCR primers (forward, F, and reverse, R) hybridize to the DNA template for amplification. The region between the primer hybridization site and the tandem repeats can be referred to as the "intervening sequence." In this hypothetical example, assuming the F and R primers are 20 bp each and the intervening sequences upstream and downstream of the core repeat are both 125 bp, the overall size of the fluorescently labeled "10" allele is $(20 + 125 + 40 + 125 + 20) = 330$ bp.

One limitation of STR markers compared to VNTR markers was the need to increase the number of STR markers tested to achieve a high power of discrimination in the population. Forensic "discrimination" using VNTR markers can be determined with 5–7 markers compared to 13–15 STR markers. For

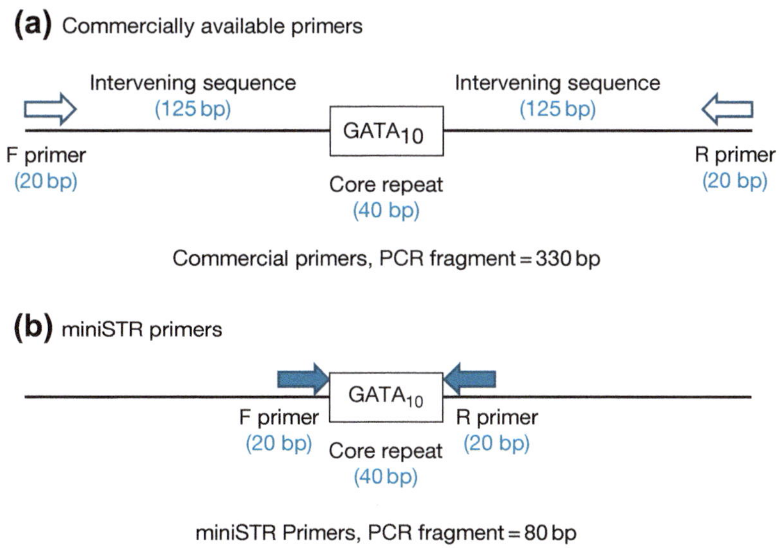

Figure 1 An example of amplification of an STR with two different primer sets. (a) With commercially available primers, the 10 GATA repeats (40 bp) are amplified with the 250 bp intervening sequences and the 40 bp primer sequences to produce an overall fragment of 330 bp. (b) With miniSTR primers, the strategy is to move the primers as close to the core repeat as possible. The miniSTR fragment would encompass the 10 GATA repeats (40 bp) and the 40 bp of the two primers to produce an overall fragment of 80 bp.

 http://dx.doi.org/10.1016/B978-0-12-800647-4.00015-1

most commercially available STR kits, the goal of the multiplex is to combine several STR markers into one reaction tube to maximize the genetic information in the sample. In a typical multiplex, the markers are arranged in either three or four dye channels, with the size range of the markers in each dye channel falling between 100 and 400 bp.

For most casework samples, the PCR amplification of STR markers is sufficient for linking the perpetrator's profile to the evidence. When samples are highly challenged or degraded, it may be impossible to obtain the full complement of markers in the commercial STR kit. Instead of a full DNA profile, a partial DNA profile is generated, which decreases the power of discrimination. For example, if only 5 or 6 of the 15 possible markers in the PCR amplify, it is possible that several hundreds of thousands (or even millions) of individuals in the population would fortuitously match the evidence.

Methods to increase the number of alleles in the profile, such as low-template DNA amplification protocols that increase the amount of DNA polymerase and the number of PCR cycles, may be useful strategies to increase the power of discrimination, but these methods require interpretational guidelines that differ from standard procedures. If the DNA is severely degraded (e.g., no DNA fragment is larger than 200 bp), aggressive amplification methods will most likely be unsuccessful for recovering the higher molecular weight markers, and the forensic scientist may need to resort to mitochondrial DNA (mtDNA) testing, which is laborious, time consuming, and has a much lower power of discrimination compared to autosomal STR testing.

The Definition of a MiniSTR

One strategy to recover genetic information from challenged samples is to amplify the region using a "miniSTR." A miniSTR is the amplification of an STR marker using primers that are as close to the repeat motif as possible. In **Figure 1(b)**, the miniSTR forward and reverse primers hybridize immediately adjacent to the repeat motif with no intervening sequences. Assuming that primers are again 20 bp, the size of this labeled PCR amplicon would be $(20 + 40 + 20) = 80$ bp, a reduction of 250 bp compared to the standard primers in the commercial kit. For the example in **Figure 1(a)**, if the DNA templates from the evidence material are all degraded to 200 bp or less, then the conventional primers would fail to amplify as the overall size of the fragment is 330 bp. The miniSTR primers in **Figure 1(b)** would successfully amplify the 10 allele to produce a result. It is important to note that barring any type of genetic variation in the intervening sequences (discussed later), the results from the miniSTR amplification should be identical to the results amplified from the conventional primers. In other words, the same genetic information is retained between the two different primer sets in **Figure 1(a) and 1(b)**.

Benefits of MiniSTRs

MiniSTRs have been demonstrated as useful for recovering genetic information from a wide variety of challenged samples. In one of the first examples of miniSTRs used for typing 48 telogen hairs, redesigned primers for the STR marker TPOX was reduced by 160 bp compared to the commercial kit. The success rate went from 18% with the commercial kit to 77% with the TPOX miniSTR primers, which is a fourfold improvement. The ability to generate autosomal STR markers from shed hairs and hair shafts represents an encouraging development for analyzing evidentiary material that is often common at crime scenes and is typically analyzed by mtDNA testing, which tends to be less informative than autosomal STR analysis.

Following the mass disaster events of September 11, 2001, Robert Shaler of the New York Office of the Chief Medical Examiner requested assistance from John Butler at the National Institute of Standards and Technology to develop miniSTR primers for the U.S. core Combined DNA Index System (CODIS) loci. Previously, Butler pioneered the development of miniSTRs for a project to rapidly genotype STR markers using matrix-assisted laser desorption/ionization time of flight mass spectrometry.

MiniSTRs were very useful for the identification of the skeletal remains recovered from the World Trade Center. According to a summary of the identification efforts four years after the attack, over one-half of the victim identifications ($\approx$850) were made with DNA testing, and of those identified, approximately 20% required miniSTRs. In addition to the increased success rates and improved statistical analyses of typing degraded skeletal remains, the International Commission on Missing Persons has used miniSTRs to sort and reassociate the comingled remains from mass graves following the conflicts after the breakup of the former Yugoslavia.

Commercially available kits of miniSTR multiplexes are available for the forensic DNA community, and, in addition to the challenged samples of degraded skeletal remains and telogen hairs, miniSTRs have been used to analyze a wide range of typical casework samples under normal conditions and have given robust results with increased genetic information compared to the conventional STR kits. In addition to the miniSTRs developed for the autosomal CODIS markers, miniSTRs have also been developed for analyzing degraded samples using non-CODIS loci, the *Y*-chromosome, and *X*-chromosomal STRs.

Given the success of miniSTR markers, the European DNA Profiling Group along with the European Network of Forensic Science Institutes in 2006 recommended that the next-generation multiplex of STR kits contain miniSTRs in addition to the loci already tested among laboratories in Europe. This decision reflected the need of the forensic DNA laboratory to resolve partial profiles from degraded stains (where miniSTRs are useful) rather than adding more polymorphic loci to increase the statistical power of discrimination for nondegraded casework material.

Limitations of MiniSTRs

Multiplexing of Markers

If the goal of generating a miniSTR marker is to make the amplicon as small as possible, then one limitation of miniSTR markers would be the limits of multiplexing. As present CE analyzers utilize four dye channels for STR markers (the fifth dye channel is dedicated to the size standard), this prevents the ability to multiplex more than six to eight loci under 150 bp. The polymorphic nature of several of the STR loci can also inhibit the ability to multiplex several loci. For example, the vWA locus has an allele spread from 10 to 24 repeats. The size of the vWA miniSTR developed for the World Trade Center identification efforts ranged from 88 to 148 bp, which prohibits the possibility of adding a second miniSTR marker to this dye channel.

The consequence of having several miniSTR multiplexes for generating a DNA profile is that more DNA extract is consumed during testing. For limited, challenged samples, this may prevent any additional testing by consummation of the sample. One method to separate overlapping loci is to add non-nucleotide mobility modifiers to the primer sequences to create space between the markers. For example, if Marker A has an upper size range of 120 bp and Marker B has a lower size range of 115 bp, it would be unwise to place these two markers in the same dye channel as there is the potential that one cannot distinguish the alleles of the two markers. If several mobility modifiers were added to the primer of Marker B (e.g., each modifier adds 2.5 bp to the amplicon), then 10 modifiers would shift the apparent size of the amplicon by 25 bp, which would place the lower size range of Marker B at 140 bp instead of 115 bp. By shifting the overlapping markers away from each other, the ability to multiplex the two markers is now possible. The mobility modifier technology is currently used in one commercially available miniSTR kit.

Concordance Issues

Another limitation of miniSTR markers is the need to establish concordance with the standard STR multiplex kit as some genetic information may actually differ between the two systems. By moving the primer sequence as close to the repeat motif as possible, it may be possible to lose some of the genetic data in the intervening sequence. An example is presented in **Figure 2**. Focusing only on one chromosome, suppose the locus has 10 tetranucleotide repeats and primer "A" is from a commercial kit.

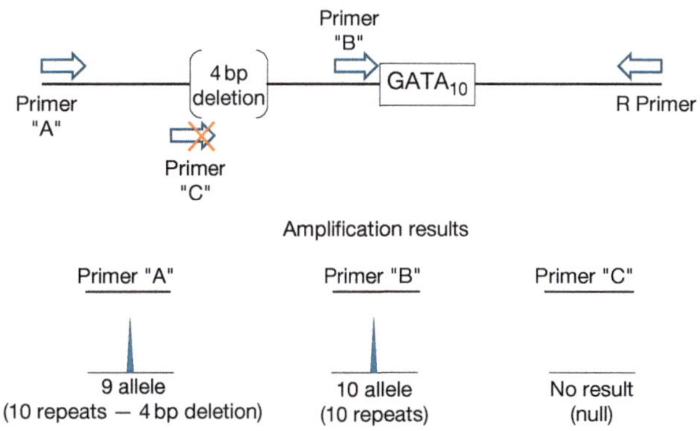

Figure 2 The importance of concordance testing with miniSTR primers. Three different PCR primers are tested for this particular marker with 10 repeats (only one chromosome is shown). Upstream of the core repeat is a 4-bp deletion. With the commercially available primer set "A," the 10 repeats appear on the electropherogram as a "9" allele as the 4-bp deletion "removes" one of the 10 repeats. With the miniSTR primer "B" adjacent to the core repeat, the 4-bp deletion is not detected and the allele would be genotyped as a "10" allele. If the miniSTR forward primer is placed upon the deletion, then no amplification may be possible as the primer sequence would not match the template DNA sequence. In this scenario (no amplification), a "null" allele is created.

Unbeknownst to the forensic scientist, in the intervening sequence between the forward primer "A" and the repeat motif is a 4-bp deletion (**Figure 2**). The consequence of this 4-bp deletion is to produce an amplicon with an apparent "9" tetranucleotide repeat (10 repeats minus 4 bp = 9 repeats). Using the conventional STR kit, this amplicon would type as a "9" allele. For the miniSTR primer "B," as the forward primer is now flanking the repeat motif, the 4-bp deletion is outside the region of amplification and therefore not detected in the PCR product: the miniSTR primer generates a "10" allele (**Figure 2**). This would create a discordant genotyping result between the commercial STR kit and the miniSTR primers at this locus.

Another potential scenario is that the miniSTR primer for this marker hybridizes within this region where the 4-bp deletion is present (**Figure 2**). In this situation, the PCR amplification efficiency could be greatly reduced (producing a relatively small peak in the electropherogram) or completely nullified (with no peak present in the electropherogram). The loss of the peak (null allele) in the electropherogram can be problematic during the analysis stage as a true heterozygous genotype (having two peaks) would appear as a homozygous genotype (only one peak) when a null allele occurs.

It is therefore important to conduct concordance testing during the validation of a new miniSTR assay to understand the degree of genetic variation within the intervening sequences of the conventional STR marker. If the genetic variant affects the primer hybridization region of the miniSTR, the commercial company may add an additional "degenerate" primer to compensate for the mishybridization.

Conclusions

Forensic scientists have occasionally considered the possibility that STRs may be replaced one day with another marker system, potentially SNPs. One major advantage to SNP testing is that the size of the PCR amplicon can be made small, typically less than 100 bp. Given the large investment in DNA databases of STR profiles, it is unlikely that SNPs will replace STRs in the near future. The emergence of miniSTRs has been a beneficial development in recovering genetic information from degraded samples and will continue to be an important tool for the forensic scientist in the future.

See also: **Biology/DNA:** DNA Extraction and Quantification; Short Tandem Repeats.

Further Reading

Biesecker, L.G., Bailey-Wilson, J.E., Ballantyne, J., et al., 2005. DNA identifications after the 9/11 World Trade Center attack. Science 310, 1122–1123.

Butler, J.M., Li, J., Shaler, T.A., Monforte, J.A., Becker, C.H., 1998. Reliable genotyping of short tandem repeat loci without an allelic ladder using time-of-flight mass spectrometry. International Journal of Legal Medicine 112, 45–49.

Butler, J.M., Shen, Y., McCord, B.R., 2003. The development of reduced size STR amplicons as tools for analysis of degraded DNA. Journal of Forensic Sciences 48, 1054–1064.

Butler, J.M., Coble, M.D., Vallone, P.M., 2007. STRs vs SNPs: thoughts on the future of forensic DNA testing. Forensic Science, Medicine, and Pathology 3, 200–205.

Coble, M.D., Butler, J.M., 2005. Characterization of new miniSTR loci to aid analysis of degraded DNA. Journal of Forensic Sciences 50, 43–53.

Dixon, L.A., Dobbins, A.E., Pulker, H., et al., 2006. Analysis of artificially degraded DNA using STRs and SNPs – results of a collaborative European (EDNAP) exercise. Forensic Science International 164, 33–44.

Gill, P., Fereday, L., Morling, N., Schneider, P.M., 2006. Letter to editor – new multiplexes for Europe: amendments and clarification of strategic development. Forensic Science International 163, 155–157.

Hellmann, A., Rohleder, U., Schmitter, H., Wittig, M., 2001. STR typing of human telogen hairs – a new approach. International Journal of Legal Medicine 114, 269–273.

Hill, C.R., Kline, M.C., Mulero, J.J., et al., 2007. Concordance study between the AmpFlSTR MiniFiler PCR amplification kit and conventional STR typing kits. Journal of Forensic Sciences 52, 870–873.

Holland, M.M., Cave, C.A., Holland, C.A., Bille, T.W., 2003. Development of a quality, high throughput DNA analysis procedure for skeletal samples to assist with the identification of victims from the World Trade Center attacks. Croatian Medical Journal 44, 264–272.

Mulero, J.J., Chang, C.W., Lagacé, R.E., et al., 2008. Development and validation of the AmpFlSTR MiniFiler PCR amplification kit: a miniSTR multiplex for the analysis of degraded and/or PCR inhibited DNA. Journal of Forensic Sciences 53, 838–852.

Müller, K., Sommerer, T., Miltner, E., Schneider, H., Wiegand, P., 2010. Casework testing of the multiplex kits AmpFlSTR SEfiler Plus PCR amplification kit (AB), PowerPlex S5 System (Promega) and AmpFlSTR MiniFiler PCR amplification kit (AB). Forensic Science International: Genetics 4, 200–205.

Opel, K.L., Chung, D.T., Drabek, J., Tatarek, N.E., Jantz, L.M., McCord, B.R., 2006. The application of miniplex primer sets in the analysis of degraded DNA from human skeletal remains. Journal of Forensic Sciences 51, 351–356.

Park, M.J., Lee, H.Y., Chung, U., Kang, S.C., Shin, K.J., 2007. Y-STR analysis of degraded DNA using reduced-size amplicons. International Journal of Legal Medicine 121, 152–157.

Parsons, T.J., Huel, R., Davoren, J., et al., 2007. Application of novel "mini-amplicon" STR multiplexes to high volume casework on degraded skeletal remains. Forensic Science International: Genetics 1, 175–179.

Relevant Websites

http://www.brighttalk.com—Webcast of A "Short" History of miniSTRs.

http://www.cstl.nist.gov—National Institute of Standards and Technology (NIST) STRBase Web page on miniSTRs.

Low-Template DNA Testing

T Caragine, K Currie, C O'Connor, and ZM Budimlija, Office of Chief Medical Examiner of the City of New York, New York, NY, USA

Glossary

Allelic drop-in A stochastic effect due to the amplification of very minor template DNA that is foreign to the main component.

Allelic dropout A stochastic effect resulting in the absence of an allele from a main component because of extreme heterozygote imbalance.

***Frye* hearing** A judicial procedure in the United States that determines the admissibility of evidence tested with a specific technique based on its general acceptance in the relevant scientific community.

Likelihood ratio The ratio of the probabilities of a set of data under two competing hypotheses.

Low-template DNA testing A more sensitive methodology of performing traditional DNA testing involving a limited quantity (or quality) of DNA, which will exhibit increased stochastic effects.

Primary transfer Standard mode of deposition of biological material from one person to an object.

Random match probability The chance of selecting a random person from a population that will have the same DNA profile as that of the evidentiary sample, showing its rarity.

Secondary transfer Transfer of biological material either from one person to a second person and then to an object that is sampled, or from one person to an object and then to a second person who is sampled directly.

Stochastic effects Random phenomena in DNA analysis such as allelic dropout, allelic drop-in, heightened heterozygote imbalance, and increased stutter, which result from amplification of nonoptimal amounts of template DNA.

Stutter Slipped-strand mispairing during DNA amplification, which is more prevalent in amplification of repeated regions.

Tertiary transfer Transfer of biological material from a person to an object, which is then handled by a second person who touches another object. This object is sampled. Alternatively, material could be transferred from one person to a second person who handles an object, which could then be touched by a third person who is sampled directly.

Validation A set of experiments that test whether procedures meet specifications for their intended use. This testing should be performed on any method before it can be implemented in forensic laboratories.

Definition

Low-template (LT) DNA testing is a more sensitive way of doing traditional DNA testing and refers to the analysis of samples that contain small amounts of DNA such as those with <100 pg of DNA. This technique is sometimes referred to as low copy number (LCN) testing, high-sensitivity (HS) testing, trace DNA, touch DNA, or contact DNA. The amount of DNA recovered from handled samples, wherein skin cells have been deposited, is generally much lower than the amounts recovered from visible biological stains (i.e., blood or semen stains). LT-DNA testing can alternatively be defined as any technique involving a limited quantity (or quality) of DNA, which will exhibit increased stochastic effects. Difficulty lies in attempting to establish a universal threshold below which LT-DNA techniques should always be used as stochastic effects increase with decreasing amounts of template DNA and span a continuous range. Nevertheless, for practical purposes, thresholds are useful in triaging samples. LT-DNA methods use the same laboratory techniques as conventional DNA testing; however, they include slight modifications that are designed to increase the DNA signal.

Applications of LT-DNA Testing

LT-DNA testing is not a new or unique technique to the forensic community and has been used throughout the scientific community for many years in many different areas. In 1996, French scientists Taberlet et al. described "reliable genotyping

 http://dx.doi.org/10.1016/B978-0-12-800647-4.00016-3

of samples with very low DNA quantities using PCR." They developed mathematical simulations to evaluate the samples amplified with low amounts of DNA compared to samples with higher amounts. Through biological experiments, they showed concordance between the two models. A year later, Findlay et al. reported using manipulation and isolation of single cells to perform genotyping using short tandem repeat (STR) analysis. They amplified DNA a large majority of the time (91%) and obtained full profiles half of the time (50%) and "usable" profiles (four or more STRs out of six) almost two-thirds of the time (64%).

Low amounts of DNA have been used in many other non-forensic applications including clinical diagnostics, oncology, and immunology. Single-cell polymerase chain reaction (PCR) can be used for preimplantation genetic diagnostics (PGD) to screen for X-linked disorders as well as for sex determination of implanted embryos. Isolation of one fetal cell from maternal blood, in some cases, negates the need for other invasive techniques such as amniocentesis or chorionic villus sampling (CVS), and facilitates treatment of genetic disorders in the early stages of gestation.

In the field of oncology, a single tumor cell variant can be isolated, amplified, and compared to normal, nontumor cells, to identify transcriptional abnormalities. Using reverse transcription PCR (RT-PCR), developmental biologists have examined gene expression patterns during cell differentiation at the very earliest stages of zygote development. Scientists were able to isolate a single cell and perform PCR to determine the expression pattern and regulation processes of certain genes. Using RT-PCR, British scientist Birgit Liss studied the gene expression of individual cells of varying types in close proximity in the brain.

More recently, Austrian scientists (using either laser microdissection or micromanipulation techniques) performed whole genome amplification on normal lymphocytes, umbilical cord blood, polar bodies and oocytes, and colorectal, renal, breast, and blood cancer cells. Cells were then screened for chromosomal abnormalities. In 2008, mutational analysis of single cancer cells showed that most of these cells shared a common origin. Furthermore, individual DNA molecules were captured in droplets to allow single-copy genetic amplification (SCGA) in a high-throughput manner.

Amplification of low amounts of DNA in forensic casework was first performed in 1999 at the Forensic Science Service (FSS) in Great Britain. As an alternative to mitochondrial DNA analysis, which cannot provide individuality due to matrilineal inheritance (through the mother), lead scientist Peter Gill and his colleagues built a framework for not only the analysis of lower amounts of DNA but also the interpretation of results obtained from such techniques. This paved the way for these techniques to be employed in crime laboratories throughout Europe, the United States, Australia, and New Zealand.

Implementation of LT-DNA Testing

In order to detect minute amounts of DNA, the following enhancement techniques are typically used: additional PCR cycles or modifications to PCR, purification of PCR products, and/or increased parameters for electrophoresis. These enhancements exaggerate stochastic effects that are inherent to all DNA testing. Effects include allelic dropouts and drop-ins, inflated peak imbalance, and/or large stutter artifacts. For example, amplification of very minor template DNA could result in the observance of an allele that is foreign to the main component, otherwise known as an allelic drop-in. For forensic evidence, this DNA may have originated either before or after the commission of a crime. Another consequence is heightened heterozygote imbalance, which at its most extreme may lead to the absence of an allele from the main component, or allelic dropout. Furthermore, if a stutter peak occurs early in PCR, its height will be taller relative to the main peak if additional cycles are used. To accommodate these phenomena, routine testing and interpretation protocols must be modified.

Forensic practitioners employ specific quality control, testing, and interpretation procedures to accommodate stochastic effects. Studies unique to each laboratory must be performed to demonstrate that these strategies generate reliable, robust, and reproducible results. These studies are a validation or a comprehensive test of procedures and interpretation policies used in forensic casework.

Through validation, a laboratory must demonstrate that they are working in an environment that has extremely low levels of background DNA. Overall precautions used in tissue culture should be employed. For example, testing should be performed in dedicated, protected work spaces in order to prevent inadvertent contamination from laboratory personnel. Proper protective attire should also be worn, which consists of full laboratory gowns, face masks that cover one's nose and mouth, gloves (double gloves for bench work and evidence exam), and hair coverings. All equipment must be routinely cleaned, both before and after each procedure and examination of each evidentiary item. One common methodology for cleaning is the use of 10% bleach followed by water and 70% ethanol. Any exogenous DNA in plasticware and water should also be removed either through irradiation with ultraviolet light or ethylene oxide fuming.

To ensure that all reagents and instruments are free of exogenous DNA and function properly, they should be tested prior to use. Moreover, controls must be evaluated with every test including extraction, purification, concentration, amplification, and separation. Positive (optimal) controls show the robustness of the test, whereas negative controls show that the results are acceptable and should be treated in the same or a more sensitive manner as actual samples. Owing to the sensitivity of the test, it is not unlikely that some DNA may be detected in negative controls. This DNA is not due to global contamination but is often tube specific. Validation studies must establish how much DNA may be detected in the negative control(s) that would not affect the results in the samples.

Another strategy to identify spurious DNA is through repetition. The extracted DNA is equally divided such that each test contains, for example, up to 100 pg of template. Although the number of repetitions employed may vary from two to four among laboratories, the common theme is that an allele must be seen at least twice to be confirmed. Alleles that do not repeat may not be attributed to a major component. It has been shown that single amplifications are misleading, and that by using this biological model, one can identify alleles that can be attributed to contributors. In addition to replicate analysis, characteristics such as heterozygote imbalance, the amplification efficiency of the loci, and increased stutter are considered when determining genotypes.

In order to confirm that results (even those from the lowest template amount of DNA used) are reproducible, notwithstanding anticipated and explained stochastic effects, LT-DNA procedures should be extensively validated. Studies are conducted with samples wherein the DNA profiles of the contributors are known. These samples should mimic forensic casework and include items from blood, bone, saliva, semen, and skin cells. Validation verifies the protocols used to deconvolute samples to ensure the accuracy of allele assignments in the presence of spurious alleles and increased stutter. Furthermore, validation should determine the precision of the quantitation assay as typically the amount of DNA dictates whether LT-DNA amplification procedures are employed.

Statistical Considerations for LT-DNA Analysis

For a random match probability calculation in LT-DNA analysis, the approach is not different than the one used in high-template (HT-DNA) analysis. This statistic is appropriate only for single-sourced samples or for deduced profiles from mixtures. Only those alleles that meet interpretation criteria should be used for the calculation. If one allele is undetermined at a locus, the random match probability can be calculated by using the "2p" rule.

For some mixed samples, the genotypes of one or more individual contributor may not be resolved. Nevertheless, DNA profiles of known samples may be compared to the results, and alleles from all replicates should be considered. If all of the alleles seen in the comparison sample's profile are seen in the mixture, the probability of inclusion can be calculated. This value indicates the number of individuals who could be contributors to the mixture as they have that same combination of alleles.

If an allele seen in a known sample's profile is not seen in the mixture results, this does not necessarily mean an exclusion as there may be scientific explanations for this absence. These include the amount of the template DNA, degradation, the number of contributors to the mixture, the amplification efficiency of the locus in question, and the length of the STR repeat. In order to put a statistical weight on this comparison, more complex calculations are required.

It is well documented that LT-DNA analysis itself is a complex process; hence, many different probabilities can be calculated. Ideally, probability models should encompass the likelihood of drop-in and dropout and should consider the frequency of alleles in unrelated as well as related populations. Likelihood ratios can be calculated for a range of scenarios from a single contributor to multiple contributors where one or more are unknown. Software that integrates allele frequencies and the probability of drop-in and locus specific dropout for a number of scenarios has been developed and recently validated in a forensic casework laboratory.

A critical factor to the likelihood ratio calculation is the number of contributors to a mixture. Determining this value is challenging without incorporating the frequency of these phenomena in another probabilistic model because of allelic dropout and drop-in. Nevertheless, models using the maximum likelihood method or empirically based criteria can be used for this estimation until more advanced software is available. Such a probabilistic model that includes all parameters is difficult to achieve; therefore, approximations may be considered given that assumptions are clearly stated.

Casework Examples

LT-DNA analysis has been used in forensic casework well over a decade, and evidence tested with this analysis has been admitted in courts of law in various countries. The technique has been extensively validated in many laboratories and thus has gained general acceptance in the relevant scientific community. The following two seminal court cases highlight this.

"The Queen versus Sean Hoey" Case (Omagh Bombing)

The Omagh bombing incident was part of a series of bombings and attempted bombings between 1998 and 2001 in Northern Ireland and London, United Kingdom. In the summer of 1998, a car bomb exploded in a busy shopping area in the District of Omagh in Northern Ireland. The explosion killed 29 and injured hundreds of people, making it the deadliest event in 30 years of violence in Northern Ireland. In 2003, the police arrested and charged an electrician, Sean Hoey.

The prosecution built their case on evidence that they believed to show a connection between the suspect and the bomb fragments found at the crime scene. The evidence was tested in two stages. Initial testing included reconstruction of the bombs and fiber comparisons. The evidence was then reexamined in 2000–2001 for DNA, using LT-DNA testing at the FSS. DNA recovered from devices from April 1998 and April 2001 yielded the same profile that matched Sean Hoey. In September 2003, as well as in November 2003, additional matches were made on additional bombing devices. However, all these devices were undetonated, and no DNA was actually detected from the detonated device from the Omagh bombing.

Unfortunately, in 1998, little precaution was taken to maintain the integrity of the evidence. The risk of DNA contamination and cross-contamination among items during the collection of evidence was high. All of these circumstances resulted in the decision of the presiding judge, Judge Weir, to dismiss the DNA evidence, stating that "items had not been collected or preserved using methods designed to ensure the high degree of integrity needed not merely for DNA examination but for the more exacting requirements of LCN DNA." The main arguments against LT-DNA testing were that the technique was not validated by experts outside of the FSS. In his judgment, Judge Weir gave a definition of validation and stated that the LCN system had not been sufficiently validated by the international scientific community. Based on sources from the Crown Prosecution Service (CPS), this case resulted in a temporary 3-week suspension of LT-DNA testing in the United Kingdom, followed by an internal review of current FSS LT-DNA cases. This review was completed and the suspension lifted on January 14, 2008, with the CPS stating that "it had not seen anything to suggest that any current problems exist with LCN (LT-DNA)." It was stated that there is "no inherent unreliability in the LCN DNA analysis process."

Queens LT-DNA Frye Hearing

The Frye standard or Frye test, evaluates whether a technique is generally accepted in the relevant scientific community and thus determines whether evidence tested with this procedure is admissible in a court of law. The first fully completed judgment regarding the use of LT-DNA autosomal testing in the United States is the case of the People of the State of New York versus Hemant Megnath, presided by Judge Robert J. Hanophy of the Supreme Court, Queens County.

The defendant was charged with murder in the first degree for allegedly slashing the victim's throat outside her home. Megnath allegedly fled in his vehicle that was then the subject of a search warrant. Samples, some of which contained LT amounts of DNA, linked the defendant to the commission of the murder.

In the final ruling, Judge Hanophy stated: "Based upon the testimony presented at this hearing, the court makes the following findings of fact and conclusions of law .... The court also finds that the credible evidence presented at the hearing established that the Office of the Chief Medical Examiner (OCME) validation studies regarding LCN DNA typing yielded reliable and reproducible results in 100% of the samples tested. The court finds that the OCME has properly developed interpretation protocols for LCN DNA testing based upon its extensive validation studies and that when correctly performed these protocols consistently yield reliable and reproducible results ... Therefore, based upon all of the evidence presented to the court during the hearing, the court finds that the People have demonstrated by ample credible evidence that LCN DNA testing with its increased amplification cycles as performed by the New York City OCME clearly passes the standard enunciated in *Frye* and is therefore admissible at trial ..."

"Moreover, in addition to holding that the *Frye* standard of reliability has been met in this case, the court also finds that the standard enunciated in *Frye* pertains only to *novel* scientific techniques. In this case, based upon the credible evidence presented at this hearing, the court finds that LCN DNA profiling as conducted by the OCME is *not a novel* scientific technique. ... DNA testing in the forensic community has been generally accepted as reliable for many years. It has also been found to be admissible under the *Frye* standard in New York courts for over 20 years. (*See People vs. Wesley, supra*.) The analysis that is utilized in high copy number (HCN) DNA testing and which has been admitted nationally in our courts for years is basically the same type of DNA testing that is used when LCN DNA testing is performed by the OCME. ..."

"Since the LCN DNA method of testing as performed by the OCME is basically the same technique as HCN DNA testing, with the exception of its increased amplification cycles, the court finds that LCN DNA testing as performed by the OCME is not a *novel* scientific technique for the purposes of the *Frye* inquiry. ... Indeed, both the LCN and HCN forms of DNA testing require the same steps to be taken. These steps, namely extraction, quantitation, amplification, and electrophoresis, are virtually identical in both HCN and LCN DNA testing. Similarly, the same issues such as stutter, allelic drop-out or drop-in occur in both forms of testing as well. In fact, the OCME has prepared and followed interpretation protocols for both HCN and LCN DNA testing to compensate for these scientific phenomena when and if they occur. These protocols were developed by the OCME based upon its validation studies and based upon similar protocols that have been used globally by other forensic scientists who perform HCN and LCN DNA testing..." At trial, all evidence was presented, and the defendant was subsequently found guilty.

Other Case Examples

LT-DNA testing has been used in current casework, cold cases, and post conviction testing, and in a wide variety of case types including homicides, assaults/sexual assaults, property crimes, arsons, hate crimes, missing persons investigations, and the identification of human remains. LT-DNA profiles have been generated from many types of handled evidence including items that have been handled extensively or briefly by an individual(s). These items include cars, air bags, doorknobs, windowsills, tools, jewelry, keys, lighters, matches, letters, envelopes, pens, sides of bottles, weapons, and shrapnel from explosive devices. Fingerprints (both fresh and archived) have also yielded profiles. Moreover, foreign DNA has been identified on ligatures such as ropes, cords, and tape, as well as on clothing. The exact location where the assailant came in contact with the clothing is helpful to target testing.

Although the main application of LT-DNA testing in criminal casework involves items that were potentially handled or touched, it has also been used on old, degraded, or otherwise compromised body fluid samples. An example of a case where LT-DNA testing was done on one such sample involved the alleged sexual assault of a woman in New York City. In 2005, a woman went out drinking with friends, later separated from her friends and met a group of men. She left with one of the men looking for a party. During that time, she allegedly was raped. When she reunited with her friends, she had a physical altercation with one of them, but the fight was stopped when she declared that she was previously sexually assaulted.

A rape kit was taken, which was negative for semen, but there were bite marks found on the woman's arm and shoulder; based largely on the testimony of the woman, the accused man was convicted of sexual assault and sentenced to 20 years in prison. He still maintained his innocence and requested examination of the swabs from the bite mark. LT-DNA testing revealed only female DNA and the profile generated was consistent with that of the woman's friend. The woman subsequently confessed that the sexual assault never occurred, and the conviction was overturned in 2010.

Additional Considerations

The weight of any evidence depends on the context of the case, and DNA is no exception. A DNA analyst may determine the type of body fluid/material that was deposited, the amount of DNA recovered, and the source of the sample. However, the age of a sample and the manner in which it was deposited (either directly or indirectly) are indeterminable. Studies have been performed, nevertheless, to determine how likely DNA can be transferred from one person to another and from people to objects.

The amount of DNA deposited or recovered from an object depends on a number of factors such as whether a person washed their hands prior to handling the object, the number of people who touched the object, how the object was stored after it was handled, and the amount of time prior to testing. The ability of an individual to deposit his/her DNA on an object has been assessed in a study by British scientists Lowe et al., where they evaluated the "shedder type" of an individual based on the ability to detect a DNA profile on an object after it had been handled. If a full profile could be obtained, even after hand washing, these people were labeled as "good shedders" as opposed to "poor shedders" where only a partial DNA profile was obtained.

There are several theoretical methods of transfer. Primary transfer is the standard mode of deposition from one person to an object. If a person touches the handle of a knife and then his/her DNA is recovered from that handle, that would be a mode of primary transfer. Secondary transfer refers to either the transfer of DNA from an individual directly to another individual who then handles an object that is sampled or from a person to an object that is then touched by another person who is swabbed or sampled. For example, person A shakes hands with person B and then person B handles a firearm. Intuitively, one would expect to recover less of person A's DNA than person B's from the firearm. Tertiary transfer involves the transfer of DNA from a person to an object that is then handled by a second person who touches another object. This object is then sampled. Alternatively, DNA could be transferred from one person to a second person who handles an object that could then be touched by a third person who is then sampled directly. For instance, person A touches a doorknob and person B touches the same doorknob and then a knife. The question is whether person A's DNA can be detected on the handle of the knife.

Studies have shown that although DNA from skin cells may be detected through secondary transfer, the extent of this transfer is limited to certain situations. For example, in order to detect the DNA of the first person, the second person had to touch the item immediately following contact with the first person. If any items were handled in between, the DNA of the first person was likely to be deposited on those items. In many cases, the original person could not be associated to the sample. If the DNA of the first person was found, samples were always mixed, and the person was typically a minor contributor.

Regarding tertiary transfer, the introduction of another object in the sequence reduces the chance of detecting the first person. Studies demonstrate that if a random object and nonintimate individuals were used, the first person could not be associated with the sample although a few alleles were seen, which were seen in the profile of the first individual. If any time elapsed between handling of the first and second objects, alleles such as these were not apparent. These studies suggest that it is highly unlikely that a person could be associated with an item through tertiary transfer.

In jurisdictions where LT-DNA analysis is employed in forensic casework, it has proven to be a valuable tool to identify the source of DNA recovered from objects at crime scenes. As with all scientific techniques, laboratories must thoroughly validate LT-DNA protocols to ensure that their individual procedures are reliable and robust. Owing to the possibility of allelic dropout and drop-in, statistical methodologies for nondeduced mixtures should include the probability of these phenomena. Both qualitative and quantitative results should be carefully considered on the basis of the context of the case. Overall, LT-DNA testing expands the capability of investigations and resolves samples that were previously inconclusive.

See also: **Biology/DNA:** Basic Principles; Bayesian Networks; DNA—Statistical Probability; DNA Extraction and Quantification; **Forensic Genetics:** History; Mixture Interpretation (Interpretation of Mixed DNA Profiles with STRs Only); Next-Generation Sequencing Technologies; Short Tandem Repeats; **Biology/DNA/Methods/Analytical Techniques:** Capillary Electrophoresis in Forensic Genetics.

Further Reading

Balding, D.J., Buckleton, J., 2009. Interpreting low template DNA profiles. Forensic Science International: Genetics 4, 1–10.

Benschop, C.C., van der Beek, C.P., Meiland, H.C., van Gorp, A.G., Westen, A.A., Sijen, T., 2011. Low template STR typing: effect of replicate number and consensus method on genotyping reliability and DNA database search results. Forensic Science International: Genetics 5, 316–328.

Buckleton, J., 2009. Validation issues around DNA typing of low level DNA. Forensic Science International: Genetics 3, 255–260.

Caragine, T., Mikulasovich, R., Tamariz, J., et al., 2009. Validation of testing and interpretation protocols for low template DNA samples using AmpFℓSTR® Identifiler®. Croatian Medical Journal 50, 250–267.

Findlay, I., Quirke, T.P., Frazier, R., Urquhart, A., 1997. DNA fingerprinting from single cells. Nature 389, 555–556.

Gill, P., Buckleton, J., 2010. A universal strategy to interpret DNA profiles that does not require a definition of low-copy-number. Forensic Science International: Genetics 4, 221–227.

Gill, P., Kirkham, A., Curran, J., 2007. LoComatioN: a software tool for the analysis of low copy number DNA profiles. Forensic Science International 166, 128–138.

Gill, P., Whitaker, J., Flaxman, C., Brown, N., Buckleton, J., 2000. An investigation of the rigor of interpretation rules for STRs derived from less than 100 pg of DNA. Forensic Science International 112, 17–40.

Hahn, S., Zhong, X.Y., Troeger, C., Burgemeister, R., Gloning, K., Holzgreve, W., 2000. Current applications of single-cell PCR. Cellular and Molecular Life Sciences 57, 96–105.

Haned, H., Pène, L., Sauvage, F., Pontier, D., 2011. The predictive value of the maximum likelihood estimator of the number of contributors to a DNA mixture. Forensic Science International: Genetics 5, 281–284.

Lowe, A., Murray, C., Whitaker, J., Tully, G., Gill, P., 2003. The propensity of individuals to deposit DNA and secondary transfer of low level DNA from individuals to inert surfaces. Forensic Science International 129, 25–34.

Mitchell, A., Ducasse, N., Tamariz, J., Wong, A., Prinz, M., Caragine, T., 2011. Evaluating dropout and drop-in rates for statistical analysis of compromised samples. Proceedings of the American Academy of Forensic Sciences.

van Oorschot, R.A., Ballantyne, K.N., Mitchell, R.J., 2010. Forensic trace DNA: a review. Investigative Genetics 1, 14.

Petricevic, S., Whitaker, J., Buckleton, J., et al., 2010. Validation and development of interpretation guidelines for low copy number (LCN) DNA profiling in New Zealand using the AmpFlSTR SGM Plus multiplex. Forensic Science International: Genetics 4, 305–310.

Taberlet, P., Griffin, S., Goossens, B., et al., 1996. Reliable genotyping of samples with very low DNA quantities using PCR. Nucleic Acids Research 24, 3189–3194.

Tamariz, J., Wong, A., Perez, J., Prinz, M., Caragine, T., October 2009. Investigation of the detection of DNA through secondary and tertiary transfer. In: 20th International Conference on Human Identification, Las Vegas, Nevada, pp. 12–15.

Tvedebrink, T., Eriksen, P.S., Mogensen, H.S., Morling, N., 2009. Estimating the probability of allelic drop-out of STR alleles in forensic genetics. Forensic Science International: Genetics 3, 222–226.

Relevant Websites

http://cps.gov.uk—The Crown Prosecution Services of England.
http://www.denverda.org—Denver District Attorney's office.
http://www.cstl.nist.gov—Information on Low Template/Low Copy Number DNA Testing on STRbase.
http://www.nyc.gov—New York City Office of Chief Medical Examiner.
http://www.nydailynews.com—New York Daily News.
http://business.timesonline.co.uk—The Times of London newspaper online.

X-Chromosome Markers

V Pereira and L Gusmão, IPATIMUP, Porto, Portugal

Abbreviations

DNA Deoxyribonucleic acid
GHEP-ISFG Spanish- and Portuguese-speaking working group of the ISFG
Indel Insertion deletion polymorphism
ISFG International Society for Forensic Genetics
LD Linkage disequilibrium
PAR Pseudoautosomal region
PD Power of discrimination
SNP Single nucleotide polymorphism
STR Short tandem repeat

Glossary

Exclusion power Power of a given marker or a set of markers to exclude a random individual of the population from biological paternity.
Genetic drift Random fluctuation of allele frequencies in a locus. The strength of genetic drift is different according to the size of the population—the effect is stronger in small populations. In the long run, genetic drift contributes to loss of genetic variation in a population.
Haplotype Combination of different loci alleles on a chromosome that are transmitted/inherited together.
Likelihood ratio Statistical test that calculates how many more times a certain observation is more likely to occur, comparing two different alternative scenarios.
Linkage disequilibrium Nonrandom association of alleles at two or more loci, located on the same or in different chromosomes.
Power of discrimination Power of a given marker or set of markers to distinguish between two random individuals of a population.
Random match probability Probability that a random DNA sample has the same profile as the DNA sample obtained from the evidence.

The X-Chromosome

Origin and Evolution

The X-chromosome is one of the sex chromosomes in humans. With around 155 million base pairs and 1100 genes, it represents about 5% of the total human genome that comprises 20,000–25,000 genes.

The two sex chromosomes originated from an ancestral autosomal pair (**Figure 1**). Around 300 Mya, this pair of autosomes started to accumulate differences and suffered structural and functional changes throughout the evolution, originating two different chromosomes: X and Y.

Even though they have a common origin, the X- and the Y-chromosomes followed different evolutionary paths: the Y-chromosome has lost most of its genomic material and does not suffer recombination in 95% of its extension, while the X-chromosome still retains traces of its autosomal past, suffering recombination along its entire length during female gametogenesis. Homology between the two chromosomes is still present in the telomeric pseudoautosomal regions (PAR 1 and PAR 2; **Figure 1**).

Characteristics

The particular characteristics of the X-chromosome make it an interesting subject for genetic studies. Many genetic conditions

 http://dx.doi.org/10.1016/B978-0-12-800647-4.00017-5

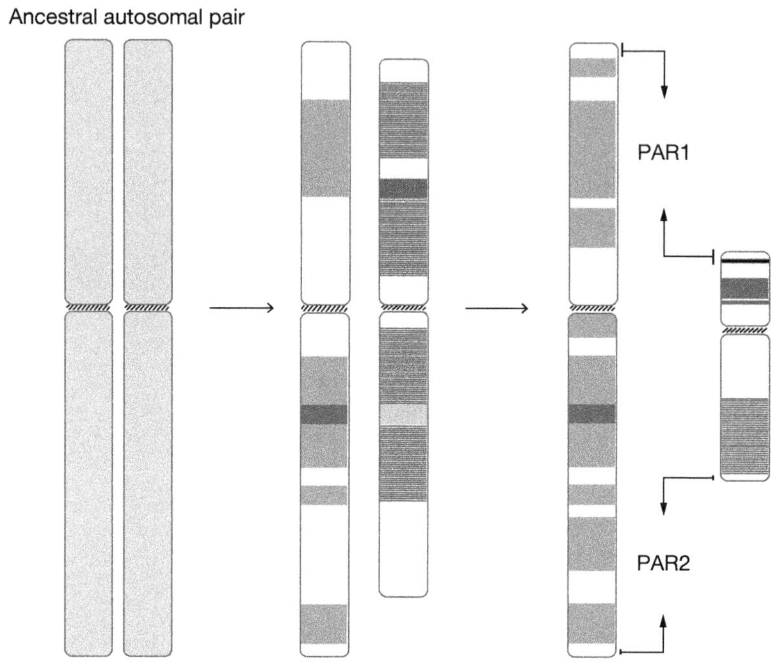

Figure 1 Evolution of the sex chromosomes.

have already been described as being related to mutations in specific genes on the X-chromosome. Hemophilia is a classic example of an X-chromosome-associated disease, among others.

In the last decade, interest in the study of the X-chromosome markers as tools for forensic and population genetic studies has been growing, as this can help to detect underlying patterns of genetic differentiation that are not usually captured by the traditionally analyzed autosomal markers.

Humans have one pair of the sex chromosomes, but the number of X-chromosomes present in each cell varies between males and females. Females have two copies, while males have one X-chromosome and one Y-chromosome. Therefore, men inherit their X-chromosome from their mothers, whereas women inherit one X-chromosome from each parent (**Figure 2**). The paternal X-chromosome they receive does not suffer recombination (except in the PARs) and is transmitted directly to the daughters. The maternal X-chromosome contains combined information from the two X-chromosomes present in the mother.

Given the difference in copy number in males and females, the study of the X-chromosome in men allows direct access to their haplotypes. As recombination only occurs in females, in each generation, only two-thirds of X-chromosomes recombine. The X-chromosome is thus disproportionately influenced by female demography, making the study of the X-chromosome particularly useful for detecting subtle differences between the two genders.

In a population with equal numbers of female and male individuals, there will only be three X-chromosomes for every four autosomes present. Furthermore, for every three X-chromosomes in a population, one will be paternally and two maternally inherited. This will lead to clear differences not only in the recombination but also in the mutation rates between the two, as in the X-chromosome the rates will be lower due to the higher mutation rate in male gametogenesis.

Owing to these characteristics, and also due to its younger age, the diversity on the X-chromosome is expected to be lower than on the autosomes. As a consequence, and looking at it from a population genetics point of view, the effects of selection, genetic drift, or substructure in a given population are more pronounced. The same is observed in the linkage disequilibrium (LD) patterns. LD can be defined as the nonrandom association of alleles at two or more loci. Several factors are responsible for breaking the extent of LD in a chromosome, such as the physical distance between the markers and recombination and mutation rates. Given that recombination only occurs in females, only one-half of the X-chromosomes in a population will recombine in each generation, and therefore it will necessarily take more time to break down LD by recombination. As a result, LD is greater when compared to the autosomes, and the size of regions with a single genetic history is larger, making it a better and more accurate tool to detect patterns of LD in populations.

The comparative analysis between the autosomes and the X-chromosome can also be used to reveal differences in demographic histories, migration, and breeding patterns of females and males. The usual studies of gender-biased demographic events compare information obtained from the Y-chromosome and mitochondrial deoxyribonucleic acid (mtDNA) markers. Unlike mtDNA and Y-chromosome analyses that inform about the history of female or male lineages, respectively, the X-chromosome allows the simultaneous study on both genders, making it an ideal system for studying population genetic differences between males and females regarding mutation rates and patterns of recombination. Owing to recombination, the X-chromosome is composed by a block-like pattern with different chromosomal regions being informative of distinct genetic histories, unlike uniparental markers that are transmitted as a single locus and where all the markers share the same genealogic history.

X-Chromosome Markers in Forensic Genetics

As previously mentioned, the X-chromosome combines some of the desirable features of autosomes and uniparental markers (Y-chromosome and mtDNA) and its particular characteristics make it an important tool in population and forensic genetic studies.

Forensic genetics is largely based on population genetic studies. The presentation of forensic genetic evidence in court is done in the face of uncertainty, with likelihood ratios that statistically compare, the probabilities of a certain observation under two alternative hypotheses with the random population serving as background.

The bulk of forensic genetic casework is related to three main areas: analysis of trace samples, individual identification, and establishment of biological relationships in paternity testing or other kinship analysis.

The following section presents some of the situations where the use of the X-chromosome markers can answer some of the challenges that cannot be solved by any other kind of genetic marker, and situations where it can serve as a complement of autosomal data analysis.

Analysis of Trace Samples

Autosomal markers are the method of choice for trace and stain analyses in forensic routine casework. They can give a reliable answer in most of the situations because of the high power of discrimination (PD) of the currently available kits.

The utility of X-chromosome markers in the analysis of trace samples and the PD of such markers varies, depending not only on the sex of the individual but also on the nature of the trace/mixture.

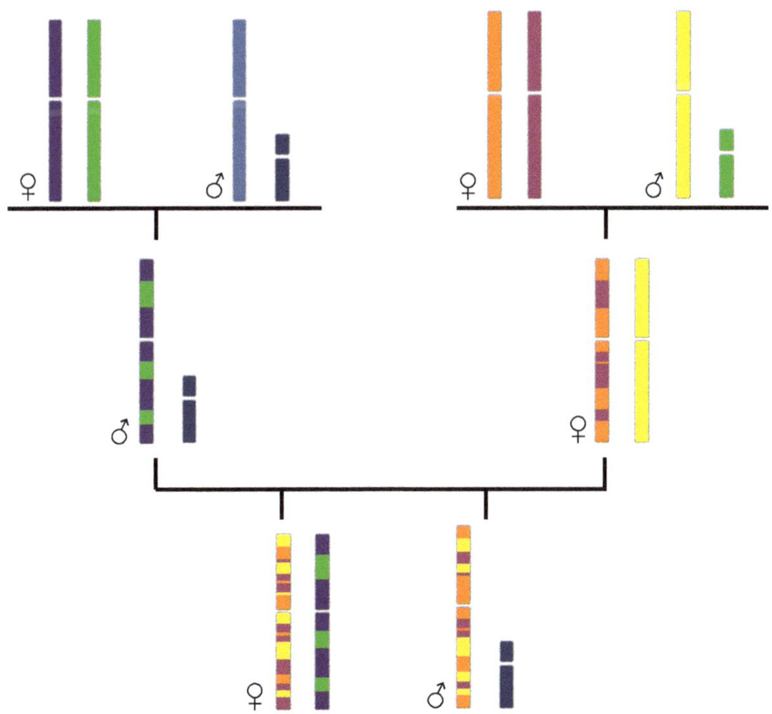

Figure 2 Genetic transmission of X- and Y-chromosomes.

If female traces are to be searched in a female background (female epithelial cells under a woman's fingernails, for instance), then the information given by the X-chromosome yields the same results as autosome analysis, with no gain in the PD.

When male traces ought to be searched on male background, the use of X-chromosome markers is not advisable, as with only one X-chromosome to be analyzed, only one allele by locus will be used, and, therefore, the PD value will be lower.

In mixed samples where a female and male individual are being investigated, the advantage of using the X-chromosome occurs in situations where there is a female trace to be identified in a male background contamination. In this case, the PD of the X markers will be higher than the autosomes. The probability of having all the female alleles included in the male profile means that the female has to be homozygous for all the systems considered, which has a low probability of occurrence for forensic-selected markers with high diversity.

As mentioned previously, in situations where a male profile is searched in a female background, it is not advisable to use the X-chromosome, as the probability of the male profile being included within the female alleles is high.

As a last remark, X-chromosome analysis can also be useful in traces collected from old and degraded samples, where most of the autosomal data may be missing. It can also be used in individual identification in victims of mass disasters, where limited amounts of DNA are available and family relationships must be established based on few genetic markers.

Paternity Cases and Kinship Testing

As for the trace samples, most of the routine casework presented to forensic practitioners regarding paternity cases involving trio constellations can be easily solved with autosomal markers.

The use of the X-chromosome can be very efficient and give additional information in father–daughter or mother–son relationships.

Owing to its mode of inheritance, the analysis of X markers on father–son relationships has no use whatsoever. On the other hand, in a situation where the two alleged fathers are father and son, the analysis of the X-chromosome can be more helpful than the autosomes as they will not share identical X-chromosome alleles by descent.

Female individuals that have the same father will share the same paternal X-chromosome. X-chromosome markers can then resolve relationships involving two sisters or half-sisters, helping to consider or exclude paternity more efficiently than autosomes.

Genealogical and pedigree reconstruction over several generations is also one of the potential applications of the X-chromosome markers, as long as the X-chromosome lineages are not interrupted by father–son relationships.

The main field where the study of X-chromosome markers can contribute the most is in paternity cases where the putative father is not immediately available and his closest relatives must be analyzed instead. The power of exclusion of autosomal markers decreases, and in this situation, the analysis of X-chromosome markers can be more informative, especially if the putative paternal grandmother is available for genotyping. As males will inherit their X-chromosome from the mother, the putative father's haplotype (that he will then pass to his daughter) can be inferred from the paternal grandmother.

As an example, a case is presented where the access to the putative paternal grandmother can be more informative (**Figure 3**). In the absence of the putative paternal grandfather (I), autosomal short tandem repeats (STRs) can be insufficient, although uncles V and VI are available. Even in their absence, the analysis of X-STRs from the grandmother (II) is enough to resolve the kinship and determine whether IV and VII are related, as II contains all the alleles present in the putative father, IV.

In more common situations, where there is no information available from the grandparents, the profile from the paternal grandmother can be reconstructed using V and VI. The analysis will be more informative, as more sons/daughters are used to reconstruct the complete profile from II.

Even though the study of the X-chromosome for population and forensic genetics is still very recent compared to the currently established autosomal protocols, the described situations confirm the potential of using the X-chromosome markers in forensic genetics and their importance in resolving some of the challenges that could not be answered otherwise. From individual identification to paternity testing and kinship analysis, the X-chromosome has proven to be an important and valuable tool.

Different types of markers have been identified along the X-chromosome specific portion, which are now available for multiple applications. Depending on the aim, markers that are more or less apart from each other, showing different degrees of

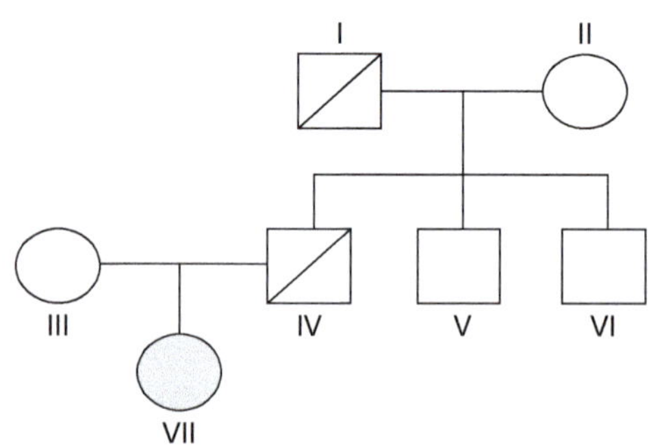

Figure 3 Example of a case where the data from the X-chromosome was more informative than the autosomal data.

association and presenting varied population diversity levels (usually related with mutation rates), can be selected.

Genetic Markers

Variation among individuals is the core of all forensic and population genetic studies. From its early days, genetic analysis has come a long way since its first approach with the "classical markers." Early population and human identification studies were done using the blood-type information of individuals, or with protein and enzymatic markers. The development of molecular biology, and more importantly the development of polymerase chain reaction in 1983, was responsible for a shift in the original focus of the studies to a new generation of "molecular markers" where DNA polymorphisms assume a position of prominence. DNA polymorphisms are usually defined as naturally occurring changes in the DNA sequence among individuals where at least two alleles have a frequency of more than 1% in the population.

Restriction fragment length polymorphisms were the first to be used in human identification studies, but in the last decades, the development and miniaturization of new technologies has made it possible to study other kinds of genetic markers, such as microsatellites or STRs, single nucleotide polymorphisms (SNPs), and insertion/deletion markers (Indels) among others.

Owing to their specific characteristics, different information can be extracted from the different types of markers, and it is important to assess their adequacy according to the goal of the study.

This chapter presents a brief review of the characteristics of the most commonly used genetic markers, in the light of their current application to the X-chromosome.

Short Tandem Repeats

STRs are DNA sequences composed by small tandem repetitions (usually 2–6 bps) whose number varies between individuals.

It is estimated that STRs occur every 10,000 nucleotides, representing around 3% of the total human genome variation. Even though they are spread throughout the genome, the majority of STRs are located in noncoding regions. These markers are selectively neutral and highly polymorphic (with average mutations rates around 2.1×10^{-3}), which renders them a high PD. They can also be genotyped using simple and fast typing techniques.

STRs can be divided into simple or complex, according to the repetitive motive they present. The complexity of the motive and its size has repercussions on the mutation rates and the number of different alleles. Several studies showed that an increase in the length also translates into an increase of point mutations that split the initial motive into smaller ones, and this can be understood as an evolutionary mechanism to control the average size of the fragment.

For all the characteristics already mentioned, the analysis of STRs has become the method of election when assessing genetic diversity in populations.

Although a vast number of STR loci have been described for autosomes and the Y-chromosome in mammals in general, and particularly in humans, just very recently has science focused on the potential of X-chromosome study.

Several human X-chromosome STR multiplexes have been described. A multiplex consisting of 10 markers has been developed as a result of collaborative work carried out by the Spanish and Portuguese Speaking Working Group of the ISFG (GHEP-ISFG).

Commercial kits are also available. The one currently in use amplifies 12 markers simultaneously, plus amelogenin for gender determination (**Figure 4**).

There is an increase in the publication of data concerning X-STRs, but further studies are still needed on allele frequency distributions, mutation rates, and LD in order to continue to establish reference population databases.

Single Nucleotide Polymorphisms

SNPs are single base substitutions that are present in the genome. The majority of SNPs is bi-allelic, but tri-allelic and tetra-allelic SNPs have also been reported.

The advantages of using SNPs in forensic casework and population genetic studies lie in their abundance in the genome—approximately 85% of the human genetic variation can be attributed to SNPs.

Compared to STRs, these markers have lower mutation rates (approximately 2×10^{-8}), and are thus more stable, making them more suitable to use in kinship analyses and in circumstances where pedigree/lineage reconstruction is needed.

SNPs can also be amplified in short fragments of around 60–80 bps. This makes them very useful in old samples with low-quantity DNA template and/or in degraded samples where the available DNA is fragmented. In these situations, the analysis of SNPs is more likely to produce better results than STR genotyping.

The fact that most SNPs are bi-allelic decreases their informativity per locus when compared to the STRs ($\sim$10–13 SNPs are necessary to get the same discrimination power as an STR). Even though ultimately SNPs will not replace the currently used STRs, they can be used as a complementary tool, increasing the information available.

Depending on the characteristics, location in the genome, and the genetic diversity of a certain SNP within and among populations, SNP analysis can be used in individual identification, phenotypic inference, and ancestry or lineage studies.

The International HapMap project is one of the most important studies that report common genetic variants that

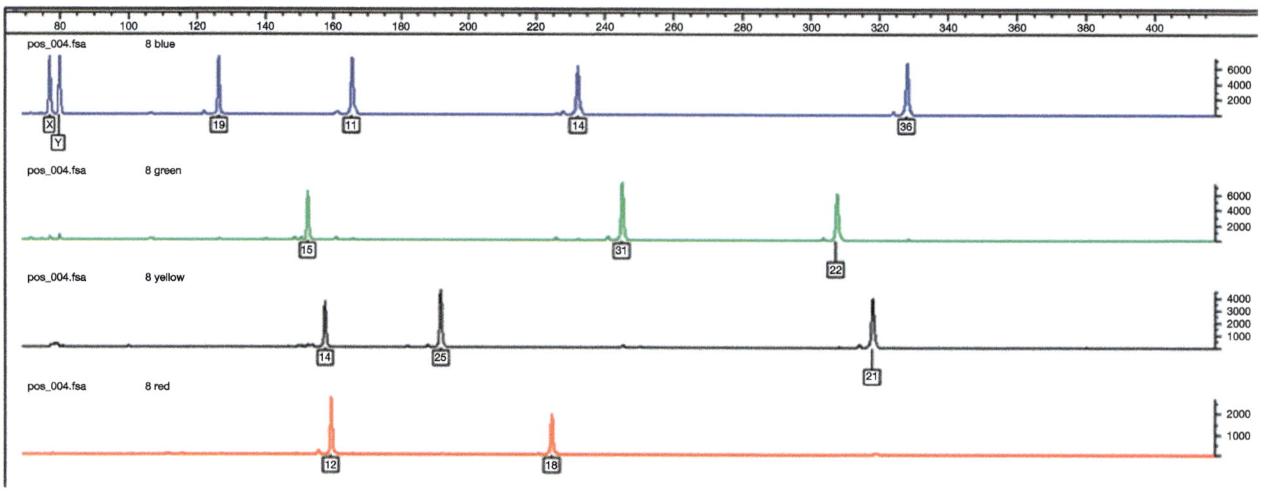

Figure 4 Electropherogram showing the genetic profile of a male individual analyzed for 12 X-chromosome STRs plus amelogenin.

occur in different human populations. Already in phase III, the HapMap database has contributed to increase the density of known SNPs across the human genome, and has reported over 10 million nonredundant SNPs to date. The SNP database from the National Center for Biotechnology Information (dbSNP; www.ncbi.nlm.nih.gov/) currently includes over 400,000 X-chromosome-specific SNPs that have been validated and are available for multiple applications.

At the present time, minimal data on the use of X-chromosome SNP in forensic analysis has been published, although some studies have already shown their applicability in relationship testing and population characterization. This area promises to grow substantially in the upcoming years, as more automated and rapid SNP typing methodologies are developed.

Insertion/Deletion Polymorphisms

Another kind of genetic variation that has gained importance over the last few years is insertion/deletion polymorphisms or Indels.

As the name suggests, Indels are length polymorphisms created by insertions or deletions of nucleotides in the genome. They can be divided into those with multiple alleles or di-allelic. Regarding di-allelic Indels, their fragment size can vary from one base pair insertion/deletion up to hundreds of kilo-base pairs, although the largest group of di-allelic Indels varies between 3 and 15 bps.

After SNPs, Indels are reported as the most abundant DNA polymorphisms. Initial studies focusing on the mapping of Indel variation in humans showed that Indel markers represent between 16% and 25% of all sequence polymorphisms in humans. Keeping in mind that the current number of SNPs reported in dbSNP database is around 10,000,000 and increasing, it is estimated that the human genome might contain around 1.6–2.5 million unique Indel polymorphisms that occur with an average density of one every 7200 bps. Considering the size of the chromosome, the density of Indels reported for the X-chromosome is somewhat lower than the autosomal average; but if one takes into account the amount of information available for each chromosome, the values are similar to the average in the autosomes, representing around one polymorphic Indel every 5–13 kbps.

Even though Indel polymorphisms are quite abundant throughout the genome, only recently has the scientific community devoted some attention to this particular kind of marker. The advantage of using Indels in population and human identification studies lies in the fact that they combine many of the desirable features of SNPs and STRs. Their application in these fields ranges from individual identification to population characterization. Like SNPs, they are very commonly distributed in the genome, and the majority of them are unlikely to present recurrent mutations. Most Indels have originated from a single mutational event that occurred at low frequency and was subsequently stable. Also like SNPs, the amplification of short fragment Indels can be done in smaller amplicons than those of STRs, improving the chances of having good quality profiles in old and degraded samples, where STR genotyping is unlikely to succeed.

The allelic frequencies of some Indels present clear differences between the major population groups making these Indels useful as ancestry informative markers.

Like STRs, the genotyping of short fragment Indels is relatively easy and fast and can be performed using the already developed methodologies available for STR typing, without the need to use direct sequencing methods or other additional requirements. They are suitable for analysis with

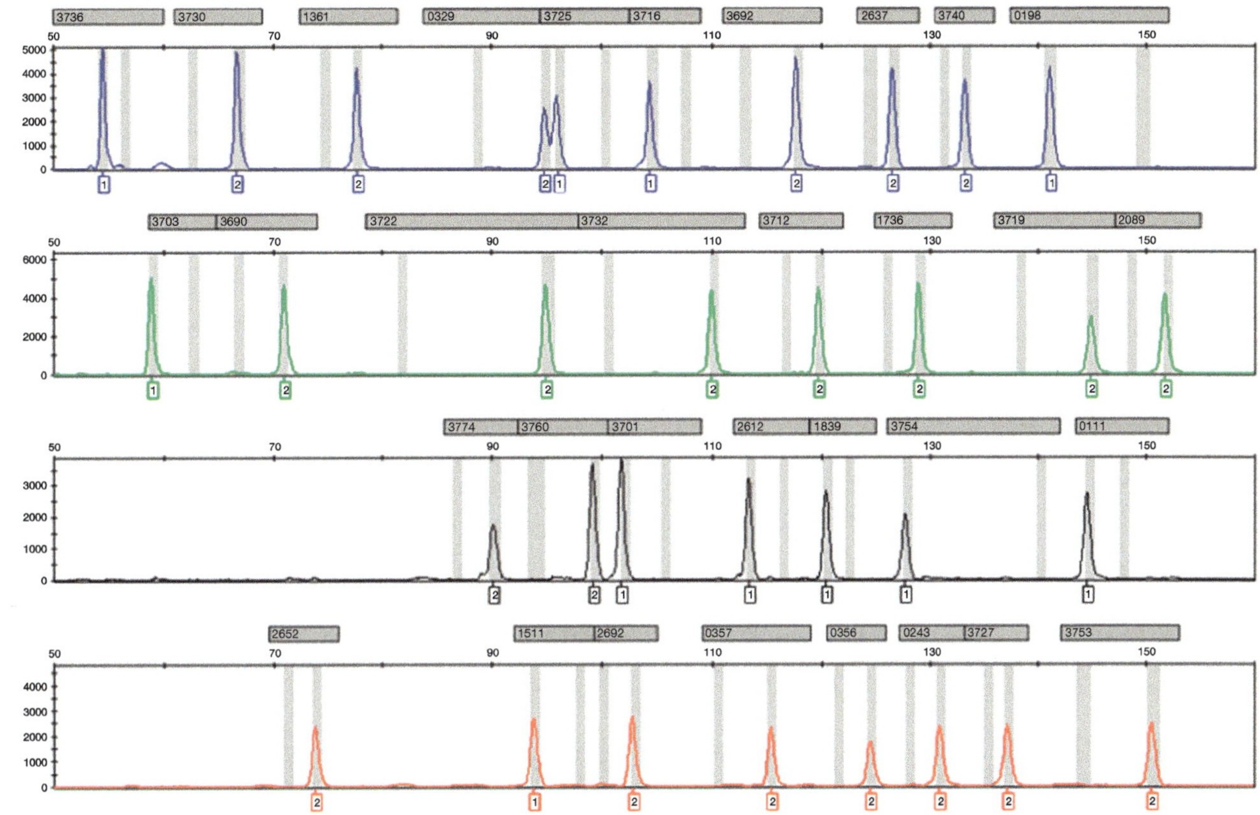

Figure 5 Electropherogram of a male individual genotyped for 33 X-chromosome Indels.

high-throughput technologies and automation of the genotyping systems.

Several studies have reported multiplexes of X-chromosome Indels that contain from 13 up to 33 markers (**Figure 5**). Data is starting to become available for European, African, Asian, and Native American populations, showing the potential of these markers for population characterization and human admixture studies.

Haploblocks

As previously stated, although SNPs are abundant throughout the genome, the analysis of SNPs still has not surpassed STR genotyping due to their lower PD per locus.

Several studies have shown that the human genome has a block-type structure, where recombination hotspots alternate with regions with strong LD. With the detection of this block-like pattern throughout the genome, a new kind of marker has become of potential forensic interest, the haploblock.

The concept is that several neighboring and tightly linked SNPs will form a block that will be inherited together, and where little or no recombination occurs between them. Even though the PD of each SNP within the block is low, when considered together as a unit, this set of linked SNPs will form haplotypes. As a result, the discriminating power will increase, and, in theory, it will be equivalent to an STR. The observed haplotypes will be then comparable to alleles in STR loci.

Some studies have already described haploblocks throughout the autosomes, but there is still some work to be done on the X-chromosome. Because of its size, it is expected that four or five blocks could be used for forensic casework.

Conclusions

In genetic identification, beyond the simplest cases of paternity testing and the comparison of genetic profiles from biological samples, situations often arise where the genetic profiles are not complete or where the interpretation of results can be quite complex.

In these situations, combining markers with specific characteristics as well as several regions of the genome with different modes of transmission (autosomes, mtDNA, Y-chromosome, and X-chromosome) has proven to be a successful technique. Several studies have already shown the usefulness of lineage markers in individual identification in diverse scenarios. X-chromosome markers have also proven their applicability in kinship testing, in situations where autosomal data cannot exclude a certain relationship between the individuals, and therefore do not provide a clear answer.

Given all the interesting features of the X-chromosome that have been constantly highlighted throughout this chapter, the application of X-chromosome markers in forensic genetics can serve as an additional research tool that can be important to unraveling some of the challenges presented in this area.

See also: **Biology/DNA:** Short Tandem Repeats; Single-Nucleotide Polymorphisms.

Further Reading

Budowle, B., Van Daal, A., 2009. Extracting evidence from forensic DNA analyses: future molecular biology directions. Biotechniques 46 (5), 339–340. 342–350.

Edelmann, J., Hering, S., Augustin, C., Szibor, R., 2009. Indel polymorphisms – an additional set of markers on the X-chromosome. Forensic Science International Genetic Supplement Series 2 (1), 510–512.

Edelmann, J., Hering, S., Augustin, C., Kalis, S., Szibor, R., 2010. Validation of six closely linked STRs located in the chromosome X centromere region. International Journal of Legal Medicine 124 (1), 83–87.

Ge, J., Budowle, B., Planz, J.V., Chakraborty, R., 2010. Haplotype block: a new type of forensic DNA markers. International Journal Legal Medicine 124 (5), 353–361.

Koboldt, D.C., Miller, R.D., Kwok, P.Y., 2006. Distribution of human SNPs and its effect on high-throughput genotyping. Human Mutation 27 (3), 249–254.

Krawczak, M., 2007. Kinship testing with X-chromosomal markers: mathematical and statistical issues. Forensic Science International Genetics 1 (2), 111–114.

Mills, R.E., Luttig, C.T., et al., 2006. An initial map of insertion and deletion (INDEL) variation in the human genome. Genome Research 16 (9), 1182–1190.

Pinto, N., Gusmão, L., Amorim, A., 2011. X-chromosome markers in kinship testing: a generalisation of the IBD approach identifying situations where their contribution is crucial. Forensic Science International Genetics 5 (1), 27–32.

Ribeiro-Rodrigues, E.M., dos Santos, N.P., et al., 2009. Assessing interethnic admixture using an X-linked insertion-deletion multiplex. American Journal of Human Biology 21 (5), 707–709.

Schaffner, S.F., 2004. The X chromosome in population genetics. Nature Reviews Genetics 5 (1), 43–51.

Szibor, R., 2007. X-chromosomal markers: past, present and future. Forensic Science International Genetics 1 (2), 93–99.

Szibor, R., Krawczak, M., Hering, S., Edelmann, J., Kuhlisch, E., Krause, D., 2003. Use of X-linked markers for forensic purposes. International Journal of Legal Medicine 117 (2), 67–74.

Tomas, C., Sanchez, J.J., Castro, J.A., Børsting, C., Morling, N., 2010. Forensic usefulness of a 25 X-chromosome single-nucleotide polymorphism marker set. Transfusion 50 (10), 2258–2265.

Weber, J.L., David, D., Heil, J., Fan, Y., Zhao, C., Marth, G., 2002. Human diallelic insertion/deletion polymorphisms. American Journal of Human Genetics 71 (4), 854–862.

Zarrabeitia, M.T., Mijares, V., Riancho, J.A., 2007. Forensic efficiency of microsatellites and single nucleotide polymorphisms on the X chromosome. International Journal of Legal Medicine 121 (6), 433–437.

Relevant Websites

www.1000genomes.org—Catalog of Human Genetic Variation.
www.chrx-str.org—Database of X-chromosome STR Markers for Forensic Purposes.
www.hapmap.org—The International HapMap Project.
www.ncbi.nlm.nih.gov/—National Center for Biotechnology Information.
www.cstl.nist.gov/strbase/—Short Tandem Repeat DNA Internet Database.

Ancestry Informative Markers

C Phillips, University of Santiago de Compostela, Galicia, Spain

Glossary

Admixture The effects of the combination of two or more populations leading to patterns of mixed variation that originally may have been common to only one contributing population.

Allele The alternative variants that create a polymorphism. Binary polymorphisms such as single nucleotide polymorphisms (SNPs) show two alleles.

Autosomes/autosomal Chromosomes that do not control gender.

Genotype A combination of two alleles sited on the maternal and paternal chromosomes (or singly in uniparentally inherited markers).

Polymorphism The presence of variant forms of a gene, nucleotide sequence, or repeated genome segment where the minor variant is found at a minimum 1% frequency.

Uniparental Variation carried on the Y-chromosome or the mitochondria that is inherited from one parent.

The First Forensic Ancestry Informative Markers: Early Use of Ancestry Informative Protein Polymorphisms Demonstrated Their Value for Investigations

As early as the 1960s, the Duffy blood group, based on serological detection of red cell antigen alleles FY*A and FY*B, was routinely used as a polymorphic marker in forensic biology laboratories. The strong association of African ancestry with the Duffy-null/negative phenotype (written Fy[a-b-] as both alleles are unexpressed due to an independent promoter variant) provided additional data from the same test that suggested a likely African ancestry component for Fy[a-b-] bloodstain donors. By the late 1970s, three additional red cell enzyme polymorphisms were used to specifically detect population diagnostic variation, comprising the hemoglobin S variant plus enzyme systems peptidase A and carbonic anhydrase. The key characteristic of these systems was an allele frequency distribution specific to Africans, that is, absent from other continental regions, albeit at relatively low 8–12% frequencies in African populations. This meant informative genotypes occurred in 22%, 21%, and 15% of Africans, respectively, yet the three tests collectively offered indicative data in 46% of cases, as shown in **Figure 1(a)**. Peptidase A protein, expressed in semen as well as in erythrocytes, allowed this system to successfully track the movements of a serial rapist active in South London and helped investigators link the crimes. This case and others indicated to scientists and investigators alike that despite a low frequency of ancestry informative genotypes, some markers could often provide robust indicators of ancestry. The Duffy system, where over 99% of genotypes are African informative, further highlights the forensic value of ancestry inference when variation is specific to a particular population group. Of course, this represents an overly simplistic view of ancestry inference for several reasons: very few polymorphisms show such clear divides between population groups; most groups are considerably less differentiated (divergent) than African–non-African population comparisons suggest; genetic differentiation between groups rapidly breaks down with the population admixture that typifies urban and postcolonial populations; and few, if any, markers are completely diagnostic of any one group—notably, Duffy-negative genotypes are absent from Khoisan Africans (**Figure 1(b)**). Now that forensic analysis is firmly in the DNA era, perhaps the most important lesson from early application of simple polymorphisms to infer that ancestry is their proven ability to give valuable investigative leads in certain circumstances, for example, when an eyewitness is absent or, of more relevance for today's forensic analyses, when no DNA database entry exists.

Y-Chromosome and Mitochondrial DNA Variation

The prompt introduction of mitochondrial DNA (mt-DNA) sequencing followed by characterization and use of Y-chromosome variation (NRY) alongside short tandem repeat

 http://dx.doi.org/10.1016/B978-0-12-800647-4.00018-7

(a)

System name	Gene	SNP identifier	% informative genotypes*	Cumulative % informative	Cumulative % uninformative
Pep A	CNDP2	rs733062	20.97	20.97	79.03
Hb S	HBB	rs334	22.03	38.38	61.62
CA II	CA2	rs2228063	15.54	47.96	52.04
Fy	DARC	rs2814778	99.56	99.77	0.23

SNP	Africa (*N* = 472)	Europe (*N* = 223)	East asia (*N* = 364)
rs733062	G: 0.111 A: 0.889	G: 0.000 A: 1.000	G: 0.000 A: 1.000
rs334	A: 0.117 T: 0.883	A: 0.000 T: 1.000	A: 0.000 T: 1.000
rs2228063	A: 0.919 G: 0.081	A: 1.000 G: 0.000	A: 1.000 G: 0.000
rs2814778	T: 0.066 C: 0.934	T: 0.990 C: 0.010	Not genotyped

(b)

	CEPH san (Khoisan Africans)	CEPH AFR	African Americans	CEPH EUR	CEPH E ASN
rs2814778	T: 1.000 C: 0.000	T: 0.034 C: 0.966	T: 0.156 C: 0.844	T: 1.000 C: 0.000	T: 1.000 C: 0.000

Figure 1 (a) Allele and genotype frequency distributions in three population groups of four previously used forensic ancestry informative polymorphisms. *Informative genotypes denote African-indicative heterozygotes and homozygotes combined. Pie chart summaries are HapMap population data. (b) Population allele frequency data of Duffy AIM-SNP rs2814778 indicating atypical frequencies in Khoisan Africans and effect of AFR–EUR admixture in African Americans. CSA = Central-South Asians (Gujarati Indians in Houston), EAS = E-ASN.

(STR) typing led to early recognition of the ancestry informative value of these two haploid markers. Each represents nonrecombining genome portions inherited uniparentally—unchanged from mother to offspring (mt-DNA) or father to son. Defining an individual's mt-DNA and NRY lineages therefore suggests shared ancestry with others carrying identical lineages and can be compared to global population surveys of lineage distributions that have become highly differentiated since migrants first left Africa. Furthermore, it may benefit forensic investigations to infer the parental ancestries of a DNA donor, particularly when each lineage is different.

Two problems arise when attempting to match an individual's uniparental lineages to particular populations. First, the mt-DNA and NRY genome portions are only a fraction of the total and may be atypical of the sum of population histories contributing to an individual's whole ancestry. The chance of finding atypical lineages increases in populations that have migrated or admixed in recent history, exemplified by Parsis—showing characteristic Iranian NRY lineages contrasting with mt-DNA lineages more typical of Gujarati. As almost everyone has some ancestry from different regions, ancestry analysis based on two markers alone risks erroneous inference from concentrating on a relatively small proportion of the genome. Second, the basis of the population specificity of particular lineages is dependent on the extent of population sampling preceding the analysis. Surveying haploid marker distributions necessitates typing all relevant variant sites at once and as one unit; therefore, much greater numbers are needed to count each haplotype, and inevitably substantial areas of a region lack surveys. Furthermore, certain lineages can become dominant and are shared across quite extensive geographic areas; notably the Y-chromosome C*(xC3c) sublineage is shared by 0.5% of all males worldwide, as it is such a dominant feature of central Asian NRY variability.

Despite these limitations, mt-DNA and NRY typing offers strong differentiation of the ancestry of two portions of a donor's DNA; therefore, a prudent measure for forensic laboratories tempted to draw ancestry inferences from haploid data is to review this variation alongside autosomal ancestry informative markers (AIMs) to provide multiple points of comparison and reduce the risk of biased ancestry inferences.

Points of Reference: Defining Populations or Ancestries, Ancestry Informativeness Metrics, Types of Autosomal AIMs, and Population Diversity Reference Panels

Defining human populations or ancestries can be a highly sensitive issue that excites strong feelings, particularly as labeling or categorizing people is a crude measure that ignores many of the most important aspects of each individual's distinctive cultural heritage. A widespread concern for ethicists is the danger that inference of ancestry in a forensic context will lead to targeting of particular communities with the burden of proof passing to members of that community when DNA profiling for elimination purposes focuses on voluntary programs screening reduced suspect groups. Many specialists advocate purely geographic terms to define an ancestry or population of origin, avoiding descriptions concentrating on visible characteristics such as "black" and "white." Other common descriptions, such as "Caucasian" or "Hispanic," though widely understood, lack geographic precision. Overall, population labels without a geographic definition often hide a large amount of heterogeneity within the group. This article uses five continental-scale descriptions (herein abbreviated): sub-Saharan African (AFR); Eurasian (EUR), comprising

European, Middle Eastern–North African, and Central-South Asian (Indian subcontinent) population groups; East Asian (E-ASN); Native American (AME); and Oceanian (OCE). These descriptions follow a broadly continental distribution of population diversity delimited by geographic barriers to large-scale population movements and repeatedly shown to match well to distributions of genetic variation. Any focus on population diversity can lose sight of a simple, universally recorded characteristic of human genetic variability: the differences between individuals within the same population describe ~85% of total variation, with differences between populations accounting for just 15%. Despite this very small proportion, there is clearly genetic variation that can be selected and built into forensically viable DNA tests.

Assessing strategies to select forensic AIMs leads to the question of how to first measure the ancestry informativeness of any given locus based on particular population comparisons. Traditionally, the population substructure metric Fst, analyzing levels of heterozygosity, is used to measure population differentiation; however, Fst works less efficiently assessing a marker's individual informativeness. Fst does not adequately reflect underlying diversity beyond pairwise population comparisons and extends poorly from binary polymorphisms such as single nucleotide polymorphisms (SNPs) to multiple-allele loci such as STRs. The very simple *delta* allele frequency differential, useful as a quick assessment of binary AIMs (δ: allele frequency in population 1 minus that in population 2), provides surprisingly good Fst approximations: $\text{Fst} \approx \delta^2$ or $\text{Fst} \approx \delta/(2-\delta)$. However, the need to properly assess any marker's ancestry informativeness has brought consensus behind using the more appropriate metric of divergence or *In*. The common nomenclature to denote three group comparisons of AFR–EUR–E-ASN is *In*3, extended to include AME, *In*4. Although reviewing ancestry informativeness metrics may seem a detail, the major constraint in forensic analyses is the input DNA available to successfully genotype marker sets; therefore, it is essential to choose the most informative loci for combination into small-scale, manageable PCR multiplexes. The most informative markers for a particular population comparison will additionally best measure levels of admixture between those populations. **Figure 2** shows the relationship between the divergence metrics δ, Fst, and *In* comparing two population groups.

The study developing the *In* divergence metric went on to compare average informativeness of different types of autosomal markers (i.e., not those of X, Y, or mt-DNA). Unsurprisingly, multiple-allele STRs had much higher *In* values than binary loci (mainly SNPs but including indels: bi-allelic insertion/deletion polymorphisms). This underlines the importance of average allele numbers per STR (those studied averaged 12.4). However, despite the great majority of binary loci being considerably less informative than all 377 STRs typed, about 1% of SNPs gave the highest *In* values of any marker. What are the implications for building viable forensic AIM sets? First, a large catalog of human SNPs offers the best chance to find the loci most differentiated between populations and therefore the best markers available. Second, though fewer indels have been described than SNPs, they offer similar possibilities and bring their own valuable characteristics to forensic analysis. Third, forensic STR data generated for identification purposes is likely to provide some ancestry information too. Since forensic STRs generally show low population divergence, this data adds value to dedicated ancestry marker sets rather than offering a viable alternative by themselves.

DNA sample panels of globally distributed populations are the most important resource for selecting AIMs but remain limited in scope and patchy in their continental focus. The most widely used panel and most comprehensive population distribution is provided by the Human Genome Diversity Panel–Center d'Etude du Polymorphisme Humain (HGDP–CEPH) comprising 949 samples in 52 populations: 7 AFR, 8 EUR, 17 E-ASN, 5 AME, and 2 OCE (plus 4 Middle East and 9 Central-South Asian). Additionally, the community resource HapMap and 1000 Genomes projects provide extensive SNP catalogs, typing continental and admixed populations, each likely to be continually extended in global coverage. To date, both projects have not characterized parental (unadmixed) AME or OCE populations. The easiest way to access and discover AIMs from the above population resources is to screen online allele frequency data. Although individual project Websites provide marker-by-marker access, a collective approach is better, whether comparing sets of SNPs, chromosome spans, or population divergent genes (e.g., pigmentation genes). Fortunately, this is possible using the *SPSmart* suite detailed in the online resources section, with the opportunity to directly download reference genotypes into all the population statistical analyses suggested in section "Statistical Analysis of AIM Genotype Data."

Autosomal AIM-SNPs

Autosomal SNPs have been the principal focus for building initial stand-alone forensic AIM sets. Despite random sets of STRs usually being more informative, searching for the most differentiated SNPs will identify the best AIMs of all, while SNPs bring considerable benefits to forensic analysis. First, there are much more extensive catalogs of SNPs than other markers, all allowing scrutiny of major group (AFR–EUR–E-ASN) differentiations. Recent genome-scale sequencing extends this catalog to SNPs with ~1% minor allele frequencies, though notably these methods are less efficient in detecting copy number variation: STRs and indels. SNPs also bring benefits from typing much shorter amplified fragments than STRs, so there is a higher quantity of intact DNA for the PCR stage. Binary polymorphisms are easier to fit into larger

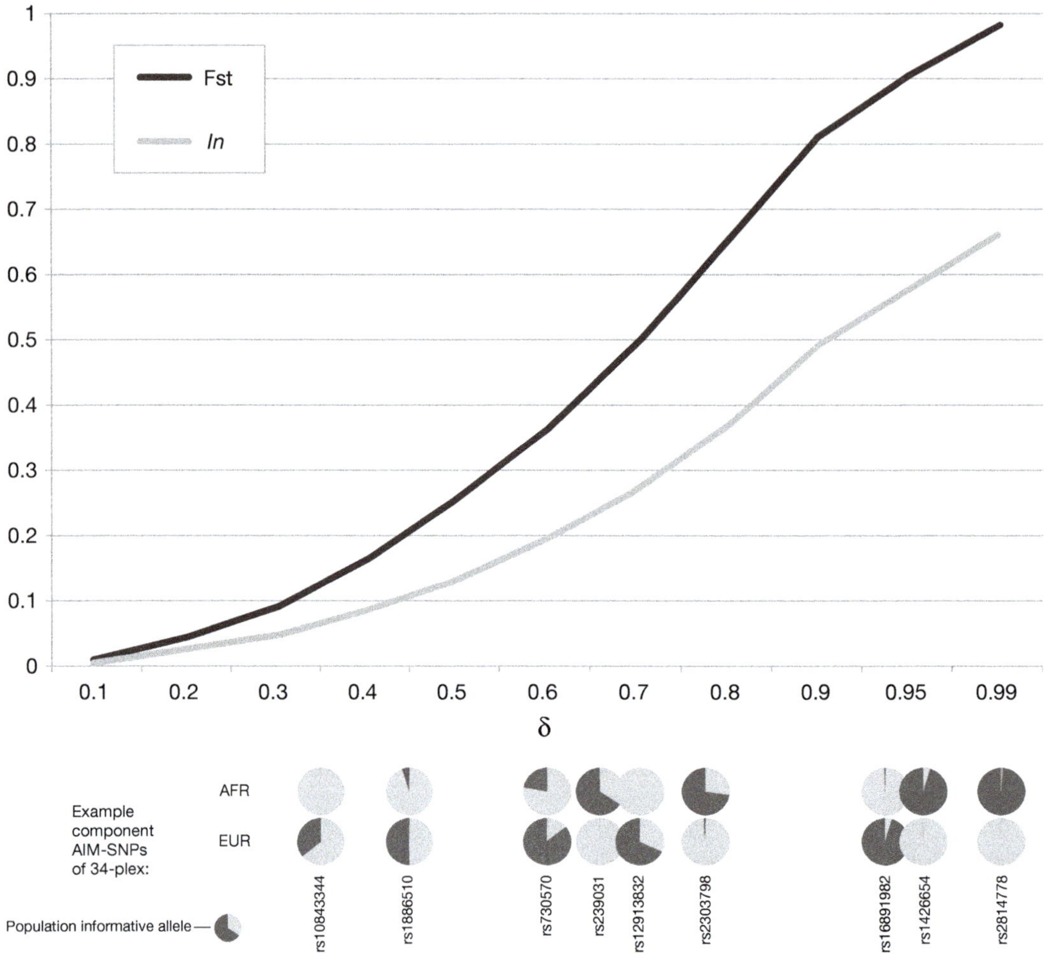

Figure 2 The relationship between Fst and *In* population divergence metrics comparing Africans and Europeans for increasing values of the δ allele frequency differential. Examples of AIM-SNP composite markers of the 34-plex forensic multiplex are aligned underneath their δ values.

multiplexes because short fragment amplification is more efficient and the allele detection stage can more easily accommodate pairs of alleles compared to larger ranges such as the 25–30 alleles of complex forensic STRs. Lastly, a range of platforms is available for genotyping SNPs, and their scope per reaction has now reached the million marker level providing the possibility of a much more detailed analysis of human population divergence. The choice of high-throughput genotyping approaches available is regularly listed as a favorable factor for adapting SNP analysis to forensic identification. However, this ignores a critical shortcoming of these techniques that restricts their potential application to forensics—the amount of input DNA required generally far exceeds the 1–20 ng typically extracted from forensic material. As ancestry analysis would normally be an adjunct to identification with STRs, there are further limits to how many reactions could be realistically added to an average DNA case. Furthermore, police investigators carry raised expectations that contact traces with subnanogram levels of DNA are well within the sensitivity limits of forensic laboratories. For this reason, two relatively small-scale multiplex AIM-SNP sets are highlighted using simple *SNaPshot* primer extension assays, typing 34 SNPs in a single test and 24 SNPs in two tests developed by Lao et al.

A third study reported a much larger 176 AIM-SNP set developed by Halder, thereby offering higher overall informativeness. However, Halder's set was designed around discontinued genotyping chemistry: the chip-based Beckman–Coulter *SNPstream* system. Although *SNPstream* showed good forensic sensitivity and could type up to 48 SNPs per reaction, it was hampered by requiring proprietary consumables/instruments as well as the need to group identical SNP substitutions and strands together into discrete PCRs (e.g., G/A, C/T, G/T, and C/A). Thus, the minimum number of reactions (not publicly reported) is likely 6–8, comprising 16G/T-A/C SNPs, 16G/C, and 147C/T-A/G. In comparison, *SNaPshot* uses established forensic DNA instrumentation and is relatively simple to adapt to different SNP sets, while showing by far the best forensic sensitivity of any current SNP typing system. The major limitation of *SNaPshot* is frequent signal peak imbalances caused by differences in the reaction dynamics of the four dye-linked terminators, making mixed-source DNA detection difficult to achieve. This is particularly important for AIM-SNP analysis where a forensic mixture comprising donors with different ancestries could easily mimic a single-source profile from an individual with admixed ancestry. Reviews of forensic AIM-SNP candidates should also take account of published marker lists, despite lacking multiplex designs or being based on singleplex Taqman genotyping. Two such SNP sets have been proposed for forensic use: 128 AIM-SNPs collated by Kosoy and 47 AIM-SNPs mainly overlapping the 24 of Lao above selected by Kersbergen.

Table 1 lists the most informative component AIM-SNPs of the above five sets ranked by *In*3 and showing *In*4, estimated using 1000 Genomes and HGDP–CEPH genotypes, respectively (Lao/Kersbergen *In*4 omitted due to missing HGDP–CEPH SNPs). Two interesting features emerge from these comparisons: marker commonality, that is, top AIM-SNPs chosen by multiple studies are confined to just two loci: rs2814778 (Duffy) or rs16891982; and most of the top 24–34 SNP components have broadly comparable *In* ancestry informativeness. These observations may partly reflect the selection strategies used. The 34-plex and Halder AIM-SNPs were accumulated over several years of searching for highly differentiated allele frequencies in online databases, whereas Lao/Kersbergen and Kosoy screened whole-genome scan (WGS) data of 10,000 and 300,000 SNPs, respectively. The comparability of the best markers in each set indicates that different AIM selection approaches can each provide informative sets; so, there are more than enough ancestry informative SNPs available to select markers that can multiplex well and provide sufficiently wide genomic distribution. The noticeably small number of extremely differentiated AIM-SNPs, for example, *In*3 0.75, not only indicates how difficult it is to find such SNPs but also reflects their absence from WGS marker sets due to a lack of association power, since these loci have almost no variability within any one population group. Lastly, there are contrasting cumulative *In*4 values between 34-plex and the two large-scale SNP sets, indicating different approaches in marker selection, with the 34-plex selected for three group differentiations but now supplemented with a 28-plex stand-alone AIM-SNP multiplex dedicated to differentiating AME populations. This follows the 2008 publication of HGDP–CEPH genotypes for over 650,000 SNPs, enabling selection of many more markers close to fixation (i.e., allele frequencies at or near 1.0 exclusively in one or more groups) in both AME and OCE groups. In summary, the prospects are good for further development of AIM-SNP multiplexes with forensic viability and scale.

Indels

Short-allele indels (1–5 nucleotide insertions, infrequently extending to >25) have recently generated interest as a simple but robust forensic marker type since they combine the best characteristics of binary polymorphisms—short amplicon lengths and mutational stability—with the best characteristics of STRs, direct typing with dye-linked PCR primers to provide balanced peak height ratios. Although the most divergent ancestry informative indels are less differentiated than the best SNPs, they exceed many STRs. This makes indels highly suitable loci for building multiplexes based on direct PCR-to-CE systems considerably more reliable than *SNaPshot* SNP typing. Two forensic AIM-indel panels have been developed: (1) a single reaction 46-plex of Pereira and (2) three 16-plex reactions of Santos. In addition to the obvious benefit of a single reaction compared to three, the AIM-indels chosen by Pereira were designed to differentiate four groups with a high overall *In*4 value, while those of Santos show weak E-ASN differentiation.

Short Tandem Repeats

It might be expected that multiallele STRs will show greater population divergence than SNPs or indels. However, STR alleles are highly unstable compared to binary loci, so new STR repeat alleles are constantly being created, while slippage size constraints lead to "allelic resonance"—high rates of diminution mutation in long alleles and high rates of addition in short alleles. Therefore, individuals with different ancestries can be identical by state, while those from the same population can show more STR differentiation than their shared ancestry would suggest. Furthermore, unless STR alleles are rare, they will not usually be lost after population isolation, although very reduced population numbers typical of founder groups can lead to a rapid rise in frequency of rare alleles by sampling effects followed by population expansion. One such example is the population-specific nine repeat allele of D9S1120, found at very low frequency in East Siberia but reaching an average 0.3 frequency in AME. It is noteworthy that this is the only example of a common population-specific STR allele, highlighting that different populations tend to share the majority of their STR variability, and divergence is characterized by relatively small frequency differences in these shared alleles. For this reason, attempts to infer ancestry from forensic STR profile data tend to show assignment error rates too high for reliable inferences from STR data alone. This is not to say

Table 1 The top 20 AIM-SNP components in four small- to medium-scale forensic ancestry tests plus the top 40 AIM-SNPs in the largest of DNAprint

		In3	*In4*
Phillips 34-plex			
1	**rs2814778**	0.865	0.783
2	rs1426654	0.833	0.562
3	**rs16891982**	0.781	0.55
4	rs3827760	0.759	0.468
5	rs881929	0.525	0.303
6	rs12913832	0.52	0.194
7	rs182549	0.515	0.157
8	rs239031	0.438	0.291
9	rs2303798	0.375	0.294
10	rs773658	0.367	0.394
11	rs2572307	0.366	0.206
12	rs722098	0.344	0.182
13	rs4540055	0.333	0.303
14	rs2065982	0.319	0.479
15	rs5997008	0.31	0.181
16	rs730570	0.307	0.217
17	rs2026721	0.305	0.275
18	rs1978806	0.304	0.218
19	rs1335873	0.297	0.289
20	rs3785181	0.26	0.212
34 SNPs *cumulative In*		**11.176**	**8.562**
Lao 24-plex			
1	**rs16891982**	0.781	
2	rs1369290	0.704	
3	rs1448484	0.654	
4	rs1478785	0.521	
5	rs2052760	0.429	
6	rs722869	0.426	
7	rs3843776	0.403	
8	rs1405467	0.388	
9	rs1876482	0.386	
10	rs1371048	0.369	(no AME allele freq. data)
11	rs1907702	0.363	
12	rs952718	0.357	
13	rs714857	0.312	
14	rs721352	0.311	
15	rs1465648	0.296	
16	rs1858465	0.292	
17	rs1461227	0.284	
18	rs1048610	0.277	
19	rs1391681	0.268	
20	rs2179967	0.195	
24 SNPs *cumulative In*		**8.276**	
Kersbergen 47 SNPs			
1	rs1369290	0.704	
2	rs1478785	0.521	
3	rs2052760	0.429	
4	rs722869	0.426	
5	rs153264	0.407	
6	rs3843776	0.403	(no AME allele freq. data)

Continued

Table 1 The top 20 AIM-SNP components in four small- to medium-scale forensic ancestry tests plus the top 40 AIM-SNPs in the largest of DNAprint—cont'd

		In3	*In4*
7	rs1405467	0.388	
8	rs725667	0.385	
9	rs1371048	0.369	
10	rs721352	0.311	
11	rs1465648	0.296	
12	rs1461227	0.284	
13	rs1048610	0.277	
14	rs1391681	0.268	
15	rs1000313	0.221	
16	rs951378	0.22	
17	rs2179967	0.195	
18	rs1823718	0.177	
19	rs950257	0.153	
20	rs1363933	0.15	
47 SNPs *cumulative In*		**8.343**	
Kosoy 128 SNPs			
1	rs4891825	0.68	0.54
2	rs11652805	0.554	0.477
3	rs3784230	0.547	0.416
4	rs10007810	0.542	0.424
5	rs9522149	0.511	0.428
6	rs260690	0.494	0.441
7	rs2416791	0.489	0.369
8	rs9845457	0.473	0.459
9	rs7554936	0.468	0.432
10	rs9530435	0.46	0.433
11	rs4908343	0.423	0.426
12	rs1040045	0.42	0.426
13	rs6548616	0.409	0.427
14	rs3745099	0.395	0.313
15	rs772262	0.39	0.334
16	rs798443	0.388	0.339
17	rs7657799	0.379	0.389
18	rs316598	0.377	0.335
19	rs7803075	0.361	0.284
20	rs4821004	0.356	0.275
128 SNPs *cumulative In*		**38.759**	**41.362**
DNAprint 178 SNPs			
1	**rs2814778**	0.865	0.783
2	rs590086	0.493	0.476
3	rs236336	0.475	0.499
4	rs984654	0.443	0.361
5	rs212498	0.422	0.349
6	rs361055	0.416	0.365
7	rs361065	0.415	0.375
8	rs6003	0.406	0.3
9	rs1337038	0.403	0.405
10	rs662117	0.402	0.322
11	rs9032	0.399	0.31
12	rs593226	0.394	0.254

Continued

Table 1 The top 20 AIM-SNP components in four small- to medium-scale forensic ancestry tests plus the top 40 AIM-SNPs in the largest of DNAprint—cont'd

		In3	*In4*
13	rs523200	0.385	0.301
14	rs2242480	0.382	0.438
15	rs1888952	0.377	0.259
16	rs595961	0.371	0.279
17	rs3176921	0.371	0.352
18	rs1800410	0.364	0.288
19	rs1415680	0.363	0.282
20	rs869337	0.349	0.405
21	rs830599	0.344	0.474
22	rs1426208	0.342	0.328
23	rs1399272	0.335	0.277
24	rs883055	0.329	0.254
25	rs1034290	0.318	0.256
26	rs913258	0.318	0.309
27	rs733563	0.312	0.226
28	rs730570	0.307	0.346
29	rs434504	0.3	0.321
30	rs67302	0.296	0.313
31	rs735050	0.295	0.245
32	rs1395579	0.29	0.237
33	rs553950	0.284	0.216
34	rs959858	0.279	0.225
35	rs285	0.278	0.21
36	rs3317	0.275	0.263
37	rs960709	0.272	0.176
38	rs721825	0.264	0.262
39	rs1375229	0.264	0.196
40	rs1528037	0.264	0.151
178 SNPs *cumulative In*		**30.967**	**31.487**

Individual marker *In*3 and *In*4 divergences are listed comparing African–European–East Asian or African–European–East Asian–American genotypes obtained from 1000 Genomes data (SPSmart: http://spsmart.cesga.es/engines.php?dataSet=engines). The cumulative values under each list represent the final divergences that can be expected with complete SNP profiles from each test. Bold rs-number SNP identifiers denote just two common loci among the alternative tests.

that STRs are completely uninformative for ancestry, as forensic STR population divergence is high enough to make combining them with other AIMs an ideal way to maximize the informativeness value of the casework genetic data as a whole.

Statistical Analysis of AIM Genotype Data

Of paramount importance in the statistical analysis of AIM data is proper consideration of the confidence limits—the levels of uncertainty associated with the ancestry inferences made. Four factors influence the degree of uncertainty of ancestry analyses: (1) the distribution of diversity among populations, (2) the AIMs used, (3) the population reference data used, and (4) the statistical methods used. Genetic diversity could be more readily gauged if global population sampling was more complete than it currently is; however, more importantly, population admixture resulting from urbanization, migration, slavery, and colonization creates far more complex distributions than the divergence patterns suggested by sample panels targeting unadmixed ancestral populations. The same complexities apply to populations on continental margins where geographic barriers are weak. Therefore, statistical tests most sensitive to admixture are the most appropriate for forensic DNA typing analyzing samples dominated by urban demographics. Furthermore, developers of forensic AIM-SNP panels have made efforts to assess the accuracy of ancestry inferences obtained from their markers. Accuracy here means how often an erroneous inference is made of standard reference samples but could include how well an individual admixture is gauged. Maximizing accuracy involves including as many AIMs close to fixation as possible, maximizing multiplex sizes, and balancing predictive power across each pairwise population comparison (E-ASN vs EUR and particularly E-ASN vs AME are especially difficult to raise). There is also some consensus on using statistical tests based on Bayesian methods, either with direct likelihood ratios between alternative populations of origin or as the analytical basis of the ubiquitous model-based clustering algorithm *Structure*. Unfortunately, detection and assessment of individual admixture is the biggest statistical problem confronting forensic ancestry inference using small-scale AIM sets.

Figure 3 outlines the Bayesian likelihood system that can be used to infer ancestry by equating likelihood of population membership with allele frequencies in each population, using example AIM-SNP rs12075. AIMs can be combined into Bayesian analyses either as single profiles that are compared to user-input reference data for the same loci (training sets) using *Snipper* (see Relevant Websites) or in joint analyses of unknowns and reference samples together in *Structure*. Alternatively, principal component analysis provides a visual representation of the divergence distances between reference population clusters, and inspection of an unknown sample's position can allow an inference of how each position/cluster is related. *Structure* can be used to provide a system for estimating the ratio of individual-level coefficients of coancestry as indicators of admixture, but this approach does not have the same capacity as analyses of population-level admixture. Kidd, analyzing the Kosoy AIM-SNP set, provides a good review of the drawbacks of *Structure* analyses, which include stochastic effects between runs, population sample size effects, incomplete geographic coverage, and AIM set deficiencies (e.g., Kosoy AIMs lack E-ASN differentiation). Unfortunately, individual admixture is common, but, more problematically, *Structure* can give patterns from intermediate populations on continental margins that mimic admixture. For example, a North African

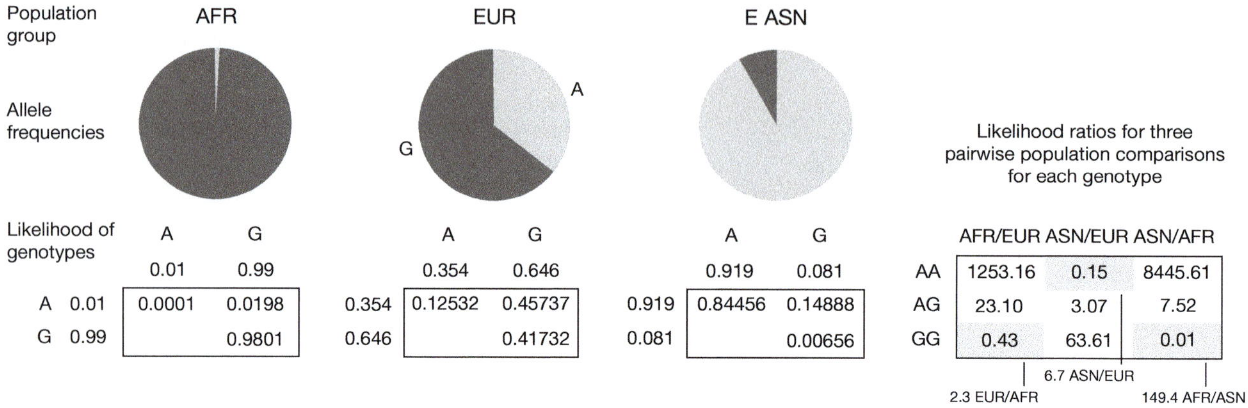

Figure 3 Illustration of the principle of Bayesian likelihood calculations shown for AIM-SNP rs12075. This statistical approach equates probability of population membership to allele frequency distributions in that population; for example, the A allele is very uncommon in AFR, so the two highest likelihood ratios for the AA genotype are for E-ASN and EUR.

analyzed in a five-group comparison that does not include North African reference samples could suggest mainly European ancestry with an African component, suggesting an individual with admixed parentage rather than ancestry from a region intermediate to the continental reference populations used. Limited reference populations force *Structure* to fit the unknown into the available patterns of genetic divergence. **Figure 4** outlines exactly the same circumstances described above using a partial 34-plex SNP profile and the 46-plex indel panel described in section "Indels." Such limitations emphasize the importance of drawing together as much genetic information as possible and dedicating resources to collating the widest possible population reference data. Lastly, rising computer power allows multiple *Structure* runs to be easily made to establish population metric confidence limits by reaching stabilized standard deviation estimates; this generally takes 25–30 runs to achieve.

Developments on the Horizon: Expanding Human SNP Catalogs, Combining Marker Types, Further Differentiation of Continental Population Groups, and X-Chromosome Markers

At the time of writing, forensic ancestry inference is gathering pace and raising interest with investigators often guided by unreliable eyewitness accounts. Therefore, it is appropriate to highlight improvements in genetic ancestry analysis already underway or soon to be introduced.

First, the 1000 Genomes project has provided an extended human SNP catalog able to collate rare variation (close to 1% minor allele frequencies) in a growing range of populations. As whole-genome sequencing becomes more routine, forensic DNA analysis can make use of this expanding data resource. It is worth noting that tri-allelic SNPs, often showing high ancestry informativeness (two are included in 34-plex), are not detected by next-generation sequencing methods—a lost opportunity to expand knowledge of their genomic distribution and population variability.

Forensic ancestry inference greatly benefits from the use of all available genetic data, and appropriately all three statistical systems outlined above accept multiple and binary allele data together. STR data considerably boost the informativeness of even the best binary AIMs, and, since all autosomal markers are independent, their combination provides increased reliability to the statistical inferences of ancestry. **Figure 5** shows that component *In*3 values for four different marker sets are remarkably similar. Since each marker type brings particular advantages to analysis of the same DNA, their combination to build a fuller picture of a donor's ancestry overcomes shortcomings of any one multiplex. To allow combination of different markers in *Snipper*, users can now upload allele frequency-based training sets as well as genotypes and their likelihoods then combined to provide an overall value.

In addition to small SNP multiplexes, the possibility of using large-scale WGS SNP arrays promises greatly increased population resolution, with prospects to go to a greater depth of differentiation than continental-scale population comparisons. Two 2008 studies showed that populations within Europe could be differentiated across reduced geographic scales ranging from 300 to 1000 km. A more realistic target for improved resolution in the immediate future could be the differentiation of European, Middle East–North African, and South Asian subpopulations of Eurasia. While Europeans and South Asians can be differentiated with small-scale additional AIM-SNP multiplexes, North African–Middle East populations are too closely related to Europeans for reliable differentiation. Therefore, subcontinental

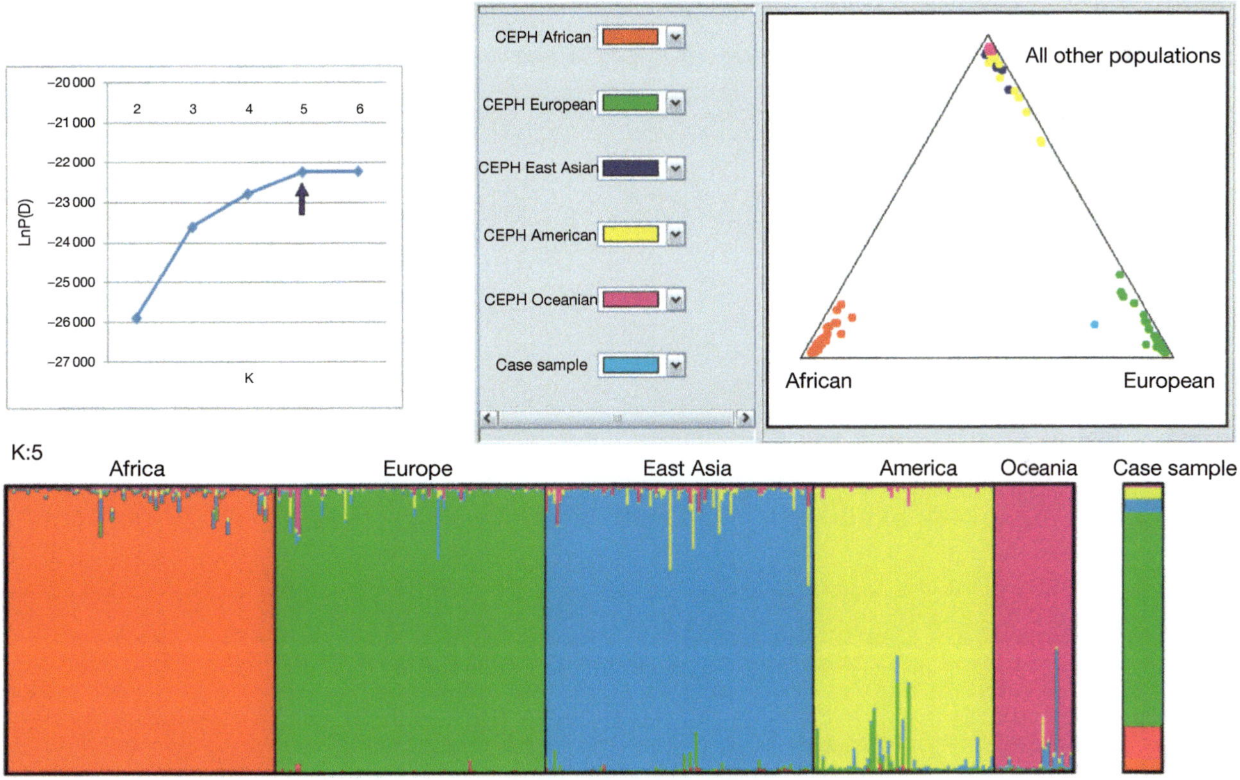

Reference populations	Africa	Europe	East Asia	America	Oceania	Number of individuals
	Membership proportions					
CEPH Africa	0.974	0.005	0.008	0.005	0.008	93
CEPH Europe	0.003	0.969	0.01	0.008	0.01	93
CEPH East Asia	0.003	0.009	0.953	0.021	0.013	93
CEPH America	0.003	0.025	0.015	0.95	0.007	63
CEPH Oceania	0.003	0.004	0.032	0.009	0.951	28
Case sample	0.157	0.751	0.046	0.041	0.005	1

Membership proportions of sample are: 75.1% EUR, 15.7% AFR

Figure 4 Structure analysis of a forensic DNA sample in an identification case. Structure identifies groups or clusters of samples based on distinctive allele frequency distributions. An unknown sample is compared to the reference allele frequencies obtained here from the HGDP–CEPH panel for 26 AIM-SNPs and 46 AIM-indels. Multiple analyses identify the optimum number of clusters: K, in this case five, where the probability value plateaus. The triangle plot positions the sample (light blue) in relation to CEPH samples where proximity to the vertex corresponds to the highest probability of membership (shown as overall values for each population in the table). Examination of the membership proportions of the sample can be interpreted as indications of coancestry in the individual or admixed parentage. This suggests mainly European ancestry with a minor African admixture component. In fact, the sample ancestry was consequently shown to be North African, a population not used as a reference in this analysis. Furthermore, North Africans are too closely related to Europeans to be adequately differentiated using the 72 AIMs typed in the analysis.

differentiation awaits developments to increase multiplex scale and detection limits in forensic SNP typing.

Lastly, X-chromosome variation has been largely overlooked for ancestry analysis. The three-fourths of chromosome population size and reduced recombination have created strong patterns of population divergence in a larger proportion of markers than equivalent autosomes. Furthermore, X AIMs in males can provide additional indicators of the ancestry of the maternal lineage alongside mt-DNA analysis.

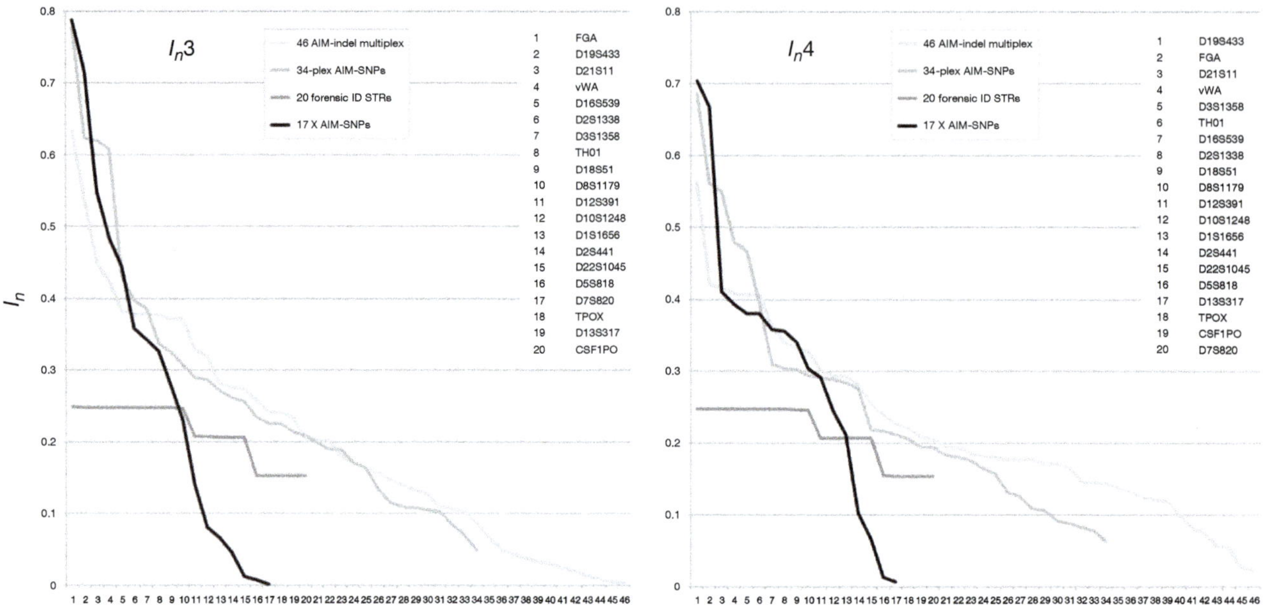

Figure 5 Ranked divergence values, *In*3 and *In*4, of component loci in forensic multiplexes: AIM-indel 46-plex, AIM-SNP 34-plex, 20 core forensic identification STRs, and X-chromosome AIM-SNPs 17-plex under development in the author's laboratory. The informativeness order of the 20 component STRs is individually listed. Plots show the autosomal SNPs, X SNPs, and indels combined into ancestry informative multiplexes that are highly comparable, with marginally improved AME differentiation from certain AIM-indel components. Additionally, STRs routinely used for forensic identification have higher *In*4 ancestry informativeness than almost half of the other set's components.

Acknowledgments

The author would like to thank Carla Santos, Antonio Salas of the Forensic Genetics Unit, USC, and Rui Pereira of IPATIMUP, Oporto, for helpful and enlightening discussions.

See also: **Biology/DNA:** DNA—Statistical Probability; Future Analytical Techniques: DNA Mass Spectrometry; Mitochondrial DNA; Short Tandem Repeats; Single-Nucleotide Polymorphisms; X-Chromosome Markers.

Further Reading

Jobling, M.A., Hurles, M.E., Tyler-Smith, C., 2004. Human Evolutionary Genetics. Garland Science, New York.

Kersbergen, P., van Duijn, K., Kloosterman, A.D., den Dunnen, J.T., Kayser, M., de Knijff, P., 2009. Developing a set of ancestry-sensitive DNA markers reflecting continental origins of humans. BMC Genetics 10, 69.

Kidd, J.R., Friedlaender, F.R., Speed, W.C., Pakstis, A.J., De La Vega, F.M., Kidd, K.K., 2011. Analyses of a set of 128 ancestry informative single nucleotide polymorphisms in a global set of 119 population samples. Investigative Genetics 2, 1.

Kosoy, R., Nassir, R., Tian, C., et al., 2009. Ancestry informative marker sets for determining continental origin and admixture proportions in common populations in America. Human Mutation 30, 69–78.

Phillips, C., Prieto, L., Fondevila, M., et al., 2009. Ancestry analysis in the 11-M Madrid bomb attack investigation. PLoS One 4 e6583.

Phillips, C., Rodriguez, A., Mosquera-Miguel, A., et al., 2008. D9S1120, a simple STR with a common Native American-specific allele: forensic optimization, locus characterization and allele frequency studies. Forensic Science International Genetics 3, 7–13.

Phillips, C., Salas, A., Sánchez, J.J., et al., 2007. Inferring ancestral origin using a single multiplex assay of ancestry-informative marker SNPs. Forensic Science International Genetics 1, 273–280.

Rosenberg, N.A., Li, L.M., Ward, R., Pritchard, J.K., 2003. Informativeness of genetic markers for inference of ancestry. American Journal of Human Genetics 73, 1402–1422.

Rosenberg, N.A., Pritchard, J.K., Weber, J.L., et al., 2002. Genetic structure of human populations. Science 298, 2381–2385.

Relevant Websites

http://alfred.med.yale.edu/—ALFRED Extensive population variation coverage of subsets of SNPs and STRs.

http://spsmart.cesga.es—popSTR Forensic STR allele frequencies of HGDP–CEPH samples.

http://mathgene.usc.es—Snipper classifier.

http://spsmart.cesga.es/—SPSmart Comprehensive SNP population data access portal.

http://pritch.bsd.uchicago.edu/; http://rosenberglab.bioinformatics.med.umich.edu/distruct.html—Structure algorithm downloads.

Mitochondrial DNA

W Parson, Innsbruck Medical University, Innsbruck, Austria

This article is a revision of the previous edition article by T. Melton and G. Sensabaugh, volume 2, pp. 499–503, © 2000, Elsevier Ltd.

Glossary

Control region The mitochondrial control region (CR) is the single, larger, noncoding portion of the mitochondrial genome. It extends 1122 bp from nucleotide position 16024–576 (relative to the rCRS). Owing to the decreased evolutionary pressure, mutations accumulate more rapidly there, which is why the CR represents the most discriminative region in the mtDNA and is primarily targeted for forensic purposes.

Haplogroup Haplogroups are clusters of similar haplotypes that share a common ancestor. Mitochondrial DNA haplogroups are named using letters and numbers in alternating order, for example H1b, and are characterized by signature mutations through which they are related. For H1b, the signature pattern is 16189C 16356C 16362C 263G 315.1C (relative to the rCRS in the control region). See Phylotree for a curated archive of mitochondrial haplogroup names and mutations.

Haplotype A haplotype is composed of genetic markers (sequences or single nucleotide positions) that are inherited together and do not undergo recombination. Mitochondrial DNA haplotypes usually consist of sequence segments of the control region and in some cases contain single nucleotide information from the coding region. They are usually reported relative to the rCRS.

Mutation In general, mutations are sudden and spontaneous changes in genomic sequences. It has become practice to call differences between two sequences as mutations. In that way, differences of an mtDNA haplotype with respect to the rCRS are sometimes also referred to as mutations, which is not true, when the sequences are only distantly related to the rCRS, and, thus, they are not directly linked by mutations.

Phylogeny Phylogeny describes the evolutionary relatedness of organisms/individuals. Owing to its maternal mode of inheritance, mtDNA is inherited along a phylogeny. The relatedness between individuals is effectively displayed in trees and networks.

Quasi-median network Here, a quasi-median network (QMN) is a graphical representation of tabular mtDNA haplotypes that can be used to depict intraspecific phylogenies. QMNs have proven useful for pinpointing data idiosyncrasies and are therefore used for a posteriori quality control of mtDNA haplotypes.

Revised Cambridge Reference Sequence (rCRS) The rCRS is the corrected version of the first sequenced human mtDNA. It represents the standard reference sequence to which mtDNA sequences are reported as haplotypes. The rCRS can be found on GenBank under accession number NC_012920.

Structure and Basics

Mitochondria are organelles with a superior function in the physiological energy household of the cell. They are the only cell particles in animals to harbor extrachromosomal DNA in the form of mitochondrial DNA (mtDNA), which differs in size, structure, and genetics from the DNA in the nucleus. mtDNA is organized in ringlike structures that are present in the mitochondria as supercoiled double-stranded molecules with an "external" purine-rich H (heavy) and an "internal" pyrimidine-rich L (light) strand. It is usually observed that H-strand-derived sequence raw data (generated with reverse sequencing primers) tend to display higher background noise and are often more difficult to sequence than forward L-strand sequences, which plays an important role in the forensic context, as discussed below.

The structure of mtDNA was determined in the late 1960s, with the first human sequence published in 1981. Twelve years later, this sequence was corrected at 11 positions and has since been referred to as the revised Cambridge Reference Sequence (rCRS). The rCRS contains 16,568 bp, which are numbered from nucleotide position (ntp) 1 within the control region

 http://dx.doi.org/10.1016/B978-0-12-800647-4.00019-9

(CR) to ntp 16569 in a clockwise manner. This numbering derives from the earlier version of the first sequence where one base was mistakenly introduced between ntps 3106 and 3107. In order to avoid confusion with already generated data, the rCRS was corrected by introducing an N-designation at ntp 3107, which is why every other sequence differs by a 3107del to the rCRS. Instead of reporting the entire string of nucleotides, the scientific community has agreed to call human mtDNA sequences relative to the rCRS for better legibility with the specification of the reading frame (terminal points of the sequenced fragment excluding primer). A reader then knows that, for example, 16069T 16126C (16024–16365) describes a sequence, which harbors a T at ntp 16069 and a C at ntp 16126 among otherwise identical nucleotides within the range of ntps 16024 and 16365 relative to the rCRS. This practicable annotation is also known as mtDNA haplotype or mtDNA profile and finds its way into mtDNA reports and databases. Since the precise point of insertions and deletions (in terms of their origin from an evolutionary perspective) cannot be unambiguously determined in a consecutive sequence of identical bases, more than one rCRS-coded alignment is possible. In the forensic setting, this may have an impact on reporting and database-querying issues (see the section "mtDNA Alignment–Phylogenetic Perspectives").

The mitochondrial genome (mtGenome) includes 37 genes that are densely packed in the coding region (577–16023), whereas the CR (16024–16576) represents the single major noncoding part of the mtDNA (**Figure 1**). The latter spans over a range of 1122 bp and includes the vast majority of polymorphic positions owing to a reduced evolutionary pressure. Early sequence studies used the two so-called hypervariable segments HVS-I (16024–16365) and HVS-II (73–340) that have been targeted for population studies and the analysis of forensic samples. It is discussed later that this separate amplification and sequencing analysis harbors the inherent problem of sample mix-up of hypervariable segments between samples in addition to the decreased discrimination power compared to the analysis of the entire CR. HVS-I and -II analysis is therefore no longer state of the art and should be replaced by the analysis of the entire CR.

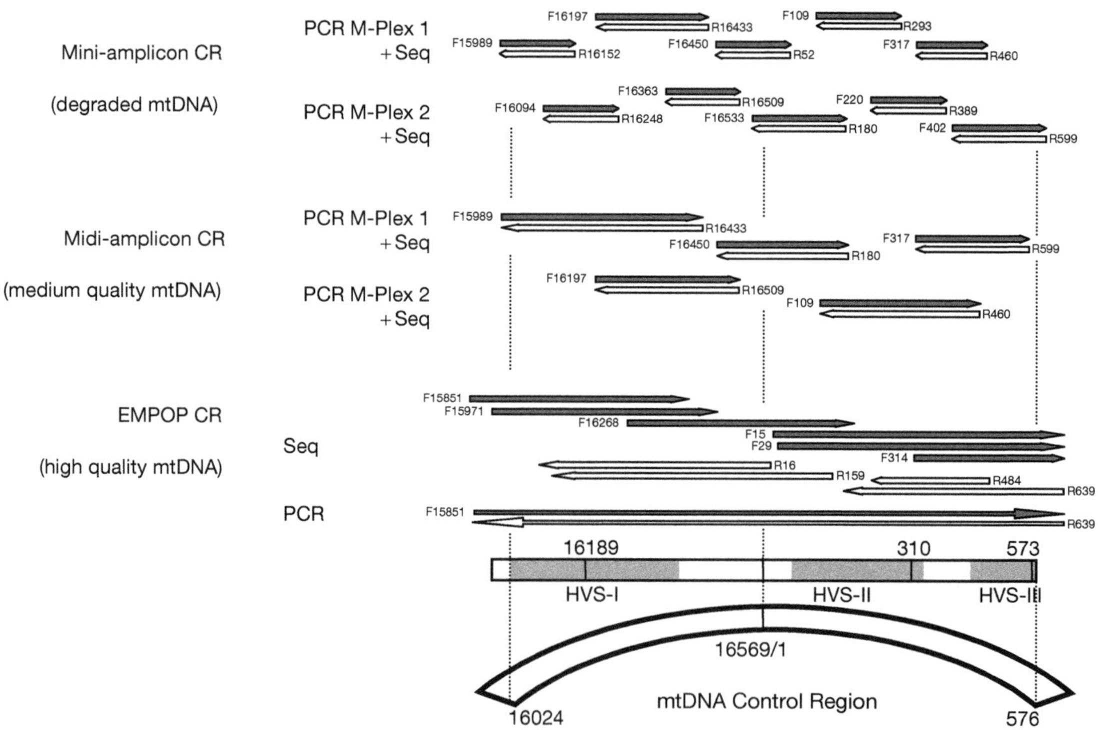

Figure 1 Scheme of the mtDNA control region with three different amplification and sequencing strategies that are applied depending to the degradation state of the available mtDNA. All three strategies lead to consensus sequences with fully double-stranded coverage. Primer designations refer to the three prime ends; primer sequences can be found in the references below. Reproduced from Eichmann, C., Parson, W., 2007. Molecular characterization of the canine mitochondrial DNA control region for forensic applications. International Journal of Legal Medicine 121, 411–416; Parson, W., Bandelt, H.J., 2007. Extended guidelines for mtDNA typing of population data in forensic science. Forensic Science International: Genetics 1, 13–19; Berger, C., Parson, W., 2009. Mini-midi-mito: sequencing strategy of mtDNA to the degradation state of crime scene samples. Forensic Science International: Genetics 3, 149–153.

Biology and Genetics

In contrast to chromosomal DNA, which is present as two parental copies in the nucleus, a cell contains up to multiple thousand copies of mtDNA. According to the endosymbiotic theory, mitochondria derive from archeobacteria, which built a structural and functional association with the cell. Some of the features of the mitochondrial molecule are remnants of this past, such as the independent replication to the nuclear DNA (nDNA) and the deviating translation code. However, extensive transfer of mtDNA into the nucleus has occurred throughout evolution and is still ongoing, which becomes evident in the form of so-called *numts* (nuclear elements of mtDNA).

Human mtDNA is believed to be inherited solely via the maternal lineage, although paternal leakage and a doubly uniparental mode of transmission are established in some animal species. There are at least two mechanisms by which the inheritance of paternal mtDNA is prevented in humans. First, mitochondria in the sperm cell are outnumbered by those in the egg by at least three orders of magnitude (50–100 in sperms vs 100,000–200,000 in the oocyte). Second, in mammals, sperm mitochondria are tagged by ubiquitin, which leads to proteolytic digestion in early embryonic development. It has been suggested that the exclusively uniparental pathway has evolved to both mitigate lethal intermitochondrial gene conflicts and prevent the inheritance of sperm mtDNA damaged by free radicals. The analysis of large pedigrees and mother–child pairs has thus far confirmed the maternal mode of inheritance; and while both paternal leakage and recombination of human mtDNA have been proposed, the underlying data and/or methods applied in most of these studies have been challenged. However, in a single yet unrefuted study of a male patient suffering myopathy, paternal transmission of mtDNA was observed. The muscle tissue of the patient showed a mixture of the mtDNA of both parents. The paternal contribution differed from the mtDNA of the father by a 2 bp deletion, which was associated with the disease. Other tissues of the patient as well as tissues of other family members did not show the paternal haplotype.

Assuming that paternal leakage may still represent the very rare exception in mtDNA transmission, the observed variation in human mtDNA can only be explained by de novo mutations in germ line cells that eventually become fixed within descendant individuals through the action of an intergenerational genetic bottleneck. Genuine mixtures of mtDNA molecules within single individuals have been described for humans and are known as heteroplasmy. For instance, the observation of point (sequence) heteroplasmy at ntp 16169 in the otherwise identical sequences of the putative remains of Tsar Nicholas II and those of his brother Georgij Romanov substantiated maternal relatedness and supported the identification of the remains of the Romanov family (**Figure 2**). In medical genetics, point heteroplasmy plays an important role in the diagnosis of mitochondrial-based diseases because pathogenic mutations

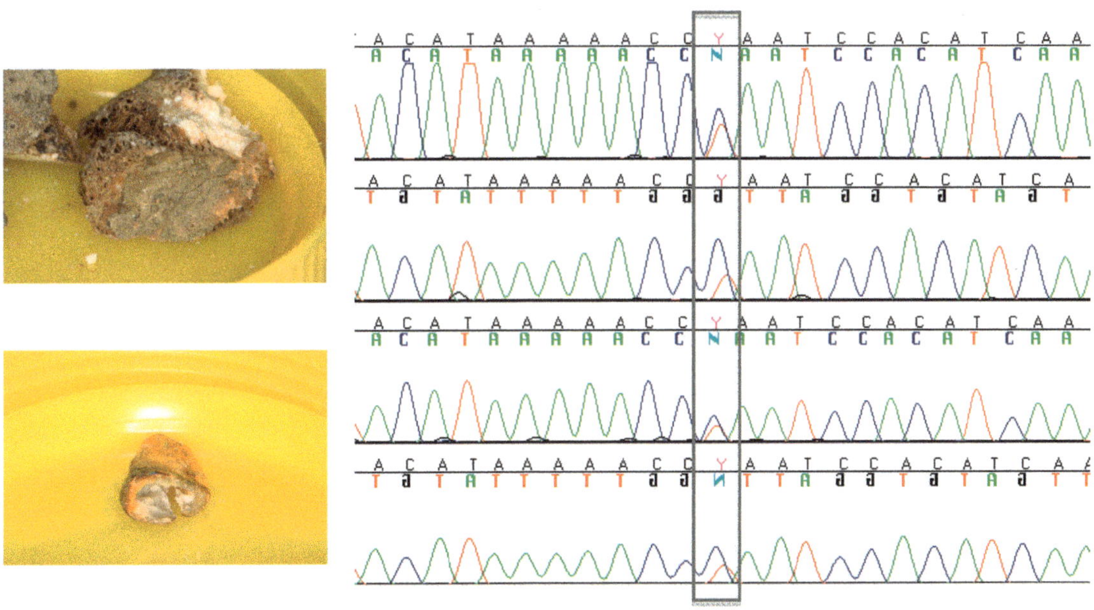

Figure 2 Photos and corresponding sequence raw data of a calcaneus fragment (above) and a partial tooth (below) of Tsar Nicholas II. Point heteroplasmy at ntp 16169. Modified from Coble, M.D., Loreille, O.M., Wadhams, M.J., et al., 2009. Mystery solved: the identification of the two missing Romanov children using DNA analysis. PLoS ONE 4, e4838.

are rarely present in homoplasmic form. Rather they must exceed a critical threshold in the mixture with the wild-type allele before a disease phenotype develops. It has recently been established that nonpathogenic point mutation mtDNA heteroplasmy is common. Extensive CR sequencing analyses of more than 5000 population samples showed heteroplasmy in 6% of individuals, but with the vast majority displaying the mixture exclusively at single sites (**Table 1**). Only very few sequences featured point heteroplasmy at two or three positions (0.14% and 0.02%, respectively) and cloning analysis showed that in all of these cases, the constituent haplotypes (three or four molecules, respectively) differed from one another at a single position only. Also, there was a clear tendency for heteroplasmy to occur at known evolutionary hotspots, for example, at ntps 16093, 152, 146, and 204 with exceptions only at positions 214 and 215. Heteroplasmy, when encountered in forensic samples, requires special attention for interpretation and evidence reporting (see the section "Practical Aspects of Forensic mtDNA Testing").

Table 1 List of positions in the mtDNA control region at which heteroplasmy was observed more than once in a total of 5015 investigated haplotypes

Position	*Trn*	*Trv*	*Position*	*Trn*	*Trv*
16093	42	—	16182	—	3
152	20	—	228	2	1
146	18	—	16184	2	1
204	18	—	64	2	—
195	10	—	183	2	—
16189	9	—	198	2	—
150	8	—	207	2	—
215	8	—	227	2	—
16183	—	8	16129	2	—
214	7	—	16168	2	—
16192	7	—	16169	2	—
16519	7	—	16173	2	—
151	4	—	16256	2	—
16092	4	—	16278	2	—
16311	4	—	16290	2	—
16362	4	—	16291	2	—
153	3	—	16301	2	—
189	3	—	16309	2	—
194	3	—	16355	2	—
199	3	—	16399	2	—
234	3	—	16111	1	1
16261	3	—	16190	1	1
16294	3	—	16234	1	1
16390	3	—	16266	1	1

Trn, transition; Trv, transversion.
Source: Reproduced from Irwin, J., Saunier, J., Niederstätter, H., et al., 2009. Investigation of point heteroplasmy in the human mitochondrial DNA control region: A synthesis of observations from over 5000 global population samples. Journal of Molecular Evolution 68, 516–527.

The Role of the Phylogeny in Forensic mtDNA Testing

Basics of the mtDNA Phylogeny

The maternal mode of mtDNA inheritance determines the evolution of the molecule along a phylogeny. Mutations accumulated along the radiating lineages of the human phylogeny and left footprints that are still visible and discernible on a subcontinental scale today. Haplotypes that share specific mutations are clustered in haplogroups (hg) that are named with an alternating order of letters and numbers in descending hierarchical order. They can display discrete geographic distributions, such as, for example, hg U5b3. This haplogroup is determined by the CR mutations 228A and 16304C on top of the U5-specific motif 73G 263G 315.1C 16192T, and 16270T. While hg U5 is typical for populations from western Eurasia and can be found at appreciable frequencies from Europe to Central Asia, hg U5b3 is primarily observed on the island of Sardinia, with spurious traces around the Mediterranean coast (**Figure 3**). This type of phylogeographic information can be useful in the forensic context when the geographic origin of an unknown sample is under investigation. However, it is important to keep in mind that these forms of phylogeographic inference pertain to the mtDNA lineage and not to the sample or individual specifically. Likewise, inferences of biogeographic ancestry based on the abundance of uniparental lineages are not necessarily linked to visible phenotypes, as is sometimes mistakenly perceived.

Error Rates in Forensic mtDNA Testing—The Role of the Phylogeny

The developments in mtDNA quality control in the past decade have shown that the phylogeny plays an important role in the discovery of sequencing and transcription errors in mtDNA data. There was increasing evidence in the early 2000s that mtDNA datasets in forensic, medical, and population genetics harbored ambiguous data. This, in turn, led to high profile discussions about the credibility of published mtDNA data in general and their application in forensic testing in particular. Recent developments in the field of next-generation sequencing technologies demonstrate that the problems are not limited to the era of Sanger sequencing but continue to surface also with the introduction of new sequencing technologies. There is no other genetic marker in forensics in which errors become so highly visible. This is due to the fact that mtDNA evolution—characterized by lacking recombination and relatively low mutation rates (compared to STRs)—portrays distinctive sequence patterns. Errors result in haplotypes that stand out.

In an effort to assess how common mtDNA sequencing errors occurred, the forensic community initiated proficiency tests in which a relatively small number of blind samples were analyzed in ring tests. Those experiments revealed an alarming error rate of up to 30% of wrongly reported mtDNA

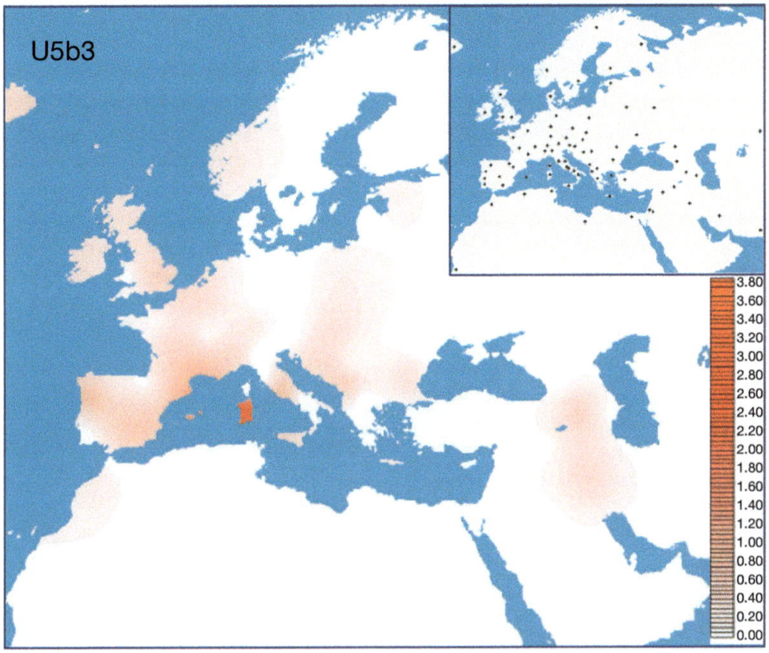

Figure 3 Spatial frequency distribution of mtDNA haplogroup U5b3 and geographical locations of populations surveyed. Reproduced from Pala, M., Achilli, A., Olivieri, A., Kashani, B., Perego, U., Sanna, D., Metspalu, E., Tambets, et al., 2010. Mitochondrial haplogroup U5b3: a distant echo of the epipaleolithic in Italy and the legacy of the early Sardinians. American Journal of Human Genetics 84, 814–821, with permission.

haplotypes. The main causes were transcription errors, phantom mutations, and artificial recombination. Transcription errors include reference bias (fallback to the reference sequence, e.g., 152T instead of 152C), transposed digits (e.g., 16039 instead of 16093), base mis-scoring (e.g., 152A instead of 152C), and base shift (e.g., 16279 instead of 16278). Phantom mutations comprise all sorts of artifacts that are associated with the laboratory process and lead to ambiguous base calls in sequence raw lane data such as, for example, signals due to unincorporated dyes, elevated baseline, compression artifacts, mobility shifts, and footprints of earlier versions of the sequencing polymerases, which were misinterpreted by software or user. All of the above-mentioned causes and artifacts can be identified and resolved by generating haplotypes with high quality sequence data that meet forensic guidelines, that is, the application of optimal chemistry and instrument conditions, fully redundant sequence coverage that is preferably, but not exclusively, produced with forward and reverse sequencing primers; multiple forward (or reverse) sequencing reactions, often from different primers, may also be used to confirm sequence data. Generally speaking, the quality of the raw sequence data dictates the type of coverage required to ensure unambiguous consensus haplotypes. Only artificial recombinants, the mix-up of separately amplified and sequenced hypervariable segments between samples, cannot be detected or avoided by appropriate raw data. These can only be detected by consulting the phylogeny, as artificial recombinants result in implausible haplotypes. They can, however, be prevented by an adequate laboratory strategy that employs supervision at critical handling steps. As a consequence of the blind test results, new amplification and sequencing protocols were developed that target the entire CR and therefore not only increase the discrimination power of mtDNA testing compared to HVS-I and -II analysis but also prevent artificial recombination and phantom mutations as a result of long, largely overlapping sequencing strands (**Figure 1**). Since the results of the blind tests indicated that manual transcription represents the most error-prone step in data handling, electronic transfer of data and a posteriori quality control of the data is critical. A robust method for detecting idiosyncrasies in mtDNA data is the application of quasi median networks (for explanation and an example, see elsewhere in this encyclopedia).

mtDNA Alignment—Phylogenetic Perspectives

As mentioned above, mtDNA variation is usually recorded relative to the rCRS. While this is straightforward for the vast majority of ntps, it has proven to be difficult for short sequence stretches that display length variation. Demonstrated by an even simpler scenario, the insertion of a nucleotide adjacent to an identical neighbor cannot be aligned in an unambiguous way, as 5′ as well as 3′ alignments are feasible. As an example, an additional T residue adjacent to the T at ntp 310, which is itself surrounded by C residues, could be called as 309.1T or 310.1T. There is no experimental solution to this problem as sequencing analysis does not capture the required information. That is why early guidelines recommended a 3′ alignment rule to harmonize nomenclature. Still, mtDNA sequences were observed that allowed for more than one single alignment. Take as example 16189T (rCRS) that is surrounded by two small C-stretches (5 Cs up and 4 Cs downstream). Two transitions at ntps 16188 and 16189 could be called 16188T 16189C, which is however identical to the alignment 16188del 16193.1C. Since different representations of the same sequence motif may result in situations where a haplotype is missed in a database search, consistent representation of identical motifs is important in the forensic context.

In an attempt to achieve one unique alignment for all mtDNA haplotypes, rules were defined on the basis of a most parsimonious binary alignment to the rCRS, with hierarchical priorities to resolve ties. Although intended to facilitate and standardize mtDNA alignment, the rules have not routinely been applied in practice. However, as our general understanding of worldwide mtDNA diversity has increased, there are now many cases for which the evolution/origin of previously ambiguous sequence motifs (e.g., the 16188T 16189C vs 16188del 16193C) can be determined. As a result, a phylogenetic approach to mtDNA alignment and nomenclature has been proposed (and is today still used by EMPOP, see elsewhere in this encyclopedia) where alignment is based on the phylogeny of mtDNA. Mutational events are inferred through comparison to the nearest known evolutionarily related sequences and therefore nomenclature is based on scientific grounds rather than a rule-based approach. In addition, by reflecting the evolutionary history of the mtDNA molecule, the phylogenetic approach allows for an estimation of the true genetic distance between the sequence and its nearest relatives. Most importantly, the phylogenetic approach extends on the convention of mtDNA annotation in related fields such as population genetics and medical genetics, between which data are shared with the forensic community on a regular basis.

A disadvantage with respect to database searches is the requirement that a forensic practitioner would need to be cognizant of the details of the phylogenetic annotation used in the database. Furthermore, it cannot be excluded that the nomenclature for a particular sequence motif may change over time, as additional phylogenetic knowledge is gained concerning the evolutionary history of the mutation events in question. Two major developments have taken place to overcome these limitations for forensic practice. First, a new search engine (SAM) has been developed and implemented in EMPOP that performs sequence queries independent of the haplotype alignment by converting all sequences into unaligned nucleotide strings that are then compared. This solution guarantees that database sequences are not missed due to different alignment, which is very important for retrieving objective database search results. Second, an Internet-based library of established mtDNA haplogroups with corresponding signature mutations (Phylotree) was developed. It is based on established methods of phylogenetic inference and is updated on a regular basis as new mtDNA data becomes available. Phylotree is useful for identifying the haplogroup status of the haplotype in question, and this in turn permits both quality checks of the mtDNA data and inferences of phylogenetic or geographic information.

Practical Aspects of Forensic mtDNA Testing

mtDNA has found a vital niche in forensic DNA testing. Its abundance in the cell is much higher (up to several thousand copies) than nDNA (four template copies for polymerase chain reaction), which correspondingly increases the chances that some copies of it survive in highly degraded forensic samples. Therefore, mtDNA testing permits the successful analysis of samples that would otherwise give no molecular result with commonly employed nuclear STR tests. Further, even distant maternally related individuals can provide a comparative reference sample to test for relatedness, and thus human identification (mostly in conjunction with other evidence) is feasible across large pedigrees with mtDNA markers. These advantages led to the application of mtDNA in crime casework where degraded samples and samples with insufficient nDNA are to be tested. Also, mtDNA analysis was found useful for the identification of human remains where both inaccessible nDNA and lack of direct comparative samples is evident. Both applications are briefly discussed in the following sections.

mtDNA Analysis for Criminal Investigations

Hair is one of the most ubiquitous pieces of evidence found at crime scenes. While living keratinocytes in the hair bulb contain nuclei and thus allow for successful STR analysis, the formation of keratinocytes in hair fibers is associated with a process that involves the breakdown of the nucleus and its DNA. There seem to be interindividual differences in DNA removal that are not yet fully understood, with some telogenic hair showing detectable traces of nDNA while the majority does not. As a result, nDNA typing is generally quite difficult with telogenic hair. Successful mtDNA typing, however, has been reported in a very high number of hair samples (>92%).

In analogy to population samples, it is also desirable to achieve full CR sequence coverage in hair (and other crime scene specimens), but full CR amplicons are unlikely to be successful in these cases. Therefore, novel multiplex strategies have been developed that amplify short overlapping segments (mini-amplicons) in a manner that the entire CR is fully captured by forward and reverse sequence strands (**Figure 1**).

It is relevant to know how much mtDNA is present in an extract from a forensic sample. Often, a maximum amount of the DNA extract is used for amplification of challenging samples or an mtDNA concentration is estimated on the basis of a nDNA quantification result, which can, however, often be misleading. It has proven useful to apply mtDNA-specific quantification assays—that are unfortunately not yet commercially available on a broad basis but need to be set up by the individual laboratories—in order to determine the quantity and quality (extent of degradation) of the DNA. The resulting data provide important information to define an appropriate strategy for downstream analysis (**Figure 1**).

Point heteroplasmy

Point heteroplasmy seems more frequent in hair (12% in HVS-I/II) than in blood and buccal cells (6% for the entire CR). Systematic studies confirmed earlier single observations that mtDNA sequences between hairs of an individual can differ. The differences between hairs that were described in these cases covered a spectrum that ranged from hairs with varying heteroplasmic mixture ratios with opposed dominant variants to hairs with apparently homoplasmic states of both variants. It has been suggested that the mitochondrial load in hair mainly derives from keratinocytes and to a smaller extent from melanocytes, which, lacking mitosis, continue to produce mitochondria during the life cycle and therefore represent a bottleneck through which heteroplasmic ratios can be shifted. This would also explain why heteroplasmic switches in hair shaft portions are observed on a regular basis rather than gradual changes along the length of the hair. Alternatively, de novo mutations may contribute to the pool of heteroplasmic observations. In fact, the majority of affected positions concur with those known as evolutionary hotspots; that is, affected positions (mutations) often coincide with fast mutating sites. In addition, the magnitude of mutational segregation within hair samples has been shown to be tractable. Heteroplasmy along any given hair shaft follows predictable patterns of increasing rarity with increasing heteroplasmic and homoplasmic differences.

From a practical standpoint, and as a result of these findings, it has been recommended that two independent portions of a single unknown hair should be analyzed, if available. This would not only address issues of heteroplasmy along the length of the hair but would also serve to minimize artifacts due to contamination. In cases where similar haplotypes are found between evidence and reference samples, the analysis of multiple reference hairs may also be helpful. It is important to note that the interpretation of mtDNA evidence from hairs needs to follow different argumentation compared to other tissues (see the section "Interpretation of mtDNA Evidence").

Length heteroplasmy

Length heteroplasmy describes the coexistence of multiple sequence lengths in the mtDNA of a sample. It is observed on a much more frequent basis than point heteroplasmy, at least given the detection limits of current sequencing approaches. The vast majority of length heteroplasmy occurs in the homopolymeric sequence segments such as the well-known C-stretches around ntps 16189, 310, and 573 in the mitochondrial CR. The mechanisms for the development of length heteroplasmy seem to be different at these three positions. The T residue at ntp 16189 in HVS-I separates two shorter C-tracts (5 and 4C residues in the rCRS, respectively) that merge to an uninterrupted stretch of 10 Cs when a transition at ntp 16189 is present. Depending on the phylogenetic background, this can occur at frequencies between 20% and 80% of the analyzed samples (e.g., 16189C is a basic signature mutation of hg B that can reach high frequencies in Eastern Asian and Native American populations). It has been determined that length heteroplasmy in C-stretches usually arises with more than eight consecutive C residues, as the polymerase seems to produce additional variants at that level and above. Therefore, haplotypes showing 16189C and no other transition between 16183 and 16193 are almost always associated with pronounced length heteroplasmy with a strong tendency toward the formation of longer variants (up to 15C residues).

In contrast, length heteroplasmy in the C-stretch of HVS-II around position 310 is usually triggered by insertions of C residues between ntps 302 and 310, which increase the number of consecutive C's to eight or more (the rCRS harbors seven Cs in this segment). Similar to HVS-I, longer heteroplasmic variants are then observed. The frequency of length heteroplasmy here has been found to be between 40% and 70%, although it should be noted that many studies do not report this phenomenon at all. Transitions at ntp 310 are relatively rare (and mostly hg-specific, e.g., hg U4a2). However, when they do occur, they are accompanied by a reduction of the overall length of the heteroplasmic length variants, which is in contrast to the previously mentioned slippage events that extend the length of the C-stretch. The mechanisms of this difference at ntp 310 have not yet been fully explored. The formation of length heteroplasmy around position 573 (HVS-III) is rare and often hg-specific. The mechanism is similar to the one described for the C-stretch between ntps 302 and 310, and the formation of the length variants is driven by insertions of C residues between ntps 567 and 574.

Generally, differences in length heteroplasmy between otherwise identical mtDNA haplotypes are not regarded as criteria for exclusion, as it is known that hair and other tissues such as blood, buccal cells, or bone of an individual can display divergent patterns. In some laboratories, it is routine practice to not even record it. The collection of "forensic data" in EMPOP reports the dominant type when multiple length heteroplasmic variants are present.

mtDNA Analysis in Human Identification

Large-scale human identification efforts involve the investigation of missing persons, victims of natural catastrophes (e.g., tsunami, earthquakes, and thunderstorms), victims from war episodes, as well as victims of terrorist attacks and accidents. The analysis of autosomal STRs is generally the prime choice in human ID cases, as the excellent power of discrimination of nDNA markers serves the purpose very well. However, the most challenging samples often require the analysis of mtDNA. Furthermore, mtDNA data are extremely useful when only maternally related individuals are available as reference to which the DNA results of unknown samples need to be compared. Also, the success rates in obtaining useful mtDNA haplotypes from those specimens that gave no or insufficient nDNA information are reported to be quite high (84%). The rate of point heteroplasmy was found to be similar to hair samples (10%).

Interpretation of mtDNA Evidence

A typical forensic scenario involves the analysis of questioned and reference samples, followed by a determination as to whether or not the mtDNA haplotypes recovered from those specimens are consistent. In this context, a determination of consistent suggests that the haplotypes (and thus questioned and reference sample) originate from the same maternal lineage. If so, the mtDNA haplotype in question is searched against mtDNA databases to determine its relative rarity and assess the statistical weight of the mtDNA evidence. As discussed before, tissues typically targeted with mtDNA markers, such as hair, may present slightly different mtDNA molecules compared to tissues that often serve as reference material, such as blood or buccal cells. It is therefore important to define interpretation rules that take this variation into account.

It has previously been defined that identical mtDNA sequences, as well as mtDNA sequences that differ only by heteroplasmic variation, cannot be excluded as deriving from a common maternal lineage regardless of the tissue involved.

It seems further settled that two or more differences between mtDNA sequences (barring differences in the homopolymeric sequence stretches) exclude the samples as originating from a common maternal lineage. Careful analysis of the differing positions is important especially in tissues such as hair that show increased variation.

mtDNA sequences that differ only by a single mutation are more difficult to evaluate and therefore sometimes lead to inconclusive results. Taking the tissue variability into consideration, two mtDNA sequences may then still belong to the same matrilineage, especially if one of the involved samples is hair. The evaluation of the actual position is then of crucial importance—a difference at a rapidly evolving position may still comply with maternal relatedness of the two samples, whereas a difference at a stable position may be indicative of different maternal backgrounds. A very probative solution, if possible, is to extend the analysis range to other parts of the CR or the coding region. This has been successfully performed in many cases.

While the body of data has grown immensely in the past decade and will likely continue to do so with the introduction of faster sequencing technologies in the future, one may never be able to achieve an easy-to-define interpretation system for sequences that differ by single mutations, just as the variation in some tissues is unpredictable. However, new technical achievements may allow for a more comprehensive analysis range in the future that would restrict difficult constellations to a minimum.

Acknowledgments

Jodi Irwin (AFDIL, Rockville) and Harald Niederstätter (GMI, Innsbruck) are greatly acknowledged for their helpful comments on the manuscript. In addition, the author would like to thank Hans-Jürgen Bandelt (University of Hamburg), Arne Dür (University of Innsbruck), Sabine Lutz-Bonengel (University of Freiburg), Thomas Parsons (ICMP, Sarajevo), Lourdes Prieto (Police Madrid), and the scientific staff at the GMI Innsbruck for their continuous support and discussion on mtDNA matters.

See also: **Biology/DNA:** Internet Accessible Population Databases: YHRD and EMPOP.

Further Reading

Bandelt, H.-J., Richards, M., Macauley, V. (Eds.), 2006. Human Mitochondrial DNA and the Evolution of Homo sapiens (Nucleic Acids and Molecular Biology). Springer, Berlin, Heidelberg, New York.

Berger, C., Parson, W., 2009. Mini-midi-mito: adapting the amplification and sequencing strategy of mtDNA to the degradation state of crime scene samples. Forensic Science International: Genetics 3, 149–153.

Coble, M.D., Loreille, O.M., Wadhams, M.J., et al., 2009. Mystery solved: the identification of the two missing Romanov children using DNA analysis. PLoS One 4, e4838.

Eichmann, C., Parson, W., 2007. Molecular characterization of the canine mitochondrial DNA control region for forensic applications. International Journal of Legal Medicine 121, 411–416.

Forster, L., Forster, P., Gurney, S.M., et al., 2010. Evaluating length heteroplasmy in the human mitochondrial DNA control region. International Journal of Legal Medicine 124, 132–142. Erratum in: International Journal of Legal Medicine 124, 319.

Holland, M.M., Parsons, T.J., 1999. Mitochondrial DNA sequence analysis – validation and use for forensic casework. Forensic Science Review 11, 21–50.

Irwin, J., Saunier, J., Niederstätter, H., et al., 2009. Investigation of point heteroplasmy in the human mitochondrial DNA control region: a synthesis of observations from over 5000 global population samples. Journal of Molecular Evolution 68, 516–527.

Lutz-Bonengel, S., Sänger, T., Parson, W., et al., 2008. Single lymphocytes from two healthy individuals with mitochondrial point heteroplasmy are mainly homoplasmic. International Journal of Legal Medicine 122, 189–197.

Melton, T., Dimick, G., Higgins, B., Lindstrom, L., Nelson, K., 2005. Forensic mitochondrial DNA analysis of 691 casework hairs. Forensic Science International 50, 73–80.

Niederstätter, H., Köchl, S., Grubwieser, P., Pavlic, M., Steinlechner, M., Parson, W., 2007. A modular real-time PCR concept for determining the quantity and quality of human nuclear and mitochondrial DNA. Forensic Science International: Genetics 1, 29–34.

Pala, M., Achilli, A., Olivieri, A., et al., 2009. Mitochondrial haplogroup U5b3: a distant echo of the epipaleolithic in Italy and the legacy of the early Sardinians. American Journal of Human Genetics 84, 814–821.

Pala, M., Achilli, A., Olivieri, A., Kashani, B., Perego, U., Sanna, D., Metspalu, E., Tambets, et al., 2010. Mitochondrial haplogroup U5b3: a distant echo of the epipaleolithic in Italy and the legacy of the early Sardinians. American Journal of Human Genetics 84, 814–821.

Parson, W., Bandelt, H.J., 2007. Extended guidelines for mtDNA typing of population data in forensic science. Forensic Science International: Genetics 1, 13–19.

Szabo, S., Jaeger, K., Fischer, H., et al., 2012. In situ labeling of DNA reveals interindividual variation in nuclear DNA breakdown in hair and may be useful to predict success of forensic genotyping of hair. International Journal of Legal Medicine 126, 63–70.

Tully, G., Bär, W., Brinkmann, B., et al., 2001. Considerations by the European DNA profiling (EDNAP) group on the working practices, nomenclature and interpretation of mitochondrial DNA profiles. Forensic Science International 124, 83–91.

Tully, G., Barritt, S.M., Bender, K., et al., 2004. Results of a collaborative study of the EDNAP group regarding mitochondrial DNA heteroplasmy and segregation in hair shafts. Forensic Science International 140, 1–11.

Underhill, P.A., Kivisild, T., 2007. Use of Y chromosome and mitochondrial DNA population structure in tracing human migrations. Annual Review of Genetics 41, 539–564.

van Oven, M., Kayser, M., 2008. Updated comprehensive phylogenetic tree of global human mitochondrial DNA variation. Human Mutation 2, E386–E394.

Relevant Websites

http://www.empop.org—EMPOP.
http://www.ncbi.nlm.nih.gov—GenBank.
https://www.mitomap.org—Mitomap.
http://www.phylotree.org—Phylotree.

Microbiology and Bioterrorism

P Roffey, Forensic and Data Centres, Australian Federal Police, Canberra, ACT, Australia

Nomenclature

B. anthracis *Bacillus anthracis* (genus species), the binomial system for naming of species.

CFU Colony forming units, a measure of the viable number of bacteria or fungi in a sample.

Glossary

16S typing A procedure for characterizing isolates of prokaryotic species and strains using the sequence of the 16S rRNA gene.

Binary fission A form of asexual reproduction in prokaryotes in which a cell divides, giving rise to two daughter cells, each containing an identical copy of the genetic material.

Clonal A descriptive term meaning a cell or cells derived from an asexual ancestry.

Cytopathic effect A change in the microscopic appearance of cells, especially in tissue culture, after being infected with a virus.

Enzyme-linked immunosorbent assay An immunoassay that uses an enzyme chemically linked to an antibody or antigen as a marker for the detection and/or quantification of an antigen or antibody in a sample.

Eukaryote A single-celled or multicellular organism for which the cells contain a distinct membrane-bound nucleus in which the genetic material is carried.

Horizontal gene transfer A process through which an organism receives genetic material from another organism that is not their ancestor. Commonly, the new genetic material creates a trait or traits that were not previously observed in the original recipient.

Immunoassay A laboratory technique that uses the specificity of binding between an antigen and its homologous antibody to identify and/or quantify an antigen or antibody in a sample.

Immunofluorescence An immunoassay that uses an antibody chemically linked to a fluorescent dye to detect and/or quantify an antigen or antibody in a sample.

Locus (genetic locus) A location within the genome of an organism.

Microbial forensics A scientific discipline dedicated to the analysis of microorganisms and/or toxins for attribution purposes.

Mitosis A form of asexual reproduction in eukaryotes in which the nucleus divides, giving rise to two daughter nuclei identical to the original nucleus. Normally mitosis occurs immediately prior to cell division.

Multilocus sequence typing A procedure for characterizing isolates of prokaryotic species and strains using the sequences of internal fragments, 400–500 nucleotides in length, of several constitutive genes (i.e., genes involved in basic cell function).

Multiple locus variable number tandem repeat analysis A procedure for characterizing isolates of prokaryotic species and strains using the length variation at several variable number tandem repeat loci on the genetic material of an organism.

Mutation A change in the DNA sequence of the genetic material of an organism. Commonly, this creates a character or trait that is not found in the parental type.

Personal protective equipment Specialized clothing, equipment, or substances worn by employees to protect against health and safety hazards.

Polymerase chain reaction A biochemical technique that is used to amplify a short sequence of DNA (or RNA) for analysis, even from samples containing only minute quantities of DNA or RNA.

Prokaryote An organism, normally microscopic and unicellular in nature, which is characterized by the absence of a distinct membrane-bound nucleus and other membrane-bound organelles.

 http://dx.doi.org/10.1016/B978-0-12-800647-4.00020-5

Recombination A process through which genetic material is broken and joined to other genetic material, resulting in new combinations of genetic material.

Single-nucleotide polymorphism analysis A procedure for characterizing DNA sequence variation that occurs at a single nucleotide on the genetic material of an organism.

Single-nucleotide repeat typing A procedure for characterizing length variation in a genome due to the number of times one kind of nucleotide is repeated at a locus.

Variable number tandem repeat locus A location in a genome where a short nucleotide sequence is organized as a tandem repeat and that often varies between isolates by the number of repeats of the nucleotide sequence.

Introduction

The intentional release of *Bacillus anthracis* in the United States in 2001 demonstrated the vulnerability of society to acts of bioterrorism. This event, and of course the coincidental attacks on the U.S. World Trade Center Towers, spurred a flurry of effort to reduce gaps in our capability to preempt, prevent, react to, investigate, and recover from acts of bioterrorism and to minimize our vulnerability. This effort continues today. In the decade since, effort has largely focused on testing, improving, extending, and integrating the capabilities of the agencies involved in the prevention and response to public emergencies such as threats of bioterrorism.

Bioterrorism (and Its Impact)

By definition, bioterrorism is the use, or threatened use, of biological agents by states, organizations, or individuals to intimidate or coerce a government, civilian population, or persons to further political or social objectives. This is distinguished from biocrime, which refers to the use, or threatened use, of biological agents to further individual criminal objectives. Biocrimes include acts such as deliberate infection or intoxication of individuals with intent to harm, incapacitate, or intimidate. Biowarfare refers to the military use of biological agents. A fourth category of bioincident sometimes used is bioaccident, which refers to the unintentional release of biological agents. The boundary between biocrime and bioaccident is difficult to distinguish if an unintentional release is associated with a crime (e.g., when an outbreak of disease occurs as a result of an illegal importation). This article focuses on the application of microbiology to the prevention and investigation of acts of bioterrorism; however, much of what is presented is equally applicable to biocrimes, biowarfare, and bioaccidents.

The use of biological agents for warfare and other malicious purposes has existed for thousands of years, but its potential as a terrorist instrument has been more fully appreciated by governments following the 2001 U.S. anthrax letters. Not surprisingly, the threat of bioterrorism elicits enormous public fear; after all, our historical records are littered with descriptions of mass casualties from disease epidemics such as smallpox, influenza, and plague. These are the same pathogens that have the potential to be used by terrorists. In addition, the potential for economic loss through both stock losses and sale and export restrictions from biological agents targeted against crops and livestock cannot be understated. Good examples are the animal diseases, such as foot and mouth disease, bovine spongiform encephalitis, and brucellosis, and the plant diseases, such as *Puccinia* rust and *Tilletia* smuts.

Biological Agents

The term biological agent refers to any pathogen or toxin that can be used for malicious purposes. Not surprisingly, the list of potential biological agents is formidable, spanning pathogens and toxins from diverse evolutionary origins. Included are species of fungi, protozoa, bacteria, viruses, viroids, and prions and toxins from plants, animals, fungi, algae, and bacteria. Thankfully, most are low- to moderate-risk agents. With that said, the list comprising the highest risk agents alone is still daunting. At this current time, the U.S. Select Agents and Toxins list identifies approximately 80 different pathogens and toxins that are considered in the higher risk category. The resources, knowledge, skills, and technologies required to detect, identify, and characterize the pathogens and toxins within this list alone are well beyond the normal range of activities of individual microbiologists or laboratories. The application of microbiology as a forensic science must integrate the skills of microbiologists from law enforcement, public health, specialists, and research laboratories in order to fulfill the comprehensive investigation that is required for legal proceedings.

Microbiology as a Forensic Science

Microbiology is a long-established scientific discipline that up until this century had rarely been used as a forensic science. Its traditional roots are in medicine and public health, veterinary science, agriculture, biotechnology, industry, and research. The demands on these laboratories are very different from those involved in criminal investigations; hence, laboratories that agree to be involved in forensic investigations have to implement quite significant change in practice in order to meet investigative and legal obligations. For example, the procedures normally used in a medical laboratory for the identification of pathogens from clinical samples may need to be adapted to suit forensic samples, may need to be extended to provide the information required to satisfy the investigation, may require more extensive validation in order to withstand the rigor of legal scrutiny, and/or may need to be adapted to satisfy the legal obligations for evidence management. Laboratory design, management, security, and accreditation may also need to be altered, adapted, or extended to meet the same legal obligations. Conversely, law enforcement agencies and forensic laboratories have had to introduce new practices to allow the safe collection of environmental samples and traditional forensic evidence from contaminated crime scenes and to introduce new procedures for the transport, triage, receipt, storage, and handling of contaminated evidence. Many law enforcement agencies and forensic facilities have specifically built new laboratories to accommodate contaminated evidence and have employed microbiologists to establish forensic procedures for the detection and presumptive identification of biological agents in the field and in the laboratory.

Like all forensic disciplines, the point at which microbiology begins to contribute to a criminal investigation is dependent on the circumstances of the case. Unlike most other forensic disciplines, clinical presentations may well be the trigger for criminal investigations. For example, a covert release of a biological agent may not be detected until links are made between victims, a pattern of illness is identified, an unusual number or type of presentations occurs, or as a discovery through retrospective epidemiological investigations. In these instances, the clinical, microbiological, and epidemiological examinations that were conducted prior to law enforcement involvement will be crucial to the criminal investigation and may form the cornerstone of the investigation and subsequent prosecution. With that said, most threats of bioterrorism are overt in nature, such as when associated with a threatening letter or phone call. Intended targets may be specific (e.g., a government representative) or random (e.g., citizens in a shopping mall). Sadly, there is evidence for all of these different modes of attack in our recent history, but thankfully, the vast majority have had limited success, have been unsuccessful, or have been hoaxes. The 2001 U.S. anthrax letters are an excellent example of how microbiology is applied in the investigation of an act of terrorism.

The 2001 U.S. Anthrax Letters

Between October 4 and November 20, 2001, 22 people in the United States developed anthrax. Eleven of these individuals contracted inhalational anthrax whereas the remaining 11 individuals developed cutaneous anthrax. Five of the inhalational anthrax victims died from their infection. Initiated as a public health investigation, it quickly became a criminal investigation led by the Federal Bureau of Investigation (FBI) when it was suspected that the infections were most likely a result of one or more deliberate mailings of letters contaminated with *B. anthracis*. Subsequently, letters containing *B. anthracis* were discovered in New York and Washington, DC, addressed to Tom Brokaw of NBC News, the *New York Post*, and the U.S. Senators Tom Daschle and Patrick Leahy. A fifth envelope was mailed to the America Media, Inc., building in Florida; however, this envelope was never recovered. Additional letters are believed to have been mailed to other media organizations in New York as inferred from the pattern of infection; however, these letters were also not recovered. The scientific analyses that were central to the investigation required the involvement of 29 government, university, and commercial laboratories. Over the course of this investigation, the scientific field known as "microbial forensics" emerged. Not surprisingly, it became the conduit through which the investigation was channeled and, combined with physicochemical analyses, it narrowed the search for the possible origins of the anthrax powders used in the attacks, which in turn provided the crucial leads used to reveal potential suspects.

The key microbiological findings that contributed to the investigation were as follows:

1. The four envelopes that were recovered contained extraordinarily high concentrations of *B. anthracis* spores (4.6×10^{10} to 2.1×10^{12} CFU per gram). The spore preparations in the letters sent to the *New York Post* and Tom Brokaw of NBC News (i.e., the New York letters) were of high purity, and the spore preparations in Senator Daschle and Senator Leahy letters (i.e., the Washington letters) were of exceptionally high purity. This indicated that the perpetrator had knowledge of *B. anthracis* spore production protocols.
2. The high concentration of spores in the preparations would have placed the perpetrator at considerable risk of inhalational anthrax. It was highly likely that the perpetrator would have used personal protective equipment (PPE), would have a means of containment (e.g., biological safety cabinet), and/or would have practiced some form of prophylaxis through administration of antibiotics and/or vaccination.
3. The spore preparations were not "weaponized." Silica, a substance added to spore preparations to enhance aerosolization, was found in the preparations but was later shown to be incorporated into the spore coat; hence, it was more likely a natural phenomenon than a form of weaponization.
4. Sampling of 621 U.S. Postal Service drop boxes that fed into the Trenton mail processing facility (i.e., the facility

corresponding to the postmark on the letters) only found *B. anthracis* spores in one mailbox. This was identified as likely to be the mailbox from which all of the known attack letters were mailed.

5. The Senator Leahy letter was located in one of 642 trash bags of unopened mail that were collected from the Senate buildings after the Senator Daschle letter was discovered. It was located using an innovative sampling protocol designed to eliminate the need to sift through each piece of mail to find contaminated mail. Swab sampling from each of the 642 bags identified 20 bags that contained higher than trace levels of *B. anthracis*. Air sampling of each of these 20 bags identified one bag that was orders of magnitude more contaminated than others. It was this bag that contained the letter addressed to Senator Leahy and was subsequently shown to contain a quantity of powdered *B. anthracis* spores.
6. The New York letters both contained *Bacillus subtilis* as a minor constituent of the powders. The Washington letters did not contain *B. subtilis*. Whole genome sequencing of the isolate from the *New York Post* letter showed a high similarity (98%), but not identity, to the published sequence of the standard laboratory strain *B. subtilis* 168. Polymerase chain reaction (PCR) assays were developed against 23 loci in the evidentiary strain that differed from the reference strain. The *B. subtilis* isolates from the New York letters were identical to each other at all 23 loci, indicating that they were the same strain. This and differences in the physicochemical properties of the materials from the Washington and New York letters indicated that the Washington and New York letters contained materials from two different spore preparations.
7. *Bacillus anthracis* isolates were collected from the 4 envelopes, 17 clinical specimens, and 106 environmental specimens taken from locations along the mail path of the implicated letters. The isolates were identified as the Ames strain. Whole genome sequencing confirmed that it had not been genetically engineered. Although insufficient to identify the source, the identification of the *B. anthracis* in the letters as the Ames strain provided evidence that the source of the strain in the letters was likely to be a laboratory. The Ames strain is uncommon in nature; hence, the source material used in the letters was unlikely to have been acquired from nature.
8. The Ames strain was originally isolated from a dead cow in Texas in 1981 and transported to the U.S. Army Medical Research Institute for Infectious Diseases (USAMRIID) laboratory at Fort Detrick in Frederick, MD. Over time, the Ames strain was shared with a number of domestic and international laboratories. The FBI assembled a repository of over 1070 Ames strain samples from 20 laboratories, which included 3 overseas laboratories. These laboratories were identified to have had the Ames strain in their inventory prior to the attacks. Of the 1070 samples, 1059 were viable. The attributes within the samples in the repository were compared against the characteristics in the evidentiary samples.
9. The *B. anthracis* present in the envelopes was shown to be a mixture of multiple distinct colony morphological types (i.e., morphotypes). The specific genetic sequences associated with these morphotypes provided a means through which relationships among evidentiary samples could be assessed. More specifically, these genetic sequences could be used to exclude potential sources of the *B. anthracis* found in the letters.
10. The genetic tests targeted to these unique sequences provided strong evidence that the *B. anthracis* spores present in each of the four envelopes originated from the same source.
11. The genetic tests targeted to the unique sequences in the morphotypes identified only two samples in the repository that had the same genetic sequences as the mailed material. Subsequent investigations revealed that both originated from a flask containing *B. anthracis* spores, identified as number RMR-1029, housed at a USAMRIID laboratory at Fort Detrick. Physicochemical tests demonstrated that material within flask RMR-1029 could not be the immediate source of the material in the letters but it could have been the seed material used for the production of the material found in the letters.
12. The identification of the laboratory and flask from which the seed material originated narrowed the search for the perpetrator to the individuals who had access to flask RMR-1029 at the USAMRIID laboratory at Fort Detrick and ultimately led investigators to identify Dr Bruce Ivins as the perpetrator.

Dr Ivins was a senior microbiologist working in the U.S. government anthrax vaccine program at the USAMRIID laboratory at Fort Detrick. Dr Ivins took his own life before charges could be filed; hence, the science behind the investigation was never subjected to the scrutiny of the judicial system. Interestingly, a review of the scientific approaches used during the FBI's investigation of the anthrax letters by the National Academy of Science (NAS) was critical of some components of the microbiological investigation and some of the conclusions drawn. In balancing these criticisms, the NAS recognized that the investigation required the application of new scientific procedures developed specifically for the investigation and that although state-of-the-art procedures were used at the time, the rapid advances in technology that had occurred over the period of the investigation had superseded some of the procedures used earlier in the investigation.

The microbiological analyses conducted during the investigation of the 2001 U.S. anthrax letters was only one component of one of the largest and most complex criminal investigations in history. Nevertheless, the importance of the microbiological investigations must not be understated because it was ultimately the guiding hand behind the investigation. It is the first comprehensive application of microbiology as a forensic science and a model for future applications.

The Application of Microbiological Procedures to the Forensic Sciences

Incidents of bioterrorism and biocrimes present a particular challenge to forensic investigations by the very nature of the crime itself. The potential presence of infectious or toxic agents dramatically complicates the performance of forensic procedures. In order to minimize risk, basic principles of good microbiological practice and microbial containment must be overlaid across all forensic procedures and of course all forensic evidence. A host of safety precautions are conducted in order to minimize personal exposure and to reduce risk of disease. Examples of such precautions are as follows:

- Remote manipulation (e.g., robotic manipulation).
- PPE (e.g., air-purifying respirators, protective garments, and disposable gloves).
- Barrier protection (e.g., cordons, glove boxes, biological safety cabinets, and high containment laboratories).
- Physical removal of contamination (e.g., the filtration of spores from a DNA extract, personnel decontamination showers).
- Inactivation of contamination prior to examination (e.g., gamma irradiation of exhibits).
- Minimization of aerosol generation (e.g., through excessive traffic, unnecessary movements, and use of high-risk procedures such as centrifugation, homogenization, and vacuuming); handling samples as liquid rather than powder significantly reduces aerosol risk.
- The use of disposable equipment and consumables.
- Minimization of workspace clutter.
- Use of aseptic technique for transfer and handling of microorganisms.
- Decontamination of work areas (e.g., disinfection, chemical deactivation, and vaporous hydrogen peroxide sterilization).
- Appropriate waste disposal (e.g., autoclaving).
- Standard laboratory hygiene practices (e.g., hand washing).
- Prophylaxis (e.g., vaccination and/or antibiotics).

Although necessary, the application of these principles can be a major hindrance to aspects of the forensic investigation. For example, the use of appropriate PPE and clothing reduces dexterity, movement, field of vision, and comfort, and it can severely limit examination time. Novel solutions are often required for seemingly simple problems. A classic example is the photography of a postal barcode on a processed envelope. The dye used in the imprinted barcode is only visible when activated by ultraviolet (UV) light. Under normal conditions, the barcode is photographed using a standard crime scene camera mounted with a UV flash. A contaminated envelope contained within a Class 3 biological safety cabinet presents a significant impediment to photography. Using the camera outside of the cabinet is problematic because the UV flash cannot penetrate the cabinet window; however, if used inside of the cabinet, the camera and data storage card will be contaminated. The solution is to use remote data transfer or remote flash activation. In hindsight, these solutions are simple; however, they can present a major dilemma when time is critical. Where possible, these restrictions should be identified preemptively and solutions should be found.

To forensic microbiologists, the principles listed above are second nature; however, to other forensic scientists, these must be learned and practiced. The resourcing of trained personnel and equipment for rare events such as bioterrorism and biocrimes is a major burden to governments, but it is an expectation of modern society in developed countries.

The Microbiological Investigation of Bioterrorism

Suspected incidents of bioterrorism trigger concurrent forensic investigations from public health and law enforcement. The public health investigation aims to identify the causative agent, its source, and potential victims so that appropriate treatment, control, and preventative measures can be implemented. The law enforcement forensic investigation seeks a more detailed characterization of the agent in its quest to attribute the causative agent to a perpetrator. Both are essential to the criminal investigation.

Journalism's "Five Ws, one H" concept of information gathering applies equally to the forensic investigation of acts of bioterrorism. This concept, immortalized in the children's book by Rudyard Kipling, *The Elephants Child* (1902), personifies the six fundamental questions that the forensic investigation seeks to address:

> *I keep six honest serving-men*
> *(They taught me all I knew);*
> *Their names are What and Why and When*
> *and How and Where and Who.*

Not surprisingly, the identification of the agent is of high priority in the forensic investigation. Armed with this knowledge, strategies that minimize risk to forensic personnel while maximizing the collection of relevant evidence can be implemented. A variety of field tests are available to assist with the identification of the agent on site. These include both generic tests for the detection of biological molecules and specialized tests for the detection of specific pathogens and toxins. Field tests are generally designed to provide rapid but presumptive identification of a very limited number of biological agents and more often than not are undertaken by personnel with minimal microbiology training.

Confirmatory-level identification is laboratory based, and the expertise to conduct these analyses resides squarely within the public health laboratories. The agent is first isolated and then identified through a series of traditional microbiological techniques. For bacteria, these include techniques such as culture, colony morphology, microscopy (cell morphology and staining reactions; e.g., gram, capsule, and spore staining), motility, sugar metabolism, fatty acid profiling, volatile organic acid profiling, biochemical testing, serotyping, phage typing, and antibiotic resistance patterns. For viruses, these include techniques such as cell cytopathic effects, host cell susceptibility, and immunoassays (e.g., enzyme-linked immunosorbent assay methods and immunofluorescence). This approach is more generic, providing an opportunity for detection of a much wider range of biological agents than that afforded by current field tests. In both viral and bacterial diagnostic laboratories, species-specific molecular tests such as PCR are commonly used to reinforce diagnoses from traditional methodology. Collectively, confirmatory-level identification is generally to the species level.

The remit of public health laboratories includes the tracing of outbreaks; hence, specialist public health laboratories have additional methodologies to further characterize pathogens. Methodologies such as 16S typing, multiple locus variable number tandem repeat analysis, single-nucleotide polymorphism analysis, single-nucleotide repeat typing, and multilocus sequence typing provide data that can be used to assess evolutionary relationships between evidentiary samples and reference strains. As technologies improve and costs reduce, there is little doubt that whole genome sequencing will also be incorporated into the routine methodology of specialist public health laboratories; however, at present, this capability still largely resides in research and commercial laboratories. Together, these molecular methodologies provide a hierarchical approach to resolving relationships. The identity of evidentiary samples is revealed through phylogenetic grouping with reference samples. This is how the *B. anthracis* within the 2001 U.S. anthrax letters was identified as the Ames strain. Even if evidentiary samples are not perfectly matched with any of the reference samples, the degree of similarity between them and the reference samples can be used to predict the nearness of the ancestral relationship between them and close relatives. The ancestral relationship in turn provides information on origin. Using the 2001 U.S. anthrax letters as an example, the identification of the *B. anthracis* as the Ames strain provided strong evidence that it was a laboratory strain and was unlikely to have been isolated from nature.

Bacteria, which are prokaryotes, are clonal in nature. They replicate by a process known as binary fission, a process equivalent to mitosis in eukaryotes, in which each daughter cell receives an identical copy of the genome. The variation seen between strains is caused by mutation, horizontal gene transfer, and recombination. These biological processes allow bacteria to adapt to altered or new environments. The clonal nature of bacteria is exploited when inferring evolutionary relationships (as described above); however, it is the differences that provide the signatures of individuality. It is likely that the material used in a bioterrorism event will contain a number of dynamic and adaptive clones that are distinctive for that preparation and hence can be used to trace evidentiary material to a particular preparation. This is how the material within the 2001 U.S. anthrax letters was traced to flask RMR-1029 at the USAMRIID laboratory at Fort Detrick. Viruses have a similar pattern of evolution; hence, similar processes can be used to trace origins to a particular preparation or host.

Returning to the Five Ws, one H concept of information gathering (*what, why, when, how, where* and *who*), the importance of microbiology in guiding the criminal investigation is evident. The identification of the agent (*what*) and its individual characteristics can be used to trace the origin of the agent (*where* and *who*) and may provide evidence of opportunity and motive (*who* and *why*). It may also be able to give clues as to when it was acquired, when it was prepared, and when it was disseminated; how it was prepared, how it was stored, and how it was disseminated; and where it was manufactured. Knowledge of the manufacturing process reveals the type of equipment and consumables that would have been used in the production process (*what*) and hence where these may have been resourced and the skills and experience of the creator (*who*). It can also indicate the type of prophylaxis (*what*) that may have been required to avoid infection or the type of illness the perpetrator may have experienced during preparation or dissemination (*who*).

Final Remarks

The incorporation of microbiology into criminal investigations has been and remains an arduous task. Traditional forensic sciences such as fingerprinting, ballistics, DNA profiling, and crime scene examination were purpose built to assist criminal investigations, whereas at the present time, the forensic application of microbiology is secondary to the primary function of most of the laboratories that are involved. This is because the facilities and expertise required to analyze microbiological specimens is largely outside of the scope of "normal" forensic laboratories and "normal" forensic practitioners. Rather, the microbiological investigation largely relies on the cooperation of nonforensic laboratories and in particular, the public health and research laboratories. The imposed procedural obligations, resourcing, and preparations required to provide these services is a major burden to these laboratories but is an absolute necessity if perpetrators of crimes such as bioterrorism are to be brought to justice.

See also: **Biology/DNA:** Future Analytical Techniques: DNA Mass Spectrometry; Introduction to Nonhuman DNA Typing; Next-Generation Sequencing Technologies; Short Tandem Repeats; Single-Nucleotide Polymorphisms; **Chemistry/Trace/Forensic Geosciences:** Crime Scene Considerations; **Investigations:** Contamination; Crime Scene Analysis and Reconstruction; Major Incident Scene Management; Packaging; Preservation; **Management/Quality in Forensic Science:** Health and Safety; **Methods:** Analytical Light Microscopy; Microscopy (Electron).

Further Reading

Beecher, D.J., 2006. Forensic application of microbiological culture analysis to identify mail intentionally contaminated with *Bacillus anthracis* spores. Applied and Environmental Microbiology 72, 5304–5310.

Budowle, B., Beaudry, J.A., Barnaby, N.G., Giusti, A.M., Bannon, J.D., Keim, P., 2008. The role of law enforcement response and microbial forensics in investigation of bioterrorism. Croation Medical Journal 48, 437–449.

Budowle, B., Schutzer, S.E., Breeze, R.G., Keim, P.S., Morse, S.A. (Eds.), 2011. Microbial Forensics, second ed. Academic Press, Burlington.

Cummings, C.A., Bormann Chung, C.A., Fang, R., et al., 2010. Accurate, rapid and high-throughput detection of strain-specific polymorphisms in *Bacillus anthracis* and *Yersinia pestis* by next-generation sequencing. Investigative Genetics 1, 5.

Jones, S.W., Dobson, M.E., Francesconi, S.C., Schoske, R., Crawford, R., 2005. DNA assays for detection, identification, and individualization of select agent microorganisms. Croation Medical Journal 46, 522–529.

Keim, P., Pearson, T., Okinaka, R., 2008. Microbial forensics: DNA fingerprinting of *Bacillus anthracis* (anthrax). Analytical Chemistry 80, 4791–4800.

Popovic, T., Glass, M., 2003. Laboratory aspects of bioterrorism-related anthrax—from identification to molecular subtyping to microbial forensics. Croation Medical Journal 44, 336–341.

Rasko, D.A., Worsham, P.L., Abshire, T.G., et al., 2011. *Bacillus anthracis* comparative genome analysis in support of the Amerithrax investigation. Proceedings of the National Academy of Sciences of the United States of America 108, 5027–5032.

Van Ert, M.N., Easterday, W.R., Simonson, T.S., et al., 2007. Strain-specific single-nucleotide polymorphism assays for *Bacillus anthracis* Ames strain. Journal of Clinical Microbiology 45, 47–53.

Relevant Websites

http://www.justice.gov—Amerithrax Investigative Summary. United States Department of Justice. (2010).

http://www.nap.edu—Review of the Scientific Approaches Used during the FBI's Investigation on the Anthrax Letters. National Research Council (2011).

http://www.selectagents.gov—National Select Agent Registry. Select Agent and Toxins List (2011).

Key Terms

Admixture, AIMs, Ancestry, Ancestry informative markers, Anthrax, Bacteria, Biocrime, Bioterrorism, Divergence, DNA technology, Duffy, Forensic science, Forensics, Haploblocks, Haplogroup, Haplotype, Heteroplasmy, HGDP-CEPH, Indels, Insertion deletion polymorphisms (Indels), Kinship analysis, Microbial forensics, Microbiology, mtDNA, Paternity testing, Pathogen, Phylogeny, Population genetics, Public health, Sequence, Short tandem repeats (STRs), Single-nucleotide polymorphisms (SNPs), SPSmart, STRs, Structure, Toxin, Trace samples, Virus, X-chromosome.

Review Questions

1. Why is quantitation important to DNA quality procedures?
2. What are the main methods for DNA extraction?
3. How is the extraction of DNA from bones and teeth different from fluids or soft tissues?
4. What was involved in the selection of short tandem repeats (STRs) for forensic use?
5. List and describe some of the irregularities of DNA extraction and related methods.
6. List the advantages and disadvantages of short tandem repeats (STRs) and single-nucleotide polymorphisms (SNPs). Which method is better and why?
7. What are "select agents and toxins"?
8. What is a mini single tandem repeats and what are the benefits of using them?
9. What is concordance testing and why is it important?
10. Define low-template DNA testing. Why is there a difficulty in saying what it is or it is not?
11. What are some of the concerns in low template DNA work? How are these concerns addressed?
12. What are the statistical considerations for low template DNA work? What about drop-in and drop-out?

13. Read over the casework examples about low-template DNA. What are the common themes and concerns?
14. Beyond their origins, what are the structural differences between the X- and Y-chromosomes? What are the implications for analysis and interpretation?
15. What is the definition of a polymorphism?
16. Do ancestry markers have a role in forensic analysis and investigations? If so, what are they?
17. What is an indel? What role might they play in forensic biology?
18. Describe the mitochondrial genome and structure. What makes it amenable to analysis in a forensic setting?
19. What is heteroplasmy? What concerns are there in forensic interpretations of mitochondrial DNA given heteroplasmy?
20. How does traditional forensic science assist with biothreat investigations?

Discussion Questions

1. Forensic DNA methodology is complex and requires a chain of techniques to complete a case. What are the quality and science issues in deciding on an analytical workflow? How can scientists work toward scientifically valid "better practices" based on what other laboratories do, the literature, and legal requirements?
2. In a National Institute of Justice-funded study in Los Angeles, Y-chromosome testing to determine the presence of male DNA and conventional serology had comparable success rates in leading to positive short tandem repeat results. What are the strengths and weaknesses of using one or the other in casework, taking time, personnel, cost, and specificity into consideration?
3. What are the issues related to doing low-template DNA work? How does the layout of a facility affect these issues? How could a laboratory decide if they should do low-template work?
4. What role does mitochondrial DNA have in forensic work? What does it do that other methods cannot? Could that information be generated in other ways or is mitochondrial DNA the only way to get at that information?
5. Most forensic laboratories do not have the facilities to handle biothreats such as *Bacillus anthracis* or *Yersenia pestis.* How can forensic laboratories prepare themselves for incidental exposure to biothreats such as these? How might partnerships with public health laboratories or federal facilities support these preparations?

Additional Readings

Butler, J.M., Coble, M.D., Vallone, P.M., 2007. STRs vs SNPs: thoughts on the future of forensic DNA testing. Forensic Science, Medicine, and Pathology 3, 200–205.
Kidd, K.K., Speed, W.C., Pakstis, A.J., Furtado, M.R., Fang, R., Madbouly, A., Maiers, M., Middha, M., Friedlaender, F.R., Kidd, J.R., 2014. Progress toward an efficient panel of SNPs for ancestry inference. Forensic Science International: Genetics 10, 23–32.
Linch, C.A., Whiting, D.A., Holland, M.M., 2001. Human hair histogenesis for the mitochondrial DNA forensic scientist. Journal of Forensic Sciences 46, 844–853.
Markotic, A., Le Duc, J., Smith, J., 2014. Bioterrorism and forensic microbiology. In: Primorac, D., Shanfield, M. (Eds.), 2014. Forensic DNA Applications: An Interdisciplinary Perspective, vol. 293. CRC Press, Boca Raton, FL.

Section 4. Interpretation

Making sense of DNA results has never been simple. The methods are complicated, the statistics are abstruse, and the actual biological evidence—the molecule, the alleles, the loci—cannot be seen. It is a teaching moment for the jury, and the forensic scientist must be adept at examples, analogies, and explanations to make sense of the process and the outcomes. The statistical and probabilistic nature of forensic DNA interpretation are what make it so powerful and place it on something of a pedestal among forensic sciences. Despite the fact that DNA interpretation is not immune to bias (Dror and Hampikian, 2011), or perhaps because of it, the interpretation of DNA results must be accurate and properly conveyed to the trier of fact.

DNA—Statistical Probability

BS Weir, University of Washington, Seattle, WA, USA

Introduction

Human individualization based on the genome exploits the fact that everyone except for identical twins is genetically distinguishable. Moreover, human genetic material is found in every nucleated cell in the body and can be recovered from samples as diverse as bone, blood stains, ear wax, or shaver clippings. DNA may be recovered from very old samples that have been well preserved, and DNA signatures may be preserved even over successive generations.

The very genetic nature of DNA evidence that makes it of such value to forensic science also brings particular problems in interpretation. One problem is that as more and more genetic loci are used for DNA profiles, the proportion of a population who might be expected to share a particular profile becomes less. There comes a point where any attempt to quantify the probability of seeing a profile strains credulity. Certainly numbers such as one in several trillion fall into that range. Another problem is that the genetic constitution of a population is dependent on previous generations. Immediate family members are likely to have similar DNA profiles, but even apparently unrelated members of a population have a shared evolutionary history. Therefore, conveying the evidentiary strength of matching DNA profiles requires the use of both probability and genetics.

Probability

Although the term "probability" features prominently in describing DNA evidence, the meaning of the term is often left unclear. Indeed, there are several possible approaches to defining probability. A classical definition is based on the notion of the proportion of times an event will occur in repeated opportunities for occurrence. When the probability that a well-shuffled deck of cards will have an ace on top is said to be 1 in 13, there is an implicit understanding that the event will be seen in one-thirteenth of any number of shufflings of the deck. When a weather forecaster says there is a 70% probability of rain that day, the meaning is less clear. Maybe the current conditions have led to rain in 70% of previous occasions, but the listeners will need to make a decision about taking an umbrella on the basis of their understanding of this figure. The personal element is even clearer in a courtroom when a prosecutor asks a jury to convict the defendant because the probability of guilt is so high as to be beyond reasonable doubt. The probabilities attached to DNA profiles cannot be interpreted as population proportions when they are very much smaller than one over the population size. They might be interpreted as personal measures of uncertainty, or they might be explained as being the result of a set of prescribed calculations. However, even such calculations necessarily have some subjectivity on the part of the person performing the calculations.

Laws of Probability

However probability is defined, it must obey a set of rules in order to be useful. Suppose there is interest in some event, H: that the card on top of a well-shuffled deck is an ace, or that it will rain today, or that the defendant is guilty. There is some information, I, about the event: the deck has 4 aces among the

 http://dx.doi.org/10.1016/B978-0-12-800647-4.00021-7

52 cards, or the weather forecaster is very good, or the evidence against the defendant is very strong. The probability of H, given the information I, is written as Pr $(H|I)$, and it satisfies the three "Laws of Probability."

The first law says that probabilities are numbers between 0 and 1 (inclusive) and that the probability of a certain event is 1. In symbols,

$$0 \leq \Pr(H|I) \leq 1$$

$$\Pr(H|H) = 1$$

The second law says that the probability of either of two mutually exclusive events G, H happening is the sum of the separate probabilities for G and H. In the card example, the events G, "The face card is a king," and H, "The face card is an ace" are mutually exclusive because they cannot both occur. Likewise, "rain" and "no rain" or "The defendant is the source of DNA" and "The defendant is not the source of the DNA" are pairs of mutually exclusive events. In symbols,

$$\Pr(G \text{ or } H|I) = \Pr(G|I) + \Pr(H|I)$$

From the first law, this implies that the probability of the defendant either being the source of a DNA sample or not being the source, given the evidence, is 1.

The third law gives the probability of both of two events, G and H, occurring. The joint probability is the probability that the first of them occurs multiplied by the probability of the second given that the first has occurred. The "first" and "second" labels are arbitrary; therefore, symbolically,

$$\begin{aligned}\Pr(G \text{ and } H|I) &= \Pr(G|I)\Pr(H|G,I) \\ &= \Pr(H|I)\Pr(G|H,I)\end{aligned}$$

For the card example, suppose G is "The top card is a face card" and H is "The top card is an ace." For a standard deck of cards,

$$\Pr(G|I) = 16/52 \ \Pr(H|G,I) = 1/4 \ \Pr(G \text{ and } H|I) = 1/13$$
$$\Pr(H|I) = 1/13 \ \Pr(G|H,I) = 1 \ \Pr(H \text{ and } G|I) = 1/13$$

If the knowledge of one event having occurred does not affect the probability of another event, the two events are said to be independent. When events G, H are independent,

$$\Pr(G \text{ and } H|I) = \Pr(G|I)\Pr(H|I)$$

Bayes' Theorem

The Laws of Probability can be used to derive a result that is central to the interpretation of DNA evidence. From the third law, for any two events G, H,

$$\begin{aligned}\Pr(H|G,I) &= \frac{\Pr(H \text{ and } G|I)}{\Pr(G|I)} \\ &= \frac{\Pr(G|H,I)\Pr(H|I)}{\Pr(G|I)}\end{aligned}$$

The second expression is the simplest form of "Bayes' theorem," and it allows for the probability of an event given a second event to be expressed in terms of the probability of the second event given the first. In other words, there has been a transposing of the condition from $H|G$ to $G|H$. This transposition requires knowledge of the separate probabilities of G and H.

The law can be written in an "odds form" by rewriting it for the event $\overline{H}$: "not H,"

$$\Pr(\overline{H}|G,I) = \frac{\Pr(G|\overline{H},I)\Pr(\overline{H}|I)}{\Pr(G|I)}$$

and then dividing the first expression by the second,

$$\frac{\Pr(H|G,I)}{\Pr(\overline{H}|G,I)} = \frac{\Pr(G|H,I)}{\Pr(G|\overline{H},I)} \times \frac{\Pr(H|I)}{\Pr(\overline{H}|I)}$$

The probability of an event divided by the probability of not that event is called the odds, so $\Pr(H|I)/\Pr(\overline{H}|I)$ is the "prior odds" of H (i.e., the odds prior to knowledge of event G). After the acquisition of knowledge that event G has occurred, the ratio $\Pr(H|G,I)/\Pr(\overline{H}|G,I)$ is the "posterior odds" of H. In equation form,

$$\text{Posterior odds} = \text{LR} \times \text{Prior odds}$$

where the ratio of the two conditional probabilities $\Pr(G|H,I)$ to $\Pr(G|\overline{H},I)$ has been termed the "likelihood ratio" (LR).

Forensic Probabilities

This formal language of probability theory has an immediate application for the interpretation of DNA evidence. Although the ultimate question in a trial concerns the guilt or innocence of the defendant, attention here is focused on just the DNA evidence. A common situation is where DNA is recovered from a biological sample left at the scene of a crime, and there is reason to believe the sample is from the perpetrator of the crime. DNA is also extracted from a blood or saliva sample from a suspect in the crime and is found to have the same profile as the crime sample. The events G and H are as follows:

G: The DNA profiles of the suspect and crime sample (are the same).
H: The crime sample is from the suspect.
$\overline{H}$: The crime sample is not from the suspect.
I: Other information relevant to the probabilities of G and H.

If the suspect is charged with being the perpetrator and becomes the defendant in a trial, then the court is going to be interested in the probability of the defendant being the perpetrator given the evidence of a DNA match. Bayes' theorem makes it clear that this can be calculated only if some prior probability can be assigned. An extreme view might be that, prior to the DNA evidence, the defendant had the same probability $(1/N)$ as anyone else in the population of being the perpetrator. For a population of size N, the prior odds would be $(1/N)]/[1 - (1/N)] = 1/(N - 1) \approx 1/N$. The posterior odds would be LR/N.

It is not customary to present prior odds in criminal trials, although they are routinely used in civil paternity disputes. For that situation, it is customary (if illogical) to assume the alleged father has a 50% probability of being the father before DNA evidence is collected. The prior odds are then 1, and the posterior odds are the same as the LR, which is known as the "paternity index." In criminal trials, the problem of assigning odds can be avoided by presenting only the LR, and the forensic scientist can testify that the DNA evidence (G) is LR times more likely if the defendant is the source of the crime sample (event H) than if some other person is the source of the crime sample (event $\overline{H}$).

DNA LRs

Calculation of the LR is clarified by considering the nature of the DNA evidence G in some more detail. The evidence can be considered to be the events that profiles G_C of the crime sample and G_S of the suspect are both of type A.

$$G : G_C = \mathcal{A} \text{ and } G_S = \mathcal{A}$$

From the third law of probability,

$$\begin{aligned}\Pr(G|H, I) &= \Pr(G_C = \mathcal{A} \text{ and } G_S = \mathcal{A}|H, I)\\ &= \Pr(G_C = \mathcal{A}|G_S = \mathcal{A}, H, I)\Pr(G_S = \mathcal{A}|H, I)\end{aligned}$$

$$\Pr(G|\overline{H}, I) = \Pr(G_C = \mathcal{A}|G_S = \mathcal{A}, \overline{H}, I)\Pr(G_S = \mathcal{A}|\overline{H}, I)$$

Therefore, the LR is

$$\text{LR} = \frac{\Pr(G_C = \mathcal{A}|G_S = \mathcal{A}, H, I)}{\Pr(G_C = \mathcal{A}|G_S = \mathcal{A}, \overline{H}, I)} \times \frac{\Pr(G_S = \mathcal{A}|H, I)}{\Pr(G_S = \mathcal{A}|\overline{H}, I)}$$

Now the DNA profile of the suspect was determined at the moment of conception of that person and cannot be influenced by whether or not the person left the crime sample; therefore, $\Pr(G_S = \mathcal{A}|H, I) = \Pr(G_S = \mathcal{A}|\overline{H}, I) = \Pr(G_S = \mathcal{A}|I)$. The LR reduces to

$$\text{LR} = \frac{\Pr(G_C = \mathcal{A}|G_S = \mathcal{A}, H, I)}{\Pr(G_C = \mathcal{A}|G_S = \mathcal{A}, \overline{H}, I)}$$

Further simplification follows from the assumption that the DNA typing system is sufficiently reliable and that two samples from the same person will be found to match. When the suspect is the perpetrator (event H), the crime sample must therefore be of type A if it is known that the suspect is of type A; therefore, $\Pr(G_C = A \mid G_S = A, H, I) = 1$ and

$$\text{LR} = \frac{1}{\Pr(G_C = \mathcal{A}|G_S = \mathcal{A}, \overline{H}, I)}$$

A final simplification follows from assuming that the DNA profiles from two different people (the perpetrator and the suspect when $\overline{H}$ is true) are independent; therefore, $\Pr(G_C = \mathcal{A}|G_S = \mathcal{A}|\overline{H}, I) = \Pr(G_C = \mathcal{A}|I)$ and

$$\text{LR} = \frac{1}{\Pr(G_C = \mathcal{A}|I)}$$

This last equation is the initial way DNA evidence was presented. Only the probability with which an unknown person would have the profile is needed. The information I may contain information about the population to which that person belongs. A profile probability of 1 in 1 million can be regarded as giving an LR of 1 million. The evidence would be 1 million times more likely if the suspect is the source of the DNA than if some other person is the source.

It needs to be stressed that the results in this section apply only to the situation in which the DNA evidence refers to material left at the crime scene by the perpetrator, and there is no DNA evidence at the scene that does not provide a match to the profile of the suspect. For example, if the evidence refers instead to a bloodstain found on the clothing of the suspect, and the stain has a DNA profile matching that of the victim, then additional factors need to be considered: What is the probability that the victim's blood would be transferred during the crime? What is the probability that the suspect would have non-self blood on his or her clothing? What is the probability that non-self blood on the suspect's clothing would match that of the victim?

Nature of DNA Profiles

To quantify the evidentiary strength of a matching DNA profile, it is necessary to decompose the profile into its component parts. DNA profiling examines the two "alleles" a person receives, one from each parent, at a number of "loci." There are several possible allelic types at each forensic short tandem repeat (STR) locus, and a person may have two copies of the same type and therefore be homozygous at a locus, or they may have two different alleles and therefore be heterozygous. As an example, consider the collection of STR loci used by CODIS. For locus TPOX, the population proportion for the 9, 10 genotype is estimated as $2p_{9_{\text{TPOX}}}p_{10_{\text{TPOX}}}$, where $p_{9_{\text{TPOX}}}$ and $p_{10_{\text{TPOX}}}$ are the frequencies of TPOX alleles 9, 10. For locus FGA, the proportion for the 19, 19 genotype is $p^2_{19_{\text{FGA}}}$, where $p_{19_{\text{FGA}}}$ is the frequency of FGA 19 alleles. At each locus, these products estimate the probability with which a random person in the population would have that "genotype." It has been assumed that the two alleles received by an individual at one locus are independent. To combine information over loci, it is further assumed that alleles at different loci are independent, and the products for each locus are multiplied together. For the two-locus profile in this example, the "product rule" calculation gives

$$\Pr(G_C = \mathcal{A}|I) = 2p_{9_{\text{TPOX}}}p_{10_{\text{TPOX}}}p^2_{19_{\text{FGA}}}$$

Dependent Profiles

For a crime in which it is known that the perpetrator must have a DNA profile of type A because the evidentiary sample had that type, it is natural to consider the profile probability (i.e., the probability of a random person in the population having that type). This is the quantity $\Pr(G_C = A|I)$ given at the end of the previous section. However, the evidential value of the sample needs to take into account the fact that there is a person (the defendant) who has already been seen to have that profile. The quantity of forensic interest is the match probability (i.e., the conditional probability), $\Pr(G_C = \mathcal{A}|G_S = \mathcal{A}, \overline{H}, I)$, and this can be quite different from $\Pr(G_C = A \mid I)$.

Effect of Relatives

The largest effect of dependencies between the DNA profiles of two people is when they are related. Relatives have the possibility of receiving the same genetic material from their common ancestors and, therefore, of having the same DNA profile. Some common values for the conditional probabilities are shown in **Table 1**, where p_i is the population frequency of allele A_i. To put the effect into perspective, numerical values of $\text{LR} = 1/\Pr(G_C = \mathcal{A}|G_S = \mathcal{A}, \overline{H}, I)$ are shown for the situation when all alleles have a frequency of 0.1. The effects of relatives are less for larger frequencies; however, in all cases, the LRs are reduced when the alternative to the suspect being the DNA source is that a relative of the suspect is the source.

Effect of Population Structure

If a locus has 5 alleles, then there are 15 possible pairs of alleles, or genotypes, at the locus. For 10 such loci, the number of possible genotypes is 576 billion. The number of possible profiles greatly exceeds the size of the world population, and the profile probability of any profile is small. However, the match probability is greater than the simple product rule calculation after that profile has been seen once already. This is because of the dependency among profiles imposed by evolution. Individuals C and S may share a DNA profile simply because they belong to a finite population. Although they may not be in the same family, they each have (at most) 2^n ancestors n generations ago, and this number quickly exceeds the population size. Any two people may have some ancestors in common, and this leads to a nonzero probability of shared profiles. This probability is greater for smaller populations.

The theory currently used by forensic scientists to accommodate this evolutionary perspective rests on the following argument. If the allele frequencies in a subpopulation are known, then the probability of an unknown person C having a certain DNA profile is estimated by the product rule using those allele frequencies. This calculation does not use the knowledge that S has already been seen to have the profile. However, the usual situation is that allele frequencies are not available for the subpopulation. This may be for practical difficulties in taking a sample from that group, or it may be because the subpopulation is not well defined. Instead, allele frequencies are available (or can be estimated) for the whole population. Taking an average over subpopulations of the conditional probability $\Pr(G_C = \mathcal{A}|G_S = \mathcal{A}, \overline{H}, I)$ leads to the following single-locus results for homozygotes A_iA_i or heterozygotes A_iA_j:

$$\begin{aligned}\Pr(G_C &= A_iA_i|G_S = A_iA_i, \overline{H}, I)\\ &= \frac{[2\theta + (1-\theta)p_i][3\theta + (1-\theta)p_i]}{(1+\theta)(1+2\theta)}\end{aligned}$$

Table 1 Effects of family relatedness

Genotype A	*Relationship*	$\Pr(G_C = \mathcal{A}\|G_S = \mathcal{A}, \overline{H}, I)$	*LR*
A_iA_j	Full siblings	$(1 + p_i + p_j + 2p_ip_j)/4$	3.3
	Parent and child	$(p_i + p_j)/2$	10.0
	Half siblings	$(p_i + p_j + 4p_ip_j)/4$	16.7
	Uncle and nephew[a]	$(p_i + p_j + 4p_ip_j)/4$	16.7
	First cousins	$(p_i + p_j + 12p_ip_j)/8$	25.0
	Unrelated	$2p_ip_j$	50.0
A_iA_i	Full siblings	$(1 + p_i)^2/4$	3.3
	Parent and child	p_i	10.0
	Half siblings	$p_i(1 + p_i)/2$	18.2
	Uncle and nephew[a]	$p_i(1 + p_i)/2$	18.2
	First cousins	$p_i(1 + 3p_i)/4$	30.8
	Unrelated	p_i^2	100.0

[a]Or uncle and niece, aunt and nephew, aunt and niece.

Table 2 Effects of population structure

		LR			
		$\theta = 0$	$\theta = 0.001$	$\theta = 0.01$	$\theta = 0.03$
$p = 0.01$	Heterozygote	5000	4152	1295	346
	Homozygote	10,000	6439	863	157
$p = 0.05$	Heterozygote	200	193	145	89
	Homozygote	400	364	186	73
$P = 0.10$	Heterozygote	50	49	43	34
	Homozygote	100	96	67	37

$$\Pr(G_C = A_iA_j | G_S = A_iA_j, \overline{H}, I) = \frac{2[\theta + (1-\theta)p_i][\theta + (1-\theta)p_j]}{(1+\theta)(1+2\theta)}$$

In these equations, θ is a measure of population structure. It can be considered as a measure of the variability of allele frequencies over subpopulations: the variance of the frequency of A_i over subpopulations is $\theta p_i(1 - p_i)$. It is also a measure of the relatedness of two alleles in the same subpopulation—the probability that two alleles in a subpopulation have a single ancestral allele. Some numerical consequences of allowing for population structure are shown in **Table 2**, in which all alleles have the same frequencies p.

One of the difficulties with this theory is in assigning a value to θ. If observations were available from a series of subpopulations within a population, then it is possible to estimate $(\theta - \phi)/(1 - \phi)$, where ϕ is the probability that two alleles in the whole population have a single ancestral allele. The quantity ϕ is often assumed to be zero, so that it is θ being estimated from subpopulation data. However, it is the lack of subpopulation data that has made the "θ-formulation" necessary in the first place, and the usual procedure is to assign a value, such as 0.03, to θ. It needs to be stressed that the equations apply on average for any subpopulation within the population.

Database Searches

There are now many large-scale databases of forensic DNA profiles, including those used by CODIS. These may be used to search for possible perpetrators or their relatives in cases in which there are no suspects or to seek evidence for links between different crimes. They could also be used to validate the statistical procedures used in this discussion.

Within-Database Comparisons

A database of 2000 (or 2 million) profiles allows for comparisons to be made between 1 million (or 1 trillion) pairs of profiles. Therefore, rare events may be found, including the event that two profiles are found to match. The matching is for any profile, as opposed to a prespecified particular profile, and this is an illustration of the "birthday problem," which states there is greater than 50% chance of finding two people in a group with the same birthday once the group size exceeds 23. The chance that two people will have a particular birthday is much smaller. This logic leads to the prediction that it is virtually certain that there are two people in the United States with the same 13-locus STR profile.

Cold-Hit Interpretation

When suspects are identified because their profiles in a database are found to match a crime-scene profile, there has been a suggestion that the strength of the DNA evidence should be downweighted. If the database has 1 million profiles, then an LR of 1 billion should be reduced to 1000 (1 billion divided by 1 million). The probability of finding a match will certainly increase as the database size increases and, indeed, finding a match is certain once the database includes the profiles of everyone. Although the prior probabilities that suspects identified by database searches change with database size, the LRs expressing the strength of the DNA evidence against the suspect(s) so identified are not changed by the size of the database.

Familial Searching

If a database profile is very similar to, but not exactly the same as, a crime-scene profile, then the possibility that it is from a close relative of the perpetrator is raised. Such familial searching has led to some successes in the cases or parent–offspring and full-sibling relationships. Familial searches can be guided by LRs that compare the probability of a database profile if it was from a relative of specified degree to the source of the query profile (using the equations in **Table 1**) to the probability that it was from a person unrelated to the source. Difficulties arise because the LRs may be higher by chance for those not related than for true relatives, and high stringency levels are needed to avoid the need to investigate large numbers of false positives. Familial searching is analogous to remains identification (e.g., after mass disasters such as the World Trade Center bombings).

Conclusion

The interpretation of matching DNA profiles often relies on some statements of probability. These statements refer to the chance of an unknown person having the profile given that a known person has been seen to have the same profile. A simple approach is to ignore the conditioning on the known person and use an estimate of the population frequency of the profile. However, this ignores the possibility that the known and unknown persons are related either by being in the same family or by being in the same population.

Further Reading

Beecham, G.W., Weir, B.S., 2011. Confidence intervals for DNA evidence likelihood ratios. Journal of Forensic Science S1, S166–S171.

Bieber, F., Brenner, C., Lazer, D., 2006. Finding criminals through DNA of their relatives. Science 312, 1315–1316.

Brenner, C.H., Weir, B.S., 2003. Issues and strategies in the DNA identification of World Trade Center victims. Theoretical Population Biology 63, 173–178.

Buckleton, J.S., Krawczak, M., Weir, B.S., 2011. The interpretation of lineage markers in forensic DNA testing. Forensic Science International: Genetics 5, 78–83.

Evett, I.W., Weir, B.S., 1998. Interpreting DNA Evidence: Statistical Genetics for Forensic Science. Sinauer, Sunderland, MA.

Laurie, C., Weir, B.S., 2003. Dependency effects in multi-locus match probabilities. Theoretical Population Biology 63, 207–219.

National Research Council, 2009. Strengthening Forensic Science in the United States: A Path Forward. National Academy Press, Washington, DC.

Weir, B.S., 1996. Genetic Data Analysis II. Sinauer, Sunderland, MA.

Weir, B.S., 2004. Matching and partially-matching DNA profiles. Journal of Forensic Science 49, 1009–1014.

Weir, B.S., 2007. The rarity of DNA profiles. Annals of Applied Statistics 1, 358–370.

Relevant Websites

http://www.fbi.gov—The Federal Bureau of Investigation: Laboratory Services, Combined DNA Index System.

Significance

SJ Walsh, Australian Federal Police, Canberra, ACT, Australia

Glossary

Allele frequency The frequency of occurrence of an STR allele in a particular population dataset, used in estimating the significance of a DNA profile match.

F_{ST} A parameter, sometimes known as the coancestry coefficient, used in the subpopulation model to accommodate for subpopulation effects on the significance of a DNA profile match.

Hardy–Weinberg equilibrium A theory to describe the association of alleles at a locus, which assumes independent association of alleles within and between loci.

Likelihood ratio An estimate made up of the ratio of two conditional probabilities that is used to introduce scientific evidence under Bayes' theorem.

Population database Collections of DNA profile data from individuals who have been grouped according to their ethnicity or biogeographic ancestry.

Product rule Simple method for estimating the significance of a DNA profile match, which relies on an assumption of Hardy–Weinberg and Linkage equilibria.

STRs Short tandem repeats or microsatellites.

Subpopulation model Approach for estimating the significance of a DNA profile match that accommodates for subpopulation effects.

Introduction

Forensic DNA profiling using conventional autosomal short tandem repeat (STR) markers typically relies on a comparison between a profile derived from an item of evidence (usually originating from a crime scene) and a profile derived from an individual (who is somehow associated with the matter under investigation). When the profiles under comparison correspond, this indicates that the donor of the known sample may also be the source of the profile derived from the evidence item. The question remains as to what significance, or evidential weight, can be placed on this particular scientific observation, and, more importantly, what inference can be drawn from it regarding the involvement of a particular individual in the matter under investigation? Evaluating this question is extremely complex and requires a forensic biologist to apply interpretation skills that are grounded in an array of disciplines including population genetics and statistics. This challenge is exacerbated when the profile itself is complex, such as in the case of mixed-, partial-, or low-template DNA profiles. The inherent difficulty of this aspect of forensic DNA profiling has meant that the attempts to address the issue of significance have been, and remain in some instances, the source of ongoing scientific debate. In addition, this aspect of forensic DNA profiling has been a source of considerable confusion and conjecture within the legal system. Notwithstanding these contextual challenges, accurate assessment of the weight of the DNA evidence is central to its admissibility in courts of law.

A Brief Summary of Approaches to Estimating the Significance of DNA Evidence

Throughout the history of their application, forensic DNA profiling techniques have targeted panels of highly polymorphic (or hypervariable) loci. As such, the profiles produced from these techniques are known to be highly discriminating from individual to individual. Demonstrating this level of discrimination (essentially the significance of the DNA evidence) typically begins with a survey of the distribution of the alleles and genotypes observed in a population sample. In the early years of forensic DNA profiling, these population samples comprised profiles from 100 to 200 individuals who had been assigned to major population groups, such as Caucasians. The assignment of ethnicity was usually based on self-declaration or appearance. The frequencies of alleles and genotypes observed in these population samples were tested using foundation population genetic tests such as tests for within- and between-locus independence. The results of within- and between-locus independence testing were usually extrapolated to infer concordance or otherwise with Hardy–Weinberg and linkage equilibria, respectively. Departures from Hardy–Weinberg and/or linkage equilibria were rarely observed in the data tested, leading to the view that the association between the alleles and genotypes was independent. This meant that the significance of observing a particular DNA profile match could be estimated by multiplying allele frequencies across the loci profiled using a technique known as the "product rule," a method that relies on the assumption of Hardy–Weinberg and linkage equilibria. This approach had long been applied in blood grouping analysis, which in many respects was the forerunner to forensic DNA profiling and had been utilized under very similar circumstances.

The assessment of the significance of DNA evidence using the product rule was controversial and led to the admissibility of this statistical interpretation approach being challenged. In some highly significant legal cases (such as *People v Castro* in the United States and *R v Tran* and *R v Lucas* in Australia), these challenges were accepted as legitimate and the statistical interpretation evidence was excluded. The successful challenges emerged from the basis of population genetics and the view that known human population genetic effects were not adequately addressed through the product rule approach, and, therefore, the estimates of the significance of the DNA evidence were flawed and were likely to have an inherent bias in favor of the prosecution. The level of scientific debate, significant enough to be referred to as the "DNA wars," meant that this aspect of the DNA profiling evidence failed the general acceptance admissibility criteria for expert scientific evidence and was excluded. Attempts were made to introduce the scientific data itself (the DNA profile) without an estimate of its significance or evidential weight; however, these were also unsuccessful, as courts felt that without an estimate of significance, jurors would have no sound basis upon which to weigh the strength of the evidence and this would lead to speculation and the potential for the prejudicial effect to outweigh the actual probative value of the evidence. It is important to also bear in mind that the introduction of DNA profiling (or DNA fingerprinting as it was then known) into the criminal justice system had been accompanied by considerable fanfare regarding its revolutionary potential as an evidential tool.

A number of enduring practical effects emerged from this formative period. First, superior courts in a number of countries had ruled that the initial methods for estimating the significance of DNA evidence were inadmissible. This led to significant efforts worldwide to determine a more comprehensive approach to the issue that would address the concerns raised by the broader scientific community. Second, courts had also made it patently clear that forensic DNA evidence would be inadmissible if there was not an accompanying estimate of the strength or significance of the observed DNA results. This accentuated the need to resolve the scientific issues, but it also established the requirement to estimate the statistical strength of forensic DNA evidence in all matters where those results were required to be presented in evidence.

Having now placed the requirement of estimating the significance (or weight) of DNA results as central to its admissibility as evidence, the development of more refined and flexible approaches began to receive considerable attention from the forensic, population genetic, and statistical communities. The issue was also the subject of high level reviews that sought to establish standards and benchmarks that would stabilize practices within the field and reassure the legal sector. The results of this period of development were the emergence of probabilistic models based on Bayesian principles. In summary, Bayes' theorem allows one to consider what you already know and see how much new evidence changes your assessment of the overall evidence. It relies on considering any given proposition by ascertaining the prior probability (or likelihood) of its occurrence and then measuring the influence of new evidence to arrive at the posterior probability (or likelihood) of the hypothesis. The new evidence is presented as a likelihood ratio (LR), which has a multiplication effect on the prior probability.

The use of Bayes' theorem in the context of forensic evidence interpretation is widely accepted in the international forensic community. The court is interested in one question: How much does the scientific evidence alter the probability that the accused is guilty or innocent? Under these circumstances, the Bayesian approach has distinct advantages over other estimates, if for no other reason than that it forces the scientist to think within the framework of the legal process and answer questions based on the function of the DNA profile as an item of evidential significance.

The basics of the statistical approach commonly applied in this area are as follows:

Consider that a suspect has been charged and the court must now assess the probability of his guilt $Pr(G)$, given the evidence E presented before it, $Pr(G|E)$. The scientist can only provide information related to the probability of the evidence $Pr(E)$. For the purpose of this discussion, E refers to the DNA profiling result requiring assessment—typically, that the defendant's profile G_S matches the crime scene profile G_{CS}.

The significance of the DNA evidence is estimated by evaluating the likelihood of observing the DNA profiling result, given two alternative hypotheses that could explain its occurrence. Typically, these are referred to as the prosecution hypothesis (H_p) and the defense hypothesis (H_d). A generic example of H_p is that the defendant *is* the source of the crime scene profile. Conversely, a generic example of H_d is that the defendant is not the source of the crime scene profile and that it has originated from an unrelated individual who, by coincidence, shares the same DNA profile as the defendant. These hypotheses are generic, but a significant benefit of this approach is that the hypotheses can be altered to better reflect the circumstances of the case. This gives this method great flexibility.

The ratio of these two probabilities is called the likelihood ratio. Mathematically, this is expressed as:

$$LR = \frac{\Pr(E|G_{CS}, G_S, H_p)}{\Pr(E|G_{CS}, G_S, H_d)}$$

where E is the DNA profiling result, G_{CS} is the genotype of the crime stain, G_S is the genotype of the defendant, H_p is the prosecution hypothesis, and H_d is the defense hypothesis.

The most widely applied approach that follows the principles outlined above is the subpopulation model of Balding and Nichols. An added advantage of this method is that it incorporates a means to accommodate for population genetic effects occurring as a result of genetic drift. The subpopulation model addresses many of the shortcomings of the product rule that had resulted in the early legal controversies. For example, the subpopulation model expressly rejects the assumption of the Hardy–Weinberg and linkage equilibria (at the population level) and therefore does not rely on an assumption of independence. Employing the subpopulation model requires the evaluation and use of a parameter sometimes known as the coancestry coefficient, or F_{ST}. Estimating F_{ST} requires the collection and analysis of subpopulation data and an appreciation and understanding of the population genetic relationships that exist within and between such groups. Therefore, an inherent advantage of the subpopulation model is the integration of population genetic understanding within the methodology, as it requires a deeper level of awareness and application of population genetics to be a routine aspect of the forensic DNA profiling field. Having a model that accommodates for population genetics embedded within a Bayesian framework that allows for flexible assessment of the relevant hypotheses is a powerful interpretation model that is commonly thought of as a gold standard within the forensic sciences.

To derive the formulae necessary to calculate a DNA likelihood ratio (or match probability, if taking the inverse) under this framework, Balding and Nichols presented an altered form of Wright's sampling formula. This equation can be used in all common casework circumstances to estimate the probability of observing the next allele in the probative genotype. Mathematically, it is expressed as:

$$\frac{(x\theta + (1-\theta)p_a)}{(1+(n-1)\theta)}$$

where x is the number of times the allele under consideration (a) has been observed, n is the total number of alleles observed, p_a is the frequency of allele a in the relevant population, and θ is the coancestry coefficient (or F_{ST}).

From the sampling formula, it is possible to derive likelihood ratio equations for the vast majority of common circumstances encountered in forensic DNA casework, such as single-source stains, mixed profiles, and disputed parentage and kinship investigations. This approach, therefore, forms the basis of the statistical methodology applied in casework.

Practical Application of Estimates of the Significance of DNA Evidence

The evolution of fundamental approaches for evaluating the significance of DNA profiling evidence, such as the subpopulation model, established a basis for evidence interpretation that resolved the major early legal concerns such that admissibility challenges to this evidence began to abate. However, as the forensic DNA profiling field is such a dynamic and rapidly changing one, evidence interpretation methods have also had to undergo constant revision, refinement, and extension, and, after doing so, they have naturally been subjected to further legal scrutiny. In the following sections, the major elements of change and scrutiny are summarized as an indication of the evolution of this already complex area.

Source of Population Data and Understanding the Influence of Population Genetics

When evaluating the DNA profiling results, the generic alternate proposition to explain a match observed between a profile arising from a crime stain and the profile of a sampled individual is that there is another individual, who has not been sampled and would also match the crime stain profile, by chance. This immediately invokes the wider population, which, given our understanding of modern human population genetics, cannot be considered as a homogeneous single population but as a collection of subpopulations that have diverged over time and through factors such as genetic drift have developed distinguishable genetic distributions at the subpopulation level. A natural question arising from these two starting points (that someone in the population may also have a matching profile and that the population is made up of subpopulations) is which subpopulations would be the most relevant to consider, and what would be the implications of selecting the wrong ones? Clearly, this question needs to be considered in relation to the agreed elements of the matter at hand and is not something that can be unilaterally decided in the forensic DNA laboratory. On occasion, such questions have substantial gravity in a criminal trial, and it may be necessary for a forensic scientist to utilize population data from remote collections. Fortunately, through the wide-scale applicability of these issues, a very large amount of population data has been compiled and tested by forensic institutions. Another means to accommodate such issues is through an assessment of a more appropriate value for F_{ST}. This parameter can represent the genetic distance between two populations diverging as a result of genetic drift, and, as such, increasing the value for F_{ST} in the equations that lead to the significance estimate can compensate for potential disparities between the selected subpopulation and the unknown true offender. In standard reporting protocols, major subpopulations residing in the region are sampled, tested, and applied as a matter of routine in the generation of significance estimates. The estimates also incorporate a value for F_{ST} that is reflective of the population genetic testing of these assembled data sets and other information arising from the understanding of modern human population genetics.

Estimating significance using an approach such as the subpopulation model seeks to accommodate aspects of modern human population genetics that may influence the estimate. This is done in a range of ways. First, the hypotheses chosen to evaluate the significance of the DNA evidence should reflect any relevant considerations that may assist the court or inquiry. For example, if there is reason to consider the proposition that the crime stain was left by a relative of the matching individual, the consideration would drastically alter the value of the final estimate but can be directly evaluated by altering the hypotheses accordingly. Second, the population data relied on in the calculations must have been collected, analyzed, and reported to a standard that is accepted by the forensic community. This process aims to ensure that significant population genetic features of the data are observed and, hence, can be accommodated through thoughtful application of the model. Finally, as recognition of the fact that our understanding of modern human population genetics at the level relevant for this purpose is still emerging, scientists must ensure that collection, profiling, and analysis occur as an ongoing process, particularly when novel markers are being considered or introduced.

Complex Profiles—Mixtures

The continuing improvement in the sensitivity and robustness of modern DNA profiling techniques has seen their application within the law enforcement context increase and broaden over time. It is possible to recover a probative DNA profile from as few as 50 cells left behind on an evidence item. This is one of the inherent strengths of forensic DNA profiling evidence; however, it is also a characteristic that leads to the observation of mixed DNA profiles, or profiles that have originated from more than one individual. Typically, the observation that the DNA profile is mixed heightens the complexity of the profile interpretation and the estimation of evidential significance. In lay terms, the observation of a mixed DNA profile reduces the overall strength of the evidence against a matching defendant, as the presence of additional DNA increases the number of possible donors who could also have contributed to the stain. Mixed profiles can vary considerably in their complexity and can therefore be approached in a range of ways. Some approaches seek to simplify the interpretation by making certain assumptions regarding the profile, such as the binary method that often requires an assumption regarding the number of contributors. These methods are sometimes criticized for including subjective, or opinion-based, aspects that taken to their extreme may lead to a nonconservative estimate. Some approaches seek to simplify the interpretation by making no assumptions at all, such as the probability of inclusion or random-man-not-excluded approach. These methods ignore a substantial amount of the scientific data available and as a result can be less accurate. Representative bodies such as the International Society for Forensic Genetics (ISFG) have assisted scientists by producing recommendations on how to approach the interpretation of complex profiles such as mixtures.

Complex Profiles—Partial- or Low-template DNA Profiles

Partial, or incomplete, DNA profiles also commonly occur in forensic casework. Because there is some data absent from the evidential profile, its significance, accordingly, is reduced. In addition, the profile is usually incomplete because of the lack of good-quality DNA in the starting sample, and this may cause stochastic or technical artifacts to also be present in the profile to a greater degree than would be the case in an optimum sample. Partial profiles only complicate the estimate of significance when there is ambiguity over the genotype designation at an individual locus. Standard methods have been extended to accommodate the inclusion of partial loci in the overall estimate.

Profiles derived from low-template samples are also commonplace in forensic science and can often represent the most critical evidence available in a case. For example, in a cold case where evidence from a historic matter is being reexamined, the DNA material would have been subject to substantial degradation and decay. This in turn compromises the ability to retrieve a profile, and, often, analysis results in a profile that is partial and/or has stochastic artifacts. Because of the importance of such evidence, techniques have been developed (such as low-copy-number profiling) that further increase the sensitivity of DNA profiling methods and increase the probability of obtaining a usable profile. A side effect of these techniques is that they can exacerbate the likelihood and magnitude of stochastic artifacts, and, therefore, their interpretation has required the development of advanced approaches that model the behavior of profile components and accommodate these additional variables in the estimate of significance.

Nonautosomal Markers

Methods for estimating the significance of profiles arising from testing of nonautosomal DNA markers (such as mitochondrial

DNA sequences or Y-chromosome STRs) are generally less evolved than those applied to routine autosomal STR profiles. The distinguishing genetic features of nonautosomal profiles prevent the direct application of statistical methods derived for autosomal STRs; however, some similarities apply. While nonautosomal profiles (or haplotypes) are shared with little to no variation among members of a maternal (in the case of mtDNA) or paternal (in the case of Y-STRs) lineages, it is still necessary to understand the frequency of occurrence of observed haplotypes within relevant subpopulations. Collection and analysis of subpopulation data is in fact more necessary for forensic laboratories utilizing nonautosomal markers, as they are more subject to microdifferentiation at the subpopulation level and this requires understanding and consideration as a component of the estimate of significance. Population data sets of mtDNA or Y-STR haplotypes are queried to determine the number of times the evidential haplotype appears. In most cases, the count of observations itself is presented as the estimate of significance, as application of more advanced probabilistic or Bayesian methods is very complex.

Estimating Significance Following a DNA Database Search

The strength of the DNA evidence resulting from an intelligence database match is often presented without any mention that the match was initially obtained from a database. It is usually not in the defendant's interest to let a jury know that he or she has a sample on the DNA database, as a negative inference may be drawn. The question of whether searching a DNA database for a match affects the significance of the evidence has been discussed extensively and forcefully in the literature. The issue also affects any search among suspects whether they are on a database or not. Unfortunately, there is much confused writing and it has at times proven very difficult for courts to make a reasoned decision in the face of quite divergent scientific views. One school of thought on this issue recommends that an adjustment be made to the estimate of significance if the identification of the defendant followed from a DNA database search. This adjustment suggests reducing the likelihood ratio estimate (or increasing, in the case of a DNA match probability) by a factor equal to the number of people in the database (N). Using a simple example of a DNA database containing the profiles of 100,000 individuals and a profile with a likelihood ratio of 1,000,000, this would result in an adjusted likelihood ratio of 10 being reported to the court. This approach is often referred to as the Np rule, where Np indicates that the random match probability p is multiplied by the size of the database, N. The conservativeness of this recommendation increases as N increases, and the proposal loses logical appeal. For example, if the database were to hold the profiles of the entire world, and there was only one matching individual, it would logically provide an irrefutable association, yet should Np be employed, the discriminating power of the match would be reduced by a factor of 7 billion and would be reported as something entirely unconvincing. The alternative school of thought follows Bayesian reasoning to demonstrate that the significance is in fact strengthened by the identification of a matching profile following a DNA database search. This is because in conducting such a search, all nonmatching individuals in the database have been excluded, thereby increasing the significance of the evidence against the remaining matched individuals (relative to the circumstance where they had been compared directly without employing a DNA database search).

See also: **Behavioral:** Interpretation; DNA—Statistical Probability; Low-template DNA Testing; Mixture Interpretation (Interpretation of Mixed DNA Profiles with STRs Only); Parentage Testing and Kinship Analysis; **Foundations:** Overview and Meaning of Identification/Individualization; Statistical Interpretation of Evidence: Bayesian Analysis; The Frequentist Approach to Forensic Evidence Interpretation.

Further Reading

Aitken, C.G.G., Taroni, F., 2004. Statistics and the Evaluation of Evidence for Forensic Scientists, second ed. Wiley, Chichester.

Balding, D.J., 2005. Weight of Evidence for Forensic DNA Profiles. Wiley, Chichester.

Balding, D.J., Donnelly, P., 1995. Evaluating DNA profile evidence when the suspect is identified through a database search. Journal of Forensic Sciences 41, 603–607.

Balding, D.J., Nichols, R.A., 1994. DNA profile match probability calculation: how to allow for population stratification, relatedness, database selection and single bands. Forensic Science International 64, 125–140.

Buckleton, J.S., Curran, J.M., Walsh, S.J., 2006. How reliable is the sub-population model in DNA testimony? Forensic Science International 15, 144–148.

Buckleton, J.S., Krawczak, M., Weir, B.S., 2011. The interpretation of lineage markers in forensic DNA testing. Forensic Science International: Genetics 5, 78–83.

Buckleton, J.S., Triggs, C.M., Walsh, S.J., 2005. Forensic DNA Evidence Interpretation. CRC, Boca Raton, FL.

Curran, J.M., Walsh, S.J., Buckleton, J.S., 2007. Empirical testing of estimated DNA frequencies. Forensic Science International: Genetics 1, 267–272.

Evett, I.W., Jackson, G., Lambert, J.A., 2000. More on the hierarchy of propositions: exploring the distinction between explanations and propositions. Science & Justice 40, 3–10.

Evett, I.W., Weir, B.S., 1998. Interpreting DNA Evidence. Sinauer Associates, Sunderland, MA.

Gill, P., Brenner, C.H., Buckleton, J.S., et al., 2006. DNA Commission of the International Society of Forensic Genetics: recommendations on the interpretation of mixtures. Forensic Science International 160, 90–101.

Gusmão, L., Butler, J.M., Carracedo, A., et al., 2006. DNA Commission of the International Society of Forensic Genetics (ISFG): an update of the recommendations on the use of Y-STRs in forensic analysis. Forensic Science International 157, 187–197.

Kaye, D.H., 2010. The Double Helix and the Law of Evidence. Harvard University Press, Cambridge, MA.

NRC, 1992. National Research Council Report: DNA Technology in Forensic Science. Report of the National Academy Press, Washington, DC.

NRC_II, 1996. National Research Council Report: The Evaluation of Forensic DNA Evidence. Report of the National Academy Press, Washington, DC.

Robertson, B., Vignaux, G.A., 1997. Interpreting Evidence: Evaluating Forensic Science in the Courtroom. Wiley, Chichester.

Weir, B.S., 2004. Matching and partially matching profiles. Journal of Forensic Sciences 49, 1009–1014.

Weir, B.S., Cockerham, C.C., 1984. Estimating F-statistics for the analysis of population structure. Evolution 38, 1358–1370.

Relevant Websites

http://www.strdna-db.org—Autosomal STR DNA (database).
http://www.empop.org—EMPOP (European mtDNA Population Database).
http://www.isfg.org—International Society for Forensic Genetics.
http://www.mitomap.org—MITOMAP (A human mitochondrial DNA database).
http://www.cstl.nist.gov—Short Tandem Repeat DNA Internet Database.
http://www.yhrd.org—Y-STR Haplotype Reference Database (YHRD).

The Frequentist Approach to Forensic Evidence Interpretation

JM Curran, University of Auckland, Auckland, New Zealand

Glossary

Probability A quantity between 0 and 1 that represents the chance of an event occurring. Probabilities may sometimes be expressed as percentages, or as odds, without loss of information. A probability may also be used to express a degree of belief that an event will occur. Such probabilities are often referred to as "subjective."

Probability (density) function A probability function describes the probabilities associated with the values of a discrete random variable. When the random variable is a continuous measurement, such as time or length, then a probability density function describes the density associated with a particular outcome. Density refers to the height of the curve. For a continuous random variable, the probability of an event is given by the area under the probability density curve.

Random experiment A situation in which the outcome is not known in advance. One may know what the possible outcomes are, but the exact outcome is not known until the experiment is conducted.

Random variable A variable that measures the outcome of a random experiment. One may know the range of possible values that a random variable may take on, but not the actual value until the experiment has been conducted.

Sample The word sample in the statistical sense means a set, or group, of objects or measurements taken from a larger population. In this article, sample means a set of (representative) objects taken from the crime scene source or recovered from a suspect.

Specimen The word specimen is used to avoid confusion with the word sample. A specimen in this chapter means a smaller part, or subsample, of some evidential source. For example, one may refer to a specimen of paint from the scene. This embodies the fact that one does not have a choice when selecting a specimen; therefore, one cannot be sure that the specimen is representative of the source.

Common questions in forensic science are "Did this evidence come from this crime scene?" or "Does this blood come from that man?" The answers to these questions become probabilistic when the circumstances become less than certain. Statistical inference provides the tools and the framework in which probability can be addressed. Questions like those above are often called "questions of common source" and have been addressed with a variety of statistical frequentist techniques. These techniques are best illustrated with an example.

Example

The following example is taken from the field of forensic glass evidence interpretation.

A window is broken during the commission of a crime. Several hours later, a suspect is apprehended. Six small fragments of glass are recovered in a search of the suspect's clothing, footwear, and headgear. Random samples of six fragments of glass are taken from the crime scene window. The glass recovered from the suspect is called the "recovered" (or questioned) sample (or specimen), and the glass taken from the scene is called the "control" sample. The refractive indices (RIs) of each fragment in each sample were determined and are given in **Table 1**.

In the ensuing sections, some summary statistics derived from the data in **Table 1** will be useful.

Table 1 The RIs of a control and recovered sample of glass

Control	*Recovered*
1.529077	1.529049
1.529085	1.529108
1.52912	1.529118
1.529133	1.529141
1.529135	1.529146
1.529189	1.529153

 http://dx.doi.org/10.1016/B978-0-12-800647-4.00023-0

Range Tests

Range tests broadly describe a class of methods that compare measurements made on evidence recovered from a suspect to the range of the control source. The range of a set of measurements is defined at the interval from the minimum observed value to the maximum observed value. For example, the range can be expressed as an interval or as a length given by the difference of the maximum and the minimum (e.g., 0.000112). The interval definition is used in this entry.

The simplest range test compares the recovered measurements in sequence to the control sample range. If a measurement falls outside of the control range, then it is deemed not to have originated from the control source. In the glass example, the smallest recovered RI measurement (1.529049) falls below the smallest control measurement; therefore, this fragment is deemed not to have come from the scene. The minimum observed in the control sample above and the maximum observed in the following control sample below are the remainder of the recovered measurements; therefore, these fragments are deemed to have come from the control source. That is, in this example, five of the six recovered fragments found on the suspect are said to have come from the crime scene. The choice of language in this example is deliberately simple to illustrate the technique rather than provide a comprehensive statement about the strength of the evidence. A weaker statement might be that the control and recovered fragments have common physical characteristics.

This type of range test is easily extended to the multivariate situation. The need for this extension arises in situations in which multiple measurements are made on different attributes of the same object. For example, elemental analysis techniques are commonly used in forensic science. These techniques simultaneously measure the concentrations of a number of chemical elements in a specimen. The criterion for making a statement of common source, or of similar characteristics, is that all of the measurements made on the recovered specimen must fall within the range observed in the control sample. An example is shown in **Table 2**. The recovered sample measurement for zirconium (99) falls outside of the range observed in the control sample; therefore, this measurement would be said not to have come from the control source.

Range tests such as those described above are very simple to carry out and require no sophisticated computation of any sort. However, they are very susceptible to outliers. In the statistical sense, outliers are measurements that are considerably different from the bulk of the measurements. Outliers may arise from true measurement error, misclassification, contamination, or simply by chance.

Most statisticians do not use the range as an estimate of the spread or variability of a set of measurements in any other context than simple description. Most formal statistical procedures that require a measure of variability use the sample standard deviation. This idea motivates a set of improved range tests that are sometimes called two-sigma (2σ) or three-sigma (3σ) rules.

In the simple range test, the recovered measurements are compared to an interval defined by the minimum and maximum observed values in the control sample. A 2σ rule is used to modify the control interval to the interval defined by the control mean plus or minus twice the control standard deviation; that is, $(\bar{x}_C - 2s_C, \bar{x}_C + 2s_C)$, where $\bar{x}_C$ and s_C are the mean and standard deviation of the control sample. If a 3σ rule is used, then the interval is defined by $\bar{x}_C \pm 3s_C$. Using the summary statistics in **Table 3**, the 2σ control interval is

$$\begin{aligned}\bar{x}_C \pm 2s_C &= \big(1.529077 - 2 \times 4.04 \times 10^{-5},\\ &\quad 1.529077 + 2 \times 4.04 \times 10^{5}\big)\\ &= (1.529042, 1.529204)\end{aligned}$$

The choice of two or three is motivated by what is known in statistics as the 68-95-99.7, σ-2σ-3σ, or the empirical rule, which states that for normally distributed data, approximately 68% of the observations lie within 1 standard deviation of the mean, approximately 95% of the observations lie within 2 standard deviations of the mean, and approximately 99.7% of the observations lie within 3 standard deviation of the mean. In the forensic glass example, all of the observations lie within 2 standard deviations of the mean (i.e., within the 2σ interval). Although 2σ rules have better statistical properties, the sequential comparison of the recovered measurements to the control intervals has an unacceptably high false exclusion rate, in which the probability of declaring at least one measurement in a set of n_r measurements to be from a different source when they are indeed from the same source is given by

$$P = 1 - (1 - \alpha)^{n_r}$$

Table 2 An example of a range test with elemental concentration data

	Fe	*Mn*	*Ba*	*Sr*	*Zr*	*Cr*
Control minimum	1978	53	166	143	70	1494
Control maximum	2322	62	200	169	90	1771
Recovered	2320	62	192	166	99	1766

Table 3 Summary statistics for the control and recovered measurements

Statistic	*Control*	*Recovered*
Minimum	1.529077	1.529049
Mean ($\bar{X}$)	1.529123	1.529119
Maximum	1.529189	1.529153
Standard deviation(s)	4.04×10^{-5}	3.84×10^{-5}

The value of α is 0.05 or 0.003 depending on whether a 2σ or 3σ rule is being used. This issue is known as a multiple comparison problem and occurs in many situations in statistics. Several practitioners claim that false inclusions rather than false exclusions are the more serious problem. That is, if a recovered item is said to have a common source with the control measurements when it is truly from a different source, then the evidence may implicate the defendant in a crime he or she did not commit. In theory, the more different the control and recovered measurements, the lower is the chance of a false inclusion. However, in practice, small sample sizes, which are common in forensic science, can badly affect the statistical properties of all approaches. In statistical terms, such tests are said to have low power. This means they have a poor probability of detecting a true difference when one exists. Both arguments have some validity, but neither is important because the frequentist approach does not consider the evidence with respect to the alternative hypothesis.

2σ rules may be used with multivariate data. The idea is easily extended by calculating 2σ or 3σ intervals for each variable measured in the control sample. If a measurement made on the recovered sample falls outside of any of the control sample intervals, then a statement of common source is not made. The extra comparisons, incurred by the extra measurements made on each item, compound the multiple comparison problem. Theoretically, this could be overcome by calculating a confidence ellipsoid for the control, which is the multivariate equivalent of the interval. However, in practice, this is almost never done.

The shortcomings of range tests may be addressed by using summary statistics on the samples, such as the sample means, rather than the individual measurements. This approach has the advantage that it is less susceptible to outliers, it is less susceptible (but not immune) to multiple comparison problems, and it uses as much information as possible from the data in a single step. Such approaches usually fall into the framework of formal statistical hypothesis tests.

Formal Hypothesis Tests

The frequentist hypothesis-testing framework is commonly used in the scientific literature. It has been used in a number of forensic disciplines to statistically address the issue of common source. This approach typically revolves around the comparison of the two sample means with respect to the observed variation in the samples.

However, most statistical hypothesis tests follow the same general steps:

1. Ask a question.
2. Formulate your question statistically; that is, find a statistic you think might answer your question.
3. Propose a null hypothesis.
4. Propose an alternative hypothesis.
5. Calculate your test statistic.
6. Calculate the P value.
7. Interpret the P value.

These steps use terms that require a brief definition. The null hypothesis is generally the hypothesis of no difference or no change. It means that any difference or change could easily be explained by random chance alone. It is a hypothesis that represents the statement "These measurements are (statistically) indistinguishable" or "These measurements come from the same source." It is important to note that the second statement is not accurately reflected by the null hypothesis. The alternative hypothesis, although not formally included in the computation, is the hypothesis of difference or change. The test statistic is a summary number that may be calculated from the observed data. The P value is defined in words as "the probability of observing a test statistic as large as, or larger than, the one observed if the null hypothesis is true." If X is any test statistic and X_0 is the value of an observed statistic in a particular case, then the P value can be written statistically as

$$P = \Pr(X \geq X_0 | H_0 \quad \text{true})$$

If the P value is small, then the correct interpretation is that the test statistic is unlikely to have occurred by random chance alone if the null hypothesis is true. In this situation, it is common to say that "the null hypothesis is rejected." If the P value is small, it is incorrect to assume that the result would be more likely if the alternative hypothesis were true. It is incorrect to make this assumption because no part of the calculation makes any reference to the alternative hypothesis; therefore, the result might be equally unlikely under the alternative hypothesis. If the P value is large, then the correct interpretation is that the test statistic is likely to have occurred by random chance alone if the null hypothesis were true. Again, any interpretation that then infers that the result is unlikely under the alternative hypothesis is incorrect. The P value is not the probability that the null hypothesis is true.

Significance Levels and Small or Big Values

The definition of what constitutes a small or large value is arbitrary, but it is related to the acceptable risk of rejecting the null hypothesis when it really is true. This type of mistake is called a type I error. In practice, if the P value is less than 0.05 or 0.01, then it is deemed to be small. The choice of these numbers is arbitrary, but they can be crudely interpreted as being "less than 1 chance in 20 (or 1 chance in 100)" of making an incorrect decision (on average, if the null hypothesis is true). The caveats in the brackets in the previous sentence are quite important and are often overlooked.

The critical values 0.05, 0.01, etc., are called the significance of the test in the Neyman–Pearson orthodoxy and is usually denoted as α. The significance is, specifically, the probability of making a type I error that the user is prepared to accept. Acceptance of this probability is not dictated by the test, but by the cost associated with making an incorrect decision. In science, $\alpha = 0.05$ is typically used. However, in legal situations, it may be preferable to use $\alpha \leq 0.01$. This is often viewed as complying with Blackstone's ratio. English jurist William Blackstone said: "(It is) better that 10 guilty persons escape than that one innocent suffer," although if $\alpha = 0.01$, then the ratio is 100:1 rather than Blackstone's 10:1. However, decreasing the value of α is not without consequence. The smaller the value of α, the harder it becomes to reject the null hypothesis when it is false or, equivalently, to detect a difference when one truly exists. That is, the significance of a test α has a complementary relationship with the probability of making a type II error, β. β is the probability of a false acceptance, or the probability of deciding that the null hypothesis is true when in fact the alternative is true. The quantity $1-\beta$ is called the power of a test. As α decreases, β increases and, correspondingly, the power of the test is reduced.

The significance of a test is often stated in a number of different ways. People alternatively use α, $1-\alpha$, $100 \times \alpha\%$, and $100 \times (1-\alpha)\%$. That is, statements such as "the test was significant at the 0.05, 0.95, 5%, and 95% level" all occur frequently in the scientific literature. The original Neyman–Pearson framework defined α as the significance level; however, the intention of the alternatives given above is usually understood. If a P value is smaller than the significance level (α), then the test is often said to be significant at the α level. Correspondingly, if the P value is greater than the significance level, then the test is said to be not significant at the α level.

Hypothesis tests are more easily understood when referring to specific tests rather than in general terms. The two-sample t test has a long tradition in scientific literature and has been used in forensic science. It is discussed in the next section.

The Two-Sample *t* Test

The two-sample t test is often used to test the hypothesis that the control sample and the recovered sample come from distributions with the same mean and variance. The inference in this situation is that if the fragments do come from distributions with the same mean and variance, then they are indistinguishable and therefore may have a common source. This is often incorrectly interpreted as "the recovered fragments come from the crime scene."

The two-sample t test compares the difference in the sample means to the difference that one would expect by random variation, or chance, alone. The idea is to make a probability statement about the difference in the true, but unknown, means of the sources that the samples come from. If the means are the same, then one can say that "the recovered sample cannot be distinguished from the control scene."

Formally, let the n_c measurements on the control sample be denoted x_i, $i = 1, \ldots, n_c$, and the n_r measurements on the recovered sample be denoted y_j, $j = 1, \ldots, n_r$. The control sample is assumed to have come from a normal distribuation with mean μ_c and standard deviation σ_c. Similarly, the recovered sample is assumed to have come from a normal distribution with mean μ_r and standard deviation σ_r. This is expressed as $x_i \sim N(\mu_c, \sigma_c)$ and $y_j \sim N(\mu_r, \sigma_r)$. The traditional (pooled) two-sample t test formally tests the null hypothesis that the distribution means are the same under the explicit assumption that $\sigma_c = \sigma_r = \sigma$ (and therefore that the sample standard deviations are each an estimate of the common standard deviation σ):

$$H_0 : \mu_c = \mu_r \text{ or equivalently } H_0 : \mu_c - \mu_r = 0$$

The alternative hypothesis is that the distribution means are different:

$$H_1 : \mu_c \neq \mu_r \text{ or equivalently } H_0 : \mu_c - \mu_r \neq 0$$

To test the null hypothesis, a test statistic is compared to the distribution of values one would expect to observe if the null hypothesis is true. For the two-sample t test, the test statistic is given by

$$T_0 = \frac{\bar{x} - \bar{y}}{\sqrt{\left(\frac{1}{n_c} + \frac{1}{n_r}\right)\frac{(n_c-1)s_c^2 + (n_r-1)s_r^2}{n_c + n_r - 2}}}$$

where $\bar{x}, \bar{y}, s_c$, and s_r are the sample means and sample standard deviations of the control and recovered samples, respectively. The significance of the test is evaluated by comparing the observed value of T_0 to the distribution of values one would observe if the null hypothesis is true, or the null distribution. For the two-sample t test, this is the Student's t distribution and is parameterized by its degrees of freedom. The degrees of freedom, $\text{df} = n_c + n_r - 2$, reflect the sample size, and in some sense the amount of information that is available. The comparison of the observed test statistic to the null distribution is summarized by the P value.

For the two-sample t test, this becomes

$$P = \Pr(T \geq T_0 | H_0 \quad \text{true})$$

The absolute value of the test statistic is used here because it makes no difference whether the recovered mean is smaller or larger than the control mean, merely the fact that it is different. It is important to note that the equal variance assumption can be relaxed. There are occasional circumstances in which this is a sensible option. This version of the t test is known as Welch's t

test. The formula for the test statistic has a different denominator, and the formula for the degrees of freedom is much more complicated, but bounded by min $(n_c, n_r)-1$ and $n_c + n_r-2$.

The pooled two-sample t test can be illustrated using the glass example. The observed test statistic is

$$\begin{aligned} T_0 &= \frac{\bar{x}-\bar{y}}{\sqrt{\left(\frac{1}{n_c}+\frac{1}{n_r}\right)\frac{(n_c-1)s_c^2+(n_r-1)^2 s_r^2}{n_c+n_r-2}}} \\ &= \frac{1.529123-1.529119}{\sqrt{\left(\frac{1}{6}+\frac{1}{6}\right)\frac{(6-1)\left(4.04\times10^{-5}\right)+(6-1)(3.84\times10^{-5})^2}{6+6-2}}} \\ &= \frac{4\times10^{-6}}{2.278\times10^{-5}} \\ &= 0.1756 \end{aligned}$$

H_0, the P value, is calculated using a t distribution with $n_c + n_r-2 = 6 + 6 - 2 = 10$ degrees of freedom. This is easily done in Microsoft Excel using the TDIST function, or in R using the pt function. The resulting P value is 0.86. This is a large P value, and "on average one would expect a result like this approximately 86 times in 100 by random chance alone." That is, this result is extremely likely to have occurred by random chance alone; hence, H_0 cannot be rejected. Note that, unlike the range test, this procedure does not omit the smallest recovered RI value. This information is included in both the recovered mean and, more importantly, in the recovered standard deviation. The inclusion of this fragment will increase the recovered variability and make it (slightly) harder to reject the null hypothesis. Some practitioners are bothered by this and use range-like tests to exclude observations from the evidence evaluation. Such practice can lead to dangerously misleading conclusions if no account is taken of the omitted information.

It is not entirely necessary to calculate a P value in this example because this test statistic can be interpreted as "the observed difference is approximately 0.18 standard deviations away from the mean when the null hypothesis is true. If the observed difference was more than 2 standard deviations away from the mean, then we would start to suspect that it was unlikely to have occurred by random chance alone. Given that 0.18 is much smaller than 2, we would intuit that the observed difference can be attributed to random variation."

The two-sample t test has a multivariate analog known as Hotelling's T^2. This test has been used in forensic science, but it is relatively uncommon. It is more common to perform tests on each variable. This approach is subject to the multiple testing problems discussed earlier. Hotelling's T^2 avoids such issues and takes into account the potential correlations between measurements. However, it does have large sample size requirements, which traditionally have been problematic.

Confidence Intervals

Hypothesis tests have a very rigid interpretation in that the user makes a decision to either accept or reject the null hypothesis based on the P value. Such an approach leads to what Ken Smalldon called the "fall-off-the-cliff effect." Consider a situation in which the P value is 0.049 and the criterion for rejection is 0.05. In this case, the scientist would reject the null hypothesis. However, if the P value were 0.051, then the scientist would accept the null hypothesis. That is, a tiny change in the numbers leads to a complete reversal of the decision. Such logic is extremely hard to justify to the court. In some situations, an alternative is to present a confidence interval.

To form a confidence interval, the scientist must choose a confidence level. The confidence level is directly analogous to the significance level for a (two-tailed) hypothesis test. The confidence level is usually stated as a percentage of the form $100 \times (1-\alpha)\%$. For example, if $\alpha = 0.05$, then this is referred to as 95% confidence level, and the resulting interval as a 95% confidence interval. Confidence intervals also have a confidence statement attached to them. That is, the scientist may state that they are $100 \times (1-\alpha)\%$ confident that the interval contains the true value of interest. Note that this is not a statement of probability. Confidence refers to the ideas of repeated sampling or infinite populations that are the foundation of the frequentist philosophy of statistics. The confidence level refers to the random nature of the interval rather than the behavior of a specific interval.

In general, confidence intervals take the form

$$\hat{\theta} \pm z_\alpha^* \mathrm{se}(\hat{\theta})$$

The quantity θ is referred to as the quantity of interest. It may be a mean, a difference in means, a proportion, a difference in proportions, an odds ratio, or even a likelihood ratio. It is not a restrictive list, and it is application-specific. The quantity $\mathrm{se}(\hat{\theta})$ is called the standard error of the estimate. It is the estimated standard deviation of the quantity of interest. The value z_α^* is a multiplier chosen from an application-specific statistical distribution that reflects the confidence level. In general, the smaller the value of α, the larger the value of z_α^* will be. Confidence intervals for many standard situations can be found in most undergraduate statistics texts.

A confidence interval for the glass example is given here for illustration. In general, a $100 \times (1-\alpha)\%$ confidence interval for the difference in the two means is given by

$$\bar{x}-\bar{y} \pm t_{\mathrm{df}}^*(1-\alpha/2)\mathrm{se}(\bar{x}-\bar{y})$$

Under the assumption that the samples come from populations with the same variance, the standard error of the difference in the means is given by

$$\mathrm{se}(\bar{x}-\bar{y}) = \sqrt{\left(\frac{1}{n_c}+\frac{1}{n_r}\right)\frac{(n_c-1)s_c^2+(n_r-1)s_r^2}{n_c+n_r-2}}$$

which is the denominator of the test statistic in the two-sample t test. This makes sense when one considers that the hypothesis essentially compares the observed difference to the estimated variability in the difference. This formula is considerably simpler when the assumption of equal variances is dropped:

$$\mathrm{se}(\bar{x}-\bar{y}) = \sqrt{\frac{s_c^2}{n_c}+\frac{s_r^2}{n_r}}$$

However, the formula for the degrees of freedom, given by Welch's approximation, is more complicated (and not given here). The critical value is the $100(1-\alpha/2)$ percentile of Student's t distribution with $n_c + n_r - 2$ degrees of freedom (assuming equal variances for both populations). This can be calculated using a handbook of statistical tables, the Microsoft Excel function TINV, or the R function qt.

Therefore, a 95% confidence interval for the glass example is given by

$$\begin{aligned} &4 \times 10^{-6} \pm 2.228 \times 2.277 \times 10^{-5} \\ &= \left(-4.7 \times 10^{-5}, 5.5 \times 10^{-5}\right) \end{aligned}$$

The confidence interval contains 0, which is the hypothesized difference (recall H_0: $\mu_c - \mu = 0$). This means that if a P value were calculated, then it would be greater than 0.05. In general, if a $100 \times (1-\alpha)\%$ confidence interval contains the hypothesized value of interest, then the associated P value from a hypothesis test will be greater than α (for a two-tailed test), and if the interval does not contain the hypothesized value of interest, then the P value will be less than α (for a two-tailed test).

Controversies and Issues

There has been considerable criticism in the forensic science and legal literature over the last 30 years regarding the appropriateness of frequentist approaches to the interpretation of evidence, and the relevance of frequentist methods in legal proceedings. Such discussion would seem to be at odds with the last 100 or so years in many fields of science, in which frequentist methods are on the whole the accepted standard for judging experimental success.

Most of the controversy is summarized by a statement given by Robertson and Vignaux, which says that a significant hypothesis test does not answer the question the court is interested in. The court wants to know "How much more (or less) likely does this piece of evidence make it that the accused is guilty?" On the other hand, a significance test tells the court, "What is the probability that I would observe this result (match) by chance alone?" Robertson and Vignaux succinctly called this "the right answer to the wrong question." Proponents of the Bayesian approach, also known as the likelihood ratio approach, or the logical approach, believe that the evidence must be evaluated with respect to at least two competing hypotheses. Such a belief is not actually at odds with the Neyman–Pearson school of hypothesis testing, but in the Bayesian approach, the alternative hypothesis explicitly enters the probability calculations.

There are also more fundamental criticisms that stem from the definitions of probability. Within the field of statistics, there are two schools of inference that are known as Bayesian and frequentist. These names of these schools relate, in general, to the Bayesian and frequentist definitions of probability.

The frequentist definition of probability, as the name suggests, depends on the long-term frequency of an event.

In the frequentist approach to inference, the inference relies on the concept of either an infinite population or repeated sampling. In addition, the parameters of a model, or values about which the scientist wishes to make an inference, are generally regarded as fixed but unknown. The data are regarded as random. This means that statements are made about the random nature of the data rather than the unknown parameters. The practical consequence of this is that it should prevent the scientist from making statements about the probability of a hypothesis being true, or about a confidence interval containing the true value with a certain probability. However, in practice, such statements are still made.

By contrast, the Bayesian definition of probability is that it is a measure of belief.

In Bayesian inference, the parameters of interest are regarded as random and unknowable and the data as fixed. In the Bayesian framework, assumptions about the unknown parameters are represented by prior probabilities or beliefs, and these are updated with additional information—the data to yield posterior probabilities. This means that a scientist using Bayesian techniques can make statements about the probability of hypotheses, or probability about credible intervals containing the true value. Credible intervals are the Bayesian equivalent of confidence intervals.

It may be of some interest that it is not completely necessary to accept the Bayesian definition of probability to use the Bayesian approach.

See also: **Foundations:** Statistical Interpretation of Evidence: Bayesian Analysis.

Further Reading

Aitken, C.G.G., Taroni, F., 2004. Statistics and the Evaluation of Evidence for Forensic Scientists, second ed. Wiley, Chichester.

Balding, D.J., 2005. Weight-of-Evidence for Forensic DNA Profiles. Wiley, Hoboken, NJ.

Curran, J.M., 2010. Introduction to Data Analysis with R for Forensic Scientists. CRC Press, Boca Raton, FL.

Curran, J.M., Hicks, T.N., Buckleton, J.S., 2000. Forensic Interpretation of Glass Evidence. CRC Press, Boca Raton, FL.

Evett, I.W., Weir, B.S., 1998. Interpreting DNA Evidence: Statistical Genetics for Forensic Scientists. Sinauer Associates, Sunderland, MA.

Hair, J.F., Black, W.C., Babin, B.J., Anderson, R.E., 2009. Multivariate Data Analysis, seventh ed. Pearson Prentice Hall, Upper Saddle River, NJ.

Lucy, D., 2005. Introduction to Statistics for Forensic Scientists. Wiley, Chichester.

Moore, D.S., McCabe, G.P., 2006. Introduction to the Practice of Statistics, fifth ed. W.H. Freeman, New York.

Robertson, B., Vignaux, G.A., 1995. Interpreting Evidence: Evaluating Forensic Science in the Court Room. Wiley, Chichester.

Wild, C.J., Seber, G.A.F., 2000. Chance Encounters: A First Course in Data Analysis and Inference. Wiley, New York.

Statistical Interpretation of Evidence: Bayesian Analysis

CGG Aitken, The University of Edinburgh, Edinburgh, UK
F Taroni and A Biedermann, The University of Lausanne, Lausanne-Dorigny, Switzerland

Glossary

Bayes' theorem Bayes' theorem is a consequence of the basic laws of probabilities and can be applied for revising beliefs about uncertain propositions in the light of new evidence. In judicial contexts, reasoning according to Bayes' theorem is used in order to examine whether particular evidence strengthens or weakens a case. More generally, Bayes' theorem provides a standard for logically correct reasoning under uncertainty.

Likelihood ratio A likelihood ratio is defined by a ratio of two conditional probabilities: the probability of the evidence given each of two mutually exclusive and competing propositions. In forensic science applications, the likelihood ratio is used as an expression for the meaning of scientific evidence and as a measure for its probative value.

Probability Probability is a measurement device for uncertainty. In one of its most widespread interpretations, it serves the purpose of expressing an individual's personal degrees of beliefs about uncertain propositions. Probability is governed by several axiomatic laws that constitute a fundamental framework for inductive logic.

Introduction

Bruno de Finetti, a pioneering subjective probabilist, considered that the role of probability theory in inductive logic is to show how the evaluations of probabilities of future events are to be modified in the light of observed events, and that this translates, in the mathematical formulation of induction, the meaning of the phrase "to learn from experience." Forensic scientists, as an illustrative example, routinely face inductive reasoning when they seek to evaluate or interpret the meaning of items of scientific evidence. This directs attention to Bayes' theorem, which, in essence, formalizes induction.

In Bayesian analysis, all available information is used in order to reduce the extent of uncertainty associated with an inferential problem. As new information is obtained, it is combined with any previous information, and this forms the basis for statistical procedures. The formal mechanism used to combine new information with previously available information is generally known as Bayes' theorem. Bayes' theorem involves the use of probabilities because probability can be thought of as the coherent language of uncertainty. At any given point in time, the scientist's state of information about some uncertain event (or quantity) can be represented by a set of probabilities. When new information is obtained, these probabilities are revised in order that they may represent all of the available information. The idea of "revising" probabilities is not one that should be interpreted as a "correction." An updated probability is not a correction or a better evaluation of an initial probability, but solely a different probability, because it is conditioned by a new (extended) state of information.

Thus, the statistical evaluation and interpretation of evidence relies on a rule that relates the dependencies amongst uncertain events through conditional probabilities. This rule enables one to specify the value of evidence in the sense of the effect that evidence has on beliefs in an issue, such as the guilt or innocence of a defendant. The underlying ideas can be applied to categorical and continuous data. They can also be applied to situations in which there are no, or limited, data but in which there are subjective opinions. They are used to ensure a logical and coherent structure to the evaluation of items of evidence.

Bayes' Rule

The Bayesian approach is named after the Reverend Thomas Bayes, a nonconformist preacher of the eighteenth century. To him is attributed an important rule that shows how uncertainty

 http://dx.doi.org/10.1016/B978-0-12-800647-4.00024-2

about an event, say R, can be changed by the knowledge of another event, say S:

$$\Pr(R|S) = \Pr(S|R)\Pr(R)/\Pr(S)$$

where Pr denotes probability and the bar | denotes the conditioning. Thus, $\Pr(R|S)$ is the probability that R occurs, given that S has occurred. Probabilities are values between 0 and 1. The value 0 corresponds to an event that is impossible to happen, and 1 corresponds to an event that is certain to happen. Probabilities are most appropriately interpreted as subjective—in the sense of "personal"—expressions of degrees of belief held by an individual. As such, they reflect the degree of imperfection of an individual's knowledge. Such belief is graduated: as evidence accumulates, one can believe in the truth of an event more or less than before, one can believe more in the truth of a given event than in the truth of another event, etc. The fundamental principle in this interpretation is that the degrees of belief of a rational individual obey the rules of probability. Therefore, probability represents the quantified judgment of a particular individual. Because a probability is a measure of a degree of belief rather than a long-run frequency (as suggested by other interpretations of probability), it is perfectly reasonable to assign probability to an event that involves a nonrepetitive situation. This makes the interpretation of probability, based on measures of belief, particularly useful for judicial contexts.

An alternative version of Bayes' rule is its odds form, where $\overline{R}$ denotes the complement of R so that $\Pr(\overline{R}) = 1 - \Pr(R)$. The odds in favor of R are then $\Pr(R)/\Pr(\overline{R})$, denoted $O(R)$, and the odds in favor of R given that S has occurred are denoted $O(R|S)$. The odds form of Bayes' rule is then

$$O(R|S) = \frac{\Pr(S|R)}{\Pr(S|\overline{R})} \times O(R)$$

In forensic science, S, R, and $\overline{R}$ are generally replaced in the odds form of Bayes' rule by E, H_p, and H_d, where E is the scientific evidence, H_p is the hypothesis proposed by the prosecution, and H_d is the hypothesis proposed by the defense. Thus, one has

$$O(H_p|E) = \frac{\Pr(E|H_p)}{\Pr(E|H_d)} \times O(H_p)$$

The left-hand side of the equation is the odds in favor of the prosecution hypothesis after the scientific evidence has been presented. This is known as the *posterior odds*. The odds $O(H_p)$ are known as the *prior odds* (i.e., odds prior to the presentation of the evidence). The factor that converts prior odds to posterior odds is the fraction

$$\frac{\Pr(E|H_p)}{\Pr(E|H_d)}$$

known as *Bayes' factor*. In forensic contexts, it is regularly termed the "likelihood ratio" and abbreviated by V, short for "value." It can take values between 0 and ∞. A value greater than 1 provides support to the prosecution's hypothesis H_p, and a value less than one favors the defense's hypothesis H_d. Evidence for which the value is 1 is neutral in that the evidence is not relevant for discriminating between the two hypotheses of interest. Note that if logarithms are used, the relationship becomes additive. This has a very pleasing intuitive interpretation of weighing evidence in the scales of justice, and the logarithm of Bayes' factor is known, after the works of the statistician I. J. Good, as the "weight of evidence." It is not necessary for the propositions in the terms denoted $O(R)$ and $O(R|S)$ above to be complementary; the rule still holds. Thus, the prosecution and defense hypotheses do not need to be complementary.

The probative value of scientific evidence is assessed by determining a value for Bayes' factor. The proper task of forensic scientists is the determination of that value. The role of judge and jury will be that of assessing the prior and posterior odds. Scientists can inform recipients of expert information on how their prior odds are altered by the evidence, but scientists cannot by themselves assign a value to the prior or posterior odds. In order to assign such a value, all of the other evidence in a case has to be considered.

The terms "evaluation" and "interpretation" are sometimes considered synonyms, but it is helpful to conceive of a distinction. "Evaluation" is the determination of a value for Bayes' factor. "Interpretation" refers to the meaning attached to their value.

The Value of Evidence

The evaluation of scientific evidence may be thought of as the assessment of a comparison. This comparison is between qualities (such as genetic traits) or results of measurements (such as refractive indices of glass fragments) of crime-related (recovered) material and of control (potential source) material. For the assessment of scientific evidence, it is widely accepted that the forensic scientist should consider at least a pair of competing hypotheses, in the context habitually denoted H_p and H_d, to illustrate their description of the fact under examination. These hypotheses are formalized representations of the framework of circumstances. Their formulation is a crucial basis for a logical approach to the evaluation of evidence. A classification developed mainly by researchers in the United Kingdom during the late 1990s, referred to as a "hierarchy of propositions," considers three main categories or levels. It involves the so-called "source," the "activity," and the "crime" level.

Categorical Data and Discrete Hypotheses

Source-Level Evaluation

The assessment at source level depends on analyses and measurements on the recovered (of unknown origin) and control (of known origin) samples. The value of a trace (or a stain) under source-level propositions, such as "Mr. X's pullover is the source of the recovered fibers" and "Mr. X's pullover is not the source of the recovered fibers" (so that another clothing is the source of the trace), does not need to take account of anything other than the analytical information obtained during laboratory examination. The probability of the evidence under the first hypothesis (numerator of Bayes' factor) is considered from a comparison between two samples (the recovered and the control) assuming they have come from the same source. The probability of the evidence under the second hypothesis (denominator of Bayes' factor) is considered by comparison of the characteristics of the control and recovered samples in the context of a relevant population of alternative sources. The population from which the source may be thought to have come is called the relevant population.

Consider a scenario in which n textile fibers have been left at the scene of the crime by the person who committed the crime. A suspect has been arrested, and it is desired to establish the strength of the link between the suspect and the crime. A comparison between the results of measurements of the physical/chemical characteristics of the questioned fibers and those of a sample taken from the suspect's pullover is made by a forensic scientist. The two hypotheses of interest are H_p, the fibers recovered from the suspect's pullover, and H_d, the fibers recovered from some garment other than that of the suspect. The evidence E has two parts: y, the characteristic Γ, say, of the recovered fibers, and x, the characteristic Γ, say, of the defendant's pullover. If the recovered fibers and the defendant's pullover have different (incompatible) characteristics, then the suspect's pullover would not be investigated in further detail.

Let I denote the background information. For example, this could include (eyewitness) evidence concerning the type of garment worn by the criminal. The value of the evidence is then

$$\frac{\Pr(E|H_p, I)}{\Pr(E|H_d, I)} = \frac{\Pr(x, y|H_p, I)}{\Pr(x, y|H_d, I)} = \frac{\Pr(y|x, H_p, I)}{\Pr(y|x, H_d, I)} \times \frac{\Pr(x|H_p, I)}{\Pr(x|H_d, I)}$$

Consider two assumptions:

The characteristics of the defendant's pullover are independent of whether his pullover is the source of the recovered fibers (H_p) or not (H_d); thus, $\Pr(x|H_p, I)c = \Pr(x|H_d, I)$.

If the defendant's pullover was not the source of the recovered fibers (H_d), then the evidence about the fibers at the crime scene (y) is independent of the evidence (x) about the characteristics of the defendant's pullover; thus, $\Pr(y|x, H_p, I) = \Pr(y|H_d, I)$.

Hence,

$$V = \frac{\Pr(y|x, H_p, I)}{\Pr(y|H_d, I)}$$

The scientist knows, in addition, from data previously collected (population studies) that fiber type Γ occurs in $100\gamma\%$ of some relevant population, say Ψ.

Assuming that the defendant's pullover is the source of the recovered fibers, the probability that the recovered fibers are of characteristic Γ, given the defendant's pullover is the source and is of characteristic Γ, is 1. Thus, the numerator of V is 1. Alternatively, it is assumed that the suspect's pullover was not the source of the recovered fibers. The relevant population is deemed to be Ψ. The true donor of the recovered fibers is an unknown member of Ψ. Evidence y is to the effect that the crime fibers are of characteristic Γ. This is to say that an unknown member of Ψ is Γ. The probability of this is the probability that a fiber donor drawn at random from Ψ has characteristic Γ, which is γ. Thus,

$$V = \frac{1}{\gamma}$$

This value, $1/\gamma$, is the value of the evidence of the characteristics of the recovered fibers when the garment donor is a member of Ψ. Given that γ is a value between 0 and 1, Bayes' factor is greater than 1; therefore, the evidence is said to be a value $1/\gamma$ times more likely if the suspect's pullover was the source of the recovered fibers than if it were not. Qualitative scales have been proposed, and they are intended to make it easier to convey the meaning of the numerical value of the evidence. However, there is ongoing discussion about the degree to which this target has been achieved.

Activity-Level Evaluation

The hierarchical level relates to an activity. It requires that the definition of the hypotheses of interest include an action. For example, such hypotheses could be "Mr. X sat on the car driver's seat," and "Mr. X never sat on the car driver's seat." The consequence of this activity—the sitting on a driver's seat—is a contact between the driver and the seat of the car. Consequently, a transfer of material (i.e., fibers in this example) may be expected. Therefore, the scientist needs to consider more detailed information about the case under examination. It relates to the transfer and persistence of fibers on the car driver's seat. This demonstrates that activity-level hypotheses cannot be addressed without a framework of circumstances.

For the sake of illustration, consider the following scenario. A crime has been committed during which the blood of a victim has been shed. A suspect has been arrested. A single blood stain of genotype Γ has been found on an item of the suspect's clothing. The suspect's genotype is not Γ. The victim's genotype is Γ. There are two possibilities:

T_0: The blood stain came from some background source.

T_1: The blood stain was transferred during the commission of the crime.

As before, there are two hypotheses to consider:

H_p: The suspect assaulted the victim.
H_d: The suspect did not assault the victim (for example, but taken to mean he is not involved in any way whatsoever with the victim).

The evidence E to be considered is that a single blood stain has been found on the suspect's clothing and that it is of genotype Γ. The information that the victim's genotype is Γ is considered as part of the relevant background information I. A general expression of the value of the evidence then is $V = \Pr(E|H_p, I)/\Pr(E|H_d, I)$.

Consider the numerator first and event T_0 initially. This supposes "a contact" between the suspect and the victim, but no blood transfer to the suspect. This is an event with probability $\Pr(T_0/H_p, I)$. Also, a stain of genotype Γ must have been transferred by some other means, an event with probability $\Pr(B, \Gamma)$, where B refers to the event of a transfer of a stain from a source (i.e., a background source) other than the crime scene (here the victim).

Next, consider T_1, the event of blood transfer to the suspect, an event with probability $\Pr(T_1|H_p, I)$. Given T_1, H_p, and the genotype Γ of the victim, it is certain that the transferred stain is Γ. This assumes also that no blood has been transferred from a background source.

Let $t_0 = \Pr(T_0|H_p, I)$ and $t_1 = \Pr(T_1|H_p, I)$ denote the probabilities of no stain or one stain being transferred during the course of the crime. Let b_0 and b_1, respectively, denote the probabilities that a person from the relevant population will have zero blood stains or one blood stain on clothing. Let γ denote the probability that a stain acquired innocently on the clothing of a person from the relevant population will be of genotype Γ. This probability may be different from the proportion of individuals in the general population which are of type Γ. Then, $\Pr(B, \Gamma) = \gamma b_1$ and the numerator can be written as $t_0\gamma b_1 + t_1 b_0$. This expresses that the presence of a stain of type Γ depends on the probability of there being no transfer (t_0), times there being such a stain as background ($b_1\gamma$), plus the probability of transfer of such a stain (t_1), times the probability of there being no such stain beforehand (b_0).

Now consider the denominator, where it is supposed that the suspect and the victim were not "in contact." The presence of the stain is then explained by chance alone. The denominator then takes the value $\Pr(B, \Gamma)$, which equals γb_1.

In summary, the value of the evidence is thus

$$V = \frac{t_0\gamma b_1 + t_1 b_0}{\gamma b_1}$$

Extensions to cases involving transfer in the other direction (e.g., from perpetrator to scene/victim rather than from scene/victim to perpetrator), or generalizations involving n stains and k groups, are available in the specialized literature on the topic.

Crime-Level Evaluation

At the "crime level," hypotheses are closest to those of interest to the jury. A formal development of the likelihood ratio under crime-level hypotheses shows that two additional parameters are of interest: (1) one concerns material that may be "relevant," meaning that it came from the offender (it is relevant to the consideration of the suspect as a possible offender) and (2) the other concerns the recognition that if the material is not relevant to the case, then it may have arrived at the scene from the suspect for innocent reasons.

Consider the following two hypotheses of interest:

H_p: The suspect is the offender.
H_d: The suspect is not the offender.

Notice the difference between these hypotheses and those of the previous sections on source or activity level. At source level, the hypotheses referred to the suspect being, or not being, the donor of the recovered trace found at the crime scene. Now, the hypotheses are stronger because they specify the suspect as a possible offender.

In the formal development of the likelihood ratio, a link is needed between what is observed (i.e., the stain at the crime scene) and the hypotheses according to which the suspect is or is not the offender. The connection is made in two steps. The first is the consideration of a hypothesis that the crime stain came from the offender and the alternative hypothesis that the crime stain did not come from the offender. If it is assumed that the crime stain came from the offender, then the second step is the consideration of a hypothesis that the crime stain came from the suspect and the alternative that the crime stain did not come from the suspect.

Developing the likelihood ratio in view of these two pairs of hypotheses introduces the concepts of (1) "relevance probability," usually denoted r and (2) "innocent acquisition probability," usually denoted as a. The resulting expression of the value of the evidence takes the following form:

$$V = \frac{r + \gamma'(1-r)}{\gamma r[a + (1-a)\gamma'](1-r)}$$

Note the difference between two possible expressions γ and γ' of the rarity of the corresponding characteristic. In fact, γ' is the probability that the crime stain would be of a given type if it had been left by an unknown person who was unconnected with the crime. The population of people who may have left the stain is not necessarily the same as the population from which the criminal is assumed to have come. However, for DNA evidence, it may be acceptable to assume $\gamma = \gamma'$.

Continuous Data and Discrete Hypotheses

A seminal paper in 1977 by Dennis Lindley showed how Bayes' factor could be used to evaluate evidence given by continuous data in the form of measurements. The measurements used by Lindley by way of illustration were those of the refractive index of glass. There were two sources of variation in such measurements: the variation within a window and the variation between different windows. Lindley showed how these two sources of variation could be accounted for in a single statistic. He was also able to account for the two factors that are of importance to a forensic scientist: (1) the similarity between the recovered and control sample and (2) the typicality of any perceived similarity. When the data are in the form of continuous measurements, Bayes' factor is a ratio of probability density functions rather than a ratio of probabilities.

Consider a set **x** of control measurements and another set **y** of recovered measurements of a particular characteristic, such as the refractive index of glass. For this example, **x** would be a set of measurements of refractive indices on fragments of a broken window at the crime scene and **y** a set of measurements of refractive indices on fragments of glass found on a suspect. If the suspect was at the crime scene, then the fragments found on him could have come from the window at the crime scene. If he was not there, then the fragments have come from some other, unknown, source.

The quantitative part of the evidence concerning the glass fragments in this case can be denoted by $E = (\mathbf{x}, \mathbf{y})$. Bayes' factor is then written as follows:

$$V = \frac{f(\mathbf{x},\mathbf{y}|H_p, I)}{\mathbf{x},\mathbf{y}|H_d, I}$$

Bayes' theorem and the rules of conditional probability apply to probability density functions $f(\cdot)$ as well as to probabilities. The value of the evidence V may be rewritten—following the argument presented in the section on discrete data—as

$$V = \frac{f(\mathbf{y}|\mathbf{x}, H_p, I)}{f(\mathbf{y}|H_d, I)}$$

This formulation of the expression for V shows that for the numerator the distribution of the recovered measurements, conditional on the control measurements as well as I, is considered. For the denominator, the distribution of the recovered measurements is considered over the distribution of the whole of the relevant population. The denominator is called the "marginal distribution" of the recovered measurements in the relevant population.

In a Bayesian approach, the characteristic of interest is parameterized, for example by the mean. Denote the parameter by θ. This parameter may vary from source (window) to source (another window).

Consider the two propositions to be compared are as follows:

H_p: The recovered sample is from the same source as the control sample.

H_d: The recovered sample is from a different source than the control sample.

The measurements **x** are from a distribution with parameter θ_1, say, and the measurements **y** are from a distribution with parameter θ_2, say. If **x** and **y** come from the same source, then $\theta_1 = \theta_2$, otherwise $\theta_1 \neq \theta_2$. In practice, the parameter θ is not known and the analysis is done with the marginal probability densities of **x** and **y**. The above equation for V can be rewritten as

$$V = \frac{\int f(\mathbf{y}|\theta) f(\mathbf{x}|\theta)\pi(\theta)\mathrm{d}\theta}{\int f(\mathbf{x}|\theta)\pi(\theta)\mathrm{d}\theta \int f(\mathbf{y}|\theta)\pi(\theta)\mathrm{d}\theta}$$

For those unfamiliar with these kinds of manipulations, Bayes' theorem applied to conditional probability distributions is used to write $f(\theta|\mathbf{x})$ as $f(\mathbf{x}|\theta)\pi(\theta)/f(\mathbf{x})$. The law of total probability with integration replacing summation is used to write $f(\mathbf{x})$ as $\int f(\mathbf{x}|\theta)\pi(\theta)\mathrm{d}\theta$. Note that $\pi(\theta)$ represents the prior distribution on the unknown parameter. Therefore, Bayes' factor does not depend only upon the sample data. It is the ratio of two weighted likelihoods.

Often, the distributions of $(\mathbf{x}|\theta)$ and $(\mathbf{y}|\theta)$ are assumed to be normal, with θ representing the mean, varying from source to source, and the variance is assumed to be constant from source to source. Those assumptions can be relaxed and (1) various possibilities can been assumed for the distribution of $(\mathbf{x}|\theta)$, $(\mathbf{y}|\theta)$, and θ, and (2) a three-level hierarchical model (variance assumed not constant) can be considered. Moreover, developments for multivariate data are also possible.

Principles of Evidence Evaluation

Three principles arise from the application of the ideas outlined so far. First, the evaluation is meaningful only when at least one alternative hypothesis is addressed. Therefore, the distribution of the data has to be considered under (at least) two hypotheses, typically that of the prosecution and that of the defense.

The second principle is that evaluation is based on consideration of probabilities of the evidence, given a particular issue is assumed true, $\Pr(E|H_p)$ and $\Pr(E|H_d)$.

The third principle is that the evaluation and interpretation of the evidence is carried out within a framework of circumstances. It has to be conditioned on the background information I.

The application of those principles guarantees some desiderata in the scientist's attitude in evaluating and offering evidence, such as balance, transparency, robustness, and added value. The degree to which the scientist succeeds in meeting these criteria crucially depends on the chosen inferential framework that may be judged by the criteria of flexibility and logic.

Interpretation

Continuous Data and Continuous Hypotheses

So far, the outline focused on categorical (or continuous) data and discrete hypotheses, but Bayesian analysis also deals with situations involving continuous hypotheses. In particular, it may happen that scientists encounter continuous propositions. A typical instance of this is the situation in which a parameter, such as a mean, needs to be estimated. As an example, suppose that a random sample, $x = (x_1, \ldots, x_n)$, is available. For example, this may be the case in which a scientist is interested in blood alcohol concentration on the basis of a series of n measurements taken from a given individual arrested by traffic police.

Suppose further that the data follow a normal distribution with unknown mean, θ, and known variance, σ^2. Suppose also that there is some background information available so that some values of θ seem more likely a priori. Then, assuming a conjugate normal prior distribution for the parameter of interest (i.e., the mean θ, having a mean μ and a variance τ^2), it can be shown that the posterior density is still normally distributed, $N(\mu(x), \tau^2(x))$, with

$$\text{mean } \mu(x) = \frac{\frac{\sigma^2}{n}}{\frac{\sigma^2}{n} + \tau^2}\mu + \frac{\tau^2}{\frac{\sigma^2}{n} + \tau^2}\bar{x} \text{ and}$$

$$\text{variance } \tau^2(x) = \frac{\frac{\sigma^2}{n}\tau^2}{\frac{\sigma^2}{n} + \tau^2}$$

The posterior mean is a weighted average of the prior mean μ and the sample mean $\bar{x}$, with weights proportional to the variances corresponding to the prior distribution and the sampling distribution. Comparable lines of reasoning can be invoked to approach situations involving unknown variances, alternative distributions, and data distributions.

Pitfalls of Intuition

The Bayesian approach to the interpretation of evidence enables various errors and fallacies to be exposed. The best known of these are the prosecutor's and defender's fallacies. As an example, consider a crime in which a blood stain is found at the scene and it is established that it has come from the criminal. Only for sake of illustration, consider that the stain has a profile that is present in only 1% of the population. It is also supposed that the size of the relevant population is 200,000. A suspect is identified by other means and his blood is found to be of the same profile as that found at the crime scene.

The prosecutor argues that, because the blood profile is present in only 1% of the population, there is only a 1% chance that the suspect is innocent. There is a 99% chance that he is guilty. The defense attorney argues that, because 1% of 200,000 is 2000, the suspect is only one person in 2000. There is a probability of 1/2000 that he is guilty. This is then used to argue that the blood group is, therefore, of little probative value and not very helpful in the case.

Consideration of the odds form of Bayes' rule explains these fallacies. Denote the blood evidence by E and let the two competing hypotheses be H_p, the suspect is guilty, and H_d, the suspect is innocent. Then, the odds form of Bayes' rule is that (omitting I from notation)

$$\frac{\Pr(H_p|E)}{\Pr(H_d|E)} = \frac{\Pr(E|H_p)}{\Pr(E|H_d)} \times \frac{\Pr(H_p)}{\Pr(H_d)}$$

Bayes' factor is $\Pr(E|H_p)/\Pr(E/H_d) = 1/0.01 = 100$. The posterior odds are increased by a factor of 100.

Consider the prosecutor's statement. It claims that the probability of guilt, after presentation of the evidence, is 0.99. In formal terms, this corresponds to $\Pr(H_p|E) = 0.99$ and, hence, $\Pr(H_d|E) = 0.01$. The posterior odds are 99, which is approximately 100. V is also 100. Thus, the prior odds are 1 and $\Pr(H_p) = \Pr(H_d) = 0.5$. For the prosecutor's fallacy to be correct, the prior belief is that the suspect is just as likely to be guilty as innocent.

The defense argues that the posterior probability of guilt $\Pr(H_p|E)$ equals 1/2000 and, hence, $\Pr(H_d|E)$ equals 1999/2000. The posterior odds are 1/1999, which is approximately 1/2000. Because the posterior odds are bigger by a factor of 100 than the prior odds, the prior odds are 1/200,000, or the reciprocal of the population size. The defense is arguing that the prior belief in guilt is approximately 1/200,000. This could be expressed as a belief that the suspect is just as likely to be guilty as anyone else in the relevant population. The fallacy arises because the defense then argues that the evidence is not relevant. However, before the evidence was led, the suspect was 1 of 200,000 people; after the evidence was led he is only one of 2000 people. Evidence that reduces the size of the pool of potential criminals by a factor of 100 is surely relevant.

Other errors have been identified. The "ultimate issue error" is another name for the prosecutor's fallacy. It confuses the probability of the evidence if a defendant is innocent with the probability he is innocent, given the evidence. The ultimate issue is the issue proposed by the prosecution of which it is asking the court to find in favor. The "source probability error" is to claim the defendant is the source of the evidence. This would place the defendant at the scene of the crime but would not, in itself, be enough to show that he was guilty. The "probability (another match) error" consists of equating the rarity of a characteristic with the probability that another person has this characteristic. The "numerical conversion error" equates the reciprocal of rarity of the corresponding characteristic to the number of people that have to be examined before another person with the same characteristic is found.

More generally, high values for the evidence provide strong support for the prosecution's case. However, they are not sufficient in themselves to declare a defendant guilty. The prior odds have to be considered as well. Very high values for the evidence, when combined with very small values for prior odds, may produce small values for the posterior odds. This may be the case when the suspect has been selected as a result of a database search and when there is little or no other evidence against the suspect.

See also: **Biology/DNA:** Bayesian Networks; DNA—Statistical Probability; **Foundations:** Overview and Meaning of Identification/Individualization.

Further Reading

Aitken, C.G.G., Lucy, D., 2004. Evaluation of trace evidence in the form of multivariate data. Journal of the Royal Statistical Society: Series C (Applied Statistics) 53, 109–122.

Aitken, C.G.G., Taroni, F., 2004. Statistics and the Evaluation of Evidence for Forensic Scientists. John Wiley & Sons, Chichester.

Bozza, S., Taroni, F., Raymond, R., Schmittbuhl, M., 2008. Probabilistic evaluation of handwriting evidence: likelihood ratio for authorship. Journal of the Royal Statistical Society: Series C (Applied Statistics) 57 (3), 329–341.

Evett, I.W., 1984. A quantitative theory for interpreting transfer evidence in criminal cases. Journal of the Royal Statistical Society: Series C (Applied Statistics) 33, 25–32.

Evett, I.W., 1987. Bayesian inference and forensic science: problems and perspectives. Statistician 36, 99–105.

Evett, I.W., Lambert, J.A., Buckleton, J.S., 1998. A Bayesian approach to interpreting footwear marks in forensic casework. Science Justice 38, 241–247.

Evett, I.W., Weir, B.S., 1998. Interpreting DNA Evidence. Sinauer, Sunderland, MA.

Good, I.J., 1991. Weight of evidence and the Bayesian likelihood ratio. In: Aitken, C.G.G., Stoney, D.A. (Eds.), The Use of Statistics in Forensic Science. John Wiley & Sons, Chichester, pp. 85–106.

Koehler, J.J., Chia, A., Lindsey, S., 1995. The random match probability in DNA evidence: irrelevant and prejudicial? Jurimetrics Journal 35, 201–219.

Lindley, D.V., 1997. A problem in forensic science. Biometrika 64, 207–213.

Robertson, B., Vignaux, G.A., 1995. Interpreting Evidence: Evaluating Forensic Science in the Courtroom. John Wiley & Sons, Chichester.

Schum, D.A., 2001. Evidential Foundations of Probabilistic Reasoning. Northwestern University Press, Evanston.

Taroni, F., Bozza, S., Biedermann, A., Garbolino, P., Aitken, C.G.G., 2010. Data Analysis in Forensic Science: A Bayesian Decision Perspective. John Wiley & Sons, Chichester.

Taroni, F., Champod, C., Margot, P., 1998. Forerunners of Bayesianism in early forensic science. Jurimetrics Journal 38, 183–200.

Thompson, W.C., Schumann, E.L., 1987. Interpretation of statistical evidence in criminal trials: the prosecutor's fallacy and the defence attorney's fallacy. Law and Human Behaviour 11, 167–187.

Thompson, W.C., Taroni, F., Aitken, C.G.G., 2003. How the probability of a false positive affects the value of DNA evidence. Journal of Forensic Sciences 38, 47–54.

Parentage Testing and Kinship Analysis

RW Allen, Oklahoma State University, Tulsa, OK, USA

Glossary

Conditional probability One of the terms needed for probability calculations using Bayes' theorem, normally the likelihood ratio calculated from genetic test results.
Deficiency case Term used to describe a parentage test that lacks a known parent.
Likelihood ratio The numerical statement of the weight of the evidence favoring the opinion that the alleged parent is the true parent of the child.
Maternity index The name given to the likelihood ratio produced in a case of questioned maternity.
Obligate allele An allele observed in a child that had to be inherited from the parent whose identity is in question.
Paternity index The name given to the likelihood ratio calculated in a case of questioned paternity.
Posterior probability The probability produced using Bayes' theorem reflecting the level of certainty that an included alleged parent is the true parent of a child.
Prior probability A term incorporated into Bayes' theorem that reflects the probability of parentage that existed before genetic testing was performed.
VNTR The term used to describe hypervariable genetic markers consisting of short sequences of tandem repeated nucleotides in chromosomal DNA.

History of Parentage Testing

The first documented case of disputed parentage can be found in the Old Testament in Kings I, Chapter 3, verses 16–27 in the story of King Solomon. Two women in a household gave birth to children at about the same time and one child died. The mother of the child who died switched her dead child for the living child while its mother slept and then claimed the living child as her own. When faced with adjudicating this case, Solomon ordered the living child to be cleaved in half and each mother to be given one half of the child. The true mother, hearing the King's ruling, begged the King not to kill her child but rather to rule the thieving mother to be the child's true parent, thereby sparing its life. Solomon accepted the woman's plea but ruled she was the child's true mother and ordered the thief to be put to death.

Parentage testing has changed significantly since the time of King Solomon. Judges do not order children to be halved or alleged parents to be punished by death. More appropriately, decisions regarding the true parentage of a child incorporate the results of genetic marker testing considered within the framework of Mendel's laws in deciding who is and who is not the true parent of a child.

The field of parentage testing began in the 1950 and 1960s with the analysis in paternity trios of red blood cell antigens as genetic systems that were well characterized, could be detected with readily available serological reagents, and routine tests were performed in blood banks around the country. Because of the rather weak discriminatory power associated with testing for red cell antigens of the ABO, MN, and Rh systems, blood typing had as its goal, at that time, the exclusion of an alleged father who was falsely accused.

The widespread use of genetic testing in matters of disputed parentage expanded during the 1960s and 1970s because of a dramatic rise in illegitimacy. During this 10-year period, about 1.7 million children were born out of wedlock. In addition to the absolute number of illegitimate children born during this period, the rate of illegitimacy was increasing, thus further exacerbating the problem. One significant social consequence of the rise of illegitimacy was a financial strain on the welfare program Aid to Families with Dependent Children (AFDC), designed to provide war widows with additional income to help support their dependent children. The dramatic rise in single-parent families due to delinquent fathers, together with a general feeling that a child has a need and right to a legal relationship with his/her father, led to the enactment of the Child Support Enforcement Act in 1974, which aimed to reduce welfare costs by collecting support for families from delinquent parents and to impose family responsibility.

Paralleling the social/legislative developments surrounding disputed parentage was the discovery in the

1970s of the human leukocyte antigen (HLA) system and the development of routine tissue typing methods. For the first time, it was not only possible to exclude a high proportion of falsely accused men (~98%), but the discriminatory power of the HLA system afforded laboratories the possibility of calculating probabilities of paternity for men who could not be excluded as fathers in paternity suits. With the wider use of testing, the need for standardization in the field was formally recognized by the American Medical Association and the American Bar Association. The American Association of Blood Banks (AABB), the organization representing the blood banks and transfusion services in which much of the testing for parentage was performed, also recognized the need for standardization in the field. In recognition of this need, a Committee on Parentage Testing was formed in 1978 and tasked with cultivating a consensus among experts that could form the basis for an accreditation program. In 1984, an accreditation program for parentage testing laboratories was initiated by the AABB. In 2009, the ninth edition of the *Standards for Parentage Testing Laboratories* was published by the AABB, reflecting the ever-changing technology associated with the field.

Technical Considerations

Two technological advances have had a dramatic impact on the field of parentage testing. One, HLA testing, was principally responsible for the evolution of inclusionary statistical calculations associated with testing. The second major advance came in the mid-1980s with the discovery of hypervariable DNA polymorphisms that could be revealed using restriction fragment length polymorphism (RFLP) analysis. Variable number tandem repeat (VNTR) loci, visualized using RFLP methods, exhibited levels of polymorphism comparable to the HLA system and had other advantages as well. One advantage was that the scope of acceptable sample types was broadened. No longer was freshly procured blood an absolute must for testing as in the case of HLA typing. Blood stains, tissue samples, and even buccal swabs could now be used as a source of material for testing. Second, a single Southern blot of restricted DNA from a parentage trio could be sequentially hybridized to multiple probes detecting different VNTR loci, producing a very powerful test battery for the relationship in question. This advantage over other genetic testing technologies was perhaps the main driving force promoting the use of DNA typing among laboratories.

In 1992 with the publication of the second edition of the *Standards for Parentage Testing Laboratories*, the AABB officially recognized the value and widespread use of DNA typing in the field, and the first laboratories became accredited to this technology. Thus, RFLP analysis for questioned parentage was the first DNA typing technology to be covered under an accreditation program. Soon to follow were standards and accreditation for the analysis of small tandem repeat (STR) loci. By 2002, 90% of laboratories reported using STR typing as their principal technology, a testament to the efficiency and effectiveness of STR versus RFLP analyses for performing testing in a cost-effective manner.

The Methods Used in Parentage Testing

The STR typing methods in widespread use among parentage testing laboratories are essentially those used by forensic DNA typing laboratories to produce profiles from reference or convicted felon samples. The most commonly obtained samples are buccal swabs, although, in some cases, "forensic type samples" must be used as a source of DNA for analysis. Such cases include products of conception in rape cases and bone for laboratories engaged in the identification of human remains. Laboratories may also occasionally be asked to identify the source of evidentiary samples recovered in missing person cases through family relatedness analysis.

Extraction of DNA from the typical parentage samples follows extraction methodologies that are widely used in forensic laboratories. Special sample types such as bone require additional steps such as pulverization and demineralization; however, standard DNA extraction methods are ultimately applied to the pretreated samples to liberate and recover DNA present. Once DNA has been recovered, quantitation may be required, although, when dealing with buccal swabs collected from normal healthy individuals, quantitation is often not necessary because of the predictability of DNA recovery using some extraction technologies.

Recovered DNA is then subjected to amplification of a collection of STR loci targeted in currently available multiplex STR typing kits such as Identifiler (Applied Biosystems, Inc., Foster City, CA) or Powerplex 16 (Promega Corporation, Madison, WI). These multiplex kits provide a very high discriminatory power for parentage testing applications (**Table 1**).

In a recent publication from Hill et al., an STR multiplex was described that simultaneously co-amplified 26 STR loci. Although at first blush this might seem to be overkill, establishing or refuting family relationships when the only individuals available for testing are distantly related can be problematic and require more loci to be examined.

Once produced, amplified STR products are generally separated by size using a capillary electrophoresis platform that is part of a genetic analyzer. Inasmuch as the process for producing electropherograms is the same for parentage testing as for forensic DNA testing, it will not be discussed here. Instead, data analysis in scenarios involving questioned parentage is the focus of this discussion and differs significantly from the typical analysis performed in the forensic DNA laboratory.

Table 1 Discriminatory power associated with small tandem repeat (STR) loci in the identifiler multiplex kit

Discriminatory power associated with common multiplex kits[a]		
Locus	*Probability of identity*[b]	*Probability of exclusion*[c]
CSF1PO	0.119	0.475
D2S1338	0.033	0.636
D3S1358	0.111	0.557
D5S818	0.119	0.518
D7S820	0.078	0.56
D8S1179	0.083	0.615
D13S317	0.081	0.47
D16S539	0.087	0.553
D18S51	0.035	0.647
D19S433	0.056	0.543
D21S11	0.051	0.608
FGA	0.033	0.644
THO1	0.105	0.581
TPOX	0.151	0.482
VWA	0.079	0.604
Cumulative values	$\sim 2 \times 10^{-18}$	>99.99%

[a]Numbers shown represent averages across the major population groups (i.e., White, Black, Hispanic, and Native American). The 15 STR loci shown below are all co-amplified along with the amelogenin locus as members of the AmpflSTR Identifiler® multiplex DNA typing kit (Applied Biosystems, Foster City, CA).
[b]The chance two unrelated individuals, selected at random from the population, would have the same STR phenotype for the locus in question.
[c]Chance of excluding a randomly selected individual as the parent of a child, when the known parent is also tested. Exclusion probabilities will decrease significantly in one-parent cases.

Analysis of the Typical Parentage Trio

Perhaps the most commonly encountered scenario in parentage testing involves a trio of individuals—a known parent of the child, the child, and an alleged parent. Often, this scenario will involve questioned paternity and the testing will be initiated by a mother or the state, both of who want to compel the father to help provide financially and emotionally for the child.

The typical trio is also the most straightforward to analyze statistically because each member has been tested; therefore, the collection of genetic markers can be directly compared. Mendel's laws require half of the alleles in the child's sample to be traceable to each true parent. Thus, one allele in the child's profile for a given marker must match an allele in the known parent, which allows the other allele in the child's profile to be compared directly with the collection of alleles detected in the alleged parent's DNA. The title "known parent" also defines the assumptions used in the statistical analysis of results leading to the calculation of a likelihood ratio (LR) in an inclusion case that reflects the weight of the evidence favoring the alleged parent as the true parent of the child. The LR may be called many things, including the paternity index (in cases of questioned paternity), maternity index (in cases of questioned maternity), sibling index (in cases of questioned sibship), etc. However, the reader should understand that in each case, the term refers to an LR that is a numerical statement of weight regarding the questioned relationship.

Consider the following pedigree and STR test results in the case of disputed paternity:

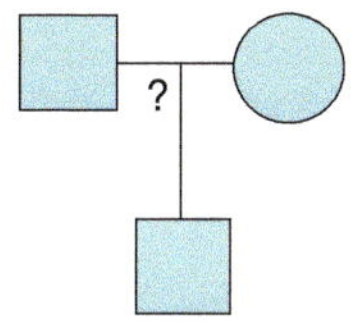

Locus	*Small tandem repeat alleged father*	*Phenotypes child*	*Mother*
D8S1179	12,14	10,12	10,13
D21S11	29,32.2	29	29,30
D7S820	12	10,12	10,12

STR typing results for three loci reflecting different states of zygosity and allele sharing in the trio are shown. The alleged parent shares at least one allele with the child at each locus; moreover, the allele shared is one of the possible obligate alleles for each marker. For example, at the D8S1179 locus, the known parent (the mother in this case) shares allele 10 with the child. On the basis of the assumption that the known parent is a true parent, allele 12 must, therefore, have been inherited from the parent whose identity is questioned. The alleged parent has allele 12 in his profile; therefore, he is included among a pool of possible parents. In assigning weight to the inclusion, two hypotheses will be compared to calculate the LR: H0 and H1. H0 estimates the likelihood or probability of the alleged parent:child:known parent trio if the alleged father is the true father of the child (i.e., the chance of producing a child who looks like this child through a mating of the alleged father with the mother). Because the mother is heterozygous, her chance of passing allele 10 to a child is 50% or 0.5. Likewise, because the alleged father is heterozygous, his chance of passing allele 12 to the child is also 0.5. If either the alleged father or mother were homozygous for an obligate allele in the child, then their chance of allele transmission would double from 0.5 to 1.0. The probability of the mother passing allele 12 is zero, as is the probability of the alleged father passing allele 10. Therefore,

$$\begin{aligned} \text{H0} &= \left(0.50_{\text{Allele 10 from Known Parent}}\right) \\ &\quad \times \left(0.50_{\text{Allele 12 from Alleged Parent}}\right) \\ &\quad + \left(0_{\text{Allele 12 from the Known Parent}}\right) \\ &\quad \times \left(0_{\text{Allele 10 from the Alleged Parent}}\right) \\ &= 0.25 \end{aligned}$$

The counterhypothesis (H1) predicts the likelihood of the results if the alleged parent is not the true parent of the child (i.e., the probability of producing a child who looks genetically like this child through a mating of the mother with an unknown, untested, random man of the same ethnicity as the alleged father). This random man must harbor allele 12 in his profile (because allele 12 is the obligate allele), and his probability of transmitting allele 12 to the child is defined by its population frequency. If allele 12 has a frequency of 0.097 and allele 10 a frequency of 0.140, then

$$\begin{aligned}H1 &= (0.50_{\text{Allele 10 from Known Parent}})(0.097_{\text{Allele 12 from RM}}) \\ &\quad + (0_{\text{Allele 12 from Known Parent}})(0.140_{\text{Allele 10 from RM}}) \\ &= 0.0485 \text{ (where RM is the "Random man")}\end{aligned}$$

Thus, the LR for the D8S1179 test result thus becomes a mathematical comparison of the probabilities of the H0 and H1 hypotheses:

$$LR = H0/H1 = 0.25/0.0485 = 5.16$$

Given the test results observed at the D8S1179 locus, the results are a little over five times as likely if the alleged parent is the true parent of the child versus someone unrelated to the alleged parent, of the same ethnic group, and random in the population. Stated perhaps more meaningfully, the probability of producing a 10, 12 child from a mating of the alleged and known parent is favored by a factor of 5.16-fold over the probability of producing the child from a mating of the known parent with a randomly selected, untested, and unrelated individual of the same ethnic background.

Locus	*D21S11 alleged father*	*Phenotypes child*	*Mother*
D21S11	29,32.2	29	29,30

Consider the test results for the D21S11 locus:

The mother shares allele 29 with the child (who is homozygous for allele 29), defining another copy of allele 29 in the child's homozygous profile as the obligate allele for the locus. The two hypotheses being compared for the D21S11 locus are identical to those expressed above and both the mother and alleged father are heterozygous for allele 29. The fact that the child is homozygous for the obligate allele will have no bearing on the calculation. Thus, the LR calculation becomes (assuming allele 29 has a frequency of 0.205):

$$\begin{aligned}LR &= H0/H1 \\ LR &= [(P_{M\text{-}29})(P_{AF\text{-}29})]/[(P_{M\text{-}29})(P_{RM\text{-}29})] \\ LR &= [(0.5)(0.5)]/[(0.5)(0.205)] \\ LR &= 0.25/0.1025 = 2.44\end{aligned}$$

Locus	*D7S280 alleged father*	*Phenotypes child*	*Mother*
D7S820	12	10,12	10,12

Consider the results for the D7S820 locus. The results for D7S820 introduce us to a new layer of complexity; that is, that the allele inherited by the child from the mother is unclear. In addition, the alleged father is homozygous for allele 12, which means his probability of transmitting it doubles to 100%.

To calculate the LR for D7S820, one must consider both possible transmissions of alleles from the mother to the child. Likewise, in the denominator (i.e., the H1 hypothesis), one must consider possible matings of the mother with random men capable of transmitting either allele 10 or allele 12 to the child. Therefore, the LR calculation becomes (assuming the allele frequency for allele 12 is 0.140 and that for allele 10 is 0.291)

$$\begin{aligned}LR = {} & [(0.5_{M\text{-}10})(1.0_{AF\text{-}12}) + (0.5_{M\text{-}12})(0_{AF\text{-}10})]/[(0.5_{M\text{-}10}) \\ & \times (0.140_{RM\text{-}12}) + (0.5_{M\text{-}12})(0.291_{RM\text{-}10})]\end{aligned}$$

$$LR = 0.5/0.2155 = 2.32$$

Now that the individual LRs for each locus has been calculated, all of the data can be combined because one is ultimately evaluating whether or not the alleged parent is capable of producing a single gamete (sperm or egg) capable of transmitting all of the necessary genetic markers to the child. Because each STR locus analyzed is independently inherited, each LR can be multiplied by every other LR to arrive at a combined value. The goal is to achieve a level of certainty regarding parentage that is compelling. Accreditation standards for parentage testing laboratories issued by the AABB (ninth edition) mandate a combined LR of at least 100 as the threshold of certainty that must be achieved, except in special circumstances.

In addition to calculating an LR, it is possible to evaluate the test results from the perspective of the random match probability typically calculated by the forensic DNA laboratory. The statistic calculated is called the RMNE (i.e., random men not excluded) and simply reflects the chance of selecting someone at random from the population and being unable to exclude them as the parent of a given child. In addition to the RMNE, the probability of exclusion (PEx) for a locus or combination of loci can be calculated, which reflects the discriminatory power of a given test or group of tests. Simply stated, the PEx is the probability that the alleged parent would have been excluded if they were falsely accused. To calculate PEx, one must first calculate the RMNE value. This, as might be expected, is proportional to the population frequency of the obligate allele(s) identified in the child. For example, for the D8S1179 locus, the obligate allele is 12, which has a population frequency of 0.097. To calculate the proportion of the population harboring allele 12 who would be included as a potential parent of the child (i.e., the RMNE), the Hardy–Weinberg equation is used to estimate homozygous and heterozygous phenotypes containing allele 12:

$$p^2 + 2pq = (0.097^2) + 2[(0.097)(1 - 0.097)] = 0.185$$

(The "1-0.097" term in the equation represents the combined frequency of all other alleles at the D8S1179 locus, except allele 12.)

Thus, 18.5% of the population would be expected to harbor allele 12 and, therefore, be included as a possible parent of the child. In an extension of this logic, 100% of people minus those who would be included leave a remainder of individuals who would not have allele 12 in their profile and, therefore, be excluded. In this case, 81.5% of the population would be excluded, which represents the PEx for the D8S1179 locus in this case. Of special note is the fact that the PEx value is calculated ignoring the genotype of the alleged parent. The only information needed to calculate PEx is the identity of the obligate gene in the child, deduced by comparing the profiles of the child and known parent.

Early in the use of inclusionary statistics for parentage testing, some states considered the PEx value alone for the determination of parentage. For example, legislation supporting child support enforcement activities in some states mandated that any man not excluded by a battery of genetic tests that excluded at least 95% of the population would be deemed by the state to be the true father of the child. Although this approach may seem at first glance acceptable, it does not consider the phenotypes of possible fathers of the child. Both an alleged father who is heterozygous for an obligate allele and one who is homozygous would have the same PEx value when clearly an alleged parent homozygous for an obligate allele would transmit it to children with twice the frequency of a heterozygote.

In addition to reporting LR values in parentage cases, a probability of parentage must appear on reports from accredited laboratories. The probability of parentage is another way to express the weight of the evidence supporting the opinion of parentage and is calculated using Bayes' theorem. Simply defined, Bayes' theorem allows for the combining of genetic and nongenetic information relevant to questioned parentage into a final statement of probability. Three terms are incorporated into Bayes' formula: the prior probability, the conditional probability, and the posterior probability. In matters of questioned relatedness, the level of certainty of the relationship, before genetic testing is performed, represents the prior probability. The prior may include evidence that the alleged and known parent were living together and acknowledged publicly that they had a sexual relationship during the period of conception. However, after genetic testing (representing the conditional probability), if the alleged parent is excluded, the level of certainty regarding parentage will be modified downward (i.e., one will be less convinced if the alleged parent represents the true parent of the child). The combination of the prior and conditional probabilities (represented by the LR) produces the posterior probability, reflecting the revised level of certainty regarding the relationship after incorporating the new information.

The calculation of the posterior probability involves creating a ratio comparing the evidence favoring parentage (under a given prior probability) with the probability both for and against parentage. Assume for this discussion that the alleged parent convinces a judge whether he/she was not in contact with the known parent during the period of conception. The judge could assign a prior probability of 10%. In other words, there is a low probability that the alleged parent is the true parent of the child based upon nongenetic information. However, the fact that genetic testing did not exclude the alleged parent and, moreover, has produced a combined LR of 100 will surely modify the 10% level of certainty. The posterior probability calculation would take the following form:

$$\begin{aligned} W_{10} &= [(0.10_{\text{Prior for}})(100_{\text{LR}})]/[(0.10_{\text{Prior for}})(100_{\text{LR}}) \\ &\quad + (0.90_{\text{Prior against}})] \\ &= 10/10.9 = 0.917, \text{ or } 91.7\% \end{aligned}$$

The term W_{10} refers to the posterior probability calculated using a prior of 10%.

Therefore, a probability of 91.7% reflects the current level of conviction that the alleged parent is the true parent of the child. It must be stressed that the probability reported represents an opinion as evidenced by the fact that it is impossible to produce a probability of parentage equal to 100% for an alleged parent, no matter how much inclusionary genetic testing is performed. Look at what happens to the posterior probability if the judge, knowing that the alleged and known parents were together on a largely uninhabited island during the period of conception, assigns a prior probability of 90%:

$$\begin{aligned} W_{90} &= (0.90)(100)/[(0.90)(100) + (0.10)] = 90/90.1 \\ &= 0.9989, \text{ or } 99.89\% \end{aligned}$$

Clearly, a much higher level of certainty regarding the parentage of the child is produced under a 90% prior for the same LR of 100. Most relatedness testing laboratories assign a prior probability of 50% unless instructed by the court to do otherwise. The reason for choosing 50% relates primarily to the neutrality of the laboratory, basing the posterior probability strictly on the genetic test results alone. The relationship

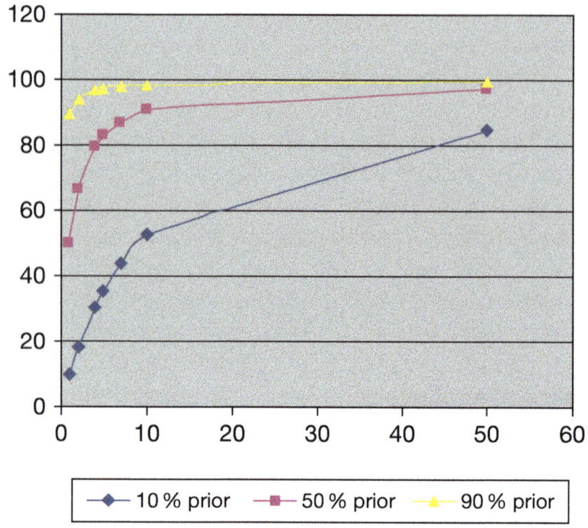

Figure 1 Relationship of posterior probability (*y*-axis) and LR (*x*-axis), displayed under three different prior probabilities.

probability and LR is shown graphically (the abscissa reflects the LR calculated and the ordinate reflects the posterior probability of parentage; **Figure 1**).

Cases Lacking a Known Parent

Often, a laboratory will be asked to perform relatedness testing in a situation in which a known parent is not available to provide a sample for analysis. The consequence of not having a known parent for the analysis is to typically reduce the LRs for each system tested, often forcing a laboratory to do more testing to achieve a compelling result. Consider the pedigree and STR test results shown in the table as follows:

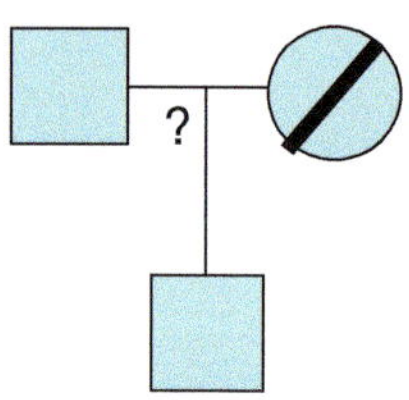

Locus	*Small tandem repeat* *alleged father*	*Phenotypes* *child*	*Mother*
D8S1179	12,14	10,12	Not tested
D21S11	29,32.2	29	Not tested
D7S820	12	10,12	Not tested

In this scenario, the known parent (the mother) has not been tested, but the alleged parent shares at least one allele with the child at each of the three loci shown and is, therefore, included as a possible true parent. To calculate an LR, both alleles in the child must be considered as possible obligates and in calculating the LR.

The hypotheses compared in the LR are H0 (the probability of producing the child from a mating of the alleged parent and an unknown, random mother) versus H1 (the probability of producing the child from a mating of parents who are unrelated and are both random in the population). For each calculation, one must assign a "random mother" who is phenotypically related to the child and one must consider her probability of transmitting either obligate allele to the child.

Locus	*D8S1179* *alleged father*	*Phenotypes* *child*	*Mother*
D8S1179	12,14	10,12	Not tested

For example, for the D8S1179 locus (the frequencies of alleles 10 and 12 are 0.097 and 0.140, respectively, and RM stands for random man and RMom for random mother)

$$LR = [(P_{AF\text{-}12})(P_{RMom\text{-}10}) + (P_{AF\text{-}10})(P_{RMom\text{-}12})]/[(P_{RM\text{-}12})(P_{RMom\text{-}10}) + (P_{RM\text{-}10})(P_{RMom\text{-}12})]$$

$$LR = [(0.5)(0.097) + (0)(0.140)]/[(0.140)(0.097) + (0.097) \times (0.140)]$$

$$LR = (0.0485 + 0)/[(2)(0.140)(0.097)] = 0.0485/0.0272 = 1.78 \text{ (LR with Mother} = 5.16)$$

The LR calculation considers two possible matings between the AF and a random mother, separated by the plus sign in the numerator.

The denominator of the calculation reflects the chance the child was produced by a mating of parents, both of who are random using the same logic.

Note how the H1 expression can be reduced to 2(0.097)(0.140), which is the same as the $2pq$ portion of the Hardy–Weinberg equation predicting the frequency of the child's heterozygous phenotype.

Locus	*D21S11* *alleged father*	*Phenotypes* *child*	*Mother*
D21S11	29,32.2	29	Not tested

For the D21S11 locus, the child is homozygous for allele 29. Whereas the zygosity of the child had no consequence for the LR calculation when the mother was tested, in a deficiency case, zygosity does have an effect on the magnitude of the

LR. For the D21S11 locus (assuming an allele frequency of 0.205 for allele 29),

$$\begin{aligned} H0 &= (0.50_{AF\text{-}29})(0.205_{RMom\text{-}29}) = 0.103 \\ H1 &= (0.205^2) = 0.042 \\ LR &= 0.166/0.042 = 2.44 \end{aligned}$$

If one compares the LR in the test lacking the mother with the LR for the test in which she was included, then one will notice that the values are the same. This seems contradictory to the statement that tests lacking a known parent will almost always produce LR values that are lower. However, recall that the values are lower because of the ambiguity in the origin of alleles in the child's profile. In the case of the D21S11 results, there is no ambiguity in the origin of alleles because the child is homozygous for allele 29; one copy had to have originated from the untested mother, leaving the second copy as the obligate from the father.

Locus	D7S280 alleged father	Phenotypes child	Mother
D7S820	12	10,12	Not tested

For the D7S820 locus, the alleged father is homozygous for one of the possible obligate alleles in the child's profile; thus, the transmission frequency for allele 12 to the child has doubled from 0.5 to 1.0:

$$\begin{aligned} LR &= [(1.0_{AF\text{-}12})(0.291_{RMom\text{-}10}) + (0_{AF\text{-}10})(0.140_{RMom\text{-}12})]/ \\ &\quad [(2)(0.291)(0.140)] \\ LR &= (0.291 + 0)/0.082 = 3.55 \quad \text{(LR with Mother} = 2.32) \end{aligned}$$

Parentage testing can also help identify unknown victims of crime or accident. Consider a skeleton found in an isolated area for which the identity is unknown. DNA extracted from the remains could be subjected to STR typing and the results compared with profiles from surviving family members. Consider the following pedigree involving remains from an unknown "Jane Doe" compared with a husband and wife who have a missing daughter:

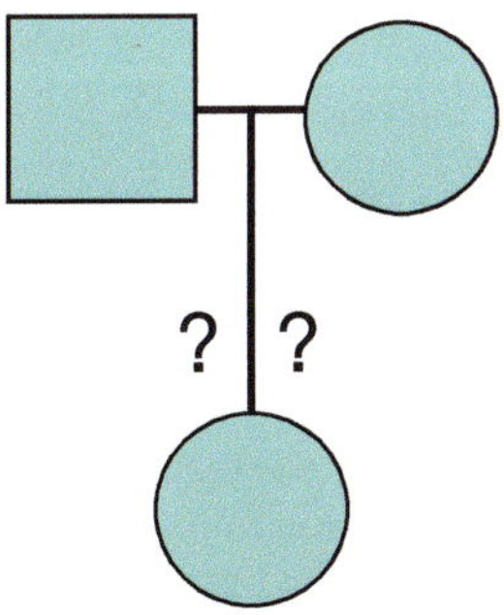

Locus	Small tandem repeat alleged father	Phenotypes child	Alleged mother
D8S1179	12,14	10,12	10,13
D21S11	29,32.2	29	29,30
D7S820	12	10,12	10,12

In this scenario, both parents are alleged; therefore, there are no assumptions in the analysis that revolve around a known parent. The H0 hypothesis would become "what is the probability of the STR profiles in the alleged parents and Jane Doe if the alleged parents are the true mother and father of Jane Doe?" The H1 hypothesis becomes, "What is the probability of the STR profiles in the alleged parents and Jane Doe if she is unrelated to; *BOTH* alleged parents and is random in the population?" For the results at the D8S1179 locus,

$$\begin{aligned} LR &= [(0.5_{AM\text{-}10})(0.5_{AF\text{-}12})]/[(2)(0.097)(0.140)] \\ LR &= 0.25/0.0272 = 9.19 \end{aligned}$$

Notice how the numerator has not changed from the typical paternity test in which the mother participated in the testing. What has changed is the H1 hypothesis, which mandates that the remains be unrelated to *BOTH* the alleged mother and alleged father and be random in the population, represented by the phenotype frequency for the locus in question.

Locus	D7S820 alleged father	Phenotypes child	Alleged mother
D7S820	12	10,12	10,12

As was the case for the D7S820 results discussed earlier, the alleged mother and child are phenotypically identical; therefore, all possible breeding scenarios must be considered in the calculation. The LR calculation takes the following form:

$$\begin{aligned} LR &= [(0.5_{AM\text{-}10})(1.0_{AF\text{-}12}) + (0.5_{AM\text{-}12})(0_{AF\text{-}10})]/ \\ &\quad [2(0.291)(0.140)] \\ LR &= 0.5/0.082 = 6.10 \end{aligned}$$

Graphical representations shown in **Figure 2** are the LR values for parentage tests in the three scenarios; that is, paternity with a known mother (labeled w/M), paternity without a known mother (labeled wo/M), and parentage with both maternity and paternity alleged (labeled AF and AM). Note how the LR values are generally larger in the remains identification cases because of the change in the H1 hypothesis in the LR calculation (**Figure 2**).

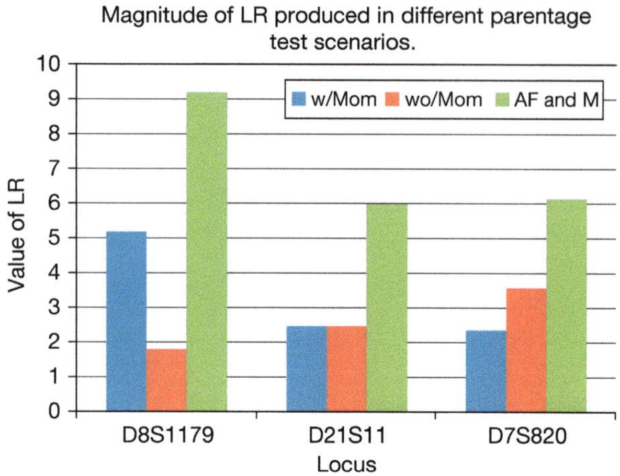

Figure 2 Magnitude of LR produced in different parentage test scenarios.

Special Types of DNA Testing

In some cases, autosomal STR markers will fail to produce a compelling LR in a questioned relationship. In such cases, analysis of DNA markers with special patterns of inheritance may be informative. Using STR markers located on the Y chromosome (Y-STRs) or single nucleotide polymorphisms (SNPs) associated with mitochondrial DNA (mtDNA), a laboratory can investigate the familial relatedness of an alleged family member with the male and female family lines, respectively.

Y-STRs exhibit levels of variability within male members of the population comparable to variability of autosomal STR markers. Multiplex Y-STR typing kits are marketed that amplify as many as 17 STR loci on the Y chromosome. Products amplified from male DNA are compatible with capillary- or gel-based platforms for electrophoretic separation and allele detection, and collectively exhibit high levels of discriminatory power. However, one must remember that the samples being compared must all be from male donors for test results to be obtained. Moreover, the males being compared must allegedly belong to a common male family line. For example, consider the following pedigree for which Y-STR typing is being considered:

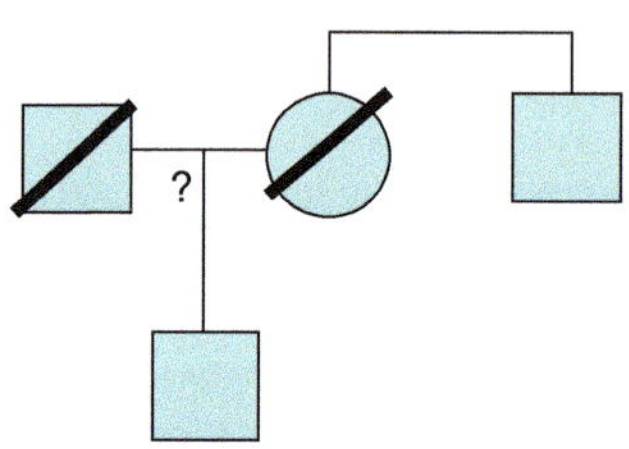

In this pedigree, although males are the source of Y chromosomal DNA being tested, the reference male is the mother's brother and thus will be descended from a different male lineage than the man who is questioned as the father of the child. In such a case, the child will likely exhibit a different linear array of Y-STR alleles (called the haplotype) than his maternal uncle; thus, results should not be interpreted as exclusionary.

Consider the following pedigree:

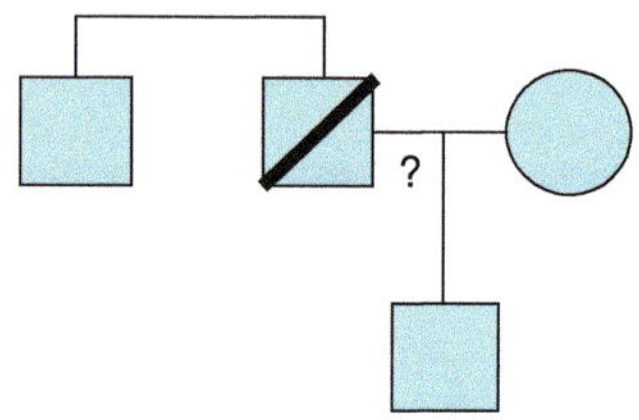

In this case, the paternal uncle will be a suitable donor for testing.

Calculations using Y-STRs are performed using haplotype frequencies rather than individual allele frequencies because the markers are tightly linked on the single Y chromosome. Haplotype frequency databases exist and are available from several sources for use in calculations in which the LR is calculated by $1/n$, where n equals the frequency of the obligate haplotype in the population.

Whereas Y-STRs are descended along the male line, mtDNA polymorphisms are inherited through the maternal lineage. Regardless of your sex, your complement of mtDNA markers was inherited from your mother. mtDNA polymorphisms are typically single nucleotide substitutions located within two specific regions of the mitochondrial genome known as the D-loop, which harbors hot spots for SNP-type variability.

Like Y-STRs, mtDNA polymorphisms are defined as haplotypes containing SNP polymorphisms that vary from a reference sequence originally obtained at Cambridge University in the United Kingdom that was arbitrarily chosen as the benchmark sequence to which all other sequences are compared. Also akin to Y-STRs, consideration must be given to carefully select family reference samples allegedly within the maternal lineage. When compared to STR typing, both on the Y chromosome and among autosomal loci, mtDNA is much less powerful for relationship testing.

Mutations and How to Deal with Them

About once in every 500–1000 parentage tests, an isolated result inconsistent with parentage will be encountered. Such inconsistencies occur in the face of overwhelming additional testing that provides a compelling probability that the alleged parent is the true parent of the child. The high degree of variability exhibited by STR loci derives from a somewhat high level of genetic instability and their predisposition to being misreplicated during meiosis. Ultimately, such misreplication events produce gametes harboring STR alleles that differ from their parent, usually by a single repeat within the tandem array. If such sperm or eggs are involved in conception, offspring will be produced exhibiting an STR profile that differs from their true parent.

When a mutation is encountered in a parentage test, it must be incorporated somehow into the overall statistical result. STR mutations are rare events; thus, a mismatch between alleged parent and child is more likely evidence of nonparentage than parentage with a mutation. Several methods exist to fairly incorporate an inconsistent result into the overall LR calculation. One is simply to assign the mutation rate as the LR value. Thus, if a locus has a mutation rate of 0.001 and a mismatch is observed, the value 0.001 is simply incorporated as the LR value for that locus. The problem with this approach is that it does conform to the typical method of comparing two hypotheses in an LR. In a more appropriate approach, the two hypotheses compared are H0 (the chance that the tested man is the father of the child and a mutation has occurred to produce the mismatched allele inherited by the child (defined by the mutation rate, μ)) versus the alternative hypothesis H1 (the chance that the tested individual is not the child's parent (defined by the probability of the locus in question to exclude someone who is falsely accused)). Thus, the LR is calculated as follows:

$$\mathrm{LR} = \mu/\mathrm{PEx}$$

Because a typical STR locus has a mutation rate of 0.001 and the typical PEx for an STR locus is 60%, LRs will average about 0.002, which will often mandate that the laboratory perform additional testing to produce a combined LR of $\geq$100. Although this approach is closer to the typical method for calculating an LR, it does not consider the transmission of alleles from the parents to the child. Still a third approach for calculation of the LR does consider transmission probabilities.

Consider the following pedigree and STR test results:

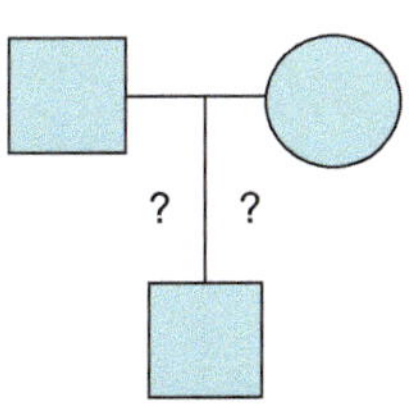

Locus	*Alleged parent*	*Child*	*Known parent*
D3S1358	17,19	17,22	16,22
D21S11	32,32.2	32,33.2	30,33.2
FGA	24,28	24,30	29,30
D8S1179	10,12	10,14	14,16
D5S818	10,12	9,13	9,10

For all systems shown in the pedigree, the alleged parent harbors an obligate allele with the exception of the D5S818 locus. At this locus, the obligate allele is 13 and the alleged parent exhibits allele 12 as the closest to the obligate in size. Research has shown that 90–95% of all STR mutations exhibit changes to the tandem array that either add or remove a single repeat. Thus, allele 12 is the most likely candidate precursor allele in the alleged parent that underwent a mutation to become allele 13 in the child. Statistical treatment of this inconsistent result is most appropriately treated as described by Brenner (see http://www.dna-view.com) as follows (assume that the frequency of allele 13 is 0.1 and the mutation rate is 0.00,116 for the D5S818 locus):

Probability of allele 13 from the AF

$$\begin{aligned} &= \left[\left(0.5_{\text{Allele 12 rather than allele 10}}\right)\left(\mu_{\text{Mutation rate}}\right)\right. \\ &\quad \times \left(0.5_{\text{Increasing in size rather than decreasing in size}}\right) \\ &= (\mu/4)\left(0.5_{\text{transmission of 9 from Known Parent}}\right) = \mathrm{H0} \end{aligned}$$

H1 in the LR calculation would reflect the probability of the child from a mating of the known parent and a random, unrelated individual of the same ethnic/racial background. Therefore,

$$\begin{aligned} \mathrm{H1} &= \left(0.5_{\text{transmission of 9 from Known Parent}}\right) \\ &\quad \times \left(0.1_{\text{transmission of allele 13 from the random parent}}\right) \end{aligned}$$

$$\begin{aligned} \mathrm{LR} &= \left[(\mu/4)\left(0.5_{\text{transmission of 9 from Known Parent}}\right)\right]/ \\ &\quad \left[(0.5)(0.1)\right] = \left[(0.00116/4)(0.5)\right]/0.05 \\ &\quad = 0.000145/0.05 = 0.0029. \end{aligned}$$

Once the LR has been produced, it is incorporated into the combined LR for all loci in the normal way (i.e., it gets multiplied together with all other loci). Mutations, when they occur, generally force a laboratory to perform additional testing to produce a combined LR of $\geq$100.

Future Considerations

Whereas parentage testing has historically occurred in private laboratories and has been performed for civil purposes, the forensic community has increasingly become aware of the utility of family relatedness testing for the investigation of traditional and nontraditional crime. Recently in Los Angeles, a long-standing unsolved series of homicides were finally solved through the use of familial searching of the CODIS database. The perpetrator of the murders was the father of a felon whose profile was in the databank for a nonviolent crime he committed. Many states are now considering legislation that would allow searching of their local databases for relatives of felons as part of the investigation process. It will be important for the laboratory conducting such searches to have a good understanding of the relevance of LR values produced from potential matches. Likewise, an understanding of family relatedness analysis is critically important for the identification of human remains. Only through a good understanding of the statistical approach to such cases can one have any chance of confidently identifying those victims who, without DNA testing, may never be reunited with their families.

See also: **Biology/DNA:** Disaster Victim Identification; DNA Extraction and Quantification; Mitochondrial DNA; Short Tandem Repeats; The National Missing and Unidentified Persons System (NamUs); **Biology/DNA/Methods/Analytical Techniques:** Capillary Electrophoresis in Forensic Genetics.

Further Reading

Edwards, M., Allen, R.W., 2004. Characteristics of mutations at the D5S818 locus studied using a tightly linked marker. Transfusion 44, 83–90.

Hill, C.R., Butler, J.M., Vallone, P.M., 2009. A 26plex autosomal STR assay to aid human identity testing. Journal of Forest Science 54, 1008–1015.

Relevant Website

http://www.nas.edu—National Academies of Science.

Mixture Interpretation (Interpretation of Mixed DNA Profiles with STRs Only)

BJ Heidebrecht, Maryland State Police, Forensic Sciences Division, Pikesville, MD, USA

2013 Published by Elsevier Ltd.

Glossary

Analytical threshold The rfu value above which a peak can reasonably be declared to be a true allele. Peaks below this rfu value may be true alleles or may be background signals.

Deconvolution The determination of reasonable genetic profiles that could be contributors to a mixed DNA profile based on quantitative peak information and any interpretation assumptions.

Dropout The failure to detect one or more alleles of a contributor at a given genetic locus because of degradation and/or stochastic sampling of low quantities of template DNA.

Indistinguishable from stutter (IFS) A state that exists when the peaks in stutter position from major contributor's alleles are similar in quantitative value to that of alleles of a minor contributor. As such, it would be valid to reason the peak in question as either stutter or a heterozygous pairing with the minor allele.

Minimum expected peak height ratio threshold (MEPHR) The minimum relative ratio of heterozygous alleles in single-source samples expected to be seen, as determined by a laboratory. This value may vary based upon the amplification kit, template DNA quantity, thermal cycling parameters, electrokinetic injection parameters, and the use of any post-polymerase chain reaction cleaning procedures.

Mixture ratio The relative ratio, or percentages, of the DNA contributions of multiple individuals to a mixed DNA profile, as determined by the use of quantitative peak information.

Polymerase chain reaction Enzymatic process in which a specific region of DNA is replicated exponentially to produce many copies of the template sequence.

Probabilistic genotype interpretation Analysis of genetic data without using analytical, stochastic, or stutter thresholds. Such analysis requires computer-based quantitative interpretation for the analysis of the number of contributors, mixture ratios of the contributors, overall quantity of DNA present, polymerase chain reaction stutter, relative amplification, degraded DNA, dye separation, and background noise. The final determination of this interpretation model is a comparison of which genotypes are more or less likely to be present in the evidential data.

Stochastic threshold The rfu value above which an apparent homozygote can reasonably be declared to be a true homozygote. An apparent homozygote below this rfu value may have dropout of the sister allele to the detected allele.

Unambiguous allele A peak defined by the analyst as a true allele in the mixture; one that is unreasonable to define as an artifact such as stutter or spectral pull-up.

Introduction

Using defined thresholds is common in forensic science, and it is a practical, although not ideal, decision. However, it should be kept in mind that applying such thresholds is somewhat arbitrary because it is based on the degree of confidence one wishes to apply when defining the thresholds, and that there will be cases in which true data lie beyond these thresholds. Therefore, the principles listed here, based upon models using defined thresholds, are applicable to the point at which an analyst can come to a "reasonable" decision regarding the interpretation of the DNA mixture.

The general approach to mixture interpretation should include the following elements:

1. A general overview of the data prior to the examination of any single locus to make determinations of the number of contributors detected, the possibility of determining a ratio of contributors, and to make determinations about the presence of a distinct major contributor(s).
2. Identification of alleles that are below the stochastic threshold and therefore might have dropout at that locus.
3. Identification of alleles that are above the stochastic threshold but may still involve dropout of an associated heterozygous allele.
4. Examination of loci without unambiguous minor alleles to determine whether the minor contributor(s) is reasonable to be considered masked by the major contributor(s) or might be completely unrepresented by the detected alleles

 http://dx.doi.org/10.1016/B978-0-12-800647-4.00026-6

5. Analysis of the mixture for peaks that may be alleles indistinguishable from stutter (IFS).
6. Reevaluation of the contribution to the mixture that is foreign to the intimate contributor for possible dropout and IFS if performing an interpretation that utilizes the assumption of an individual being intimate to the sample.
7. Attempt to resolve the mixture to single genotype pairs using mixture deconvolution.
8. Comparison with any reference standards that are to be considered probative to the mixture to make a determination of inclusion, exclusion, or inconclusive.

Determining the Number of Contributors

DNA evidence is generally considered to have originated from more than one contributor if three or more unambiguous alleles are present at one or more loci (excepting triallelic loci) and/or the peak height ratios (PHRs) in loci with only two unambiguous alleles are below the laboratory's minimum expected peak height ratio (MEPHR) threshold (excepting primer site mutations).

Generally, the minimum number of contributors to a mixed sample can be determined based on the locus that exhibits the greatest number of unambiguous alleles. For example, if no more than four alleles are detected per locus, then the analyst can be reasonably confident that the evidence originated from only two contributors. However, it must be noted that there exists the possibility of a mixture of three contributors containing no more than four alleles at all examined loci. Further examination of the possible genotype combinations and their calculated PHRs, as compared to the laboratory's MEPHR threshold, must be undertaken to discount the probability of three or more contributors (**Figure 1**).

On the basis of the number of unambiguous alleles and the varying peak heights of the alleles, it is possible that a reasonable determination as to the number of contributors cannot be made. In such instances, it is appropriate to rely on the locus that exhibits the greatest number of unambiguous alleles to determine a minimum number of contributors present. For example, if a maximum of six alleles are detected in any given locus, then the analyst can be reasonably confident that the evidence originated from at least three contributors.

Determining a Ratio of Contributors

If a reasonable assumption as to the number of contributors can be made, then it may be possible to determine the relative ratio, or percentage, of each of the contributors to the mixture using quantitative peak information. The quantitative intensity, commonly expressed as relative fluorescent units (rfu) of the DNA typing results of a mixture, will generally be proportional to the relative contribution of each contributor to the mixed biological sample. Thus, the rfu values of the detected alleles can be utilized to calculate an approximate ratio of DNA contributions of individuals to the mixture.

If the mixture has been assumed to comprise only two contributors, then any loci with four unambiguous alleles can be used as a foundation to make a determination of the ratio of the two contributors. Utilizing the assumption that both of the contributors will be heterozygous, all potential genotype combinations can be tested against the laboratory's MEPHR threshold. If more than one genotype pair combination meets the laboratory's MEPHR threshold, then the mixture is close to a 1:1 ratio of contributors. If only one genotype pair combination meets the laboratory's MEPHR threshold, then the ratio of contributors at this locus can be estimated as being the sum

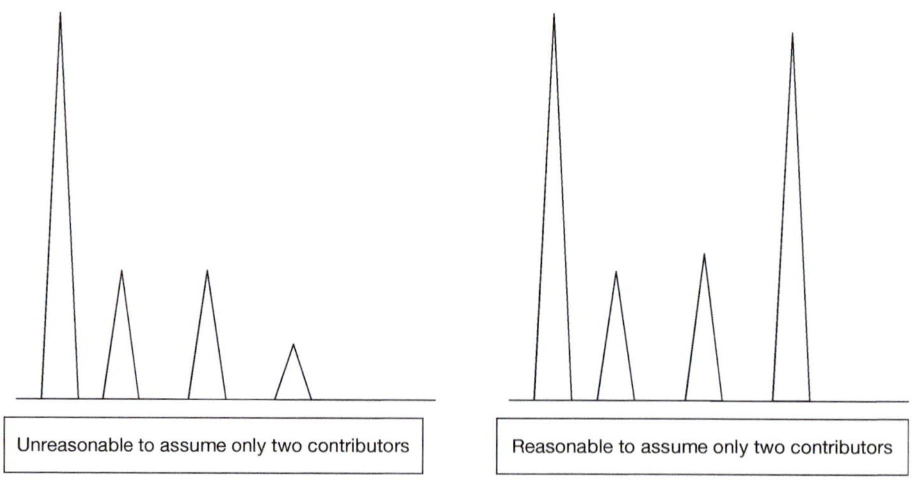

Figure 1 Determining the number of contributors.

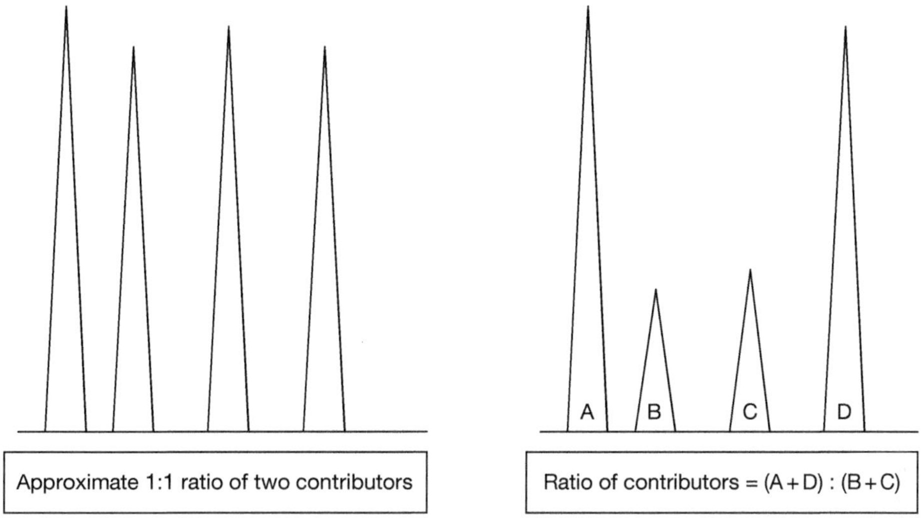

Figure 2 Determining a ratio of contributors in a two-person mixture.

of the rfu values for the two more significant alleles as compared to the sum of the rfu values for the two less significant alleles (**Figure 2**). The possibility that stutter may be influencing the rfu values of the less significant alleles, skewing the PHR of the minor contributor and ratio of contributors, should be considered.

If the mixture has been assumed to comprise only two contributors, then any loci with three unambiguous alleles might be used to further refine the determination of the ratio of the two contributors. Because it is possible to have one allele dropping out from a two-person mixture when only three alleles are detected, the possibility of dropout must be investigated prior to determining if a three-allele locus is suitable for use in the determination of a ratio of contributors. If one of the alleles is at or below the stochastic threshold, the possibility exists that one allele at this locus may be unrepresented by the detected alleles. Given this possibility, such loci should not be included in the calculations for determining a ratio of contributors. If all alleles are above the stochastic threshold, then the possibility that stutter from a significant allele could be causing the minor allele to be reported as above the stochastic threshold should be considered (see below for further discussions regarding stochastic thresholds). If the minor allele is of a similar quantitative value as stutter from a significant allele, then this stutter position peak may be IFS (see below for further discussions regarding peaks being IFS) and such loci should not be included in the calculations for determining a ratio of contributors because an accurate determination of the contribution of the lesser contributor cannot be made. If, after taking into account the stochastic threshold and minor alleles being in stutter position and peaks being IFS, it can still be concluded that the three unambiguous alleles are fully representative of the mixed DNA profiles of both contributors, then the genotype combinations may be homozygous/heterozygous (no allele sharing) or may be heterozygous/heterozygous (one shared allele). All such genotype combinations can be tested against the laboratory's MEPHR threshold and the original ratio of contributors as determined by examination of the four-allele loci.

Similar examination of two-allele loci can also be performed with the genotype pairs including the possibility that both alleles may be shared, only one allele may be shared, or both contributors may be homozygous. In addition, given the fact that only two alleles are detected, the possibility that one contributor may be partially or completely unrepresented by the detected alleles must also be considered when determining if a locus is suitable for use in determining a ratio of contributors.

After a ratio of contributors has been calculated for several loci, the possibility that one of the contributors may be experiencing degradation of their DNA profile must be considered to determine if continuing the analysis using a ratio of contributors will be appropriate. If the low-molecular-weight loci indicate that the ratio of contributors is close to 1:1, but the high-molecular-weight loci indicate that the ratio of contributors is close to 10:1, then this would indicate that one of the contributor's DNA is degraded. As such, it may not be appropriate to define a ratio of contributors for the mixture as a whole. The issue would become even more complicated if one contributor is a significant contributor at low-molecular-weight loci but is the lesser contributor at the high-molecular-weight loci.

Although the above information was provided for mixtures comprising only two contributors, it may be possible to perform similar examinations on mixtures concluded to comprise only three contributors.

If the number of contributors to the mixture cannot be reasonably defined, then it may still be possible to define a single major contributor, or a mixture of contributors, distinct from a multitude of minor contributors. This separation of major and minor contributor(s) should be based upon a clear distinction between the rfu values of the alleles purported to belong to the major and minor contributors to discount the possibility of allele sharing between minor contributors creating a false major profile. As the number of possible contributors present in the mixture increases, this separation should be even more distinct because the possibility increases that allele sharing could cause a false major profile.

Alleles below the Stochastic Threshold

The purpose of a stochastic threshold is to define a point at which the possibility that a detected allele may be experiencing dropout of its heterozygous sister allele below the analytical threshold must be considered reasonable. Thus, without any additional information regarding a mixture, any loci having alleles with rfu values below the stochastic threshold must be considered as having data that are not fully representative of all contributors to the mixture. With additional information, the analyst can alter this original assumption and potentially define a locus as reasonable to have data that are fully representative of all contributors to the mixture.

If a reasonable decision can be made to determine the number of contributors to a mixture, the number of alleles detected at a locus can be used to reason if dropout should be considered. For example, if the mixture is reasoned to involve only two contributors, and four alleles are detected at a locus, then it is reasonable to conclude that both contributors are fully represented, regardless of the stochastic threshold. In addition, the laboratory's MEPHR can be utilized to reason if dropout should be considered. For example, if the mixture is reasoned to involve only two contributors, and three alleles are detected at a locus, then pairing one of the detected alleles with an undetected sister allele leaves two alleles as a genotype pair that can then be compared to the MEPHR to determine if this is a reasonable decision.

Alleles above the Stochastic Threshold

Stochastic thresholds are defined based upon a sample being a single source. Issues of shared alleles and the influence of stutter are not considered when examining single-source samples. However, when analyzing mixtures, such issues could artificially inflate the rfu value of an allele such that it is detected above the stochastic threshold while it might truly have an undetected sister allele. The analyst's interpretation as to the number of contributors, the ratio of contributors, and the laboratory's MEPHR should be used to examine this issue further. If the analyst cannot reason why stutter or allele sharing is not significantly influencing the rfu value of an allele above the stochastic threshold, then dropout must still be considered a possibility (**Figure 3**).

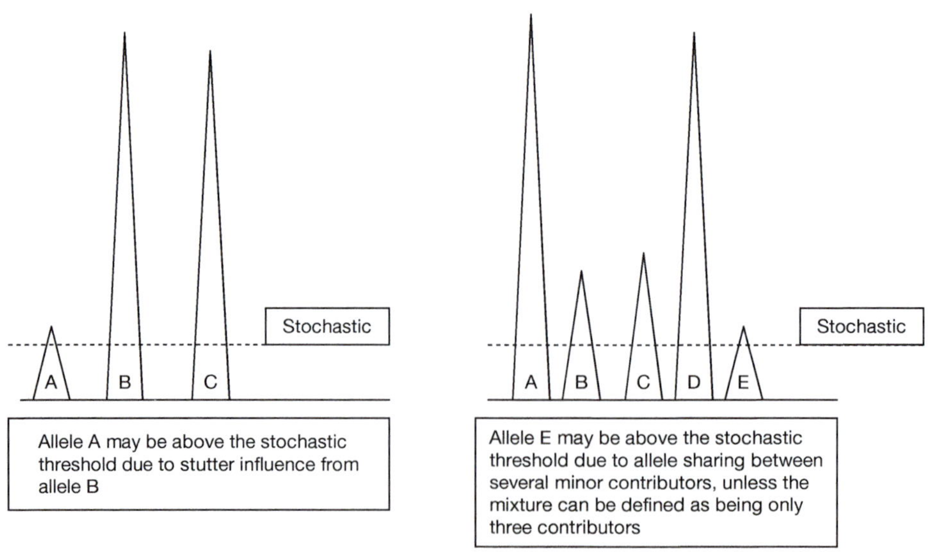

Figure 3 Cautions about stutter and allele sharing influences in regard to the stochastic threshold.

Loci without Unambiguous Minor Alleles

Mixtures reasoned to be consisting of only two contributors may show from one to four alleles at any given locus. When there are four detected alleles, it can be assumed that no dropout is occurring. When there are three detected alleles, it can be assumed that one allele may be undetected based upon the above-listed information regarding the stochastic threshold. However, when only one or two alleles are detected, the possibility that one entire genotype may be undetected must be examined.

If the mixture has demonstrated a consistent ratio of contributors across various loci, then this information can be used in the interpretation. Loci with high rfu values and a close ratio of contributors are unlikely to be experiencing dropout; allele sharing is a more reasonable assumption. Loci with moderate rfu values and a disparate ratio of contributors are more likely to be experiencing dropout; the ratio of contributors may suggest that the minor contributor's alleles would be expected to be below the stochastic threshold and, therefore, may not be reliably amplifying (**Figure 4**).

The laboratory's MEPHR should also be utilized in making the determination that a minor contributor may be experiencing dropout. If the detected alleles meet the laboratory's MEPHR, then it is equally possible that the minor contributor may be sharing allele(s) with the major contributor, or may be experiencing some degree of dropout. However, if the detected alleles do not meet the laboratory's MEPHR, then it is unreasonable to assume that the minor contributor is completely unrepresented by the detected alleles; some degree of allele sharing must be occurring to cause the imbalance in the PHR of the major contributor (**Figure 5**).

In addition, the overall rfu value of the minor contributor should be considered. If the rfu values of the minor contributor are below the stochastic threshold at several genetic loci, the possibility of dropout becomes more reasonable. If the rfu values of the minor contributor are significantly above the stochastic threshold, dropout becomes less reasonable; allele sharing is a more reasonable assumption. Degradation of the minor contributor should be considered when using this information because this could skew the interpretation.

The final challenge to loci without unambiguous minor alleles is that one piece of information may indicate that allele sharing is a more reasonable assumption whereas another piece of information may indicate that dropout is a more reasonable assumption. Declaring that dropout is a possibility will ultimately be statistically conservative toward a defendant who is fully represented by the detected alleles. However, this decision will then also not exclude certain genotypes as being possible contributors that would be excluded if the conclusion were to be that all contributors are represented by the detected alleles.

Although the above information was provided for mixtures comprising only two contributors, it may be possible to perform similar examinations on mixtures concluded to be comprising three or more contributors.

Indistinguishable from Stutter

In mixed-source samples, it is possible that the alleles of the minor contributor(s) are in a position one repeat shorter than

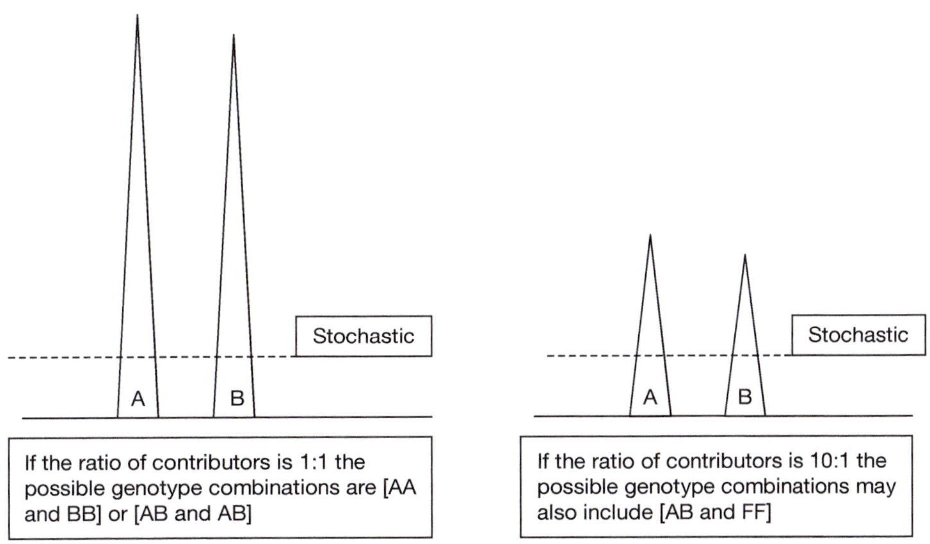

Figure 4 Using the ratio of contributors to determine if alleles may be undetected.

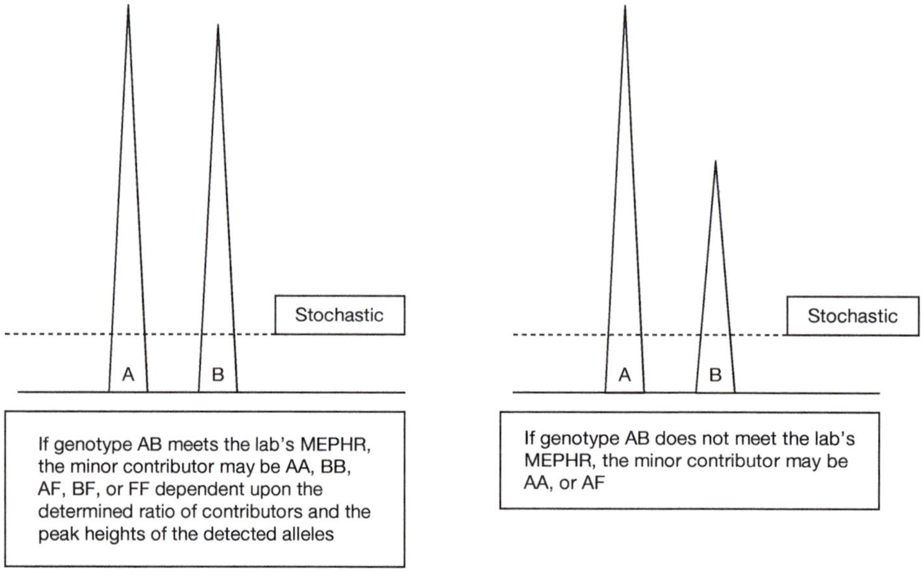

Figure 5 Using peak height ratio expectations to determine if alleles may be undetected.

the major contributor(s). If such an allele also happens to be of an intensity such that the rfu value falls below the stutter expectations for that locus, it is possible that the true composition of the mixture may be misinterpreted. Evidence samples that have minor contributor(s) alleles of similar rfu values to the stutter peaks of the major contributor(s) should be reanalyzed with analysis settings such that stutter thresholds are not applied, while maintaining all other analysis settings. Any new data may then be compared to the other minor peaks of the mixture to categorize the questionable data as stutter or to maintain the designation as IFS.

If the rfu of the peak in question is at or above the laboratory's MEPHR when compared with a single (possibly homozygous) unambiguous minor component allele within that locus, it is possible that this peak in question is either stutter as it meets the expectations of a stutter peak, or a heterozygous allele to the single minor allele as it also meets the expectations of heterozygosity for the minor contributor. Because the true amount of stutter that is occurring in this specific amplification and at this specific allelic bin cannot be determined, the true composition of this peak cannot be determined. As such, the peak in question must be designated as IFS.

When performing the calculation to determine if the peak in question meets the laboratory's MEPHR when compared to a minor component allele, it is important to note that the PHR calculation is not the lesser rfu value divided by the greater. The calculation must be performed as the rfu value of the peak in question divided by the rfu of the unambiguous minor allele. Performing the calculation in this manner may produce a result of greater than 100% and will prevent a PHR calculation that does not meet the MEPHR, but that could be explained by the peak in question having rfu values from both stutter and a minor contributor allele.

If the number of contributors to the mixture can be reasoned, then this information can be utilized to discount the determination of IFS and therefore distinguish the peak in question as being solely stutter. If the number of unambiguous alleles present in the mixture is maximized by the number of contributors, then the possibility that any peaks in stutter position could be true alleles of the minor contributor(s) could only be explained by the presence of a triallelic individual. Because such occurrences are rare, the more reasonable explanation is that the peak in question is solely stutter. If the number of contributors to the mixture cannot be reasoned, then it is possible that every peak in stutter position, above the analytical threshold, may be a true heterozygous or homozygous allele of the minor contributor(s).

It must be noted that once a locus has been determined to have the possibility of dropout, further investigation into the possibility of peaks being IFS is irrelevant. The statistics that would be applied to include undetected alleles will also include alleles that may be masked by being in stutter position (**Figure 6**).

Interpretations That Utilize the Assumption of an Individual Being Intimate to the Sample

It is reasonable to assume that DNA typing results obtained from an intimate sample will contain the DNA of the

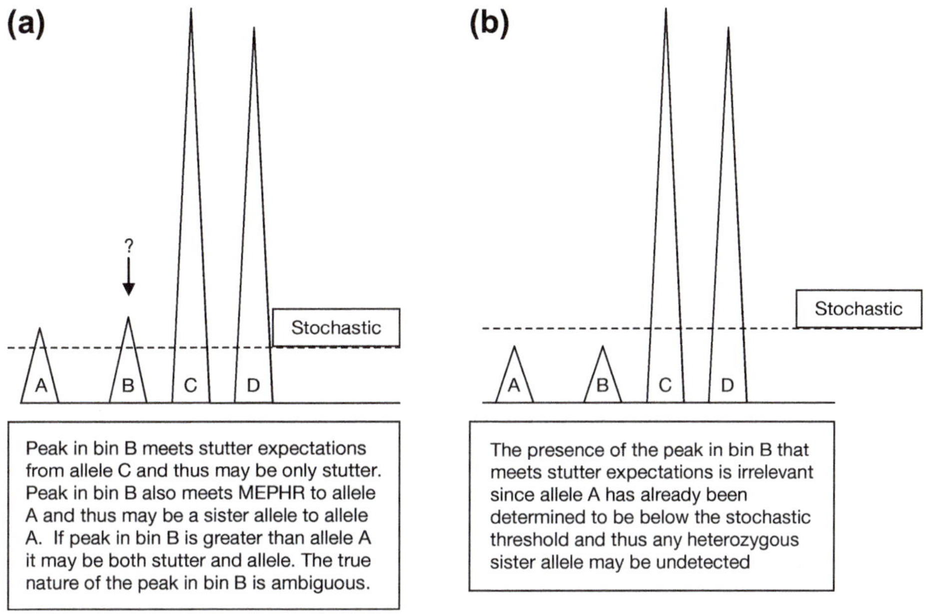

Figure 6 (a) Examining peaks in stutter position to distinguish as stutter or define as "indistinguishable from stutter" (IFS). (b) Examining a peak as IFS in regard to the stochastic threshold. (a) Adapted from Gill, P., et al., 2006. DNA commission of the International Society of Forensic Genetics: recommendations on the interpretation of mixtures. Forensic Science International 160, 90–101, with permission.

individual from whom the sample was taken. On the basis of the assumption of a "known contributor," refinements to the interpretation of a mixture may be made regarding the potential for dropout and peaks being designated as IFS. The assumption of a known contributor is only appropriate when such an assumption is nonprobative to the investigation of the evidence.

Evaluation of IFS in Regard to the Presence of a Known Contributor

Considering that the issue of IFS is solely the province of the minor contributor(s), if the known contributor is consistent with the predominant alleles in the mixture, no refinements to the interpretation of peaks being IFS may be made. However, if the known contributor is consistent with being a minor contributor, the DNA profile of the known contributor can be compared against the ambiguous peaks.

Mixtures with a single minor contributor that is consistent with the known contributor

If declaring an ambiguous peak as a potential true allele of the minor contributor would create a minor contributor profile that is not consistent with the known contributor, then this would reject the assumption of the known contributor as being the minor contributor. As such, the ambiguous peak can reasonably be defined as being solely stutter. Prior to such rejection of the designation of IFS, the analyst should be confident that their assumption is reasonable.

Mixtures with a defined number of minor contributors including one that is consistent with the known contributor

If declaring an ambiguous peak as a potential true allele of the minor contributors would create a mixture of minor contributors that exceeds the maximum number of expected alleles, given the presence of the known contributor, then this would reject the assumption of the known contributor as being one of the minor contributors and/or reject the assumption as to the number of defined minor contributors. As such, the ambiguous peak can reasonably be defined as being solely stutter. Prior to such rejection of the designation of IFS, the analyst should be confident that their assumptions are reasonable.

Evaluation of Dropout in Regard to the Presence of a Known Contributor

Considering that the issue of dropout is associated with DNA profiles with low rfu values, if the known contributor is consistent with robust alleles, then no refinements to the interpretation of dropout may be made. However, if the known contributor is consistent with being present at stochastic levels, then the DNA profile of the known contributor can be compared against the loci where dropout may be occurring.

Mixtures with a single minor contributor that is consistent with the known contributor

If declaring that "dropout is reasonable in the profile of the minor contributor" would create a minor contributor profile that is not consistent with the known contributor, then this would reject the assumption of the known contributor as being the minor contributor. As such, the possibility of dropout can be declared as unreasonable; the profile of the known contributor is fully represented by the detected alleles. Prior to such rejection of the possibility of dropout, the analyst should be confident that their assumption is reasonable.

Mixtures with a defined number of minor contributors including one that is consistent with the known contributor

If declaring that "dropout is reasonable in the minor contributors" would create a mixture of minor contributors that exceeds the maximum number of expected alleles, given the presence of the known contributor, then this would reject the assumption of the known contributor as being one of the minor contributors and/or reject the assumption as to the number of defined minor contributors. As such, the possibility of dropout can be declared as unreasonable; the profiles of the minor contributors are fully represented by the detected alleles. Prior to such rejection of the possibility of dropout, the analyst should be confident that their assumptions are reasonable (**Figure** 7).

Mixture Deconvolution

Once an evidentiary DNA profile has been interpreted for the number of contributors, the ratio of contributors, the presence of a "known contributor," the possibility of dropout, and the presence of IFS, it may be possible to utilize this information to make reasonable determinations as to the genetic profiles of the probable contributors. The concept of mixture deconvolution is to examine all of the different possible genotype combinations that could pair together to create the detected results and then eliminate genotype combinations as unreasonable until only a single genotype combination remains as a reasonable explanation of the evidence.

In order to define a genotype combination as unreasonable, the analyst must first determine what would be considered as reasonable divergences from a perfect model. For example, if an average ratio of contributors across the mixture was determined to be approximately 3:1, would a genotype combination that requires the contributors to be at a 4:1 ratio to produce the evidence be considered reasonable?

Mixture deconvolution works best when the ratio of contributors is close. At a disparate ratio of contributors, it may be impossible to distinguish between allele sharing and imbalanced alleles of a heterozygote that still meet the laboratory's MEPHR. Mixture deconvolution can also be more

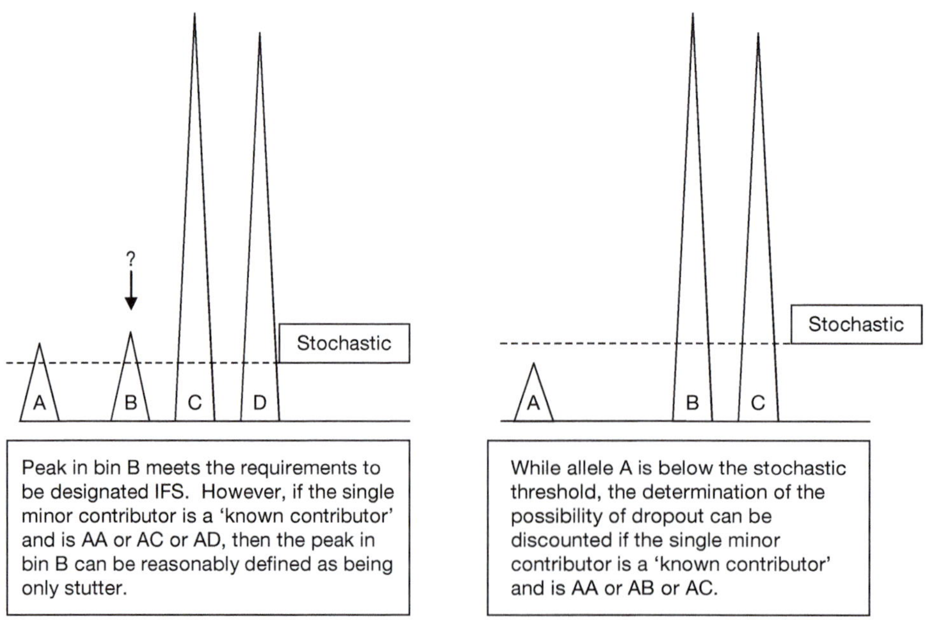

Figure 7 Use of a known contributor's profile to refine the interpretations of the possibility of dropout and peaks that are "indistinguishable from stutter." Adapted from Gill, P., et al., 2006. DNA commission of the International Society of Forensic Genetics: recommendations on the interpretation of mixtures. Forensic Science International 160, 90–101, with permission.

useful when one of the contributors can be assumed to be a "known contributor" because this will further eliminate genotype pairs that would otherwise be considered reasonable without such an assumption (**Table 1**).

Probative Comparisons

Although it may be likely that the DNA profile of a probative reference standard has been generated and analyzed prior to

Table 1 Example for a locus with four alleles, assuming the existence of only two contributors

Allele	*Relative fluorescent units (rfu)*
1	1000
2	500
3	980
4	475

First contributor				*Second contributor*			
Genotype	*rfu*	*Peak height ratio (PHR) (%)*	*Contribution (%)*	*Genotype*	*rfu*	*Peak height ratio (PHR) (%)*	*Contribution (%)*
(1,3)	(1000,980)	98	67	(2,4)	(500,475)	95	33
(2,4)	(500,475)	95	33	(1,3)	(1000,980)	98	67
(1,2)	(1000,500)	50	51	(3,4)	(980,475)	48	49
(2,3)	(500,980)	51	50	(1,4)	(1000,475)	48	50
(1,4)	(1000,475)	48	50	(2,3)	(500,980)	51	50
(3,4)	(980,475)	48	49	(1,2)	(1000,500)	50	51

On the basis of the laboratory's minimum expected peak height ratio (MEPHR), the most likely combinations would be one contributor having alleles 1 and 3, and the second contributor having alleles 2 and 4.

The total rfu of the contributor of alleles 1 and 3 is $(1000 + 980) = 1980$.

The total rfu of the contributor of alleles 2 and 4 is $(500 + 475) = 975$.

Therefore, the first contributor is donating approximately twice the amount of DNA to the mixture as the second contributor $(1980/975 = 2.03)$.

Example for a locus with two alleles, assuming there are only two contributors, on the basis of an average ratio of contributors of 2:1

Allele	*rfu*
1	749
2	1414

First contributor				*Second contributor*			
Genotype	*rfu*	*PHR (%)*	*Contribution (%)*	*Genotype*	*rfu*	*PHR (%)*	*Contribution (%)*
(2,2)	(707,707)	100	65	(1,1)	(374,374)	100	35
(1,2)	(749,707)	94	67	(2,2)	(353,353)	100	33
(1,1)	(374,374)	100	35	(2,2)	(707,707)	100	65
(2,2)	(565,565)	100	52	(1,2)	(749,282)	38	48
(1,2)	(499,942)	53	67	(1,2)	(249,471)	53	33
(1,2)	(374,1414)	26	83	(1,1)	(187,187)	100	17
(1,1)	(299,299)	100	28	(1,2)	(149,1414)	11	72

On the basis of the laboratory's MEPHR, and a comparison to the average ratio of contributors, the most likely combinations would be one contributor being homozygous (2,2) and the second contributor homozygous (1,1). However, it is also reasonable that one contributor may be heterozygous (1,2) and the second contributor homozygous (2,2).

Having both contributors heterozygous (1,2) or having one contributor heterozygous (1,2) and the second contributor homozygous (1,1) may not meet the laboratory's MEPHR and/or may be outside of a reasonable range around the expected ratio of contributors; therefore, they may be unreasonable genotype pair combinations.

Additional genotype combinations that include undetected alleles are not shown in this example but should also be considered during the evaluation.

the interpretation of the evidence profile, it must be noted that the interpretation of the mixed DNA profile to this point has been performed completely independent of any comparison to a probative reference standard. Because it is only alleged as to the presence of the probative individual in the mixed DNA profile, it would be inappropriate to have interpreted the evidence with an assumption of the probative individual being present.

On the basis of the comparison of the probative reference standard to the interpreted DNA mixture, one of three conclusions can be made: (1) The mixture contains insufficient information to draw a conclusion as to the sources of the evidence, (2) the mixture contains sufficient information within at least one genetic locus to conclude that the probative individual can be excluded as one of the sources of the detectable DNA, and (3) the mixture contains sufficient information within at least one genetic locus to conclude that there is insufficient information to exclude (i.e., can include) the probative individual as one of the sources of the detectable DNA.

Future Considerations for DNA Mixture Interpretation

What has been discussed here is an interpretation process based upon the use of thresholds. Discussions abound about the appropriateness of such a process because it is based upon yes/no decision points in defining signal detected by the capillary electrophoresis instrument as an allele (analytical threshold) and as a true homozygous profile (stochastic threshold). Because such decision points are based on the degree of confidence one wishes to apply when defining the threshold, a more complete process would include a sliding scale of confidence in the data. A peak at a certain rfu point would not be declared to be uninterpretable, but the confidence in the peak being an allele could be modeled with a probabilistic genotype interpretation. A single allele at a certain rfu point would not be declared to be 100% likely to have dropout of a sister allele, but the confidence in the zygosity of the single allele could be modeled with a probabilistic genotype interpretation. Although such calculations may be possible with the use of appropriate software applications, there will still likely be a point at which the evidence contains too many contributors, is too degraded, or is of too limited quantity to ultimately be useful in the prosecution of a criminal matter.

See also: **Biology/DNA:** DNA—Statistical Probability; Short Tandem Repeats; **Biology/DNA/Methods/Analytical Techniques:** Capillary Electrophoresis in Forensic Genetics.

Further Reading

Budowle, B., Chakraborty, R., Van Daal, A., 2010. Authors' response. Journal of Forensic Sciences 55 (1), 269–272.
Gill, P., Buckleton, J., 2010. Commentary on Budowle et al. mixture interpretation: defining the relevant features for guideline for the assessment of mixed DNA profiles in forensic casework. Journal of Forensic Sciences 55 (1), 265–268.
Gill, P., Brenner, C.H., Buckleton, J.S., et al., 2006. DNA commission of the International Society of Forensic Genetics: recommendations on the interpretation of mixtures. Forensic Science International 160, 90–101.
Paoletti, D.R., Doom, T., Crane, C., Raymer, M., Crane, D., 2005. Empirical analysis of the STR profiles resulting from conceptual mixtures. Journal of Forensic Sciences 50, 1361–1366.
Perlin, M.W., Sinelnikov, A., 2009. An information gap in DNA evidence interpretation. PLoS One 4 (12), e8327.
SWGDAM, 2010. SWGDAM Interpretation Guidelines for Autosomal STR Typing by Forensic DNA Testing Laboratories. http://www.fbi.gov/hq/lab/html/codis_swgdam.pdf.

Relevant Website

http://www.cstl.nist.gov—Short Tandem Repeat DNA Internet DataBase.

Ancestry Informative Markers

C Phillips, University of Santiago de Compostela, Galicia, Spain

Glossary

Admixture The effects of the combination of two or more populations leading to patterns of mixed variation that originally may have been common to only one contributing population.

Allele The alternative variants that create a polymorphism. Binary polymorphisms such as single nucleotide polymorphisms (SNPs) show two alleles.

Autosomes/autosomal Chromosomes that do not control gender.

Genotype A combination of two alleles sited on the maternal and paternal chromosomes (or singly in uniparentally inherited markers).

Polymorphism The presence of variant forms of a gene, nucleotide sequence, or repeated genome segment where the minor variant is found at a minimum 1% frequency.

Uniparental Variation carried on the Y chromosome or the mitochondria that is inherited from one parent.

The First Forensic Ancestry Informative Markers: Early Use of Ancestry Informative Protein Polymorphisms Demonstrated Their Value for Investigations

As early as the 1960s, the Duffy blood group, based on serological detection of red cell antigen alleles FY*A and FY*B, was routinely used as a polymorphic marker in forensic biology laboratories. The strong association of African ancestry with the Duffy-null/negative phenotype (written Fy[a-b-] as both alleles are unexpressed due to an independent promoter variant) provided additional data from the same test that suggested a likely African ancestry component for Fy[a-b-] bloodstain donors. By the late 1970s, three additional red cell enzyme polymorphisms were used to specifically detect population diagnostic variation, comprising the hemoglobin S variant plus enzyme systems peptidase A and carbonic anhydrase. The key characteristic of these systems was an allele frequency distribution specific to Africans, that is, absent from other continental regions, albeit at relatively low 8–12% frequencies in African populations. This meant informative genotypes occurred in 22, 21, and 15% of Africans, respectively, yet the three tests collectively offered indicative data in 46% of cases, as shown in **Figure 1(a)**. Peptidase A protein, expressed in semen as well as in erythrocytes, allowed this system to successfully track the movements of a serial rapist active in South London and helped investigators link the crimes. This case and others indicated to scientists and investigators alike that despite a low frequency of ancestry informative genotypes, some markers could often provide robust indicators of ancestry. The Duffy system, where over 99% of genotypes are African informative, further highlights the forensic value of ancestry inference when variation is specific to a particular population group. Of course, this represents an overly simplistic view of ancestry inference for several reasons: very few polymorphisms show such clear divides between population groups; most groups are considerably less differentiated (divergent) than African–non-African population comparisons suggest; genetic differentiation between groups rapidly breaks down with the population admixture that typifies urban and postcolonial populations; and few, if any, markers are completely diagnostic of any one group—notably Duffy-negative genotypes are absent from Khoisan Africans (**Figure 1(b)**). Now that forensic analysis is firmly in the DNA era, perhaps the most important lesson from early application of simple polymorphisms to infer is that ancestry is their proven ability to give valuable investigative leads in certain circumstances, for example, when an eyewitness is absent or, of more relevance for today's forensic analyses, when no DNA database entry exists.

Y-Chromosome and Mitochondrial DNA Variation

The prompt introduction of mitochondrial DNA (mt-DNA) sequencing followed by characterization and use of

 http://dx.doi.org/10.1016/B978-0-12-800647-4.00027-8

(a)

System name	Gene	SNP identifier	% informative genotypes*	Cumulative % informative	Cumulative % uninformative
Pep A	CNDP2	rs733062	20.97	20.97	79.03
Hb S	HBB	rs334	22.03	38.38	61.62
CA II	CA2	rs2228063	15.54	47.96	52.04
Fy	DARC	rs2814778	99.56	99.77	0.23

SNP	Africa (*N*=472)	Europe (*N*=223)	East asia (*N*=364)
rs733062	G: 0.111 A: 0.889	G: 0.000 A: 1.000	G: 0.000 A: 1.000
rs334	A: 0.117 T: 0.883	A: 0.000 T: 1.000	A: 0.000 T: 1.000
rs2228063	A: 0.919 G: 0.081	A: 1.000 G: 0.000	A: 1.000 G: 0.000
rs2814778	T: 0.066 C: 0.934	T: 0.990 C: 0.010	Not genotyped

(b)

Figure 1 (a) Allele and genotype frequency distributions in three population groups of four previously used forensic ancestry informative polymorphisms. *Informative genotypes denote African-indicative heterozygotes and homozygotes combined. Pie chart summaries are HapMap population data. (b) Population allele frequency data of Duffy AIM-SNP rs2814778 indicating atypical frequencies in Khoisan Africans and effect of AFR–EUR admixture in African Americans. CSA, Central-South Asians (Gujarati Indians in Houston); EAS, E-ASN.

Y-chromosome variation (NRY) alongside short tandem repeat (STR) typing led to early recognition of the ancestry informative value of these two haploid markers. Each represents nonrecombining genome portions inherited uniparentally: unchanged from mother to offspring (mt-DNA) or father to son. Defining an individual's mt-DNA and NRY lineages therefore suggests shared ancestry with others carrying identical lineages and can be compared to global population surveys of lineage distributions that have become highly differentiated since migrants first left Africa. Furthermore, it may benefit forensic investigations to infer the parental ancestries of a DNA donor—particularly when each lineage is different.

Two problems arise when attempting to match an individual's uniparental lineages to particular populations. First, the mt-DNA and NRY genome portions are only a fraction of the total and may be atypical of the sum of population histories contributing to an individual's whole ancestry. The chance of finding atypical lineages increases in populations that have migrated or admixed in recent history, exemplified by Parsis: showing characteristic Iranian NRY lineages contrasting with mt-DNA lineages more typical of Gujarat. As almost everyone has some ancestry from different regions, ancestry analysis based on two markers alone risks erroneous inference from concentrating on a relatively small proportion of the genome. Second, the basis of the population specificity of particular lineages is dependent on the extent of population sampling preceding the analysis. Surveying haploid marker distributions necessitates typing all relevant variant sites at once and as one unit; therefore, much greater numbers are needed to count each haplotype and inevitably substantial areas of a region lack surveys. Furthermore, certain lineages can become dominant and are shared across quite extensive geographic areas—notably the Y-chromosome C*(xC3c) sublineage is shared by 0.5% of all males worldwide, as it is such a dominant feature of central Asian NRY variability.

Despite these limitations, mt-DNA and NRY typing offers strong differentiation of the ancestry of two portions of a donor's DNA; so, a prudent measure for forensic laboratories tempted to draw ancestry inferences from haploid data is to review this variation alongside autosomal ancestry informative markers (AIMs) to provide multiple points of comparison and reduce the risk of biased ancestry inferences.

Points of Reference: Defining Populations or Ancestries, Ancestry Informativeness Metrics, Types of Autosomal AIMs, and Population Diversity Reference Panels

Defining human populations or ancestries can be a highly sensitive issue that excites strong feelings, particularly as labeling or categorizing people is a crude measure that ignores many of the most important aspects of each individual's distinctive cultural heritage. A widespread concern for ethicists is the danger that inference of ancestry in a forensic context will lead to targeting of particular communities with the burden of proof passing to members of that community when DNA profiling for elimination purposes focuses on voluntary programs screening reduced suspect groups. Many specialists advocate purely geographic terms to define an ancestry or population of origin, avoiding descriptions concentrating on visible characteristics such as "Black" and "White."

Other common descriptions such as "Caucasian" or "Hispanic," though widely understood, lack geographic precision. Overall, population labels without a geographic definition often hide a large amount of heterogeneity within the group. This article uses five continental-scale descriptions (herein abbreviated): sub-Saharan African (AFR), Eurasian (EUR)—comprising European, Middle Eastern-North African, and Central-South Asian (Indian subcontinent) population groups—East Asian (E-ASN), native American (AME), and Oceanian (OCE). These descriptions follow a broadly continental distribution of population diversity delimited by geographic barriers to large-scale population movements and repeatedly shown to match well to distributions of genetic variation. Any focus on population diversity can lose sight of a simple, universally recorded characteristic of human genetic variability: the differences between individuals within the same population describe ~85% of total variation, with differences between populations accounting for just 15%. Despite this very small proportion, there is clearly genetic variation that can be selected and built into forensically viable DNA tests.

Assessing strategies to select forensic AIMs leads to the question of how to first measure the ancestry informativeness of any given locus based on particular population comparisons. Traditionally, the population substructure metric Fst, analyzing levels of heterozygosity, is used to measure population differentiation; however, Fst works less efficiently assessing a marker's individual informativeness. Fst does not adequately reflect underlying diversity beyond pairwise population comparisons and extends poorly from binary polymorphisms such as single nucleotide polymorphisms (SNPs) to multiple-allele loci such as STRs. The very simple *delta* allele frequency differential, useful as a quick assessment of binary AIMs (δ: allele frequency in population 1 minus that in population 2), provides surprisingly good Fst approximations: $Fst \approx \delta^2$ or $Fst \approx \delta/(2 - \delta)$. However, the need to properly assess any marker's ancestry informativeness has brought consensus behind using the more appropriate metric of divergence or *In*. The common nomenclature to denote three group comparisons of AFR–EUR–E-ASN is *In*3, extended to include AME, *In*4. Although reviewing ancestry informativeness metrics may seem a detail, the major constraint in forensic analyses is that the input DNA available to successfully genotype marker sets; therefore, it is essential to choose the most informative loci for combination into small-scale, manageable PCR multiplexes. The most informative markers for a particular population comparison will additionally best measure levels of admixture between those populations. **Figure 2** shows the relationship between the divergence metrics δ, Fst, and *In* comparing two population groups.

The study developing the *In* divergence metric went on to compare average informativeness of different types of autosomal markers (i.e., not those of X, Y, or mt-DNA). Unsurprisingly, multiple-allele STRs had much higher *In* values than binary loci (mainly SNPs but including indels: bi-allelic insertion/deletion polymorphisms). This underlines the importance of average allele numbers per STR (those studied averaged 12.4). However, despite the great majority of binary loci being considerably less informative than all 377 STRs typed, about 1% of SNPs gave the highest *In* values of any marker. So, what are the implications for building viable forensic AIM sets? First, a large catalog of human SNPs offers the best chance to find the loci most differentiated between populations and therefore the best markers available. Second, though fewer indels have been described than SNPs, they offer similar possibilities and bring their own valuable characteristics to forensic analysis. Third, forensic STR data generated for identification purposes are likely to provide some ancestry information too. Since forensic STRs generally show low population divergence, these data add value to dedicated ancestry marker sets rather than offering a viable alternative by themselves.

DNA sample panels of globally distributed populations are the most important resource for selecting AIMs but remain limited in scope and patchy in their continental focus. The most widely used panel and most comprehensive population distribution is provided by the Human Genome Diversity Panel–Centre d'Etude du Polymorphisme Humain (HGDP–CEPH) comprising 949 samples in 52 populations: 7 AFR, 8 EUR, 17 E-ASN, 5 AME, and 2 OCE (plus four Middle East and nine Central-South Asian). Additionally, the community resource HapMap and 1000 Genomes projects provide extensive SNP catalogs, typing continental and admixed populations, each likely to be continually extended in global coverage. To date, both projects have not characterized parental (unadmixed) AME or OCE populations. The easiest way to access and discover AIMs from the above population resources is to screen online allele frequency data. Although individual project Web sites provide marker-by-marker access, a collective approach is better, whether comparing sets of SNPs, chromosome spans, or population divergent genes (e.g., pigmentation genes). Fortunately, this is possible using the *SPSmart* suite detailed in the online resources section, with the opportunity to directly download reference genotypes into all the population statistical analyses suggested in Section "Statistical Analysis of AIM Genotype Data."

Autosomal AIM-SNPs

Autosomal SNPs have been the principal focus for building initial standalone forensic AIM sets. Despite random sets of STRs usually being more informative, searching for the most differentiated SNPs will identify the best AIMs of all, while SNPs bring considerable benefits to forensic analysis.

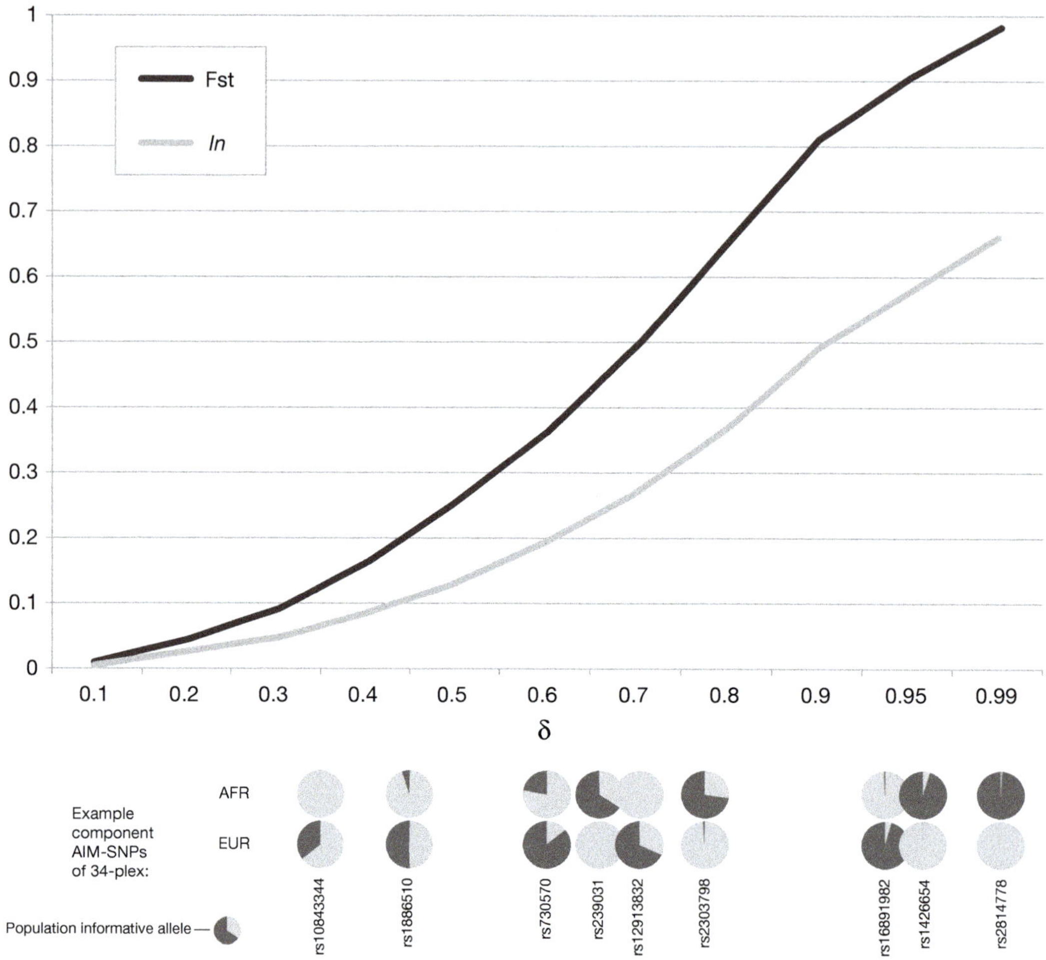

Figure 2 The relationship between Fst and *In* population divergence metrics comparing Africans and Europeans for increasing values of the δ allele frequency differential. Examples of AIM-SNP composite markers of the 34-plex forensic multiplex are aligned underneath their δ values.

First, there are much more extensive catalogs of SNPs than other markers, all allowing scrutiny of major group (AFR–EUR–E-ASN) differentiations. Recent genome-scale sequencing extends this catalog to SNPs with ~1% minor allele frequencies, though notably these methods are less efficient in detecting copy number variation: STRs and indels. SNPs also bring benefits from typing much shorter amplified fragments than STRs, so there is a higher quantity of intact DNA for the PCR stage. Binary polymorphisms are easier to fit into larger multiplexes because short fragment amplification is more efficient and the allele detection stage can more easily accommodate pairs of alleles compared to larger ranges such as the 25–30 alleles of complex forensic STRs. Lastly, a range of platforms are available for genotyping SNPs and their scope per reaction has now reached the million marker level providing the possibility of a much more detailed analysis of human population divergence. The choice of high-throughput genotyping approaches available is regularly listed as a favorable factor for adapting SNP analysis to forensic identification. However, this ignores a critical shortcoming of these techniques that restricts their potential application to forensics—the amount of input DNA required generally far exceeds the 1–20 ng typically extracted from forensic material. As ancestry analysis would normally be an adjunct to identification with STRs, there are further limits to how many reactions could be realistically added to an average DNA case. Furthermore, police investigators carry raised expectations that contact traces with subnanogram levels of DNA are well within the sensitivity limits of forensic laboratories. For this reason, two relatively small-scale multiplex AIM-SNP sets are highlighted using simple *SNaPshot* primer extension assays, typing 34 SNPs in a single test and 24 SNPs in two tests developed by Lao et al.

A third study reported a much larger 176 AIM-SNP set developed by Halder, thereby offering higher overall informativeness. However, Halder's set was designed around discontinued genotyping chemistry: the chip-based Beckman–Coulter *SNPstream* system. Although *SNPstream* showed good forensic sensitivity and could type up to 48 SNPs per reaction, it was hampered by requiring proprietary consumables/instruments as well as the need to group identical SNP substitutions and strands together into discrete PCRs (e.g., G/A, C/T, G/T, and C/A). Thus, the minimum number of reactions (not publicly reported) is likely 6–8, comprising 16G/T-A/C SNPs, 16G/C, and 147C/T-A/G. In comparison, *SNaPshot* uses established forensic DNA instrumentation and is relatively simple to adapt to different SNP sets, while showing by far the best forensic sensitivity of any current SNP typing system. The major limitation of *SNaPshot* is frequent signal peak imbalances caused by differences in the reaction dynamics of the four dye-linked terminators, making mixed-source DNA detection difficult to achieve. This is particularly important for AIM-SNP analysis where a forensic mixture comprising donors with different ancestries could easily mimic a single-source profile from an individual with admixed ancestry. Reviews of forensic AIM-SNP candidates should also take account of published marker lists, despite lacking multiplex designs or being based on singleplex Taqman genotyping. Two such SNP sets have been proposed for forensic use: 128 AIM-SNPs collated by Kosoy and 47 AIM-SNPs mainly overlapping the 24 of Lao above selected by Kersbergen.

Table 1 lists the most informative component AIM-SNPs of the above five sets ranked by *In*3 and showing *In*4, estimated using 1000 Genomes and HGDP–CEPH genotypes, respectively (Lao/Kersbergen *In*4 omitted due to missing HGDP–CEPH SNPs). Two interesting features emerge from these comparisons: marker commonality, that is, top AIM-SNPs chosen by multiple studies are confined to just two loci: rs2814778 (Duffy) or rs16891982 and most of the top 24–34 SNP components have broadly comparable *In* ancestry informativeness. These observations may partly reflect the selection strategies used. The 34-plex and Halder AIM-SNPs were accumulated over several years of searching for highly differentiated allele frequencies in online databases, whereas Lao/Kersbergen and Kosoy screened whole-genome scan (WGS) data of 10 000 and 300 000 SNPs, respectively. The comparability of the best markers in each set indicates that different AIM selection approaches can each provide informative sets; so, there are more than enough ancestry informative SNPs available to select markers that can multiplex well and provide sufficiently wide genomic distribution. The noticeably small number of extremely differentiated AIM-SNPs, for example, *In*3 0.75, not only indicates how difficult it is to find such SNPs but also reflects their absence from WGS marker sets due to a lack of association power, since these loci have almost no variability within any one population group. Lastly, there are

Table 1 The top 20 AIM-SNP components in four small- to medium-scale forensic ancestry tests plus the top 40 AIM-SNPs in the largest of DNAprint

		In3	*In4*
Phillips 34-plex			
1	**rs2814778**	0.865	0.783
2	rs1426654	0.833	0.562
3	**rs16891982**	0.781	0.55
4	rs3827760	0.759	0.468
5	rs881929	0.525	0.303
6	rs12913832	0.52	0.194
7	rs182549	0.515	0.157
8	rs239031	0.438	0.291
9	rs2303798	0.375	0.294
10	rs773658	0.367	0.394
11	rs2572307	0.366	0.206
12	rs722098	0.344	0.182
13	rs4540055	0.333	0.303
14	rs2065982	0.319	0.479
15	rs5997008	0.31	0.181
16	rs730570	0.307	0.217
17	rs2026721	0.305	0.275
18	rs1978806	0.304	0.218
19	rs1335873	0.297	0.289
20	rs3785181	0.26	0.212
34 SNPs cumulative In		**11.176**	**8.562**
Lao 24-plex			
1	**rs16891982**	0.781	
2	rs1369290	0.704	
3	rs1448484	0.654	
4	rs1478785	0.521	
5	rs2052760	0.429	
6	rs722869	0.426	
7	rs3843776	0.403	
8	rs1405467	0.388	
9	rs1876482	0.386	
10	rs1371048	0.369	(No AME allele frequency data)
11	rs1907702	0.363	
12	rs952718	0.357	
13	rs714857	0.312	
14	rs721352	0.311	
15	rs1465648	0.296	
16	rs1858465	0.292	
17	rs1461227	0.284	
18	rs1048610	0.277	
19	rs1391681	0.268	
20	rs2179967	0.195	
24 SNPs cumulative In		**8.276**	
Kersbergen 47 SNPs			
1	rs1369290	0.704	
2	rs1478785	0.521	
3	rs2052760	0.429	
4	rs722869	0.426	
5	rs153264	0.407	

Continued

Table 1 The top 20 AIM-SNP components in four small- to medium-scale forensic ancestry tests plus the top 40 AIM-SNPs in the largest of DNAprint—cont'd

		In*3*	In*4*
6	rs3843776	0.403	(No AME allele frequency data)
7	rs1405467	0.388	
8	rs725667	0.385	
9	rs1371048	0.369	
10	rs721352	0.311	
11	rs1465648	0.296	
12	rs1461227	0.284	
13	rs1048610	0.277	
14	rs1391681	0.268	
15	rs1000313	0.221	
16	rs951378	0.22	
17	rs2179967	0.195	
18	rs1823718	0.177	
19	rs950257	0.153	
20	rs1363933	0.15	
47 SNPs *cumulative In*		**8.343**	
Kosoy 128 SNPs			
1	rs4891825	0.68	0.54
2	rs11652805	0.554	0.477
3	rs3784230	0.547	0.416
4	rs10007810	0.542	0.424
5	rs9522149	0.511	0.428
6	rs260690	0.494	0.441
7	rs2416791	0.489	0.369
8	rs9845457	0.473	0.459
9	rs7554936	0.468	0.432
10	rs9530435	0.46	0.433
11	rs4908343	0.423	0.426
12	rs1040045	0.42	0.426
13	rs6548616	0.409	0.427
14	rs3745099	0.395	0.313
15	rs772262	0.39	0.334
16	rs798443	0.388	0.339
17	rs7657799	0.379	0.389
18	rs316598	0.377	0.335
19	rs7803075	0.361	0.284
20	rs4821004	0.356	0.275
128 SNPs *cumulative In*		**38.759**	**41.362**
DNAprint 178 SNPs			
1	**rs2814778**	0.865	0.783
2	rs590086	0.493	0.476
3	rs236336	0.475	0.499
4	rs984654	0.443	0.361
5	rs212498	0.422	0.349
6	rs361055	0.416	0.365
7	rs361065	0.415	0.375
8	rs6003	0.406	0.3
9	rs1337038	0.403	0.405
10	rs662117	0.402	0.322
11	rs9032	0.399	0.31

Continued

Table 1 The top 20 AIM-SNP components in four small- to medium-scale forensic ancestry tests plus the top 40 AIM-SNPs in the largest of DNAprint—cont'd

		In*3*	In*4*
12	rs593226	0.394	0.254
13	rs523200	0.385	0.301
14	rs2242480	0.382	0.438
15	rs1888952	0.377	0.259
16	rs595961	0.371	0.279
17	rs3176921	0.371	0.352
18	rs1800410	0.364	0.288
19	rs1415680	0.363	0.282
20	rs869337	0.349	0.405
21	rs830599	0.344	0.474
22	rs1426208	0.342	0.328
23	rs1399272	0.335	0.277
24	rs883055	0.329	0.254
25	rs1034290	0.318	0.256
26	rs913258	0.318	0.309
27	rs733563	0.312	0.226
28	rs730570	0.307	0.346
29	rs434504	0.3	0.321
30	rs67302	0.296	0.313
31	rs735050	0.295	0.245
32	rs1395579	0.29	0.237
33	rs553950	0.284	0.216
34	rs959858	0.279	0.225
35	rs285	0.278	0.21
36	rs3317	0.275	0.263
37	rs960709	0.272	0.176
38	rs721825	0.264	0.262
39	rs1375229	0.264	0.196
40	rs1528037	0.264	0.151
178 SNPs *cumulative In*		**30.967**	**31.487**

Individual marker *In*3 and *In*4 divergences are listed comparing African–European–East Asian or African–European–East Asian–American genotypes obtained from 1000 Genomes data (SPSmart: http://spsmart.cesga.es/engines.php?dataSet=engines). The cumulative values under each list represent the final divergences that can be expected with complete SNP profiles from each test. Bold rs-number SNP identifiers denote just two common loci among the alternative tests.

contrasting cumulative *In*4 values between 34-plex and the two large-scale SNP sets, indicating different approaches in marker selection, with the 34-plex selected for three group differentiations but now supplemented with a 28-plex stand-alone AIM-SNP multiplex dedicated to differentiating AME populations. This follows the 2008 publication of HGDP-CEPH genotypes for over 650 000 SNPs—enabling selection of many more markers close to fixation (i.e., allele frequencies at or near 1.0 exclusively in one or more groups) in both AME and OCE groups. In summary, the prospects are good for further development of AIM-SNP multiplexes with forensic viability and scale.

Indels

Short-allele indels (1–5 nucleotide insertions, infrequently extending to >25) have recently generated interest as a simple but robust forensic marker type since they combine the best characteristics of binary polymorphisms—short amplicon lengths and mutational stability—with the best characteristics of STRs, direct typing with dye-linked PCR primers to provide balanced peak height ratios. Although the most divergent ancestry informative indels are less differentiated than the best SNPs, they exceed many STRs. This makes indels highly suitable loci for building multiplexes based on direct PCR-to-CE systems considerably more reliable than *SNaPshot* SNP typing. Two forensic AIM-indel panels have been developed: a single reaction 46-plex of Pereira and three 16-plex reactions of Santos. In addition to the obvious benefit of a single reaction compared to three, the AIM-indels chosen by Pereira were designed to differentiate four groups with a high overall *In*4 value, while those of Santos show weak E-ASN differentiation.

Short Tandem Repeats

It might be expected that multiallele STRs will show greater population divergence than SNPs or indels. However, STR alleles are highly unstable compared to binary loci, so new STR repeat alleles are constantly being created, while slippage size constraints lead to "allelic resonance": high rates of diminution mutation in long alleles and high rates of addition in short alleles. Therefore, individuals with different ancestries can be identical by state, while those from the same population can show more STR differentiation than their shared ancestry would suggest. Furthermore, unless STR alleles are rare they will not usually be lost after population isolation, although very reduced population numbers typical of founder groups can lead to a rapid rise in frequency of rare alleles by sampling effects followed by population expansion. One such example is the population-specific nine repeat allele of D9S1120—found at very low frequency in East Siberia but reaching an average 0.3 frequency in native Americans. It is noteworthy that this is the only example of a common population-specific STR allele, highlighting that different populations tend to share the majority of their STR variability, and divergence is characterized by relatively small frequency differences in these shared alleles. For this reason, attempts to infer ancestry from forensic STR profile data tend to show assignment error rates too high for reliable inferences from STR data alone. This is not to say that STRs are completely uninformative for ancestry, as forensic STR population divergence is high enough to make combining them with other AIMs an ideal way to maximize the informativeness value of the casework genetic data as a whole.

Statistical Analysis of AIM Genotype Data

Of paramount importance in the statistical analysis of AIM data is proper consideration of the confidence limits—the levels of uncertainty associated with the ancestry inferences made. Four factors influence the degree of uncertainty of ancestry analyses: (1) the distribution of diversity among populations, (2) the AIMs used, (3) population reference data used, and (4) the statistical methods used. Genetic diversity could be more readily gauged if global population sampling was more complete than it currently is; however, more importantly, population admixture resulting from urbanization, migration, slavery, and colonization creates far more complex distributions than the divergence patterns suggested by sample panels targeting unadmixed ancestral populations. The same complexities apply to populations on continental margins where geographic barriers are weak. Therefore, statistical tests most sensitive to admixture are the most appropriate for forensic DNA typing analyzing samples dominated by urban demographics. Furthermore, developers of forensic AIM-SNP panels have made efforts to assess the accuracy of ancestry inferences obtained from their markers. Accuracy here means how often an erroneous inference is made of standard reference samples but could include how well an individual admixture is gauged. Maximizing accuracy involves: including as many AIMs close to fixation as possible, maximizing multiplex sizes, and balancing predictive power across each pairwise population comparison (E-ASN vs EUR and particularly E-ASN vs AME are especially difficult to raise). There is also some consensus on using statistical tests based on Bayesian methods: either with direct likelihood ratios between alternative populations of origin or as the analytical basis of the ubiquitous model-based clustering algorithm *Structure*. Unfortunately, detection and assessment of individual admixture is the biggest statistical problem confronting forensic ancestry inference using small-scale AIM sets.

Figure 3 outlines the Bayesian likelihood system that can be used to infer ancestry by equating likelihood of population membership with allele frequencies in each population, using example AIM-SNP rs12075. AIMs can be combined into Bayesian analyses either as single profiles which are compared to user-input reference data for the same loci (training sets) using *Snipper* (see Relevant Websites) or in joint analyses of unknowns and reference samples together in *Structure*. Alternatively, principal component analysis provides a visual representation of the divergence distances between reference population clusters and inspection of an unknown sample's position can allow an inference of how each position/cluster is related. *Structure* can be used to provide a system for estimating the ratio of individual-level coefficients of coancestry as indicators of admixture, but this approach does not have the same capacity as analyses of population-level admixture. Kidd, analyzing the Kosoy AIM-SNP set, provides a good review of

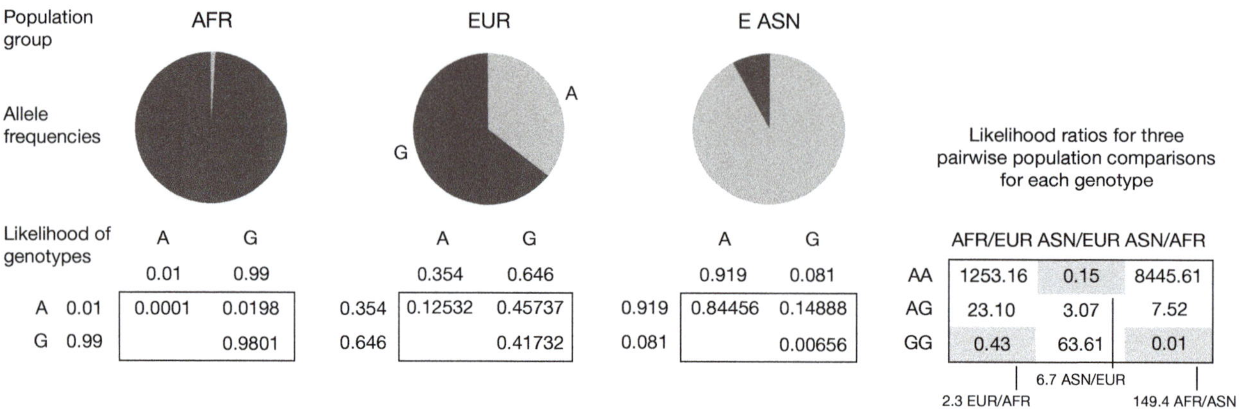

Figure 3 Illustration of the principle of Bayesian likelihood calculations shown for AIM-SNP rs12075. This statistical approach equates probability of population membership to allele frequency distributions in that population; for example, the A allele is very uncommon in AFR, so the two highest likelihood ratios for the AA genotype are for E-ASN and EUR. AFR, sub-Saharan African; E-ASN, East Asian; EUR, Eurasian.

the drawbacks of *Structure* analyses which include stochastic effects between runs, population sample size effects, incomplete geographic coverage, and AIM set deficiencies (e.g., Kosoy AIMs lack E-ASN differentiation). Unfortunately individual admixture is common, but, more problematically, *Structure* can give patterns from intermediate populations on continental margins that mimic admixture. For example, a North African analyzed in a five-group comparison that does not include North African reference samples could suggest mainly European ancestry with an African component suggesting an individual with admixed parentage rather than ancestry from a region intermediate to the continental reference populations used. Limited reference populations force *Structure* to fit the unknown into the available patterns of genetic divergence. **Figure 4** outlines exactly the same circumstances described above using a partial 34-plex SNP profile, and the 46-plex indel panel is described in section "Indels." Such limitations emphasize the importance of drawing together as much genetic information as possible and dedicating resources to collating the widest possible population reference data. Lastly, rising computer power allows multiple *Structure* runs to be easily made to establish population metric confidence limits by reaching stabilized standard deviation estimates—this generally takes 25–30 runs to achieve.

Developments on the Horizon: Expanding Human SNP Catalogs, Combining Marker Types, Further Differentiation of Continental Population Groups, and X-Chromosome Markers

At the time of writing, forensic ancestry inference is gathering pace and raising interest with investigators often guided by unreliable eyewitness accounts. Therefore, it is appropriate to highlight improvements in genetic ancestry analysis already underway or soon to be introduced.

First, the 1000 Genomes project has provided an extended human SNP catalog able to collate rare variation (close to 1% minor allele frequencies) in a growing range of populations. As whole-genome sequencing becomes more routine, forensic DNA analysis can make use of this expanding data resource. It is worth noting that triallelic SNPs, often showing high ancestry informativeness (two are included in 34-plex), are not detected by next-generation sequencing methods—a lost opportunity to expand knowledge of their genomic distribution and population variability.

Forensic ancestry inference greatly benefits from the use of all available genetic data and appropriately all three statistical systems outlined above accept multiple and binary allele data together. STR data considerably boost the informativeness of even the best binary AIMs and, since all autosomal markers are independent, their combination provides increased reliability to the statistical inferences of ancestry. **Figure 5** shows that component *In*3 values for four different marker sets are remarkably similar. Since each marker type brings particular advantages to analysis of the same DNA, their combination to build a fuller picture of a donor's ancestry overcomes shortcomings of any one multiplex. To allow combination of different markers in *Snipper*, users can now upload allele frequency-based training sets as well as genotypes and their likelihoods then combined to provide an overall value.

In addition to small SNP multiplexes, the possibility of using large-scale WGS SNP arrays promises greatly increased population resolution, with prospects to go to a greater depth of differentiation than continental-scale population

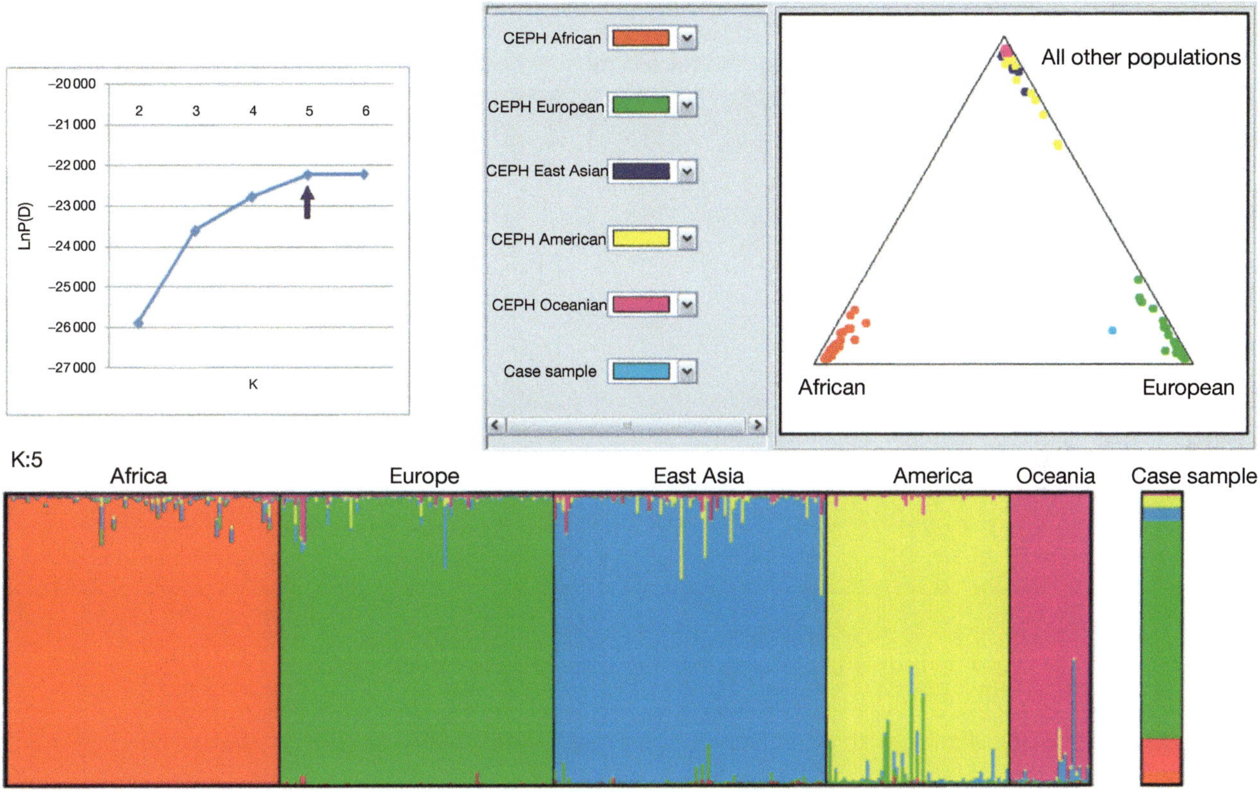

Reference populations	Membership proportions: Africa	Europe	East Asia	America	Oceania	Number of individuals
CEPH Africa	0.974	0.005	0.008	0.005	0.008	93
CEPH Europe	0.003	0.969	0.01	0.008	0.01	93
CEPH East Asia	0.003	0.009	0.953	0.021	0.013	93
CEPH America	0.003	0.025	0.015	0.95	0.007	63
CEPH Oceania	0.003	0.004	0.032	0.009	0.951	28
Case sample	0.157	0.751	0.046	0.041	0.005	1

Membership proportions of sample are: 75.1% EUR, 15.7% AFR

Figure 4 Structure analysis of a forensic DNA sample in an identification case. Structure identifies groups or clusters of samples based on distinctive allele frequency distributions. An unknown sample is compared to the reference allele frequencies obtained here from the HGDP–CEPH panel for 26 AIM-SNPs and 46 AIM-indels. Multiple analyses identify the optimum number of clusters: K—in this case five, where the probability value plateaus. The triangle plot positions the sample (light blue) in relation to CEPH samples where proximity to the vertex corresponds to the highest probability of membership (shown as overall values for each population in the table). Examination of the membership proportions of the sample can be interpreted as indications of coancestry in the individual or admixed parentage. This suggests mainly European ancestry with a minor African admixture component. In fact, the sample ancestry was consequently shown to be North African—a population not used as a reference in this analysis. Furthermore, North Africans are too closely related to Europeans to be adequately differentiated using the 72 AIMs typed in the analysis.

comparisons. Two 2008 studies showed that populations within Europe could be differentiated across reduced geographic scales ranging from 300 to 1000 km. A more realistic target for improved resolution in the immediate future could be the differentiation of European, Middle East–North African, and South Asian subpopulations of Eurasia. While Europeans and South Asians can be differentiated with small-scale additional AIM-SNP multiplexes, North African–Middle

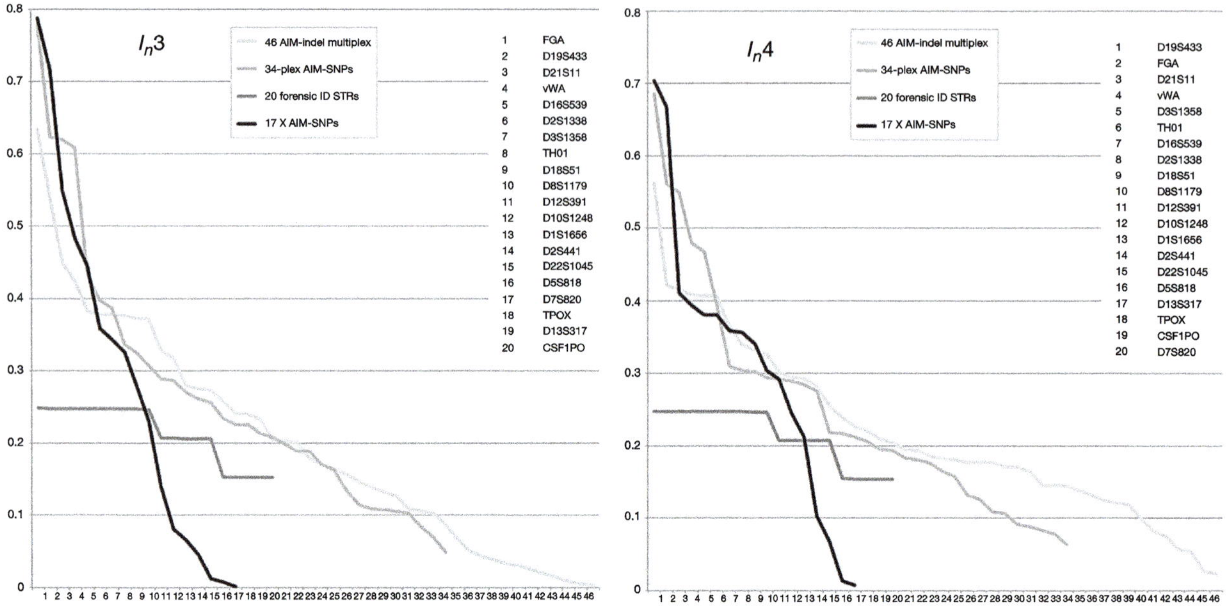

Figure 5 Ranked divergence values, *In*3 and *In*4, of component loci in forensic multiplexes: AIM-indel 46-plex, AIM-SNP 34-plex, 20 core forensic identification short tandem repeats (STRs), and X chromosome AIM-SNPs 17-plex under development in the author's laboratory. The informativeness order of the 20 component STRs is individually listed. Plots show the autosomal SNPs, X SNPs, and indels combined into ancestry informative multiplexes which are highly comparable—with marginally improved AME differentiation from certain AIM-indel components. Additionally, STRs routinely used for forensic identification have higher *In*4 ancestry informativeness than almost half of the other set's components.

East populations are too closely related to Europeans for reliable differentiation. Therefore, subcontinental differentiation awaits developments to increase multiplex scale and detection limits in forensic SNP typing.

Lastly, X-chromosome variation has been largely overlooked for ancestry analysis. The ¾ chromosome population size and reduced recombination have created strong patterns of population divergence in a larger proportion of markers than equivalent autosomes. Furthermore, X AIMs in males can provide additional indicators of the ancestry of the maternal lineage alongside mt-DNA analysis.

Acknowledgments

The author would like to thank Carla Santos, Antonio Salas of the Forensic Genetics Unit, USC, and Rui Pereira of IPATIMUP, Oporto for helpful and enlightening discussions.

See also: **Biology/DNA:** DNA – Statistical Probability; Future Analytical Techniques: DNA Mass Spectrometry; Mitochondrial DNA; Short Tandem Repeats; Single-Nucleotide Polymorphisms; X-Chromosome Markers.

Further Reading

Jobling, M.A., Hurles, M.E., Tyler-Smith, C., 2004. Human Evolutionary Genetics. Garland Science, New York.

Kersbergen, P., van Duijn, K., Kloosterman, A.D., den Dunnen, J.T., Kayser, M., de Knijff, P., 2009. Developing a set of ancestry-sensitive DNA markers reflecting continental origins of humans. BMC Genetics 10, 69.

Kidd, J.R., Friedlaender, F.R., Speed, W.C., Pakstis, A.J., De La Vega, F.M., Kidd, K.K., 2011. Analyses of a set of 128 ancestry informative single- nucleotide polymorphisms in a global set of 119 population samples. Investigative Genetics 2, 1.

Kosoy, R., Nassir, R., Tian, C., et al., 2009. Ancestry informative marker sets for determining continental origin and admixture proportions in common populations in America. Human Mutation 30, 69–78.

Phillips, C., Prieto, L., Fondevila, M., et al., 2009. Ancestry analysis in the 11-M Madrid bomb attack investigation. PLoS One 4, e6583.

Phillips, C., Rodriguez, A., Mosquera-Miguel, A., et al., 2008. D9S1120, a simple STR with a common native American-specific allele: forensic optimization, locus characterization and allele frequency studies. Forensic Science International. Genetics 3, 7–13.

Phillips, C., Salas, A., Sánchez, J.J., et al., 2007. Inferring ancestral origin using a single multiplex assay of ancestry-informative marker SNPs. Forensic Science International. Genetics 1, 273–280.

Rosenberg, N.A., Li, L.M., Ward, R., Pritchard, J.K., 2003. Informativeness of genetic markers for inference of ancestry. American Journal of Human Genetics 73, 1402–1422.

Rosenberg, N.A., Pritchard, J.K., Weber, J.L., et al., 2002. Genetic structure of human populations. Science 298, 2381–2385.

Relevant Websites

http://alfred.med.yale.edu/– ALFRED Extensive Population Variation Coverage of Subsets of SNPs and STRs.

http://spsmart.cesga.es – popSTR Forensic STR Allele Frequencies of HGDP–ceph Samples.

http://mathgene.usc.es – Snipper Classifier.

http://spsmart.cesga.es/– SPSmart Comprehensive SNP Population Data Access Portal.

http://pritch.bsd.uchicago.edu/; http://rosenberglab.bioinformatics.med.umich.edu/distruct.html – Structure Algorithm Downloads.

Forensic DNA Phenotyping: DNA Testing for Externally Visible Characteristics

M Kayser, Erasmus MC University Medical Center, Rotterdam, The Netherlands

Definition, Motivation, and Principle

Forensic DNA phenotyping (FDP) is a relatively young field of forensic genetics and includes, in its widest sense, the extraction of information on human phenotypes through molecular analysis from biological crime scene samples. Although in its current definition, FDP usually involves DNA analysis of externally visible characteristics (EVCs), in principle, also non-visible phenotypes, such as disease traits and their risks or behavioral traits, can potentially be extracted from the DNA of biological crime scene samples and can potentially provide forensically relevant information. Furthermore, also other biomarkers, such as RNA or methylated DNA, are potentially useful for phenotype prediction from crime scene samples. Often, DNA-based inference of biogeographic ancestry (or genetic ancestry testing) is grouped into FDP, but the assumption that the geographic region(s) where the genetic ancestors of a person originated is manifested in the person's appearance does not always hold true. Although this assumption may indeed be justified if the geographic region of genetic ancestry reflects one, and only one, of the few regions harboring people of distinct appearance (such as Europeans), it is difficult for the many geographic regions reflecting transition zones of appearance traits (such as the Middle East), or for the many geographic regions with strong appearance resemblances (such as some regions of sub-Saharan Africa with some regions of Oceania). Extrapolating human appearance information from DNA-based biogeographic ancestry information is very difficult, if not impossible, for people of mixed genetic origins (with ancestors from different geographic regions). Currently, there is no scientific understanding about the relationship between genetic admixture and appearance trait manifestation whatsoever. However, genetic ancestry testing can indeed provide useful information for forensic investigations without extrapolating appearance, and has already found its niche within forensic genetics during recent years.

FDP naturally evolved out of the realization that there is a general limitation in conventional forensic DNA profiling, namely that persons unknown to the investigating authorities are usually not identifiable through this approach. As long as police investigations are not 100% successful in providing the true suspect, and as long as forensic DNA (profile) databases are not large enough to fully represent the criminal population, including all the first-time criminals, there always will be forensic cases where the evidence DNA profile does not match that of a known suspect. In such cases, mass screenings through conventional autosomal STR profiling may help, but in reality these are only applied occasionally, due to ethical, legal, economic, and other concerns. In contrast to the early days of forensic DNA analysis, by now the message has even spread to the criminal population that participating in DNA dragnets will result in identification, making this approach less and less successful. Ways to improve the success rate of DNA mass screenings are in the application of familial searches using autosomal STRs or, in the case of male perpetrators, more successfully using Y-chromosomal STRs, to identify the nonparticipating suspect through STR profile similarities with participating biological relatives. However, such advanced DNA dragnets are controversially discussed as they violate the law in many countries that allow refusal to testify against ones blood relatives. Clearly, the most efficient way of increasing the success rate of conventional forensic DNA profiling is by increasing the size of forensic DNA databases. Although such databases are constantly growing in many countries, due to various political, societal, and economic reasons, it is unrealistic to expect them to become fully representative of the criminal part of the population, not to speak of the establishment of a universal DNA database for forensic use.

If forensic cases that do not reveal STR (or SNP) profile matches wish to be solved with the help of crime scene samples, additional information potentially stored in the samples that may help finding its unknown donors must be explored. One of the most obvious human characteristics is appearance and it can easily be imagined that EVC information of an unknown sample donor extracted directly from the crime scene sample would be highly useful for investigative intelligence purposes in finding such a person, as it would allow concentration of the investigation in a particular direction. FDP is expected to provide knowledge currently provided by eye witnesses in case they are available. However, FDP can be applied to all cases where suitable biological material is available from the crime scene, but only in a subset of cases eye witnesses are available. Moreover, it is expected that those EVCs that finally will be applied in practical FDP can be predicted more accurately through molecular means than through eye witness memories, because the latter are known to be considerably error-prone and EVCs with established low molecular prediction accuracies are unlikely to be applied. Furthermore,

 http://dx.doi.org/10.1016/B978-0-12-800647-4.00028-X

FDP allows the attachment of a statistical estimation to the predicted EVC, indicating how likely it is that the EVC information is indeed correct; this crucial information currently cannot be provided with eye witness statements as the necessary empirical evidence is missing. Hence, FDP potentially has various advantages over currently used eye witness reports in the search for unknown suspects.

The strongest limitations of FDP revolve around the lack of knowledge about the genetic basis of human appearance in general. More is known about the genetics of numerous human disease traits than about the genetic factors determining human appearance. This may come as a surprise, especially when realizing that the very same technologies such as parallel genotyping of hundreds of thousands (currently up to more than one million) of single nucleotide polymorphisms (SNPs) through microarrays, and the very same analytical approaches, such as genome-wide association studies (GWASs), that are frequently applied with success to identify genes underlying disease traits can also be applied for finding genes involved in EVCs. However, GWASs are expensive and need specially educated technical and scientific staff—requirements that can be afforded within well-funded medical genetic research, but often not in limited-funded anthropological or forensic research. Anecdotal knowledge about the appearance resemblance of family members indicates that human appearance is largely determined by genetic factors, although at least some EVCs are additionally influenced by environmental factors. The last 5 years have seen exciting progress, most successfully provided through GWAS, in the identification of genes involved in a few EVCs such as pigmentation traits and body height. Once SNPs are identified to carry statistically significant trait association, additional statistical approaches and additional replication testing are needed to establish their predictive value for a given phenotypic trait. Once the most EVC-predictive DNA markers have been identified, genotyping assays must be developed and subsequently need to be forensically validated for demonstrating that they meet the specific quality requirements of forensic DNA analysis. This chain-of-exploration, combined with limited research activities in this particular field of nonmedical human genetics, has led to the current situation, with only one forensically validated DNA test being available for practical FDP.

The Proof-of-Principle: Eye Color Prediction from DNA

The identification of genes involved in human eye (iris) color variation goes back at least 10 years, but it was really the use of the GWAS approach with its first application to human pigmentation traits in the late 2000s that improved human knowledge about the genetic determination of human eye color significantly. Currently, about two handfuls of genes are known with confirmed eye color association, each gene usually being supported by various SNPs. Additional genes, albeit with expectedly smaller effect size than the currently known ones, are still expected to become identified. Hence, the common public opinion that blue-eyed parents can only sire blue-eyed children, and brown-eyed parents only brown-eyed children, cannot be true (as rare anecdotal knowledge also indicates) because this would require a single-gene (or two) scenario with a dominant–recessive inheritance pattern. However, in the majority of cases, blue-eyed parents indeed have blue-eyed children and brown-eyed parents have brown-eyed children, which is caused by the fact that two neighboring genes *OCA2* and *HERC2* acting together in a regulatory relationship have a much stronger influence on eye color variation than any of the other genes involved. Although the additional genes only have a minor impact on eye color, they can explain (often in combination with each other) why sometimes the eye color of children is different from that of their biological parents.

Knowledge on eye color genes from GWAS and other mapping approaches has already been taken one step further, and the most eye color-predictive SNPs have been identified from association data. It was demonstrated in a large sample set of thousands of Dutch Europeans with varying eye colors and by using several dozen eye color-associated SNPs that 15 SNPs from eight genes provide overall prevalence-adjusted prediction accuracies of over 0.9 for blue and brown eye color using a statistical measure AUC (area under the receiver characteristic operating curves) that runs from 0.5 for random prediction to 1 for completely accurate prediction. Six of these SNPs (rs12913832, rs1800407, rs12896399, rs16891982, rs1393350, and rs12203592) of six genes (*HERC2*, *OCA2*, *SLC24A4*, *SLC45A2*, *TYR*, and *IRF4*, respectively) cover almost all of the eye color prediction accuracy achieved in this study. A single multiplex genotyping assay called IrisPlex has been developed for these six SNPs based on chemistry and lab equipment commonly available in forensic institutions. Together with the published article, a statistical tool has been made available for estimating eye color prediction probabilities from IrisPlex genotypes that accesses model parameters obtained from thousands of Dutch Europeans. **Figure 1** demonstrates an illustrative example of the overall power of the IrisPlex system in accurately predicting blue and brown eye color from DNA. The eye color of 3 of the 40 people used for illustrative purposes could not be predicted correctly from their DNA using IrisPlex, with two of them having similarly low probabilities for all three eye color categories not allowing any conclusion, and one being predicted incorrectly. As a further step toward practical forensic application, the IrisPlex assay has been taken through forensic developmental validation, demonstrating that it is highly sensitive, requiring less DNA than commercially available STR kits, performs successfully in various forensically relevant sample types, and provides concordant results in independent laboratories. Hence, overall, the IrisPlex assay meets the agreed quality standards in forensic DNA analysis. An IrisPlex study

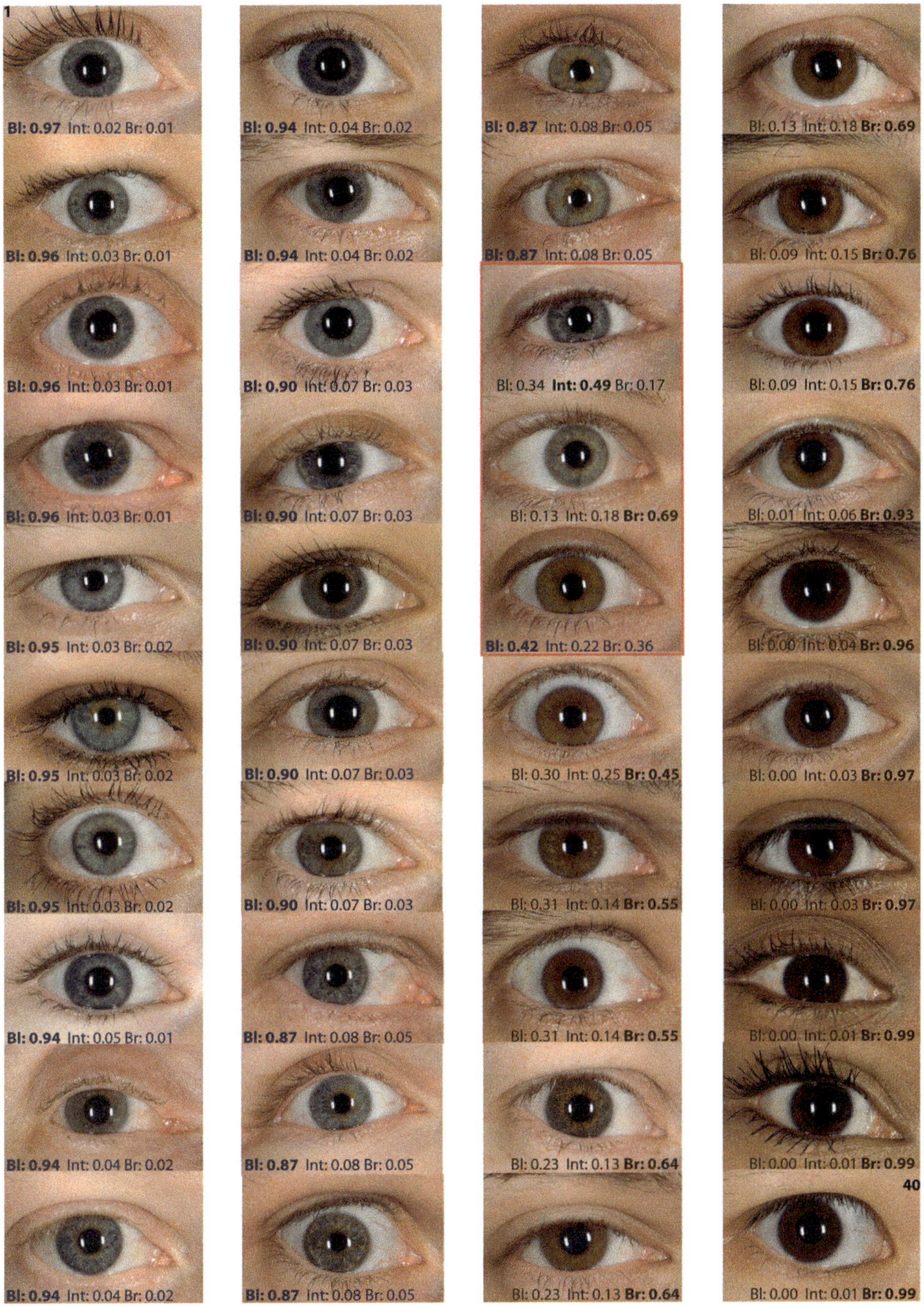

Figure 1 Illustrative example of DNA-based eye color prediction using the IrisPlex system. Eyes of 40 volunteers are ordered according to the IrisPlex probabilities for blue, intermediate, and brown eye color starting with the highest probability for blue eye color in the upper-left corner and the highest probability for brown eye color in the lower-right corner. Visual inspection of phenotypic eye color was not considered in the ordering of the eye images. The red box marks the two individuals for whom IrisPlex eye color prediction was not informative because the three eye color probabilities are similar, and the one individual for whom the prediction was incorrect. Reproduced from Walsh, S., Liu, F., Ballantyne, K., et al., 2011. IrisPlex: a sensitive DNA tool for accurate prediction of blue and brown eye color in the absence of ancestry information. Forensic Science International: Genetics 5, 170–180.

using large datasets from populations around Europe is currently under way for evaluating the IrisPlex prediction model.

Some of the IrisPlex SNPs are associated with eye color variation and are unlikely to be causal. A potential problem with the use of associated but not causal SNPs for prediction purposes is that the genetic association may be geographically restricted, leading to a disturbing effect of geography on the reliability of the predictive outcomes. This is especially crucial when associated SNPs are applied to predict a trait that has a geographically restricted distribution such as eye color. Eye color variation is only found in people of (at least partial) European biogeographic ancestry or those from regions geographically close to Europe, whereas outside this region, people usually have brown eye color, representing the ancestral state in humans. The European evolutionary history of eye color variation makes it probable that SNP alleles associated with nonbrown eye colors in Europeans are also found in non-Europeans who express brown eye color, which indeed has been observed for some of the IrisPlex SNPs in a worldwide study. However, the combined use of all six IrisPlex SNPs in the overall prediction model resulted in the prediction of non-brown eye colors only in regions where eye color variation is known (i.e., Europe and neighboring regions such as the Middle East and Western Asia), and brown was the only eye color predicted in all of the worldwide regions where only brown eye color is known (i.e., East Asia, Oceania, sub-Saharan Africa, Native America). This indicates that the IrisPlex system provides accurate eye color prediction probabilities independent of biogeographic ancestry.

Additional SNPs other than the six included in the IrisPlex system have been proposed to be predictive of eye color. However, either they do not provide additional independent information due to genetic linkage to IrisPlex SNPs, or they do not provide any practically useful accuracy improvement for blue and brown eye color prediction already available with the IrisPlex system, or they are unlikely to provide any eye color information at all because they were ascertained from the combined data of Europeans and non-Europeans. Applying a broad geographic approach for finding predictive markers for a geographically restricted trait such as eye color bears the risk of interpreting results as eye color informative that in reality rather reflect continental biogeographic ancestry. Future studies may provide currently unknown SNPs to further improve the already high prediction accuracy of the IrisPlex system for blue and brown eye color and/or to provide similarly high prediction accuracies for additional eye color categories such as green. Future research may also show if one can finally overcome the currently followed categorical approach of DNA-based eye color prediction, aiming to predict from DNA, the various grades of eye color from the lightest gray to the darkest black. Recently, new eye color genes have been identified that show association with continuous eye color, which raises the expectation that more detailed eye color prediction from DNA may be feasible in the future. Such a continuous approach to DNA-based eye color prediction would not only increase the level of detail of eye color prediction but would also avoid the potential complication with categorical prediction in that different investigating officers, for example, when being told that the sample donor is of blue eyes with 98% probability and 99% accuracy as obtained through FDP such as with the Iris-Plex System, may have different shades of blue in mind when searching for the unknown suspect. Practical outcomes of such a continuous prediction approach could be matching color charts or color printouts both produced from the genetic information obtained through FDP.

Additional Appearance Traits with Emerging Genetic and Predictive Knowledge

In comparison to eye color, much less knowledge is available for any other EVC regarding predictive DNA markers and molecular tools. After eye color, genetic knowledge on hair color is currently perhaps the most advanced among all EVCs. Various genes have recently been identified for hair color using GWAS, many of which overlap with genes contributing to eye color variation, as may be expected given the relationship between both pigmentation phenotypes in Europeans. One noticeable exception is the *MC1R* gene, which greatly determines red hair (and to a lesser degree other hair colors such as blond), but seem to have no, or only a very minor, effect on eye color variation. In fact, SNPs from the *MC1R* gene were proposed for red hair prediction by the United Kingdom's Forensic Science Service in the early 2000s, using scientific knowledge previously accumulated. However, it took a further 10 years for advances in hair color genetics to provide a large number of hair color-associated SNPs that have now been tested for their predictive effect on various hair color categories. A model including 11 SNPs (rs12913832, rs12203592, rs1042602, rs4959270, rs28777 and rs16891982, rs683, rs1800407, rs2402130, rs12821256, and rs2378249) from 10 genes (*HERC2, IRF4, TYR, EXOC2, SLC45A2, TYRP1, OCA2, SLC24A4, KITLG,* and *ASIP*), together with the two compound markers MC1R_r and MC1R_R each including different sets of rare SNPs from the *MC1R* gene, provides AUC values of over and up to 0.9 for red and black, as well as over 0.8 for blond and brown hair color in hundreds of Polish Europeans expressing various hair colors. Furthermore, this model differentiated between similar hair color categories such as red and blond-red as well as blond and dark-blond. Recently, the HIr-isPlex System has been introduced, which represents a single multiplex assay considering all these hair color DNA variants and the IrisPlex SNPs, altogether 24 DNA markers, for the simultaneous prediction of eye and hair color from DNA. As with eye color, additional SNPs have been proposed to be useful for hair color prediction, for example, from joined analyses of people from different continental biogeographic ancestry; however, their effect seems to be one of the biogeographic ancestry rather than of hair color. Future research in finding additional SNPs for hair color prediction is still needed, especially for the currently least-accurately predictable blond and brown hair colors, and—as with eye color—moving from categorical to continuous prediction would be beneficial also for hair color to increase the level of detail and to avoid practical problems during police investigations. One issue that needs to be considered in future hair color prediction attempts is the age-depend change of hair colors such as from blond during childhood to darker colors during adulthood. Age-depended hair color change currently is not yet understood on the molecular level and thus is not considered with the currently available list of hair color predictive DNA variants.

Many of the genes involved in eye and hair color are also expected to be involved in skin color variation, as suggested by the correlation between the three pigmentation traits in Europeans, and confirmed by the genetic data available thus far. However, as people from Asia or Africa have uniform dark eyes and hair but can have differences in skin color, genes involved in skin color variation that do not affect eye and hair coloration can also be expected. Although some SNPs have been suggested for skin color prediction already, not enough is yet known about the genetic determination of the full spectrum of human skin color variation, which in fact is expressed in people from different continental regions. Future studies using alternative approaches to GWAS for finding additional skin color genes, such as expression or methylation studies, will be required to deliver more skin-color predictive biomarkers.

Currently, for other EVCs, genetic knowledge is even less advanced. Some first genes have been identified for male baldness in Europeans (*AR*, 20p11), straight hair in Europeans (*TCHH*), and thick hair in Asians (*EDAR*). However, for most EVCs, currently nothing is known about the underlying genes. One noticeable EVC exception, where considerable progress about associated SNPs and genes have been made over the last 5 years but the knowledge is still not advanced enough to allow practical FDP, is human body height or stature. The notion that human height is largely inheritable goes back 125 years to the groundbreaking discovery by the Englishman, Sir Francis Galton, that children's body height can be estimated from mid-parental height. Later, it was estimated from comparisons between monozygotic and dizygotic twins that about 80% of human height variation is heritable. Although applying linkage and candidate-gene approaches to normal height did not provide breakthroughs, these methods did identify genes involved in rare medical syndromes with strong height manifestations such as Marfan syndrome. It again was the GWAS approach that provided genes and SNPs associated with body height. Height GWASs also demonstrated; however, that phenotypic effect sizes of the SNPs found to be statistically significant in their trait association are very small, such as only a few millimeter height change per each SNP. It, therefore, was not surprising that a dedicated genetic height prediction study using data from all height-associated SNPs (~50) available at the time in thousands of Dutch Europeans revealed an AUC of only 0.65 (where 0.5 indicates random prediction). Recall that AUCs for some eye and hair colors are above 0.9, where 1 means completely accurate prediction. Currently, about 180 genetic loci are known that are statistically significant in their association with human body height. This was established in the largest GWAS meta-analysis ever done thus far, involving more than 180 000 individuals. However, these 180 genetic loci together explain only ~10% of the height variation of these 180 000 people. Although no dedicated prediction analysis has been published yet using this most recent genetic knowledge, it can be expected that the height prediction accuracy achievable with all currently available SNPs is still too low for practical FDP. Hence, many more height-predictive DNA markers need to be identified, and are highly expected to exist given the large amount of still missing heritability, before DNA-based height prediction may become practically feasible.

The currently available EVC examples (but also those known from disease traits) demonstrate that the genetic complexity of a trait, together with the amount of heritability and the environmental contribution, determines not only how easy it is to find the most relevant genes involved and to develop highly predictive DNA markers, but also how many predictive markers are eventually needed to obtain prediction accuracies high enough for practical FDP applications and thus how easy it will be to develop a DNA prediction tool. If the genetic complexity of an EVC (or any other trait) is low, while heritability is high and environmental contributions are low, the most relevant genes can be identified with reasonable efforts. This scenario usually leads to a relatively small number of highly predictive DNA markers identified, for which currently available multiplex genotyping technology suitable for forensic DNA analysis such as SNaPshot can be used to develop DNA tools that can be forensically validated and made available for practical FDP; for example, the currently available IrisPlex and HIrisPlex Systems for eye and hair color prediction. If, however, the genetic complexity of an EVC is high while heritability is high and environmental contributions are low, the search for determining genes and associated SNPs is complicated by the small individual effect size requiring very large studies, and the number of predictive markers needed to achieve reasonable accuracies usually is high, with body height as one example. Consequently, once the knowledge is finally established from hundreds or thousands of predictive SNPs, genotyping technologies that allow the parallel analyses of these large numbers of genetic markers are needed that must also meet the specific requirements for forensic DNA analysis. However, such technologies are currently not available. Obviously, any nongenetic contributions cannot be covered by a predictive DNA test; hence, EVCs with low heritability and high environmental contribution are unlikely to be predicted accurately from DNA or any other molecular data.

Outlook: The Near and Distant Future of FDP

Various ongoing scientific and technological developments raise the expectation that DNA-based prediction of more EVCs than eye and hair color will eventually become available with suitable forensically validated tools for practical FDP application with skin color being one likely example. Furthermore, there are additional gene-mapping activities currently under way on additional EVCs, such as male baldness, hair morphology, and body height, which will serve as a prerequisite for developing predictive DNA markers and forensically validated molecular tools if the accumulated genetic knowledge allows the prediction accuracy needed for practical applications. Hence, the near future will see a growing list of such group-specific EVCs predicted from the DNA of crime scene samples. Such DNA tools will allow the disclosing of an appearance group that the unknown crime scene sample donor is likely to belong to, resulting in the possibility of a more concentrated police investigation in the search for unknown perpetrators by lowering the number of potential suspects. This FDP-guided shortlist of potential subjects would then be presented for conventional DNA profile analysis in search of a match with the evidence profile. FDP involving group-specific EVCs is not expected to be applied to the bulk of forensic cases because conventional police investigation, in combination with existing and growing forensic DNA databases, will deliver sample donor identification through conventional DNA profiling in a large number of cases. However, its facility will lie in the unsolved cases, that is, those that cannot be solved with conventional means including no matches in conventional DNA profiling, which concern police and relatives of victims. Here, FDP involving group-specific EVCs is expected to provide investigative help, especially when the number of EVCs predictable from crime scene samples with high enough accuracy will grow further, as can be expected from ongoing scientific activities.

At the end of the day, however, it is the individual-specific human appearance that is anticipated to be fully conveyed by FDP, as only knowledge on individual-specific appearance can in principle provide individual identification. It is appealing and not scientifically unjustified to speculate about such a future development. If indeed individual-specific appearance of an unknown sample donor can be predicted from a biological crime scene sample, the obtained phantom facial picture can be provided to the police for matching with their database of ID card/passport photographs, allowing the retrieval of the name and address of the person in question. If this becomes true, forensic DNA (profile) databases, with all their costs, efforts, and limitations, can be buried in oblivion. The current reality, however, is that individual-specific appearance prediction from DNA, or other biomarkers, represents pure science fiction, as almost nothing is known about the genes determining facial morphology. On the one hand, the identical faces of monozygotic twins (at least for parts of their life) indicate that genetics must play the major role in determining (almost) all individual-specific facial morphology. On the other hand, immense scientific work will be needed to understand the genetics underlying facial morphology and, once understood, to develop predictive biomarkers and, if predictive enough, molecular tools validated for forensic application. Activities have been started to map the genetic architecture of the human face such as by the International Visible Trait Genetics (VisiGen) Consortium. In a recent GWAS carried out by the VisiGen Consortium in almost 10,000 Europeans, five genes have been identified with involvement in facial shapes. Three of them (*PRDM16*, *TP63*, and *PAX3*) have been implicated previously by other approaches in vertebrate craniofacial development and disease, of which one (*PAX3*) was reported earlier with involvement in facial morphology in a GWAS study on children. The remaining two genes (*C5orf50* and *COL17A1*) potentially represent completely new players in the molecular networks governing facial development. From these first studies it seems, as may be expected, that the genetic complexity of the human face is high, as the identified DNA variants only have small effects. Continued and intensified research on the genetics and molecular biology of human appearance will be needed and will eventually show if drawing a reasonably accurate facial phantom picture solely from a biological crime scene sample will eventually become a reality, or will remain fiction in the CSI-type television shows.

Acknowledgments

The author wishes to express his gratitude to those members of his department who carry out various work on identifying genes and predictive biomarkers for human appearance traits, and on developing and forensically validating molecular tools for human appearance prediction in future forensic applications. Susan Walsh and Ruud Koppenol are particularly acknowledged for their contributions to establish Figure 1, and Susan additionally for useful language comments on the manuscript. The author's scientific work on the genetics and prediction of human appearance traits is funded in parts by the Netherlands Forensic Institute (NFI), the Erasmus MC University Medical Center Rotterdam, and the Netherlands Genomics Initiative (NGI)/Netherlands Organization for Scientific Research (NWO) within the framework of the Forensic Genomics Consortium Netherlands (FGCN).

See also: **Biology/DNA:** Ancestry Informative Markers; Single-Nucleotide Polymorphisms.

Further Reading

Branicki, W., Liu, F., van Duijn, K., et al., 2011. Model-based prediction of human hair colour using DNA variants. Human Genetics 129, 443–454.

Kayser, M., de Knijff, P., 2011. Improving human forensics through advances in genetics, genomics and molecular biology. Nature Reviews Genetics 12, 179–192.

Kayser, M., Schneider, P.M., 2009. DNA-based prediction of human externally visible characteristics in forensics: motivations, scientific challenges, and ethical considerations. Forensic Science International: Genetics 3, 154–161.

Koops, B.J., Schellekens, M., 2008. Forensic DNA phenotyping: regulatory issues. Columbia Science and Technology Law Review 9, 158–202.

Lango Allen, H., Estrada, K., Lettre, G., et al., 2010. Hundreds of variants clustered in genomic loci and biological pathways affect human height. Nature 467, 832–838.

Liu, F., van Duijn, K., Vingerling, J.R., et al., 2009. Eye colour and the prediction of complex phenotypes from genotypes. Current Biology 19 (5), R192–R193.

Liu, F., van der Lijn, F., Schurmann, C., et al., 2012. A genome-wide association study identifies five loci influencing facial morphology in Europeans. PLoS Genetics 8 (9), e1002932.

Sulem, P., Gudbjartsson, D.F., Stacey, S.N., et al., 2007. Genetic determination of hair, eye and skin pigmentation in Europeans. Nature Genetics 39 (12), 1443–1452.

Walsh, S., Lindenbergh, A., Zuniga, S.B., et al., 2011. Developmental validation of the IrisPlex system: determination of blue and brown iris colour for forensic intelligence. Forensic Science International: Genetics 5, 464–471.

Walsh, S., Liu, F., Ballantyne, K., et al., 2011. IrisPlex: a sensitive DNA tool for accurate prediction of blue and brown eye colour in the absence of ancestry information. Forensic Science International: Genetics 5, 170–180.

Walsh, S., Liu, F., Wollstein, A., et al., 2012. The HIrisPlex system for simultaneous prediction of hair and eye colour from DNA. Forensic Science International: Genetics 7 (1), 98–115.

Bayesian Networks

F Taroni and A Biedermann, The University of Lausanne, Lausanne-Dorigny, Switzerland

Introduction

Almost 30 years ago, Bayesian networks have been developed in the field of artificial intelligence as a framework that should assist researchers and practitioners in applying the theory of probability to inference problems of more substantive size and, thus, to more realistic and practical problems. Since the late 1980s, Bayesian networks have also attracted researchers in forensic science, and this tendency has considerably intensified throughout the last decade. There is now a considerable body of scientific literature that reports on Bayesian networks as a tool that can be used to study, develop, and implement probabilistic procedures for evaluating the probative value of particular items of scientific evidence in forensic science. Within this context, evaluative issues that pertain to forensic DNA profiling evidence hold an important position because this is one of the main categories of evidence whose assessment has been studied through Bayesian networks. The scope of topics is large and includes almost any aspect that relates to forensic DNA profiling. Typical examples are inference of source (or "criminal identification"), relatedness testing, database searching, and special trace evidence evaluation (such as mixed DNA stains or stains with low quantities of DNA).

Bayesian Networks

Preliminaries

Based on the elements of graph and probability theory, Bayesian networks can roughly be defined as a pictorial representation of the dependencies and influences (represented by arcs) among variables (represented by nodes) deemed to be relevant for a particular probabilistic inference problem. Since the early 1980s, Bayesian networks have gained increased acceptance in the field of expert system technology, which focuses on the study of knowledge bases associated to inference engines. Notably through their ability to coordinate principal probabilistic inference tasks, such as deduction (or prediction) and induction, Bayesian networks are now considered to be a general representation scheme for uncertainty in knowledge. Although graphical approaches to represent probabilistic information have already been discussed in the first half of the nineteenth century, it is now generally agreed that the seminal works of Judea Pearl in the 1980s have initiated the development of the formalism known today as Bayesian networks.

The name "Bayesian networks" is among the most frequently encountered designations. According to the field of application, a variety of other terms—some with possible nuances in definitional details—may be encountered. Among these terms are "Bayes nets," "Bayesian belief networks," "Bayesian expert systems," "graphical probabilistic networks," "probabilistic network models," or "causal networks." For example, the term "belief" in "Bayesian belief networks" is sometimes emphasized to point out that the probabilistic assignments used in a given model reflect degrees of personal belief of the individual who conducts a given probabilistic modeling and inference process. In yet other contexts, the notion of "causality" is sometimes used. This stems from the fact that the links between the nodes of a Bayesian network can be interpreted as causal relationships, even though the definition of Bayesian networks does not refer to causality and there is no requirement that the links represent causal impact.

Definition and Properties

Bayesian networks are a combination of graph theory, which is used to provide a qualitative model structure, and probability theory, which is used to characterize the nature and strength of the relationships that reign within a model. More formally, a Bayesian network covers the following elements:

- A finite collection of random variables that are represented by nodes. Each of these nodes has a finite set of mutually exclusive states. In the context, these may also be called "outcomes."
- A set of directed edges that connect pairs of nodes.
- The set of variables and the set of directed edges are combined in such a way that a directed acyclic graph is obtained, that is, a graph where no loops are permitted.
- Node probability tables are associated with each variable of a network. The probability table of a variable A that receives entering edges from variables B_1, ..., B_n contains conditional probabilities $\Pr(A|B_1, \ldots, B_n)$, whereas a variable A with no entering edges from other variables contains unconditional probabilities $\Pr(A)$. The term "unconditional" refers here only to the absence of an explicit conditioning on other variables (nodes) in a network. Strictly speaking, a probability of the kind $\Pr(A)$ is also

 http://dx.doi.org/10.1016/B978-0-12-800647-4.00029-1

considered as conditional because there is always contextual information, habitually denoted by I, which is used when quantifying $\Pr(A)$. This implies that $\Pr(A)$ should be written more correctly as $\Pr(A|I)$, but I is often omitted to reduce notational burden.

The nodes of a Bayesian network represent propositional variables of interest, that is, very generally speaking, statements or assertions that such and such is the case. This may be an outcome or a state of nature. It is assumed that personal degrees of belief can be assigned to these states. Propositions are basic intellectual attributes formed by an individual during the course of a reasoning task. A proposition can be thought of as referring to states of affairs. Most often, the actual state may not be known with certainty. For example, there may be uncertainty about the truth or otherwise of the proposition according to which a crime stain has been left by the offender. Within a Bayesian network, such a proposition is conceptualized in terms of a node, whose states represent the truth and the falsity of that proposition. The degree of belief maintained in each of these states is expressed numerically, that is, in terms of probabilities. These probabilities are organized in that node's probability table.

The mutually exclusive states of a variable are also referred to as the "domain" of the variable. The domain of a variable may take one of different forms that will determine that variable's subtype. Examples include {red, green, blue} for a labeled variable, {T, F} for a Boolean variable (with "T" and "F" denoting "true" and "false," respectively), $\{-2, 1, 4, 5, 7.34, 8\}$ for a numbered variable, and $\{]-\infty; 0],]0; 10],]10; 100]\}$ for an interval node. Note that the last node type is usable for specifying the intervals over which a continuous quantity can be implemented in a discrete form.

The arrows in a Bayesian network represent relationships that correspond to a property that an expert modeler assumes to hold within the context of an inference problem at hand. If a network is properly constructed, then a directed edge from a node A to a node B signifies that A has a direct influence on B. As an intuitively appealing way of presentation, the links between nodes are sometimes interpreted as "causal relationships." It is important to note, however, that the definition of Bayesian networks does not refer to causality and there is no requirement that the links represent causal impact. Broadly speaking, the links in a network represent probabilistic relevance relationships.

A distinctive feature of Bayesian networks is their incorporation of probability in terms of tables, associated with each node. This allows for interpreting the nature and the strengths of the relationships between a network's different graphical constituents. The node tables can accommodate probabilities from a variety of different sources. Among the most common sources are personal probabilities from human experts and (statistical) data from, for example, databases or the literature. Node probability tables can thus be considered as a means of interfacing a model to data. Besides, probability tables can also be completed by the use of mathematical expressions by exploiting various variable subtypes as described earlier.

An important property of Bayesian networks is the encoding of collections conditional independence assumptions and the representation of probability distributions. For the purpose of illustration, consider a distribution Pr defined on n discrete variables ordered arbitrarily as $A_1, A_2, \ldots, A_n$. Using the product rule, the joint distribution $\Pr(A_1, A_2, \ldots, A_n)$ can be decomposed as follows, also known as the "chain rule":

$$\Pr(A_1, A_2, \ldots A_n) = \left[\prod_{i=2}^{n} \Pr(A_i|A_1, \ldots, A_{i-1})\right] \Pr(A_1)$$

A more economic representation of a joint probability distribution can be obtained if one is capable of specifying variables that are not "sensitive" to all predecessors but only to a certain subset of those predecessors. Stated otherwise, a variable A_i may be independent of all other predecessors once a selected group of predecessors of A_i, called "parents" (par) of A_i, is known. In such a case, the product of the above equation can be rewritten in a shorter form: $\Pr(A_i|\text{par}(A_i))$. Now, if the conditional independencies in a Bayesian network hold for the collection of variables $A_1, A_2, \ldots, A_n$, then the Bayesian network provides a representation of the joint probability distribution $\Pr(A_1, A_2, \ldots, A_n)$ in terms of the product of all specified potentials, that is,

$$\Pr(A_1, A_2, \ldots, A_n) = \prod_{i=2}^{n} \Pr(A_i|\text{par}(A_i))$$

where $\text{par}(A_i)$ represents the set of parental variables of A_i. The latter equation is called the "chain rule for Bayesian networks" and formally defines what a Bayesian network means: a representation of the joint probability distribution for all the variables.

A key task operated by Bayesian network consists of the processing of newly acquired information; that is, calculating the conditional probabilities of the states of the nodes in the network given that the values of some of the nodes have been observed. It is customary to denote the latter as "evidence variables" and the former as "query variables." Broadly speaking, the term "evidence" can be interpreted as information that is available to a particular individual and that is thought to be incorporated into the system of beliefs maintained by that individual. In forensic contexts, such "information" may consist of one or more propositions whose actual state becomes certain for the individual conducting the inference task (e.g., when a scientist decides that there is a "match" between evidential and reference material). This would then provide the basis for reasoning about other propositions that have a bearing on an inference problem of interest. There may also be occasions in which "information," or "evidence," may be of a more technical nature, such as numerical data generated by an experimental procedure (e.g., a number of glass fragments collected on a suspect's clothing or, in the context of DNA evidence, detected alleles of genotypes). Such numerical data may directly qualify as input data that can be accommodated by a Bayesian network (e.g., by means of a numbered node). Evidence on a variable thus corresponds to a statement of the certainties of that variable's states. If it is known with certainty in which state a variable is, then the evidence is called "hard" and the node is said to be "instantiated." Alternatively, an instantiated variable may also be referred to as an "observed" variable. Generally, evidence that is not "hard" is called "soft." One can also talk about evidence in terms of a function. For a variable with discrete states, for example, an evidence function that assigns a zero probability to all but one state may be said to provide hard evidence.

In Bayesian networks, evidence is processed according to Bayes' theorem. This represents one of the main points of interest for the study of Bayesian networks for probabilistic inference in forensic science. A convenient graphical illustration of this property amounts to a two-node network, involving the two binary variables H and E, in terms of the following representation: $H \rightarrow E$. A very common, general instance that can be represented in this way is the evaluation of a screening test where E refers to the result of the test (which may be either positive or negative) and H is the proposition about which one is uncertain. For example, one may be uncertain about whether or not a trace is human blood or whether or not an unknown powder contains something illegal. On observing that E holds, one seeks to calculate $\Pr(H|E, I)$, where I denotes additional contextual information. To apply Bayes' theorem for this task, that is, $\Pr(H|E) = \Pr(H, E)/\Pr(E)$, the following calculations are needed (omitting I for shortness of notation): (1) $\Pr(H, E) = \Pr(H)\Pr(E|H)$ and (2) $\Pr(E) = \Pr(E|H)\Pr(H) + \Pr(E|\overline{H})\Pr(\overline{H})$. Notice that calculation (2) invokes the so-called extension of the conversation rule.

In the above computation, evidence on E is "forwarded" to H against the direction of the arc that holds between these two nodes. It is important to note that within Bayesian networks, propagation is also possible along the direction of the arcs. To continue the example introduced above, propagation along the direction of the arc $H \rightarrow E$ means to calculate the probability of E given H, or $\Pr(E|H)$ for short. What happens during the passage from $\Pr(E)$ to $\Pr(E|H)$ can be seen in (2). This relationship states that for assessing the uncertainty about E, uncertainty in relation to H needs to be accounted for. When H becomes "known," this means that $\Pr(H) = 1$ and $\Pr(\overline{H}) = 0$. Consequently, (2) reduces to $\Pr(E|H)$, and this is just the respective value that has been specified in the conditional probability table of node E.

This description of probabilistic calculations that can be handled within Bayesian networks is informal and based solely on a local network fragment. Since the beginning of the development of Bayesian networks, researchers and practitioners have sought ways to automate these calculations, notably through computerized implementations. This was considered to be an essential step to be achieved if the approach is to be of use for real-world applications. A collection of algorithms are now available that allow calculations to be made in an efficient manner. These approaches have since then been implemented in academically and commercially available Bayesian network software.

Bayesian Networks for Probabilistic Inference in Forensic Science

"Early" Uses of Bayesian Networks for Particular Case Modeling

One of the first studies, in print, on Bayesian networks applied to forensic case settings was published in the late 1980s in the *Journal of the Forensic Science Society*. It focuses on a hypothetical murder scenario (see **Figure 1**) where the authors show how a network approach might be applied to cases involving several, possibly complicated, interrelated issues. They provide a detailed discussion on how (1) relevant propositions can be extracted from a scenario, (2) relationships between propositions are represented qualitatively in terms of a directed graph, and (3) subjective beliefs are incorporated as probabilities and used for inference.

Bayesian Networks for Generic Patterns of Inference

Instead of focusing on a particular scenario, as outlined in the previous section, it is also possible to pursue a modeling approach that aims at a standard analysis of recurrent patterns of inference concerning scientific evidence. This perspective

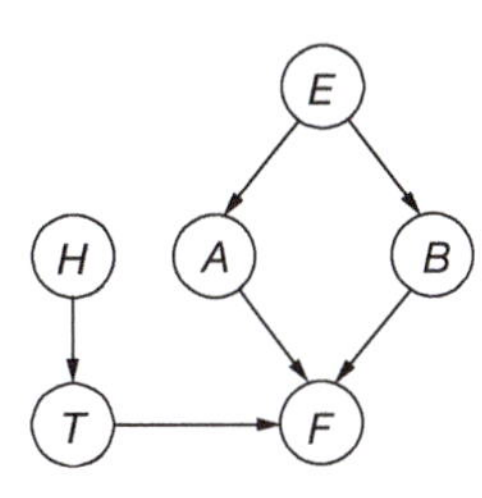

Figure 1 Bayesian network for a hypothetical murder case. The nodes are defined as follows: *A*, "X" committed the murder; *B*, "Y" committed the murder; E, eyewitness evidence of a row between "X," "Y" and the victim some time before the crime was committed; F, fibers from a jacket similar to one found in the possession of "X" are found at the scene of the crime; *H*, "Y" drives the car of "X" regularly; *T*, "Y" picks up fibers from jacket of "X." Reproduced from Aitken, C.G.G., Gammerman, A.J., 1989. Probabilistic reasoning in evidential assessment. Journal of the Forensic Science Society 29, 303–316, with permission from Elsevier.

concentrates on some more generic and fundamental issues that forensic scientists should account for if they seek to evaluate their evidence in the light of propositions that are of judicial interest. That is, the modeling concentrates on aspects of case settings that determine the general pattern of inference (e.g., the relevance of evidence), irrespective of situational detail. **Figure 2(a)** shows an example for such a Bayesian network, used for evaluating "one-trace" cases involving transfer from the offender to the scene. It includes parameters such as

- the rarity of the compared characteristics among members of the relevant suspect population,
- the possibility that the stain would have been left by the suspect, even though he was innocent of the offense, or
- the relevance of the crime stain for the case (i.e., the probability that the stain has a true connection with the offender).

A more formal definition of the various nodes is given in **Table 1**.

Figure 2(b) shows a more refined representation of a situation in which one seeks to draw an inference about *S*, the proposition according to which the suspect is the source of a crime stain. A particular aspect of this model is a distinction between (a) a true, but actually unobserved, correspondence between the profiles of the crime stain and a reference sample from the suspect (node *M*) and (b) an observed (or reported) correspondence by the scientists. This distinction allows the incorporation of a probability for a false positive. This situation, a false positive, occurs when a report states a correspondence when in fact the crime stain and the suspect have different profiles.

Figure 2(c) is also amenable for an inference about the proposition *M* but extends to the additional item of information *D* that a certain number of profiles in a database were

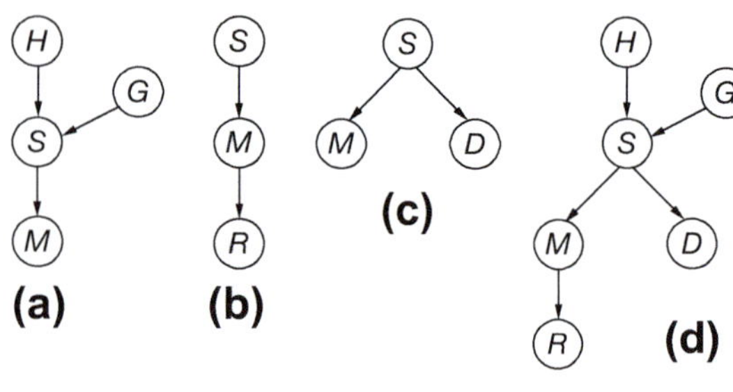

Figure 2 Bayesian network fragments for (a) one-trace one-offender cases (involving transfer from the criminal to crime scene), (b) the problem of laboratory error, (c) results of a database search. Model (d) shows a combination of the network fragments (a–c). The definition of the nodes is as given in **Table 1**. Reproduced from Taroni, F., Biedermann, A., Garbolino, P., Aitken, C.G.G., 2004. A general approach to Bayesian networks for the interpretation of evidence. Forensic Science International 139, 5–16, with permission from Elsevier.

Table 1 Definition of the binary nodes used in the Bayesian networks shown in **Figure 2**

Node	*Definition*
H	The suspect is the offender
S	The crime stain came from the suspect
G	The crime stain came from the offender
M	The suspect's blood and the crime stain have matching
R	Reported match between suspect's profile and the profile of the crime stain
D	The other (N − 1) profiles of the database do not match

found to be different from that of the crime stain. This is a relevant supportive item of information that exerts distinct support for the proposition that the suspect is the source of the crime stain, in the same way as is learning about a match *M* between the profiles of the suspect and the crime stain.

It is important to mention that all three Bayesian networks, **Figure 2(a–c)**, have a probabilistic underpinning that agrees with published likelihood ratio formulae that seek to assess the probative value of DNA evidence in the respective situations. A further aspect worth mentioning is that these network fragments can also be logically combined so as to lead to the model shown in **Figure 2(d)**. This model allows for a joint evaluation of the various aspects considered in the separate local network fragments. This illustrates that Bayesian networks play an important role for coherent representation of complicated patterns of evidence. In particular, it is possible to address inference problems on a more local level first and then using the fragments thus constructed for reasoning on a problem of higher complexity. Above all, however, a model remains a probabilistic interpretation of a real phenomenon (or, more generally, an inference problem) that is constructed at a given level of acceptable approximation. It does not amount to a claim of "true model."

Advanced Bayesian Network Approaches for Assessing DNA Evidence

Representation of genotypes

In the previous sections, a single discrete node was generally used for representing the outcomes of DNA analyses (e.g., the proposition according to which the crime stain and the suspect's blood "correspond" with respect to their DNA profile). In the simplest case, this perspective amounts to a two-node network fragment in which knowledge about the state of an observational variable, such as *E* (e.g., short for "DNA match"), is used for drawing an inference about propositions according to which the "matching" suspect is (is not) the source of the crime stain. If the latter propositions are represented by *H*, the Bayesian network would take the structure $H \rightarrow E$.

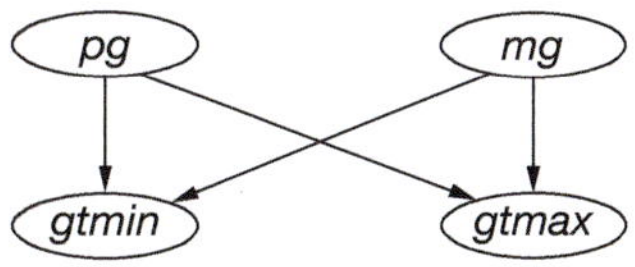

Figure 3 Representation of an individual's genotype as the minimum (*gtmin*) and maximum (*gtmax*) of the two parental gene nodes *pg* and *mg*, inherited via the paternal and maternal line, respectively. Reproduced from Dawid, A.P., Mortera, J., Vicard, P., 2007. Object-oriented Bayesian networks for complex forensic DNA profiling problems. Forensic Science International 169(2–3), 195–205, with permission from Elsevier.

Besides these formative and coarse modeling approaches, considerable additional research has been devoted to the application of Bayesian networks to inference problems involving the results of DNA analyses. An important direction of research in that area focuses on basic representational schemes, usable as repeatable modules in analogous situations. These submodels are more fine-grained network fragments focusing on individual genes, rather than on full genotype representations. An example of this is a network with the converging connection $mg \rightarrow gt \leftarrow pg$, where node gt represents a genotype that is modeled as a logical combination of the alleles inherited from the mother and father. These parentally inherited genes are represented by the nodes mg and pg, to be read "maternal gene" and "paternal gene," respectively. A gene A, for instance, can take one of several different forms, also called alleles. Suppose there are n alleles at gene A. These alleles may be denoted $A_1, A_2, \ldots, A_n$ at a given locus. In the Bayesian network $mg \rightarrow gt \leftarrow pg$, the states A_1, A_2, and A_x are assumed for nodes mg and pg. The third state, A_x, accounts for all unobserved alleles $A_3, \ldots, A_n$. The possible states of the genotype node gt may then be defined as A_1A_1, A_1A_2, A_1A_x, A_2A_2, A_2A_x, and A_xA_x, which are all the logical combinations of pairs of alleles.

For a more general ready-to-use representation, one might want to specify, for each parental gene pg and mg, the full repertory of alleles at a given locus. However, this may lead to a rapid increase in the size of the probability table for the node gt. This can be avoided by separating the node gt into two distinct nodes $gtmin$ and $gtmax$, as shown in **Figure 3**. These two nodes represent, respectively, the minimum and the maximum of the two parental gene nodes pg and mg.

Relatedness testing

The application of the more detailed modeling approach for genotypes, outlined in the previous section, can be illustrated in the context of a scenario of disputed paternity. Consider that a certain male, denoted as the putative father pf, is supposed to be the father of a certain child c. DNA profiles are available on the mother m, the putative father pf, and the child c. The entity of interest is the likelihood ratio for the proposition that the putative father pf is the true father tf, noted $tf = pf?$, given knowledge about the child's genotype cgt and the mother's genotype mgt. The paternity pedigree corresponding to this inference problem is shown in **Figure 4(a)**. A representation of this disputed paternity case in terms of a Bayesian network is shown in **Figure 4(b)**. There would be a Bayesian network of this kind for each genetic marker that has been analyzed. These networks can be analyzed separately and the resulting likelihood ratios combined subsequently. An alternative way of

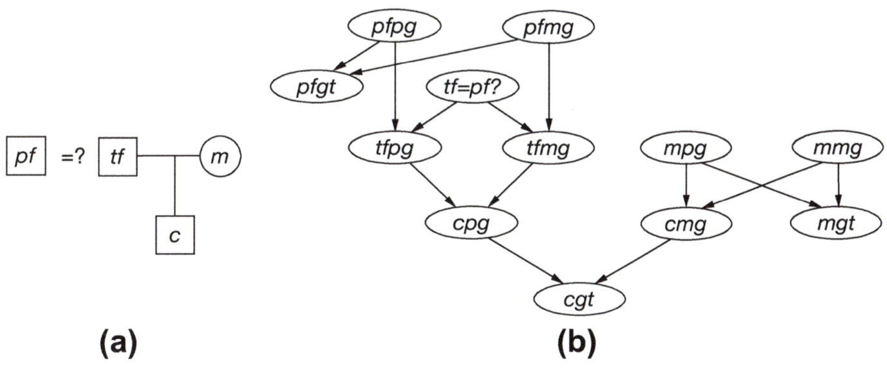

Figure 4 Different representations of a case of disputed paternity: (a) paternity pedigree (with squares representing males and circles females, *pf* denoting the putative father, *tf* denoting the true father, *m* denoting the mother, and *c* denoting the child) and (b) a Bayesian network. For the Bayesian network, *tfpg*, *tfmg*, *mpg*, and *mmg* denote the paternal *p* and maternal *m* (in second place) genes of the true father *tf* and the mother *m* (in first place); *cpg* and *cmg* denote the child's paternal and maternal genes, respectively; *pfpg* and *pfmg* denote the putative father's paternal and maternal genes, respectively; *pfgt*, *mgt*, and *cgt* denote the genotypes of the putative father, the mother, and the child, respectively; and *tf* = *pf*? takes two values in answer: "yes" or "no" as to whether the true father is the putative father. Reproduced from Dawid, A.P., Mortera, J., Pascali, V.L., van Boxel, D., 2002. Probabilistic expert systems for forensic inference from genetic markers. Scandinavian Journal of Statistics 29, 577–595, with permission from Wiley.

proceeding consists of combining the single-locus networks within a single "top-level" network, in the context also called "supernetwork."

The Bayesian network depicted in **Figure 4(b)** allows one to obtain the same results as with classic arithmetic calculus of Essen-Möller under the Hardy–Weinberg assumption of independence. One might thus be tempted to conclude that there is no real gain by working with Bayesian networks, as there is indeed no need to develop new methods for problems that can be solved by simple algebra. However, the very aim of proposing the network shown in **Figure 4(b)** is different. It provides a solid basis for evaluating DNA evidence and serves as a starting point for approaching more complex problems that accompany the evaluation of forensic DNA evidence, such as missing data (i.e., when profiling data of some individuals are unavailable), additional data (e.g., from a related person, if available), or mutation.

Inference of source for crime stains

Besides relatedness testing, the network approach to inference based on typing results for genetic markers, as presented in the previous sections, is also very helpful for addressing evaluative questions about crime stains. **Figure 5** illustrates this in terms of a full numerically specified example in which the profile of a crime stain is assumed to correspond to the profile of a suspect. The analysis focuses on a hypothetical marker with alleles A_1, A_2, and A_x, as defined previously. The population proportions for A_1 and A_2 have been set to 0.05. In **Figure 5**, the

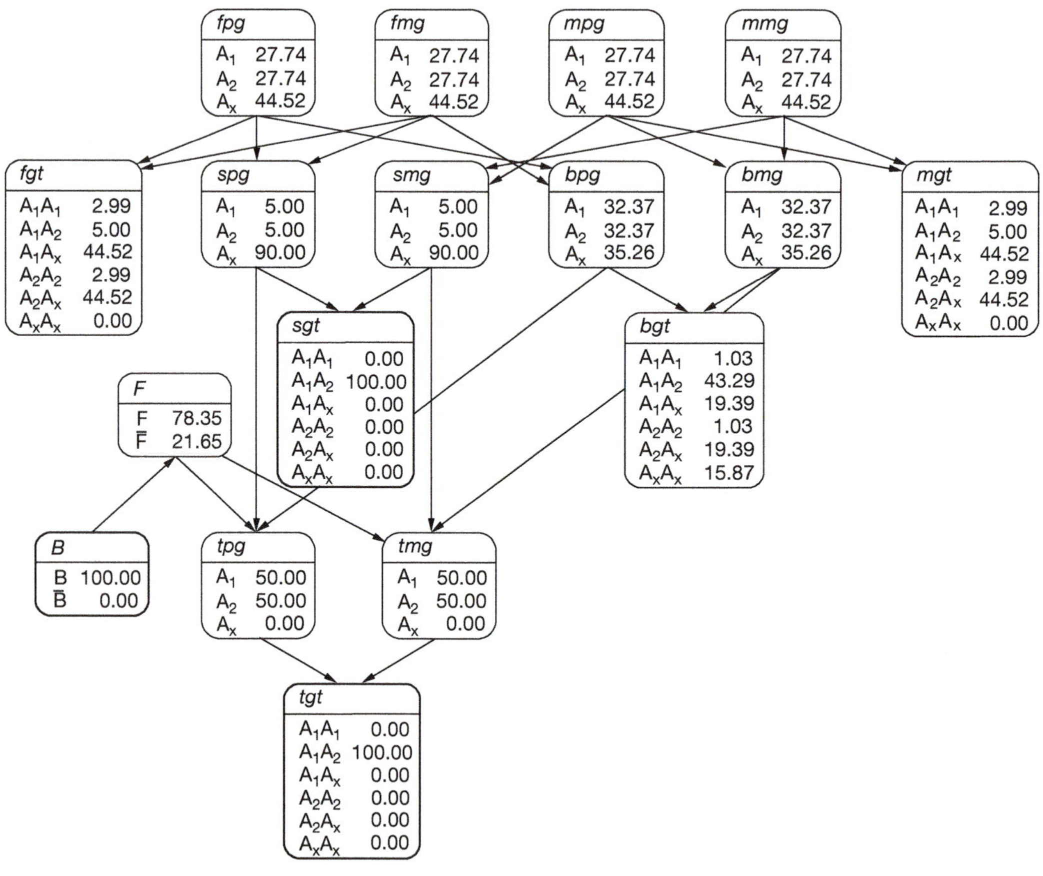

Figure 5 Bayesian network for evaluating DNA typing results in a one-stain scenario when the alternative proposition at the source level is that the suspect's brother left the stain. The nodes *B*, *tgt*, and *sgt* are instantiated, meaning that the suspect is assumed to have a brother and that information is available about the genotype of the suspect and the crime stain. Node *F* is the source node, with two states, *F*, the suspect is the source of the crime stain, $\bar{F}$, a brother of the suspect is the source of the crime stain. Node *B* has two states: *B*, the suspect has a brother, and $\bar{B}$, the suspect does not have a brother. Nodes *fpg*, *fmg*, *mpg*, *mmg*, *spg*, *smg*, *bpg*, *bmg*, *tpg*, and *tmg* are gene nodes, with three states, states A_1, A_2, and A_x. Nodes *fgt*, *mgt*, *sgt*, *bgt*, and *tgt* are genotypic nodes. Note that *f* denotes father, *p* paternal, *m* mother (if in first place) or maternal (if in second place), *s* suspect, *b* brother, and *t* trace (if in first place). Instantiated nodes are shown with a bold border. Reproduced from Taroni, F., Aitken, C.G.G., Garbolino, P., Biedermann, A. 2006. Bayesian Networks and Probabilistic Inference in Forensic Science. Wiley, Chichester, with permission from Wiley.

node *F* displays the posterior probability that the suspect is the source of a crime stain (which is found to have the profile A_1A_2), given that the suspect has the same DNA profile as the crime stain, whereas the alternative proposition is that a brother of the suspect—unavailable for testing—is the source of the crime stain. Besides, this network could also readily be extended to incorporate the possibility that a random member of the general population is the source of the crime stain.

Conclusions

Despite the various compelling capacities of the Bayesian network formalism, the manual model construction may often be a painstaking process, in particular, for larger applications. As a means to overcome such difficulties, Bayesian networks have been extended to "object-oriented Bayesian networks." The idea behind this approach is to define generic "classes" of networks, particular nodes of which (so-called "instances") can be used, as required, in place of nodes in other networks. The object-oriented Bayesian network language thereby allows one to describe inference problems in terms of interrelated objects. This currently represents a major direction of research in Bayesian networks for inference from genetic markers. This approach is also helpful for combining typing results from several genetic markers.

More generally, Bayesian networks represent a powerful graphical approach for evidence evaluation (also other than DNA) in judicial contexts. Compared to most previously developed graphical methods, the use of Bayesian networks offers the additional advantage of incorporating probability theory as a coherent measure of uncertainty. Moreover, computerized systems currently exist that can perform calculations over a number of variables with varying dependency structure. More recent developments, in particular, the extension to object orientation, have further increased the capacity of Bayesian networks to deal with the level of complication that is associated with real-case settings involving DNA evidence. Bayesian networks thus represent a complementary contribution to the body of analytical techniques that are needed to approach inference problems in accordance with probability theory, both conceptually and practically.

See also: **Biology/DNA:** DNA – Statistical Probability; **Foundations:** Overview and Meaning of Identification/Individualization; Statistical Interpretation of Evidence: Bayesian Analysis.

Further Reading

Aitken, C.G.G., Gammerman, A., 1989. Probabilistic reasoning in evidential assessment. Journal of the Forensic Science Society 29, 303–316.
Biedermann, A., Taroni, F., 2006. Bayesian networks and probabilistic reasoning about scientific evidence when there is a lack of data. Forensic Science International 157, 163–167.
Dawid, A.P., Evett, I.W., 1997. Using a graphical method to assist the evaluation of complicated patterns of evidence. Journal of Forensic Sciences 42, 226–231.
Dawid, A.P., Mortera, J., Pascali, V., van Boxel, D., 2002. Probabilistic expert systems for forensic inference from genetic markers. Scandinavian Journal of Statistics 29, 577–595.
Dawid, A.P., Mortera, J., Vicard, P., 2007. Object-oriented Bayesian networks for complex forensic DNA profiling problems. Forensic Science International 169, 195–205.
Evett, I.W., Gill, P.D., Jackson, G., Whitaker, J., Champod, C., 2002. Interpreting small quantities of DNA: the hierarchy of propositions and the use of Bayesian networks. Journal of Forensic Sciences 47, 520–530.
Garbolino, P., Taroni, F., 2002. Evaluation of scientific evidence using Bayesian networks. Forensic Science International 125, 149–155.
Jensen, F.V., Nielsen, T.D., 2007. Bayesian Networks and Decision Graphs. Springer, New York.
Kjaerulff, U.B., Madsen, A.L., 2008. Bayesian Networks and Influence Diagrams: A Guide to Construction and Analysis. Springer, New York.
Mortera, J., Dawid, A.P., Lauritzen, S.L., 2003. Probabilistic expert systems for DNA mixture profiling. Theoretical Population Biology 63, 191–205.
Neapolitan, R.E., 2004. Learning Bayesian Networks. Pearson Prentice Hall, Upper Saddle River, NJ.
Pearl, J., 1982. Reverend Bayes on inference engines: a distributed hierarchical approach. In: Proceedings of the National Conference on Artificial Intelligence (AAAI'82). Morgan Kaufmann, Pittsburgh, pp. 133–136.
Pourret, O., Naïm, P., Marcot, B., 2008. Bayesian Networks: A Practical Guide to Applications. Wiley, Chichester.
Taroni, F., Aitken, C.G.G., Garbolino, P., Biedermann, A., 2006. Bayesian Networks and Probabilistic Inference in Forensic Science. Wiley, Chichester.
Taroni, F., Biedermann, A., Garbolino, P., Aitken, C.G.G., 2004. A general approach to Bayesian networks for the interpretation of evidence. Forensic Science International 139, 5–16.

Key Terms

Admixture, AIMs, Allele frequency, Ancestry, Ancestry informative markers, Bayes' factor, Bayes' rule, Bayes' theorem, Bayesian inference, Bayesian networks, Biological eye witness, Body height, Categorical data, Conditional probability, Confidence intervals, Continuous data, Cousins, Databases, Database search, Deconvolution, Degree of belief, Divergence, DNA, DNA evidence, DNA probability, DNA typing, Duffy, Evidence evaluation, Evidence interpretation, Externally visible characteristic (EVC), Eye color, Facial morphology, Fallacy, False positive result, Forensic DNA phenotyping (FDP), Frequentist inference, FST, Genome-wide association study (GWAS), Graphical model, Hair color, HGDP—CEPH, Human appearance, Human remains identification, Hypothesis testing,

Indels, Indistinguishable from stutter, Inference, Interpretation, Laws of Probability, Likelihood ratio, Major contributor, Mixture, Mixture ratio, Number of contributors, Parentage testing, Peak height ratios, Physical trait, Population database, Population genetics, Population structure, Posterior probability, Prior probability, Probability, Probability theory, Product rule, Range tests, Relatedness, Relationship testing, Siblings, Single nucleotide polymorphisms (SNPs), Small tandem repeat testing, SPSmart, Statistics, Stochastic threshold, STRs, STR Subjective probability, Structure, Subpopulation model, Theta, Uncertainty, X chromosome.

Review Questions

1. What is "frequentist inference"?
2. What is a range test? How is it used? What is "the cliff problem"?
3. What is the empirical rule? When is it used? When can it *not* be used?
4. When does the value of α (alpha) vary? How is this determined?
5. What is the null hypothesis? What is the alternative hypothesis?
6. What can be said if the *P* value is low? What cannot be said? Why?
7. What are some of the problems using the two-sample *t* test? If Hotelling's T^2 avoids these issues, then why is it not used more often in forensic science?
8. What is θ? What part does it play in confidence intervals?
9. What is Bayes' rule? What is it based upon?
10. If Bayes' rule is based on "subjective—in the sense of 'personal'—expression of degrees of belief held by an individual," then is it appropriate for use in science? Why or why not?
11. What are likelihood ratios? How do they differ from Bayes' rule?
12. If background population frequencies are not known, can likelihood ratios still be used?
13. What are prior odds? What are posterior odds?
14. What is the "prosecutor's fallacy"? What is the "defender's fallacy"? How do these relate to the work of a forensic scientist?
15. How is forensic DNA testing used in parentage testing? Why would this be a *forensic* analysis?
16. What is the parentage trio? How are likelihood ratios used to determine parentage?
17. Can parentage be tested for if a parent is missing? How?
18. How is the number of contributors in a mixture determined? How is the ratio of each determined?
19. How are contributors sorted from stutter? What are the potential problems in this process?
20. What are the conclusions that can be drawn from the comparison of a probative reference standard to the interpreted DNA mixture?

Discussion Questions

1. Why are statistics even needed in forensic science?
2. How would you explain the frequentist approach to a jury? How would you explain the Bayesian approach to the same jury?
3. If the frequentist approach "does not answer the question the court is interested in", that is, guilty or innocence, then does the Bayesian approach answer this question? Should any statistical approach in forensic science answer this question? Is this the responsibility of the laboratory?
4. Mathematical methods are capable of very specific sorting, and artificial intelligence has already crept into software applications. Is it possible that some mixtures will *never* be able to be sorted out statistically? Why or why not?
5. Draw a decision tree outlining how to address mixtures and in what order to ask what questions.

Additional Readings

Bright, J.A., Curran, J.M., Buckleton, J.S., 2014. The effect of the uncertainty in the number of contributors to mixed DNA profiles on profile interpretation. Forensic Science International Genetics 12, 208–214.

Carboni, I., Iozzi, S., Nutini, A.L., Torricelli, F., Ricci, U., 2014. Improving complex Kinship Analyses with additional STR loci. Electrophoresis. http://dx.doi.org/10.1002/elps.201400080.

Christensen, A.M., Crowder, C.M., Ousley, S.D., Houck, M.M., 2014. Error and its meaning in forensic science. Journal of Forensic Sciences 59 (1), 123–126.

Kelly, H., Bright, J.A., Buckleton, J.S., Curran, J.M., 2014. A comparison of statistical models for the analysis of complex forensic DNA profiles. Science and Justice 54 (1), 66–70.

Steele, C.D., Balding, D.J., 2014. Statistical evaluation of forensic DNA profile evidence. Annual Review of Statistics and Its Application 1, 361–384.

Section 5. Professional Issues

Dean Gialamas, past president of the American Society of Crime Laboratory Directors, has said that "Ethics mean nothing to me. Ethics is knowing right from wrong and prisons are filled with people who know that; they chose badly. What is needed is integrity, the will to do what's right." Headlines proclaim the end of forensic science because of failures on the part of organizations or people who choose the wrong thing: stealing drugs, falsifying reports, lying during testimony, fudging science. Listing them would be depressing and, using Gialamas's perspective, pointless: We already know they chose poorly. The real question is, how to get people to choose well, to do what is right? It starts with education and understanding the connection between what a scientist does in the laboratory and the effect that has on individuals and society. In fraud investigations, the acronym "ABC" is used, meaning fraud can originate with a single bad Apple, a bad Barrel of apples, or a bad Crop of them. Again, from Gialamas's view, it could also mean a bad farmer, a manager who sends the wrong messages, does not do what is right for the organization or its employees, and lets bad actions slide. Which of these is the worst? Hard to say, because they each can lead to the downfall of a laboratory or a discipline.

Forensic DNA analysis carries a special burden because of its use in exonerating the wrongfully convicted. In fact, the first use of DNA profiling in a criminal investigation led to an exoneration, that of Richard Buckland in the United Kingdom (BBC News, 2009). An entire network of groups devoted to reviewing and retesting forensic evidence in claims of innocence, The Innocence Network, has yielded the exoneration of hundreds of people. The ethical implications are astounding and, as forensic science moves forward, these lessons learned must be incorporated into our practices and profession.

As a profession, forensic science needs to see outside its historically limited perspective and look to other professions for insight, advice, and models to improve its standing and reputation. "The way we've always done it" does not work anymore and is an insufficient answer for what ails forensic science. If forensic science does not take itself seriously, why would anyone else? This section lays out basic issues every forensic scientist faces, as an individual, an employee of an organization, and a member of a professional community.

"DNA pioneer's 'eureka' moment". 2009. *BBC News*. September 9. Online at: http://news.bbc.co.uk/2/hi/programmes/newsnight/8245312.stm.

Crime Scene to Court

K Ramsey and E Burton, Greater Manchester Police Forensic Services Branch, Manchester, UK

Glossary

T1/2/3 CSI Skill tiers defined for crime scene investigation officers, with 1 being the most basic level of training (usually volume crime offences only), 2 being the range of volume, serious and major crime investigations, and 3 being trained in crime scene management/the coordination of complex investigations.

CBRN Chemical, biological, radiation, and nuclear incidents.

L2 Level 2 investigations, specific skills required, for example, covert operations, deployment and substitution of items, and forensic markers.

CCTV Closed circuit television (cameras or evidence from).

HTCU High-tech crime unit (examination of hardware/software/data/images from any system or device).

VSC/ESDA Video spectral comparison: the analysis of inks, primarily in fraudulent documents; Electro static detection analysis: the examination of (writing) indentations on paper.

NaBIS National Ballistic Intelligence Service (UK).

LCH Local Clearing House (firearms).

NCA National Crime Agency (UK).

CPS Crown Prosecution Service (UK).

NOS National Occupational Standards.

CPD Continuous professional development.

 http://dx.doi.org/10.1016/B978-0-12-800647-4.00030-8

Introduction

A multitude of disciplines evolved within forensic science during the twentieth century, resulting in highly specialized fields of evidential opportunities to support criminal investigations. Many of the more traditional disciplines, for example, footwear analysis and blood pattern interpretation, now have well-established principles and methodologies that have been proven in a criminal justice context; developments in these areas are largely confined to technical support systems and information sharing through databases. The very rapid rate of development of DNA profiling techniques during the 1980s and 1990s led to the emergence of national and international DNA databases; however, the pace of change has now been significantly reduced. Conversely, the end of the twentieth century and the early part of the twenty-first century have seen an explosion of new forensic evidence types that are less established in court—disciplines such as CCTV, mobile phones, computer analysis, and the use of digital images and social media are collectively referred to as e-forensics.

Owing to the highly specialized nature of each forensic discipline and the varied rate of evolution, forensic science effectively represents a composite of interrelated, and often distinct, opportunities to support criminal investigations.

Most current models of forensic service delivery, especially where part of a wider organization, for example, police forces and enforcement agencies, have arisen over time by bolting on additional elements and clustering together within related fields. If the current capability of forensic science were to be designed from scratch as an effective entity, it is certain that a more integrated, and hence effective, structure would be proposed.

In addition, there has been a professionalization of forensic science in the workplace and increasing requirements for regulation; as recently as the 1980s, crime scene investigation, for example, was widely undertaken by police officers and was largely restricted to recording/recovering visible evidence; this was used in a limited capacity to support that particular investigation without scope for wider intelligence development. Now, crime scene investigation is predominantly undertaken by specialist staff employed exclusively to undertake these duties.

To practice in a forensic discipline, specialized training, qualifications, and competency levels are required. The range of evidence types that have potential to support investigations has widened considerably. Some disciplines lend themselves to cross-skilling.

Public expectations of what forensic science can deliver have been heightened by highly popular mainstream television programs, both documentary and fictional. Often, the expectation of what can be delivered exceeds what is either possible or financially sensible. This leads to a requirement on service providers and users to make informed (evidential and financial) decisions regarding the best use of forensic evidence in support of investigations.

This article considers options to optimize the use of forensic evidence types recovered from crime scenes in the context of the different models available to criminal justice systems; the concept of integrated case management is outlined and discussed.

Task

The task is to bring together all potential forensic evidential opportunities, holistically review their significance to the investigation, prioritize the progression of work, deliver the best evidence to the court for testing (complying with all continuity, integrity, and quality requirements), and ensure the best value for money when determining spending on forensic evidence.

Internationally, there are variable constraints and opportunities due to the different criminal justice models and the commercial market situation at state/regional and country levels.

Models

1. All forensic evidence sourced within a law enforcement agency, for example, a police laboratory.
2. All forensic evidence provided by external specialists contracted to a law enforcement agency.
3. Composite of (a) and (b).

Forensic Strategies

The recovery of evidence from the crime scene is only the start of the forensic process. Once the evidence has been collected, packaged, and preserved, it needs to be analyzed in order to provide meaningful information to the investigation and subsequently the courts.

Forensic examinations are carried out in order to implicate or eliminate individuals and also to establish what has occurred during the commission of an offense or incident.

Deciding what analysis is required can be a complex process. Some of the issues for consideration include the following:

- Is it necessary to examine all the evidence that is recovered?
- Should every possible test be carried out?

In an ideal world, it would be preferable to carry out every possible analysis; however, in reality, it is likely that this will be neither practicable nor financially viable. In addition, carrying out every possible analysis would overload forensic laboratories.

When making decisions about what forensic analysis should be carried out, it is vitally important that consideration be given to both the potential prosecution and defense cases. An impartial approach must be taken to assessing examination requirements. It is often not necessary to carry out an examination of every item of evidence recovered, but examinations should be directed to where value could potentially be added to an investigation.

A forensic strategy should be developed around every case where forensic evidence plays a part, which may relate to an overall case or to an individual item of evidence. A forensic strategy should be developed in a holistic manner taking into account all potential evidence types and should direct and coordinate the forensic examinations/analyses that are required.

Forensic strategies can be developed in different ways by one or more of the following:

- Investigating officer
- Crime scene investigator (CSI) or crime scene manager
- Forensic scientist/forensic specialist
- Forensic submissions officer (this is a role that can be variably named such as forensic advisor, scientific support manager, etc.; it describes an informed individual within a police force or law enforcement agency who uses knowledge and expertise to advise on forensic analysis and who has decision-making authority and control of the budgetary spending)
- Legal representative
- Pathologist.

Forensic strategies are generally initially developed and applied by individuals involved in the prosecution aspects of a crime. Although this is the case, it is vitally important that a balanced and unbiased approach be taken to the development of a strategy and consideration given to information that may support the defense case as well as the prosecution case. Examinations that are likely to add value or provide information to an investigation (irrespective of whether they will support or weaken the prosecution case) should be carried out, and all results must be disclosed to the defense team. Defense should also be given the opportunity to carry out any review of strategies, examination processes, and/or results that they require and be provided with access to any items of evidence that they want to examine themselves in order to build the defense case.

In order to develop the forensic strategy and make appropriate decisions about which forensic examinations will be of value to the investigation, the following are necessary:

- To be able to gather as much information as possible about the circumstances of the case
  - Circumstances of evidence recovery
  - Accounts given by victim(s), witnesses, suspect(s), etc.
- To have an understanding and knowledge of forensic science and its application to investigations.

A forensic strategy meeting is a useful way of ensuring that all relevant parties are aware of the full circumstances of the case and enables a "multiagency" discussion about the processing of all exhibits to optimize evidential potential in a comprehensive and coordinated manner.

It can often be the case that police officers do not have a full understanding or knowledge of forensic science, likewise forensic scientists historically have had a relatively poor understanding of police and investigative processes; this can lead to miscommunication and confusion in relation to the application of forensic science to meet investigative needs. A joint approach to the development of forensic strategies helps to improve the communication and understanding on a case-by-case basis.

A formal forensic strategy meeting is often required only in more serious cases; however, the general approach can be applied to any investigation. Even in the simplest cases, it is often beneficial for discussions to take place between the investigating officer, the CSI, the forensic advisor/budget holder/decision maker, and the prosecutor. Alternatively, generic strategies can be implemented, for example, for a particular crime type or *modus operandi.*

When assessing the potential examination of a particular item and the development of a forensic strategy, the requirements of the investigation are the primary concern, and consideration should be given to the following issues:

- The type and nature of the item/exhibit
- The context of the item
  - Exactly where and when it was recovered
  - Condition of the item (wet, damaged, etc.)
- The integrity of the item
  - Has it been appropriately recovered, handled, packaged, and preserved?
  - Is the security and continuity of the item intact?
- The potential evidence that may be obtained from the item, for example, DNA, fingerprints, fibers, footwear marks
- The information these evidence types may provide to the investigation
- Whether this potential information is likely to add value to the investigation
  - Is it possible that new information will be provided?
  - Is it possible that an account given by a witness, victim, or suspect will be supported or refuted?
  - Will the information help to establish what has occurred?
- Whether there is a conflict between potential evidence types, and if so, which evidence type will be of most value under the circumstances

  - For example, swabbing/taping for DNA may damage fingerprints, but where the DNA is likely to be at low levels and requires specialized low-template DNA analysis, the presence of DNA may not necessarily prove contact with an item, whereas fingerprints will always prove that contact has occurred
- The chance of success, that is, obtaining a result/information of value to the investigation (this may be inclusive or exclusive).

Much work has historically been completed in relation to developing and understanding the success rates relating to DNA profiling; however, relatively little work has been undertaken to fully understand the success rates associated with other forensic evidence. This is largely because other evidence types, such as fibers, gunshot residue, footwear marks, etc., are generally more complex to interpret than DNA. In relation to DNA profiling, success rates are generally based on the chances of obtaining a DNA profile; however, with the other evidence types, the value of the outcome very much depends on the circumstances of the investigation. For example, when searching an item of clothing taken from a suspect for glass, the absence of glass or the presence of glass could both be of value to the investigation depending on the circumstances. The presence of glass on the clothing that matches control sample(s) from the crime scene is only of value if its presence cannot be accounted for in any legitimate way; conversely, the absence of glass on the item of clothing may lead to a conclusion that the suspect was not involved in the offense, depending on the circumstances of the offense and arrest.

In addition to being able to understand and evaluate the chances of being able to obtain a meaningful result, it is also vital that the value of the overall contribution to the entire case is understood. This involves being able to understand the value and contribution of the forensic examination to the detection of the offense as well as the outcome of the court process. This is an even more difficult issue to evaluate and understand than the chances of being able to obtain a forensic test result.

Because the value of forensic evidence is so dependent on the individual case circumstances, decisions about examinations must be made on an individual case basis. There have been recent developments in some agencies/forces to better understand the chances of success of different types of forensic evidence and the value to investigations; this will help to better inform decisions about evidential potential and examination viability as well as assist in achieving value for money. This approach is best described as *forensic effectiveness*.

The forensic strategy should also take into account the timescales associated with the investigative process and the criminal justice system, and it should be ensured that forensic analysis can meet the requirements of the criminal justice process, including court dates and any requirements to disclose appropriate information to the defense team(s).

Each police force/law enforcement agency will have its own approach to the submission of exhibits for forensic examination/analysis. Irrespective of whether the analysis is carried out in an internal police laboratory, external commercial company, or government owned laboratory, these approaches can be applied to all examinations and all evidence types.

These approaches help to ensure that decisions are based on scientific knowledge, viability, and evidential value taking into account all aspects of the investigation. They will help ensure that the best evidence is obtained while considering value for money and that it can be applied to any investigation irrespective of the seriousness of the offense or the scale of the investigation.

Integrated Case Management

The concept and use of forensic strategies in directing investigations is not new but is often limited by the evolved structure of forensic disciplines within investigative agencies. Classically, DNA and fingerprint evidence from volume crimes will be independently submitted at the same time by different routes, and this often results in wasted effort/spending and duplicated results. The development and use of forensic intelligence has been variable. Emerging thinking includes organizational redesign of forensics to better integrate with related functions such as intelligence collection, targeted deployment of resources, and prioritized forensic submissions.

The concept of integrated case management draws together informed operational deployment (e.g., of crime scene investigators) followed by a more holistic approach to submissions for testing. The strategy takes greater account of supporting intelligence and desired outcomes. Regular reviews and trigger points are included for the staged submission of potential evidence, and communication with investigators is enhanced, allowing for a more responsive and directed investigation.

Ultimately, the production of *intelligent identifications* can be better achieved by having an integrated process that links the enforcement priorities, available resources, potential forensic evidence, intelligence, and prosecutor requirements; this model provides flexibility to respond to changing demands and gives an increased likelihood of efficient and effective spending on forensic support to investigations. There is no single way to achieve this, but an illustration of how to rethink some of the traditional silo-based forensic disciplines is provided in **Figure 1**.

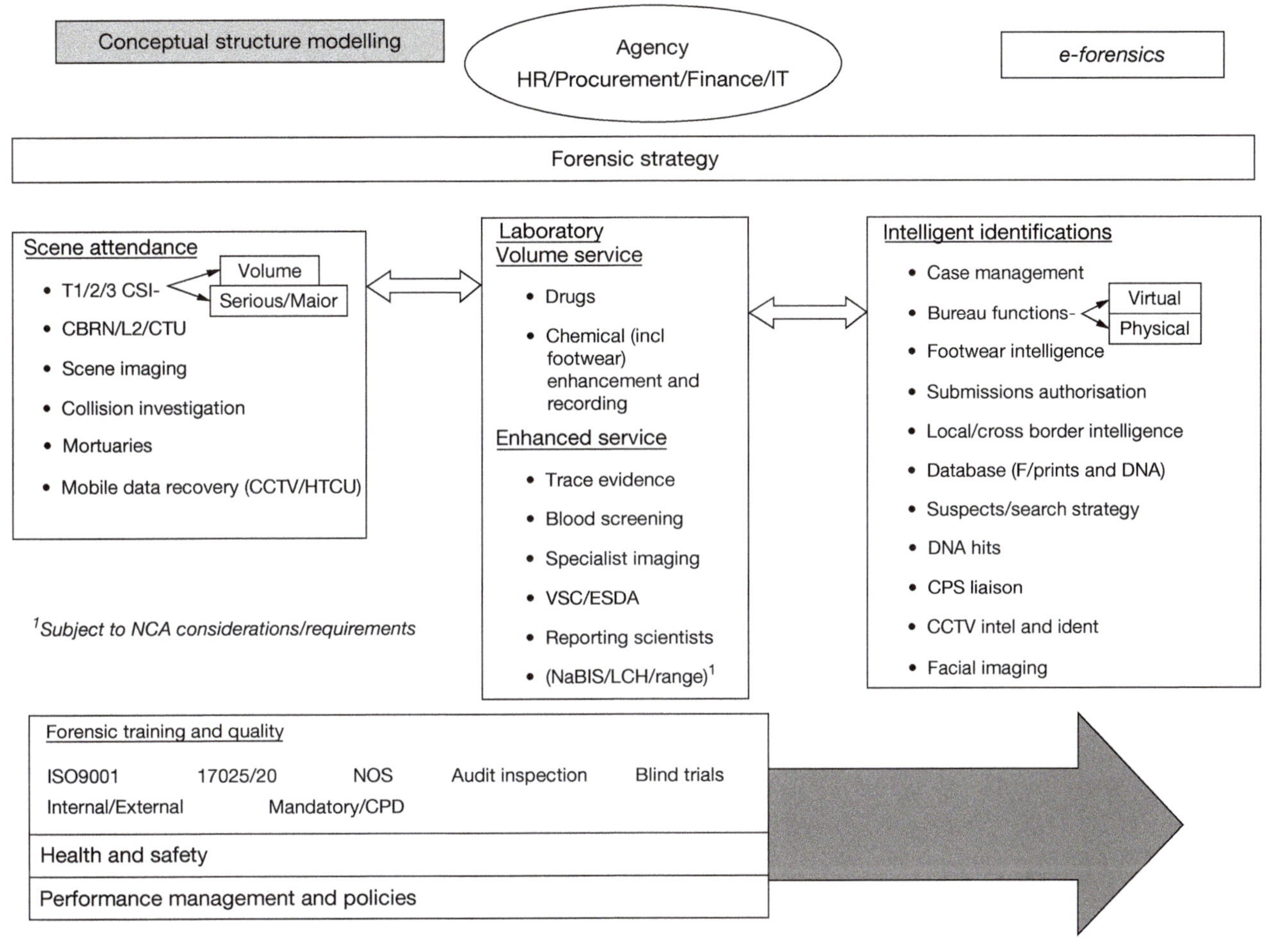

Figure 1 Conceptual structure modeling.

Summary

The single biggest challenge to the forensic science community during the twenty-first century is to modernize delivery of integrated services in support of investigations. This must:

- build on the previous development of each discipline;
- accommodate the new and emerging technological disciplines;
- meet the regulatory requirements;
- reflect the changing workforce and skills; and
- deliver the best evidence to courts in support of investigations.

See also: **Foundations:** Forensic Intelligence; History of Forensic Sciences; Principles of Forensic Science.

Further Reading

Faigman, et al., 2006. Modern Scientific Evidence: The Law and Science of Expert Testimony. Thomson Reuters.
Fisher, B.A.J., Fisher, D.R., 2012. Techniques of Crime Scene Investigation, eighth ed. CRC, Boca Raton, FL.
Houck, M., Crispino, F., McAdam, T., 2013. The Science of Crime Scenes. Elsevier.
Innocence Project, 2011. http://www.innocenceproject.org/Content/Facts_on_PostConviction_DNA_Exonerations.php (accessed 10.03.11).
Kirk, P.L., 1974. In: Thornton, J.L. (Ed.), Crime Investigation, second ed. Wiley, New York (1985 reprint edn. Malabar, FL: Krieger Publishing Company).
NAS, 2009. Strengthening Forensic Science in the United States: A Path Forward. NAS Report: Committee on Identifying the Needs of the Forensic Sciences Community. National Academies Press, Washington, DC.
White, P., 2010. Crime Scene to Court: The Essentials of Forensic Science. Royal Society of Chemistry, Cambridge, ISBN 978-1-84755-882-4.

Forensic Laboratory Reports

J Epstein, Widener University School of Law, Wilmington, DE, USA

There is no precise formula, dictated by law or science, as to what a forensic laboratory report must contain when it reports test results or analysis outcomes. Its content may be determined by the individual examiner's predilections, internal laboratory policy, the law of the jurisdiction, accreditation organization standards, or the reason(s) for its production. What can be said with certainty is that by understanding the current criticism of the practice of producing forensic laboratory reports and trends in standards for reports, and by considering the use to which the report may be put in the court process and the legal and ethical commands regarding reporting and, more generally, the duties of the forensic scientist, a model for forensic laboratory reports can be identified.

Before discussing these factors, it bears mention that the term *report* itself lacks clarity, as it may refer to the complete case file documenting the examination or just to the compilation of results. Herein, *report* denotes the latter—the document prepared for the consumer (the investigator, counsel, or court official who directed that the examination and testing be conducted). Even this report may vary in degree of detail, as there can be the summary report advising the requesting party of the outcome; a more formal report prepared for disclosure to the court or opposing counsel as part of pretrial discovery; an amplification of the initial discovery-generated report when it is determined that the expert will in fact testify; and a report that will be presented in lieu of actual testimony. Additional documentation may include an administrative or dispositional report detailing the receipt or return of the item(s) sent for analysis.

What must also be acknowledged is that the expert's role in the adjudicative process is in some ways defined by whether the system is adversarial, with the expert being called by the party seeking to establish a point, as in the United States; or inquisitorial/"common law," where the expert is a court witness, presumed to be neutral, and without allegiance to a particular party, as in France, Belgium, and Germany. These demarcations are not always adhered to, as American law permits a trial judge to appoint and take testimony from a "court" expert under Federal Rule of Evidence 706, and in some cases involving offenses of fraud and falsification, France permits competing experts. These differing roles, however, do not alter the necessary components of a forensic laboratory report, and, as is detailed following, both ethical and legal considerations as well as a commitment to the role of science may require the report to be neutral and to acknowledge any limitations and/or weaknesses.

Contents of a Report—A "Science" Standard

At least in the United States, there has been substantial criticism of forensic laboratory reporting. This is found in *Strengthening Forensic Science: A Path Forward*, the 2009 report of the National Research Council (NRC) of the National Academy of Sciences. After reporting that forensic laboratory reports lack precise terminology, the report concluded that most laboratory reports do not meet the standard it proposed:

> As a general matter, laboratory reports generated as the result of a scientific analysis should be complete and thorough. They should describe, at a minimum, methods and materials, procedures, results, and conclusions, and they should identify, as appropriate, the sources of uncertainty in the procedures and conclusions along with estimates of their scale (to indicate the level of confidence in the results). Although it is neither appropriate nor practicable to provide as much detail as might be expected in a research paper, sufficient content should be provided to allow the nonscientist reader to understand what has been done and permit informed and unbiased scrutiny of the conclusion.

This criticism does not stand in isolation. A 2011 British court decision also expressed concern over the sufficiency of detail and documentation in a forensic (latent print) prosecution. After noting the failure of the examiner to contemporaneously record "detailed notes of his examination and the reasons for his conclusions[,]" the court added that [t]he quality of the reports provided by the Nottinghamshire Fingerprint Bureau for the trial reflected standards that existed in other areas of forensic science some years ago, and not the vastly improved standards expected in contemporary forensic science.

The NRC standard is more detailed than that of various forensic organizations. ASCLD/LAB, for example, requires that only written reports be generated for "all analytical work" and must contain conclusions and opinions and a clear communication of "the significance of associations made."

Other standards address the need for full documentation, but do not distinguish between a laboratory's bench notes and the final product. For example, the International Organization for Standardization's ISO/IEC Standard 5.10.5 requires that "the laboratory shall document the basis upon which the opinions and interpretations have been made" without

 http://dx.doi.org/10.1016/B978-0-12-800647-4.00031-X

specifying where that information is to be recorded. Similar language is used for ballistics reports, as recommended by the Scientific Working Group on firearms (SWGGUN) requiring that "[w]hen opinions and interpretations are included, the laboratory shall document the basis upon which the opinions and interpretations have been made. Opinions and interpretations shall be clearly marked as such in the test report."

Yet, the more detailed mandate urged by the NRC report is not unique. Scholars and agencies have articulated similar or at least substantial standards. A 2004 publication of the Royal Society of Chemistry (RSC) suggested the following information as appropriate for inclusion in an expert report:

- A summary of the event to contextualize the scientific test(s)
- An outline of the scientific work conducted
- A list of items examined
- Description of the work performed
- A statement interpreting the findings
- An overall conclusion.

The RSC text also urges that the report identify the assistants in the testing and the role each played and include appendices with tables or similar displays of test results.

For DNA analysis, the Federal Bureau of Investigation's standards for DNA laboratories require reports to include a description of the evidence examined and of the technology, results and/or conclusions, and a "quantitative or qualitative interpretative statement."

One final scientific issue regarding the contents of a report is the concern over bias. Research has shown that information received by the analyst might affect his/her judgment, as when the examiner receives domain-irrelevant information such as the fact that the suspect whose fingerprints are being examined "confessed to the crime" or when the verification is not "blind." Documentation of such information in a laboratory report (or the bench notes) is one responsive action, as is an internal laboratory policy to reduce analyst or verifier exposure to potentially biasing information.

Contents of Report: Legal Standards

That which science requires is to some extent mirrored in legal requirements for expert reports. These vary from nation to nation, and within nations when states or regions have their own authority to legislate criminal practice.

In the United Kingdom, Rule 33.3, Criminal Procedure Rules 2010 mandates contents of a full report, that is, one for submission in court, as follows:

1. The findings on which they have relied in making the report or statement;
2. Details of which of the findings stated in the report or statement are within their own knowledge, which were obtained as a result of examinations, measurements, tests, etc., carried out by another person and whether or not those examinations, measurements, tests, etc., were carried out under the expert's supervision;
3. The identity, qualifications, relevant experience, and any certification of the person who carried out the examination, measurement, test, etc.;
4. Details of any statements of fact, literature, or other information upon which they have relied, either to identify the examination or test requirements, or which are material to the opinions expressed in the report or statement or upon which those opinions are based;
5. A summary of the conclusions and opinions reached and a rationale for these;
6. A statement that if any of the information on which their conclusions or opinions are based changes, then the conclusions or opinions will have to be reviewed;
7. Where there is a range of opinion on the matters dealt with in the report or statement, a summary of the range of opinion, and reasons for the expert's own opinion;
8. Any information that may cast doubt on their interpretation or opinion; and
9. If the expert is not able to give an opinion without qualification, what the qualification is.

Much less specific is the legislated mandate for federal criminal prosecutions in the United States. Under Federal Rule of Criminal Procedure 16, the government must permit the defense to inspect and to copy or photograph the results or reports of any scientific test or experiment and must produce before trial a written summary of any proposed expert testimony that describes the witness's opinions, the bases and reasons for those opinions, and the witness's qualifications. Defense counsel in criminal cases has a reciprocal disclosure requirement. Despite the seeming generality of these terms, American courts have at times interpreted them to require some greater detail in the reports, such as underlying documentation.

In the United States, an additional requirement derived from the Constitution's guarantee of due process of law may affect what must be included in a laboratory report issued by a police or other government agency. The prosecution must disclose information that is "favorable to the accused" and "material either to guilt or to punishment" as well as "evidence that the defense might have used to impeach the Government's witnesses by showing bias or interest." This extends to "evidence affecting credibility[.]" This information is generally denominated "Brady material."

The applicability of these rules to official (police or state) laboratories is settled. The U.S. Supreme Court has held that the disclosure obligation extends to police agencies working with the prosecution, and this has been extended to forensic examiners. Hence, in a report or some other communication, a forensic examiner in government employ must ensure that Brady material is disclosed.

What remains to be defined are the terms *exculpatory* or *impeachment* information. The core of each is easily described. Evidence is exculpatory if it tends to reduce the degree of guilt or question proof of culpability; impeachment information is proof of a bias or interest, or otherwise information that could be used to contradict or attack the credibility of the analyst or report. This type of disclosure parallels that of forensic laboratory reports imposed by the United Kingdom's evidence code. The code requires inclusion in the report of "a summary of the range of opinion and reasons for the expert's own opinion; [] any information that may cast doubt on their interpretation or opinion; and if the expert is not able to give an opinion without qualification, what the qualification is."

Reports: Stand-alone Evidence or Support for a Testifying Expert

Whether a laboratory report may stand on its own as evidence in a trial, or instead must be accompanied by testimony of the forensic analyst, is a function of the law of the jurisdiction in which the case is tried. In the United States, a prosecution expert's report may not be admitted on its own, as this is deemed to violate the defendant's right to confront adverse witnesses. The Supreme Court in Melendez-Diaz versus US held that a certificate of analysis fell within the core class of testimonial statements because it was a solemn "declaration or affirmation made for the purpose of establishing or proving some fact." In the 2011 follow-up of the Melendez-Diaz decision, the Court further held that another lab analyst may not come in to testify to the report's contents, at least where the other analyst neither supervised nor observed the initial testing. (This applies only to prosecution expert reports, as in the United States only the defendant has a guarantee of the right to confront witnesses. Admissibility of a defense forensic report without examiner testimony would be determined by the state's rules of evidence but is generally unheard of.)

At the same time, the confrontation right does not mean that the analyst must testify. A state may create a notice and demand statute under which the prosecution notifies the defendant of its intent to use an analyst's report as evidence at trial, after which the defendant has a specified period of time in which to demand the expert's live testimony. A defendant's failure to "demand" waives the need for the analyst's presence and allows use of the report. As well, an accused may always agree to stipulate to the report's content, eliminating the need for any live testimony.

The Melendez-Diaz approach is not followed uniformly on an international basis. Canada permits proof by means of an expert report, without live testimony, where the proponent of the report has provided it to the opposing party and the trial court recognizes the author as a legitimate expert. The court retains discretion to mandate the expert's appearance for cross-examination. Australia's Evidence Act of 1995 similarly authorizes expert proof by certificate, but the opposing party may require the offering side to "call the person who signed the certificate to give evidence." In the United Kingdom, expert reports are themselves admissible as evidence, subject to the judge's discretion in requiring the analyst or examiner to appear.

Ethical Considerations and Forensic Reports

The decision of what to include in a forensic laboratory report, beyond that required by law or by science, may be informed by ethical considerations. Forensics organizations often have ethical codes, but they may be silent as to the particulars of report writing. Illustrative is the Code of the American Board of Criminalistics, which only asserts general obligations such as "[e]nsure that a full and complete disclosure of the findings is made to the submitting agency[.]" Other codes may not mention reporting at all but instead address only the delivery of information without distinguishing between the written report and a courtroom presentation of evidence. An exception is that of the Australian and New Zealand Forensic Science Society, Inc., which requires that a report be nonpartisan when results are ambiguous. "Where test results or conclusions are capable of being interpreted to the advantage of either side in a legal proceeding, each result or conclusion should be given weight according to its merit."

Ethical considerations may also be imposed by law. In the United Kingdom, the expert is deemed to hold only one allegiance, that to the court, regardless of the party who retained the individual. Specific ethical obligations are imposed for written reports. First, where there is a range of opinion, the expert must summarize the various positions. Second, if the opinion rendered cannot be given without qualification, the expert must disclose that and state the qualifying aspects or concerns.

Conclusion

Within and across nations, there is no clear standard for forensic reports intended for court use, except where prescribed by law. What should be manifest is that the more detailed the report, and thus the more it is capable of rigorous assessment by an independent expert evaluator, the more credibility will be attributed to both the results and the examiner.

See also: **Legal:** History of the Law's Reception of Forensic Science; Legal Aspects of Forensic Science; Legal Systems: Adversarial and Inquisitorial; **Management/Quality in Forensic Science:** *Sequential Unmasking*: Minimizing Observer Effects in Forensic Science; **Professional:** Ethics.

Further Reading

Codes of Practice and Conduct for Forensic Science Providers and Practitioners in the Criminal Justice System 44–45 (United Kingdom), December 2011. http://www.homeoffice.gov.uk/publications/police/forensic-science-regulator1/quality-standards-codes-practice?view=Binary.

Dror, I.E., Cole, S., 2010. The vision in "blind" justice: expert perception, judgment and visual cognition in forensic pattern recognition. Psychonomic Bulletin and Review 17 (2), 161–167.

Dror, I.E., Rosenthal, R., 2008. Meta-analytically quantifying the reliability and biasability of forensic experts. Journal of Forensic Sciences 53 (4), 900–903.

National Research Council, 2009. Strengthening Forensic Science in the United States: A Path Forward. National Academies Press, Washington, DC. http://www.ncjrs.gov/pdffiles1/nij/grants/228091.pdf.

Quality Assurance Standards for Forensic DNA Testing Laboratories, 2009. Standard 11.2. http://www.cstl.nist.gov/strbase/QAS/Final-FBI-Director-Forensic-Standards.pdf.

Reviewing Historical Practices of Forensic Science Laboratories, September 29, 2010. http://www.ascld.org/.

Rothwell, T., 2004. Presentation of expert forensic evidence. ch. 15. In: White, P. (Ed.), Crime Scene to Court: The Essentials of Forensic Science, second ed. RSC, Cambridge, pp. 430–432.

Spencer, J.R., 2002. Evidence European Criminal Procedures. Ch. 15. Cambridge University Press, New York, pp. 632–635.

Relevant Websites

http://www.criminalistics.com/ethics.cfm—American Board of Criminalistics, Rules of Professional Conduct.

http://www.ascld.org/—The American Society of Crime Laboratory Directors.

http://www.ascld-lab.org/—The American Society of Crime Laboratory Directors Laboratory Accreditation Board.

http://www.afte.org/AssociationInfo/a_codeofethics.htm–Association of Firearms and Toolmarks Examiners, AFTE Code of Ethics.

http://www.anzfss.org.au/code_of_ethics.htm—Australian and New Zealand Forensic Science Society.

http://www.forensicdna.com/Media/Bias_FS.htm—An extended list of articles on the issue of bias in forensic examinations.

http://www.iso.org/iso/home.html—International Organization for Standardization.

http://www.swggun.org/swg/index.php?option=com_content&view=article&id=25:transition-from-ascldlab-legacy-to-isoiec- 17025&catid=10:guidelines-adopted&Itemid=6—SWGGUN, Transition from ASCLD/LAB Legacy to ISO/IEC 17025.

http://webarchive.nationalarchives.gov.uk/+/http://www.justice.gov.uk/criminal/procrules_fin/contents/rules/part_33.htm—United Kingdom, Criminal Procedure Rules 2010.

Health and Safety

N Scudder and B Saw, Australian Federal Police, Canberra, ACT, Australia

Glossary

Clandestine laboratory (Clan Labs) Setting up of equipment or supplies for the manufacture of illegal compounds such as drugs or explosives.

Confined space An enclosed or partially enclosed space that is not intended or designed primarily for human occupancy, within which there is a risk of one or more of the following: (1) an oxygen concentration outside the safe oxygen range; (2) a concentration of airborne contaminant that may cause impairment, loss of consciousness, or asphyxiation; (3) a concentration of flammable airborne contaminant that may cause injury from fire or explosion; or (4) engulfment in a stored free-flowing solid or a rising level of liquid that may cause suffocation or drowning.

Dynamic risk management The continuous assessment of risk in the rapidly changing circumstances of an operational incident, in order to implement the control measures necessary to ensure an acceptable level of safety.

Hazard The potential for a substance to cause adverse effects.

Hierarchy of control measures Ranking of measures taken to prevent or reduce hazard exposure according to effectiveness, from the most effective measures that eliminate hazards to the least effective, which achieve only limited protection.

OHS policy A policy document indicating an organization's commitment to OHS, its intentions, objectives, and priorities, and identifying roles and responsibilities.

Risk The likelihood of injury or illness arising from exposure to any hazard(s) and the magnitude of the adverse effect.

Occupational Health and Safety Policy

Legislation in many countries places the onus of responsibility on employers to provide a healthy and safe working environment under occupational health and safety (OHS) legislation and common law. Employers should ensure that all managers, supervisors, and staff are aware of their OHS responsibilities. Management leadership can positively influence OHS outcomes for an organization.

Workplace health and safety is an ongoing process. Subject to the legislative requirements of each jurisdiction, in most instances a documented OHS policy is required. The development of such a policy requires the commitment of both staff and management. Once commitment has been achieved, the OHS policy should be developed with involvement from all stakeholders, and promulgated.

The OHS policy should:

- articulate the organization's commitment to OHS;
- indicate that sufficient resources (both financial and personnel) will be provided to promote and maintain OHS standards and meet OHS requirements;
- outline the organization's intentions, objectives, and priorities (OHS);
- describe in broad terms the means by which the objectives will be met;
- identify the roles and responsibilities of management, supervisors, and staff in meeting OHS requirements; and
- be signed off by the most senior manager of the organization, reflecting the importance of the policy.

The OHS policy should be reviewed periodically to ensure its currency.

The OHS policy is, however, only one part of an appropriate OHS strategy for a forensic organization. The OHS policy must be underpinned by risk assessments and incident/accident reports that enable the organization to assess its OHS exposure, to meet legislative requirements such as reporting obligations, and to respond to risks appropriately.

An organization can develop a list of the main hazards that its staff are likely to be exposed to in the course of their duties, utilizing OHS reports, incident/accident reports, and previous risk assessments. Prioritizing the main health and safety issues allows the organization to develop appropriate action plans to meet the objectives of its OHS policy.

 http://dx.doi.org/10.1016/B978-0-12-800647-4.00032-1

Forensic organizations may consider integration of some OHS requirements with their quality assurance system. Many laboratories effectively use their quality system to embed OHS requirements in their documented procedures, to review OHS hazards as part of a periodic audit program, or to manage elements of their OHS action plans through their corrective action system. OHS, like quality, can then be viewed as an important yet integrated component of an effective management system.

Risk Assessments

Once potential OHS hazards have been identified, forensic organizations should evaluate the likelihood of injury from the interaction to the hazard and the magnitude of the adverse effect. The process of risk assessment will be very useful for managing potential OHS hazards within the facility and the expected external work environment. The purpose of the risk assessment process is to ensure that all workplace hazards have been identified, recorded, assessed, controlled, and reviewed. The desired outcome of this process is to eliminate, as far as practicable, the risk of injury or illness to personnel, damage to property, and damage to the environment. The process of developing risk assessment is often better suited to the known work environment. An OHS assessment of an office or a laboratory can quickly identify specific hazards that may require attention. Obviously, this works well for the office and laboratory environment within one's control; however, each external scene will be different.

It is important that the range of potential hazards in external crime scenes and work environments is considered. While some risks can be grouped and managed collectively, the specific hazard and risk mitigation and control will vary from scene to scene given the circumstances. Given this, forensic practitioners should have an ability to undertake dynamic risk assessments, or "risk on the run" as it is known in some jurisdictions.

Dynamic Risk Management

Dynamic risk assessments are conducted by a forensic practitioner as part of the attendance and examination process. In some instances, such as attendance at a clan lab, a person may be designated as the site safety officer and have carriage of this as well as health and safety for all personnel at the site. Practitioners should be trained to assess the risk given the circumstances at the time, considering the actual hazards present at a crime scene.

A designated forensic practitioner or site safety officer should undertake a quick reconnaissance of the crime scene to ensure the safety of forensic practitioners and others working at the scene. A review of the scene should be repeated whenever the situation at the scene changes. This could involve a visual inspection without entering the crime scene, and asking a number of questions, for example:

- Does the crime scene involve structures that are now unstable?
- Has confirmation been obtained from the fire brigade or other emergency responders that power, gas, and water to the site have been turned off?
- Is there adequate shelter so that practitioners can rest without succumbing to environmental stressors such as heat, cold, wind, or rain?

It is important to close the loop and incorporate any strategic elements of each dynamic risk assessment in OHS policy and planning. After each incident, any relevant information obtained during the dynamic risk assessment should be recorded and collated for strategic analysis.

Hierarchy of Control Measures

Within OHS, there is a "hierarchy of control" designed to mitigate or resolve a risk deemed unacceptably high. The hierarchy of control is a sequence of options that offer a number of ways to approach the hazard control process. Various control options may be available. It is important to choose the control that most effectively eliminates the hazard or minimizes the risk in the circumstances. This may involve a single control measure or a combination of different controls that together provide the highest level of protection that is reasonably practicable:

1. Eliminate the hazard. If this is not practical, then:
2. Substitute the hazard with a lesser risk. If this is not practical, then:
3. Isolate the hazard. If this is not practical, then:
4. Use engineering controls. If this is not practical, then:
5. Use administrative controls, such as safe work practices, instruction, and training. If this is not practical, then:
6. Use personal protective equipment (PPE), such as gloves, eye protection, boots, and respirators.

It is important that management and staff discuss and consult, where possible, during all phases of the hazard identification, risk assessment, and risk control process.

Examples

1. If an organization is considering purchasing a piece of analytical equipment, and two products have the same capabilities but substantially different noise levels during operation, the organization may consider the noise level of the equipment and opt for the quieter system. This example demonstrates the principle of eliminating the hazard at source, which is the most effective control measure, when compared to training and provision of PPE such as hearing protection.

2. In the case of a fire scene of a building, applying a hierarchy of control approach, it is first necessary to consider the elimination or substitution of hazards. At a fire scene, this is not possible. It is, however, possible to isolate the scene to prevent danger to the public and to maintain the integrity of the scene. Power, water, and gas to a building should be disconnected prior to entering the site. A structural engineer's opinion may be necessary prior to entry to the building. Safe entry and exit to the site can be established. Other administrative controls, such as briefing practitioners and maintaining records of the entry and exit of personnel, may be applied. Finally, practitioners can be prevented from entering the fire scene unless utilizing the appropriate PPE.

Specific Laboratory Hazards

The likely hazards within a laboratory environment include the following.

Chemicals

Chemical exposure may occur through inhalation, skin absorption, or direct ingestion and, once absorbed, are either stored in a particular organ or tissue, metabolized, or excreted. The effect of a chemical on a person is dependent on a number of factors such as duration and frequency of exposure, concentration of the chemical, and an individual's metabolism. A synergistic effect may occur when the undesirable effects of one substance are intensified if exposure has occurred to another substance.

Some nanomaterials exhibit different chemical properties compared to what they exhibit on a macroscale. As this is a relatively new field, there is insufficient knowledge regarding the hazards posed by nanomaterials. The potential hazards associated with nanomaterials may include increased reactivity because of their increased surface-area-to-volume ratio, the ability to cross some of the body's protective mechanisms, and the lack of the body's immunity against such small particles. Because of this lack of knowledge, the suggested control strategy to be used when working with nanomaterials should be "as low as reasonably achievable" (ALARA) approach to reduce exposure.

The effects of chemicals on the body may be categorized:

- poisonous or toxic chemicals are absorbed into the body and exert either an acute or short-term effect, such as headache, nausea, or loss of consciousness, or a long-term effect such as liver or kidney damage, cancer, or chronic lung disease;
- corrosive chemicals burn the skin, eyes, or respiratory tract;
- irritants can inflame the skin or lungs, causing conditions such as dermatitis or bronchitis;
- sensitizers may exert long-term effects, especially to the skin (such as contact dermatitis) and to the respiratory tract (such as occupational asthma) by inducing an allergic reaction; and
- explosive or flammable substances pose immediate danger of fire and explosion, causing damage to the body through direct burning, or through inhalation of toxic fumes emitted during combustion.

Safety data sheets (SDS), also known as material safety data sheets (MSDS), are designed to provide relevant information regarding the identity, physical characteristics, safe storage, use, disposal, first-aid treatment, and spill management of substances that are handled in the workplace. The information includes whether the substance is deemed to be a hazardous and/or a dangerous goods item. At a minimum, the SDS should be consulted before the first use of a chemical or other substance within a laboratory, or if practitioners are unfamiliar with the product. Copies of SDS should be retained according to legislative requirements. In some jurisdictions, electronic SDS management systems can allow an efficient way of accessing up-to-date SDS information.

Sharps

Sharps are objects that have sharp edges or points that have the potential to cut, scratch, or puncture the skin. Sharps can cause physical injury and have the potential to introduce infectious and toxic agents through skin wounds. Examples include hypodermic syringes and needles, knives, or broken glasswares.

All forensic practitioners have a responsibility to handle and package sharps safely. Particular care should be given to ensuring that sharps are appropriately labeled when packaged. Sharps such as knives could, for example, be packaged in clear plastic tubes, making it easier for a person opening the item to identify the contents and the direction the sharp item is facing. Forensic labs should be encouraged to develop policies that encourage forensic practitioners and others that submit items to develop safe-packaging procedures.

Biological Material

Examples of "biological material" commonly encountered in forensic examinations include body tissue, blood, and body fluids (urine, saliva, vomit, pus, seminal fluid, vaginal fluid, and feces). Biological material is potentially hazardous as it may contain infectious agents such as viruses, bacteria, fungi, and parasites that cause a variety of communicable diseases.

Hair, fur, and items of clothing that have been in close contact with humans or animals may also harbor parasites such as fleas or nits.

When examining plant material such as cannabis, consideration should be given to the presence of *Aspergillus* sp. mold. If the *Aspergillus* spores are inhaled into the lungs, a serious, chronic respiratory or sinus infection can result. If mold is visible, the cannabis should be treated as a biological and respiratory hazard.

It is impossible to determine the prevalence of infectious or communicable diseases in the environment in which forensic practitioners work. Consequently, practitioners should adhere to recommended procedures for handling biological material and adopt an approach known as the "standard precautions." This approach requires practitioners to assume that all biological material is a potential source of infection, independent of diagnosis or perceived level of underlying risk.

Vaccinations should be offered for practitioners. The types of vaccinations given may depend on whether work is confined to the laboratory or whether work is performed in the field, as well as whether forensic practitioners are likely to be deployed overseas where other diseases may be more prevalent.

Firearms

Forensic practitioners may retrieve firearms from crime scenes. All personnel who may be required to handle firearms, either in the field, in the laboratory, or in support roles such as property or exhibit stores should be trained in how to render a firearm safe. As with the standard precautions, it is important to consider all firearms as potentially loaded and adopt the practice of never pointing a firearm in the direction of another person, even after it has been rendered safe.

Firearms examiners, who undertake firearms investigations including test firing and bullet recovery, will be exposed to hazards such as noise and lead. They should have their hearing and blood lead levels monitored on a regular basis to ensure that hearing protection is being worn and is functioning correctly and that any exposure to lead from the firearms is quickly identified and addressed.

Computer Forensics Laboratory

Computer forensic examiners specialize in obtaining, analyzing, and reporting on electronic evidence stored on computers and other electronic devices. Crimes involving a computer can range across the spectrum of criminal activity, from child pornography to theft of personal data to destruction of intellectual property. Potential hazards involve static postures, occupational overuse, and stress from viewing graphic images.

Some suggestions to minimize the stress from viewing graphic images are as follows:

- psychological assessment before and after viewing graphic material, and periodically;
- exposure to only one medium, for example, visual material only, rather than examining both sound and visual material simultaneously;
- specifying limits as to the amount of time spent examining explicit material in a day; and
- ceasing any examination of explicit material at the end of their shift, to allow themselves time to refocus attention away from this stressor.

Electrical/Machinery

Forensic laboratories use a wide range of electrical equipment and machinery. Practitioners need to ensure that any inherent risk from electric shock is mitigated. The use of residual current devices (safety switches) is an appropriate strategy, as is visual inspection and periodic testing and tagging of power cords, to detect obvious damage, wear and other conditions that might render it unsafe by a person qualified to do so under the legislation in effect in the jurisdiction.

Fume Cupboards

Fume cupboards are integral to minimizing the risk of exposure to chemical and biological hazards. Not all fume cupboards are suitable for all hazards. Fume cupboards should be maintained and inspected periodically. During maintenance, attention should be given to:

- The fume cupboard itself, including flow rates and replacement of absorbents or filters.
- In the case of externally vented fume cupboards, the ductwork and location of external vents. This is particularly important during any building maintenance or refurbishment.

Fume cupboards must be used for all operations that have the potential to release hazardous fumes, mists, or dusts.

- Before commencement of work, ensure that the fume cupboard is clean and free from contamination.
- Ensure the minimum of equipment is stored in the fume cupboard and is placed toward the back of the cupboard to reduce disturbance to the air flowing into the fume cupboard.
- Lower the sash as far as practicable during use to improve fume containment.

Recirculating fume cabinets rely on filtration or absorption to remove airborne contaminants released in the fume cabinet before the exhaust air is discharged back into the laboratory. They are suitable for light-to-moderate use with a known range of substances. The range of substances for which each cabinet can be used is limited by the need for compatibility with the chemicals in use as well as with the particular type of absorbent or filter fitted to the cabinet.

Robotics

The introduction of automated robotic platforms has significantly enhanced the efficiency of forensic analysis. The use of robotics is becoming more common and is very useful for a range of repetitive laboratory tasks. Besides saving time, robotics overcomes the need for repetitive work involved in pipetting, eliminating musculoskeletal injuries.

Hazards associated with robotics include the risk of exposure to the chemicals used in the work, electrocution, and cutting, stabbing, or shearing from the moveable parts of the robot. The interlocks on the robots should not be bypassed.

X-rays

X-rays are used in analytical and imaging instrumentation. Potential exposure to X-rays is generally localized to specific parts of the body, usually the hands or fingers. Depending on the X-ray energies delivered, effects may range from erythema (redness) at point of exposure, blood changes, cancer, through to death. Depending on the legislative requirement in each country, practitioners working with X-ray equipment may be required to use dosimeters to assess radiation dose.

Lasers

Lasers span the visible and nonvisible electromagnetic spectrum and have many applications in forensic science, including Raman spectroscopy. Lasers are generally classified according to the level of risk they represent. Damage from laser beams can be thermal or photochemical. The primary sites of damage are the eyes and skin. Hazards associated with laser work may include:

- fire,
- explosion,
- electrocution, and
- inhalation of contaminants from laser interactions.

Precautions for use of lasers include:

- Display the class of laser in use.
- Appropriate protective eyewear with side protection and appropriate attenuation for the wavelength(s) in use must be worn.
- Interlocks on the laser should not be bypassed.
- Keep the laser beam path away from eye level whether one is seated or standing.

High-Intensity Light Sources

High-intensity light sources such as the Polilight® provide a range of colored light bands and white light for forensic work:

- Care should be taken that high-intensity white light is not directed onto any object at short distances from the end of the light guide, as this can cause severe heat damage to the object and may result in a fire.
- The light beam should never be directed at eyes as the light can cause permanent damage.

Manual Handling

Manual handling refers to any activity that involves lifting, lowering, carrying, pushing, pulling, holding, restraining, or the application of force. Only a very small number of manual handling injuries are caused by the lifting of heavy weights alone. Actions such as reaching, twisting, bending, or maintaining static postures contribute to injury affecting the muscle or skeletal systems of the body. These musculoskeletal injuries predominantly involve the neck, back or shoulder or arm muscles, tendons, ligaments, or joints.

Injuries may be caused from activities such as maintaining static postures while working at fume cupboards, repetitive keyboard and mouse work, pipetting, and prolonged use of comparison microscopes.

Some preventative strategies include:

- Seeking further assistance to have the activities assessed to minimize the manual handling risks inherent in the activity.
- Planning tasks so that rest breaks are scheduled.
- Choosing the best tools for the tasks.
- Alternate hands while using a mouse, if possible.

There is a move to make instruments smaller and more portable for use at crime scenes. While this has significant benefits, including potentially reducing the number of exhibits collected, moving equipment can also raise manual handling concerns.

General Laboratory Management

Housekeeping is important in laboratories. It is important to maintain clear passageways, have proper labeling of chemicals, clean and uncluttered work areas, and appropriate storage. The handling of powders is a potentially hazardous operation, and good housekeeping can help minimize airborne contamination from spilled materials. Having a planned preventative maintenance program and regular inspections of the workplace, plant, and equipment are essential for the smooth running of the laboratory.

Handling of Exhibits in Court

Each evidential item must be appropriately packaged and sealed, if this is not already the case, before it is exhibited in court. Items such as clothing that are normally stored in paper may need to be repackaged in clear plastic, allowing the item to remain sealed and minimizing the risk of cross-contamination when handled in court. Caution should be exercised against opening exhibits in court, in case any hazards such as mold or irritant fumes are released.

Hazards in the Field

Forensic practitioners are often required to work or train in the field. Consideration should be given to managing hazards that may affect practitioners, including:

- environmental hazards such as heat, cold, humidity, or wet weather, the terrain, and fauna or flora at the scene;
- the type of operation, for example, working in a clandestine laboratory (clan lab) often involves quite specific hazards;
- the possible presence of offenders or other security risks such as booby traps at a scene; and
- the availability of first aid and emergency response domestically and overseas.

The risks from these hazards should be considered within the scope of the exercise or operation. Some possible responses to hazards, which may be considered in a dynamic risk assessment, include:

- designating a location for emergency equipment, such as a crime scene vehicle, and ensuring that disinfectants, antiseptics, and a first aid kit are easily accessible;
- planning an emergency exit from the scene and ensuring that this is communicated to all personnel present;
- establishing a decontamination point if there is exposure to chemical or biological material;
- the use of appropriate PPE including sunglasses, sunscreen, and hats when working outdoors;
- depending on the external temperature, work activity, duration, and PPE worn, practitioners should have access to shade for rest and adequate fluids if required during hot weather to prevent heat stress. The wearing of PPE including chemical suits and respirators requires longer and more frequent periods of rest break for recovery in hot temperatures and humid environments;
- in cold weather, provision should be made to have adequate warm clothing and a sheltered area; and
- the risk of animal or dog bites while attending a crime scene should not be discounted. If practitioners are searching in vegetated areas, the risk of snake or tick bites should be considered, along with possible exposure to plants such as poison ivy or stinging nettles.

Confined Spaces

Forensic practitioners may have to enter confined spaces. Due to the high risks associated with entering the confined space, many jurisdictions mandate that entry into a confined space must not be made until a confined-space permit has been issued. Practitioners must receive specific training before work or entry into confined spaces.

Chemical Biological and Radiological and Nuclear Incidents

Forensic practitioners may be required to attend a chemical biological and radiological and nuclear (CBRN) incident. CBRN incidents where forensic practitioners may attend and conduct examinations include:

- chemical (warfare agent, toxic industrial chemical);
- biological (weaponized agent, natural disease);
- radiological (discrete, or wide area contamination); and
- nuclear.

Depending on the response agency protocol in place, forensic practitioners may be working closely with the fire brigade and other emergency first responders. Entry must not be made into the "warm" or "hot" zone of the scene without consultation with the other emergency first responders.

Clan Labs

Clan labs pose a significant threat to the health and safety of police officers, forensic practitioners, the general public, and the environment. There are many hazards associated with clan labs including:

- flammable materials and/or explosive atmosphere;
- acutely toxic atmospheres;
- leaking or damaged compressed gas cylinders; and
- traps and hazards deliberately set to cause injury or death to police and other responders.

As a result of the frequency at which clan labs are encountered and the severe and variable risks associated with the investigation, many jurisdictions have developed specific policies and procedures concerning clan lab investigations.

For forensic practitioners to deal with clan labs requires a high level of fitness as well as technical expertise. Practitioners must understand:

- illicit drug chemistry;
- how to neutralize the risks of explosions, fires, chemical burns, and toxic fumes;
- how to handle, store, and dispose of hazardous materials; and
- how to treat medical conditions caused by exposure.

Practitioners must also wear full protective equipment including respirators and may be required to move equipment at the clan lab in the process of collecting evidence. The storage and handling of unknown chemicals from clan labs or seizures should also be considered. Preliminary identification should take place, before its storage or disposal.

When unknowns such as "white powders," chemicals (in liquid, solid, or gas state) or biological materials are encountered in the field, it is prudent to be cautious and obtain up-to-date intelligence to shed more light on what is at the scene. It may be an explosive material or contain anthrax spores or ricin or something as innocuous as talc.

Some precautions include:

- wearing the appropriate level of protective clothing/equipment for the activity;
- avoiding direct contact with the substance, even if only in small quantities;
- not smelling or tasting anything from the scene;
- noting physical characteristics such as color, form, and consistency;
- where it is safe to do so, looking for hazard symbols on packaging or labels if available; and
- seeking specialist advice if unable to identify the substance.

Potential Hazards during an Overseas Deployment

Forensic practitioners can be required to work overseas to assist with large-scale disasters. An example was the Thailand Tsunami Victim Identification process involving forensic practitioners from 30 countries working to recover and identify bodies. Forensic practitioners need to be mindful of hazards likely to be encountered during an overseas deployment depending on the location, magnitude of the operation, and how many practitioners are deployed. Some hazards to be considered include:

- climatic demands;
- remote and sometimes dangerous terrain;
- different cultural sensitivities;
- security requirements;
- different levels of infrastructure support at the locality;
- logistics, including the transport of large quantities of equipment, manual handling, setting up, and packing up;
- different hygiene levels;
- diseases that can be transmitted by insect and or animal vectors;
- the possibility of infectious diseases; and
- asbestos and other hazards in buildings.

Work-Related Stress

Practitioners at work may experience work-related stress. There are some specific stressors unique within forensic work. Forensic practitioners may experience workplace-related stress due to their attendance at morgues, violent crime scenes, disaster victim identification, or from requirements to view explicit or graphic material or images.

Indicators of stress include changes in eating habits, tiredness due to changes in sleep patterns, frequent absences from work, reduced productivity, and problems with concentration, motivation, and morale. Physical symptoms may include headaches, abdominal pains, diarrhea, constipation, high blood pressure, insomnia, anxiety state, and depression.

Many organizations offer programs to provide assistance to employees, including counseling to help practitioners to deal with work-related stress or resilience training to manage work–life balance.

See also: **Management/Quality in Forensic Science:** Principles of Quality Assurance; Risk Management; Principles of Laboratory Organization.

Further Reading

Clancy, D., Billinghurst, A., Cater, H., 2009. Hazard identification and risk assessment – understanding the transition from the documented plan to assessing dynamic risk in bio security emergencies. World Conference on Disaster Management, Sydney, Australia. http://www.wcdm.org/.

Furr, K., 2000. Handbook of Laboratory Safety, fifth ed. CRC Press, Florida.

Green-McKenzie, J., Watkins, M., 2005. Occupational hazards: law enforcement officers are at risk of body fluid exposure. Here's what to expect if it happens to you. Law Enforcement Magazine 29 (9), 52–54, 56, 58.

Hanson, D., 2007. Hazardous duty training officers to tackle hazmat emergencies. Law Enforcement Technology 34 (4), 80–85.

Haski, R., Cardilini, G., Bartolo, W., 2011. Laboratory Safety Manual. CCH Australia Ltd, Sydney.

Horswell, J., 2000. The Practice of Crime Scene Investigation. CRC Press, Florida.

Jackel, G., 2004. The High Cost of Stress. AUSPOL: The Official Publication of the Australian Federal Police Association and ALAJA, 14–37.

Mayhew, C., 2001a. Occupational health and safety risks faced by police officers. Australian Institute of Criminology. Trends and Issues in Crime and Criminal Justice 196, 1–6.

Mayhew, C., 2001b. Protecting the occupational health and safety of police officers. Australian Institute of Criminology. Trends and Issues in Crime and Criminal Justice 197, 1–6.

Rothernbaum, D., 2010. Exposed: an officer's story. Clan Lab Safety Alert 7 (2), 1–2.

Smith, D., 2005. Psychosocial occupational health issues in contemporary police work: a review of research evidence. Journal of Occupational Health and Safety, Australia and New Zealand 21 (3), 217–228.

Tillman, C., 2007. Principles of Occupational Health and Hygiene: An Introduction. Crows Nest: Allen & Unwin.

Whitman, M., Smith, C., 2005. The culture of safety: no one gets hurt today. Police Chief LXXII (11), 2024–2627.

Winder, C., 2011. Hazard Alert: Managing Workplace Hazardous Substances. CCH Australia Ltd, Sydney.

Witter, R., Martyny, J., Mueller, K., Gottschall, B., Newman, L., 2007. Symptoms experienced by law enforcement personnel during methamphetamine lab investigation. Journal of Occupational and Environmental Hygiene 4, 895–902.

Relevant Websites

http://www.ccohs.ca/oshanswers/occup_workplace/labtech.html—Canadian Centre for Occupational Health and Safety (CCOHS).

http://www.ccohs.ca/oshanswers/occup_workplace/police.html—What Do Police Do?.

http://www.cdc.gov/niosh/—Centers for Disease Control and Prevention (CDC).

http://www.forensic.gov.uk/html/company/foi/publication-scheme/health-and-safety/—Forensic Science Service, Health and Safety.

http://www.hse.gov.uk/services/police/index.htm—Health and Safety Executive (HSE).

http://www.londonhealthandsafetygroup.org/archive.html—London Health and Safety Group.

http://www.osha.gov/—Occupational Safety & Health Administration.

http://www.police.qld.gov.au/Resources/Internet/rti/policies/documents/QPSForensicServicesHealth_SafetyManual.pdf—Health and Safety Manual, Police Forensic Services, Queensland Police.

Accreditation in Forensic DNA Analysis

R Decorte, KU Leuven, Leuven, Belgium; University Hospitals Leuven, Leuven, Belgium

Glossary

Accreditation Procedure in which an external agency formally recognizes a laboratory or an individual to be competent for performing specific tasks.

Accuracy The degree of correlation between a measured value and an accepted reference value or the value obtained by a previous method.

Audit A systematic and independent review in order to determine if the activities and results conform to established standards.

Calibration A series of tests under specified conditions to demonstrate that an instrument or device produces results within specified limits by comparison to those produced by a traceable standard.

Certification Procedure in which a third party provides written proof that a product, a process, or a service meets certain requirements.

Precision The repeatability or reproducibility of individual measurements expressed as standard deviation (SD) or relative standard deviation (CV).

Probe A short single-stranded DNA segment that is tagged with a reporter molecule (radioactive phosphorus or nonradioactive biotin) and complementary to a given target in the genome.

Proficiency test A test to evaluate the competence of the technicians and the performance of a laboratory; tests can be blind in which the lab does not know that it is being tested, or open so that the technicians are aware they are being tested; internal proficiency tests are organized by the laboratory itself, while external proficiency tests are organized by an external agency independent of the laboratory.

Quality assurance Systematic procedures implemented by the laboratory to ensure accuracy and reliability of the tests performed.

Quality control Internal procedures used to monitor the quality of the tests performed; external established standards or known test reagents (positive and negative) can be used as controls.

Reference material A generic term for a substance or material whose property values are known and fixed, and are certified by an external organization.

Reproducibility The precision of the methodology to produce results under different conditions or at different time points.

Sensitivity Capacity of the test to detect small quantities of a substance.

Specificity The degree of uniformity of the response to the substance in question.

Validation A series of tests performed to check if a methodology or instrument meets certain predefined criteria set by the laboratory or the company that provides the test or instrument.

Introduction

In 2010, it was 25 years ago that Alec Jeffreys published his paper describing the use of DNA analysis in an immigration case. DNA fingerprinting (as it was called) was an important step forward in forensic identification, and over several decades, forensic DNA technology has become a major tool in the fight against crime. As with any new technology introduced to forensic evidence analysis, DNA fingerprinting or profiling (as we call it now) was challenged in the early days in the courtroom, especially in the United States. One of the most fundamental aspects of American jurisprudence is the adversarial system where the two parties, prosecutor and defense, confront the jury and the judge with the evidence for and against the defendant. This judicial system uses several standards to evaluate the admissibility of new or novel scientific evidence in court. In the first U.S. criminal case (*State of California v. Andrews,* 1988) where DNA profiling was presented, the results of DNA analysis performed by Lifecodes Corporation were admitted, but the statistical evidence was

 http://dx.doi.org/10.1016/B978-0-12-800647-4.00033-3

excluded because the prosecution could not validate it. In a retrial (after a hung jury), the court admitted both pieces of evidence applying the "Rule 702 reliability test" and the "Downing relevance test." The latter standard was established in 1985 and gave the court the possibility to exercise a pretrial hearing in case of a serious question concerning the reliability of the evidence. In another case (*State of New York v. Castro*, 1989), the admissibility of DNA evidence was critically questioned. Lifecodes Corporation analyzed a bloodstain on the suspect's watch (Joseph Castro) and the DNA profile of the victim matched that from the bloodstain. The defendant swore that the blood was his own, which the prosecutor wanted to counterattack with the DNA evidence. After a pretrial hearing where different expert witnesses from both the prosecution and the defense presented a review of the DNA evidence, the New York Supreme Court decided that the DNA identification theory and practices are generally accepted in the scientific community, and that forensic DNA identification evidence meets the "Frye standard." However, the Court ruled the inadmissibility of the DNA evidence because Lifecodes did not use generally accepted scientific techniques for obtaining their results. Several flaws were observed in their procedures, including probe contamination, inappropriate controls, and inconsistent matching rules. This case highlighted the need for standardization of practices and uniformly accepted methods for quality assurance (QA).

The need for QA was further emphasized by proficiency studies in 1987 and 1988 conducted by the California Association of Crime Laboratory Directors in which a high rate of false positives (incorrect sample loading and sample mixing) and false negatives (inability to identify a mixture) were reported due to laboratory error. The Federal Bureau of Investigation (FBI) responded in 1988 by creating a Technical Working Group on DNA Analysis Methods, or Scientific Working Group on DNA Analysis Methods (SWGDAM) since 1999 in order to establish peer-consensus standards for forensic DNA testing. Over the years, this group has established guidelines for QA, proficiency testing, and interpretation, and has sponsored several interlaboratory studies. By 1989, the number of questions (e.g., legal, ethical, and reliability) concerning forensic DNA typing has risen to such an extent that the National Research Council (NRC) of the National Academy of Sciences (NAS) volunteered to address the general applicability and appropriateness of DNA technology in forensic science including issues of standardization and data management. A first report (NRC I) appeared in 1992 with recommendations in six separate areas: technical considerations, statistical interpretation, laboratory standards, data banks and privacy, legal considerations, and social and ethical issues. The committee's recommendation concerning laboratory error was: "Laboratory errors should be measured with appropriate proficiency tests and should play a role in the interpretation of results of forensic DNA typing." Furthermore, in a reaction to a newspaper article published by the *New York Times* about the report, the NRC responded: "We regard the accreditation and proficiency testing of DNA typing laboratories as essential to the scientific accuracy, reliability, and acceptability of DNA typing evidence in the future. Laboratories involved in forensic DNA typing should move quickly to establish quality-assurance programs." It was not until 1998 that the DNA Advisory Board (DAB; established by the FBI after approval of legislation (DNA Identification Act) in the U.S. Congress in 1994) came with separate but overlapping sets of QA standards for forensic DNA testing laboratories and convicted offender DNA databasing laboratories. The DAB also stated that there is a need for a mechanism to ensure compliance with these standards. They recommended that forensic laboratories performing forensic DNA analysis seek accreditation to demonstrate compliance with the standards and, therefore, ensure quality control (QC).

The requirement for accreditation of forensic DNA typing laboratories has been embedded in specific legislation concerning forensic DNA analysis in several countries and is one of the requirements in these countries for conducting forensic DNA analysis in criminal cases. However, many countries, such as the United States, do not have a mandatory system but rely on voluntary accreditation. In February 2009, the NAS in the United States released a report, "Strengthening Forensic Science in the United States. A Path Forward," that was critical of the forensic system in the United States. The report pointed, with the exception of DNA analysis, to a lack of consistency in procedural standards, training, accreditation, and overall research in forensic fields such as fingerprint, firearm identification, and analysis of bite marks, blood spatter, hair, and handwriting. The NAS report also formulated some recommendations, especially mandatory accreditation and certification for forensic laboratories and their personnel.

Accreditation or Certification?

Establishing a QA system in a laboratory should help to ensure that the results provided by the laboratory and its personnel are reliable and accurate. This can be achieved by implementing and maintaining a quality management system that describes in detail the efforts the laboratory takes for obtaining reliable results and for reducing the chance of error, but which also should lead to improvements in the laboratory and personnel processes. External assessment of this quality system by an impartial authority can lead to accreditation or certification if the quality system meets defined standards of performance, competence, and professionalism. An individual forensic expert can only be certified if he or she meets criteria concerning education, training, and competence, which can be demonstrated by documentation and examination. Individual certification has certain advantages for the legal system as it proves the competence to report DNA typing results or present and discuss these results in court. However, it is inadequate to evaluate the competence of the laboratory that provides the results. Certification of individual experts can be voluntary (e.g., American Board of Criminalistics in the United States) or mandatory (e.g., Netherlands Register of Court Experts) as part of legal requirements.

A laboratory can become certified or accredited if it meets predefined standards. According to a 2004 survey conducted by the European Network of Forensic Science Institutes (ENFSI), 17 members out of 53 were accredited, the majority (14) according to ISO/IEC 17025 standards or "national regulation." ISO/IEC is a joint initiative of the International Organization for Standardization (ISO), a network of national standards institutes in 162 countries, and the International Electrochemical Commission (IEC). Two ENFSI members reported that they were accredited according to ISO 9001:2000 and ISO 9002 standards that have been developed by ISO. These ENFSI laboratories were apparently not aware that they were not accredited but "certified according to ISO 9001" (ISO 9002 was replaced by ISO 9001 in 2000). ISO 9001 (current version 2008) is an international standard providing a set of requirements for a quality management system with the purpose to satisfy client needs. A certificate can be obtained after a successful audit performed by an external agency accredited for performing these assessments.

ISO/IEC 17025 (current version 2005) is a standard that specifies the general requirements of competence for a laboratory or institution to carry out tests and/or calibrations, including sampling. It is applicable to any laboratory that performs testing or calibration activities irrespective of the scientific field where the laboratory is active. Regulatory and safety requirements (e.g., laboratory safety) on the operation of laboratories are not covered by ISO/IEC 17025. Compliance with these requirements is regulated locally. Laboratories that comply with ISO/IEC 17025 will also operate in accordance to ISO 9001. However, certification only for ISO 9001 does not demonstrate the competence of the laboratory to produce reliable and reproducible results. Accreditation, according to ISO/IEC 17025, is a more comprehensive approach to assure the reliability of the test results and is also seen as the international standard for forensic laboratories. Accreditation of forensic DNA testing is mandatory in several countries around the world because of specific requirements in DNA legislation. On November 30, 2009, the European Council Justice and Home Affairs (Council Framework Decision 2009/905/JHA) reached an agreement on a framework regarding mandatory accreditation of forensic service providers carrying out laboratory activities in fingerprinting and DNA profiling. The purpose of this framework is to ensure that forensic laboratory results obtained in one European Union (EU) member state are recognized by the law enforcement authorities in all other EU member states. This decision also means that a common international standard (ISO/IEC 17025:2005) is introduced for forensic service providers within the EU, but this standard will not apply to any measures taken outside a laboratory (e.g., sampling at the scene of crime). EU member states should implement these decisions in their legislations by November 30, 2013, for DNA profiling and by November 30, 2015, for dactyloscopic data.

In the United States, accreditation has been mostly voluntary except for some states (New York, Texas, and Oklahoma). In 1982, the American Society of Crime Laboratory Directors/Laboratory Accreditation Board (ASCLD/LAB) offered a voluntary forensic laboratory accreditation program known as the "Legacy Program." This program contained statements of principles describing acceptable levels of performance and the criteria of evaluation. These criteria were divided into essential (91 standards that directly affect and have a fundamental impact on the laboratory or the processed evidence), important (45 standards that are key indicators of the overall quality of the laboratory but do not directly affect the product or the evidence), and desirable (16 standards that have the least effect on the product or the processed evidence and will improve the professionalism of the laboratory). A forensic laboratory was accredited by the ASCLD/LAB Board of Directors if it met 100% of the essential criteria, 75% of the important criteria, and 50% of the desirable criteria. In 2009, the ASLCD/LAB announced that it would no longer accredit laboratories through its Legacy Program. Instead, ISO/IEC 17025:2005 compliance (ASLCD/LAB International) is endorsed and all labs previously accredited by ASLCD are required to comply with the international standard no later than March 31, 2014. The criterion rating system of the Legacy Program has been abandoned by ASCLD/LAB, and each lab should comply now with the numbered requirements of ISO/IEC 17025:2005. As of June 7, 2012, ASCLD/LAB has accredited 390 forensic laboratories including 17 international (Singapore, Canada, New Zealand, Malaysia, and Hong Kong) and 24 private laboratories, with 216 laboratories accredited under the "International Testing Program." Forensic Quality Services Inc. (FQS; the ANSI (American National Standards Institute)—ASQ (American Society for Quality) National Accreditation Board acquired FQS Inc. on November 29, 2011) is another accreditation body in the United States that has provided accreditation to ISO/IEC 17025 since 2004. Up to June 2012, 60 laboratories have been accredited by FQS.

The quality system of the FBI laboratory relies on the requirements described in ISO/IEC 17025:2005 in addition to supplemental standards of ASCLD/LAB. These standards can be helpful in the process of setting up a QA program in a forensic laboratory as the requirements in ISO/IEC 17025 are stated in general terms. However, the ASCLD/LAB standards cannot create additional criteria to ISO/IEC 17025 but can be used as a guideline for the interpretation of the requirements. Other forensic laboratories use the ILAC Guide

19:2002 "Guidelines for Forensic Science Laboratories" as a guide to implement an ISO/IEC 17025 quality system. In addition to these guidelines, forensic laboratories can also use the recommendations of the Paternity Testing Commission (PTC) of the International Society of Forensic Genetics (ISFG). In 2002, the PTC formulated explanations and recommendations for paternity testing laboratories concerning certain requirements of the ISO/IEC 17025 standard.

A Short Guide to Accreditation for ISO/IEC 17025

Accreditation is a process of comparison and evaluation of a (forensic) laboratory's operations against the requirements (e.g., ISO/IEC 17025:2005; **Table 1**). It relies on QC and QA. QC refers to measures taken to ensure that the laboratory analysis and interpretation meets a specified standard. QA refers to measures taken by the organization (laboratory) to monitor, verify, and document its performance, and to minimize the occurrence of error. The QA system includes internal procedures (e.g., redundant testing), regular external proficiency testing, and regular internal and external auditing of laboratory operations. A laboratory audit might be the evaluation of certain procedures (internal) or the entire operation of a laboratory (external). Records of the assessment describe the findings of the audit and may lead to a course of corrective actions that have to be taken in order to resolve any problem or deficiency in the standard requirements observed during the audit. The findings of the audit are graded, which reflects the type of action (immediately, within a certain period, or none) a laboratory has to take in order to resolve the remarks made. The laboratory has to present a "plan of action" with defined deadlines for resolving the remarks and will get its accreditation only after approval of this plan by the audit team. Accreditation is limited in time (3–5 years) and is controlled annually by the same audit team that did the inspection for the first application for accreditation. A laboratory can extend its accreditation, which is obtained after a full inspection usually by a new team of assessors.

Establishing a QA system in a laboratory is the first step toward accreditation. While only 17.3% of the European forensic institutes in the 2004 survey of ENFSI were accredited according to ISO/IEC 17025, 50% of the institutes had a QA system available and another 44.2% were in the process of development. A QA system should at least have good documentation of all processes in the laboratory, including validated and documented procedures (standard operating procedures or SOP), tested reagents, calibrated equipment, appropriate control samples, and detailed documentation of the operations, results, and interpretations. In particular, a good QA system focuses on minimizing the risk of errors and establishing methods for detecting errors. Having a QA system in place is a good starting point on the track to accreditation as many aspects of the ISO/IEC 17025 requirements might be already covered (**Table 1**). Some of these aspects are trivial but others require more explanation, especially with regard to the forensic field. These items include control of records (4.12), personnel (5.2), accommodation and environmental conditions (5.3), test and calibration methods and method validation (5.4), and assuring the quality of test and calibration results (5.9).

Control of Records

In a quality system, all procedures performed from the receipt of the samples until the reporting of the results of the testing must be documented. Any action in the laboratory process should be recorded so that these actions are traceable to the person (analyst, examiner, or reporting scientist) who has performed the actions. Where appropriate, observations or test results must be preserved with photographic records (e.g., examination of evidence objects), printed or electronic scans (e.g., electropherograms of DNA profiles). Manual corrections should be recorded and documented through interpretation guidelines. In general, the information in these records should be such that another competent person can evaluate and interpret the data in the absence of the examiner/analyst who has done the analysis. This independent evaluation of the results has been implemented in most forensic laboratories in order to assure the validity of the interpretation of the results. This process should be documented and the records should indicate who has done these controls. All these aspects are similar to the chain of custody of evidence objects and must assure that any review of the laboratory case records allows reconstructing the process each evidence object has gone through in the laboratory.

Personnel

ISO/IEC 17025 requires that the laboratory defines the minimum requirements of the different staff members, including qualifications (e.g., education), job description, and a documented training program for new staff. Local regulations may require that staff members, who are responsible for reporting the results, must be certified according to certain criteria. Both DAB and ISFG (PTC) have made recommendations concerning laboratory directors, technical managers, or scientists who are authorized to sign reports: (1) education should be at least at the level of a master's degree in the relevant area (e.g., biology or human genetics for DNA analysis) and (2) experience of at least 3 years in a competent forensic (or paternity) DNA testing laboratory must be demonstrated. The PTC also included that experience must be documented with at least 100 reports covering all major aspects of paternity testing. In addition, the DAB recommends for examiners/analysts a minimum bachelor's degree, at least 6 months of forensic DNA laboratory experience, and successfully completing

Table 1 Key categories of requirements in ISO/IEC 17025:2008

1. Scope—general requirements for the competence of the laboratory to carry out tests/calibrations, including sampling
2. Normative references—cited references with regard to standards
3. Terms and definitions—clarification of terms and definitions
4. Management requirements
   - 4.1 Organization—the laboratory must meet the requirements of ISO/IEC 17015, the needs of the customer/client, the regulatory authorities, or the organizations providing recognition
   - 4.2 Quality system—the laboratory shall establish, implement, and maintain a quality system appropriate for the activities of the laboratory
   - 4.3 Document control—the laboratory shall establish and maintain procedures to control documents (design, approval, and changes) that are part of the quality system (quality manual, operation manuals, standard operating procedures (SOP), etc.)
   - 4.4 Review of requests, tenders, and contracts—the laboratory shall establish procedures and policies so that both clients/customers and laboratory understand the requirements and that the laboratory has the capacity to perform the work
   - 4.5 Subcontracting of tests and calibrations—any subcontracting should be performed by a competent subcontractor after informing the client/customer
   - 4.6 Purchasing services and supplies—the laboratory shall establish procedures and policies for the selection and purchasing of supplies and services that can affect the quality of the tests of the laboratory
   - 4.7 Service to the client—requesting customer feedback (positive and negative) in order to improve the quality system and the service to the client
   - 4.8 Complaints—the laboratory shall establish procedures and a policy for the resolution of complaints received internally (personnel) and externally (clients)
   - 4.9 Control of nonconforming testing and/or calibration—the laboratory shall establish procedures and a policy to deal with testing/calibration that do not conform to the SOP of the laboratory or the agreed requirements of the client
   - 4.10 Corrective action—the laboratory shall establish a procedure and policy (including the designation of appropriate authorities) for implementing corrective action when problems are identified (nonconforming work or departures from the policies in the quality system); the procedure should include an analysis of the cause, selection, and implementation of the corrective action, monitoring of the corrective actions, and need for additional internal auditing
   - 4.11 Preventive action—procedures must be in place to direct preventive actions against nonconformances, either technically or against the quality system; any preventive action should be covered with action plans for implementation and monitored to reduce the likelihood of the occurrence of such a nonconformance and to take advantage of the opportunities
   - 4.12 Control of records—the laboratory shall establish and maintain procedures concerning records (quality and technical) including identification, collection, access, storage, maintenance, and disposal

Continued

Table 1 Key categories of requirements in ISO/IEC 17025:2008—cont'd

   - 4.13 Internal audits—the laboratory shall have a predetermined schedule and procedure to conduct periodic internal audits; all elements of the quality system should be covered, including all testing activities
   - 4.14 Management reviews—the laboratory's top management is required to review the performance of the quality system and testing systems periodically according to a predefined schedule to ensure the suitability and effectiveness of the system, and to introduce necessary changes and improvements; ISO/IEC 17025 directs a number of topics that must be covered during the review
5. Technical requirements
   - 5.1 General—the laboratory shall take account of factors that can influence the correctness and reliability of the tests performed or to be developed
   - 5.2 Personnel—the management of the laboratory is required to ensure the competence of the personnel that operate the equipment, perform the tests, or write the reports; a training program should be established that is relevant to the work performed
   - 5.3 Accommodation and environmental conditions—a laboratory must provide an environment that will facilitate the correct performance of the testing
   - 5.4 Test and calibration methods and method validation—a laboratory must use appropriate methods and procedures, including methods for sampling, in order to assure correct results; methods that have been appropriately validated and published are recommended
   - 5.5 Equipment—the laboratory must have the necessary equipment to accomplish the correct sampling and measurement, and to assure the correct performance and accuracy of the tests
   - 5.6 Measurement traceability—equipment used for tests should be calibrated; calibrations or measurements should be traceable to international standards; reference materials must be traceable to certified reference materials (if possible)
   - 5.7 Sampling—the laboratory shall have a sampling plan and procedures for sampling when part of a substance or a sample is used for testing
   - 5.8 Handling of test and calibration items—the laboratory shall establish procedures for the transportation, receipt, handling, protection, storage, retention, and disposal of test items including provisions to protect the integrity of the test, and to protect the interests of the laboratory and the client
   - 5.9 Assuring the quality of test and calibration results—a laboratory should have quality control procedures for checking and monitoring the validity of the tests
   - 5.10 Reporting the results—a laboratory should report the results of all tests including all the information requested by the client and necessary for the interpretation of the test results; results should be reported accurately, clearly, unambiguously, and objectively, and opinions and interpretations must be clearly marked in the report

a qualifying test; whereas for technicians, a training program and successfully completing a qualifying test with respect to their job responsibilities would be required. In addition, the laboratory must have a policy for training and education in order to keep the competence of the personnel at the level of current and future developments. The efficiency of these actions should be monitored. The ENFSI DNA working group has also published a Concept Training Document with minimum recommendations for training and competence testing of staff.

Accommodation and Environmental Conditions

Owing to the sensitive information of forensic evidence analysis, it is inevitable that the laboratory facilities and evidence storage must be properly secured and that access is restricted. Special care is needed in order to prevent cross-contamination, which can be done by physical separation of different activities or separating analysis processes, for example, reference samples are processed (DNA analysis) by analysts who do not examine evidence objects. In addition, the examination of evidence objects in a single forensic case might need separate examination in space or in time (e.g., evidence objects from the suspect versus evidence objects from the victim). As current forensic DNA analysis methods rely on DNA amplification (PCR), it is necessary to take steps to prevent contamination with PCR products by dividing the laboratory into at least three different work areas: examination of the evidence objects and DNA isolation (pre-PCR), work areas for PCR setup (pre-PCR), and work areas for handling of PCR products (post-PCR). Special attention must be given to the avoidance of contamination from post-PCR areas to pre-PCR areas. This can be accomplished by using strict procedures for organization of the laboratory work: an analyst who starts the day in a post-PCR work area cannot do any work in a pre-PCR area the same day, while the reverse is still possible if the analyst continues his/her work in the post-PCR area after working in a pre-PCR area. The ISFG (PTC) has recommended that a laboratory should have procedures for monitoring potential contamination from PCR products, which also includes validated decontamination procedures. With respect to contamination, it is also necessary to focus on procedures for monitoring (and decontamination) of disposable plasticware and reagents used in the analysis procedures.

Test and Calibration Methods and Method Validation

A laboratory performing forensic DNA testing should use methods, including methods for sampling, that are appropriate for the analysis. The ISFG (PTC) has recommended using DNA systems for which proficiency testing is available and the population distribution data is available. Laboratory-developed methods and nonstandard methods, including equipment and software (commercially available or in-house developed), should have been validated before they can be used in routine casework. This does not mean that commercially developed test kits, which have been validated (developmental) by the manufacturer, can be used by a forensic laboratory without further validation. A laboratory should always do an internal validation of these kits in order to ensure that the laboratory is able to reproduce the specifications (e.g., sensitivity and specificity) set by the manufacturer on equipment used by the laboratory. The validation process should start with a written procedure of the analysis (draft version of a SOP), setting objectives for the validation, and defining requirements for accepting the validation. The results must be analyzed appropriately (including statistical evaluation) after the experimental procedures, and formally reported with a conclusion (e.g., acceptance, rejection, and additional validation necessary) concerning the validation. Typical studies of internal validation of DNA systems (short tandem repeats or STRs) in forensic testing include determining reproducibility, precision for sizing the alleles, sensitivity, and mixture studies. The ISFG (PTC) has recommended the following for validation of methods: (1) using reference standards or reference materials; (2) comparison of results achieved with other methods; (3) interlaboratory comparisons and (4) systematic assessment of the factors influencing the results; and (5) assessment of the uncertainty of the results based on scientific understanding of the theoretical principles of the method and practical experience. The ENFSI DNA working group has also published a list of minimum criteria that could serve as a guideline in the validation of various aspects of DNA profiling.

Assuring the Quality of Test and Calibration Results

A laboratory must have procedures for monitoring the quality of the procedures and test results, including calibration of equipment used in the analytical procedures. Calibration should be traceable to international standards or by using certified reference materials. A laboratory should use proper positive and negative controls in its analytical procedures where positive controls are (preferably) traceable to international standards or certified reference material. The National Institute of Standards and Technology in the United States provides reference materials for DNA profiling (STR and mtDNA) and DNA quantitation that can be used for validations or for monitoring the performance of the lab. Laboratories should participate in interlaboratory comparisons or proficiency testing programs. The laboratory should set up an internal QC or testing program if certain methods or DNA systems are not covered in these external programs. This also includes the type of samples for which a laboratory has obtained accreditation. Bones, tissue samples, and hair are typical samples not included in external proficiency DNA testing programs. The laboratory should analyze these samples at least once a year in order to evaluate the lab's performance in typing these samples. Typically, some samples that have been analyzed previously are typed a second time by the analyst without knowledge of the previous results for these samples.

Both DAB and ISFG (PTC) have recommended participating in a proficiency testing program at least twice a year. Blind proficiency testing is generally considered the best way to evaluate the performance of a laboratory. They are, however, difficult to set up if the laboratory does not know that it is part of a testing program. In this case, it requires cooperation from official authorities (police and/or justice) in order to disguise the test as a "routine" case, which may lead to ethical and legal problems. For this reason, current blind proficiency testing programs are based on the distribution of standard material to all participants in the program and on a grading system of the test results. There are several providers of forensic proficiency testing programs of which Collaborative Testing Services Inc. (CTS) and the German DNA profiling group (GEDNAP) are used by most forensic laboratories in the United States and Europe, respectively. CTS, since 1978, is a commercial provider of proficiency tests in several fields of forensic testing and is recognized by ASCLD/LAB. The DNA test samples are usually two reference bloodstains and two questioned stains. Laboratories are requested to report the test results, including DNA profiles and body fluid identification (only when information given with the samples does not include the source of the cell material), and to give an interpretation (inclusion, exclusion, or inconclusive) based on the test results. After evaluation of the results of the participating laboratories, an extensive report with the results of all the participants is made available. GEDNAP is the German-speaking group of the EDNAP group, which was established in 1989 with the aim to harmonize DNA profiling in Europe. The blind trial of GEDNAP is organized by the Institute for Forensic Medicine in Münster (Germany) with the following aims: (1) standardization of methods and procedures; (2) standardization of nomenclature; (3) evaluation of the competence of the laboratories to obtain correct results; and (4) elimination of errors in typing. Each participant in the program receives two series of samples each consisting of three reference samples and four questioned samples. The questioned samples are designed to reflect real casework samples with respect to type, size, and material. Laboratories are requested to give information concerning the analytical procedures used and the DNA profiles obtained, including the raw data. The laboratory will receive a report in which every allele call has been graded: (1) no errors; (2) mixture not detected; (3) error in typing but would not be reported; and (4) error in typing, which would be reported. Type 4 errors are considered to be true errors in the final evaluation, and the laboratory receives a certificate for the DNA systems, which were correctly typed. The results of internal QCs and from proficiency testing must be analyzed by the lab in order to report the performance of the laboratory. Any observed problem or error should lead to planned actions in order to correct the problem or prevent it from happening again.

See also: **Biology/DNA:** Forensic DNA Advisory Groups: DAB, SWGDAM, ENFSI, and BSAG; History of the International Society for Forensic Genetics – ISFG; **Legal:** Legal Systems: Adversarial and Inquisitorial.

Further Reading

Budowle, B., Bottrell, M.C., Bunch, S.G., et al., 2009. A perspective on errors, bias, and interpretation in the forensic sciences and direction for continuing advancement. Journal of Forensic Sciences 54, 798–809.

Butler, J.M., 2009. Fundamentals of Forensic DNA Typing. Elsevier Academic Press, San Diego.

Committee on DNA Technology in Forensic Science, National Research Council, 1992. DNA Technology in Forensic Science. National Academy Press, Washington.

Committee on DNA Forensic Science: An update, National Research Council, 1996. The Evaluation of Forensic DNA Evidence. National Academy Press, Washington.

Committee on Identifying the Needs of the Forensic Science Community, Committee on Science, Technology, and Law Policy and Global Affairs, Committee on Applied and Theoretical Statistics, Division on Engineering and Physical Sciences, 2009. Strengthening Forensic Science in the United States: A Path Forward. National Academy Press, Washington.

Gill, P., Rowlands, D., Tully, G., et al., 2010. Manufacturer contamination of disposable plastic-ware and other reagents – an agreed position statement by ENFSI, SWGDAM and BSAG. Forensic Science International: Genetics 4, 269–270.

Malkoc, E., Neuteboom, W., 2007. The current status of forensic science laboratory accreditation in Europe. Forensic Science International 167, 121–126.

Morling, N., Allen, R., Carracedo, A., et al., 2002. Paternity Testing Commission of the International Society of Forensic Genetics. Recommendations on genetic investigations in paternity cases. International Journal of Legal Medicine 117, 51–61.

Rand, S., Schürenkamp, M., Brinkmann, B., 2002. The GEDNAP (German DNA profiling group) blind trial concept. International Journal of Legal Medicine 116, 199–206.

Rand, S., Schürenkamp, M., Hohoff, C., Brinkmann, B., 2004. The GEDNAP blind trial concept part II. Trends and developments. International Journal of Legal Medicine 116, 199–206.

Relevant Websites

www.ctsforensics.com—Collaborative Testing Services, Inc.—Proficiency testing.

www.dna.gov/lab_services/—DNA Initiative—Services for Laboratories.

www.enfsi.org—European Network of Forensic Science Institutes—Documents concerning training and validation.

www.gednap.de—German DNA Profiling Group—Stain Commission & GEDNAP Proficiency Tests.

www.ilac.org—International Laboratory Accreditation Cooperation—Accreditation Bodies.

www.iso.org—International Organization for Standardization—ISO/IEC 17025:2005.

www.cstl.nist.gov/strbase/—National Institute of Standards and Technology—Lab Resources.

www.nist.gov—National Institute of Standards and Technology—Standard Reference Material.

Measurement Uncertainty

Ted Vosk, Criminal Defense Law Firm, Kirkland, WA, USA

Abbreviations

b_{ias} Bia
$\bar{y}_c$ Bias corrected mean measured value
Y_b Best estimate of "true" measurand value
μ_c Combined uncertainty
k Coverage factor
U Expanded uncertainty
X Input quantities
ε_m Maximum total error
$\bar{y}$ Mean measured value
$f(X_1,X_2,\ldots,X_N)$ Measurement function
ε Measurement error
y Measured value
$Y_{99\%}$ Measurand value with 99% level of confidence
ε_{ran} Random error
μ_r Relative standard uncertainty
$\partial f/\partial x_i$ Sensitivity coefficients
σ Standard deviation
μ Standard uncertainty
ε_{sys} Systematic error
Y 'True' measurand value
$\boxplus$ Unspecified method for combining ε_{sys} and ε_{ran}

Glossary

Bias The quantitative characterization of systematic error.
Combined uncertainty The standard uncertainty associated with the final measurement result determined by "adding" up the standard uncertainties associated with each of the individual sources of uncertainty.
Coverage factor A positive, real number that when multiplied by a measurement's combined uncertainty yields the expanded uncertainty. The coverage factor determines the level of confidence associated with a coverage interval.
Coverage interval An interval about the best estimate of a measurand's "true" value that will contain those values believed to be attributable to the measurand with a specified level of confidence.
Expended uncertainty Measure of uncertainty obtained by multiplying a measurement's combined uncertainty by a coverage factor. It defines the half width of a coverage interval.
Level of confidence The probability, defined as a degree of belief, that the "true" value of a measurand lies within the range defined by a coverage interval.
Measurand The quantity whose value is sought to be determined by a measurement.
Measurement function A function that describes the relationship between the measurand value and those quantities required to determine it.
Quantity Physical properties subject to measurement, such as length, time, weight, and concentration.
Random error The inherent unpredictable fluctuation in measured values under fixed conditions.
Sensitivity coefficients The partial derivatives of a measurement function that describe how the measurand's value varies with changes in the values of the input quantities.
Standard uncertainty Measurement uncertainty expressed as the standard deviation of a frequency or belief based probability distribution.
Systematic error The tendency of a set of measurements to consistently (on average) underestimate or overestimate the "true" value of a measurand by a given value or percentage.
Uncertainty The quantitative characterization of the dispersion of values that, based on one's universe of information concerning a measurement, are believed to be reasonably attributable to a measurand.

 http://dx.doi.org/10.1016/B978-0-12-800647-4.00034-5

Measurement

Measurement constitutes a specific category of scientific investigation. It is an empirical process whereby a researcher seeks to determine the numerical magnitude attributable to some physical/phenomenological quantity of interest referred to as the "measurand." Many naively consider measurement to be a mechanical process whereby the quantity of interest is sensed/probed by a measuring instrument yielding directly the value attributable to the measurand. This mechanical activity is simply one step in the overall measurement process. Alone, it does not tell us what we want to know about the value(s) attributable to a measurand. Rather than a passively mechanical process of probing and discovery, measurement is more completely understood as an empirically grounded, information-based inference requiring active input from the researcher before any value can be attributed to a measurand. Measurement uncertainty identifies in an explicit, quantitatively rigorous manner the limitations governing the rational inferences that can be made concerning the value(s) attributable to a measurand based on the results of measurement.

Measurement to Meaning

Measurement Error and Error Analysis

What does a measurement result mean? In other words, given a measured value y, what value(s) can actually be attributed to a measurand? Lay people often interpret the value reported by a measurement as representing the singular "true" value attributable to a measurand (**Figure 1**):

$$Y = y \quad [1]$$

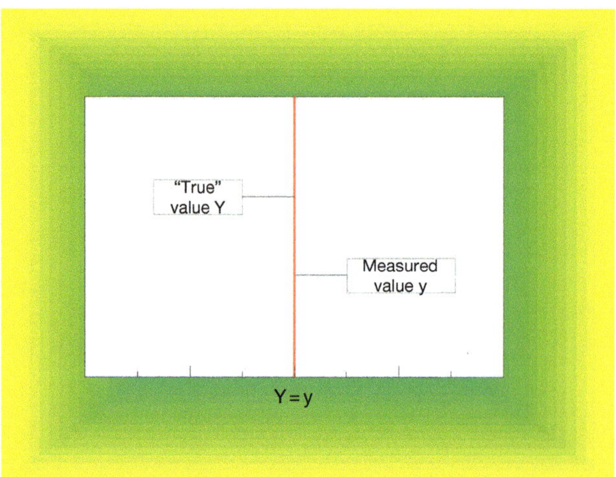

Figure 1 Measurement as singular "true" value.

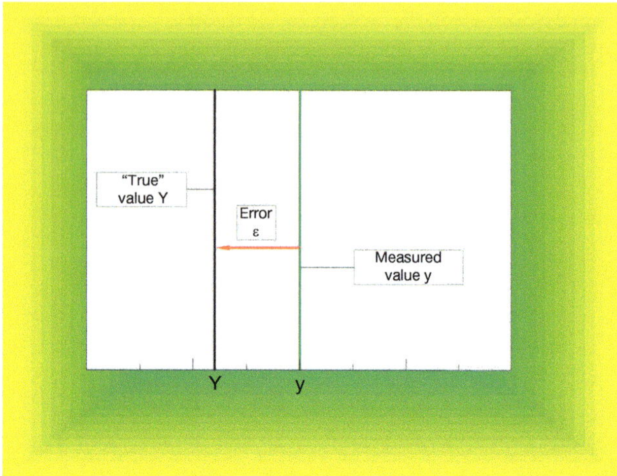

Figure 2 Measurement in reality inherent error.

Science has long realized, however, that "error" is an inherent characteristic of measurement distinguishing measured values from the "true" quantity values sought to be determined (**Figure 2**).

Error analysis is the traditional approach to the interpretation of measurement results. It is based on the premise that if the error associated with a measurement can be determined, then a measurand's "true" value can also be determined:

$$Y = y - \varepsilon \quad [2]$$

There are two types of errors associated with every measurement: random and systematic. Systematic error is the tendency of a method/instrument to yield values that are consistently (on average) artificially inflated or depressed with respect to the "true" values of the quantities being measured. It is quantitatively characterized as bias (**Figure 3**).

The identification of systematic error can be one of the most difficult aspects of the measurement process. The reason is that if one is measuring an unknown quantity, the measured values themselves provide no basis for concluding that they are systematically offset from the measurand's "true" value. Thus, one can never know whether all systematic errors associated with a measurement have been identified. Some sources of systematic error can be identified and quantified through measurement of reference materials. Even when rigorously determined in this manner, however, the magnitude of the bias can never be exactly known.

Random error is the unpredictable/random fluctuation in measured values under fixed conditions. It introduces inherent variability into the measurement process, placing a fundamental limitation on the repeatability of measured results. For many common situations, the random variation in a measurement's results can be approximately characterized by a Gaussian (normal) distribution (**Figure 4**).

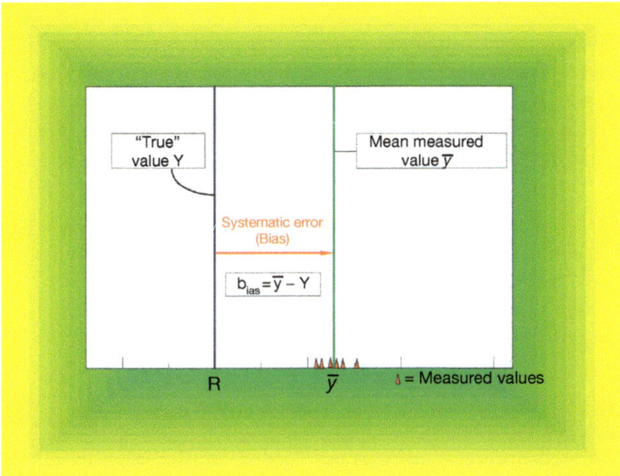

Figure 3 Systematic error and bias.

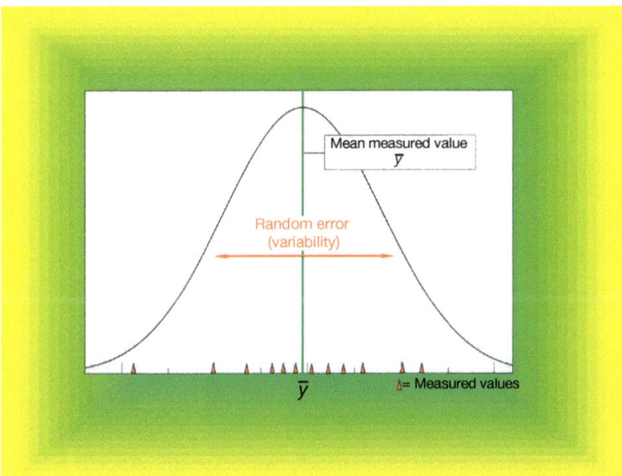

Figure 4 Random error and variability.

Random error is quantitatively characterized by a set of measurement's standard deviation:

$$\sigma_y = \sqrt{\frac{\sum_{i=1}^{n}(y_i - \bar{y})^2}{n-1}} \quad [3]$$

The standard deviation provides a measure of the variability of individually measured values about their mean. If there is significant variability, the standard deviation will be large. If variability is slight, the standard deviation will be small.

Systematic and random errors describe aspects of the *physical state of a measurement*. It is not always clear whether an error should be categorized as systematic or random, and the determination may be context dependent. Taken together, they

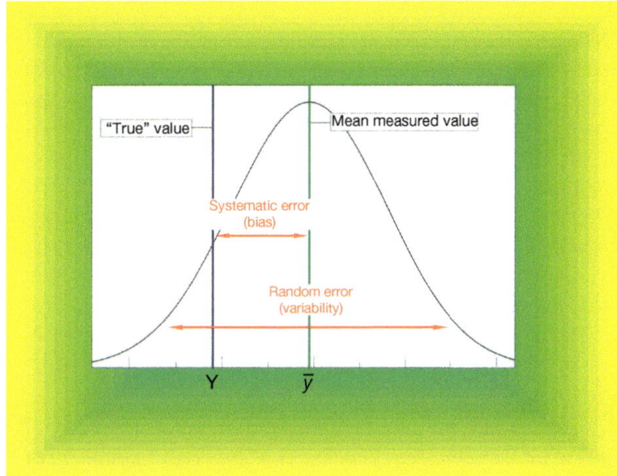

Figure 5 Measurement error.

constitute what is formally known as "measurement error" (**Figure 5**).

The total error associated with a measurement can never be absolutely determined, that is, it is unknowable. As a result, error analysis can never supply a measurand's "true" value. Instead, the goal of error analysis is to identify, minimize, and eliminate *as best as possible* all identifiable sources of error so as to provide an estimate of a measurand's value that is *as close as possible* to its "true" value (**Figure 6**).

This requires some method for combining systematic and random components of error to obtain a characterization of a measurement's total error:

$$\varepsilon = \varepsilon_{sys} \boxplus \varepsilon_{ran} \quad [4]$$

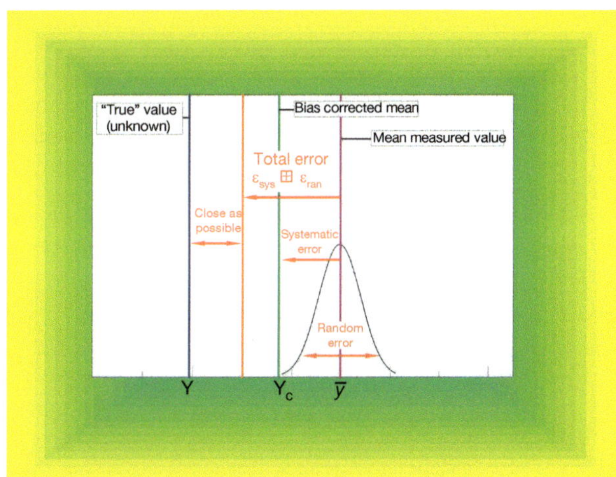

Figure 6 Error analysis estimate as close as possible.

To understand where this leads, one must have an idea of the mathematical underpinnings of error analysis. Error analysis is grounded in frequentist statistical theory, which defines probability in terms of relative frequency of occurrence. This means that the probability that a particular condition will be found to exist is determined by how frequently it occurs within the universe of all possible events. Although these probabilities can seldom be known because the universe of all possible events can seldom be completely known, they can be "objectively" estimated as the relative frequency of occurrence over sample data sets. What is critical is that in error analysis, the estimation of probabilities is "objectively" based solely on statistical sampling according to the frequentist paradigm.

The analysis of random error fits well within the frequentist paradigm. On the other hand, except in limited circumstances, the evaluation of systematic error does not. Because systematic and random errors are different in nature, each requires distinct treatment. There is no rigorously justifiable manner within the frequentist paradigm by which systematic and random errors can be combined to yield a statistically meaningful estimate of a measurement's total error.

Due to the frequentist underpinnings of error analysis, the best it can provide is an upper limit on a measurement's total error. This bounded error is often expressed as some linear combination of the bias and standard deviation associated with a measurement:

$$\varepsilon_{\mathrm{m}} = b_{\mathrm{ias}} + 3\sigma \quad [5]$$

This places a bound on the maximum separation expected between a measured and "true" value. It does not, however, denote how close together the two values are *actually* expected to lie. In other words, it tells us the worst a measurement result could be without any indication of how good it actually is. Moreover, the meaning of this bounded error is vague, as it fails to tell us how probable it is that a measured value lies within the prescribed range of the measurand's "true" value. Given a measured value y, the best error analysis provides is an incompletely defined estimate of the maximum separation between a measured value and a "true" value. It cannot tell us the values that are likely to be attributable to the measurand given a particular measured value.

The Meaning of Meaning

A significant epistemological question surrounds any scientific proposition: Is a scientific proposition intended to describe some physical state of the universe itself or simply to describe our state of knowledge about such a physical state? If it is the former, the direct object of the proposition is an external fully independent reality. If it is the latter, the direct object of the proposition is an internal cognitive position that is information dependent. Many claim that if scientific propositions are to be objectively meaningful, they must fall into the first category. Others counter that regardless of the objective content of scientific propositions, they necessarily reside in the second category as all we can ever actually claim to know is our internal cognitive state, not some independent external reality.

Although seemingly esoteric, the position adopted can have practical implications. It may change not only the interpretation of scientific statements but also the manner in which they can be investigated. And so it is with scientific measurement. When a measurement result is reported, is it to be interpreted as a statement about the physical state of a measurand? Or, is it simply an expression of our state of knowledge about the measurand's physical state? And what are the practical implications of the choice made?

Measurement error is an aspect of the *physical state* of a measurement. It is related to a measurand through error analysis that purports to convey the bounds of its actual *physical state* through the determination of a bounded error. Where a precise estimate of a measurand's actual value is not critical, the bounded error may provide a result with sufficient meaning to be useful. Where a measurand's actual value is important, however, this level of meaning may be inadequate. If possible, one would like to understand the meaning of a measured value in terms of how it maps into those values that are *likely* to be attributable to the measurand.

Measurement Uncertainty

The New Paradigm

Measurement uncertainty addresses the shortcomings of error analysis by fundamentally redefining the way measurement is interpreted and providing a quantitative metric for mapping measured values into those believed to be reasonably attributable to a measurand. In this new paradigm, error is replaced as the focus of analysis by a new entity: uncertainty. This is not a matter of mere semantics. Uncertainty and error are completely distinct concepts. While measurement error concerns the actual *physical state of* a measurand, measurement uncertainty relates to the *state of knowledge about* the measurand.

This does not mean that those phenomena formerly understood as systematic and random errors are ignored. To the contrary, they are fully encompassed within the uncertainty framework. What they represent, however, has been reconceptualized to overcome the limitations inherent in frequentist philosophy. Central to the uncertainty paradigm is the alternative Bayesian notion of probability as a degree of belief. That is, probability is defined by how strongly one believes a given proposition. This formulation permits consideration of information about a measurand beyond that cognizable in frequentist theory and provides a common basis for its analysis whether statistically or nonstatistically based.

In the uncertainty paradigm, as in error analysis, a measurand's "true" value is unknowable. However, this is not due to the physical phenomenon of irreducible error but to the impossibility of our ever possessing perfect knowledge concerning a measurand's state. Uncertainty focuses on this limitation interpreting a measurement result as a probability distribution that characterizes one's state of knowledge about a measurand's value. While measurement error as a physical phenomenon is as unknowable as a measurand's "true" value, the characterization of a result as a probability distribution in this manner permits a result's uncertainty to be rigorously determined.

When a measurement is performed, it always takes place against a backdrop of existing information about the measurement to be made and the measurand itself. Some of this information may be in the form of statistically obtained data, while some may be based on other sources such as general knowledge of the behavior and properties of relevant materials, methods, and instruments. When a measurement is performed, the discrete value obtained adds to our universe of information and updates our state of knowledge concerning the measurand. Because our information is necessarily incomplete, our knowledge concerning the measurand remains fuzzy. Given the information possessed, the discrete value obtained represents a packet of values dispersed about the measured result, all of which are believed to be attributable to the measurand with relative degrees of conviction (**Figure** 7).

It is the identification of probabilities as degrees of belief that transforms this packet of values into a probability distribution. In this context, the meaning of a measured value corresponds to a probability distribution characterizing the relative likelihood of the values believed to be attributable to a measurand based on the totality of currently available information (**Figure** 8).

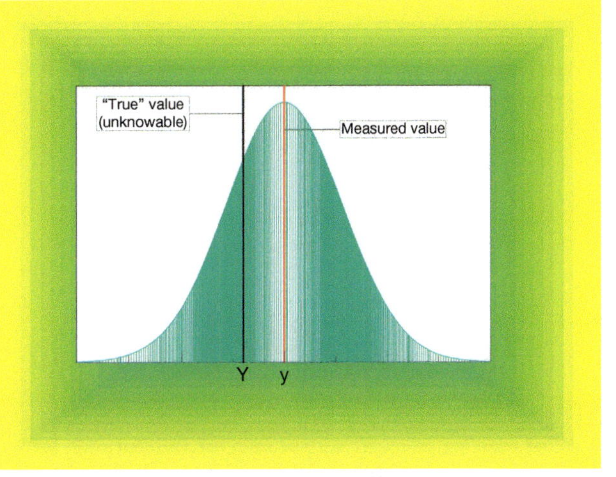

Figure 8 Measurement as probability distribution.

This distribution completely specifies our state of knowledge concerning the values attributable to a measurand. Moreover, it delineates in a mathematically rigorous manner how a measured value, y, maps into those values believed to be attributable to a measurand. By doing so, it also determines the inferences that can be made concerning a measurand's value based on the values measured.

As an example, given a measured value, the distribution permits one to determine the probability that a measurand's value lies within any given range of values. In this context, one can think of the probability associated with the distribution as being equal to the area under the curve representing it. The probability that a measurand's value lies within a specified range is given by the proportion of the area under the curve spanning the range in question to the total area under the curve (**Figure** 9).

Given a measured value, y, the question of what values can *reasonably* be attributed to a measurand involves two

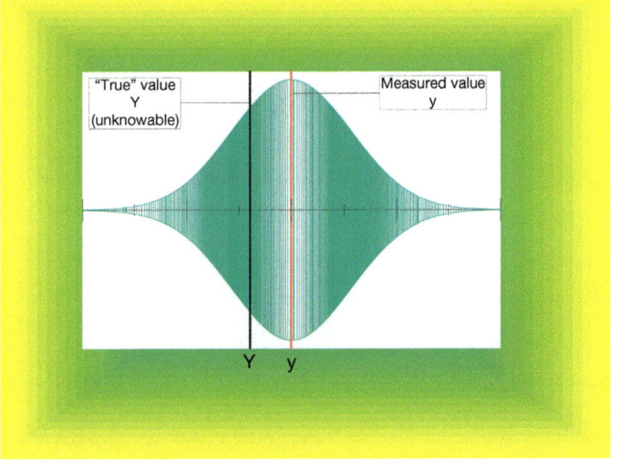

Figure 7 Measurement as packet of values.

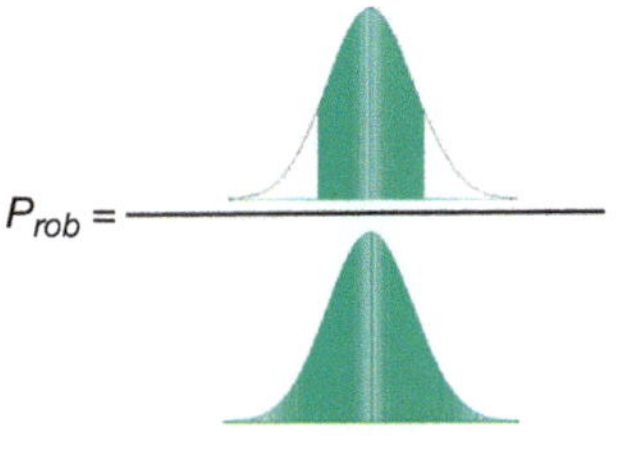

Figure 9 Probability = ratio of areas under curve.

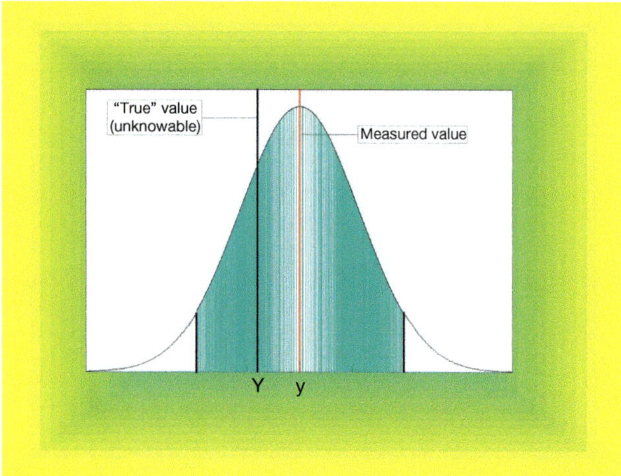

Figure 10 Values reasonably attributable to measurand.

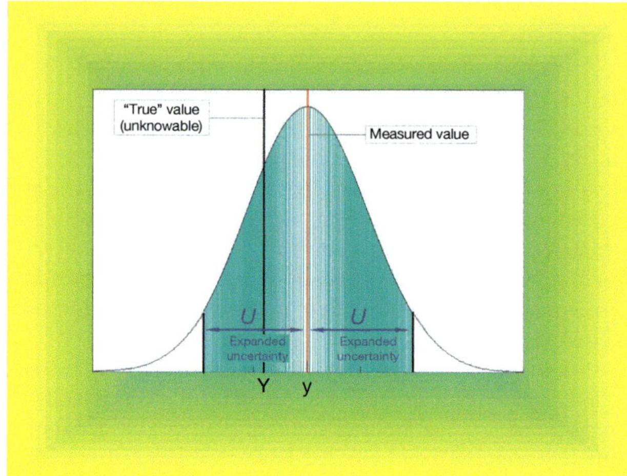

Figure 11 Expanded uncertainty.

competing considerations. First, we want to exclude values that, although possible, are highly improbable. Second, we need to include enough values so that there is a significant probability that the measurand's value is actually among those considered. The measurement's probability distribution provides a conceptually straightforward way of accomplishing this. Simply slice off the tails of the distribution while including enough of its middle so that the area of the remaining region represents a significant probability that the measurand's value lies within it (**Figure 10**).

From this, we can obtain a range of values reasonably attributable to a measurand, along with an associated probability that the value of the measurand lies within it. This defines the uncertainty of a measurement. Measurement uncertainty is the quantitative characterization of the dispersion of values that, based on the universe of information concerning a measurement, are believed to be *reasonably* attributable to a measurand. The half-width of this range of values is known as a result's expanded uncertainty, *U* (**Figure 11**).

The expanded uncertainty defines what is known as a "coverage interval" about a measured value. The coverage interval conveys the set of quantity values reasonably attributed to the measurand along with the specific probability that its "true" value actually lies within this range. The probability is referred to as the interval's associated "level of confidence." Coverage intervals having an associated level of confidence between 95% and 99.7% are typically selected (**Figure 12**):

Coverage interval

$$y - U < Y_{99\%} < y + U \quad [6]$$

Coverage Interval versus Confidence Interval

Coverage intervals and confidence intervals are distinct tools and should not be confused. A coverage interval is a metrological concept based on Bayesian analysis. In this framework, parameters of interest can be treated as random variables so that they can be the subject of probabilistic statements without logical inconsistency. The level of confidence associated with a coverage interval refers to the probability, understood as a degree of belief, that a measurand's value lies within the interval.

A confidence interval is a statistical concept based on frequentist methodology. In this framework, the stochastic nature of the investigation lies entirely in the sampling process, not the parameter value. Accordingly, the level of confidence associated with a confidence interval does not associate a probability with the measurand value. Rather, its object is the interval itself. If one were to conduct multiple sets of measurements and generate a confidence interval for each set, the level of confidence tells you the proportion of these intervals that would be expected to cover/overlap a measurand's value (**Figure 13**).

There are two types of uncertainties: type A and type B. Unlike the two types of errors, type A and type B uncertainties are not distinguished by the nature of their source. Instead, they are defined by the manner in which they are determined. Type A uncertainty refers to the uncertainty that has been determined by statistical (frequentist) methods utilizing observed frequency distributions. Type B uncertainty refers to the uncertainty that has been determined by nonstatistical means relying on knowledge, experience, and judgment to create belief-based a priori distributions.

Type A evaluations are often referred to as "objective" and type B as "subjective." However, this does not mean that type B evaluations are any less real or valid than type A.

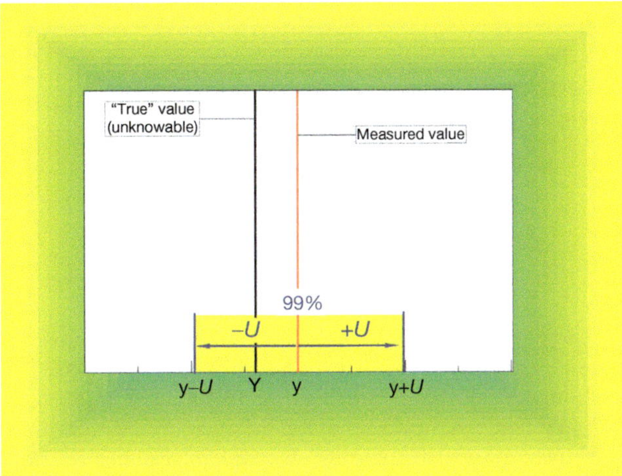

Figure 12 Coverage interval.

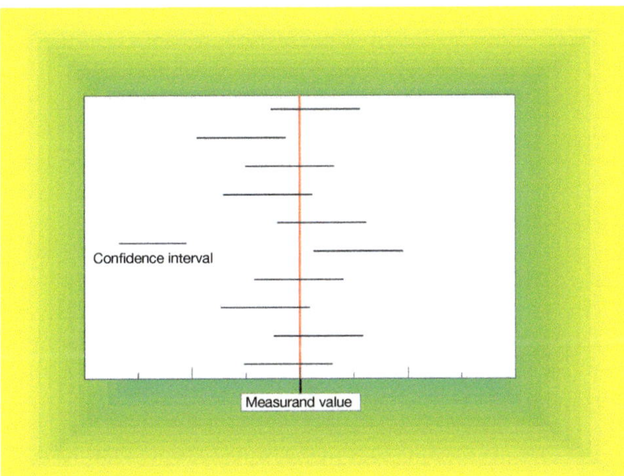

Figure 13 Interpretation of a confidence interval.

Both evaluations rely on accepted notions of probability. Nor is one approach necessarily superior to the other. Whether type A or type B analysis yields better results is context dependent.

Regardless of the approach employed to determine them, a foundational tenant of this paradigm is that the uncertainties themselves do not differ in nature. Once determined, all distributions are interpreted in the Bayesian manner, representing models of our state of knowledge quantified according to degree of belief. This permits type A and type B uncertainties to be treated on equal footing as standard deviations of the distributions they are based on, providing rigorous justification for their combination into a "combined uncertainty" using traditional methods of analysis.

The importance of this lies in the fact that a measurement's uncertainty is usually made up of the combination of uncertainties from several distinct sources. To understand the significance, recall the inability of error analysis to combine systematic and random errors in a rigorously justifiable manner to determine a measurement's total error. To avoid confusion, in the context of uncertainty, systematic errors are referred to as "systematic effects." For pedagogical purposes, systematic effects were not included in the above discussion. Nonetheless, the determination of uncertainty assumes that every measurement has been corrected for significant systematic effects.

What the uncertainty paradigm permits us to do, regardless of the nature of a systematic effect or how it has been quantified, is to treat it as a probability distribution. When this is done, the distribution's expectation yields the required systematic correction (hereinafter referred to as bias) and its standard deviation characterizes the uncertainty associated with the bias. Treated in this manner, systematic effects and their associated uncertainties are placed on equal footing with measured values and their associated uncertainties, so that those phenomena formerly understood as systematic and random errors can now be combined in a logically consistent and rigorously justifiable manner. In general, the evaluation of the uncertainty arising from systematic effects may be either type A or type B.

Returning to the above discussion, it can now be seen that the uncertainty paradigm naturally incorporates systematic effects into the mapping of measured values to those believed to be attributable to a measurand (**Figure 14**).

The correction shifts the position of the probability distribution along the axis of values, while the uncertainty associated with the correction will modify the shape of the distribution.

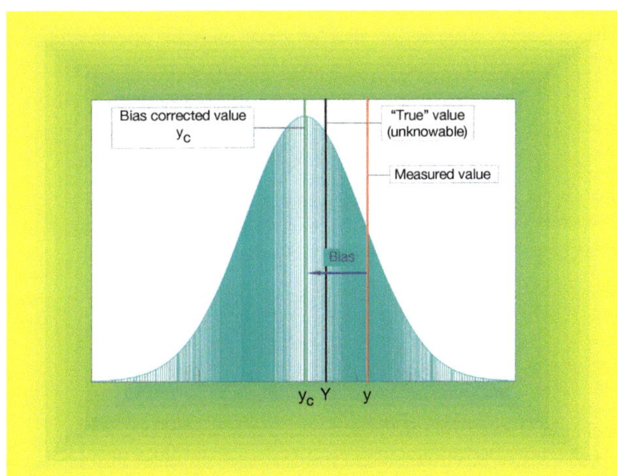

Figure 14 Mapping measurement to "reality."

As would be expected, this will shift the coverage interval in the direction of the correction as well.

Something that must be considered at this point is that given the inherent variability of measured values, it is seldom acceptable to base the determination of a measurand's value on a single measurement. Good practice requires acquisition of multiple measured values combined to determine their mean. The *best estimate* of a measurand's "true" value is then given by the *bias corrected mean* of the measured values:

$$\begin{aligned} \text{Best estimate} &= \text{bias corrected mean} \\ Y_\text{b} &= \bar{y}_\text{c} \end{aligned} \quad [7]$$

It is a fundamental principle of measurement that where the actual value of a measurand is important, as a result is not complete and cannot be properly interpreted unless it has been corrected for bias and is accompanied by a quantitative statement of its uncertainty. Accordingly, a complete measurement result consists of the best estimate of the measurand's "true" value accompanied by its uncertainty:

$$\begin{aligned} \text{Measurement result} &= \text{best estimate} \pm \text{uncertainty} \\ Y_{99\%} &= Y_\text{b} \pm U \end{aligned} \quad [8]$$

$$\begin{aligned} &\text{Coverage interval} \\ &Y_\text{b} - U < Y_{99\%} < Y_\text{b} + U \end{aligned} \quad [9]$$

Measurement Uncertainty: A Forensic Example

The value of a measurand can be critical to the determination of certain criminal matters. For example, some states define the offense of driving under the influence of alcohol (DUI) by an individual's "true" breath alcohol concentration (BrAC). The measurement of BrAC, like any other scientific measurement, is accompanied by uncertainty. Thus, by themselves, the values reported by a breath test machine tell us little about an individual's "true" BrAC and whether they have actually committed a crime. Consider tests administered to two different individuals on different instruments in a state where DUI is defined by a BrAC of 0.08 g/210 l (**Figures 15 and 16**).

Blank test	.000
Internal standard	Verified
Subject sample	.084
Blank test	.000
External standard	.082
Blank test	.000
Subject sample	.081
Blank test	.000

Figure 15 Identical measurement results, different measurement meaning: Breath analysis.

Blank test	.000
Internal standard	Verified
Subject sample	.084
Blank test	.000
External standard	.079
Blank test	.000
Subject sample	.081
Blank test	.000

Figure 16 Breath analysis.

Each test reports identical BrAC values in excess of the state's per se limit with a mean value of 0.0825 g/210 l. Without more, these "breath test tickets" clearly seem to indicate that the BrACs in question exceed the legal limit. Moreover, given that the external standard readings are both reading true, there is actually no way to distinguish between these two tests.

The two tests' uncertainties reveal a different picture though. Despite identically measured values, the uncertainty of each, expressed as coverage intervals, is different (**Figures 17 and 18**).

Clearly, the computed uncertainty associated with test 1 is greater than that associated with test 2. Moreover, further examination reveals that the likelihood that each individual's BrAC is actually less than 0.08 g/210 l is nearly 20% and 10% for tests 1 and 2, respectively (**Figures 19 and 20**).

Thus, not only do these "identical" tests not have identical meanings, but also each represents a sizable likelihood in the context of reasonable doubt that the BrACs in question are less than the relevant limit. Proper interpretation of these results clearly requires knowledge of their uncertainty.

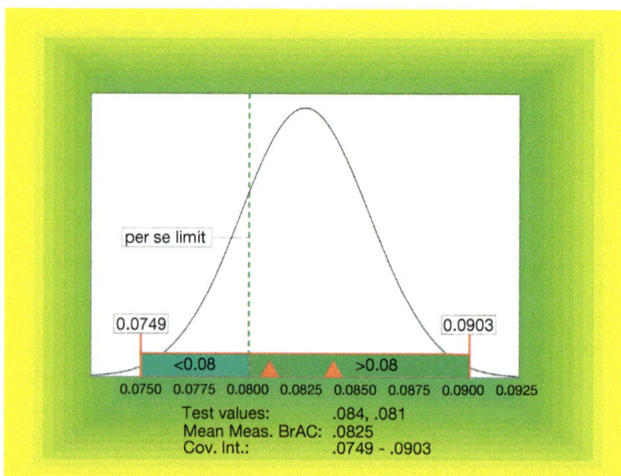

Figure 17 BrAC test 1.

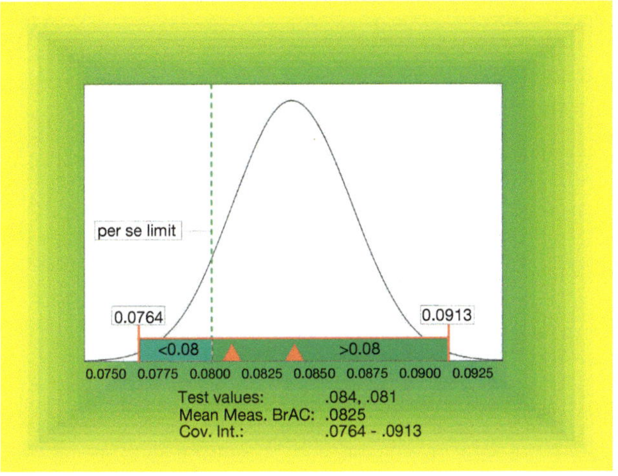

Figure 18 BrAC test 2.

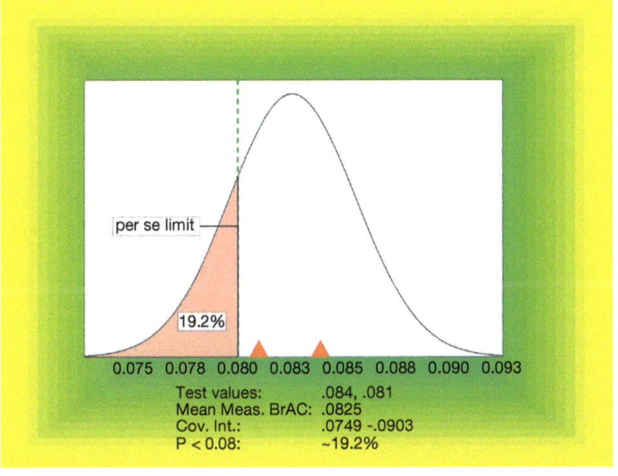

Figure 19 BrAC test 1.

Determining Measurement Uncertainty

There are several different methods for determining a measurement's uncertainty. The first step in each is to identify and quantify all systematic effects and appropriately correct for each.

The second step is typically the identification of relevant sources of uncertainty. A common way to document these is through a cause-and-effect diagram, which depicts each source of uncertainty and their relationship to each other and the final result (**Figure 21**).

When all the quantities on which a measured value depends can be varied simultaneously, a result's uncertainty can be determined, directly using statistical methods. Except for the

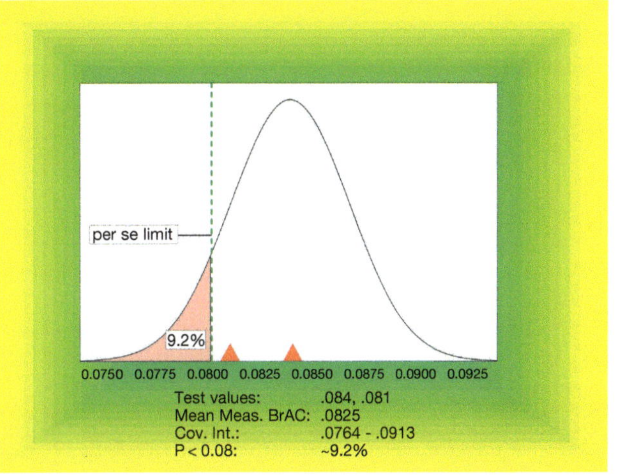

Figure 20 BrAC test 2.

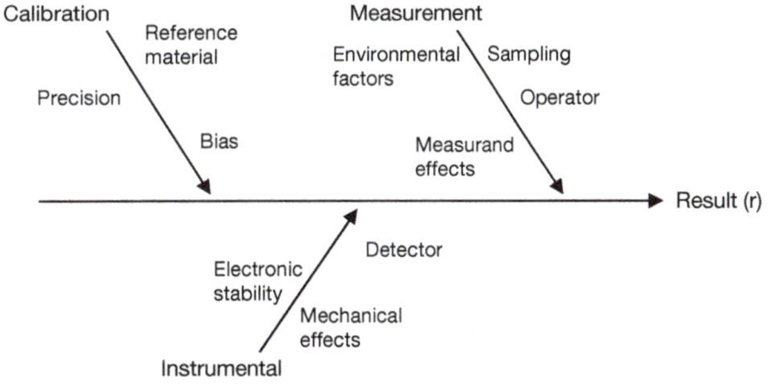

Figure 21 Cause-and-effect diagram.

simple measurements, however, this approach is typically not practical.

Generally, then, the next step is to determine the magnitude of each of the relevant uncertainties. Each is quantified as a standard deviation and referred to as a "standard uncertainty":

$$\text{Standard uncertainty} \quad \mu \equiv \sigma \tag{10}$$

The relative standard uncertainty is the ratio of the standard uncertainty to the best estimate of the measurand value. It can be useful when combining or comparing uncertainties of separate measurements:

$$\text{Relative standard uncertainty} \quad \mu_{r_y} = \frac{\mu_y}{|Y_b|} \tag{11}$$

For some measurements, each source of uncertainty may be associated with the measurement as a whole and manifest itself independently as a direct effect on the final result. Such is the case with direct measurements. In these circumstances, a result's "combined uncertainty," μ_c, is given by the root-sum-square (rss) of the standard uncertainties:

$$\mu_c = \sqrt{\sum_{i=1}^{n} \mu_i^2} \quad [12]$$

Most measurements are indirect in nature, determining a measurand's value through its relationship to other measured quantities. The most common method of determining uncertainty in these circumstances is discussed in the *Guide to the Expression of Uncertainty in Measurement* (the GUM). Application of the GUM requires that a measurement be modeled as a mathematical function, referred to as the measurement function:

$$\text{Measurement function} \quad Y = f(X_1, X_2, \ldots, X_N) \quad [13]$$

This function describes the relationship between the measurand value and those quantities required to determine it. For example, if the measurand is the volume of a cylinder, the measurement function might be given as:

$$V(r,h) = \pi r^2 h \quad [14]$$

The combined uncertainty of the measurand is determined by "adding" up the individual standard uncertainties using the method of "propagation of uncertainty":

$$\mu_c = \sqrt{\sum_{i=1}^{N}\left(\frac{\partial f}{\partial x_i}\cdot \mu_{x_i}\right)^2 + 2\sum_{i=1}^{N-1}\sum_{j=i+1}^{N}\frac{\partial f}{\partial x_i}\cdot\frac{\partial f}{\partial x_i}\cdot \mu_{x_i x_j}} \quad [15]$$

If each of the input quantities is independent, the expression simplifies to:

$$\mu_c = \sqrt{\sum_{i=1}^{N}\left(\frac{\partial f}{\partial x_i}\cdot \mu_{x_i}\right)^2} \quad [16]$$

For the volume of a cylinder, the combined uncertainty would be given by the expression:

$$\mu_{cv} = \sqrt{(2\pi r h \mu_r)^2 + (\pi r^2 \mu_h)^2} \quad [17]$$

Propagation of Uncertainty: Applied to Measurement Functions with Independent Input Quantities

1. Measurement function:

$$Y = a \cdot X \quad [18]$$

$$Y_b = a \cdot x_b \quad [19]$$

$$\mu_y = a \cdot \mu_x \quad [20]$$

2. Measurement function:

$$Y = X^n \quad [21]$$

$$Y_b = x_b^n \quad [22]$$

$$\mu_{r_y} = \frac{\mu_y}{|Y_b|} = \left|n\right| = \frac{\mu_x}{|x_b|} \quad [23]$$

3. Measurement function:

$$Y = X - W + \cdots + Z \quad [24]$$

$$Y_b = x_b - w_b + \cdots + z_b \quad [25]$$

$$\mu_y = \sqrt{\mu_x^2 + \mu_w^2 + \cdots + \mu_z^2} \quad [26]$$

4. Measurement function:

$$Y = \frac{X \times \cdots \times W}{Z \times \cdots \times Q} \quad [27]$$

$$Y_b = \frac{x_b \times \cdots \times w_b}{z_b \times \cdots \times q_b} \quad [28]$$

$$\mu_{r_y} = \frac{\mu_y}{|Y_b|} = \sqrt{\left(\frac{\mu_x}{x_b}\right)^2 + \left(\frac{\mu_w}{w_b}\right)^2 + \cdots + \left(\frac{\mu_z}{z_b}\right)^2 + \left(\frac{\mu_q}{q_b}\right)^2} \quad [29]$$

The expanded uncertainty is obtained by multiplying the combined uncertainty by a coverage factor, *k*:

$$\text{Expanded uncertainty} \quad U = k\mu_c \quad [30]$$

The coverage factor determines the coverage interval's level of confidence. It is commonly based on a *t*-distribution. Where a measurement's degrees of freedom are sufficiently large, the level of confidence bestowed by a given coverage factor is approximately that associated with a Gaussian distribution (**Figure 22**).

The coverage factor is typically chosen to yield a level of confidence of 95% or greater. For the volume of a cylinder, the expanded uncertainty yielding a 99% level of confidence would be given by the expression:

$$U = 2.576\sqrt{(2\pi r h \mu_r)^2 + (\pi r^2 \mu_h)^2} \quad [31]$$

k	:	%
1	:	68.27
1.645	:	90
1.96	:	95
2	:	95.45
2.576	:	99
3	:	99.73

Figure 22 Coverage factors and levels of confidence: Gaussian distribution.

For the GUM to apply, the distribution characterizing a final result must not depart appreciably from normality. Where this is not the case, or where a measurement function is complicated or unknown, a more general approach to the determination of uncertainty is based on the *propagation of distributions*. Instead of determining the standard uncertainty of each input quantity and combining them, the distributions characterizing the quantity value of each input quantity are directly combined to construct the distribution characterizing our state of knowledge of the measurand's value (**Figure 23**).

The standard deviation of the final distribution yields a result's standard uncertainty. It should be noted that the resultant distribution and, hence, its uncertainty (coverage interval) need not be symmetric about the mean. The Monte Carlo method, a computer-based iterative simulation process, is an example of this approach.

A final approach to the determination of uncertainty is the top-down method, so-called because it focuses on the measurement process as a whole instead of its detailed breakdown into distinct sources of uncertainty. It utilizes overall reproducibility estimates, based on measurement trials, as a direct estimate of the uncertainty associated with a measurement method. This approach is often utilized where a measurement function is complicated or unknown. Although each has its advantages, in certain circumstances, the GUM and top-down approaches can be used together to determine the uncertainty of a measurement where desirable.

Meaning Requires Uncertainty

Scientific measurement provides a powerful tool for investigating physical phenomena. No matter how good a measurement is, we can never know the "true" value of the quantity of interest. Error analysis focuses on the measurand itself, with the intent of providing a value that is as close as possible to its "true" value. What it actually provides is an ill-defined upper limit on a measurement's total error, revealing the worst a measured value might be without conveying how good it actually is. Uncertainty analysis focuses on our state of knowledge about a measurand, providing a quantitative mapping of measured values into those values believed to be actually and reasonably attributable to the quantity of interest. This conveys the meaning of a result by rigorously defining and constraining the inferences that can be drawn from it. Accordingly, where the actual value of a measurand is important, a result is not complete and cannot be properly interpreted unless it is accompanied by a quantitative statement of its uncertainty.

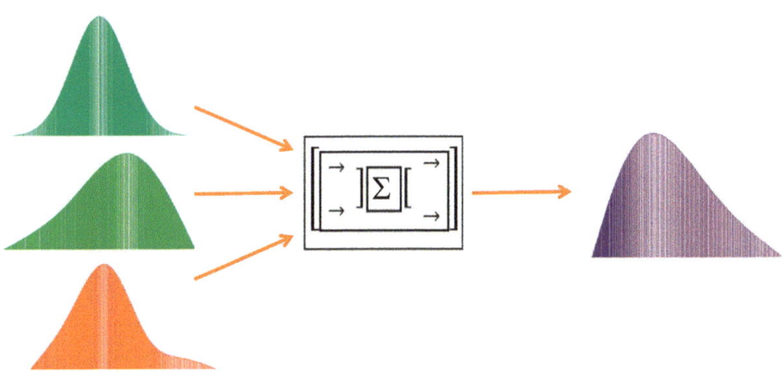

Figure 23 Propagation of distributions.

See also: **Foundations:** Statistical Interpretation of Evidence: Bayesian Analysis; The Frequentist Approach to Forensic Evidence Interpretation; **Legal:** Legal Aspects of Forensic Science; **Methods:** Chemometrics; **Toxicology:** Interpretation of Results; **Toxicology/Alcohol:** Breath Alcohol.

Further Reading

Ehrlich, C., Dybkaer, R., Wöger, W., 2007. Evolution of philosophy and description of measurement. Accreditation and Quality Assurance 12, 201–218.

Estler, W.T., 1999. Measurement as inference: fundamental ideas. CIRP Annals 48 (2), 611–631.

EURACHEM, 2000. Quantifying Uncertainty in Analytical Measurement (2000) QUAM:2000.1. EURACHEM. www.eurachem.org.

EURACHEM, 2007. Measurement Uncertainty Arising from Sampling: A Guide to Methods and Approaches. EURACHEM. www.eurachem.org.

ISO, 2004. Guidance for the Use of Repeatability, Reproducibility and Trueness Estimates in Measurement Uncertainty Estimation ISO/TS 21748. ISO, Geneva.

JCGM, 2008. Evaluation of Measurement Data – Guide to the Expression of Uncertainty in Measurement (GUM) JCGM 100:2008. ISO, Geneva.

JCGM, 2008. Evaluation of Measurement Data – Supplement 1 to the 'Guide to the Expression of Uncertainty in Measurement' – Propagation of Distributions Using a Monte Carlo Method JCGM 101:2008. ISO, Geneva.

JCGM, 2008. International Vocabulary of Metrology – Basic and General Concepts and Associated Terms (VIM) JCGM 200:2008. ISO, Geneva.

JCGM, 2009. Evaluation of Measurement Data – An Introduction to the 'Guide to the Expression of Uncertainty in Measurement' and Related Documents JCGM 104:2009. ISO, Geneva.

Kacker, R., Sommer, K., Kessel, R., 2007. Evolution of modern approaches to express uncertainty in measurement. Metrologia 44, 513–529.

Kirkup, L., Frenkel, B., 2006. An Introduction to Uncertainty in Measurement: Using the GUM (Guide to the Expression of Uncertainty in Measurement). Cambridge University Press, New York.

NIST, 1994. Guidelines for Evaluating and Expressing the Uncertainty of NIST Measurement Results NIST 1297. National Institute of Standards and Technology, Gaithersburg, MD.

Vosk, T., 2010. Trial by numbers: uncertainty in the quest for truth and justice. NACDL Champion 56, 48–56 (reprinted with permission in The Voice for the Defense 40(3), 24–33 (2011)).

The Innocence Project

KA Findley, University of Wisconsin Law School, Madison, WI, USA

Overview of the Innocence Project and Innocence Network

The Innocence Project is a pro bono legal services organization affiliated with the Cardozo Law School at Yeshiva University in New York City, devoted to utilizing postconviction DNA testing to exonerate wrongly convicted innocent individuals and to reforming the criminal justice system to minimize the risks of wrongful convictions. The Innocence Project is actually just one—one of the first and the most prominent—of a growing network of independent innocence projects dedicated to exonerating wrongly convicted individuals with compelling new evidence of their innocence. Under a licensing agreement with the Innocence Project, many of those projects bear variations of the name "Innocence Project," such as the Innocence Project Northwest (in Seattle, WA), the Wisconsin Innocence Project, and the Innocence Project New Orleans (to mention just a few). Others operate under other names such as the Center on Wrongful Convictions (in Chicago), the Michigan Innocence Clinic, and the North Carolina Center on Actual Innocence.

Although all operate independently, these projects have formed an affiliation organization known as the Innocence Network. As of June 2011, the Innocence Network counted 66 projects in its membership, 55 in the United States and 11 more in Canada, Great Britain, Ireland, Australia, New Zealand, and the Netherlands, with new organizations being formed in other regions of the world as well.

Some of these projects follow the model of the flagship Innocence Project in New York and handle only cases in which DNA evidence is available to prove innocence. A larger number of projects now accept cases in which other types of evidence, in addition to DNA, can also be found or developed to prove innocence. Recently, a few projects have formed that handle only the latter types of cases—non-DNA-based claims of evidence.

Because the various innocence organizations are independent and are created in various locations under various circumstances, they do not follow any one set or prescribed organizational structure. Many projects are affiliated with law schools and operate as clinical programs in which law students work on cases under clinical faculty (attorney) supervision, investigating and litigating the claims of innocence. Others operate as independent nonprofit organizations that provide internships for law students from a number of separate law schools within a geographical area. Still others have no real law-school affiliation and instead operate either as stand-alone nonprofit legal organizations or as collectives of pro bono private attorneys. As a requirement for membership in the Innocence Network, however, all must have dedicated staff and must agree never to charge clients for their services.

Not all innocence organizations provide direct legal representation to prisoners who claim to be innocent. Some are instead investigation projects that do not themselves provide legal representation to prisoners, such as undergraduate criminal justice programs or investigative journalism projects. When such projects develop compelling new evidence of innocence, they typically refer the cases to pro bono attorney organizations or otherwise arrange legal representation for the wrongly convicted individuals. Still another new type of project provides support services to exonerees after their release from prison.

History

Beginnings of a New Movement

The Innocence Project formally opened its doors in New York in 1992. The Innocence Project, however, was not the first such organization devoted to proving the innocence of imprisoned individuals. Centurion Ministries in Princeton, New Jersey, had been doing that work for approximately 10 years, beginning in the early 1980s, and might be the first of such organizations. Centurion Ministries was created by James McCloskey, a former business executive who turned to the ministry, as an outgrowth of his chaplaincy work. Centurion Ministries, which remains active today, is not a traditional legal services organization. It has no legal staff but instead focuses on in-depth factual investigations to find the evidence that can prove innocence. Once sufficient evidence of innocence has been found, Centurion Ministries hires or otherwise arranges legal counsel to litigate the claims of innocence.

The emergence of the Innocence Project, however, marked a dramatic new awakening in the criminal justice system to the reality and magnitude of the problem of wrongful convictions. The Innocence Project launched this new era—variously described as "the innocence movement," the "innocence revolution," and the "age of innocence"—primarily through the power of DNA evidence. The DNA exonerations, for the first time in the history of the criminal justice system, began to generate a surprisingly large and growing pool of cases in which we knew with near certainty, based upon scientific analysis, that the criminal justice system had erred. The DNA exonerations put to rest the myth that the wrongful conviction of an innocent person was an "unreal dream." At the same time that the DNA cases proved beyond dispute the reality of error, it attached real human names and faces to the problem of wrongful convictions; it generated stories of real people whose lives had been destroyed by misfiring of the criminal process, stories that powerfully moved the public, the courts, and policy makers alike.

Barry Scheck and Peter Neufeld, two New York lawyers, led the way in utilizing DNA to exonerate the innocent in the early days of forensic DNA analysis. Drawing on their experiences in high-profile cases in which prosecutors had begun to use DNA, Scheck and Neufeld realized the potential for DNA to prove innocence as well. The two created the Innocence Project in 1992, at a time when there had only been five DNA exonerations of wrongly convicted individuals in the United States (or anywhere else, for that matter). A year later, in 1993, a group of volunteers formed the Association in Defense of the Wrongly Convicted, launching the innocence movement in Canada. Nineteen years after creation of the Innocence Project, as of June 2012, the number of known DNA exonerations in the United States had grown to 292, largely, although not entirely, as a result of the work of innocence organizations across the country. At least 135 additional individuals had been exonerated by innocence projects using evidence other than DNA, and an untold number of individuals had been exonerated by non-DNA evidence by attorneys outside the Innocence Network.

New Projects and Emergence of the Innocence Network

In the following years, several additional innocence organizations formed, starting in Washington, Illinois, Wisconsin, and California. In 2000, Scheck and Neufeld, joined by *New York Times* writer Jim Dwyer, published their influential book *Actual Innocence* that told the story of many of the first DNA exonerations, and, for the first time, in a comprehensive way, sought to analyze the sources of error in these DNA-proven wrongful convictions. The book identified eyewitness identification error as the most frequent contributor to false convictions, joined by false confessions, flawed forensic science evidence, perjured jailhouse informants or "snitch" testimony, prosecutorial and police misconduct, and inadequate defense counsel. In addition, Scheck, Neufeld, and Dwyer charted a course for the future of the innocence movement, setting a goal of establishing innocence projects across the country "that will represent clients in DNA and non-DNA cases," and of creating an Innocence Network.

In 2003, leaders from a number of the nation's emerging innocence organizations formed a steering committee to work on creating the Innocence Network envisioned by Scheck, Neufeld, and Dwyer. In 2005, the Innocence Network was formally organized, with a board of directors elected by the membership. As of 2011, 66 innocence organizations had joined the network, most in the United States, but 11 scattered among Canada, the United Kingdom, Ireland, Australia, New Zealand, and the Netherlands. In the United Kingdom, the Innocence Network UK, which as an entity is a member of the Innocence Network, is itself an umbrella organization for over 20 member projects in universities. In the spring of 2011, the Innocence Network hosted its first international innocence conference, which drew participants from virtually all regions of the world and foretold likely further expansion beyond these English-speaking common-law countries.

The Educational Mission

Place in Clinical Legal Education

Many, although not all, innocence organizations in the United States operate as law-school-based clinical educational programs. Beginning in the 1960s, clinical programs have become an increasingly important part of legal education in the United States. Through clinical programs, law students learn to become lawyers in part by representing real clients in real cases, under the supervision and instruction of licensed clinical faculty.

Legal educators soon learned that innocence cases offer uniquely rich and challenging contexts for pedagogy. Even more so than many other clinical programs, innocence organizations involve students in extensive fact investigation. They offer a learning model that is quite different from the traditional law-school focus on appellate opinions, in which the facts are presented as a given or even insignificant. At the same time, innocence cases provide a valuable opportunity to examine the criminal justice system from the back end, by deconstructing cases that have already been tried and appealed, and in which the system failed. Moreover, the size, complexity, and unpredictability of innocence cases pose challenges to clinical teaching methodology, while at the same time they offer opportunities for students to learn about complex criminal litigation. In this way, innocence cases share certain characteristics with civil rights and other large-scale litigation projects that are sometimes undertaken in law-school clinical settings.

Undergraduate Education

The formal education mission extends beyond law schools. One of the earliest innocence organizations, the Medill School of Journalism Innocence Project at Northwestern University in Evanston, Illinois, is an undergraduate journalism program in investigative journalism, as are more recently created projects such as the Justice Brandeis Innocence Project at the Schuster Institute for Investigative Journalism at Brandeis University, and the Innocence Institute of Point Park University in Pittsburgh. Still other projects, such as the Northern Arizona Justice Project and the Downstate Illinois Innocence Project, provide educational opportunities for students in other educational programs, such as criminal justice or legal and policy studies.

The Policy Mission

Lessons from the Innocence Cases

A central goal of the innocence movement has been to draw lessons from the wrongful convictions that can lead to reforms to minimize the risk of false convictions. Examining the DNA exonerations in particular has revealed several recurring causes of factual error in criminal cases.

Among the recurring contributors to wrongful convictions, eyewitness error is by far the most prevalent, occurring in 76% of the first 250 DNA exoneration cases. Eyewitness error typically does not involve untruthful witnesses, but rather well-meaning, honest witnesses who are simply mistaken about their memory of the perpetrator or the crime. Considerable psychological research has demonstrated the fallibility of eyewitnesses and identified factors that can contribute to eyewitness error. Eyewitness memory is susceptible to contamination and distortion by suggestive police identification procedures or postincident information and may be impaired initially by the conditions under which the crime occurred.

False confessions are also prominent among the causes of wrongful convictions, present in 16% of the first 250 DNA exonerations. Although it is counterintuitive to imagine that an innocent person would confess to a crime he or she did not commit, the DNA exonerations demonstrate the reality of false confessions. High-pressure, confrontational police interrogation tactics, such as those included in the Reid technique of interrogation (which is taught in some form in most police jurisdictions in the United States), which are believed to be effective at eliciting confessions from the guilty, also can induce innocent people to confess. Social science research suggests that, under such interrogation tactics, false confessions can be the product of rational choices.

Jailhouse informer or "snitch" evidence, present in 21% of the first 250 DNA exonerations, typically involves testimony offered by individuals who are themselves in trouble with the law and claim that the defendant confessed or made incriminating statements to them. Courts have long recognized that such witnesses are very unreliable, both because their criminal background suggests that they might have little regard for the truth and more importantly because they have an incentive to fabricate in the hope of obtaining benefits from the state in return.

Numerous wrongful convictions have also rested in part upon fraudulent or mistaken forensic science. Forensic evidence was offered in more than 70% of the first 250 cases in which DNA later exonerated the defendant. According to Brandon Garrett, in those cases with forensic testimony, 61% of the cases involved improper or scientifically unsupported testimony.

Police and prosecutorial misconduct involves overreaching in a variety of contexts. The most common type of prosecutorial misconduct involves failure to comply with the constitutional mandate that prosecutors must disclose to the defense all material exculpatory evidence in their possession. In part, a prosecutor's failure to comply with this mandate reflects the very difficult demands that the adversary system imposes on prosecutors. For a prosecutor whose responsibility to convict the accused naturally encourages him or her to view the evidence in an inculpatory light, it expects a great deal to require that same prosecutor to simultaneously view the evidence from the defendant's perspective and to recognize its exculpatory value.

Finally, inadequate defense counsel is a frequent cause of wrongful convictions. Indigent legal services are chronically underfunded, and the result frequently is inadequate defense investigation and a lackluster challenge to the state's case at trial. When the defense is inadequate, the adversarial system fails to function as designed to weed out erroneous charges or to protect the innocent.

Preventing and Remedying Wrongful Convictions

Increasing awareness in the criminal justice system of the problem of wrongful convictions has also led to a heightened interest in reforms to reduce the rate of such errors. Policy makers have become interested in reforms to prevent wrongful convictions, not just because each such case is an injustice to the wrongly convicted but also because they recognize that every time an innocent person is wrongly convicted, the true perpetrator eludes prosecution. A variety of official commissions and policy-making bodies, sometimes dubbed "innocence commissions," have been created in a number of jurisdictions to examine the wrongful conviction cases and develop recommendations for reforms to minimize such errors.

Minimizing eyewitness error

To date, most progress in implementing reforms designed to minimize wrongful convictions has been made in the areas of eyewitness error and false confessions. In particular, extensive psychological research has produced a well-developed series of recommendations for improving eyewitness identification procedures. A number of law enforcement agencies throughout the country are now implementing some or all of these recommendations. Some of these reforms are being adopted voluntarily by law enforcement; in other instances, the reforms are mandated by new statutes or court rulings.

Some of the more significant eyewitness identification reforms include ensuring that witnesses are properly instructed that the perpetrator might not be present in any given lineup or photo array, so that the witness does not feel compelled to pick someone in every case; properly selecting lineup or photo array "fillers" (nonsuspects) so that the suspect does not stand out; presenting no more than one suspect in any given lineup or photo array; conducting the identification procedure in a "double blind" manner—meaning that neither the witness nor the detective administering the procedure knows which individual is the suspect—so that the detective cannot even inadvertently cue the witness as to whom to pick; and presenting photographs or lineup members sequentially, rather than simultaneously, so that the witness must rely on absolute judgments drawn from memory, rather than relative judgments based on comparing one lineup member or photograph to the others.

Guarding against false confessions

The most significant reform designed to prevent false confessions is a requirement that all custodial interrogations be electronically recorded from start to finish. Recording serves several purposes. It deters police from engaging in improper coercive tactics or feeding crime-related information that can produce false confessions. It also creates a clear record of what was said and done, so that lawyers, judges, and juries can more fully and accurately consider the reliability of any statements elicited during an interrogation, and indeed help fact finders accurately determine what the suspect said, in their own words, without interpretation or paraphrasing by police witnesses. Electronic recording also protects police from spurious claims of misconduct in the interrogation room and produces powerful evidence to help convict the guilty when a suspect freely and convincingly confesses or incriminates himself in a recording that can be played for the jury.

Model statutes

On a variety of topics, the Innocence Project has also produced model statutes, and has worked with legislatures around the country to encourage their adoption. Model statutes address such matters as:

- Requiring states to preserve biological evidence after conviction
- Creating a right to postconviction DNA testing in cases in which test results favorable to the defendant might provide a basis for overturning the conviction
- Improving eyewitness identification procedures
- Mandating electronic recording of custodial interrogations of suspects
- Providing or improving compensation packages available to exonerees
- Creating forensic oversight commissions.

Federal legislation

At the federal level, the Innocence Project actively worked to pass the Justice for All Act of 2004, which President George W. Bush signed into law on October 30, 2004. That Act includes the Innocence Protection Act, which, among other things, grants federal inmates the right to petition a federal court for DNA testing to support a claim of innocence and encourages states—through the power of the purse—to adopt measures to preserve evidence and make postconviction DNA testing available to inmates seeking to prove their innocence. The Justice for All Act also includes provisions that assist death-penalty states with efforts to create effective systems for the appointment and performance of qualified counsel, together with better training and monitoring for both the defense and prosecution. It provides substantial funding to states for increased reliance on DNA testing in new criminal investigations, increases the amount of compensation available to wrongfully convicted federal prisoners, and expresses the idea of Congress that all wrongfully convicted persons should be reasonably compensated.

In 2009, the National Academy of Sciences (NAS), the preeminent scientific authority in the United States, issued a groundbreaking report on the status of forensic sciences in the United States. The NAS concluded that the forensic science system in the United States was in disarray—fragmented, inadequately regulated, and poorly grounded in science. Central to its call for reform was its recommendation that the federal government create a National Institute of Forensic Sciences to encourage research, provide oversight, and establish standards for forensic science evidence in the United States. The Innocence Project has since then been actively involved in efforts to implement this and the other recommendations of the NAS.

Amicus briefs

Finally, the Innocence Network and its member projects have become active, through the Network's Committee on Amici and Policies, in producing amicus briefs in state and federal litigation on issues related to wrongful convictions. Numerous Innocence Network and individual project briefs have been filed in the United States Supreme Court, many federal circuit courts of appeals, and various state supreme courts, and intermediate appellate courts. Innocence Network briefs are frequently cited in decisions by these courts and have been influential in numerous court decisions.

See also: **Biology/DNA:** Basic Principles; Forensic Genetics: History; **Legal:** DNA Exonerations; History of the Law's Reception of Forensic Science; Legal Aspects of Forensic Science; **Professional:** National Academy of Sciences (NAS).

Further Reading

Committee on Identifying the Needs of the Forensic Sciences Community, 2009. Strengthening Forensic Science in the United States: A Path Forward. National Academy of Science, Washington, DC.

Doyle, J.M., 2010. Learning from error in American criminal justice. The Journal of Criminal Law and Criminology 100, 109–147.

Findley, K.A., 2006. The pedagogy of innocence: reflections on the role of innocence projects in clinical legal education. Clinical Law Review 13, 231–278.

Findley, K.A., 2008. Toward a new paradigm of criminal justice: how the innocence movement merges crime control and due process. Texas Tech Law Review 41, 133.

Garrett, B.L., 2008. Judging innocence. Columbia Law Review 108, 55–142.

Garrett, B.L., 2011. Convicting the Innocent: Where Criminal Prosecutions Go Wrong. Harvard University Press, Cambridge, MA.

Gould, J.B., 2009. The Innocence Commission: Preventing Wrongful Convictions and Restoring the Criminal Justice System. New York University Press, New York.

Gross, S.R., et al., 2005. Exonerations in the United States, 1989 through 2003. The Journal of Criminal Law and Criminology 95, 523–560.

Medwed, D.S., 2003. Actual innocents: considerations in selecting cases for a new innocence project. Nebraska Law Review 81, 1097–1151.

Scheck, B.C., Neufeld, P.J., Dwyer, J., 2000. Actual Innocence: Five Days to Execution and Other Dispatches from the Wrongly Convicted. Doubleday, New York.

Siegel, A.M., 2005. Moving down the wedge of injustice: a proposal for a third generation of wrongful convictions scholarship and advocacy. American Criminal Law Review 42, 1219.

Stiglitz, J., Brooks, J., Shulman, T., 2002. The Hurricane meets the paper chase: innocence projects new emerging role in clinical legal education. California Western Law Review 38, 413–431.

Suni, E.Y., 2002. Ethical issues for innocence projects: an initial primer. University of Missouri-Kansas City Law Review 70, 921–969.

Zalman, M., 2011. An integrated justice model of wrongful convictions. Albany Law Review 74, 1465–1524.

Relevant Websites

http://www.innocencenetwork.org—Innocence Network.
http://www.innocenceproject.org—Innocence Project.

DNA Exonerations

KA Findley, University of Wisconsin Law School, Madison, WI, USA

Glossary

ABO blood typing A commonly used genetic typing test that uses antibodies to detect variations on the surface of human blood cells. Individuals are typed as having A, B, O, or AB blood types.

CODIS Combined DNA Index System, established by the FBI, composed of a collection of databases of DNA profiles obtained from evidence samples from unsolved crimes and known convicted offenders.

Mitochondrial DNA The DNA found in the many mitochondria found in each cell of a body. Mitochondrial DNA (mtDNA) can be used to obtain profiles from cells that have no nucleus, such as cells in hair shafts, or in degraded samples. The sequencing of mtDNA can link individuals descended from a common female ancestor.

Polymerase chain reaction (PCR) A process used in DNA identification testing in which one or more specific small regions of the DNA are copied using a DNA polymerase enzyme so that a sufficient amount of DNA is generated to permit analysis.

Restriction fragment length polymorphism (RFLP) A process used primarily in the late 1980s and early 1990s for DNA identification testing involving measuring size (fragment length) differences at specific regions of the DNA.

Short tandem repeats (STRs) Small regions of DNA that contain short segments of repeating patterns of base pairs. Thirteen STR sequences have been selected for the Combined DNA Index System (CODIS).

Discovery of Wrongful Convictions through DNA Testing

Until the early 1990s, the common wisdom in the United States was that the criminal justice system rarely, if ever, wrongly convicted innocent people. That sentiment was expressed perhaps most famously by Judge Learned Hand, who wrote in 1923 that "[o]ur procedure has been always haunted by the ghost of the innocent man convicted. It is an unreal dream." A few years later, a prosecutor in Worcester County, Massachusetts, declared, "Innocent men are never convicted. Don't worry about it. It is a physical impossibility." More recently, former U.S. Attorney General Edwin Meese quipped, "But the thing is, you don't have many suspects who are innocent of a crime. That's contradictory. If a person is innocent of crime, then he is not a suspect."

DNA has changed that perception and, in the process, has reshaped the debate about criminal justice in America. As of July 2012, 292 people had been proven innocent of serious crimes—mostly rapes and murders—by DNA testing conducted years, and sometimes decades, after they were wrongly convicted and sentenced to prison or even to death. The DNA exonerations, by creating an awareness of the fallibility of the system, have also led to hundreds of other successful efforts to exonerate individuals even where there is no DNA evidence.

Moreover, by demonstrating the reality of error in the criminal justice system with scientific certainty, the DNA exonerations created a learning opportunity—an opportunity to study the wrongful convictions and identify sources of error that can be avoided in the future. As a consequence, the DNA exonerations have led to a host of reforms intended to improve the reliability of the criminal justice system in its core function, sorting the guilty from the innocent. Those reform proposals, some of which have been adopted in various jurisdictions, typically focus on eyewitness identification procedures, electronic recording of interrogations to reduce false confessions, improved reliability and oversight of the forensic sciences, limitations on unreliable jailhouse informant testimony, and improved indigent defense services, among others.

Emergence of DNA as a Forensic Tool

In 1984, geneticist Sir Alec Jeffreys, working in his laboratory in Leicester, England, developed the first forensic DNA profiling technology, utilizing multilocus probes and a method known

 http://dx.doi.org/10.1016/B978-0-12-800647-4.00036-9

as restriction fragment length polymorphism (RFLP) analysis. Jeffreys dubbed this new forensic DNA technique "DNA fingerprinting." The age of forensic DNA technology was born.

The First Exoneration: The Pitchfork Case

The first forensic application of Jeffreys's new DNA technology simultaneously produced a conviction and an exoneration. In November 1983, the body of a raped and strangled 15-year-old girl was found lying near a footpath in the village of Narborough, England, not far from Leicester. At the time of the Narborough crime, the forensic science in such cases was standard ABO blood group analysis, or serology testing. Serology testing determined that semen recovered from the girl's body was from a type A secretor with enzyme marker PGM1+. That serology profile limited the possible sources to 10% of the adult male population. But that was all police had; they had no suspects and no leads.

Three years later, in 1986, the body of another 15-year-old girl—who had also been raped and strangled—was found in the adjoining village of Enderby, within a mile of the first rape site. As in the first case, serology analysis determined that the perpetrator was a type A, PGM1 + secretor.

This time, though, police had a suspect, a 17-year-old kitchen porter at a nearby mental hospital. The boy, who was known to be mentally slow, confessed to the second murder, but refused to confess to the first. But there was a problem: the boy was not a PGM1 + secretor. Despite the serology exclusion, the boy remained the prime suspect; the serology evidence alone was not enough to overcome the power of the confession.

Without a confession in the first case, but suspecting the boy of both crimes, police called in Dr. Jeffreys to analyze the old semen sample from the first rape/murder to see if it matched the DNA from a blood sample from the accused boy. Using a single-locus probe, Jeffreys excluded the suspect. Police then sent Jeffreys the semen sample from second murder. Again, the DNA excluded the suspect. Moreover, the DNA from the second case matched the sample from the first case. The two crimes had an apparent common perpetrator, but it was not the accused boy. Finally, police accepted the boy's innocence and released him. The world had its first DNA exoneration.

Police then sought to use the new DNA technology aggressively to solve the crime. They asked all male residents of Narborough and Enderby between the ages of 17 and 34 to supply blood and saliva samples voluntarily for analysis. Police collected nearly 5000 samples. Five hundred of those men could not be eliminated by conventional serology testing, so their samples were subjected to DNA analysis. Initially, no one matched. But police soon learned that a baker named Colin Pitchfork had convinced a fellow employee to provide blood and saliva samples in place of his own. When confronted with evidence of this deception, Pitchfork confessed and pled guilty and, subsequently, received concurrent life sentences for the two crimes. The DNA had both exonerated the wrongly accused and convicted the guilty.

The Growth of DNA Exonerations

In the late 1980s, prosecutors began to use the new technology extensively to match crime scene evidence to suspects. Soon, the defense began to realize the potential for DNA evidence to prove innocence as well.

Discovering innocents in prison

In 1989, in Illinois, Gary Dotson became the first person exonerated by DNA evidence after being wrongly convicted. Twelve years earlier, in 1977, a young woman claimed that two men had abducted her as she walked home from work, forced her into the back seat of a car, and raped her. In 1979, Dotson was convicted of aggravated kidnapping and rape of the woman and sentenced to 25–50 years in prison. The evidence against him included the victim's eyewitness identification; serology testing that revealed that swabs with semen from the rape kit included both blood groups type A and type B and that both the victim and Dotson were type B, thereby purportedly including Dotson (although it should have meant that Dotson was excluded as the source of the semen, since neither he nor the victim could have contributed the type A secretions); and forensic testimony that a pubic hair recovered from the victim's underwear was dissimilar to the victim's hair but similar to Dotson's.

In 1985, 6 years after Dotson's conviction, the victim confessed that she had fabricated the rape to hide a consensual sexual encounter with her boyfriend. The Illinois courts and governor rebuffed the victim's recantation and refused to vacate the conviction (although the governor commuted the sentence). In 1987, Dotson's lawyers asked Dr. Jeffreys for RFLP analysis, but the samples were too badly degraded to produce conclusive results. Dotson's lawyers then sent the samples to Dr. Edward Blake at Forensic Science Associates in Richmond, California, to apply another more sensitive but less discriminating technology—polymerase chain reaction (PCR) DQ Alpha testing. Those tests revealed that the sperm on the victim's underwear could not have come from Dotson but could have come from the victim's boyfriend. Dotson's conviction was overturned, and the charges were dismissed.

A second DNA exoneration followed in late 1989. Another followed a year later in 1990, and then two more in 1991. More exonerations followed swiftly thereafter, and in increasing numbers in ensuing years.

New technologies

New technologies that made testing increasingly feasible soon emerged, even with minute or degraded samples. PCR, a process roughly analogous to DNA Xeroxing, combined with short tandem repeat (STR) analysis, replaced RFLP as the dominant technology and enhanced both the sensitivity and discriminating power of DNA analysis. PCR/STR testing, for example, permitted analysts to obtain DNA profiles from some objects that a perpetrator merely touched (often referred to as "touch DNA" or "contact DNA"). At the same time, mitochondrial DNA testing (mtDNA) permitted analysis of DNA from nonnucleated cells, such as those in the shafts of hairs, and from degraded samples. Y-STR testing permitted profiling only the DNA from the male portions of a mixture, an important step in identifying small amounts of male DNA that might otherwise be masked or overwhelmed by female DNA in a vaginal swab. Other emerging technologies continue to expand the power of DNA testing.

Databasing

Development of the FBI database of DNA profiles also enhanced the ability of the criminal justice system both to identify the guilty and exonerate the innocent. The FBI database, the Combined DNA Index System (CODIS), is a collection of databases of DNA profiles obtained from evidence samples from unsolved crimes and from offenders convicted of particular crimes. CODIS has been critical in exonerating innocent people from cases where an exclusion from the crime scene evidence might not alone be enough to prove innocence.

Chaunte Ott, for example, convicted of a brutal murder of a young woman in Milwaukee, Wisconsin, would not have been exonerated but for a match in the database. Ott was convicted of murder but not sexual assault. So when DNA from the victim's vaginal swabs produced a male profile that did not match Ott, it was not enough to exonerate him; the state contended that the semen was unrelated to the crime and must have come from a prior consensual encounter. But years later, when the profile from that rape kit produced CODIS matches to DNA from the rape kits from two other women who had also been murdered in the same part of Milwaukee and in the same time period, it became apparent that the DNA was not irrelevant to the crime. That conclusion was confirmed when subsequent CODIS matches linked the DNA to a total of nine women who had been raped and murdered by a man named Walter Ellis, who became known as Milwaukee's infamous North Side Strangler. With this link to a serial killer, Ott was exonerated, freed, and compensated for his years of wrongful imprisonment.

Impact on the system

By 1996, the exonerations began to have an impact on the law enforcement and judicial communities. In that year, the United States Department of Justice, through the National Institute of Justice (NIJ) and at the direction of then Attorney General Janet Reno, published a research report examining the first 28 DNA exonerations of wrongly convicted individuals. Reflecting the reality that rape tends to produce significant biological evidence from the attacker, all 28 of these first cases involved sexual assault; in six of the cases, the victim was also murdered. The 28 defendants had served a total of 197 years in prison, an average of almost 7 years each, before being exonerated by DNA.

In response to the NIJ report, Attorney General Reno asked the NIJ to establish a National Commission on the Future of DNA Evidence to identify ways to maximize the value of DNA in the criminal justice system. In September 1999, the Commission published a report entitled *Postconviction DNA Testing: Recommendations for Handling Requests*. In that report, the Commission encouraged prosecutors and defense attorneys to cooperate on arranging postconviction DNA testing in cases where it might exonerate the defendant.

Preservation of and Access to DNA Evidence

The success of DNA as a tool to exonerate the wrongly convicted highlighted a problem with the existing system for evaluating such evidence; no rules in most states required the government to preserve biological evidence after conviction so that it would be available for future testing, and most states provided no right or mechanism for accessing such evidence for postconviction DNA testing. Beginning first in Illinois and New York, states began passing legislation providing a right to postconviction DNA testing when it might prove innocence. Other states and the federal government soon followed. Many also required preservation of biological evidence after conviction. Today, most states and the federal government require preservation, and 49 states, the federal government, and the District of Columbia provide a statutory right of access to evidence for postconviction DNA testing when it might prove innocence, although some are limited to certain offenses or time periods; only Oklahoma has yet to adopt any postconviction testing statute.

In those jurisdictions where there was no postconviction DNA testing statute, or where the statutes were for any reason inadequate, imprisoned individuals turned to another source for a right to the testing: the courts and the Due Process Clause of the Constitution. Under federal civil rights law (42 U.S.C. sec 1983), prisoners sued the states claiming that denying them access to the DNA evidence violated their due process rights. A number of courts granted relief in such cases, and some produced exonerations.

In 2009, however, in *District Attorney's Office for the Third Judicial District v. Osborne*, 129 S.Ct. 2308 (2009), the court found no due process right to testing where state law already provided an adequate opportunity to secure the test. *Osborne* recognized that state law can indeed create a due process liberty interest in accessing DNA evidence that can prove innocence. A question that remains open is how the court will assess claims that a state law does not adequately protect the opportunity for testing.

DNA Exonerations Today

The Exonerations

As of July 2012, the total number of known DNA exonerations of wrongly convicted individuals had risen to 292. As the number of innocence projects in the United States grew each year, the technology advanced and awareness of the problem of wrongful convictions increased; the number of exonerations grew steadily after 1992, peaking at 25 exonerations in 2002. Despite predictions that the rate of postconviction DNA exonerations would begin to dwindle as DNA testing was completed on most old cases, the number of exonerations each year has remained fairly constant since then, ranging between 13 (in 2004) and 23 (in 2009). The number of DNA exonerations per year is set forth in **Table 1**.

Analyzing the first 250 of these DNA exonerations, Professor Brandon Garrett found that these innocent men and women spent an average of 13 years in prison. Seventeen had been sentenced to death, and 80 were sentenced to life in prison. Approximately 98% of the 250 innocent people had been convicted of rape or rape and murder. The overrepresentation of rapes and murders among these cases could reflect a higher-than-normal error rate in such cases, given the intense public pressure on police and prosecutors to obtain a conviction in such high-profile cases. More likely, the primary reason the DNA exonerations include almost entirely rapes and rapes/murders is that sexual assaults are the crimes most likely to yield biological evidence for DNA analysis. That explanation would suggest that there might be untold numbers of individuals convicted of other crimes who are also innocent and wrongly convicted but are unable to obtain vindication through DNA testing because the cases lack testable biological evidence.

Table 1 DNA exonerations by year

Year	*DNA exonerations*
1989	2
1990	1
1991	2
1992	5
1993	4
1994	7
1995	8
1996	13
1997	9
1998	4
1999	11
2000	15
2001	19
2002	25
2003	18
2004	13
2005	19
2006	18
2007	19
2008	14
2009	23
2010	18
2011	15

Of those exonerated by DNA, 70% were minorities. In rape cases, 75% of the exonerees were black or Latino, while only 30–40% of all rapes are committed by minorities. Most rapes are committed within racial groups; 90% are committed by offenders of the same race as the victim. Yet among exonerees, nearly half of all wrongful rape convictions involved black or Latino perpetrators and white victims.

The DNA evidence in many of these cases did more than exonerate an innocent person. In 45% of the DNA exonerations, the DNA tests identified the actual rapists or murderers, many of whom had been free for years and had gone on to commit other crimes, while an innocent person sat in prison for their crimes.

Features of Wrongful Convictions

Study of the DNA exonerations has provided insights into the types of evidence and errors that create false convictions.

Eyewitness error

The most prevalent type of erroneous evidence in these cases is eyewitness error; eyewitnesses wrongly identified the accused in 76% of the first 250 cases. Typically, these eyewitnesses misidentified an innocent person not because they were lying but because they were simply mistaken. Considerable research has now confirmed the fallibility of eyewitness memory and identified police practices that can even unintentionally taint an eyewitness's memory and produce false identifications. Indeed, Garrett's review of the first 250 DNA exonerations found that in 78% of the cases, police contaminated the eyewitness identifications with suggestive methods, like giving cues—whether intentionally or not—about which lineup member was the suspect or conducting lineups where one suspect obviously stood out from the others.

Reforms to improve eyewitness accuracy are beginning to emerge from the new recognition about the seriousness of the eyewitness error problem. Many states, including New Jersey, North Carolina, Ohio, and Wisconsin, among others, are implementing social-science-based police practices designed to minimize eyewitness error. These reforms include practices like instructing eyewitnesses before an identification procedure that the real perpetrator might or might not be present, as the witness should not feel compelled to pick someone; ensuring that everyone included in a lineup or photo array fits the description of the perpetrator, so that no one stands out; conducting lineups and photo arrays in a "blind" manner, meaning that the police officer administering the test does not know which person is the suspect; presenting suspects and fillers (known innocent individuals included in the procedure to fill out the lineup or photo array) to the witness sequentially rather than simultaneously, so as to minimize the tendency to compare faces and pick the best fit, rather than only picking an individual truly recognized as the perpetrator; including only one suspect per identification procedure; presenting any one suspect to a witness only once, rather than in several repeated procedures; and accurately recording a witness's statement of confidence immediately after making an identification, before the witness receives any confirming or disconfirming feedback about his or her "pick."

Flawed forensic science evidence

Based on Garrett's study, the second most prevalent type of evidence in the first 250 DNA exonerations is forensic science evidence. Seventy-four percent of the DNA exonerations included other forensic science evidence. The forensic evidence in these cases included serology testing (as in Pitchfork and Dotson; 116 cases), microscopic hair comparison (75 cases), fingerprints (20 cases), bite mark comparison (7 cases), shoe print comparison (6 cases), and voice comparison (1 case). Garrett and Peter Neufeld have analyzed the transcripts of the testimony of forensic analysts in 153 of the DNA exoneration cases in which transcripts are available and found that the forensic testimony was invalid in 61% of the cases, either by misusing population data or by drawing conclusions unsupported by empirical data as to the probative value of the evidence. In the remaining cases, the science might have been valid but of limited utility when compared to DNA's greater ability to discriminate. Forensic testimony was invalid in virtually every category of forensic science, including 58% of the serology testimony, 39% of the hair comparison testimony, 71% of the bite mark testimony, 17% of the shoe comparison testimony, and 5% of the fingerprint testimony.

Some of these techniques, such as microscopic hair analysis, are not in wide use any longer, but the methodologies and types of testimony that went awry in these cases continue today in a variety of forensic disciplines. A landmark study by the National Academy of Sciences (NAS) carefully examined the state of forensic sciences and concluded, "With the exception of nuclear DNA analysis, ... no forensic method has been rigorously shown to have the capacity to consistently, and with a high degree of certainty, demonstrate a connection between evidence and a specific individual or source." Indeed, the NAS concluded that—again excluding DNA—"[l]ittle rigorous research has been done to validate the basic premises and techniques in a number of forensic science disciplines."

False confessions

Counterintuitively, the DNA exonerations establish that innocent people do confess to serious crimes like rapes and murders that they did not commit. Of the first 250 DNA exonerations, 16% involved false confessions. In homicides, where there is usually no surviving victim eyewitness and hence confessions become more critical to police, approximately two-thirds of the DNA exonerations involved false confessions. Almost all these false confessions included significant details of the crimes, including details not publicly known, which the police routinely claimed they had not disclosed to the suspect and that only the true perpetrator would have known. Yet research reveals that in fact, most of these confessions were contaminated by police and produced by intense interrogation tactics in prolonged interrogations that lasted hours, or even days, utilizing psychological tactics to convince the suspect to confess.

Courts, legislatures, and police departments have found that the most important first step in addressing the problem of false confessions is to require that all custodial interrogations of suspects should be electronically recorded, from start to finish, and without interruption. Such recordings protect suspects from coercive tactics and make a record when police go too far or when they contaminate the interrogations with supposedly secret crime details. At the same time, electronic recording protects police from spurious claims of misconduct in the interrogation room. Recordings of voluntary confessions also provide prosecutors with powerful evidence of guilt. To date, police in 11 states and the District of Columbia are required or encouraged to record at least some interrogations, and police in hundreds of jurisdictions around the country have begun to record voluntarily.

False informant testimony

Twenty-one percent of the first 250 DNA exonerations had informant testimony at the defendant's initial trial. Most of this testimony was provided by jailhouse informants, codefendants, or confidential informants or cooperating witnesses. These witnesses typically testified that the defendants confessed the crime to them and provided details about how they committed the crime. The criminal justice system has long known that such witnesses lack credibility because they have an incentive to fabricate evidence against the defendant, yet the system has simultaneously approved reliance on informant testimony. Potential informants know, or hope, that providing such evidence to the state will produce leniency or other benefits in their own cases. Yet the system does little to protect against such false testimony. The DNA exonerations confirm the seriousness of the threat that such testimony poses to accurate fact finding at trial and has led to some proposals for reform or greater scrutiny of such proof.

Other features of the wrongful convictions

Other common features of the wrongful convictions exposed by postconviction DNA testing include various forms of police and prosecutorial misconduct and inadequate or ineffective representation by defense counsel. Additionally, virtually every case exhibits some degree of tunnel vision—the combination of innate cognitive biases (e.g., confirmation bias and outcome bias) and institutional pressures that predispose investigators to focus on a suspect and then filter all subsequent information in the case through the lens of that early conclusion about the suspect's guilt.

Finally, the DNA exonerations tell a story of appellate failure. Very few of these innocent defendants obtained relief during the appellate review of their convictions. Most courts affirmed the convictions of these innocent defendants, and in approximately half the cases, courts commented on the strength of the evidence of guilt, while in 10% of the cases, the appellate courts called the evidence of the innocent person's guilt "overwhelming."

See also: **Anthropology/Odontology:** Odontology; Basic Principles; DNA Databases; Forensic Genetics: History; Mitochondrial DNA; Short Tandem Repeats; **Investigations:** Fingerprints; **Legal:** History of the Law's Reception of Forensic Science; Legal Aspects of Forensic Science; The Innocence Project; **Methods:** Analytical Light Microscopy; **Pattern Evidence:** Footwear Marks; Tools; **Pattern Evidence/History:** Fingerprint Sciences; **Professional:** National Academy of Sciences (NAS); **Toxicology/Alcohol:** Blood; **Toxicology/Drugs of Abuse:** Blood.

Further Reading

Connors, E., Lundregan, T., Miller, N., McEwan, T., 1996. Convicted by Juries, Exonerated by Science: Case Studies in the Use of DNA Evidence to Establish Innocence after Trial. National Institute of Justice, Washington, DC.

Findley, K.A., 2009. Innocence protection in the appellate process. Marquette Law Review 93, 591–638.

Garrett, B.L., 2008. Judging innocence. Columbia Law Review 108, 55–142.

Garrett, B.L., 2011. Convicting the Innocent: Where Criminal Prosecutions Go Wrong. Harvard University Press, Cambridge, MA.

Garrett, B.L., Neufeld, P.J., 2009. Invalid forensic science testimony and wrongful convictions. Virginia Law Review 95, 1–97.

Gross, S.R., et al., 2005. Exonerations in the United States, 1989 through 2003. Journal of Criminal Law and Criminology 95, 523–560.

Kaye, D.H., 2010. The Double Helix and the Law of Evidence. Harvard University Press, Cambridge, MA.

National Research Council and National Academy of Sciences, 1992. DNA Technology in Forensic Science. National Academy Press, Washington, DC.

Scheck, B.C., Neufeld, P.J., Dwyer, J., 2001. Actual Innocence: When Justice Goes Wrong and How to Make it Right. Signet, New York.

Thompson-Canino, J., Cotton, R., Torneo, E., 2009. Picking Cotton: Our Memoir of Injustice and Redemption. St. Martin's Press, New York.

U.S. Department of Justice, Office of Justice Programs, National Institute of Justice, and National Commission on the Future of DNA Evidence, 1999. Postconviction DNA Testing: Recommendations for Handling Requests. U.S. Department of Justice, Office of Justice Programs, National Institute of Justice, National Commission on the Future of DNA Evidence, Washington, DC.

Relevant Websites

www.innocencenetwork.org—Innocence Network.
www.innocenceproject.org—Innocence Project.

DNA Databases

PM Schneider, University of Cologne, Cologne, Germany

Glossary

Adventitious match Result of a database search with ambiguous results due to searching with a partial profile with a low discrimination power (e.g., when the random match probability is equal to or less than the size of the database), where it must be considered that matching database record(s) may not be connected to the crime.

CODIS The Combined DNA Index System is the software system that runs the U.S. National DNA Index System (NDIS), which contains the combined data of all U.S. state DNA databases.

Cold hit A person found in a DNA database search using a crime stain profile who had not been a suspect in this case based on conventional police investigations.

EDNAP group The European DNA Profiling group was introduced in 1989 by scientists from academic and governmental laboratories to carry out collaborative experiments with the aim of harmonizing forensic DNA profiling methods across Europe.

ESS loci The European Standard Set of STR loci used for database typing.

Familial searching A database search strategy aiming to identify first-degree relatives from unknown perpetrators.

NDNAD The National DNA Database in England and Wales.

Introduction

Although the history of national databases storing DNA profiles of criminal offenders and unsolved crime cases is still quite short, it is one of the greatest success stories of modern criminal investigation strategies, at least equal to the introduction of dactyloscopy. In Europe, the first national DNA database was established in England and Wales in 1995. In the United States, the Combined DNA Index System (CODIS) was gradually introduced by the FBI beginning in 1989, and was formally created by the DNA Identification Act of 1994 and launched nationally in 1998. Since then, most of the European countries as well as many countries from all over the world have introduced collections of DNA profiles from criminal cases. It has to be noted, however, that some of these databases only hold data from unsolved crime cases since the storage of offender profiles typically requires specific legislation. As there are significant differences regarding the criminal justice systems, the national databases were created on the background of a specific legal history and culture as reflected by the various national regulations that can now be found. In the countries collecting only crime scene samples, databases typically have been introduced based on existing legislation for samples obtained from routine casework.

However, there are several important issues that need to be decided when database legislation is considered. These include the criteria for adding an offender's DNA profile to the database, the decision to also include suspects (or arrestees, depending on the legislation) prior to the court proceedings, as well as convicted offenders already imprisoned at the time when the database is introduced, the time period for storing a person's profile in the database, and the handling of a person's reference DNA sample (i.e., a blood sample, a buccal swab, and/or a DNA sample extracted from blood or buccal cells) after it has been typed, that is, to retain or to destroy it.

Criteria for the Inclusion of DNA Profiles in National DNA Databases

As there is considerable diversity regarding the legal systems in the European countries, these will be used as examples to point out the relevant issues for the introduction and operation of criminal DNA databases. In most legislation, specific criteria have been defined based on the type or severity of a crime qualifying for storage of DNA profiles obtained from biological stains. Typically, capital and violent crimes as well as all types

 http://dx.doi.org/10.1016/B978-0-12-800647-4.00037-0

of sexual offenses are included in most databases. Some countries have adopted a detailed list of criminal offenses for inclusion as defined by the respective penal code (e.g., France and Norway), whereas in others, the length of the time period a convicted offender has to stay in prison is considered. These periods may vary between 1 and 5 years. Furthermore, to store a DNA profile in a database, a formal decision by a judge or investigating magistrate is required. Finally, in a number of countries no specific selection criteria exist (e.g., Austria, England/Wales, and Switzerland; see below).

There are two groups of persons that are considered for a database entry: suspects and/or arrestees in ongoing criminal investigations and convicted offenders. The inclusion of suspects is possible in England, Austria, Croatia, Slovenia, Switzerland, Germany, Finland, Denmark, the Netherlands, and Norway, but the selection criteria for suspects are rather diverse. The most stringent strategy has been implemented in England, Austria, Croatia, Slovenia, and Switzerland, where "any recordable offense" qualifies the suspect for a database entry. In most countries, however, entry criteria are based on the type of crime (Norway), as well as the length or type of expected conviction, for example, imprisonment for more than a year (Germany, Finland), 1.5 years (Denmark), 4 years (the Netherlands), or even 5 years (Hungary). The inclusion of suspects is not allowed in Belgium, Norway, and Portugal.

The inclusion of suspects at an early stage of the investigation may lead to a situation where the suspect's profile is entered into the database and generates a match with a DNA profile from another unsolved crime. This "cold hit" could then lead to a new investigation even if the charges of the initial investigation have already been dropped. Although the database record from a suspect has to be eliminated in most countries if a person has been acquitted, the new investigation related to the cold hit will of course be carried out. It is obvious that this approach will generate more hits when the "population" of potential offenders grows larger in such a database. This assumption is supported by national DNA database statistics that are exemplified for several countries (see **Table 1**). For example, in Belgium, only 47% of the database records are from offenders, and, consequently, only 38% of all database hits are person-stain hits. In countries where more than 70% of the records are from persons, at least 70% of the observed hits are between persons and stains. In England and Wales, about 10% of the population is already in the database. More than 90% of all database records are from persons, and more than 85% are person-stain hits. It has to be considered as well that offender-matched profiles from stain cases are removed, whereas the offender will remain on the database. This results in a much higher "throughput" rate for stain profiles.

For convicted offenders, the criteria are the same in all countries that also accept suspects. In some of the remaining countries, such as Norway and Belgium, a court decision is required. This is also the case in Germany, where the decision must be justified by a prognosis on the risk of future offenses. In Sweden, a conviction of at least 2 years in prison is required. In the Netherlands, a convicted offender may voluntarily offer his sample for the database, even if the conviction is for a period of less than 4 years. This illustrates that a database entry may also serve to protect the privacy of a convicted offender once he has been released from jail and has decided to obey the law. If such a voluntary sample is

Table 1 DNA database statistics of selected European countries

Country	*Population total (million)*	*Database*									
		Persons (thousand)	*Stains (thousand)*	*Database population (%)*	*Persons (%)*	*Stains (%)*	*Total hits (thousand)*	*Person hits (thousand)*	*Person hits (%)*	*Including suspects*	*Last update*
Austria	8.1	145.5	44.8	1.80	76	24	19.9	13.9	70	Y	June 2011
Belgium	10.4	21.8	24.6	0.21	47	53	4.5	1.7	38	N	June 2011
Denmark	5.5	73.9	40.2	1.34	65	35	19.6			Y	September 2011
Finland	5.4	111.9	12.4	2.07	90	10	15.6	14	90	Y	June 2011
France	59.3	1698.1	103.7	2.86	94	6	52.4	45.7	87	Y[a]	July 2011
Germany	82.4	746.9	201.9	0.91	79	21	126.9	100	79	Y	December 2011
The Netherlands	16.1	118.9	47.1	0.74	72	28	32	27.1	85	Y[a]	June 2011
Norway	4.5	22.1	6.2	0.49	78	22	2.8	2.1	75	N	June 2010
Sweden	9	99.4	33.1	1.10	75	25	42.3	30	71	Y	June 2011
Switzerland	7.8	126.6	33.1	1.62	79	21	36	29	81	Y	June 2011
England/Wales	53.7	5369	387.5	10	93	7	1659	1423	86	Y	June 2011
Total	300	8589		3.28			2056	1679	82		

[a]The law was changed after some years of operation to include suspects.

included in the DNA database and a new crime scene sample is added without generating a hit, this individual is automatically excluded from being involved in the unsolved case. In France, all cases of sexual assault as well as all serious crimes qualify for a database entry. However, the offender has to donate the sample voluntarily, as he cannot be forced due to laws protecting his physical integrity. Nevertheless, it appears that most offenders agree to have their samples taken, as they are otherwise punished by a fine for denying their sample. Another solution to this dilemma is to collect cigarette butts, hairs, or brushes from those offenders who would accept a fine, as the genetic analysis of "abandoned" samples is not prohibited by the law. Nevertheless, this practice seems to be questionable as the correct establishment of the "abandoned" sample's identity could be doubtful and prone to error or manipulation.

In England and Wales, database records are still being kept without restriction even for acquitted suspects. However, the legality of this rule was challenged by two individuals who requested their DNA samples and data records to be removed. One of the accused persons, a boy who was only 11 years old when his genetic sample was obtained, was acquitted, and in the second case involving an adult man, no charges were pressed due to a pretrial reconciliation. The request was eventually denied by the House of Lords, so that the case was brought to the European Court of Human Rights (ECtHR). This court ruled in favor of the request and observed that keeping the samples of acquitted or innocent persons without restriction is a violation of privacy rights as defined in Art. 8 of the European Convention of Human Rights. Subsequently, the British government proposed changes to accommodate the ruling of the ECtHR.

Countries not retaining database records without restrictions have mechanisms in place for their elimination. In countries where suspects are entered into the database, these records have to be eliminated once the charges have been dropped or when the suspect has been acquitted in court. Interestingly, Denmark makes a clear difference between these two scenarios: the record is eliminated immediately when the prosecution has dropped the charges (assuming the police clearly believe that the suspect is innocent), but the record remains on the database for 10 years in case of acquittal (since this may have happened only due to lack of evidence). Convicted offenders will stay forever in the database in the United Kingdom, in Austria, Finland, Norway, and Croatia (even for a period after death, as old cases may still be solved when these DNA profiles remain in the database). In the other countries, periods between 10 and 40 years are in place before a record may be eliminated. The decision may also depend on the offender's age or an individual prognosis, as in Germany, or on the severity of the crime (e.g., in Slovenia).

The third aspect to consider is the procedures for collecting and storing the reference samples from suspects and convicted offenders. All countries are now taking buccal swabs as these can be collected without the help of a physician. In a number of countries, bar-coded sampling kits have been developed, which also allow an easy anonymization procedure. Thus, the DNA profiles can be stored separately from the personal information. This is the case in most countries except for Germany where the samples are anonymized only for the typing laboratory but are stored together with the complete personal information in the police database. A major difference exists regarding the regulations to retain or destroy the reference samples after they have been typed. Samples are kept in the United Kingdom, Austria, Finland, Denmark, Hungary, Slovenia, and Croatia. Thus, it is possible to test the sample again to confirm the data when a match has been called, and before the match report is handed over to the prosecutor. In addition, samples would be available for retyping in case the number of database loci is increased. On the other hand, there are also strong arguments in favor of destroying the samples after the typing results have been obtained. Destruction efficiently prevents any unauthorized use of the samples and thus ensures the protection of genetic privacy. Furthermore, the destruction of samples does not generate additional long-term expenses for adequate sample storage. In the countries where no reference samples are kept, a fresh sample is usually requested from the suspect when a match report indicates that this person may have been involved in another crime. Thus, the investigation does not rely on the information obtained from the database, but on a fresh sample that can be used as evidence in court, if necessary.

To ensure that the typing results are stored in the database as accurately as possible, most countries have mechanisms in place that all reference samples are tested twice. In addition, the technical quality can also be ascertained by requesting that laboratories working for a national DNA database have introduced a quality management system, regularly take part in proficiency testing exercises, and are accredited according to international standards such as ISO 17025. Accreditation will become mandatory in the European Union (EU) in November 2013 for all forensic DNA laboratories following an EU Council framework decision in 2009.

Genetic Typing Systems

A major effort has been undertaken by the scientific community since 1995 to create a high level of standardization regarding the genetic typing systems. Short tandem repeat (STR) loci are forming the core of all national DNA databases. In Europe, an agreement has been obtained on a common set of STR loci, the European Standard Set (ESS) comprising the seven STR systems: THO1, VWA, FGA, D21S11, D3S1358, D8S1179, and D18S51. Shortly afterward, the Interpol Standard Set of Loci (ISSOL), which is identical to the ESS loci except for including the amelogenin locus, has been defined by Interpol. Subsequently, Interpol has also introduced an international platform for a DNA data exchange. In the United States, the FBI Laboratory, which administers the CODIS system, has implemented a common set of 13 STR loci. All seven ESS loci are part of the CODIS marker set, which in addition includes the six loci, CSF1PO, TPOX, D5S818, D7S820, D13S317, and D16S539. In Germany, the STR locus SE33 (humACTBP2) has been included from the beginning of the database operation in 1998 due to its high discrimination power.

In 2005, the European DNA Profiling Group (EDNAP) and the ENFSI DNA Working Group convened to discuss an extension of the ESS loci. It was triggered by a political process with the aim to enable a European data exchange between the EU member states. The Treaty of Prüm was signed in 2005 with the purpose of stepping up cross-border cooperation, particularly in combating terrorism, cross-border crime, and illegal migration. When massive exchanges of DNA profiles are undertaken between national databases following the implementation of the Treaty of Prüm, the seven ESS loci do not have sufficient discrimination power to avoid adventitious matches. These may occur when the power of discrimination of a DNA profile in question is insufficient (e.g., when the random match probability is equal or less than the number of persons in the database), so that it must be considered that the matching database record(s) may not be connected to the crime.

Furthermore, due to the increased sensitivity of STR typing kits, more and more crime stain samples are submitted for analysis either with low amounts of DNA or with compromised DNA quality due to degradation. Typing of such samples typically results in partial profiles with even less power of discrimination. In this situation, robust STR systems with short amplicons are quite useful, as these are more useful for typing degraded DNA samples. A recommendation from the ENFSI and EDNAP groups was adopted to add the five new loci (D1S1656, D2S441, D10S1248, D12S391, and D22S1045) to the ESS. Among these are three short amplicon STR loci (D2, D10, and D22), as well as two loci with a high discrimination power (D1 and D12). Furthermore, the three STR loci (D2S1338, D16S539, and D19S433) that are routinely typed in many forensic DNA labs are also being used for the DNA data exchange, increasing the total number of markers to 15 STR loci. Regarding the United States, an FBI CODIS Core Loci Working Group made recommendations in 2011 to expand the STR marker set by selecting loci either from the ESS or from typing kits already used for many years in the forensic community. Selection criteria were based, among others, on discrimination power, lack of association with medical conditions, and a low mutation rate to enable identification of missing persons.

Privacy Rights, Ethical Considerations, and New Directions

The introduction of DNA databases has been accompanied by a lively and sometimes controversial debate about the protection of privacy, as well as the extent to which DNA, both as a source of information as well as from the derived DNA profiles, should be investigated. It has been aptly stated in a review on the ethical context of criminal DNA databases that "there is an essential tension throughout this discursive field between a wonderment of the ability of DNA to identify the perpetrators of crime and a dread about its capacities to erode civil liberties and human rights." A major concern is related to the collection of a person's genetic sample containing the entire genomic DNA. Although a DNA sample does not constitute "personal data," and is thus not directly covered by data protection provisions, it allows to reconstruct all genetic information from an individual given that the appropriate methods are applied, such as by using the new "next generation" sequencing technologies allowing to sequence a full human genome in a couple of days. Therefore, even if the current legislation restricts the genetic information to STR typing results, which are stored in a database, there is a strong concern that indefinitely stored DNA samples could be "abused" without revealing it publicly, or in an unpredictable situation where a radical change of the political system occurs. Therefore, as described above, the majority of countries have decided to discard personal reference samples. In Switzerland, it was initially decided to keep reference samples during an evaluation period of the national DNA database. However, when the final legislation was passed, this provision was removed on the grounds of privacy protection, as well as saving significant costs for secure sample storage.

On the other hand, it has to be noted that a crime stain from an unknown perpetrator does not necessarily constitute a "private" sample. It has rather been abandoned at a crime scene and thus is not likely to be deemed worthy of protection under any appeal to the privacy of personal information. Consequently, research is underway to extract additional information such as the prediction of biogeographic ancestry, that is, the geographical region where a person has his or her genetic roots. Furthermore, scientific efforts are underway to investigate coding DNA sequences in the hope of obtaining additional clues on the identification of the perpetrator based on externally visible characteristics (EVCs), such as hair, eye and skin color, body height, or facial features, also termed "forensic DNA phenotyping" (FDP). In the Netherlands, DNA legislation was introduced in 2004 to explicitly allow for this type of genetic investigation. It may be argued that the analysis of coding sequences represents a flagrant violation of privacy rights and will open the floodgates for all other types of investigations on genetic traits in criminal investigations.

However, it is quite unlikely that a detailed "genetic photofit" picture will ever become reality, as EVCs other than pigmentation markers are highly complex genetic traits that might not become easily predictable even if the entire genome is sequenced. Genetic prediction on ECVs from a crime scene has to be based on a likelihood estimate in a range where a considerable margin of error remains. Thus, it will be useful only in cases where the STR-based DNA profile does not generate a hit in the criminal DNA database. It will then only help to narrow down the number of suspects and will have the same or a lower quality as the statement of an eyewitness. Once a particular suspect or a group of suspects has been identified, identity to or exclusion from the crime scene sample will be established using "conventional" STR typing. Therefore, it must be understood that it does not make any sense to store genetic data on EVCs in criminal DNA databases. These can only be used to provide limited intelligence on an unknown stain donor, and will be discarded once the true perpetrator has been identified by STR analysis.

Another strategy that is considered controversial in some countries, but not in others, is the search for genetic relatedness based on STR profiles in existing criminal DNA databases. This has already been carried out in some states of the United States as well as in the United Kingdom, where familial searches helped to identify unknown offenders by linking the crime scene profiles to first-degree relatives of the perpetrator whose DNA profiles were already entered into the DNA database. Whereas this approach is allowed in a number of U.S. states and in England, it is not allowed in many European countries such as Germany and France, as it would be considered not only an intrusion into privacy but also as an illegal use of genetic information derived from STR profiling. In the courtroom, testimony can be refused by a witness if a relative is accused. However, by carrying out familial searches, the individual from the database suspected to be, for example, the brother of the unknown perpetrator is used as an "unwilling informant" about his relative. It also has to be considered that the number of STR loci typed for the national databases typically has adequate power for a direct comparison but may be not large enough to establish sufficiently strong evidence to prove genetic relatedness. Obviously, there are still controversial views about the prospects and limits of DNA evidence as an intelligence source in criminal investigations when it comes to operate a national DNA database in the framework of the rather diverse criminal justice systems throughout the world.

See also: **Biology/DNA:** Accreditation in Forensic DNA Analysis; Ancestry Informative Markers; Forensic DNA Advisory Groups: DAB, SWGDAM, ENFSI, and BSAG; Forensic DNA Phenotyping: DNA Testing for Externally Visible Characteristics; Short Tandem Repeats.

Further Reading

Bieber, F.R., Brenner, C.H., Lazer, D., 2006. Human genetics. Finding criminals through DNA of their relatives. Science 312, 1315–1316.

Butler, J.M., 2012. DNA Databases: Uses and Issues. Advanced Topics in Forensic DNA Typing: Methodology. Elsevier Academic Press, New York.

Gamero, J.J., Romero, J.L., Peralta, J.L., Corte-Real, F., Guillén, M., Anjos, M.J., 2008. A study of Spanish attitudes regarding the custody and use of forensic DNA databases. Forensic Science International: Genetics 2, 138–149.

Gill, P., Fereday, L., Morling, N., Schneider, P.M., 2006. The evolution of DNA databases – Recommendations for new European STR loci. Forensic Science International 156, 242–244.

Hares, D.R., 2012. Expanding the CODIS core loci in the United States. Forensic Science International: Genetics 6, e52–e54.

Hindmarsh, R., Prainsack, B. (Eds.), 2010. Genetic Suspects: Global Governance of Forensic DNA Profiling and Databasing. Cambridge University Press, Cambridge.

Kayser, M., Schneider, P.M., 2009. DNA-based prediction of human externally visible characteristics in forensics: motivations, scientific challenges, and ethical considerations. Forensic Science International: Genetics 3, 154–161.

Martin, P.D., Schmitter, H., Schneider, P.M., 2001. A brief history of the formation of DNA databases in forensic science within Europe. Forensic Science International 119, 225–231.

Myers, S.P., Timken, M.D., Piucci, M.L., et al., 2011. Searching for first-degree familial relationships in California's offender DNA database: validation of a likelihood ratio-based approach. Forensic Science International: Genetics 5, 493–500.

Storvik, G., Egeland, T., 2007. The DNA database search controversy revisited: Bridging the Bayesian-frequentist gap. Biometrics 63, 922–925.

Williams, R., Johnson, P., 2004. 'Wonderment and dread': Representations of DNA in ethical disputes about forensic DNA databases. New Genetics and Society 23, 205–223.

Relevant Websites

http://www.fbi.gov/about-us/lab/codis—Combined DNA Index System (USA).

http://www.enfsi.eu/page.php?uid1/454—ENFSI DNA Working Group.

http://www.isfg.org/EDNAP—European DNA Profiling Group.

http://www.dnaresource.com/—Forensic DNA Database Policy.

http://www.npia.police.uk/en/8934.htm—National DNA Database in England and Wales.

http://www.nuffieldbioethics.org/bioinformation—Nuffield Council on Bioethics: The forensic use of bioinformation.

The National Missing and Unidentified Persons System (NamUs)

MM Houck, Forensic & Intelligence Services, LLC, St. Petersburg, FL, USA

Introduction

It has been estimated that there are approximately 40,000 unidentified human remains in the offices of the nation's medical examiners and coroners or that were buried or cremated before being identified. In June 2007, the Office of Justice Programs' (OJP) Bureau of Justice Statistics (BJS) confirmed that, in a typical year, medical examiners and coroners handle approximately 4400 unidentified human decedent cases, 1000 of which remain unidentified after 1 year. BJS further identified the need to improve record-retention policies. As of 2004, more than half (51%) of the nation's medical examiners' offices had no policy for retaining records—such as X-rays, DNA, or fingerprints—on unidentified human decedents. BJS also noted, however, that more than 90% of offices servicing large jurisdictions did have such a policy. Cases of missing persons 18 years old and younger must be reported, but reporting adult missing persons is voluntary. Only a few states have laws that require law enforcement agencies to prepare missing person reports on adults. Overall, there is a low rate of reporting these cases through the National Crime Information Center.

The NamUs is a national centralized repository and resource center for missing persons and unidentified decedent records. NamUs is a free online system that can be searched by medical examiners, coroners, law enforcement officials, and the general public from all over the country in the hope of resolving these cases. The Missing Persons Database contains information about missing persons, which can be entered by anyone; however, before it appears as a case on NamUs, the information is verified. NamUs provides a user with a variety of resources, including the ability to print missing persons' posters and receive free biometric collection and testing assistance. Other resources include links to state clearinghouses, medical examiners' and coroners' offices, law enforcement agencies, victim assistance groups, and pertinent legislation.

The Unidentified Persons Database contains information entered by medical examiners and coroners. Unidentified persons are people who have died and whose bodies have not been identified. Anyone can search this database using characteristics such as sex, race, distinct body features, and even dental information.

The newly added UnClaimed Persons database (UCP) contains information about deceased persons who have been identified by name but for whom no next of kin or family member has been identified or located to claim the body for burial or other disposition. Only medical examiners and coroners may enter cases in the UCP database. However, the database is searchable by the public, using a missing person's name and year of birth.

When a new missing person or unidentified decedent case is entered into NamUs, the system automatically performs cross-matching comparisons between the databases, searching for matches or similarities between cases. NamUs provides free DNA testing and other forensic services, such as anthropology and odontology assistance. The NamUs Missing Persons Database and Unidentified Persons Database are now available in Spanish.

Acknowledgment

Material provided by OJP from http://www.namus.gov.

See also: **Biology/DNA:** DNA Databases; **Investigations:** Fingerprints; **Pattern Evidence/Fingerprints (Dactyloscopy):** Identification and Classification.

Further Reading

Ritter, N., 2007. Missing persons and unidentified remains: the nation's silent mass disaster. NIJ Journal 256, 2–7. http://www.nij.gov.

Disaster Victim Identification

WH Goodwin and T Simmons, University of Central Lancashire, Preston, UK

Abbreviations

AM Antemortem
DVI Disaster victim identification
ICRC International Committee of the Red Cross
PM Postmortem
STR Short tandem repeat
VNTR Variable number tandem repeat

Introduction

In every disaster or conflict, the need to recover and identify the deceased is a matter of urgency, foremost on behalf of the psychological needs of relatives of those missing; the right to know the fate of one's missing relatives is a fundamental right and should be respected and enacted—this principle holds regardless of the circumstances that have led to the death. Alongside humanitarian needs, disaster victim identification (DVI) also addresses legal concerns regarding everything from civil suits concerning liability in an aviation, train, or ferry disaster; the need to provide death certificates for purposes of inheritance and remarriage; through to the prosecution of perpetrators of war crimes.

The scope of DVI operations has evolved significantly since the mid-1990s, when most instances centered on transport accidents involving up to a few 100 victims. Advances have been driven in part technically by developments, particularly in DNA analysis, that have increased the circumstances in which identification of human remains is possible. Politically, the response to several events of international importance in the late twentieth and early twenty-first centuries, such as conflicts in the Balkans 1991–1999, the World Trade Center attack 2001, and the pan-Asian Tsunamis 2004, focused a large amount of resource to the identification of the victims. This led to logistical and technical advances in DVI and also to higher expectations for forensic science to be used for human identification following disasters and conflicts, even when there are thousands of victims.

Disaster Classification

A disaster can be defined as an unexpected event causing death or injury to many people. Traditional considerations for activating a DVI response related to "mass disasters," where external assistance was required following a catastrophic event that overwhelmed the resources of an affected community and rendered it unable to respond adequately acting alone. There are many different types of disaster that can necessitate DVI including traffic accidents, natural disasters, technical/industrial accidents, terrorist attacks, and events that occur during conflict, both within and between countries.

In addition to the type of disaster, an important aspect when considering DVI is whether it is open or closed. Closed disasters, such as aircraft crashes, are those in which the identities of the victims are known through crew and passenger manifests (although these may not be entirely accurate in all cases); in such instances, the task of the DVI team is largely to match the identity of the remains to individuals known to be missing. In many of these cases, access to relevant antemortem (AM) information necessary for matching is also facilitated by the relative ease of locating kin, medical and dental records, and DNA samples. Open disasters are those in which the identity and even the number of the victims are unknown. Establishing who was indeed a victim can be quite complicated even in a thoroughly modern society where it may take several days or weeks, even years to resolve in a situation of limited fatalities; in the case of a natural disaster involving multiple countries or locations within a country and thousands to tens of thousands of victims of multiple nationalities, it can take years to resolve. For victims of conflict, where the number and identity of victims are unknown, individuals disappeared over several years (or decades), the location of graves has been obscured, AM records are scant or lacking in their entirety, and political will and monetary resources are slim, identification, when possible, can take decades. It should also be noted that it is possible to have a classification of combined, for example, when a plane crashes on a populated area killing people of the ground as well as those in the plane.

Management of Disaster Victim Identification

Interpol recommends that each member state should establish a permanent DVI team, with preplanning and training for disasters. In planning for and following a disaster, multiple facets of the DVI operation have to be considered, for example, initial assessment of the scope of the disaster, mapping and searching of the affected area, estimating the number of victims and degree of fragmentation, methodology to recover and transport the corpses, methodology to be used for identification, and identifying the individuals/medico-legal institutes that are to be involved in the identification process. The criteria that must be met before identifications are made must also be agreed upon prior to bodies being released to families—this becomes increasingly important with increasing numbers of victims as this augments the probability of incorrect identifications.

Another important decision is the scope of the identification process, that is, with fragmented remains what will the operation aim to identify—whole bodies only, recognizable body parts, body parts of a specific size? In cases of extreme fragmentation (e.g., plane crashes) or disruption of primary burials into secondary and even tertiary mass burials (e.g., Bosnia), it is also necessary to have a policy in place regarding how relatives of the missing will be informed when a portion of their missing person has been identified. Through this policy, relatives of the missing may, for example, elect to be notified when (1) the entire identification process has been completed and all the remains identified of the individual are collected and returned at a single time; (2) the first body part has been identified; or (3) every time a body part has been identified. This allows the relatives of the missing to assert some control over their relationship to the identification process and also decide at which point they wish to hold memorial and/or funeral services.

Principles of Identification

Identification of individuals killed in mass disasters and conflicts should be held to the same standards as identification of individuals killed (or found dead) under any other circumstance. The processes used in identifying individuals must be robust and the families of the missing must have confidence in the identification process. Decisions regarding the methods of identification to be employed are influenced by the condition of the victims, personnel involved in the identification, resources, and technology, as well as by the availability of AM comparatives. There are four widely recognized means of positive identification, whereby a single method alone can be used to make an identification; all others must be regarded as a means of presumptive identification, which can be used to support identification or generate further leads to identity, but may not in themselves "make" an identification. Fingerprints, dental/medical records (including radiographs), nuclear DNA, and unique medical identifiers are all means of primary positive identification. Visual recognition (of tattoos, facial features, birthmarks, scars, etc.), a matching biological profile generated by forensic anthropologists (age, sex, race, stature, and AM trauma/pathology), matching medical conditions identified by pathologists, facial superimposition, matching personal effects and clothing, matching identification documents, exclusion (when, for example, there is only one child among the victims), and/or matching mitochondrial DNA (mtDNA) profiles are secondary means of identification, ideally for use in support of the primary methods (**Figure 1**).

Methods of Identification

Objective Methods

Objective methods, sometimes referred to as scientific methods, if applied appropriately, can give unambiguous identifications.

Fingerprints

Identification of individuals through fingerprints is a well-established scientific method, and is routinely used worldwide. In humans, the palms and fingers are covered in skin that is thickened with ridges that helps to grip surfaces (friction ridge skin); the soles of the feet and toes are also covered with friction ridge skin. Friction ridge skin is considered to be unique and over the last 100 years of application, with millions of fingerprints used for forensic identification, only a handful of issues of misidentification have been reported, making fingerprints a powerful means of identification; importantly fingerprints remain unchanged throughout life, other than through scarring.

Several systems have been developed to classify fingerprints, all of which are based on categorization of the overall pattern, that is, loops, arches, and whorls, and then identification of distinct combinations of features within the pattern, such as bifurcations, lakes, and ridge endings. Its utility to DVI identification varies from case to case. The remains have to be fleshed and in a state of preservation that allows for prints to be taken—this may be possible even with partially decomposed and even burned remains, as fingers curl inward when exposed to fire, thus preserving the ridge details.

As with all other forms of identification, AM records also need to exist for comparison. Whether extensive AM records are available varies depending on the country or countries involved; many countries collect fingerprints from all of its citizens once they reach adulthood and this information is typically held in a national computer, which allows rapid searching—in other countries, legislation may prevent the storage of fingerprints, or

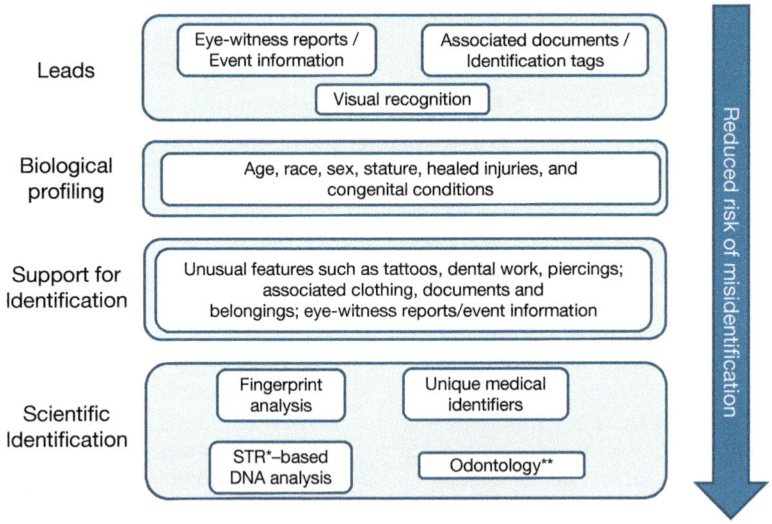

Figure 1 Identifications obtained using visual recognition or other customary means are, where possible, supported by comparing antemortem and postmortem data to allow biological profiling and collection of additional evidence to support the identification. Ideally, identifications should be supported by at least one form of scientific identification, which greatly reduces the possibility of misidentification. *, SNP-based DNA analysis could also provide scientific identification but is not widely used; **, scientific identification using odontology would normally require comparison of dental radiographs or other features that would be considered to be unique.

restrict it to those arrested in connection to a criminal offense. If no AM records are available, it may be possible to recover AM prints from the personal possessions of the missing person(s), assuming there is reliable information on who is actually missing. With a computer-based search using an automated fingerprint identification system (AFIS), a list of candidate matches can be produced in seconds; however, the algorithms are not sufficiently refined to produce exact matches and computer-generated matches have to be examined manually by an expert to establish a confirmed match.

Dental radiographs

The identification of individuals based on a comparison of AM and postmortem (PM) radiographs is, arguably, a somewhat subjective process, but one which is nonetheless recognized as a scientific means by which a positive identification may be made. While in the past, radiographic equipment may not have been available in situ and radiographers were forced to ship bulky equipment and improvise darkrooms in which to develop the films, this is no longer an obstacle. Portable digital radiographic equipment—some even hand-held—is widely available, and rapidly becoming cost-effective. If not available in the country in which the disaster or conflict has occurred, this equipment is so portable that it can be carried as hand luggage in the passenger compartment of aircraft deploying individuals to the scene.

The AM–PM matching of radiographs for identification is more widely accepted in forensic dentistry than in forensic anthropology, where the former is most often based on radiographic images of dental restorations and/or implants, which evince the unique characteristics of both the morphology of the lesion and that of the dentist's individual technique and thus afford multiple surfaces for examination (**Figure 2**); the latter relies upon matching frontal sinus,

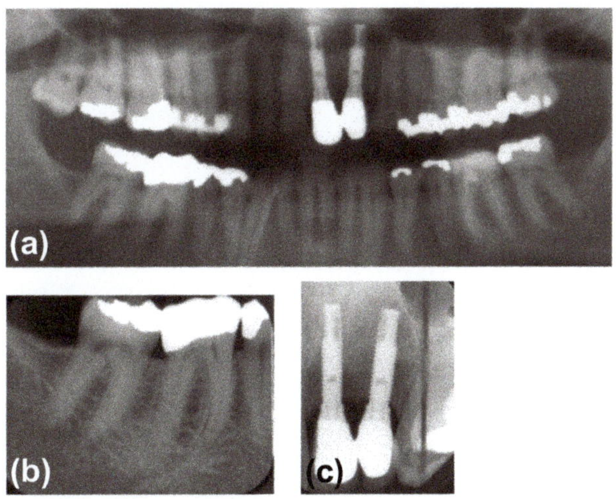

Figure 2 (a) Antemortem orthopantogram, (b) postmortem mandibular, and (c) maxillary radiographs from the same individual. Radiographs courtesy of Dr John Robson.

cranial sutures, vertebral morphology, and even bone trabecular patterns, not just the orthopedic equivalent of implants, fixators, pins, plates, screws, and artificial joints. Although the angle at which an AM radiograph is taken may cause distortion, elongation, and superimposition of features in a dental radiograph, the problem is often compounded in an orthopedic image by additional factors such as age-related changes in joint surfaces and trabecular realignment caused by the application of differing stresses due to activity level and type with age. In all radiographic comparisons, the years elapsed between when the AM image was made and the individual's death must be taken into consideration. Superimposition of the AM–PM images of restorations is a frequently used technique in conjunction with the correspondence of measurements. Again, there is somewhat better correspondence within dental images than even within internal fixators used in fracture repair, as remodeling of bone due to weightbearing contributes to the movement of implanted devices over time. Dental records themselves (e.g., notations of teeth treated, condition of teeth, etc.) are not definitive in DVI as both omissions and mistakes in recording do occur; however, such records are potentially useful when comparing large numbers of AM and PM records to establish possible matches and in providing additional support for an identification; in some contexts dental records are used when radiographs are not available.

The utility of dental radiographs tends to be limited to developed countries where individuals typically visit the dentist and radiography is commonly used as part of routine examinations or following any major dental work. The dentist normally keeps either the developed radiographs themselves, microfilm of those radiographs, or stores digital radiographic images in the patient's electronic file. When disaster victims have not been subjected to trauma that has resulted in disruption of the dentition and AM records that are available, forensic odontology is a powerful means of achieving identifications.

Nuclear DNA

Since its introduction into forensic science in 1985, DNA profiling has become a commonplace in forensic laboratories worldwide. Its primary forensic use is for the identification material recovered from scenes of crimes; however, it is also widely used in the identification of human remains, particularly following on from transport disasters, such as plane crashes.

By the early to mid-1990s, the analysis of short tandem repeats (STRs) had replaced variable number tandem repeat-based analysis. STRs had several advantages: they could be analyzed using polymerase chain reaction (PCR)-based methods, which made them much more sensitive; the alleles of STR loci are also much shorter, making the analysis of degraded material easier; several STR loci could be analyzed in one reaction and analyzed together using capillary electrophoresis, which greatly reduced the time taken to carry out the analysis; and the profiles could be broken down into a series of numbers corresponding to the number of core repeats present in each allele, which allows comparisons to be made between DNA profiles generated within a laboratory and also to compare profiles generated in different laboratories.

STRs are found throughout the genome and they are composed of short blocks of sequence that are repeated in tandem—the STRs commonly used for forensic analysis have blocks of sequence that are 4 or 5 bp long (**Figure 3**). While there are numerous STR loci in the human genome that could be used as forensic markers, around 20–25 are commonly used. These have been selected for being highly discriminating (typically having a large number of variants (alleles) that differ in the number core repeats) and for being easy to analyze using PCR-based technology. Using current methodology DNA profiles can, in principle, be generated within a few hours and produce a profile that is extremely rare, if not unique (**Figure 4**).

Because of the limited discrimination capacity of the early profiling systems, it was not until 1991 that DNA profiling was successfully employed in the identification of human remains—in this case, a murder victim in the UK. It has since been successfully applied to cases that range from the identification of individual bodies to more complex scenarios with multiple victims following, for example, air crashes, fires and explosions, terrorist attacks, natural disasters, and conflicts. A distinct advantage of DNA analysis in DVI is that all tissues contain DNA, and therefore the method will work on highly fragmented remains and enable fragments of bodies to be reassociated.

As with the other forms of identification, the use of DNA analysis in DVI will vary from context to context. Whether DNA can be recovered from the human remains depends on the degree of environmental insult, for example, if the remains have been subjected to high temperatures in excess of 200 °C or there has been a long delay in locating and recovering the remains the DNA can be highly degraded, and it may not be

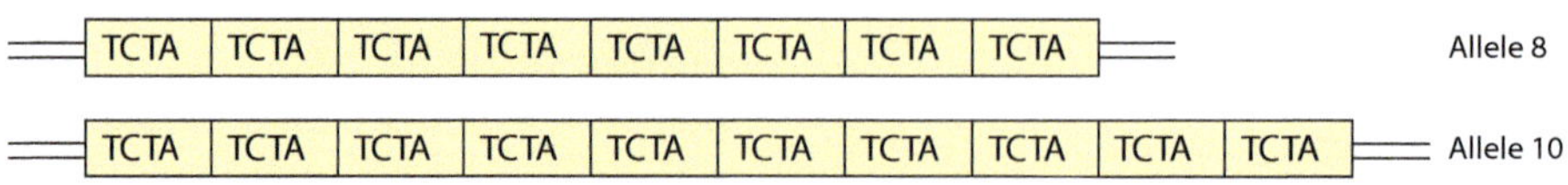

Figure 3 The structure of a short tandem repeat. This example shows the structure of two alleles from the locus D8S1179. The DNA either side of the core repeats is called flanking DNA. The alleles are named according to the number of repeats that they contain—hence alleles 8 and 10.

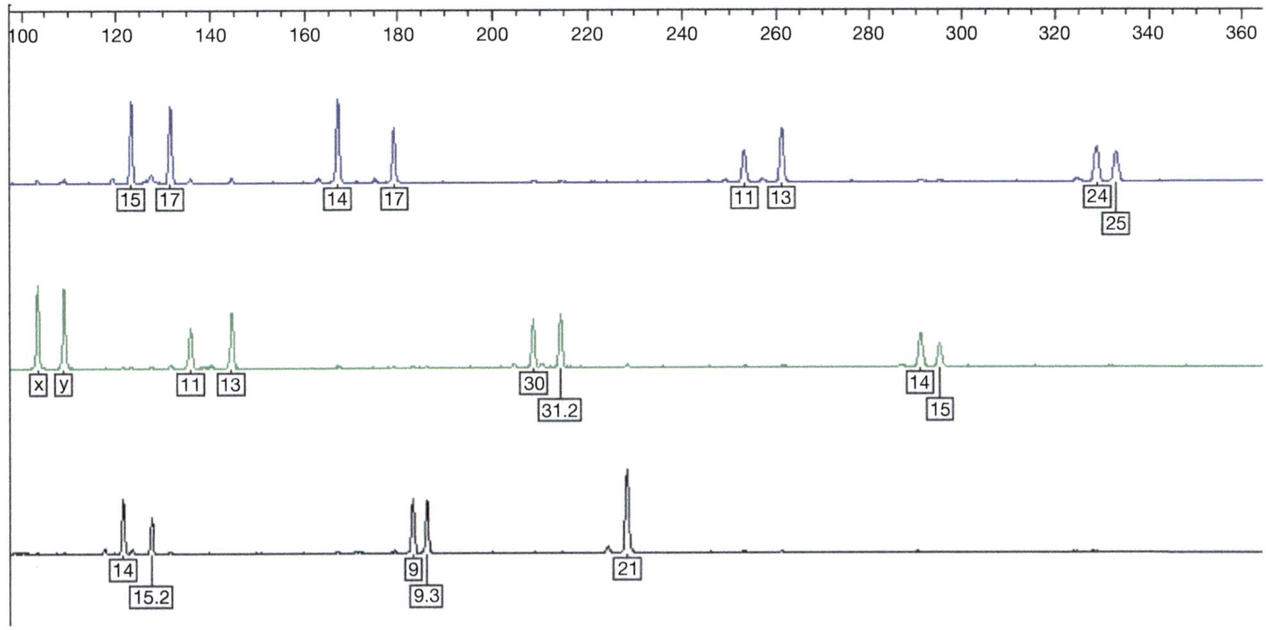

Figure 4 A DNA profile is represented by a series of peaks that can be broken down into a numerical code—the numbers correspond to the number of core repeats in each STR allele. The profile above contains the information on 10 STR loci and the amelogenin locus, which differentiates between the X and Y chromosomes—in this profile, labeled X and Y (showing that this DNA sample is from a male).

possible to generate a profile. AM data are required for comparison: this can be in the form of a direct comparison if a biological sample from the missing person is available, or more commonly by comparison to biological relatives of the missing person.

Unique medical identifiers

On occasions, PM analysis of human remains may happen upon a medical implant; typical examples are artificial joints and pacemakers. These medical devices come with a unique serial number and can allow for unambiguous identification as long as the relevant information can be located. Needless to say, identifications through this method are not common.

Data Collection

Data collection, both PM and AM, is a critical component of the DVI operation. Several agencies, both national and international, have developed forms that facilitate the systematic collection of data that can be used in the identification process. The most commonly employed system for DVI work uses the Interpol forms—these have been specifically developed for DVI work. The International Committee of the Red Cross (ICRC) has also developed AM and PM forms, which have been designed for use in postconflict scenarios (**Figure 5**). Both these systems can be computerized with the data entered into a relational database, allowing AM and PM data to be cross-searched. National authorities have also developed their own systems, for example, in the US, the Disaster Mortuary Operational Response Team (DMORT) has its own set of recording forms and database recording similar information. Obviously, the more victims and the greater the fragmentation of those individuals, the more imperative it is to computerize PM and AM records. Searching by hand through records for matches, especially when the personnel who originally recorded PM details are no longer available and memory is lacking, is a frustrating exercise.

Postmortem

The cooperation and teamwork of experts, sharing of information, and agreement concerning and adherence to criteria by which an identification will be made, are critical to the management and effective performance of any DVI team. The work flow in the morgue, and hence floor plan, should be arranged to facilitate the processing of remains as well as the communication among the various teams of experts. The technical experts involved in the collection of data will vary depending on the state of the human remains; typically teams will comprise some or all of a pathologist, who will undertake a PM examination; an anthropologist to examine skeletal material; an odontologist to take radiographs and examine the teeth; a radiographer to take whole body X-rays; a fingerprint

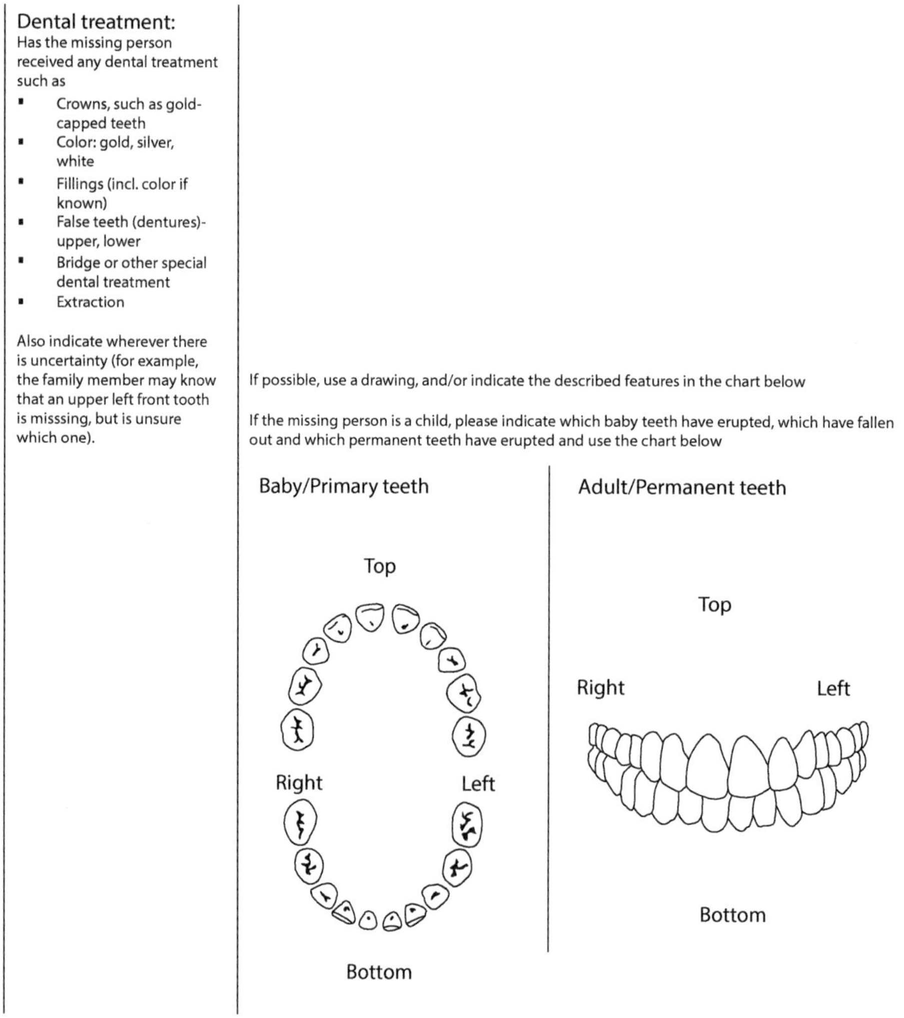

Dental treatment:
Has the missing person received any dental treatment such as
- Crowns, such as gold-capped teeth
- Color: gold, silver, white
- Fillings (incl. color if known)
- False teeth (dentures)-upper, lower
- Bridge or other special dental treatment
- Extraction

Also indicate wherever there is uncertainty (for example, the family member may know that an upper left front tooth is misssing, but is unsure which one).

If possible, use a drawing, and/or indicate the described features in the chart below

If the missing person is a child, please indicate which baby teeth have erupted, which have fallen out and which permanent teeth have erupted and use the chart below

Figure 5 A section of the antemortem data collection form developed by the International Committee of the Red Cross.

expert; and a biologist to take samples for DNA analysis. Other individuals, for example police officers and crime scene investigators, will also be involved carrying out tasks such as documenting personal belongings, clothing, taking photographs, and ensuring chain of custody for any evidential items.

Antemortem

A prerequisite to the application of any of these methods is the existence of relevant, reliable AM data. Following a mass disaster, an AM data collection interview is typically conducted with relatives of the missing. The collection of AM data is as much a specialized process as conducting a PM examination, and interviews of relatives of the missing should be performed only by trained personnel. Interviews are best performed by native speakers of the language, so in-country training of personnel should be planned. During the interview, information concerning the individual's physical description, a description of the clothing the individual was wearing, and any personal effects that were with the individual are recorded on an AM data form—this form should be compatible with the PM form to allow searching of comparable fields of information. A photograph of the missing person is collected and the existence and whereabouts of medical and dental records for that individual are noted so that these can be requested from doctors and dentists at a later date. Photographs of the victim's smiling can be also be useful as the teeth may have distinguishing morphology or features such as spots caused by hypoplasia. During this interview, if possible, DNA samples are taken and latent fingerprints are enhanced and collected from the home of the missing person. DNA samples may be direct reference samples (e.g., from the missing person's toothbrush or hairbrush) or indirect reference samples, preferably from their immediate kin (father, mother, children).

The above methods work very well in developed countries and the process above describes the situation in a country with well-developed infrastructure. However, the infrastructure of many less-developed countries does not facilitate the collection, maintenance, and storage of such relevant records that drive the DVI process for the citizenry of developed countries. In postconflict situations, even where such records may have existed at one time, they may have been destroyed during the conflict or its aftermath or have become unavailable due to political and boundary shifts. In natural or other mass disasters in less developed countries, the same may be true regarding destruction of extant records or the lack of relevant records. Furthermore, subsequent to mass disasters and conflicts, many individuals are frequently displaced internally or have become refugees in neighboring countries. This makes locating relevant kin of the missing difficult, and organizing and conducting AM interviews challenging. Whenever possible, it is recommended to avoid retraumatizing the relatives of the missing by repeated visits and questions, as these doubtless reopen wounds, doubts, and raise anxiety.

Selection of Methods for Identification

In any mass disaster, the method that can be employed successfully will be dictated according to the condition of the remains, the composition of experts in the DVI team, the technical and financial resources available, and the choices made by the team's leadership during the course of its operational mandate.

Prior to DNA analysis, comparison of dental records was the most widely used method to achieve identifications. Analysis of five disasters in the UK between 1985 and 1989 which comprised three air disasters, a capsized ferry, and a fire on an oil platform, identified that dental records had been used to identify, on average, over 80% of the recovered bodies. In more recent large-scale disasters, for example, in the World Trade Center investigations, DNA was the first choice for identification and generated the majority of identifications by a single modality (86%), dental and fingerprints combined only yielding an additional 10% of identifications. Similarly, since the inception of the International Commission for Missing Person's (ICMP) DNA laboratory in Tuzla (Bosnia), identifications from the 1992 to 1995 Bosnian conflict have been DNA-led, with secondary means of identification used, where possible, to support the DNA-based identification—as of mid-2011, over 13 000 individuals in Bosnia and Herzegovina had been identified and returned to their families. In contrast, although DNA was initially a method of first choice in the Asian Tsunami identifications in Thailand, 11 months after the tsunami 80% of foreign victims had been identified using dental comparisons—dental analysis with local victims identified 55% of Thai victims, lower than with foreign victims due to the lack of AM records in many cases. Overall, in the 15 months following the disaster, identifications had been made using dental alone, 1105; dental plus others, 1451; fingerprints alone, 670; fingerprints plus others 927; DNA alone, 27; DNA plus others 459.

There are reasons for the success ratios of the identification methods in each of the above examples. In the World Trade Center, victim fragmentation was extreme and the goal was set to identify every piece of tissue greater than or equal to 5 cm^3, thus necessitating the use of DNA. In Bosnia, lack of AM medical and dental records, commingling in secondary mass graves, and time elapsed since the deaths of the victims are but a few of the factors that dictated the reliance on DNA rather than other primary identifiers. In Thailand, important factors included that dental-based identifications could be made for many of the foreign victims relatively rapidly: many bodies were not fragmented, removing the requirement for DNA-based re-association; fingerprint analysis was successful with many Thai victims; limited in-country facilities were capable of handling the volume of DNA samples from the disaster; and decomposition of tissue was rapid in the tropical environment, making DNA analysis difficult.

Evaluation of Identification Data

The exact procedures used in the identification process vary from country to country and from scenario to scenario. Typically, identifications are made through an organization that acts as an identification commission or board; this would typically include an expert from the main disciplines involved in making identifications—investigators/crime scene investigators, fingerprint examiners, odontologists, pathologists, anthropologists, and DNA analysts—and should be presided over by the legal authority charged with issuing death certificates. In this manner, all the evidence contributing to the identification of an individual in a mass disaster is reviewed a final time by everyone who has contributed to that process, and a legal decision concerning the establishment of positive identity and repatriation of the remains to kin can be completed.

Evaluating the identification is a complex task, especially as the number of victims increases—this heightens the possibility of coincidental matches, which, if not detected, can lead to misidentifications. An often cited example where this occurred is the identification of a fire officer recovered from the World Trade Center following 9/11, who was misidentified on the basis of his clothing that identified him as a fire officer from a particular unit coupled with a rare congenital anomaly in spinal vertebra. The identification was not confirmed by any of the recognized objective methods of identification and DNA analysis later exposed the misidentification, but only after the remains had been returned to the wrong family—the rare medical condition had been shared by one of his colleagues in his unit. Such seemingly remote coincidences become more likely as the number of victims increases.

Conclusions

The requirement for governments and indeed the international community to be able to mount an effective DVI response following disasters and conflicts is widely accepted. Recent technological advances in terms of DNA analysis, portable radiographic equipment, and sophisticated computer databases that allow comparison of AM and PM data have increased the number of cases where the identification of human remains is possible. There will always be limitations as to what is possible; for example, following the World Trade Center identifications, even with an enormous effort expended, no identification could be made for over 40% of the victims, which should not distract from the success in identifying over 1500 victims. With continued improvements in technology, preparedness, and infrastructure to deal with a large number of samples in a timely fashion, there is the potential to have a greater proportion of victims identified and returned to their families following future disasters and conflicts.

See also: **Anthropology/Odontology:** History of Forensic Anthropology; Odontology; Personal Identification in Forensic Anthropology; **Biology/DNA:** DNA Extraction and Quantification; MiniSTRs; Mitochondrial DNA; Short Tandem Repeats; Single-Nucleotide Polymorphisms; The National Missing and Unidentified Persons System (NamUs); **Forensic Medicine/Clinical:** Airplane Crashes and Other Mass Disasters; **Forensic Medicine/Pathology:** Autopsy.

Further Reading

Ballantyne, J., 1997. Mass disaster genetics. Nature Genetics 15, 329–331.

Biesecker, L.G., Bailey-Wilson, J.E., Ballantyne, J., et al., 2005. Epidemiology – DNA identifications after the 9/11 World Trade Center attack. Science 310, 1122–1123.

Bowers, C.M., 2004. Forensic Dental Evidence: An Investigator's Handbook. Elsevier, Amsterdam.

Brenner, C.H., 2006. Some mathematical problems in the DNA identification of victims in the 2004 tsunami and similar mass fatalities. Forensic Science International 157, 172–180.

Dolan, S.M., Saraiya, D.S., Donkervoort, S., Rogel, K., Lieber, C., Sozer, A., 2009. The emerging role of genetics professionals in forensic kinship DNA identification after a mass fatality: lessons learned from Hurricane Katrina volunteers. Genetics in Medicine 11, 414–417.

Donkervoort, S., Dolan, S.M., Beckwith, M., Northrup, T.P., Sozer, A., 2008. Enhancing accurate data collection in mass fatality kinship identifications: lessons learned from Hurricane Katrina. Forensic Science International: Genetics 2, 354–362.

Huffine, E., Crews, J., Kennedy, B., Bomberger, K., Zinbo, A., 2001. Mass identification of persons missing from the break-up of the former Yugoslavia: structure, function, and role of the international commission on missing persons. Croatian Medical Journal 42, 271–275.

International Committee of the Red Cross, 2004. The Missing and Their Families – Documents of Reference. ICRC, Geneva.

International Committee of the Red Cross, 2009. Missing People, DNA Analysis and Identification of Human Remains. ICRC, Geneva.

Interpol, 2009. Disaster Victim Identification Guide. Interpol, Lyon.

Keough, M.E., Simmons, T., Samuels, M., 2004. Missing persons in post-conflict settings: best practices for integrating psychosocial and scientific approaches. The Journal of the Royal Society for the Promotion of Health 124, 271–275.

Morgan, O.W., Sribanditmongkol, P., Perera, C., Sulasmi, Y., Van Alphen, D., Sondorp, E., 2006. Mass fatality management following the South Asian tsunami disaster: case studies in Thailand, Indonesia, and Sri Lanka. PLoS Medicine 3, e195.

National Institute of Justice, 2005. Lessons Learned from 9/11: DNA Identification in Mass Fatality Incidents. US Department of Justice, Washington, DC.

Prinz, M., Carracedo, A., Mayr, W.R., et al., 2007. DNA Commission of the International Society for Forensic Genetics (ISFG): recommendations regarding the role of forensic genetics for disaster victim identification (DVI). Forensic Science International: Genetics 1, 3–12.

Schuller-Gotzburg, P., Suchanek, J., 2007. Forensic odontologists successfully identify tsunami victims in Phuket, Thailand. Forensic Science International 171, 204–207.

Ubelaker, D.H., Jacobs, C., 1995. Identification of orthopedic device manufacturer. Journal of Forensic Sciences 40, 168–170.

Forensic DNA Advisory Groups: DAB, SWGDAM, ENFSI, and BSAG

JM Butler, National Institute of Standards and Technology, Gaithersburg, MD, USA

Glossary

Quality assurance A system of activities whose purpose is to provide confidence to the producer or user of a product or service that it meets defined standards or quality.

Validation The process by which a method, instrument, or computer program is deemed useful for a specified purpose through rigorous evaluation before acceptance into routine use.

Introduction

With a technique as powerful as forensic DNA testing to help establish guilt or innocence in the context of criminal investigations, it is imperative that measures are in place to create confidence in the results obtained. This article provides a brief review of national- and international-level organizations that support the forensic DNA community in an advisory capacity to promote accurate and reliable testing and to assist with quality assurance measures. **Table 1** includes a summary of the major national or regional groups that govern or coordinate efforts with forensic science. **Table 2** lists some details regarding the forensic DNA advisory groups that will be covered in this article.

The United States

Concerns regarding data quality as forensic DNA testing that began to spread in the first decade of its use led to the formation of several organizations within the United States. In addition, reports by the National Research Council of the U.S. National Academies of Science in 1992 and 1996 focused on technical and statistical issues surrounding high-quality DNA results.

The Technical Working Group on DNA Analysis Methods/The Scientific Working Group on DNA Analysis Methods

The Technical Working Group on DNA Analysis Methods (TWGDAM) was established in November 1988 under FBI Laboratory sponsorship to aid forensic DNA scientists in North America. Since 1998, TWGDAM has been known as SWGDAM, which stands for the Scientific Working Group on DNA Analysis Methods. SWGDAM is a group of approximately 50 scientists representing federal, state, and local forensic DNA laboratories in the United States and Canada. A representative of the European Network of Forensic Science Institutes (ENFSI) DNA Working Group often attends as well. Meetings are held twice a year, usually in January and July. For several years, public SWGDAM meetings were held in conjunction with the International Symposium on Human Identification, sponsored each fall by the Promega Corporation. Since 2006, the public SWGDAM meeting has been held as part of the FBI-sponsored National Combined DNA Index System (CODIS) Conference.

Since the organization's inception, six individuals have served as TWGDAM or SWGDAM chair: James Kearney (FBI), Bruce Budowle (FBI), Richard Guerrieri (FBI), David Coffman (Florida Department of Law Enforcement), and Ted Staples (Georgia Bureau of Investigation). In January 2011, Anthony Onorato (FBI) was appointed by the FBI Laboratory director to be the chair of SWGDAM.

Over the years, a number of TWGDAM or SWGDAM committees have operated to bring recommendations before the entire group. These committees have included (at different times) the following topics: restriction fragment length polymorphism, polymerase chain reaction, CODIS, mitochondrial DNA, short tandem repeat (STR) interpretation, training, validation, Y chromosome, expert systems, quality assurance, missing persons/mass disasters, mixture interpretation, mass spectrometry, enhanced method detection and interpretation, and rapid DNA analysis. TWGDAM issued guidelines for quality assurance in DNA analysis in 1989, 1991, and 1995. Revised SWGDAM validation guidelines were published in 2004, and interpretation guidelines for autosomal STR typing were released in 2010. Several ad hoc working groups have

 http://dx.doi.org/10.1016/B978-0-12-800647-4.00040-0

Table 1 Organizations assisting forensic science quality assurance

Organization; year started	*Membership*	*Websites*
American Society of Crime Laboratory Directors (ASCLD); started in 1974	US federal, state, and local lab managers; not directly associated with SWGDAM but ASCLD/LAB uses the FBI quality assurance standards for DNA audits	http://www.ascld.org
European Network of Forensic Science Institutes (ENFSI); started in 1995	Sixteen working groups including one on DNA	http://www.enfsi.eu
Senior Managers of Australian and New Zealand Forensic Laboratories (SMANZFL); started in 1986	Eight specialist advisory groups (SAGs) including one on biology (BSAG)	http://www.nifs.com.au/SMANZFL/SMANZFL.html
Academia Iberoamericana de Criminalística y Estudios Forenses (AICEF); started in 2004	Represents 19 Spanish- and Portuguese-speaking countries in Europe and Latin America; has four working groups including one on forensic genetics	http://www.aicef.net/
Asian Forensic Sciences Network (AFSN); started in 2008	Five working groups including one on DNA	http://www.asianforensic.net

SWGDAM, Scientific Working Group on DNA Analysis Methods; LAB, Laboratory Accreditation Board; BSAG, Biology Specialist Advisory Group.
Information from International Forensic Strategic Alliance (IFSA) 2010 Annual Report: http://www.ascld.org/files/ifsa+cov_BAT.pdf and http://www.ifsaworldwide.org/.

Table 2 Forensic DNA advisory groups

Organization	*Membership*	*Meeting frequency/purpose*
DNA Commission of the International Society for Forensic Genetics (ISFG)	ISFG Executive Committee and selected experts; chaired by Dr Peter Gill	As needed to prepare recommendations (see http://www.isfg.org/Publications/DNA+Commission)
Scientific Working Group on DNA Analysis Methods (SWGDAM)	US and Canada federal, state, and local DNA technical leaders and invited guests (40–50 people total); subdivided into five to eight committees	Meets twice a year to develop guidelines on validation, DNA data interpretation, and other topics
European Network of Forensic Science Institutes (ENFSI) DNA Working Group	>30 European countries and invited guests (90–100 people total); subdivided into five committees	Meets twice a year along with European DNA Profiling Group (EDNAP)
Biology Specialist Advisory Group (BSAG)	Representatives of each forensic DNA lab in Australia and New Zealand (11 people total)	Meets once a year under direction of SMANZFL and with support of the Australian National Institute of Forensic Science

produced recommendations on such topics as the review of outsourced data and partial matches. SWGDAM documents are made available through *Forensic Science Communications*, an online journal sponsored by the FBI Laboratory.

DNA Advisory Board

The DNA Advisory Board (DAB) was a congressionally mandated advisory board that was created and funded by the United States Congress through the DNA Identification Act of 1994. The first meeting of the DAB was held on May 12, 1995, and chaired by Nobel laureate Dr Joshua Lederberg. The DAB consisted of 13 voting members that included scientists from federal, state, local, and private forensic laboratories; molecular geneticists and population geneticists not affiliated with a forensic laboratory; a representative from the National Institute of Standards and Technology (NIST); the chair of TWGDAM; and a judge.

The original voting members of the DAB included Joshua Lederberg (Rockefeller University), Arthur Eisenberg (University of North Texas Health Science Center), Shirley Abrahamson (Wisconsin State Supreme Court), Jack Ballantyne (Suffolk County Crime Lab), Bruce Budowle (FBI Laboratory), Ranajit Chakraborty (University of Texas Health Science Center), Bernard Devlin (Carnegie Mellon University), Marcia Eisenberg (Laboratory Corporation of America), Paul Ferrara (Virginia Division of Forensic Science), John Hicks (Alabama Department of Forensic Sciences), Margaret Kuo (Orange County Sheriff's Office), Terry Laber (Minnesota Bureau of Criminal Apprehension), and Dennis Reeder (NIST). Nonvoting members of the DAB were Phillip Reilly (Eunice Kennedy Shriver Center for Mental Retardation), Larry Presley

(FBI Laboratory), Jay Miller (FBI Laboratory), and Randall Murch (Designated Federal Employee, FBI Laboratory). A number of other individuals attended and participated in various DAB meetings over the 5 years that the group met.

The DAB was created for a 5-year period to issue quality assurance standards (QAS) for the forensic DNA community. When the DAB's responsibilities ended in 2000, SWGDAM was designated as the group responsible for offering recommendations on revisions to the QAS as needed. In 2007, SWGDAM revised the QAS for forensic DNA testing laboratories and the QAS for DNA databasing laboratories. These revised standards went into effect on July 1, 2009 after being approved by the FBI Laboratory director. Further revisions regarding data review were made at the January 2011 SWGDAM meeting and went into effect on September 1, 2011.

Forensic DNA laboratories in the United States are mandated by Congress to follow strict QAS. In October 1998 and April 1999, at the recommendation of the DAB, the FBI director issued QAS for forensic DNA testing laboratories and QAS for convicted offender DNA databasing laboratories that define how forensic laboratories are required to conduct business. These QAS were revised a decade later and went into effect on July 1, 2009, with some additional minor revisions introduced in 2011 regarding data review. The 2009 revisions also renamed the convicted offender QAS as the QAS for DNA databasing laboratories so that they would be applicable for laboratories processing offender, arrestee, and detainee specimens. US forensic DNA laboratories are governed by the QAS and regularly audited for their compliance to these standards.

There are 17 topics covered in the revised (and original) QAS: (1) scope, (2) definitions, (3) quality assurance program, (4) laboratory organization and management, (5) personnel, (6) facilities, (7) evidence/sample control, (8) validation, (9) analytical procedures, (10) equipment calibration and maintenance, (11) reports/documentation, (12) review, (13) proficiency testing, (14) corrective action, (15) audits, (16) safety, and (17) outsourcing.

The American Society of Crime Laboratory Directors and Its Laboratory Accreditation Board

The American Society of Crime Laboratory Directors (ASCLD) and its Laboratory Accreditation Board (ASCLD/LAB) play an important role in the United States as well as internationally for laboratory accreditation programs. The ASCLD/LAB motto is "quality assurance through inspection." The crime laboratory accreditation program is a voluntary program in which any crime laboratory may participate to demonstrate that its management, operations, personnel, procedures, and instruments meet stringent standards. The goal of accreditation is to improve the overall service of forensic laboratories to the criminal justice system. If a forensic laboratory is interested in becoming accredited, an ASCLD/LAB accreditation manual is available from the executive secretary for a fee. Laboratories becoming accredited in forensic biology are audited against the FBI's QAS for the laboratory operations pertaining to DNA testing. ASCLD/LAB accreditation may be under the Legacy Program or the International Program. However, no new Legacy Program applications have been processed since April 2009. Laboratories are being supported under the Legacy Program until they can transition to ASCLD/LAB-International, which accredits to ISO/IEC 17025 requirements. As of September 2011, a total of 389 crime laboratories were accredited by ASCLD/LAB although not all of them are doing DNA testing. For additional information, see ASCLD/LAB Web site.

Forensic Quality Services

Forensic Quality Services, Inc. (FQS) is a not-for-profit organization providing ISO/IEC 17025 accreditations to forensic testing laboratories in the United States. FQS is recognized by the FBI to perform QAS DNA assessments and offers training workshops on accreditation. For more information, see FQS Web site.

Europe

As with the United States, organizations have been in place in Europe since the late 1980s to help with forensic DNA analysis.

DNA Commission of the International Society for Forensic Genetics

The International Society for Forensic Genetics (ISFG) is an organization of over 1100 scientists from more than 60 countries promoting scientific knowledge in the field of forensic markers from human blood. Since 1989, the ISFG has issued recommendations on a variety of important topics in forensic DNA analysis through a DNA Commission. These recommendations have included naming of STR variant alleles and STR repeat nomenclature, mitochondrial DNA and Y-STR issues, DNA mixture interpretation, paternity-testing biostatistics, disaster victim identification, and use of animal DNA in forensic genetic investigations. For more information, see ISFG DNA Commission Web site.

European DNA Profiling Group

Another working group of the ISFG is the European DNA Profiling Group (EDNAP), which consists of members from 21 laboratories across 17 European countries along with a few invited guests from the United States and Australia. Niels Morling from Denmark is the chair of EDNAP, whose members are from university Institutes of Legal Medicine and government forensic laboratories with a focus on research. Currently, Austria, Belgium, Denmark, England, Finland, France, Germany, Greece, Ireland, Italy, the Netherlands, Norway, Portugal, Scotland, Spain, Sweden, and Switzerland are represented.

EDNAP was established in October 1988 with a goal to harmonize methods used to aid forensic DNA investigations. EDNAP meets twice a year (since 2004 in conjunction with ENFSI DNA working group meetings) and regularly organizes collaborative exercises to assess methods and examine where improvements can be made. These interlaboratory studies are published in the scientific literature and have helped establish European core loci and address new marker systems (see ISFG Web site). The Institute of Legal Medicine in Innsbruck, Austria, has developed and maintains the EDNAP mitochondrial DNA population database. For more information, see EDNAP Web site.

The European Network of Forensic Science Institutes

The ENFSI was formally started in 1995 to set standards for exchange of data between European member states and to be an accrediting body through conducting laboratory audits. Today ENFSI is recognized as the sole voice of the forensic science community within Europe. Within the ENFSI, there is a DNA working group that meets twice a year to discuss forensic DNA protocols and research in much the same fashion as SWGDAM does within North America.

The ENFSI DNA working group has five committees referred to as "workshops": (1) quality control, quality assurance, sampling kits, training, and teaching; (2) DNA analysis methods and interpretation; (3) DNA databases; (4) automation and expert systems; and (5) forensic biology. Manufacturers are permitted to participate in many of the meeting sessions and are given an opportunity to share information on their latest products.

The database committee produces an annual document on DNA database management that in April 2010 included 28 recommendations (audit questions surrounding these recommendations have been added in more recent versions). Reports and surveys of DNA database sizes in Europe are regularly conducted and shared through the ENFSI Web site. Recommendations for training of DNA staff and minimum validation guidelines were released in November 2010. An ENFSI collaborative project on Y-STR analysis of DNA mixture samples was published in 2008 and a statement issued regarding European consensus regarding DNA mixture interpretation principles was published in conjunction with EDNAP in 2007. The ENFSI DNA working group maintains a population database for determining match probabilities across European populations at their Web site.

Chairs of the ENFSI DNA working group have included Dave Werrett and Lyn Fereday from the U.K. Forensic Science Service and Ingo Bastisch from Germany's BKA (Bundeskriminalamt). Members of ENFSI come from Austria, Belgium, Bosnia and Herzegovina, Croatia, Cyprus, the Czech Republic, Denmark, Estonia, Finland, France, Germany, Greece, Hungary, Ireland, Italy, Latvia, Lithuania, Montenegro, the Netherlands, Norway, Poland, Portugal, Russia, Slovakia, Slovenia, Spain, Sweden, Switzerland, Turkey, and the United Kingdom. Invited guests from the United States, Abu Dhabi, and Australia regularly attend as well. For additional information, see ENFSI Web site.

Spanish- and Portuguese-Speaking Countries

The Academia Iberoamericana de Criminalistica Y Estudios Forenses (AICEF) serves Spanish- and Portuguese-speaking countries in Europe and Latin America and has 32 active members from 19 different countries. There are four working groups in AICEF: crime scene (CITEC), forensic genetics (GITAD), ballistics (CITBAF), and drugs of abuse (GITADA). For more information, see AICEF Web site.

Australia/New Zealand

The National Institute of Forensic Science

The National Institute of Forensic Science (NIFS), which is located in Melbourne, began in 1992 as a central organization to serve the forensic science community in Australia and New Zealand. NIFS sponsors and supports research in forensic science, assists with development and coordination of forensic science services between jurisdictions, aids training programs, and coordinates delivery of quality assurance programs. In 2008, NIFS became a directorate in the newly formed Australia New Zealand Policing Advisory Agency. NIFS works closely with the Senior Managers of Australia and New Zealand Forensic Science Laboratories (SMANZFL). For more information, see NIFS Web site.

The Senior Managers of Australia and New Zealand Forensic Science Laboratories

The SMANZFL are the directors from forensic science organizations in Australia and New Zealand who meet at least once a year in an effort "to promote leadership in the forensic sciences in the pursuit of excellence." SMANZFL is supported by eight specialist advisory groups covering biology, chemistry, document examination, field and identification sciences, toxicology, illicit drugs, and electronic evidence. For more information, see SMANZFL Web site.

Biology Specialist Advisory Group

The Biology Specialist Advisory Group (BSAG) is one of the eight specialist advisory groups of SMANZFL and is funded by NIFS to prepare recommendations for their laboratories. BSAG meets formally once a year but also holds additional meetings in person or through the Internet as needed. The BSAG has representatives from 11 organizations within Australia and New Zealand: Victoria Police Forensic Services Centre, Victorian Institute of Forensic Medicine, New South Wales Institute of Forensic Medicine, New South Wales Police Forensic Services Group, Queensland Health, Northern Territory Police Forensic Services, Western Australia's PathWest, Forensic Science South Australia, Forensic Science Service Tasmania, Australia Federal Police, and New Zealand's ESR (Environmental Science and Research). Pam Scott of the Forensic Science Service in Tasmania is the current BSAG chair. BSAG has written in support of the ISFG DNA Commission recommendations on DNA mixture interpretation and disaster victim identification. For more information, see BSAG Web site.

Asia

The Asian Forensic Sciences Network (AFSN) is the most recent regional organization formed in support of forensic sciences. Created in 2008, AFSN has five workgroups covering DNA, illicit drugs, toxicology, trace evidence, and quality assurance and standards. AFSN meets annually. As of September 2011, member institutes include representatives from Brunei Darussalam, Indonesia, Korea, Laos, Malaysia, Mongolia, People's Republic of China, Philippines, Singapore, Thailand, and Vietnam. For more information, see AFSN Web site.

International Cooperation and Coordination

At the international level, there has been a recent effort to have more cooperation across the regional groups listed in **Table 1**. In 2009, the International Forensic Strategic Alliance (IFSA) was established as a partnership between the regional networks of operational forensic laboratories including ASCLD, ENFSI, SMANZFL, AICEF, and AFSN.

While individual DNA advisory groups like SWGDAM or ENFSI typically produce their own guidelines, there have been a few instances where joint publications have been authored. In 2004, SWGDAM coauthored a position statement on single nucleotide polymorphism typing, with ENFSI emphasizing that STR markers would likely remain the primary currency for national DNA databases for the foreseeable future. In 2010, SWGDAM joined with ENFSI and BSAG in a position paper on consumable contamination concerns and potential solutions for manufacturers and consumers. This topic is continuing to be pursued through an international effort that will hopefully lead to a formal ISO (International Standards Organization) standard for forensic grade DNA-free products.

Acknowledgments

Review of this article by Dawn Herkenham and Linzi Wilson-Wilde is greatly appreciated. Forensic DNA research conducted at NIST is supported by an interagency agreement between the National Institute of Justice and the NIST Office of Law Enforcement Standards. Points of view in this document are those of the author and do not necessarily represent the official position or policies of the U.S. Department of Justice. Certain commercial equipment, instruments, and materials are identified in order to specify experimental procedures as completely as possible. In no case does such identification imply a recommendation or endorsement by the National Institute of Standards and Technology nor does it imply that any of the materials, instruments, or equipment identified are necessarily the best available for the purpose.

See also: **Biology/DNA**: History of the International Society for Forensic Genetics – ISFG; Internet Accessible Population Databases: YHRD and EMPOP.

Further Reading

Adams, D.E., Lothridge, K.L., 2000. Scientific working groups. Forensic Science Communications 2 (3), 1–4. Available at: http://www.fbi.gov/about-us/lab/forensic-science-communications/fsc/july2000/swgroups.htm.

Aronson, J.D., 2010. On trial! governing forensic DNA technologies in the USA. In: Hindmarsh, R., Prainsack, B. (Eds.), Genetic Suspects: Global Governance of Forensic DNA Profiling and Databasing. Cambridge University Press, New York, pp. 240–261.

Butler, J.M., 2012. Advanced Topics in Forensic DNA Typing: Methodology. Elsevier Academic Press, San Diego.

DNA Advisory Board, 2000. Statistical and population genetics issues affecting the evaluation of the frequency of occurrence of DNA profiles calculated from pertinent population database(s). Forensic Science Communications 2 (3). Available at: http://www2.fbi.gov/hq/lab/fsc/backissu/july2000/dnastat.htm.

FBI Quality Assurance Standards (2011). Available at: http://www.fbi.gov/about-us/lab/codis/qas-standards-for-forensic-dna-testing-laboratories-effective-9-1-2011.

Gill, P., Rowlands, D., Tully, G., Bastisch, I., Staples, T., Scott, P., 2010. Manufacturer contamination of disposable plastic-ware and other reagents – an agreed position statement by ENFSI, SWGDAM and BSAG. Forensic Science International. Genetics 4 (4), 269–270.

Gill, P., Werrett, D.J., Budowle, B., Guerrieri, R., 2004. An assessment of whether SNPs will replace STRs in national DNA databases – joint considerations of the DNA working group of the European Network of Forensic Science Institutes (ENFSI) and the Scientific Working Group on DNA Analysis Methods (SWGDAM). Science & Justice 44, 51–53.

Presley, L.A., 1999. The evolution of quality assurance standards for forensic DNA analyses in the United States. Profiles in DNA 3 (2), 10–11. Available at: http://www.promega.com/profiles.

Relevant Websites

http://www.ascld-lab.org – ASCLD/LAB.
http://www.nifs.com.au/smanzfl/SAGcriteria.pdf – BSAG.
http://www.isfg.org/EDNAP – EDNAP.
http://www.enfsi.eu/ – ENFSI.
http://www.fbi.gov/about-us/lab/forensic-science-communications/ – Forensic Science Communications.
http://www.forquality.org/ – FQS.
http://www.fsigenetics.com/ – Forensic Science International: Genetics.
http://www.isfg.org/ – International Society for Forensic Genetics.
http://www.nifs.com.au/ – NIFS.
http://www.SWGDAM.org – Scientific Working Group, DNA Analysis Methods.

Forensic Laboratory Efficiency and Funding

R Wickenheiser, Montgomery County Police Crime Laboratory, Gaithersburg, MD, USA

Abbreviations

Case One criminal offense and the collective group of evidentiary items and samples emanating from that offense which can be analyzed by a crime laboratory

Item One evidentiary item which can be sampled for analysis by a crime laboratory

Sample One portion of suspected biological material which can be analyzed by a crime laboratory

Glossary

Analytical capacity The maximum sample output of analyses a laboratory can produce.

Backlog The number of cases submitted to a crime laboratory for analysis that has not yet been completed, where a final report has not yet been issued.

CODIS (combined DNA index system) A term used synonymously with NDIS (National DNA Index System), which is the national DNA database administrated by the United States Federal Bureau of Investigation.

Forensic DNA Analysis of crime scene samples using biological materials to generate profiles and in turn link these to suspect via direct comparison or a match using a DNA database of profiles from known individuals.

Property crime Offenses committed in which items have been damaged or stolen but no physical harm has caused to an individual.

SANE (sexual assault nurse education) A program for uniformly training medical staff in the proper treatment of victims of sexual assault, including collection of sexual assault evidence through medical investigation.

UCR (Uniform Crime Reporting Statistics) UCR, collected and reported by the United States Federal Bureau of Investigation, is a compilation of the number of various crimes separated by jurisdiction, type of crime, and various other parameters.

General

Forensic DNA has the potential to revolutionize the manner in which crimes are investigated. Conventional police wisdom dictates that the first 48 h of an investigation are pivotal for solving a crime, with clearance rates dropping significantly once 72 h have passed. Television crime dramas feature this catchphrase in their titles, including "The First 48" (Arts and Entertainment Channel). While Cold Case squads are working diligently to challenge this paradigm, it follows that the most investigative resources are applied shortly after a crime is committed as suspects are developed and eliminated. Hence, the costs of conducting police investigations are front-end loaded, as a large amount of resources are exhausted at the earliest stages of the investigation. With typical North American crime lab response times of weeks to months after the commission of the crime, traditional application of forensic science provides objective corroborating evidence but results are frequently insufficiently timely to impact the cost structure of many investigations. In contrast to long response time from crime commission to forensic lab report, the actual analysis time is several hours or days for most types of forensic analyses. The largest component of response time is not the lab analysis itself, but is the time a case sits in a queue behind other cases in a backlog.

In the past, forensic science relied on a suspect sample to be supplied along with the crime scene sample. Serological analyses took days, and early DNA (restriction fragment length

 http://dx.doi.org/10.1016/B978-0-12-800647-4.00041-2

polymorphism) analysis took weeks for a case to be completed. Hence, investigations were mostly complete along with the development of viable suspects even when cases were initially sent to the crime lab. Now with databases and improvements in forensic technology, a suspect sample is no longer required, and the minimum time for analysis has been reduced to days or even hours. This revolution of analysis speed, sensitivity, and use of information technology to compare millions of suspect profiles to known individuals produces a momentous opportunity. Forensic DNA objectively includes and eliminates suspects and develops new suspects through the DNA databases that traditional investigation may not. Rapid analysis and use of databases can occur with sufficient speed so as to assist investigations at the earliest stages, when the most resources can be focused more quickly on the right suspects while eliminating the innocent from suspicion.

A cursory examination of this situation would indicate if backlogs of cases were eliminated, then case analysis could be quick enough to direct investigations. The reality, however, is that insufficient analysis capacity exists to meet the increasing demands of investigators as they discover that a quicker response is possible. As labs become quicker, more cases are submitted, quickly redeveloping a temporarily reduced backlog.

In order to focus limited resources, many crime labs have taken to limiting the number of analyses per case, items examined, or do not conduct all analysis types on all cases. Typically, crime labs are not well equipped to project future demand for their service other than to draw on past experience, nor are they able to obtain significant additional resources outside of temporary grant funding. The long-term solution is to accurately forecast the appropriate demand of cases and items and in turn match the crime lab analytical capacity to this projected demand to ensure quick completion of cases without the redevelopment of backlogs.

The use of forensic technology to solve and prevent crime through rapid analysis will require an investment in lab analytical infrastructure. In order to match analytical capacity to investigative requirements, policy makers must make a conscious decision as to which types of cases and items should be analyzed. This article outlines the forensic potential of case types and samples within cases, as well as demonstrates the value of analyzing property crime cases. Further, a "forensic fire station" model is proposed to provide rapid response to case submissions in order to maximize the cost saving through targeting investigations at the earliest stages.

Method

An accurate forecast of demand would enable policy makers to determine the level of resources appropriate for their jurisdiction to turn toward rapid DNA analysis. The Federal Bureau of Investigation (FBI) compiles detailed statistics for crimes committed in each jurisdiction in the United States, which are provided by the agencies themselves. This undertaking is known as the Uniform Crime Reporting (UCR) program. A study of model crime labs will be used to determine the portion of crimes which are effectively analyzed by forensic DNA technology. Further examination of case types will determine the optimal number of samples per case in order to reduce the demand for analysis to the lowest common denominator of samples, thereby simplifying the balancing of supply to demand.

The number of items submitted per forensic DNA case can vary widely, with major homicide cases and sexual assaults contributing significantly more DNA samples than a simple property crime. While a greater focus should be placed on major crimes against the person, very straightforward small property crime cases can be of great value in apprehending criminals at earlier stages in their career, linking crime trends, or catching a serious criminal in a lesser offense.

Many major crimes are solved through lesser crimes as major criminals frequently commit property crimes as their "day job." Analysis of property crimes is much simpler as cases average significantly less samples per case than major crimes. Property crimes have low clearance rates through traditional investigation as there are seldom witnesses, whereas they yield large hit rates using DNA databases. As higher-throughput DNA analysis has developed, cases are placed into a batch process. Lesser crimes with few samples per case can be placed with larger more serious cases in order to round out analytical batches to make best use of resources. Lesser crimes can also work as extra analytical capacity is made available between peaks of major crime demand. With fewer samples per case and larger hit rates on DNA databases, property crimes are very cost-effective means of solving crime at a potentially earlier point in a criminal's career. While property crimes bear fewer samples per case, their connection to major crimes reveals patterns that assist in solving crime sprees. Therefore, a further examination of the breakdown of samples per case will enable a more accurate projection of analytical resources.

Eight high-achieving DNA laboratories were examined and questioned regarding average number of samples analyzed per case. An examination of case submission for these high-achieving labs in relation to the UCR statistics for their jurisdiction was used to determine the ratio of case submissions to crimes committed. The most successful laboratory in this panel of successful crime labs was used as a model with respect to the submission ratio, which is the fraction of the UCR statistics that can be successfully analyzed. Detailed statistics have been developed to calculate an accurate average samples per case submissions for each type of crime. Multiplying the average samples per case for each type of case by the number of cases that can be successfully analyzed produces the number of samples which can be successfully analyzed. Finally, the sample totals for all of the different types of crime are summed to produce the demand for analysis. Once demand for analysis has been forecast, laboratory analytical capacity supply can be designed to meet the demand, hence reaping the maximum benefit from forensic technology.

Laboratory A was analyzed for output and expenses in order to provide a cursory estimate of the level of resources needed to provide rapid DNA service. The Laboratory A Biology Unit case, serology, and DNA sample output per analyst and analysis were collected. Cost savings provided by the laboratory were calculated and then compared to the cost of crime in order to assess the cost-effectiveness of rapid DNA analysis.

As outlined above, there are the four steps in forecasting the number of DNA samples that are cost effectively analyzed in a jurisdiction. First, the number of crimes for each crime type occurring in the region is obtained using the FBI UCR statistics (see **Table 1**).

In theory, the number of crimes reported represents the maximum number of cases that can be submitted and effectively analyzed by the crime laboratory. Next, examination of the panel of high-achieving crime labs is performed in order to estimate the fraction of each type of case that can be effectively analyzed by the crime laboratory (see **Table 2**).

The submission ratio gives an idea of the variation in penetration of service found in each crime lab. Clearly, there is a large gap between crimes committed and the number of cases analyzed in crime laboratories. Not surprisingly, there are a very large proportion of major crimes that are analyzed in all crime laboratories. Crime labs analyze major cases of crimes against the person as a first priority, and then move on to property crimes if there is any analytical capacity remaining. If all labs moved to the submission ratio of their highest high-achieving peer, this estimated increase would provide a starting point toward a forecast of potential future demand for lab analysis.

The submission ratio of homicide cases is above 100% in many crime labs, as demonstrated in **Table 2**. This is because suicide and attempted homicide case are often submitted, with the outcome of the case unknown until the investigation is completed. Cold cases are also submitted, further increasing the submission ratio. Therefore, it stands to reason that a submission ratio can exceed the FBI UCR statistics for a particular type of crime. Therefore, a target submission ratio of 160% will be used, which is an average submission ratio for the crime lab panel.

In the case of sexual assaults, two of the crime labs have made a particular focus on sexual assaults. Efforts have been coordinated with sexual assault nursing education (SANE) programs to ensure that all sexual assault cases are collected and analyzed. Also included in these statistics are attempted sexual assaults, thereby increasing the submission ratio above 100%. These labs can serve as a target for other crime labs in terms of a submission ratio projection. Therefore, a target of 110% submission ratio will be used for sexual assault crimes.

For the crimes of assault and robbery, the crime lab panel varied widely. A variety of reasons may underlie the variation, including knowledge base of investigators, acceptance policies of crime laboratories, proximity of investigators to the lab, and their working relationship with the crime laboratory analysts. As a result, the highest achievers will be selected for a target submission ratio. Maine State Police led the panel with a submission ratio of 3.15% for cases of assault; therefore, a target of 3.1% will be used for this crime type. Orange County led the panel with the submission ratio of 7.9% for robbery cases; therefore, 7.9% will be used as a target submission ratio for robberies.

The Orange County Sheriff-Coroner Forensic Science Services was recognized by the National Institute of Justice (NIJ) through selection as one of six pilot crime labs for a landmark study to determine the potential of using DNA to solve property crimes. The NIJ property crimes pilot project applied to the South Operations patrol area of Orange County with a population roughly one-sixth of the total county. The South Operations patrol area saw submission of 526 property crime cases in a 14-month period, which equates to a 20% submission ratio. Spurring this high submission ratio was training of law enforcement officers coupled with a dedicated police program supervisor. This police supervisor supported training, motivated officers to recognize, collect, and submit burglary evidence, and then followed up by collecting and disseminating success stories. The supervisor also assisted investigators and the lab in targeting those evidence types touched or left behind by perpetrators and those types of items most likely to yield a successful profile. This approach prevented extra work in analyzing items with a low probability of successful DNA analysis. Elimination samples were also collected immediately from home owners, should they have touched items to be examined for suspect DNA to assist interpretation of mixed samples and elimination of non-probative profiles. In the Orange County Project, DNA profiles

Table 1 2009 US and laboratory A jurisdiction crimes by type

Crime	*Number of offenses in US*	*Number of offenses in lab A jurisdiction*
Murder	15,241	13
Rape	88,097	124
Robbery	408,217	992
Aggravated assault	806,843	904
Burglary	2,199,125	3011
Motor vehicle theft	794,616	1732

2009 Uniform Crime Reporting Statistics, Crime in the United States, U.S. Department of Justice, Federal Bureau of Investigation, Criminal Justice Information Services Division, http://www2.fbi.gov/ucr/cius2009/data/table_01.html and http://www2.fbi.gov/ucr/cius2009/data/table_10_md.html.

Table 2 Submission ratio of case types by high-achieving crime laboratories

Offense	*Average (%)*	*Target (%)*	*Orange County, SO, CA (%)*	*San Diego, PD, CA (%)*	*Maine State Police, Augusta (%)*	*CBI, Denver, CO (%)*	*Minnesota State Bureau of Criminal Apprehension, St. Paul, MN (%)*	*WV State Police (%)*	*GBI, Atlanta, GA (%)*	*WA State Police, Seattle (%)*
Murder	159.98	160.00	218.18	195.59	247.37	157.01	113.60	70.67	65.83	211.58
Sexual assault	61.64	110.00	50.00	102.30	40.06	41.12	64.07	53.98	110.22	31.39
Assault	1.42	3.10	2.01	1.78	3.15	0.36	1.70	0.13	0.72	1.47
Robbery	2.60	7.90	7.89	3.00	4.11	0.57	1.75	1.29	0.20	1.95
Burglary	1.76	20.00	5.98	3.46	[a]	0.57	1.03	0.13	0.92	0.22
Motor vehicle	0.26	20.00	1.39	0.02	0.00	0.17	0.40	0.00	0.04	0.02

CBI, Colorado Bureau of Investigation; GBI, Georgia Bureau of Investigation.
[a]Maine State Police combines the statistic of robbery and burglary into one category; hence, 4.11% is for both of these crimes.

are developed in 65% of trace (touch) cases; 45% of it produces a foreign profile that is uploadable to combined DNA index system (CODIS). Once the profile is in the database, the current hit rate is 21% in terms of developing a suspect to aid the investigation.

Motor vehicle theft in particular shows tremendous promise as vehicles are often recovered, and are excellent sources of DNA. Steering wheels, door handles, shift levers, and other touched surfaces are effective targets for fingerprints and trace DNA. With both of these valuable examinations combined as offered by the Orange County Sheriff-Coroner Forensic Science Services, the potential solution rate of this type of crime is exciting. As many car thieves are recidivists and the property damage to stolen cars is very significant, the crime solving and saving potential is very large in dollar terms. Therefore, based on the success of the Orange County pilot, a target submission of 20% will be used for burglaries and auto theft cases.

In the third step, the average number of samples per case type was obtained (see **Table 3**). In order to provide a reasonable estimate of the number of evidentiary samples analyzed for each type of case, the panel of crime labs was interviewed and provided estimates. The Colorado Bureau of Investigation (CBI) was alone in its keeping of detailed submission data that

Table 3 Colorado Bureau of Investigation crime laboratory DNA section case submissions, Lakewood Laboratory

	Serology			*DNA*		
2007 Submissions	*Cases*	*Items*	*Items/case*	*Cases*	*Samples*	*Samples/case*
Homicide	165	1684	10.2	166	1238	7.5
Attempted homicide	1	18	18.0	0	0	0.0
Sexual assault	431	4947	11.5	271	1318	4.9
Aggravated assault	106	704	6.6	74	437	5.9
Kidnapping	21	174	8.3	7	34	4.9
Burglary	213	604	2.8	186	393	2.1
Auto theft	43	157	3.7	44	118	2.7
Criminal trespassing	9	24	2.7	13	15	1.2
Felony theft	17	41	2.4	12	26	2.2
Robbery	44	170	3.9	39	135	3.5
Property	8	15	1.9	4	5	1.3
Drugs	1	1	1.0	0	0	0.0
Misc	92	269	2.9	78	179	2.3
Child abuse	4	15	3.8	2	8	4.0
Average items/case			7.6			4.4
Total	1155	8823		896	3906	

Table demonstrates average number of items and samples per case type.

Table 4 Calculation of potential DNA samples for the United States: submission ratio multiplied by Uniform Crime Reporting crimes multiplied by the average sample number per case, summed for all offense types

Offense	*Submission ratio (%)*	*US crimes*	*Potential cases*	*Average sample number per case*	*Potential samples*
Murder	160.00	15,241	24,386	7.5	182,892
Sexual assault	110.00	88,097	96,907	3.1	300,411
Assault	3.10	408,217	12,655	4.1	51,884
Robbery	7.90	806,843	63,741	3.1	197,596
Burglary	20.00	2,199,125	439,825	1.8	791,685
Motor vehicle	20.00	794,616	158,923	2.7	429,093
Totals		4,312,139	796,436		1,953,561

included samples per type of case. Estimates provided by the other crime labs in the panel independently agreed with the statistics kept by CBI, thereby validating item numbers per case type as seen in **Table 3**.

As depicted in **Table 3**, there are approximately 7.5 DNA samples in each homicide case. This contrasts to 5.9 for cases of assault and 4.9 samples for case of sexual assault. Crimes against the person typically have more samples per case than property crimes, as evidenced by 3.5 samples for robbery, 2.7 for auto theft, and 2.1 samples for burglary cases.

In order to project the number of cases, the FBI UCR statistics is multiplied by the submission ratio for each crime type. The number of case samples for each type of case is then calculated by multiplying this projected case total with the average number of samples per case. A grand total of case samples is then found by summing the samples for all the case types. These calculations are demonstrated in **Table 4**.

Calculating the total potential samples is demonstrated using the crime of robbery as an example. As seen in **Table 4**, there were 806,843 robberies committed in 2009 as per the UCR statistics. If one can forecast the submission ratio as 7.9%, and the average samples per case at 3.1, then the total forecasted number of samples for robbery cases is 197,596. This calculation is conducted for each type of crime, resulting in a grand total of 1,953,561 samples in order to conduct DNA analysis US wide at the level set by top labs in the high-achieving lab panel studied.

While calculating the theoretical total of forensic DNA samples for the US is an interesting exercise, a more practical approach is to apply this method to a single laboratory, which in turn will serve as an example calculation for other jurisdictions. By following this example, jurisdictions may forecast the resources required to match the supply of lab analysis to meet demand for their own area. A hypothetical example using Laboratory A will be used to demonstrate the application of this method to forecast forensic DNA demand.

As noted in **Table 5**, there were a total of 6776 UCR statistic crimes (not including larceny) committed in the jurisdiction covered by Laboratory A in 2009. Using the submission ratios as dictated in the crime lab panel and the number of samples per case type, the total number of samples projected is 2946 annually.

Once the number of DNA samples has been forecasted, resources required to balance DNA analysis to this demand can be established. Examination of the number of samples produced per full time casework analyst can be used to determine number of employees required to balance analytical capacity to forecasted demand. **Table 6** depicts the output of two DNA analysts who were dedicated to DNA casework through a year with a small component of additional non-case-related duties.

The average output for the two full-time DNA analysts is 97 cases. These cases were comprised of an average of 247 items analyzed, which in turn yielded 304 DNA samples analyzed.

Table 5 Calculation of potential DNA samples for laboratory A

Offense	*Submission ratio (%)*	*Lab A jurisdiction crimes*	*Potential cases*	*Average sample number per case*	*Potential samples*
Murder	160.00	13	21	7.5	156
Sexual assault	110.00	124	136	3.1	423
Assault	3.10	992	31	4.1	126
Robbery	7.90	904	71	3.1	221
Burglary	20.00	3011	602	1.8	1084
Motor vehicle	20.00	1732	346	2.7	935
Totals		6776	1208		2946

Table 6 Laboratory A annual full time DNA analyst output

	Cases	*Items examined*	*DNA samples*
Analyst 1	93	236	290
Analyst 2	100	258	318
Average	97	247	304

These analysts were selected as their duties focus very largely on casework, whereas other analysts have significant other duties which would skew casework output statistics. It is noteworthy how consistent the output of the two analysts is relative to each other. While a very small sampling of analysts, it is useful as an illustration of methodology to estimate resources required to meet the 2946 sample annual projection.

Estimating the total number of analysts is provided by dividing the projected number of samples by the average output per analyst. Approximately 10 DNA analysts working full time would, therefore, be required to produce this level of output (2946/304 = 9.7). Additional tasks conducted in the Biology Unit add overhead, such as accreditation-related duties, CODIS administration, QA/QC duties, training, research and development, validation of new technology, and an extra cushion in order to stay ahead of peaks of demand. With a general estimate of 30% overhead, a total staff of 13 would be sufficient to meet full casework potential represented by the crime rate found Laboratory A's jurisdiction. With a population estimate for Laboratory A's area of 971,600 (2009 U.S. Census Bureau, Population Division), this equates to one DNA analyst per 74,738 citizens.

This level of DNA sample projection provides a starting point in order to forecast the level of analytical resources required to meet the overall demand to prevent a backlog from developing and recurring. Addition of resources often comes at the expense of other programs and therefore must be well justified. A calculation as to the cost-benefit or return on investment will provide an illustration of the tremendous value of forensic DNA.

Again, Laboratory A will be used to demonstrate the cost-benefit of using forensic DNA to solve and prevent crime. DNA database hits equate to cases where no suspect was developed in a case; hence, DNA was responsible for matching a crime scene DNA profile to the known suspect found in the database. **Table 7** depicts the DNA database hits for Laboratory A from 2002 to 2009.

The Laboratory A Biology Unit has had very good success in providing investigations with new leads on major crimes using the CODIS. The savings of investigative time and public safety are intuitively very large; however, they are difficult to quantify. Many cases have suspects and could be solved by conventional means with a greater outlay of investigative time and energy. In cases where the DNA database has matched suspects, no suspect, or a different suspect was named in these cases. As a result, considerable savings are realized in cases with a DNA database match, particularly when the recidivist (repetitive and escalating) nature of crime is factored in. Costs of cases of sexual assault have been quantified and will, therefore, be used to measure the value of the DNA service. The estimated cost of each sexual assault is $111,238 in terms of damage to the victim, lost time at work, medical cost, and expenses. There were 21 sexual assault DNA database hits in 2010. If one considers the recidivism rate of eight offenses for rapists, then the saving of the cost of crime is over $16.35 million annually.

The estimated cost of each burglary is $1500 in terms of damaged and stolen property. As the top 10% of burglars commit an estimated 232 burglaries apiece annually and some estimates place a career burglar at 200 offenses, a very conservative estimate of 20 offenses will be assumed for an average burglar/robbery offender. There were 28 burglary and 11 robbery CODIS hits for the Laboratory A in 2010 for a total of 39 hits on burglary/robbery cases. The value of these DNA database hits, therefore, translates into a savings of $1.17 million of the cost of crime annually.

Table 7 Laboratory A CODIS hits by case type

	2002	*2003*	*2004*	*2005*	*2006*	*2007*	*2008*	*2009*	*2010*	*Total*
Murder		1		1			1		1	4
Sexual assault	4	1	8	5	8	4	9	7	21	67
Assault					1				1	2
Robbery	1	1	2	2	1	6	9	8	11	41
Weapons				1		1				2
Auto theft						1	4	1	2	8
Burglary		1	5		3	4	22	16	28	79
Misc			1				1	1	2	5
Larceny			1		1		1	4	7	14
Total	5	4	17	9	14	16	47	37	73	222

The combined cost savings of major crime ($16,350,000) and property crime ($1,170,000) is $17,520,000. The cost of the Laboratory A Biology Unit has been calculated to total $724,794 annually. For each dollar spent, this translates into a savings of $24.17, or a 2417% return on investment. The savings for property crime alone justifies the DNA program, saving $1.61 for each dollar spent.

The cost of analysis of a DNA case is the same if it is done within moments of the crime occurring or 6 months later once a case works its way to the front of a backlog. The cost of added resources to provide additional analytical capacity to conduct analysis as soon as a crime is committed is more than offset by the significant return on investment demonstrated. A metaphor is operating a fire station with a backlog of fires versus providing sufficient resources to quickly respond to the next fire. The cost and timeliness of the fire dictate a quick response. With the improved speed of forensic DNA and utility of DNA databases, the paradigm has shifted to the point that running a backlog in forensic analyses while a known suspect profile sits in a database is just as wasteful.

Discussion

The cost-effectiveness of forensic DNA in solving and preventing crime has been well documented including the analysis of high volume less serious crimes. Crime labs facing large backlogs are more apt to focus on crimes against the person, while lesser offenses such as property crimes are not accepted or are given a lower priority. Increasing lab capacity will improve the response time for major crimes and permit analysis of property crimes, which benefits the system as a whole. A recent project conducted in Denver, Colorado, yielded over $90 savings in investigative and costs of crime for each $1 spent. As demonstrated in this study, property crimes typically possess less than half as many samples per case as major crimes, while DNA database hit rates on property crimes are surpassing those of major crimes. Furthermore, property crime has been found to link to violent crime in over 50% of cases, demonstrating that lower prioritization of lesser offenses may hamper investigations as a whole. Therefore, forecasting crime submissions to include property crimes makes good economic and crime-solving sense.

Forensic DNA objectively includes and eliminates suspects and develops new suspects through the DNA databases that traditional investigation may not. Eliminating a large number of suspects conclusively where a crime scene DNA profile from the perpetrator has been developed is a relatively new concept that has been used successfully in a number of major cases, including the homicides committed by Collin Pitchfork and Derrick Todd Lee. Known as "DNA dragnets," these investigations took advantage of forensic DNA technology's capabilities that are now harnessed in increasingly large databases. With DNA databases now expanding to include lesser offenses as well as arrestees, each crime scene profile is compared to very large numbers of suspects, in essence equaling a dragnet for every case. Legislative efforts coupled with computer technology have brought the power of simultaneous multiple DNA profile comparisons to every agency able to access an accredited crime lab with CODIS capability.

Lives and resources can be saved by analysis of DNA earlier in the investigation of a crime, reducing the time a criminal has available to commit new offenses on additional victims. Stopping a perpetrator early in their career increases the opportunity for intervention and rehabilitation attempts and success. Actual reduction in crime rates can result through the early apprehension of prolific repeat offenders. One prolific burglar admitted to over 1000 offenses. Removing this individual from the population resulted in an immediate reduction in the burglary rate by 40%. Property crimes in particular are highly recidivist offenses, with burglars committing in excess of 200 crimes apiece; hence, an earlier intervention will prevent future crimes.

The cost of a criminal investigation is front-end loaded, in that the majority of investigative resources are spent shortly after the crime occurs. The cost per investigator for a typical police department is estimated to be $500 per day. Meanwhile, the cost of each DNA sample analyzed has been estimated to be approximately $500. Correspondingly, if a DNA result can be provided a day earlier the potential cost savings for each investigation will increase. The cost of forensic DNA is the same per case whether done early in the investigation or later once a large proportion of investigative resources have already been expended on a case. Moving forensic DNA analysis to the front end of a case makes sense from crime prevention, investigational, and cost perspectives.

With a return on investment of over 2400% as demonstrated by the calculation with Laboratory A or $90 per $1 expenditure in Denver, having cases sit awaiting analysis while investigative resources are spent on suspects that could be easily eliminated with quick DNA analysis is wasteful. An analogy can be drawn between crime labs and providers of services that are critical in terms of response time. Fire service is modeled on quick response, as having a backlog of fires would prove to be disastrous in terms of public safety and loss of property. A backlog of DNA cases is like having a backlog of fires at the fire station. Investigative resources are being rapidly consumed while cases sit awaiting analysis.

DNA cases are currently prioritized in many crime labs, with a constant juggle of backlogged cases as cases are triaged in order to focus rare resources on the most important cases and samples. With additional capacity that is in excess of demand peaks, backlogs can be reduced to near zero. The only cases in backlog would be cases that are currently in analysis, thereby reducing response time to the time actually taken for the lab analysis and reporting itself, which can now be measured in days. With the backlog of "fires" now being eliminated, each case would begin processing shortly after arrival at the laboratory. Case processing is typically a batch process, with plates of samples and controls being taken through analytical steps as a unit. By staggering batches by starting them at different points through a week or month, priority cases and samples can be placed on the next batch, with lesser crimes filing in the openings to make best use of available resources. Through accurately forecasting demand and establishing supply just above that demand, prompt response times are assured to reap the maximum benefits of forensic technology. No longer would there be a backlog of fires at the forensic fire station.

Cost savings are not the only benefit of rapid response DNA technology. Potentially less reliable eyewitness testimony can be shored up with objective forensic evidence. Forensic DNA evidence increases guilty pleas, increases prosecution rates eightfold, and increases sentences six- to tenfold, thereby also streamlining and increasing the effectiveness of the justice system as well. More victims may also come forward as the pressure to provide testimony is reduced.

Suspect DNA profiles from property crimes not only hit to major offenders, but property crime projects have seen hit rates in excess of 40%. Investigations that utilize DNA benefit with higher identification rates, increasing the identification of suspects from 14% to 44%. The case for conducting forensic DNA analysis on all available types of crime is compelling from a cost and effectiveness standpoint.

Expenditure to provide a measured surplus of forensic analytical capacity is prudent to ensure a rapid response. The surplus of service need not be large, only enough to provide for the peak demand, while lesser calls for service can be handled in the periods of lesser demand. There are a large number of accreditation-related quality control and assurance-related activities, training, validation of new techniques, and the like that can be addressed with resources spared between demand peaks. Analysis of less time critical property crimes has been demonstrated to be a very cost-effective method of ensuring good use of analytical capacity. Accurate projections of case load characteristics will permit balancing of analytical resources to eliminate backlogs and, most importantly, prevent them from occurring, which in turn will ensure prompt response times.

Conclusion

Expansion of forensic laboratory analytical capacity is a significant undertaking that can be performed by each jurisdiction. Using the method provided in this paper provides a forecast of sample demand that can be calculated by multiplying the UCR statistic crimes with the submission ratio and average samples per case type. Once the resources are applied, and analytical capacity is in place, forensic backlogs will be eliminated and prevented from recurring. The cost-benefit of over 2400% as demonstrated by a sample laboratory provides a compelling case for the financial prudence of focusing investigative resources on the correct suspect at the earliest stages of a criminal investigation.

In summary, while the projection of future submissions of DNA cases in crimes yet to be committed is somewhat speculative, the future of solving crimes with DNA is demonstrably bright. Significant numbers of these cases can be solved, and repeat offenders stopped earlier in their careers. Continued use of DNA on major crimes is projected to remain stable, while growth in sample output will be sustained by property crime cases. Investing in forensic DNA is a wise investment that will pay big dividends in producing more effective investigations and improvements for public safety. Implications have been made regarding the additional cost of lab resources, investigators, and prosecutors that would be required to adequately address projected case demands, posing the question: Can we afford to? Conversely, when faced with the demonstrated cost-benefit of solving and preventing crime through forensic technology in human and economic terms, can we afford not to?

See also: **Behavioral:** Modus Operandi; **Biology/DNA:** DNA Databases; Laboratory Automation and LIMS in Forensics; Low-Template DNA Testing; Significance; **Forensic Medicine/Clinical:** Sexual Violence; **Foundations:** Forensic Intelligence; **Management/Quality in Forensic Science:** Effectiveness.

Further Reading

Bond, J.W., 2007. Value of DNA evidence in detecting crime. Journal of Forensic Sciences 52 (1), 128–136.

Burrows, J., Tarling, R., 2004. Measuring the impact of forensic science in detecting burglary and autocrime offenses. Science and Justice 44 (4), 217–222.

Hurst, L., Lothridge, K., 2010. DNA Evidence and Offender Analysis Measurement: DNA Backlogs, Capacity and Funding. National Institute of Justice. NCJ 230328. http://www.ncjrs.gov/pdffiles1/nij/grants/230328.pdf.

Lovrich, N.P., Pratt, T.C., Gaffney, M.J., et al., 2004. National Forensic DNA Study Report. Final Report. www.dna.gov.

Mennell, J., Shaw, I., 2006. The future of forensic and crime scene science part I. A UK forensic science user and provider perspective. Forensic Science International 157 (1), 7–12.

Nelson, M., 2010. Making sense of DNA backlogs – myths vs. reality. NIJ Journal 266. NCJ 230415. http://www.ncjrs.gov/pdffiles1/nij/230415.pdf.

Ritter, N., 2008. DNA solves property crimes (but are we ready for that?). NIJ Journal 261. http://www.ojp.usdoj.gov/nij/journals/261/dna-solves-propertycrimes.htm.

Ritter, N., 2010. Solving the problem of untested evidence in sexual assaults. National Institute of Justice NIJ Journal 267. NCJ 233284. http://www.nij.gov/journals/267/evidence.htm.

Roman, J.K., Reid, S., Reid, J., Chalfin, A., Adams, W., Knight, C., April 2008. The DNA Field Experiment: Cost-effectiveness Analysis of the Use of DNA in the Investigation of High-volume Crimes. Final report for the National Institute of Justice. National Institute of Justice, Washington, DC. NCJ 222318. http://www.ncjrs.gov/pdffiles1/nij/grants/222318.pdf.

Strom, K.J., Ropero-Miller, J., Jones, S., Sikes, N., Pope, M., Horstmann, N., 2009. The 2007 Survey of Law Enforcement Forensic Evidence Processing. National Institute of Justice. NIJ 228415. http://www.ncjrs.gov/pdffiles1/nij/grants/228415.pdf.

Summary of the Proceedings, 2010. Eliminating the rape kit backlog: a roundtable to explore a victim-centered approach. In: Summary of the Proceedings, US Dept. Of Justice, Office of Violence against Women, Washington, DC, May 11–12, 2010. http://www.ovw.usdoj.gov/docs/rape-kit-roundtable-summary-10262010.pdf.

Urban, J.K., Reid, S., Reid, J., Chalfin, A., Adams, W., Knight, C., 2008. The DNA Field Experiment: Cost Effectiveness Analysis of the Use of DNA in the Investigation of High-volume Crimes. NIJ Research Report.

Wickenheiser, R.A., 2004. The business case for using forensic DNA technology to solve and prevent crime. Journal of Biolaw and Business 7 (3), 34–50.

Zedlewski, E., Murphy, M.B., 2006. DNA analysis for "minor" crimes: a major benefit for law enforcement. NIJ Journal 253. http://www.nij.gov/journals/253/dna_analysis.html.

Internet Accessible Population Databases: YHRD and EMPOP

L Roewer, Charité – Universitätsmedizin Berlin, Berlin, Germany
W Parson, Innsbruck Medical University, Innsbruck, Austria

Glossary

AMOVA A method that measures the genetic distances between subpopulations (e.g., of a metapopulation); this can be done frequency-based (F_{st} statistics) or with taking the molecular relationship between alleles into account (Φ_{st} statistics); results can be illustrated in an MDS plot.

Discrimination capacity (DC) The number of haplotypes in a sample which can be separated by a certain number of polymorphic sites, for example, STRs or SNPs.

Haplogroup A set of mtDNA or Y chromosomal haplotypes that is defined by nonrecurrent, slowly mutating markers such as SNPs.

Haplotype The combination of allelic states of a set of polymorphic markers lying on the same DNA molecule, for example, the Y chromosome or the mitochondrial DNA.

Metapopulation A group of populations connected by ancestry and migration.

Quasi-median networks (QMN) Graphical representations of haplotypic data, permitting visual assessment of the haplotypes based on their evolutionary relationships to each other.

Y-STR A DNA sequence containing a number (usually <50) of tandemly repeated short (2–6 bp) sequences, such as $(GATA)_n$. Often polymorphic and also known as microsatellites.

Introduction to the Y Chromosome and Mitochondrial DNA Database Projects

Lineage markers have special fields of application in forensic genetics. Y chromosome analysis is very helpful in cases where there is an excess of DNA from a female victim and only a low proportion from a male perpetrator. Typical examples include sexual assault without ejaculation, sexual assault by an azoospermic (vasectomized) male, male DNA under the fingernails of a female victim, male "touch" DNA on the skin, and the clothing or belongings of a female victim. Mitochondrial DNA (mtDNA) analysis is of importance for the analyses of low target number DNA, namely from unidentified (typically skeletonized) remains, hair shafts without roots, or very old specimen where only heavily degraded DNA is available. The unusual nonrecombinant mode of inheritance of Y and mtDNA weakens the statistical weight of a match between individual samples but makes the method efficient for the reconstruction of paternal or maternal relationship, for example, in mass disaster investigations. In practice, most laboratories conduct DNA analysis according to a workflow which characterizes the sample DNA extract with regard to quantity, degradation state, or sex ratio prior to any short tandem repeat (STR) analysis, allowing the analyst to make the most informed decision on the best method to proceed. This workflow produces a lot of DNA profiles from mtDNA and Y chromosomal STRs, which do not exclude but match a person as a donor of a trace. Because statistical interpretation is obligate in forensic reporting for all kinds of DNA sequences, including linear markers, the probability that a particular genotype might occur at random in a population must be calculated and expressed in numerical terms. This inevitably requires very large databases to retrieve frequencies of the haploid profile detected in the trace. Owing to intense international collaboration within the forensic community, these databases are available, accessible via the Internet, and constructed to comply with the quality standards required for forensic reference data. The Y chromosome haplotype reference database (YHRD) was established in 1997 and went online in 2000. The database currently contains 97,575 haplotypes from 739 populations (release 37 built on June 21, 2011). About 37% of these are typed for the maximum of 17 loci as included in the AmpFℓSTR® Yfiler™ PCR Amplification Kit (**Figure 1**). The YHRD is hosted at the Department of Forensic Genetics, Institute of Legal Medicine Berlin, Charité—Universitätsmedizin Berlin, Germany. The EDNAP Mitochondrial DNA Population Database (EMPOP) was established in 1999 and went online in 2006. The database currently contains 14,847 haplotypes

 http://dx.doi.org/10.1016/B978-0-12-800647-4.00042-4

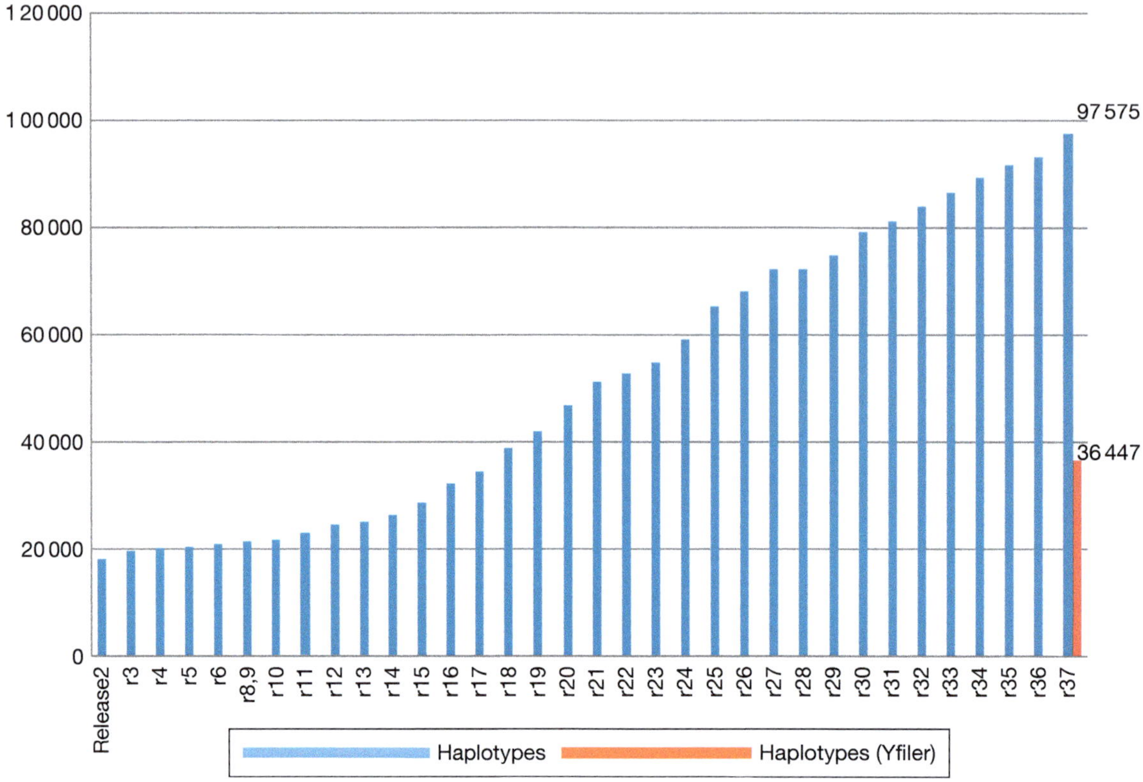

Figure 1 YHRD growth 2000–2011.

(release 5 built on July 5, 2011, **Figure 2**). EMPOP is hosted at the Institute of Legal Medicine, Innsbruck Medical University in Innsbruck, Austria.

What is the *raison d'etre* for such voluminous repositories which connect local databases to a metadatabase? The answer lies in the aforementioned nonrecombinant nature of Y chromosomes and mtDNA, which represent, in effect, a single locus. The "product rule" used to obtain frequency estimates for unlinked autosomal alleles cannot be applied to estimate the population frequency of a certain combination of fully linked alleles (haplotype). These frequencies need to be calculated and reported on the basis of the number of observation (counts) in databases, which are representatives for the population(s) of interest. Frequency estimates of a particulate haplotype thus crucially depend on the size and the content of the reference database used. To assess the representativeness of such databases, the extent of structure among populations also needs to be considered. This is particularly important for markers on the Y chromosome and mtDNA because of its haploid mode of inheritance, the reduced effective population size of the Y chromosome, and socially instituted practices as patri- or matrilocality makes them more sensitive to genetic drift than the autosomes and generates rather high between-population diversities. This more pronounced stratification has important consequences for the sampling scheme. The database representation and the reporting are explained in the following sections.

Haplotype Sampling

Essential for the YHRD and EMPOP projects is the collaborative character relying on the engagement of individual laboratories to make their data accessible and comparable via a common Internet platform and to agree on a high standard of data quality. The decentralized sampling strategy implies that each submitting group has to ascertain the sample population. This ascertainment includes informed consent documentation, measures to avoid sampling of close relatives or probands of nonlocal origin, and proper naming of the sample. Sample numbers depend on the size of the investigated population. Urban and cosmopolitan population studies should involve at least 200 individuals, whereas regional data sets should contain a minimum of 100 samples. Exceptions are valid for extremely small population sizes. Requested is also the publication of a manuscript that describes in detail the population(s)

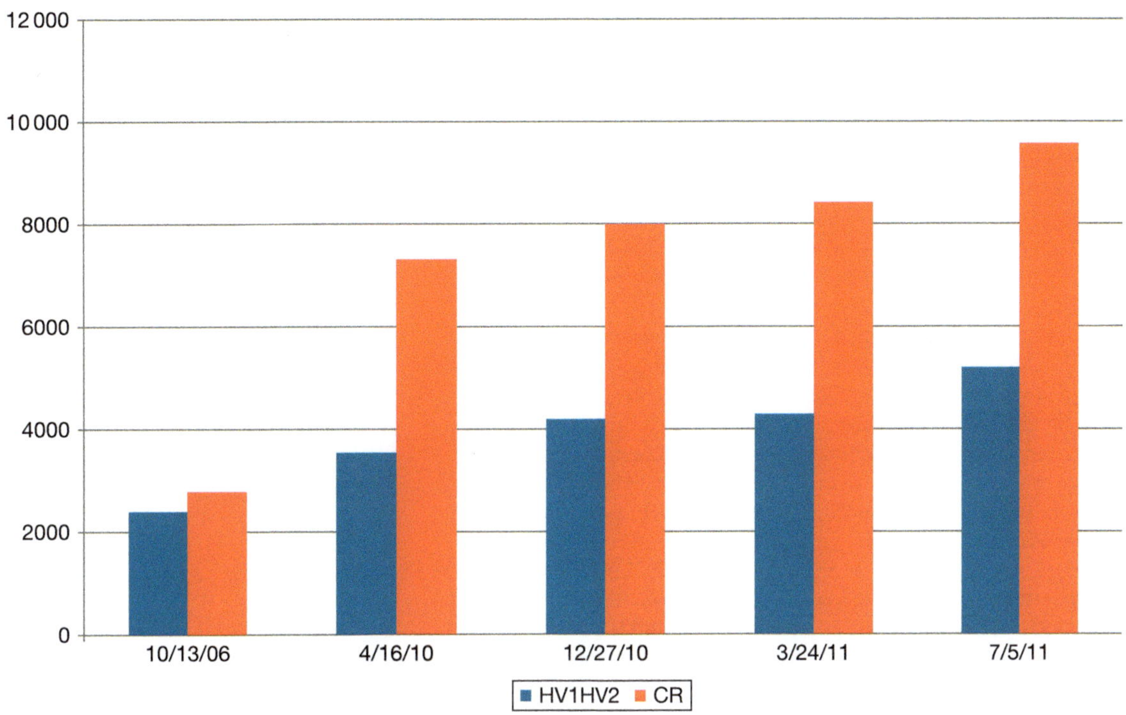

Figure 2 EMPOP growth 2006–2011.

submitted to EMPOP or YHRD and contains the original data set. This manuscript is linked via an accession number to the respective database where the population sample can be searched. The names of the population samples chosen by the submitters need to follow a ternary code to define a minimum of causal relationship: region and country (ethnic/linguistic group). If sample populations are properly described, they can be merged into the so-called metapopulations (MP). This means that geographically widespread populations that share a common genetic ancestry and are connected by migration can be joined to MPs. For example, Turks, Kalmyks (Russia), and Khalks (Mongolia) belong to the Altaic-speaking MP; US American, Australian, and South African Europeans, as well as French, Spanish, or Irish, belong to the European MP; or Han, Hui, and She belong to the Sino-Tibetan MP. The extent of homogeneity within a MP and the distance to others can be measured using the AMOVA algorithm by calculating genetic distances expressed by F_{st} or R_{st} values. It has been shown for an earlier edition of the YHRD with about 41,000 individuals that the chosen MP classification is supported by the deeply structured haplotype data deposited in the database. Both databases supply inventories of included populations that serve as guidance for the assignment of the relevant termini. However, the geographical or linguistic classification is not the only way to represent the clustered structure of Y chromosomal and mtDNA types. There is also a phylogenetic classification possible, which is based on a monophyletic, hierarchical tree defined by unique event (nonrecurrent) polymorphisms or single nucleotide polymorphism (SNPs). Each branch of the tree (haplogroup) is defined by at least one SNP. All Y chromosomes or mtDNA molecules sharing a mutation are related by descent, until a further mutation splits the branch. Haplotypes within a haplogroup may be highly similar or even "identical by descent." Thus, the haplogroup can be used as a criterion to substructure the database according to the phylogenetic descent of samples. Many haplogroups can be equated with events in human prehistory and show a geographical pattern. To accommodate the phylogenetic classification scheme, the YHRD database is continuously extended for binary Y-SNP polymorphisms and a grouping of Y-STR haplotypes according to haplogroups thus becomes feasible. Currently, 7168 Y-STR haplotypes (7.3%) have an experimentally determined haplogroup designation. The haplogroup affiliation of an mtDNA sequence is already present in the reported haplotype that is generated for forensic discrimination. Owing to the high degree of homoplasy in the mtDNA, CR haplogroup determination can be supported by coding region information (SNPs), but in the majority of samples the rough haplogroup status can be derived from control region profiles.

The Quality Assessment Scheme of YHRD and EMPOP

The quality assessment scheme is of utmost importance for the court acceptance of the reference data and the calculations adapted from these data. All institutions contributing haplotypes to the databases have to pass an obligate review to assess the quality of their data. For first submitters to YHRD, also a QC test is mandatory, which includes five blind samples that have to be correctly typed for the submitted data set. The QC results will be evaluated and certified by the YHRD curatorial board. Submitted population data for both YHRD and EMPOP will be reviewed to find (1) typographical errors, (2) mistaken nomenclature, and (3) systematic deviations to the core haplotype distributions of the MP or haplogroup. Once the lab has passed the QC and the data are evaluated, the lab receives an accession number for each submitted population sample. This accession number has to be included in the article, which will appear in one of the forensic journals (e.g., Forensic Science International: Genetics, International Journal of Legal Medicine, Legal Medicine) in the online rubric "Announcement of population data." The editors of the forensic journals closely cooperate with the database curatorial boards and have issued guidelines for the publication of population data, which have to be followed by submitting authors.

The past decade saw significant changes in how mtDNA has been investigated in the laboratory and how sequences are aligned and searched. The main motivation was a high-profile discussion on the low quality of published mtDNA data sets and an unacceptable high error rate in the early 2000s. In its first 7 years, the EMPOP project (1999–2006) primarily aimed at the identification of the sources of error in an in-depth manner and, as a consequence, laboratory protocols, documentation formats, and database logistics were adapted accordingly. Since its first release, EMPOP has not only been a resource of high-quality curated mtDNA data but also included quality control mechanisms to alert the user when ambiguous data were applied. A robust method for detecting idiosyncrasies in mtDNA data that are available via the EMPOP Web site is the application of quasi-median networks (QMNs). They essentially serve as graphical representations of tabular data, permitting visual assessment of the haplotypes based on their evolutionary relationships to each other (**Figure 3**). Since mtDNA data are characterized by a high degree of homoplasy and recurrent mutations that both make QMNs complex, specific filtering of mutations is necessary before a QMN can be calculated and drawn. The networks of reduced and condensed haplotypes are simple when the quality of data is high (**Figure 3(a), (b), (d)**). Quasi-medians represent virtual haplotypes that are not included in the sample set but required to link the sequences in the QMN. Therefore, the number of quasi-medians is augmenting with increasing phylogenetic distance of the samples, such as when, for example, mtDNA sequences from Europe (superhaplogroup N) and Africa (superhaplogroup L) are merged in one set. Errors in sequence data lead to a similar picture, as has been shown by Hans-Jürgen Bandelt and coauthors in the late 1990s. They usually lead to an increase in quasi-medians and thus indicate that review of the sequence raw data is necessary (**Figure 3(c)**). The generation of QMNs is supported by EMPOP under the "tools" section, a more detailed description of the process and examples can be found there.

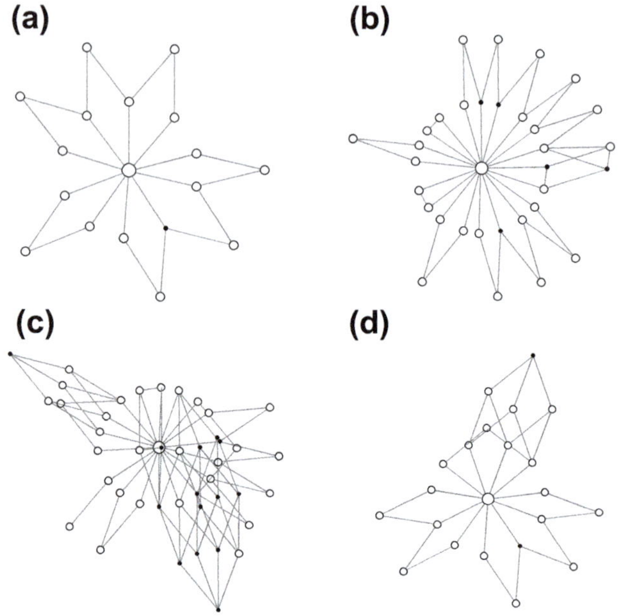

Figure 3 Depiction of four quasi-median network torsi, HVS-I (16024–16,400, filtered with hotspot_EMPOPspeedyWE). (a) Etalon torso, 202 west Eurasian haplotypes of forensic quality; (b) the addition of 31 west Eurasian high-quality sequences to the etalon has only minor effects on the display of the torso; (c) the addition of 29 sequences from a Darginian data set to the etalon increases the complexity of the torso by the introduction of 13 new quasi-medians (black dots), which indicate the presence of unobserved variation. Affected polymorphisms are transitions at 16280, 16281, and 16384, and a transversion at 16391 that all turned out as phantom mutations. (d) Removal of the phantom mutations from the data in (c) results in an inconspicuous torso.

The Tool Boxes of YHRD and EMPOP

YHRD

The YHRD can be searched for all single alleles and all allele combinations in a continuously growing and regularly updated data set. Because new releases replace the previous ones, the release number and date are an important part of the "Search result" document. The database supports the most frequently used haplotype formats (e.g., minimal haplotype = minHt, SWGDAM, Powerplex Y or Yfiler haplotype) for which differently sized databases exist. The discrimination indices in four population sets for typical haplotype formats are depicted in **Figure 4**.

At each position of the search mask, the respective allele must be entered. To facilitate the search, the scroll-down menu shows all alleles that have been observed in the database at the respective locus. Irregularly spaced STR alleles are named according to the International Society for Forensic Genetics (ISFG) recommendations. The database has a structure that can be adapted to the needs of the user allowing searches in the whole database or in subsets defined by the MP, the nationality, or the haplogroup of the sampled chromosomes. Currently, Y-STR profiles can be searched within 7 continental sets, 34 hierarchically arranged MPs, 108 countries, and 118 haplogroups (release 37 from June 21, 2011; see **Figures 5 and 6**). A query returns a printable document which includes the absolute number of matches in the tab-selected database type (MPs, continents, haplogroups) and the relative frequency value including the confidence interval limits (CILs) calculated according to the exact Clopper–Pearson method. Though very simple and easily defensible, this approach known as the counting method has limitations due to the reduced size of the database and sampling effects especially in poorly sampled populations. By clicking the tab "Frequency surveying estimates," the result page presents frequencies calculated by a Bayesian extrapolation method. This method—which is an alternative option to calculate frequencies for rare or unobserved haplotypes by counting—is applicable only for haplotypes with ≥9 STR and for 11 well-saturated reference databases representing populations of European, Asian, and

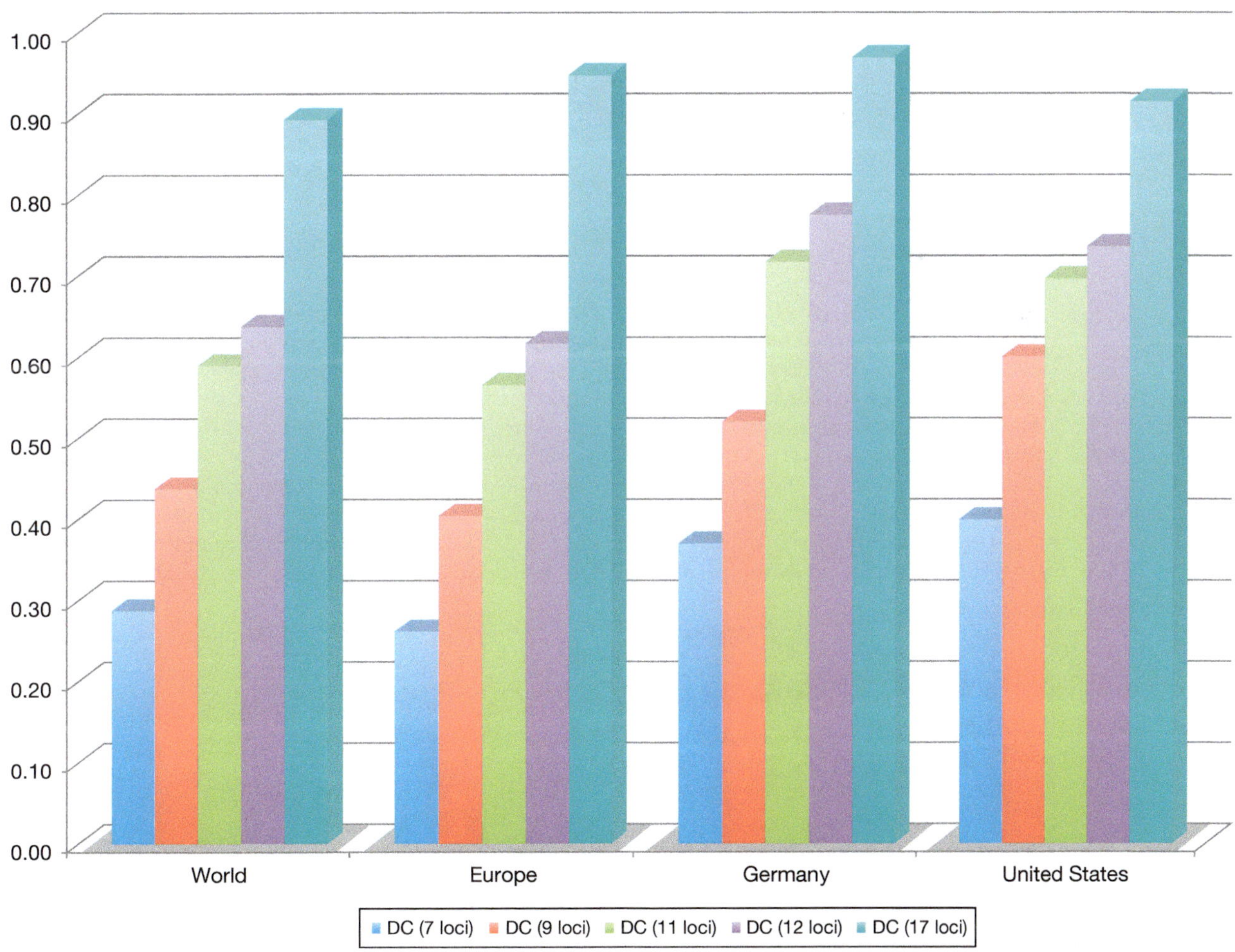

Figure 4 Discrimination capacity (DC) in different YHRD population sets (release 37).

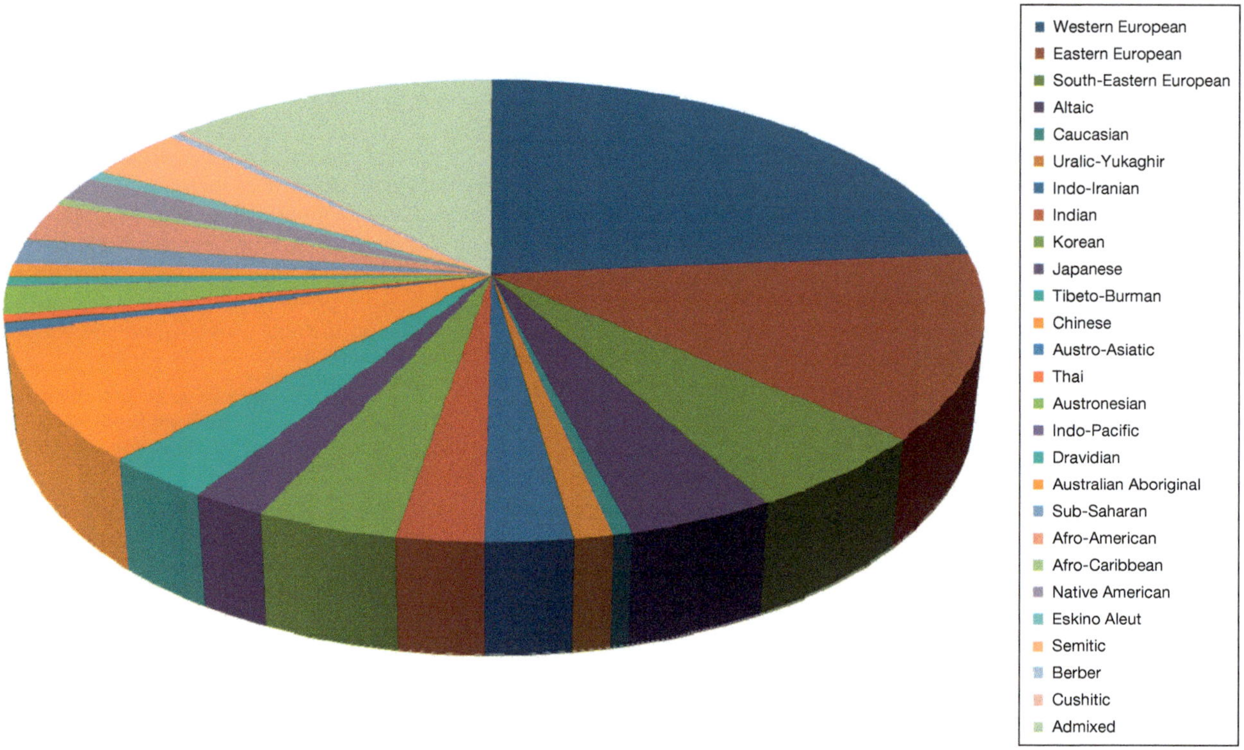

Figure 5 Representation of metapopulations in the YHRD (release 37).

African ancestry. The frequency of a haplotype in question is represented as a beta-type posterior distribution with mean (mean likelihood estimate) and mode points (maximum likelihood estimates). This posterior distribution is obtained by extrapolation from the structure and frequency of all other haplotypes in the relevant ancestral group (MP). We recommend the mean value as a robust estimator of the frequency of a rare haplotype. If the counting method is used in case of unobserved haplotypes, a truthful estimate can be retrieved either by adding the unobserved haplotype to the database $(1/n+1)$ or by using the upper CIL which is reported at the result page in case of zero observations.

Scrolling the result page further down shows a scalable and movable map on the basis of the Google Maps software, with the relative proportion of matches shown in red/blue for each geocoded sampling location. There are several tools to customize the map. Clicking a geoposition in the map opens a window with essential information on the population sample(s), including name, assigned continent, ethnicity, and MP, as well as the frequency of the searched haplotype at this

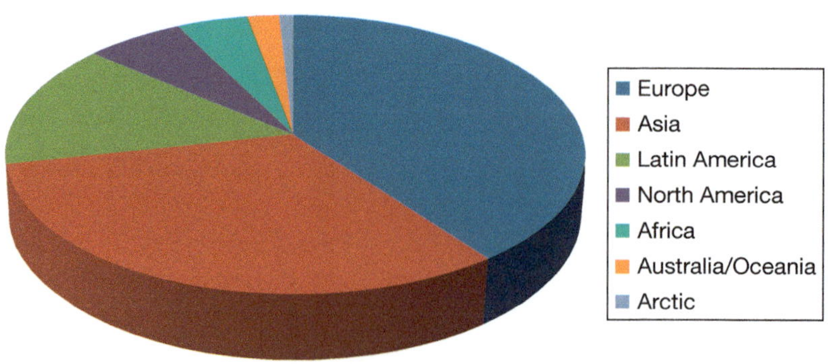

Figure 6 Representation of continents in the YHRD (release 37).

position. Further down, a table with all matched and one-step neighboring haplotypes is shown. The population summary beneath these tables finally presents the matches per single population sample ordered (in default mode) by absolute numbers. Clicking on the population name opens a window with essential information on the contributor(s) or submitting institutions. The accession numbers for this population can be clicked in this window and guide the user directly to the contributor's page presenting full reference to the sample and links to the publication(s).

For the interpretation of Y-STR evidence in cases of mixture, a tool has been implemented in the YHRD. This program allows calculating likelihood ratios for varying numbers of known and unknown contributors. The database delivers population-dependent frequencies of the haplotype profiles detected in the trace.

Furthermore, a tool to assess the extent of population substructure the AMOVA algorithm has been programmed and implemented in the YHRD database. Analysis of molecular variance (AMOVA) is a method for analyzing population variation using molecular data, for example, Y-STR haplotypes. The online tool accepts Excel files and creates entry files from it. As much as nine reference populations or population sets from the YHRD plus the test population sample can be added to the AMOVA analysis. The calculation returns a *.csv table with pairwise F_{st} or Φ_{st} plus p values as a significance test (10 000 permutations). In addition, an MDS plot is generated to illustrate the genetic distance between the analyzed populations graphically. The program lists the references for the selected population studies which facilitate the correct citation. A detailed description of the Y-STR Haplotype Reference Database (YHRD) tools is published in the manual "YHRD 3.0, Directions for use," which can be downloaded from the Web site.

EMPOP

EMPOP allows for sequence searches in two different formats, as rCRS-coded haplotype that is the common reporting format of mtDNA variation and as (FASTA-like) nucleotide sequence string that represents the output format of a raw data derived consensus sequence. Alignment and annotation of rCRS-coded haplotypes are known to be ambiguous, which means that there is more than one possible way of calling (mainly due to insertion/deletion events that can be differently aligned relative to the rCRS). To avoid that such haplotypes are mistakenly missed in a database search, the query and database sequences are turned into strings of nucleotides that are then compared (SAM) and presented relative to the rCRS again in the output. This solution guarantees that database sequences are not missed due to different alignment, which is very important for retrieving objective database search results. EMPOP is so far the only freely available database that includes this feature.

Haplotypes in EMPOP are defined by their sequence range. The query engine allows for any user-defined ranges to be searched complying with the variety of sequencing results from pristine to degraded mtDNA. In an attempt to offer highest discrimination, power haplotypes covering the entire control region are primarily loaded onto EMPOP. However, the majority of existing sequences are present in the earlier targeted HVS-I and HVS-II formats, which are also included in the database to increase the generally low representation of mtDNA haplotypes (**Figure 7**).

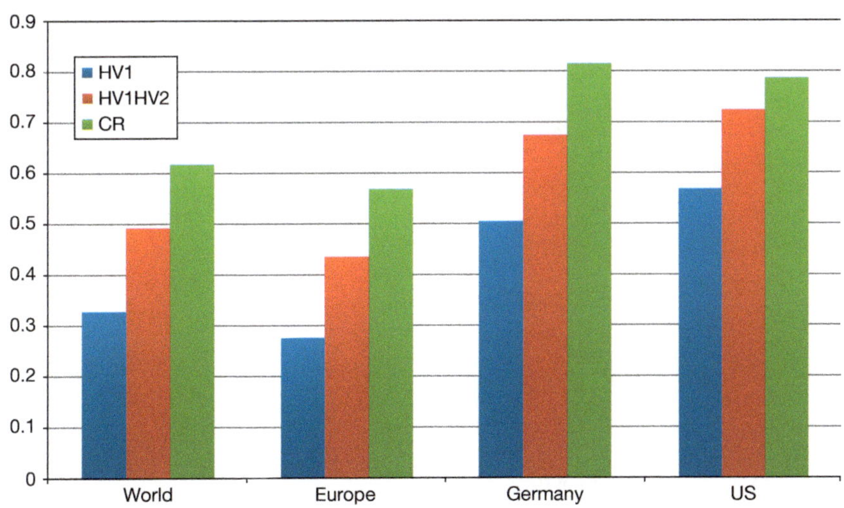

Figure 7 Discrimination capacity in different EMPOP population sets (r. 5).

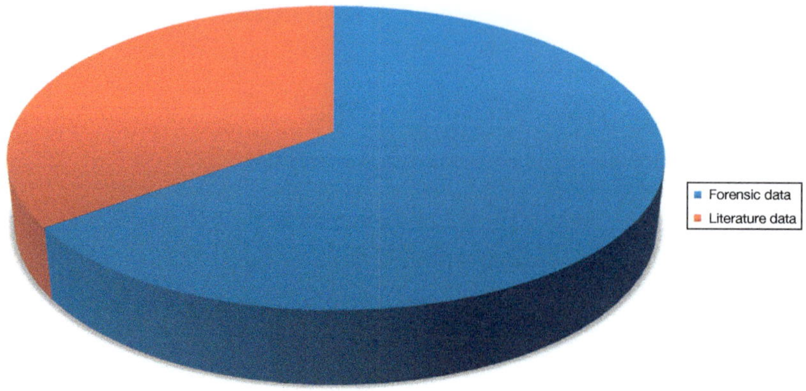

Figure 8 Representation of "forensic" and "literature data" in EMPOP.

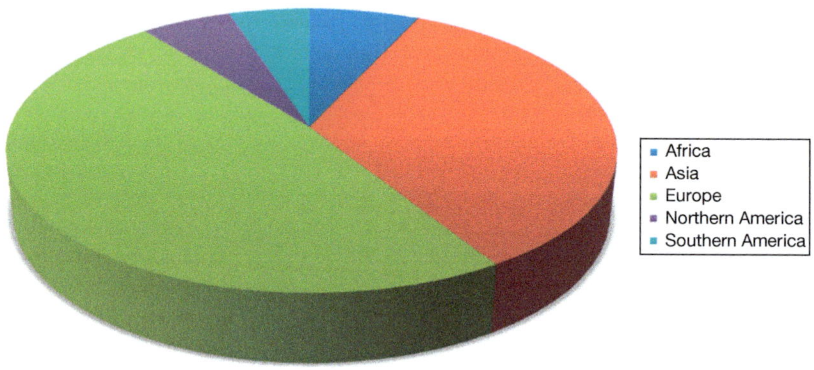

Figure 9 Representation of continents in EMPOP (r. 5).

"Forensic data" in EMPOP refer to haplotypes that are represented by and permanently linked to high-quality raw data. This allows the curator to check questionable positions any time. "Literature data" undergo the same scrutiny of quality control; however, raw lane data are either absent or do not meet the required forensic standards (i.e., sequence quality). Nevertheless, "literature data" can also be used for determining the rarity of a haplotype in a forensic setting (**Figure 8**).

The SAM addresses the issue of point heteroplasmy by differentiating literal and pattern search modes. The former restricts full matches to the presence of haplotypes with completely identical heteroplasmic positions, that is, 152Y only matches 152Y and not 152C. The latter treats mixture designations as matches with their components, that is, 152Y matches T152 and 152C and vice versa. The search engine also allows length heteroplasmy at the notorious C-tracts around positions 16189, 310, and 573 to be disregarded, which makes frequency estimates more conservative. Query haplotypes are reported by the counting method and can be specifically searched according to geographic (**Figure 9**) and MP categories. Frequency values are calculated based on the number of observations indicating lower and upper bound confidence intervals (according to the Wilson method). Unobserved haplotypes are added to the database according to the $(1/n + 1)$ method to achieve a conservative frequency estimate.

EMPOP offers a tool section that currently holds software to aid the quality check of a (new) data set (EMP TOOL). These haplotypes can be sorted according to different criteria, while plausibility and formal checks are performed.

Furthermore, online database projects with forensic relevance comprise the chromosome X database presenting X-STR frequencies, the ENFSI STR database for common autosomal STRs, and a national US database for Y-STRs.

See also: **Biology/DNA:** DNA – Statistical Probability; DNA Databases; Mitochondrial DNA; Short Tandem Repeats; X-Chromosome Markers.

Further Reading

Alonso, A., 2011. DNA Electrophoresis Protocols for Forensic Genetics. Humana, Totowa, NJ.

Bandelt, H.-J., Parson, W., 2008. Consistent treatment of length variants in the human mtDNA control region: a reappraisal. International Journal of Legal Medicine 122, 11–21.

Bandelt, H.-J., Richards, M., Macaulay, V. (Eds.), 2006. Human Mitochondrial DNA and the Evolution of *Homo sapiens* (Nucleic Acids and Molecular Biology). Springer, Berlin.

Buckleton, J.S., Krawczak, M., Weir, B.S., 2011. The interpretation of lineage markers in forensic DNA testing. Forensic Science International: Genetics 5, 78–83.

Carracedo, A., Butler, J.M., Gusmão, L., Parson, W., Roewer, L., Schneider, P.M., 2010. Publication of population data for forensic purposes. Forensic Science International: Genetics 4, 145–147.

Gusmão, L., Butler, J.M., Carracedo, A., et al., DNA Commission of the International Society of Forensic Genetics, 2006. DNA Commission of the International Society of Forensic Genetics (ISFG): an update of the recommendations on the use of Y-STRs in forensic analysis. Forensic Science International 157, 187–197.

Jobling, M.A., Pandya, A., Tyler-Smith, C., 1997. The Y chromosome in forensic analysis and paternity testing. International Journal of Legal Medicine 110, 118–124.

Parson, W., Dür, A., 2007. EMPOP – a forensic mtDNA database. Forensic Science International: Genetics 1, 88–92.

Parson, W., Roewer, L., 2010. Publication of population data of linearly inherited DNA markers in the International Journal of Legal Medicine. International Journal of Legal Medicine 124, 505–509.

Röck, A., Irwin, J., Dür, A., Parsons, T., Parson, W., 2011. SAM: string-based sequence search algorithm for mitochondrial DNA database queries. Forensic Science International: Genetics 5, 126–132.

Roewer, L., 2009. Y chromosome STR typing in crime casework. Forensic Science Medicine and Pathology 5, 77–84.

Underhill, P.A., Kivisild, T., 2007. Use of Y chromosome and mitochondrial DNA population structure in tracing human migrations. Annual Review of Genetics 41, 539–564.

van Oven, M., Kayser, M., 2008. Updated comprehensive phylogenetic tree of global human mitochondrial DNA variation. Human Mutation 2, E386–E394.

van Oven, M., Ralf, A., Kayser, M., 2011. An efficient multiplex genotyping approach for detecting the major worldwide human Y-chromosome haplogroups. International Journal of Legal Medicine 125, 879–885. http://dx.doi.org/10.1007/s00414-011-0605-2.

Willuweit, S., Caliebe, A., Andersen, M.M., Roewer, L., 2010. Y-STR frequency surveying method: a critical reappraisal. Forensic Science International: Genetics 5, 84–90.

Willuweit, S., Roewer, L., International Forensic Y Chromosome User Group, 2007. Y chromosome haplotype reference database (YHRD): Update. Forensic Science International: Genetics 1, 83–87.

Wolf, A., Caliebe, A., Junge, O., Krawczak, M., 2005. Forensic interpretation of Y-chromosomal DNA mixtures. Forensic Science International 152, 209–213.

Relevant Websites

http://strbase.org – Autosomal STR Database for European Populations.
http://www.empop.org – EDNAP Mitochondrial DNA Population Database.
http://www.chrx-str.org – X Chromosomal STR Database.
http://www.yhrd.org – Y Chromosome Haplotype Reference Database.
http://usystrdatabase.org – Y-STR Database for US Populations.

History of the International Society for Forensic Genetics—ISFG

N Morling, University of Copenhagen, Copenhagen, Denmark

The International Society for Forensic Genetics—ISFG—was founded on June 24, 1968 at a meeting at the University of Mainz, Germany, by a group of dedicated blood group serologists (**Table 1**) under the name "Gesellschaft für forensiche Blutgruppenkunde" (Society for Forensic Haemogenetics). Thus, the ISFG is a German, nonprofit society that was registered on July 31, 1968 at the District Court, Mainz, Germany (registration no. 1006).

The initial aim of the society was to establish a scientific platform for the study of genetic markers in human blood for use in forensic genetics. The number of both German-speaking and other international members increased rapidly and, in 1989, the Society was made an international society ("International Society for Forensic Haemogenetics") with German and English as the official languages. Since 1993, all presentations at the ISFG congresses have been given in English. In 1991, the name of the Society was changed to "International Society for Forensic Genetics," reflecting that almost all kinds of tissues can be typed successfully with DNA methods. The statutes of the ISFG from 2011 are shown in **Table 2**.

Executive Board of the ISFG

The board of the ISFG has five members (**Table 3**).

The ISFG presidents are listed in **Table 4**. Lists of other board members are found at http://www.isfg.org.

Honorary Members

All activities of the ISFG are unpaid and nonprofit. Many members have made very valuable contributions to the society.

Table 1 Founders of the ISFG

Dr A. Arndt-Hanser
Dr B. von Boros
Dr B. Gumbel
Prof. Dr K. Hummel
Dr H. Leithoff
Prof. Dr K. Luff
Prof. Dr F. Petersohn
Prof. Dr L. Wolff
Prof. Dr W. Zimmermann

The general assemblies have appointed a number of honorary members (**Table 5**).

Membership

In 2001, the ISFG had more than 1100 individual members from more than 50 countries. The members typically work with forensic genetics in academic institutions (universities, etc.), criminal justice, and police organizations, as well as private companies. The members' expertise includes molecular and population genetics, blood group serology, biostatistics, criminal law, medical ethics, etc. Applicants need recommendations from two members of the ISFG. The membership fee (in 2011: €60.00 per year) includes reduction of the registration fee at the biannual congresses and a subscription (print and online version) to the scientific journal "Forensic Science International: Genetics" that is affiliated with the ISFG.

Commercial companies can become corporate members to express their support for the aims of the society.

The Biannual ISFG Congresses

The most important activity of the ISFG is the international congresses that are being held biannually. The location and the president of the congress are decided by the general assembly of the ISFG. The 2007 and 2009 ISFG congresses were attended by more than 600 participants (**Table 6**).

Proceedings of the ISFG Congresses

Since 1997, the proceedings of the biannual ISFG congresses have been published in Progress in Forensic Genetics, Elsevier. Since 2007, the proceedings are freely available through Forensic Science International: Genetics Supplement Series (http://www.fsigeneticssup.com). In the period 1985–1995, the proceedings were published in Advances in Forensic Haemogenetics by Springer.

Scientific ISFG Prizes

The board of the ISFG can award scientific prizes. The scientific prize is given at the biannual ISFG congress. The prize winner is

 http://dx.doi.org/10.1016/B978-0-12-800647-4.00043-6

Table 2 Statutes of the ISFG 2011—translation from German into English

§ 1—Name and Place of Registration
The International Society for Forensic Genetics is incorporated with place of registration at Mainz.

§ 2—Aims
1. The society aims to promote scientific knowledge in the field of genetic markers in human blood. This is to be accomplished by scientific meetings of the society, meetings of regional working parties, and by scientific publications.
2. The society strives for cooperation with other scientific bodies. The society especially is always ready to assist public inquiries.

§ 3—General Usefulness
1. The society's sole scientific purpose is given in the sense of "beneficiary tax purpose" of the German Tax Code (Abgabenordnung).
2. The society does by no means pursue an economical purpose. The funds of the society may only be applied for appropriate statutory purposes. The members receive no fees in their capacity as members and also no other allowances out of the funds of the society.
3. No person may be supported in a way inappropriate to the purposes of the society or benefit of inappropriate allowances.

§ 4—Membership
1. Any academic graduate, dealing scientifically with genetic markers in human blood, can apply for full membership.
2. Corporate members (e.g., commercial companies) can be enrolled as members, but they do not have the right to vote.
3. Applications for membership must be made to the Executive Committee of the society together with references from two full members. Admission to the society is subject to the decision of the Executive Committee.
4. Membership is terminated by written notice of withdrawal, death, or by disqualification. Notice of withdrawal is given by registered letter to the Executive Committee.
5. Scientists, whose contributions are of great importance in respect to haemogenetics and any other persons who especially deserve acknowledgment by the society, can be nominated as honorary members. This is subject to the decision of the General Assembly.
6. The membership may not be used for advertising purposes.
7. Any scientifically interested person is able to become an extraordinary member without the right of voting, as far as these are not listed up in point (1).

§ 5—Executive Committee
1. The Executive Committee consists of the President, the Vice president, the Representative for all Working Parties, the Secretary and the Treasurer.
2. The General Assembly elects the Executive Committee by secret ballot and by a simple majority of votes from the membership. The Treasurer and the Secretary are elected for 4 years consecutively, the other members for the Executive Committee for 2 years. If the President is reelected the Vice president is also reelected automatically for another 2 years. Only one reelection is permitted.
3. The newly elected Executive Committee takes over its official function on the first January following the election; until then the former Executive Committee remains in office.
4. The Executive Committee is still authorized to pass resolutions, even if one member should withdraw prematurely. The required by-election then takes place at the next General Assembly.
5. The Executive Committee may invite guests for the Board Meeting.

§ 6—Authorization for Representation
Two members of the Executive Committee represent the society in the sense of § 26 BGB (German Civil Code).

§ 7—General Assembly
1. The General Assembly pays particular attention to the following:
   - Receiving of the annual report, also the annual report of the treasurer,
   - Election of members of the Executive Committee,
   - Relief of the members of the Executive Committee,
   - Appointment of honorary members,
   - Establishment of time and place of scientific conventions,
   - Decision of regulations if necessary,
   - Decision of alterations of statutes and regulations,
   - Decision of dissolvement of the society.
2. The General Assembly passes a resolution with a simple majority as long as the statutes do not read differently.
3. As a rule, the General Assembly takes place on the occasion of a scientific convention. Therefore, the Executive Committee must take known, in writing, appointed time of the convention 6 weeks in advance. A topic which does not belong or appear on the agenda can be introduced without resolution, providing three-fourth of the members are in favor of its acceptance.
4. A special General Assembly can be called by the Executive Committee. It must be called for by at least one-fourth of the members who have submitted reasons to the Executive Committee.
5. Upon the decision of the Executive Committee or upon the request of at least 100 ordinary members or upon the decision of two-third of the members present at the General Assembly a vote concerning business affairs may be carried out by letter.

(Continued)

Table 2 Statutes of the ISFG 2011—translation from German into English—cont'd

§ 8—Scientific Conferences
1. At least every 2 years a scientific conference is held.
2 Each member may bring forward proposals concerning the program. The proposals must be received by the Executive Committee at least 4 months in advance. It is up to the Executive Committee to decide the scientific subject of the papers and to choose the speakers.
3. The International Society tor Forensic Genetics can distribute every 2 years, on the occasion of the scientific congresses, the "Scientific Prize of the International Society for Forensic Genetics," according to special statutes.

§ 9—Membership Subscriptions, Auditor, Business Year
1. A yearly membership subscription is raised, which becomes due at the beginning of the calendar year and the amount of which is fixed by the General Assembly. Changes in the subscription fees become valid at the beginning of the following calendar year.
2. Honorary members are not eligible to subscription fees. For corporate members the subscription fees agreed upon are the minimum and are agreed on an individual basis by self-assessment.
3. At the end of a business year the cash account of the society is checked by two auditors elected from the General Assembly. The latter report to the General Assembly.
4. The business year is identical with the calendar year.

§ 10—Working Parties, Committees, Commissions
1. Working parties function for the exchange of experience.
2. The General Assembly can conclude the formation of working parties, committees, and commissions.

§ 11—Alterations of the Statutes
1. An application for alteration of the statutes, duly signed by at least one-fifth of the members, must be addressed to the President together with reasons 3 months before the General Assembly.
2. The Executive Committee is also entitled to propose alterations of the statutes with reasons to the General Assembly, the subject of which must be made known to the members together with the invitation to the General Assembly.
3. Alterations of the statutes are concluded by the General Assembly in accordance with § 33 BGB (German Civil Code) with a three-fourth majority of the present members. An alteration of the aims of the society is only possible with the agreement of all members.

§ 12—Dissolution of the Society
1. The dissolution of the society can only be considered after the application of the least two-third of the members has been brought before the Executive Committee within 3 months before the General Assembly takes place.

For the conclusion to dissolve the society a three-fourth majority of the present members is required.

2. When the society is dissolved, its property falls to the "Deutsche Forschungsgemeinschaft," who will use it immediately for general utility purposes. The agreement of the relevant revenue office must be obtained beforehand.

Table 3 The 2011 executive board of the ISFG

President	Prof. Dr Niels Morling, Copenhagen
Vice president	Prof. Dr Peter M. Schneider, Cologne
Secretary	Prof. Dr Wolfgang R. Mayr, Vienna
Treasurer	Leonor Gusmao, PhD, Porto
Representative of all working groups	Mechthild Prinz, PhD, New York

encouraged to give a presentation of the scientific work at the following ISFG congress (**Table 7**).

The Language-Based Working Parties

The ISFG has the following language-based working groups: Chinese, English, French, German, Italian, and Spanish–Portuguese. The working groups typically treat items of regional or national interest. Some of the working groups also offer quality control and proficiency testing exercises (http://www.isfg.org, http://www.rtw-eswg.forensic.ku.dk and http://www.gep-isfg.org/ISFG/English/portada.php).

Table 4 Presidents of the ISFG

1968–1970	Prof. Dr W. Zimmermann, Homburg/Saar
1970–1973	Prof. Dr H. Leithoff, Mainz
1974–1976	Dr K. Heindl, Nürnberg
1977–1981	Prof. Dr H.H. Hoppe, Hamburg
1982–1983	Prof. Dr C.P. Engelfriet, Amsterdam
1984–1985	Prof. Dr W. Spielmann, Frankfurt/Main
1986–1987	Prof. Dr R. Bütler, Bern
1988–1991	Prof. Dr B. Brinkmann, Münster
1992–1995	Prof. Dr W. Bär, Zürich
1996–1999	Prof. Dr B. Olaisen, Oslo
2000–2003	Prof. Dr A. Carracedo, Santiago de Compostela
2004–2007	Prof. Dr P.M. Schneider, Cologne
2008–2011	Prof. Dr N. Morling, Copenhagen
2012–	Dr Mechthild Prinz, New York City

Table 5 Honorary members of the ISFG

Prof. Dr E. Essen-Möller, Alsbäck/Lysekil, Sweden
Prof. Dr P. Dahr, Bensberg, Köln
Prof. Dr E. Krah, Heidelberg
Prof. Dr M. Krüpe, Fulda
Prof. Dr W. Zimmermann, Homburg/Saar
Prof. Dr J.-J. van Loghem, Amsterdam
Prof. Dr F. Levine, Raritan, NJ, USA
Dr R.R. Race, London
Dr R. Sanger, London
Prof. Dr O. Prokop, Berlin
Prof. Dr H. Leithoff, Mainz
Prof. Dr K. Hummel, Freiburg
Dr B. Dodd, London
Dr E. van Loghem, Amsterdam
Dr M. Pereira, London
Prof. Dr E. Schwarzfischer, München
Prof. Dr C.P. Engelfriet, Amsterdam
Prof. Dr K. Henningsen, Kopenhagen
Dr A.G. Gathof, Würzburg
Prof. Dr H.H. Hoppe, Hamburg
Prof. Dr W. Spielmann, Frankfurt/Main
Prof. Dr D.A. Hopkinson, London
Prof. Dr H. Matsumoto, Takatsuki/Osaka
Prof. Dr A. Arndt-Hanser, Mainz
Prof. Dr R. Bütler, Zollikofen
Prof. Dr A. Jeffreys, Leicester
Prof. Dr A. Fiori, Rome
Prof. Dr E. Villanueva, Granada
Prof. Dr P.J. Lincoln, London
Prof. Dr Ch. Rittner, Mainz
Prof. Dr B. Brinkmann, Münster
Prof. Dr B. Olaisen, Oslo

Table 6 ISFG congresses 1969–2011

2011 Vienna	President	Prof. Dr W.R. Mayr
2009 Buenos Aires	President	Dr E. Raimondi
2007 Copenhagen	President	Prof. Dr N. Morling
2005 Ponta Delgada (Azores)	Presidents	Prof. Dr A. Amorim and Prof. Dr F. Corte-Real
2003 Arcachon	President	Prof. Dr Ch. Doutremepuich
2001 Münster	President	Prof. Dr B. Brinkmann
1999 San Francisco	President	Prof. Dr G. Sensabaugh
1997 Oslo	President	Prof. Dr B. Olaisen
1995 Santiago de Compostela	President	Prof. Dr A. Carracedo
1993 Lido di Venezia	President	Prof. Dr A. Fiori
1991 Mainz	President	Prof. Dr Ch. Rittner
1989 New Orleans	President	Dr H. Polesky
1987 Vienna	President	Prof. Dr W.R. Mayr
1985 Copenhagen	President	Dr K. Henningsen
1983 Munich	Presidents	Prof. Dr F. Schwarzfischer and Dr A.G. Gathof
1981 Bern	President	Prof. Dr R. Bütler
1979 London	Presidents	Dr B. Dodd and Prof. Dr C.P. Engelfriet
1977 Hamburg	President	Prof. Dr H.H. Hoppe
1975 Innsbruck	President	Prof. Dr H. Reissigl
1973 Amsterdam	President	Prof. Dr J.-J. van Loghem and Prof. Dr C.P. Engelfriet
1972 Trier	President	Prof. Dr H. Leithoff
1971 Mainz	President	Prof. Dr H. Leithoff
1970 Freiburg	President	Prof. Dr K. Hummel
1969 Lübeck	President	Prof. Dr W. Zimmermann and Prof. Dr M. Krüpe

Table 7 Scientific ISFG prizes

2009	Antonio Salas, Santiago de Compostela, Spain
2007	Reinhard Szibor, Magdeburg, Germany
2005	Walther Parson, Innsbruck, Austria
2003	John Butler, Gaithersburg, MD, USA
1999	Lutz Roewer, Berlin, Germany
1997	Antti Sajantila, Helsinki, Finland & Colin Kimpton, UK National DNA Database Group, Birmingham, England
1989	Manfred Hochmeister, Bern, Switzerland
1987	Wolfgang Dahr, Cologne, Germany

The DNA Commission

Since 1989, the board of the ISFG together with invited scientists has established various ad hoc working groups called "DNA Commission of the ISFG" that have discussed important forensic genetic topics and formulated recommendations. The published recommendations have helped to establish scientific standards for new typing methods and genetic systems.

The European DNA Profiling Group

The European DNA Profiling (EDNAP) group was established in October 1988 in London at a meeting of forensic genetic scientists from European countries. The initial purpose of EDNAP was to harmonize DNA technologies for crime case investigations so that DNA results could be exchanged across the borders in Europe. In 1991, EDNAP was accepted as a working group of the ISFG. Approximately 20 European laboratories are members of EDNAP. The EDNAP group collaborates closely with the DNA Working Group of the European Network of Forensic Science Institutes. The two groups usually organize common meetings twice a year. EDNAP organizes exercises to explore the possibility of standardization of new forensic genetic methods. The results of the exercises are published and made available on the ISFG Web site (see http://www.isfg.org).

Compliance with Statutes

The ISFG membership shall not be used for advertisement purposes. For more information, please visit http://www.isfg.org.

See also: **Biology/DNA:** Forensic DNA Advisory Groups: DAB, SWGDAM, ENFSI, and BSAG.

Further Reading

Amorim, A., Corte-Real, F., Morling, N. (Eds.), 2006. Progress in Forensic Genetics 11. 21st Congress of the International Society for Forensic Genetics, Ponta Delgada, Portugal, 2005. Elsevier, Amsterdam.

Brinkmann, B., Carracedo, A. (Eds.), 2003. Progress in Forensic Genetics 9. 19th Congress of the International Society for Forensic Genetics. Münster, Germany, 28 August–1 September 2001. Elsevier, Amsterdam.

Carracedo, A., Bär, W., Lincoln, P., et al., 2000. DNA Commission of the International Society for Forensic Genetics: guidelines for mitochondrial DNA typing. Forensic Science International 110 (2), 79–85.

Doutremepuiche, Ch., Morling, N. (Eds.), 2004. Progress in Forensic Genetics 10. 20th Congress of the International Society for Forensic Genetics. Arcachon, France, 2003. Elsevier, Amsterdam.

Gill, P., Brenner, C., Brinkmann, B., et al., 2001. DNA Commission of the International Society of Forensic Genetics: recommendations on forensic analysis using Y-chromosome STRs. Forensic Science International 124, 5–10.

Gill, P., Brenner, C.H., Buckleton, J.S., et al., 2006. DNA commission of the International Society of Forensic Genetics: recommendations on the interpretation of mixtures. Forensic Science International 160, 90–101.

Gjertson, D.W., Brenner, C.H., Baur, M.P., et al., 2007. ISFG: recommendations on biostatistics in paternity testing. Forensic Science International: Genetics 1 (3), 223–231.

Gusmao, L., Butler, J.M., Carracedo, A., et al., 2006. DNA Commission of the International Society of Forensic Genetics (ISFG): an update of the recommendations on the use of Y-STRs in forensic analysis. Forensic Science International 157, 187–197.

Linacre, A., Gusmão, L., Hecht, W., et al., 2011. ISFG: recommendations regarding the use of non-human (animal) DNA in forensic genetic investigations. Forensic Science International: Genetics 5 (5), 501–505.

Morling, N., Allen, R.W., Carracedo, A., et al., 2002. Paternity Testing Commission of the International Society of Forensic Genetics: recommendations on genetic investigations in paternity cases. Forensic Science International 129 (3), 148–157.

Progress in Forensic Genetics 12. In: Morling, N. (Ed.), 2008. 22nd Congress of the International Society for Forensic Genetics. Copenhagen, Denmark, 2007, Forensic Science International Genetics Supplement Series, vol. 1(1). Available at http://www.fsigeneticssup.com/.

Progress in Forensic Genetics 13. In: Morling, N. (Ed.), 2009. 23rd Congress of the International Society for Forensic Genetics, Buenos Aires, Argentina, 2009, Forensic Science International Genetics Supplement Series, vol. 2(1). Available at http://www.fsigeneticssup.com/.

Progress in Forensic Genetics 14. In: Morling, N. (Ed.), 2011. 24th Congress of the International Society for Forensic Genetics. Vienna, Austria, 2011, Forensic Science International Genetics Supplement Series, vol. 3(1). Available at http://www.fsigeneticssup.com/.

Prinz, M., Carracedo, A., Mayr, W.R., et al., 2007. DNA Commission of the International Society for Forensic Genetics (ISFG): recommendations regarding the role of forensic genetics for disaster victim identification (DVI). Forensic Science International: Genetics 1 (1), 3–12.

Relevant Websites

http://www.gep-isfg.org – The Spanish and Portuguese-speaking Working Group of the International Society for Forensic Genetics.

http://www.isfg.org – Internal Society for Forensic Genetics.

http://www.rtw-eswg.forensic.ku.dk – English Speaking Working Group of the International Society of Forensic Genetics.

Key Terms

ABO, Accreditation, Acquittal, Alec Jeffreys, Analytical capacity, Backlog, Barry Scheck, Bayesian, Bias, BSAG, Case forecasting, Clinical legal education, CODIS, Cold hit, Colin Pitchfork, Confidence interval, Cost-benefit, Counting method, Coverage interval, Database, Defense counsel, Degree of belief, Disaster victim identification, DNA, DNA advisory groups, DNA backlog, DNA profile, EDNAP, Edward Blake, Electronic recording of interrogations, ENFSI, European data exchange, Exonerations, Exonerees, Externally visible characteristics, Extrapolation method, Eyewitness identification, False confessions, Familial searching, FBI Laboratory, Fingerprints, Forensic dentistry, Forensic DNA, Forensic odontology, Frequentist, Future submissions, Gary Dotson, Genetic privacy, Guidelines, GUM, Haplotype, History, Identification, Informants, Innocence commissions, Innocence Network, Innocence Project, International Society for Forensic Genetics (ISFG), Investigation, ISFG, Lab resources, Legislation, Match probability, Measurement, Measurement error, Metapopulation, Missing persons, Mitochondrial DNA, Mixture analysis, NAS, National Academy of Sciences, Offender, PCR, Pedagogy, Peter Neufeld, Phylogeny, Police misconduct, Policy, Population database, Population subdivision, Probability, Probability distribution, Proficiency testing, Propagation of distributions, Propagation of uncertainty, Property crime, Prosecutorial misconduct, Quality assessment scheme, Quality assurance, Quality control, Radiography, Rapid DNA analysis, Random error, Reference sample, RFLP, Serology, Short tandem repeats, Snitches, Statutes, Suspect, SWGDAM, Systematic error, Treaty of Prüm, Type A uncertainty, Type B uncertainty, Uncertainty, Wrongful convictions, Y chromosome, Y-STRs.

Review Questions

1. Are the models offered for forensic service provision suggested by Ramsey and Burton the only ones available? What other models might there be?

2. What's a "forensic strategy"? What questions are part of developing one? Why is it important to a case and to a laboratory?
3. Why is integration of forensic cases "the single biggest challenge to the forensic science community"?
4. What is currently in forensic reports? How do these differ from other scientific reports? How do they differ from published articles in peer-reviewed journals? What *should* be in forensic reports? Make a table listing each component and compare.
5. Who is the "audience" of forensic reports? The police using the technical information to investigate the case or other scientists who must review the technical information? Is it both? How does this affect the content of forensic reports? Should it?
6. How do the legal requirements of the contents of a forensic report differ between the United Kingdom and the United States?
7. Can forensic reports stand on their own (that is, without an expert's testimony)? What determines this?
8. Are there ethical obligations to the format and content of a forensic report? If so, what are they?
9. What is "Brady material"?
10. What is "OHS"? What should this policy articulate?
11. What is the difference between ISO 17025 and ISO 9001? Are they equivalent?
12. What was the first criminal case in the United States that presented DNA profiling? What is the significance of *State v. Castro*, 1989?
13. Why is good housekeeping important in a forensic laboratory?
14. What is the Innocence Project? What function in the criminal justice system does it serve? Why was it created?
15. Why is DNA such a powerful tool in wrongful convictions? Why are other forensic methods not used as much as DNA in these cases?
16. Why are nearly all wrongful convictions sexual assaults or murders?
17. What are the privacy issues associated with DNA databases? If databases help find and convict criminals, why should innocent citizens be concerned if their profile has been entered into a database?
18. What is measurement uncertainty? What are the types of uncertainty? How are they different than "errors"?
19. What are the different criteria for entrance to a DNA database in various countries? What do these differences say about those countries' criminal justice systems?
20. What is NameUS? What role does it play in the criminal justice system?

Discussion Questions

1. How should forensic examinations and analyses be "integrated"? With laboratory specialization, how can cases move through a forensic laboratory in an integrated fashion? What are the benefits to doing this? What are the problems?
2. Why are forensic reports formatted the way they are? Is there a better way to present this information? Who are they written for and who *should* they be written for?
3. Why would police and prosecutors be unwilling to consider a wrongful conviction? What professional or social pressures might be at play? What is the role of forensic science in these cases, especially if science was used to prosecute the person in the first place?
4. Why is uncertainty of measurement analytically important to forensic science? Is it important ethically? Why or why not?
5. Accreditation is an indication that a laboratory is following the minimum acceptable standards; the external assessment of a laboratory by an accrediting body is one part of a larger quality system. List some of the ways other than accreditation that a laboratory maintains quality. How does accreditation feed into these? If a laboratory already has an excellent quality system, what does accreditation mean?

Additional Readings

Cole, S.A., 2014. History of forensic science in policing. In . In: Encyclopedia of Criminology and Criminal Justice. Springer, New York, pp. 2153–2158.

de Keijser, J., Elffers, H., 2012. Understanding of forensic expert reports by judges, defense lawyers and forensic professionals. Psychology, Crime & Law 18 (2), 191–207.

Howes, L., Kirkbride, K., Kelty, S., Julian, R., Kemp, N., 2014. Forensic scientists' conclusion: how readable are they for non-scientist report-users? Forensic Science International 231 (1–3), 102–112.

Machado, H., Silva, S., 2014. "Would you accept having your DNA profile inserted in the National Forensic DNA database? Why?" Results of a questionnaire applied in Portugal. Forensic Science International: Genetics 8 (1), 132–136.

Roland, M.C., 2009. Quality and integrity in scientific writing: prerequisites for quality in science communication. Journal of Science Communications 8 (02), A04.

Siegel, J., King, M., Reed, W., 2013. The laboratory report project. Forensic Science Policy & Management 4 (3–4), 1–11.

Section 6. Additional Topics

"Prediction is very difficult, especially if it's about the future." The famed physicist, Niels Bohr, could not have been more right with his pithy quote about forecasting—it is difficult. Which methods will dominate DNA analysis in the next decade, mass spectrometry, next generation sequencing, or rapid DNA? Hard to say. What is certain is the constant broadening of DNA applications beyond the human genome. Animals, insects, plants, and microbes all have their own DNA potentials in criminal cases ranging from abuse, smuggling, counterfeits, even to homicide. Looking for a future in forensic DNA? Nonhuman DNA might be a good place to start.

Future Analytical Techniques: DNA Mass Spectrometry

W Parson, Innsbruck Medical University, Innsbruck, Austria
S Hofstadler, Ibis Biosciences Inc., Carlsbad, CA, USA

Abbreviations

ESI Electrospray ionization
FTICR Fourier transform ion cyclotron resonance mass spectrometry
HPLC High-performance liquid chromatography
ICEMS Ion-pair reversed-phase liquid chromatography electrospray ionization mass spectrometry
***m/z* ratio** Mass over charge ratio
MALDI Matrix-assisted laser desorption/ionization
miniSTR Short tandem repeat loci amplified in short fragment sizes
MS Mass spectrometry
SNP Single-nucleotide polymorphism
STR Short tandem repeat
TOF Time of flight

Glossary

Electrospray ionization (ESI) Ionization technique of biomolecules for mass spectrometry.
Gas chromatography Gas-phase separation method for volatile compounds.
High-performance liquid chromatography (HPLC) Column-based method for separating analytes based on differences in hydrophilic/hydrophobic interactions.
Matrix-assisted laser desorption/ionization (MALDI) Ionization technique of biomolecules for mass spectrometry.
miniSTR Short tandem repeat loci amplified in short fragment sizes.
Restriction fragment length polymorphism Method of differentiating DNA based on variation at sites recognized by restriction enzymes.
Short tandem repeat (STR) Repetitive repeat element used to differentiate DNA.
Single-nucleotide polymorphism (SNP) A single base change in a DNA sequence relative to a reference sequence.
Solid-phase extraction Chromatographic technique used to prepare samples for subsequent analysis by removing interfering substances.
Variable number of tandem repeats Repetitive repeat element used to differentiate DNA.

 http://dx.doi.org/10.1016/B978-0-12-800647-4.00044-8

Background

Much of the nuclear variation that has been targeted in forensic genetics is present as fragment length polymorphism. This applies to earlier restriction fragment length polymorphism-based methods, where variable number of tandem repeats alleles were discriminated on flat-bed gels with fragment sizes up to 20 kbp, as well as modern short tandem repeat (STR) loci that are separated under denaturing conditions with sizes up to 500 bp. Discernible size categories are used to number (call) STR alleles relative to sequenced reference alleles. These STR categories are used to calculate allele frequencies that form the basis of statistical evaluations. In the late 1990s, the forensic community witnessed the development of commercially available, larger STR multiplex kits containing between 10 and 15 STR markers, and the forensic experts became used to reporting STR profile frequencies beyond one in a billion. This development was also triggered by the establishment of national DNA databases that require high discrimination power to confidently identify links between unknown crime scene samples and suspects/convicted persons.

Forensic samples, for example, specimens collected at the scene of a crime, are by nature unpredictable in terms of DNA quality and quantity. They are often affected by environmental conditions that lead to DNA degradation. As a practical consequence, casework samples often yield partial STR profiles that contain only a reduced number of useful loci, mostly at low-molecular-weight ranges. Partial STR profiles are usually less discriminative and may therefore pose a problem for the practitioner when they fail to provide strong evidence in a case or result in too many adventitious matches in DNA database searches. To compensate for the reduced discrimination power, so-called miniSTR strategies were developed, where amplification primers were moved closer to the repeat region to reduce the amplified fragment size and represent alleles at lower molecular weights. This allows for an increased number of successfully typed loci and, in the case of complementing STR profiles (consensus from different STR multiplex amplifications), helps achieve the required discrimination power. This strategy is, however, restricted by the amount of available DNA. Often DNA quality and quantity are linked in crime scene samples, that is, low DNA amount goes hand in hand with some degree of degradation, which is why miniSTR analysis does not always resolve the issue. Alternatively, markers that are better suited for the successful analysis of degraded DNA, for example, single-nucleotide polymorphism (SNP) and insertion/deletion polymorphisms, were also considered but not broadly adopted by the forensic community as standard loci, mainly because of the incompatibility with the existing national DNA databases that seem to lock the selection of forensic STR loci.

Even in the early days of STR typing, so-called variant alleles were observed under nondenaturing electrophoresis conditions. Although their fragment sizes were identical to the "normal alleles," they showed slightly different migration patterns. Sequencing studies revealed that they showed variation at single, or few, nucleotide positions, which apparently affected their electrophoretic mobility. While those variants were only rarely considered as separate allele classes—they were usually lumped together with the respective categories of the normal alleles—their observation indicated the presence of additional genetic variation in STRs that remained hidden under denaturing electrophoresis conditions. Could this information be captured by alternative detection methods? And if so, would this additional discriminatory power offset the loss of information caused by partial profiles when degraded DNA is present? These questions raised interest in the application of mass spectrometry (MS)-based methods for the analysis of the forensic STR loci. In contrast to electrophoretic separation where only fragment sizes are estimated, MS-based methods result in molecular masses of the amplified DNA that can be transformed into base composition profiles. This means that not only fragment sizes but also nucleotide variation (substitutions) can be inferred, allowing for discrimination of alleles, which differ in base composition but are of identical length.

In addition to technical questions such as the overall success rates of such approaches, the overall performance of MS, and the potential to automate the process, one would certainly be interested in how much of the additional genetic variation could be detected by MS. Sanger sequencing of forensic STR alleles would theoretically capture all detectable genetic variation present in a sample but is undoubtedly too expensive and too laborious for routine samples (and in many samples not applicable). Next-generation sequencing technologies are still failing to demonstrate the reliability, especially in difficult samples, that would be required in a forensic context. Can MS-based methods compete with the performance of established electrophoresis systems? What are their benefits and limitations? These questions are addressed in the following sections, as well as the state of the art of MS-based DNA analysis in forensic science.

Mass Spectrometric Methods in Forensic Genetics

Early Work

While the early work of Butler and coworkers clearly demonstrated the applicability of matrix-assisted laser desorption/ionization–time of flight (MALDI–TOF) in the characterization of STRs, there is a notable absence of published reports in which MALDI–Fourier transform ion cyclotron resonance mass spectrometry (FTICR) was employed to characterize nucleic acids associated with forensic markers. The fact that signals from larger oligonucleotide ions derived from polymerase chain reaction (PCR) would appear at significantly higher *m*/*z* ratios, where FTICR performance is significantly degraded, has precluded the implementation of the MALDI–FTICR method to characterize STRs. Additionally, a key consideration for MALDI–FTICR relative to MALDI–TOF is the timescale over which the mass measurement takes place and the inherent delay between ion formation and ion detection. Ions that are internally excited due to the MALDI ionization process have more time to undergo metastable decay on the relatively long timescale of the FTICR measurement (100–1000 ms) compared to the much shorter timescale of a TOF detector (<100 μs). Even under relatively gentle MALDI conditions, MALDI–FTICR spectra of oligonucleotides greater than about 20 nucleotides in length often exhibit some extent of metastable decay that is typically manifested as loss of one or more neutral purine bases. However, owing to the gentle nature of electrospray ionization (ESI), the ESI–FTICR technique enjoyed early adoption as a method with which to characterize forensic DNA markers derived from both autosomal STRs and mitochondrial DNA (mtDNA).

The first ESI–FTICR analysis of an STR marker (TH01 allele 9.3) was accomplished in the late 1990s on a 4.7 T ESI–FTICR instrument, and the same platform was later employed to correctly differentiate between subtypes in the vWA locus that could not be distinguished by traditional gel-based genotyping methods. These studies also demonstrated that the relatively high mass of the PCR amplicons derived from STRs (30–60 kDa) were not particularly amenable to high-performance mass measurements on the FTICR platform. The inherent space charge limit of the trapped ion cell in combination with the added cost and complexities associated with operating the FTICR platform in a "hands-off" high-throughput modality precluded the broad adoption of ESI–FTICR instrumentation as a viable platform. The commercial availability of benchtop ESI–TOF mass spectrometers, which provided sensitivity and mass accuracies rivaling those of the FTICR platform, ushered in a new era in the mass spectrometric interrogation of DNA forensics markers and laid the foundation for broad implementation in the mainstream forensic community.

ESI–TOF: Current State of the Art

John Bennett Fenn won the Nobel Prize in Chemistry in 2002 for his development of ESI. ESI is particularly useful for the ionization of macromolecules, such as larger DNA fragments, which tend to fragment during ionization with other techniques. The last decade has seen two main approaches to the application of MS to the analysis of forensic markers, both relying on ESI–TOF–MS. The major difference between these two approaches lies in the way in which amplified PCR products are purified and prepared for ESI–MS (as outlined below). This post-PCR purification step is a critical prelude to mass spectrometric analysis as there are a myriad of buffer components (salts, dNTPs, detergents, etc.) that are required for PCR amplification but are deleterious to the performance of the mass spectrometer as they can interfere with the ionization process and result in uninterpretable mass spectra. The analysis and interpretation of the DNA data is then founded on base composition analysis. Masses derived from a mass spectrum can either be (1) compared to a "lookup" mass list derived from known sequences or base compositions or (2) converted directly to base compositions, which can either be compared to existing base compositions in a database or used to populate a new database. Final base composition assignment for a double-stranded PCR product requires Watson–Crick base pairing between the candidate base compositions for both the forward and reverse single-stranded DNA products (the number of As, Gs, Cs, and Ts of one strand must equal the number of Ts, Cs, Gs, and As of the complementary strand, respectively).

The ion-pair reversed-phase liquid chromatography electrospray ionization mass spectrometry approach

The analytical approach behind the ion-pair reversed-phase liquid chromatography electrospray ionization mass spectrometry (ICEMS) method involves the direct hyphenation of a high-performance liquid chromatography (HPLC) system with the ESI–TOF, which was developed in the early 1990s. The strategy is to load crude PCR products onto the HPLC column, where they are purified and coarsely fractionated and directly injected into the mass spectrometer. Reverse-phase chromatography proved very efficient in purifying and desalting PCR products—an important prerequisite for clean spectra and sensitive detection limits. A great deal of effort has been put into optimizing the chromatographic aspect of this approach to maximize the utility of the ICEMS method. As such, it has been shown that rods filled with octadecylated silica particles, octadecylated polystyrene/divinylbenzene particles, or monolithic polystyrene/divinylbenzene with 10–25 nM butyldimethylamine or cyclohexyldimethylamine as solvents result in improved performance. A key advantage of this approach is that, in addition to amplicon purification, HPLC also provides coarse size fractionation, which facilitates the analysis of complex amplicon mixtures as derived from multiplex PCRs. The Innsbruck group has shown that the analysis of an autosomal STR 14-plex and an mtDNA 23-plex is feasible in one multiplex reaction with typical forensic quality samples.

The Ibis approach

On the Ibis PLEX-ID platform, the mass spectrometric analysis process that follows PCR thermocycling is completely automated. Unlike the HPLC-based method described above, this approach utilizes fully automated anion exchange-based amplicon purification to remove salts, excess dNTPs, polymers, and other constituents of the PCR reaction that can form adducts or add to the chemical noise background in the mass spectra directly from 96-well PCR plates. Two internal mass standards (acidic peptides) that bracket the most informative region of the spectrum (m/z of ~726 to ~1346) are incorporated into the final desalting buffer to aid in subsequent data processing. Using a novel dual electrospray source configuration, this integrated approach allows the fully automated analysis of a PCR reaction every 30 s. Thus, a typical eight-well assay is "read" in only 4 min.

After MS, data processing is automatically triggered by the integrated runtime controller. Data processing employs custom software to (1) remove general background noise, (2) post-calibrate the raw mass spectrum, using multiple isotope peaks of the internal peptide calibrants, and (3) "deconvolve" the raw spectrum to produce a simplified spectrum consisting of mass on the X-axis and signal intensity on the Y-axis. The resulting deconvolved mass spectrum is traversed to determine mass peak positions and report final masses in a list that is imported directly into a database for storage and retrieval during sample analysis. The analysis of laboratory-derived data is encoded as configurable parameters in an automated analysis interface.

Increasing the accuracy by mass tags

To achieve unambiguous base composition determinations for PCR products up to about 130 bp, a mass assignment accuracy of approximately 25 ppm is required. Further, near-neighbor (i.e., SNP-containing) base compositions have forward and reverse strand masses that are similar to each other. For example, products with base compositions of [A46 G20 C32 T39] and [A47 G19 C31 T40]—corresponding to a G → A + T → C change—have masses that differ by approximately 1 Da for each forward and reverse strand as a G → A SNP reduces the mass by 16 Da and a T → C SNP increases the mass by 15 Da. With sufficient mass accuracy and precision, which is normally achievable with ESI–TOF–MS analysis, these possibilities can generally be distinguished (albeit not when present simultaneously within the same spectrum). However, because biochemical reactions contain noise and peak shapes are not always perfect in distribution, ambiguity at this level is possible.

With the G_{10} approach (Ibis), PCR is performed with a modified mastermix in which the normal dNTP mix is replaced with one containing normal dATP, dCTP, and dTTP and a modified version of dGTP (G_{10}) containing 10 ^{13}C atoms. These 10 "heavy" carbons change the mass of each incorporated GTP by 10 Da, and thus, in the case of the G → A and T → C double SNP offsets the masses of the two strands by ~11 Da, rather than 1 Da, making base composition assignment unambiguous (**Figure 1**). The use of this isotopically enriched nucleotide analog does not appear to impact PCR efficiency or the incorporation of GTP. Similarly, with the ICEMS approach, allele discrimination was improved by replacing dTTP by dUTP in the dNTP mix. Uracil and thymine are both complementary to cytosine, but the molecular mass of deoxyuridine is approximately 15 Da less than that of deoxythymidine, which results in improved allele discrimination.

MS-Based Genotypes and Haplotypes to Aid Forensic Analysis

Mass Spectrometric STR Analysis

There has been substantial effort in the forensics community to improve the performance and sensitivity of STR analysis from challenging samples. One strategy, commonly referred to as miniSTRs, applies shortened amplified products by moving

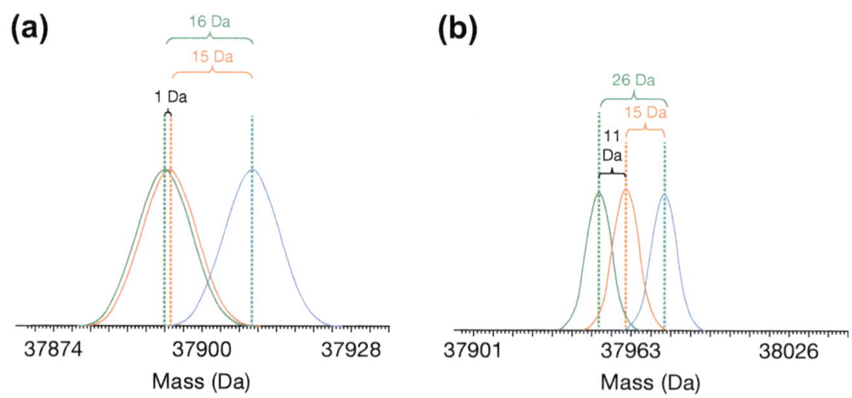

Figure 1 Utility of ^{13}C-enriched dGTP to differentiate analysis SNPs using mass spectrometry. In (a) the PCR products are generated with natural dNTPs; a G → A (green) and a T → C (red) variant produce amplicons very close in mass to each other (about 1 Da difference) but well resolved from the base allele (black). (b) When amplified with ^{13}C-enriched dGTP in place of dGTP, a G → A (green) and a T → C (red) variant from allele 14 produce amplicons separated by nearly 11 Da, which allows unambiguous assignment of each SNP variant. Note that with the use of the ^{13}C-dGTP, there is an unambiguous detection of an SNP from the base allele 14 product (black), and an unambiguous assignment of the base switch involved in the SNP.

amplification primers closer toward the repeat region. Both technologies mentioned above are actually complementary to this methodology and utilize the same approach. The reduction in amplicon sizes increases the resolution obtained during MS analysis. This approach has the following primary advantages: (1) nucleotide polymorphisms are inherently revealed during analysis; (2) prior information about nucleotide polymorphisms is not required (neither the prior characterization nor the prior localization of an SNP within a PCR product is required for it to be correctly identified); (3) no allelic ladder is required for any locus analyzed; (4) no primer labels are required (products are analyzed directly in the mass spectrometer); and (5) alleles of different loci can cross in length, and same-length alleles of one locus can be differentiated if they differ in base composition. This feature deserves explicit attention as it demonstrates that MS-based detection is amenable to DNA analysis with practically all STRs in "miniSTR mode," whereas locus spacing with CE-based multiplexes allows size reduction for only a portion of markers in a multiplex. Finally, if a novel allele with a length previously not seen is detected, a base composition can be derived directly and a very reasonable hypothesis can be made immediately about the allele structure (although sequencing is still required to ultimately confirm the sequence structure).

Let us take as an example the simple STR marker D3S1358 that is widely used in forensic genetics and is part of the core STR panels in the United States (CODIS 13) and Europe (extended European Standard Set of Loci (ESS)). Its repeat region consists of a relatively stable TAGA sequence motif that has been found to range from 8 to 20 units with frequent alleles observed at the higher molecular range (14–19 units). Even in small population studies, remarkable differences in the amount of discernible alleles have been observed between electrophoretic sizing and MS-based analysis. In less than 100 samples from Europe, a total of seven allele categories (alleles 14–20) were detected by electrophoresis with the most common alleles 15 and 16 at frequencies exceeding 20%. With MS detection, the number of discernible D3S1358 alleles increased twice as most of the frequent size categories displayed differences in their base composition profile (**Figure 2**).

Here, T–C exchanges in the repeat motif were observed as a source for the additional variability detected only by MS. Sanger sequencing confirmed the presence of CAGA (instead of TAGA) repeat units at the 3′ end of the repetitive region. This simple example shows that variation in the underlying nucleotide sequence can provide substantial additional discrimination power that is useful in the forensic context. Two immediate questions arise from this observation. What is the quantitative gain in discrimination power? Is the assumption of allele/sequence identity across various tissues in an individual still valid? There is so far no evidence to doubt the latter statement as somatic mutations, mosaicism, or chimerism have not been reported to act any differently at the level of the nucleotide sequence than they do with respect to the fragment size. This means that we would not expect significant increase in intraindividual differences (between tissues) when moving from fragment size to base composition analysis. However, this issue needs to be verified and demonstrated in the course of systematic validation studies. The first question about the gain in discrimination power is relatively easy to address once the commercial support allows for the establishment of appropriate population data to determine valid allele frequencies. Initial data has already been generated to raise appetite.

An important detail of MS-based STR typing is the fact that data generated with this technology is fully compatible with existing data generated by CE. This means that existing datasets, such as the established national DNA databases, can be used without limitations. Importantly, comparisons with older DNA results are always possible. Any technical development that employs a different set of forensic markers (e.g., SNPs, Indels) would require changes, and old data would become irrelevant.

ICEMS approach STR analysis

In 11 out of 21 forensically relevant markers, a significant increase in discrimination power was observed using ICEMS compared to CE already in small sample sizes tested (<100) indicating that nucleotide variation may be more common than anticipated (**Table 1**).

Two main sources of nucleotide variation were observed: (1) SNPs already established in the HapMap project were found in sequence regions between repeat units and (2) primers such as rs9362477:G > A in SE33 or rs11642858:A > C in D16S539 that led to the identification of new allele variants. In addition, "shuffled" repeat units were observed by ICEMS and later confirmed by direct Sanger sequencing as, for example, in vWA, where different ratios of the TCTA and TCTG repeat units were determined. This effect is even more pronounced in more complex STRs, such as D2S1338. Here, the varying number of the repeat blocks TGCC, TTCC, and TCCG led to almost twice the number of discernible alleles as compared to pure amplicon size variation.

In an effort to combine informative loci in a multiplex reaction, 13 of the autosomal STRs (vWA, D21S11, D3S1358, D16S539, D8S1179, D7S820, D13S317, D5S818, TPOX, CSF1PO, D2S441, D10S1248, and D22S1045) and the gender-specific marker amelogenin were assembled in one PCR multiplex assay (**Figure 3**) and applied to the analyses of different populations and various types of forensic samples. These experiments indicated that the STR 14-plex was on par with commercially available CE-based STR multiplexes in terms of typing success rate.

Ibis approach STR analysis

Ibis has developed an ESI–TOF-based STR assay that includes the 13 core CODIS STR loci and the sex marker amelogenin. To

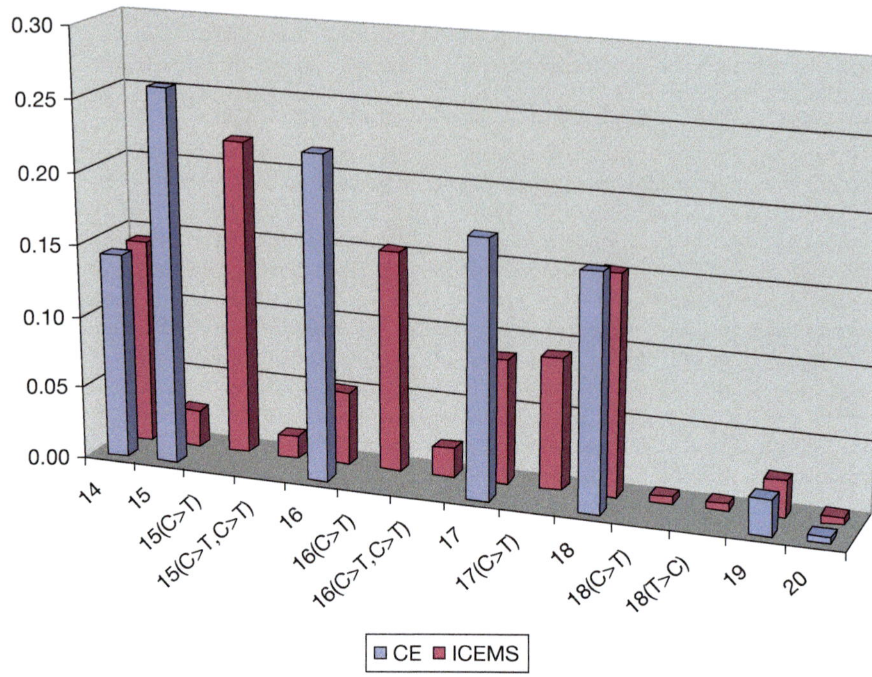


```
15            GACAGAGCAAGACCCTGTCTCA  TAGATAGATAGATAGATAGATAGATAGATAGATAGATAGATAGACAGACAGACAGATAGA    TACATG
15            GACAGAGCAAGACCCTGTCTCA  TAGATAGATAGATAGATAGATAGATAGATAGATAGATAGATAGACAGACAGACAGATAGA    TACATG
15(C>T)       GACAGAGCAAGACCCTGTCTCA  TAGATAGATAGATAGATAGATAGATAGATAGATAGATAGATAGATAGA CAGACAGATAGA    TACATG
15(C>T)       GACAGAGCAAGACCCTGTCTCA  TAGATAGATAGATAGATAGATAGATAGATAGATAGATAGATAGATAGA CAGACAGATAGA    TACATG
15(C>T)       GACAGAGCAAGACCCTGTCTCA  TAGATAGATAGATAGATAGATAGATAGATAGATAGATAGATAGATAGA CAGACAGATAGA    TACATG
15(C>T)       GACAGAGCAAGACCCTGTCTCA  TAGATAGATAGATAGATAGATAGATAGATAGATAGATAGATAGATAGA CAGACAGATAGA    TACATG
15(C>T)       GACAGAGCAAGACCCTGTCTCA  TAGATAGATAGATAGATAGATAGATAGATAGATAGATAGATAGATAGA CAGACAGATAGA    TACATG
15(C>T,C>T)   GACAGAGCAAGACCCTGTCTCA  TAGATAGATAGATAGATAGATAGATAGATAGATAGATAGATAGATAGATAGA CAGA TAGA    TACATG
15(C>T,C>T)   GACAGAGCAAGACCCTGTCTCA  TAGATAGATAGATAGATAGATAGATAGATAGATAGATAGATAGATAGATAGA CAGA TAGA    TACATG
15(C>T,C>T)   GACAGAGCAAGACCCTGTCTCA  TAGATAGATAGATAGATAGATAGATAGATAGATAGATAGATAGATAGATAGA CAGA TAGA    TACATG
```

Figure 2 Comparison of discernible D3S1358 allele categories with capillary electrophoresis (CE) and ICEMS based on 98 unrelated European samples. The conventional approach (CE) allows for the discrimination of seven allele classes (14–20), whereas the MS-based method (ICEMS) captures additional variant alleles (a total of 14 categories). Detected sequence variants for allele 15 are indicated below the graph.

Table 1 Comparison of discernible allele categories based on electrophoretic sizing (CE) and molecular mass (using the Innsbruck ICEMS approach) and the net gain in discrimination power

		Number of alleles		*PM*			*h*		
Locus	N	*CE*	*MS*	*CE*	*MS*	*Gain (%)*	*CE*	*MS*	*Gain (%)*
D5S818	98	6	15	0.141	0.032	341	0.704	0.867	23
D13S317	92	7	12	0.068	0.034	100	0.717	0.837	17
D3S1358	98	7	14	0.081	0.043	88	0.847	0.857	1
D21S11	98	11	17	0.048	0.029	66	0.857	0.929	8
D8S1179	96	9	15	0.061	0.038	61	0.865	0.906	5
vWA	99	7	16	0.069	0.048	44	0.788	0.848	8
D7S820	95	7	12	0.063	0.046	37	0.801	0.874	9
D2S1338	95	11	20	0.044	0.033	33	0.916	0.947	3
D2S441	98	7	11	0.114	0.088	30	0.806	0.837	4
D16S539	99	7	9	0.105	0.096	9	0.889	0.889	0
SE33	94	32	39	0.014	0.013	8	0.968	0.968	0

CE, capillary electrophoresis; PM, matching probability; h, heterozygosity.
Source: Pitterl, F., Schmidt, K., Huber, G., et al., 2010. Increasing the discrimination power of forensic STR testing by employing high-performance mass spectrometry, as illustrated in indigenous South African and Central Asian populations. International Journal of Legal Medicine 124, 551–558.

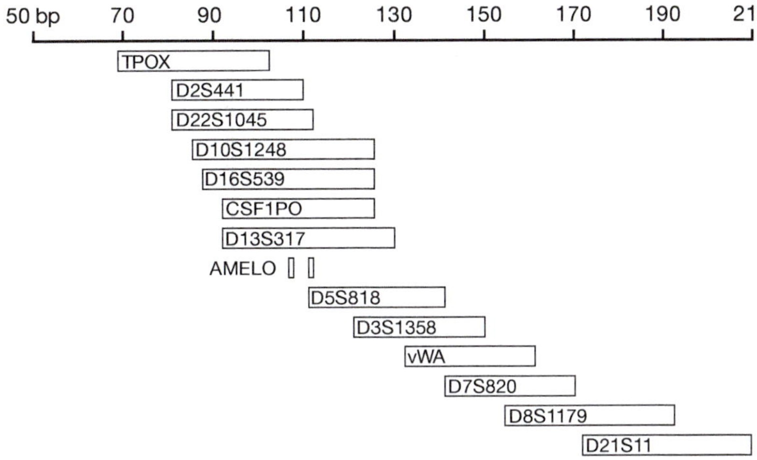

Figure 3 Scheme of an autosomal STR 13-plex with the gender-specific marker amelogenin that is coamplified in a single multiplex PCR assay. All markers reside in the low molecular size range (miniSTR), which is only achievable with MS-based detection platforms as conventional CE analysis would not allow for marker separation with current fluorescent dye technology.

explore the extent to which SNPs in the STR loci add to the allele pool (and associated resolving power) of the standard CODIS panel, a collection of more than 1000 reference samples was assembled, which had been previously typed by CE performed in the laboratories of collaborators at the FBI, AFDIL, NIST, and UNTHSC. Polymorphisms relative to reference alleles were found in 11 of the 13 loci analyzed. At nine of the 13 loci, SNPs were observed in alleles in which the number of repeats (and thus lengths) of the alleles were identical. These alleles are termed "same-length heterozygotes" as these loci would be typed homozygotic by conventional CE-based methods. In fact, based on the >1000 samples, it appears that the same-length heterozygotic prevalence is approximately 9.3%, 9.2%, and 8.76% for the loci D3S1358, D13S317, and D5S818, respectively (**Figure 4**). Four other loci (D8S1179, D21S11, vWA, and D7S820) contained same-length heterozygotic alleles more than 2.5% of the time in this sample set (**Table 2**).

Mass Spectrometric mtDNA Analysis

Ibis mtDNA control region tiling assay

Ibis developed a 24-primer multiplexed assay that amplifies human mtDNA (mtDNA) hypervariable regions 1 and 2 (HV1 + HV2) by eight triplexed PCR reactions that occupy one column of a 96-well plate (**Figures 5 and 6**). By anchoring on standardized coordinates, that is, the rCRS, any base composition profile can be directly compared to any other profile produced in this assay or to any mtDNA sequence spanning the same range of amplified coordinates. On the basis of an analysis of 1266 human mtDNA sequences from GenBank, the tiling assay retains the ability to differentiate 94.2% of the entries by one or more base composition differences. The partial loss of information comes from reciprocal SNPs (e.g., C → T + T → C) that are close enough to be contained within a single amplified region. They then produce identical base compositions for that primer pair if they are the only differences between the sequences. The assay also covers a larger coordinate space than the minimal HV1/HV2 sequencing traditionally performed in forensic laboratories (16024–16365, 73–340). For the same 1266 sequences that are distinct in sequence over the tiling coordinates, only 90.2% are discriminated by sequencing of the minimal HV1 and HV2 regions.

A key advantage of MS-based approaches relative to sequencing as applied to heteroplasmic samples is illustrated in **Figure 6**. Importantly, length heteroplasmy typically manifests as variation in the number of bases residing within a homopolymeric stretch (i.e., C-stretches). In HV1, the region in which this is most often observed, the homopolymeric stretch begins at nucleotide position number 16184. A similar region of length heteroplasmy exists in HV2, encompassing nucleotide positions 303–315 (for more details on length heteroplasmy, see elsewhere in this encyclopedia).

Direct Sanger sequencing has two key limitations when analyzing samples containing length heteroplasmy: (1) sequences that differ by the number of C residues in a homopolymeric stretch produce multiple overlapping sequence patterns that are slightly out of register; this results in an uninterpretable sequencing read after the homopolymeric stretch and (2) the contributing species to the homopolymeric profile can sometimes be difficult to be quantified effectively. Both these limitations can be overcome by ESI-MS analysis. First, the mass spectrometer is well suited to characterize

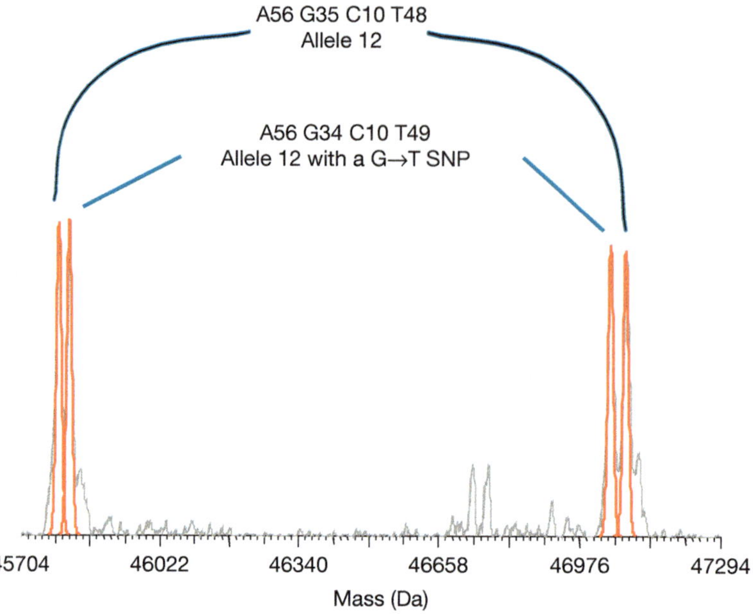

Figure 4 Illustrations of SNPs within STRs. A "same-length heterozygote." All "allele type 12" for the D5S818 marker are not equivalent; some contain a G-to-T SNP, which distinguishes them from individuals containing the "normal" allele type 12. The ESI–TOF spectrum illustrates the presence of both a base allele 12 and an allele 12 containing a G → T SNP; using the ^{13}C-enriched dGTP nucleotides results in a net mass difference of 35 Da between the same-length alleles. This sample is genotyped as homozygous 12 by Identifiler® (ABI).

Table 2 Frequency of observation of polymorphic alleles in 1033 samples typed at 13 CODIS loci using the Ibis high-throughput ESI–TOF mass spectrometry platform. An additional 391 samples were typed at the seven most polymorphic CODIS loci. Note that in six of the loci, SNPs are observed with a prevalence of >23% (confirming most polymorphic markers from the Innsbruck study with much lower sample size, **Table 1**) and that in three of the loci, more than 8% of the same-length alleles are "same-length heterozygotes"

Locus	*Number of alleles with single-nucleotide polymorphisms (SNPs)*	*Samples tested*	*Percentage of alleles with one or more SNPs*	*Number of same-length heterozygous samples*	*Percentage of samples heterozygous with same-length alleles*
D3S1358	2140	1424	75.1	132	9.3
D8S1179	1893	1423	66.5	83	5.8
D13S317	875	1424	30.7	131	9.2
D21S11	789	1422	27.7	57	4.0
vWA	762	1424	26.8	72	5.1
D5S818	666	1424	23.4	122	8.6
D7S820	250	1424	8.8	40	2.8
FGA	41	1033	2.0	1	0.1
D18S51	36	1033	1.7	4	0.4
D16S539	5	1033	0.2	0	0.0
CSF1PO	2	1033	0.1	0	0.0
AMEL	0	1033	0.0	0	0.0
THO1	0	1033	0.0	0	0.0
TPOX	0	1033	0.0	0	0.0

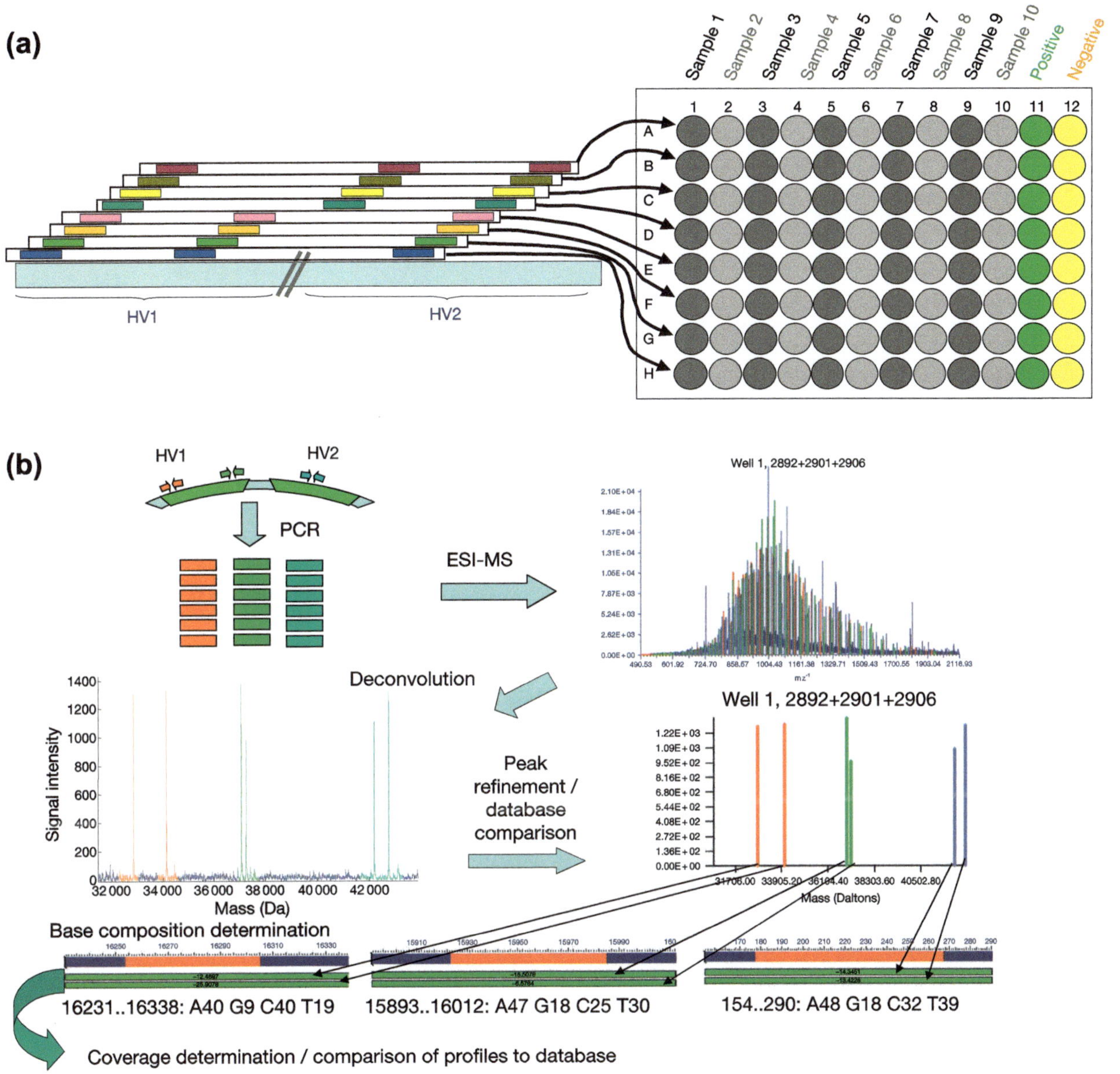

Figure 5 Overview of the mtDNA triplex tiling assay. (a) Primer pair groupings by approximate mtDNA spatial locations of grouped primers (left side) and layout of a 12-sample-per-plate assay kit plate. (b) Schematic overview outlining the analysis process for one reaction. Results of eight reactions are automatically tied together to generate a base composition profile. Each entry corresponds to a *start coordinate … stop coordinate: base composition*. In the example illustrated here, the individual has a base composition of A48 G18 C32 T39 spanning the rCRS coordinates 154–290 (bottom right of figure).

samples containing mixtures because ions at different *m/z* ratios are detected independently. Thus, the ability to detect the fragment containing the short homopolymeric stretch is independent of the ability to detect the fragment containing the long homopolymeric stretch. In MS, there is no analog to being "out of register." As illustrated in **Figure 6**, multiple fragments representing multiple genotypes within a given region will generate multiple signals (assuming nonidentical molecular masses of the genotypes). Because fragments of similar length and base composition have similar ionization efficiencies,

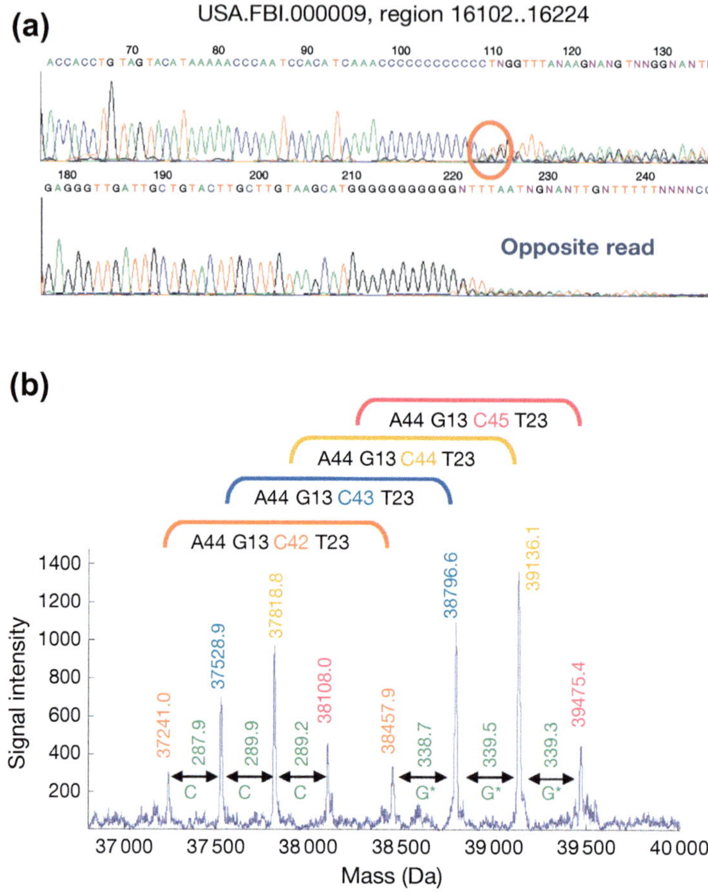

Figure 6 Effect of length heteroplasmy upon mtDNA sequencing and the mitochondrial tiling assay. Sequence analysis is severely challenged by multiple templates that differ in length. (a) Forward strand sequence electropherogram of a sequencing reaction developed by direct PCR-product sequencing from in-house saliva sample CS0033 on top. The sequence electropherogram becomes unreadable after the poly-C region because of a mixture of templates of varying length. (b) Deconvolved mass spectrum for primer pair, which amplifies coordinates 16124 … 16201 encompassing the HV1 poly-C stretch. There are four clearly resolved products that differ by single C residues in the poly-C tract. * ^{13}C-enriched dGTP was used in these reactions, adding ~10 Da to the mass of each G residue.

relative signal intensities can be used to measure the relative amounts of both genotypes in a sample.

ICEMS mtDNA haplogroup screening

An mtDNA assay for the ICEMS technology was developed by targeting 22 SNPs in the mtDNA coding region and SNP 16519 from the control region (CR), which provides a useful tool for either screening unknown samples or further typing samples that have been analyzed for the CR and require additional analysis for establishing the haplogroup status. The amplified fragments were selected in such a way that they include haplogroup diagnostic markers of mtDNA lineages representative for the West Eurasian phylogeny. Thus, a prescreening of larger population data from this subcontinental region is also feasible to assess population genetic parameters in a quick and cost-effective manner relative to Sanger sequencing. In total, the approach targeted 627 mitochondrial sites allowing for the detection of additional variation outside the primarily targeted SNPs that can be used for further discrimination. The observed power of discrimination of >98% significantly exceeds that of alternative SNP screening strategies (e.g., single-base extension). It is further observed that the 23-plex was successful in obtaining useful results for even highly degraded samples with maximum amplicon lengths below 131 bp.

Conclusions and Future Directions

MS has long been a core component of many forensics laboratories and is the tool of choice for analyzing a wide range of evidence associated with illicit drugs and their metabolites, explosives residue, toxins and adulterants, and other controlled substances. Many of these early applications of forensic MS were catalyzed by the availability of novel separation/purification techniques (gas chromatography, HPLC, SPE, etc.) coupled with highly efficient ionization methods. The studies described above, and many others published elsewhere, illustrate the power of the mass spectrometer as a core analytical platform for DNA-based forensic markers. Clearly, one of the strengths of this platform is that it is in essence a "universal detector" and has the ability to unwind complexities associated with SNPs, mixtures, and length heteroplasmies, which pose significant challenges to CE- or sequence-based methods. Commercial mass spectrometers have evolved considerably in recent years, and benchtop ESI–TOF instruments are now routinely making measurements that would have been challenging for even the most sophisticated (and expensive) mass spectrometers a mere decade ago. The forensics community is only now beginning to appreciate the additional resolving power and breadth that the MS platform provides in a forensic DNA context. Research and development activities focused on improved sample preparation and automation for MS-based analysis of DNA markers are presently underway in a number of labs around the world. It is conceivable that integrated microfluidic approaches will play a prominent role in such endeavors as will a next generation of even smaller and lower cost-integrated robotic platforms, which are directly interfaced with existing laboratory information systems.

Acknowledgments

SAH acknowledges the considerable contributions to this work by Tom Hall, Christine Marzan, David Duncan, and Kristen Boles. WP would like to thank the staff at the Institute of Legal Medicine, Innsbruck, in particular, Gabriela Huber, Harald Niederstätter, Herbert Oberacher, and Florian Pitterl for the work on the ICEMS system.

See also: **Biology/DNA:** DNA Databases; Laboratory Automation and LIMS in Forensics; Mitochondrial DNA; Short Tandem Repeats; **Biology/DNA/Methods/Analytical Techniques:** Capillary Electrophoresis in Forensic Genetics; **Methods:** Capillary Electrophoresis in Forensic Biology.

Further Reading

Hall, T.A., Budowle, B., Jiang, Y., et al., 2005. Base composition analysis of human mitochondrial DNA using electrospray ionization mass spectrometry: a novel tool for the identification and differentiation of humans. Analytical Biochemistry 344, 53–69.

Hall, T.A., Sannes-Lowery, K.A., McCurdy, L.D., et al., 2009. Base composition profiling of human mitochondrial DNA using polymerase chain reaction and direct automated electrospray ionization mass spectrometry. Analytical Chemistry 81, 7515–7526.

Hofstadler, S.A., Sampath, R., Blyn, L., et al., 2005. TIGER: the universal biosensor. International Journal of Mass Spectrometry 242 (1), 23–41.

Hofstadler, S.A., Sannes-Lowery, K.A., Hannis, J.C., 2005. Analysis of nucleic acids by FTICR MS. Mass Spectrometry Reviews 24, 265–285.

Jiang, Y., Hofstadler, S.A., 2003. A highly efficient and automated method of purifying and desalting PCR products for analysis by electrospray ionization mass spectrometry. Analytical Biochemistry 316, 50–57.

Oberacher, H., Niederstätter, H., Parson, W., 2007. Liquid chromatography-electrospray ionization mass spectrometry for simultaneous detection of mtDNA length and nucleotide polymorphisms. International Journal of Legal Medicine 121, 57–67.

Oberacher, H., Niederstätter, H., Pitterl, F., Parson, W., 2006. Profiling 627 mitochondrial nucleotides via the analysis of a 23-plex polymerase chain reaction by liquid chromatography-electrospray ionization time-of-flight mass spectrometry. Analytical Chemistry 78, 7816–7827.

Oberacher, H., Pitterl, F., Huber, G., Niederstätter, H., Steinlechner, M., Parson, W., 2008. Increased forensic efficiency of DNA fingerprints through simultaneous resolution of length and nucleotide variability by high-performance mass spectrometry. Human Mutation 29, 427–432.

Pitterl, F., Niederstätter, H., Huber, G., Zimmermann, B., Oberacher, H., Parson, W., 2008. The next generation of DNA profiling-STR typing by multiplexed PCR-ion-pair RP LC-ESI time-of-flight MS. Electrophoresis 29, 4739–4750.

Pitterl, F., Schmidt, K., Huber, G., et al., 2010. Increasing the discrimination power of forensic STR testing by employing high-performance mass spectrometry, as illustrated in indigenous South African and Central Asian populations. International Journal of Legal Medicine 124, 551–558.

Introduction to Nonhuman DNA Typing

R Labonte and H Miller Coyle, University of New Haven, West Haven, CT, USA

Abbreviations

CODIS Combined DNA Indexing System
mitotypes Mitochondrial DNA haplotypes
PCR-RFLP DNA barcoding method based on amplification of restriction enzyme digested DNA fragments
rRNA Ribosomal RNA
STR Short tandem repeat

Glossary

Capillary electrophoresis Automated DNA size separation technology.
Multiplex Combined assay for numerous short tandem repeat regions.
RAPD Random amplified polymorphic DNA; DNA fragments that generate an identifying barcode.

While human DNA testing for identification of a biological source of evidence is routine in forensic science laboratories, nonhuman DNA typing is still considered a specialty application. Nonhuman DNA can be a significant piece of associative evidence in a variety of forensic applications, ranging from animal cruelty cases to criminal cases that can help link people to crime scenes, or one person to another person. The types of nonhuman DNA that have been used in the past in forensic cases include animal DNA typing, microbial DNA typing of soil samples, and plant DNA typing. The scope of nonhuman DNA typing methods is expansive; therefore, as an introductory article, this discussion focuses on the common animal and microbial systems. Nonhuman DNA typing also encompasses wildlife applications, plants, pollens, and insects. Some of these techniques have been used for general research purposes, and many have been applied to forensic casework as well. All these techniques are currently being researched further and could have a great impact on the field of forensic science in the future.

Animal DNA Typing

In the most recent National Pet Owners Survey, the American Pet Products Association reported that approximately 62% of households within the United States have a pet, with just fewer than 39 million houses owning a cat and just over 46 million houses owning a dog (http://www.americanpetproducts.org). Since cats and dogs are so prominent in the American household, their significance in forensic casework has become recognized over the years. In particular, samples of nonhuman blood, saliva, tissue, and hair can be used for both nuclear DNA typing and mitochondrial DNA typing of animals in a diverse range of cases with both criminal and civil applications. Just like humans, animals can be the victim, suspect, or witness, depending on the type of case. The animal can be the victim in cases of animal abuse, and DNA typing is sometimes a useful tool in these investigations to confirm a particular scene where, for example, an animal was beaten. There are also cases in which an animal may need to be identified by DNA typing if the animal was stolen or the remains of the lost animal are found elsewhere. Evidence in animal abuse cases often includes tissue samples and blood samples. In cases of a missing pet, if the parents are available, samples can be collected to try to generate a known reference DNA profile by reconstructing genetic heritage, or if there are items known to have that pet's DNA (hair, saliva, etc.), these items can be used to try to generate a known DNA profile for that particular animal. This collection of known reference samples is similar to protocol for missing person casework. Canines, in particular, can also become the suspect in cases of animal attacks on humans or other animals, as well as cases where an animal gets loose and causes damage to property or individuals. In these types of cases, evidence needs to be collected that could potentially

 http://dx.doi.org/10.1016/B978-0-12-800647-4.00045-X

contain biological material from the suspect animal. This can include clothes from a human victim and swabs of the victim's skin, and if the victim is another animal, samples of fur with the potential of containing the attacker's saliva can be used, but it is important to try to sample areas where the victim's blood is not present. This is to avoid the victim DNA from becoming the predominant profile, masking the minor DNA sample of the attacker. In addition, the attacker should be examined for the presence of hairs or other materials from the victim in the mouth or the claws. Lastly, animals can play the role of a silent witness in which DNA from biological fluids or hair can help link a victim's pet to a suspect or crime scene or the suspect's pet to the victim or crime scene. Hair is the most common finding in these types of cases since the animal naturally sheds hair into the environment and hairs tend to cling to things in the surrounding areas. There are a number of laboratories that conduct animal DNA testing including QuestGen Forensics (Davis, CA) and the Veterinary Genetics Laboratory at UC Davis (Davis, CA). Although many criminal investigations may use human DNA typing to aid in an investigation, clearly animal DNA typing can be very useful in a variety of civil cases as well.

Canine DNA Typing

Canine DNA typing has been used and deemed admissible in court in a variety of types of cases including the dog as a silent witness, the dog as the suspect in the case, and the dog as the victim in cases of animal abuse. Numerous cases are summarized on the Denver DA Web site (http://www.denverda.org) and the QuestGen Forensics closed casework list on their Web site (http://www.questgen.biz). One of the earliest cases noted on the QuestGen Forensics Web site was a case that occurred in Canada in which a man and his dog were murdered and a mixed bloodstain from each victim was found on the suspect's jeans, with the nonhuman portion matching the dog. There are also cases listed using both STR and mitochondrial DNA typing techniques on hairs and bodily fluids showing the wide range of applications evidence from canines can have in forensic investigations.

Short tandem repeat typing of canine DNA samples

Canine short tandem repeat (STR) markers have been researched over the years for forensic science applications and a kit has been developed to enable forensic DNA analysts to type this species for casework. The California Department of Justice, the National Institute of Standards and Technology, the National Institute of Health, the Federal Bureau of Investigation, MMI Genomics, and Finnzymes collaborated with research scientists to create a kit for canine STR typing for forensic applications. The Finnzymes Canine 2.1 Multiplex STR Reagent Kit uses fluorescent detection technology to enable robust and reliable STR typing of canine DNA samples. The 18 STRs chosen are unlinked (physically map to different chromosomes) and the criteria for these chosen loci were similar to the human loci used in human STR testing. The kit also has a gender identification element and the zinc finger gene in canines. Dogs commonly involved in forensic cases, along with both mixed and pure breed dogs, were profiled with this kit and validated for forensic applications. The loci used in the kit were determined to have high variation, proved to be individualizing for dogs, and provided a standardized STR panel for forensic DNA analysts to use in casework involving samples from canines. There are other commercial STR kits available for canine typing; the StockMarks kit for canines is from Applied Biosystems Inc. (Foster City, CA) and contains supplies to polymerase chain reaction (PCR) amplify 10 STR markers approved by the American Kennel Club (AKC). The methods for canine DNA extraction, quantitation, amplification, separation, and detection are all easy to adapt in forensic science laboratories because these methods are already being used for human DNA analysis and other nonhuman DNA typing applications. The UC Davis Veterinary Genetics Laboratory (Davis, CA), as well as other agencies, also uses a Canine CODIS, similar to the human version, in order to help stop dog fighting crimes and form linkages between dogs and breeders. Overall, canine STRs are individualizing and useful for cases involving dog attacks and animal abuse or in situations where canine samples can help link people to crimes or crime scenes. One case on the Denver DA Web site (http://www.denverda.org) that illustrates this involved DNA testing of feces found on the bottom of shoes believed to have been worn by the suspect on the day the crime had occurred. The DNA profile generated was compared to the profile of the dog that produced the feces at the crime scene, and it was determined that the feces on the shoe came from the same animal.

Mitochondrial DNA typing of canine DNA samples

Just as with human DNA typing applications, when dog hair becomes a piece of evidence, there is not always sufficient root tissue material available for STR analysis. As a result, a less discriminating but more successful test known as mitochondrial DNA typing can be performed on these samples. Even though this test is not as good for individualization as nuclear DNA tests, it can be an important tool to make exclusions in a case by testing sequence variation within the control region, especially the hypervariable regions, of the mitochondria. One particular study experimented with a short fragment within the hypervariable region 1 that has a low mutation rate and contains single nucleotide polymorphisms and concluded that this was a good method when working with potentially degraded samples. This is important because mitochondrial DNA typing can be the method of choice when samples are degraded in order to have a better chance at obtaining a profile just as when working with highly degraded DNA or skeletal remains in human identification. Mitochondrial DNA typing of this region was also determined to be species specific and a rapid way to screen multiple samples for exclusion of potential suspect canines in a case. It is important that this test is specific to canines because cat hairs can also often be found at crime scenes, and humans are handling these samples, so this method should not be sensitive to human, feline, and canine-related species (wolves). Overall, these regions have sufficient variability and high exclusionary rates and therefore are good methods for mitochondrial DNA typing of canine hair samples. One case noted on the Denver DA Web site (http://www.denverda.org) involves a homicide in which mitochondrial DNA testing of dog hairs found on the rope and tape used to bind the murder victim yielded results that were consistent with the mitochondrial sequence of the suspect's dog. This evidence was not individualizing but was used in this case against the suspect and aided the overall investigation.

Feline DNA Typing

Feline DNA typing has been used in forensic casework, with the main focus on cases of a domestic cat playing the role of a silent witness by linking people to people, or people to scenes, or in cases of animal abuse. The first forensic case and probably one of the most famous to date involving feline DNA typing was the case of a cat named Snowball in Canada. A woman had gone missing from her home and her bloodstained car was found nearby. A bag was also found, containing bloodstained shoes and a coat lined with white hairs in the interior, nearby to the victim's home. The blood on the shoes matched that of the victim, and the hairs were determined to be consistent with cat hairs. These hairs were later typed for DNA and compared to a known reference sample from the primary suspect's cat and determined to be a match, and thus the suspect was convicted of the crime. One of the companies that performs STR and mitochondrial DNA typing on animal samples, QuestGen Forensics, notes a case in a list of closed casework from Iowa in 2003 on their Web site (http://www.questgen.biz), in which, a woman went missing and her body was found bound in fabric containing cat hairs. Mitochondrial DNA testing was performed on the cat hairs, and it was determined that the cats at the household where the fabric was believed to have come from had mitochondrial haplotypes that could not be excluded; therefore, they could be the source of the hairs on the fabric. This evidence along with other evidence resulted in the primary suspect being convicted of the crime. Other criminal and animal abuse cases have been noted involving feline DNA typing, and brief synopses of some of these cases can be found on the Denver DA Web site (http://www.denverda.org). These cases show that feline DNA typing has proven to be significant in forensic investigations in the past, this type of evidence and testing has been admissible in court, and therefore, DNA typing of feline DNA is expected to play a significant role in a variety of future forensic casework applications.

STR typing of feline DNA samples

Feline STR markers have been researched over the years, and a commercial kit has been developed to enable forensic DNA analysts to type this species for forensic applications. The National Cancer Institute's (NCI) Laboratory of Genomic Diversity and the National Institute of Standards and Technology (NIST) and Promega Corporation (Madison, WI) joined forces to develop the MeowPlex STR typing kit, with the intention of creating a multiplex assay using polymorphic tetranucleotide STR loci with characteristics consistent with those of the 13 core CODIS loci used in STR typing of human DNA. There are certain requirements to pick the candidate STR loci for a DNA typing kit for humans, and these criteria were used to choose feline STR loci as well. The loci chosen not only had to be tetranucleotide markers but also needed to be robust and reproducible, to be genetically unlinked, and to have low mutation rates and high discriminating power. Loci that meet these criteria and that follow Mendelian genetic patterns can be used in statistical calculations of significance with population databases generated for feline species. The STR markers that were chosen for this kit resulted from experiments with 22 candidate loci tested among 200 cat DNA samples representing just fewer than 30 breeds. The 11 markers chosen were determined to be highly polymorphic and robust enough for a multiplex assay necessary to obtain desirable results in future applications. Along with these markers, a gender marker for the Y chromosome in domestic cats was added in order to simultaneously determine the sex of the cat. This multiplex kit works similarly to human DNA typing kits in which a dye-labeling and capillary electrophoresis system is used to separate loci of overlapping sizes and small amounts of sample are required for typing. The PCR conditions for this assay are similar to those for human DNA typing; therefore, this is a method that can be done in a forensic laboratory where human DNA typing is already being performed for forensic casework. Quantitative PCR assays have also been researched and developed in studies in the past. Another important development came about when a population database was generated for feline STR testing as a reference for statistical analysis. The domestic cat breeds recognized by the largest registries in the United States were all sampled (buccal swab or blood sample) and typed with the polymorphic loci from the feline multiplex kit in order to generate a reference population database for feline STR typing. Fewer than 40 breeds were represented with a sample size of over 1000, and the heterozygosity values ranged from average to high for these loci within the various breeds. With the creation of this database, forensic DNA samples from felines could now be typed with a robust multiplex kit and the data could be given significance by the use of population statistics in court. Lastly, this kit was also determined to be specific to feline species and some other closely related relatives along with a few other mammals, but was not sensitive to human DNA. Another significant development in feline STR typing research has been the use of a real-time PCR assay that quantitates the amount of starting DNA template sample prior to amplification of the sample. This works a lot like the methods performed for human samples but is not species specific for felines, which is not a huge legal issue due to the lack of mixtures anticipated in these types of cases. This assay proved to be very rapid and extremely sensitive with very low quantities of DNA (23 pg). Therefore, feline STR DNA can be extracted, quantitated, amplified with a multiplex assay, and separated and detected successfully and has proven to be significantly valuable biological evidence in a number of forensic science cases.

Mitochondrial DNA typing of feline DNA samples

Mitochondrial DNA typing of felines can be used on hair samples if sufficient root material is unavailable for STR testing of feline DNA. Since it is very common for cats to shed their hairs and leave them behind on nearby surfaces in the environment they live in, many of these hairs will not contain tissue material for STR typing, and therefore mitochondrial DNA typing is the only option. The entire mitochondrial DNA genome of the domestic cat has been sequenced. In a recent study, randomly bred cats from four different regions across the United States were tested for variation across feline mitotypes to show that mitochondrial DNA typing could be useful for forensic investigations. This study discusses how although STR typing is usually preferred over mitochondrial DNA typing; the latter has been used successfully in several previous forensic investigations involving homicide. It was determined that of the 174 cat hair samples tested, 32 mitotypes were able to be differentiated, with four of the most common types seen across all four regions of the United States. The results obtained were consistent with having enough variation for forensic testing of these mitochondrial DNA sequences within the feline population and that certain results showed that substructure should not be a big issue for court acceptance. This study also suggests that there may be other variations of mitotypes across cat populations in the United States, which would give an even higher power of discrimination to mitochondrial DNA typing of felines, and these are being further researched. Another study also researched nonrepetitive areas of the control region in feline mitochondrial DNA for its use in forensic evidence databases. A significant amount of research has been conducted on feline mitochondrial DNA, and this area of nonhuman DNA typing will be further studied and utilized more often in future forensic investigations.

Implications for the Future of Animal DNA Typing in Forensic Casework

The use of canine and feline DNA typing in forensic science will continue to grow in the future and is a significant tool for assisting in investigations. Multiplex kits may be further developed by the addition of extra loci and then commercialized for use. Training programs are critical for more laboratories to begin to perform these assays on these types of samples on a routine basis. Currently, only a few specialized public laboratories and a handful of private laboratories offer this testing to law enforcement, prosecutors, or defense attorneys. The use of DNA typing of canine and feline samples in forensic casework will continue to grow in the future.

Plant DNA Typing

DNA typing of trace evidence from plant materials can be used in forensic investigations to help link suspects to crime scenes or to other people involved in a case. The Palo Verde case that occurred in Arizona in 1992 is a well-known example of when DNA typing from seeds was used to help link the suspect to the crime scene in a homicide case (http://www.denverda.org). In this case, the body of the victim was located by an area containing Palo Verde trees in which one tree at the scene contained abrasions on the bark consistent with an object backing into its surface. Two seeds were found in the bed of the suspect's pickup truck, which were later determined to be consistent with coming from that particular Palo Verde tree at the scene using randomly amplified polymorphic DNA (RAPD) technology. The plant material served as associative evidence that helped to convict the suspect in this particular case, along with other physical evidence. DNA typing of plant material has been researched extensively in recent years for its application in forensic casework. There are a number of different types of plant material that have been tested, including opium poppy, a variety of grasses and trees, as well as other plant species. In addition, *Cannabis sativa* STRs have been studied extensively for forensic application, and databases for these types of samples have been studied for use in investigations. *C. sativa* has been studied not only in drug investigations but also as a fiber type in the form of hemp. DNA typing of these types of biological samples can help form linkages in a forensic investigation, just as previously described for animal samples.

There are a variety of technologies used for plant DNA typing, and they have been applied in cases. Different types of plant materials can be extracted and purified using a combination of liquid nitrogen and a variety of available kits, complete with reagents and required materials, in order to recover DNA and attempt to remove PCR inhibitors. Some of the kits commercially available are Qiagen kits (Valencia, CA) including the DNeasy Plant Miniprep Kit, Qiagen DNeasy Plant Mini Kit, DNeasy Plant Maxi Kit, and the DNeasy 96 Plant Kit for high-throughput processing of plant samples. Other kits include the MasterPure™ Plant Leaf DNA Purification Kit and the QuickExtract™ Plant DNA Extraction Solution both by Epicentre Biotechnologies (Madison, WI) and the UltraClean Plant DNA Isolation Kit (MO BIO Laboratories, Inc., Carlsbad,

CA). Microsatellites such as STRs and short sequence repeats (SSRs) from plant material including DNA from seeds, leaves, and other trace materials can be used to compare crime scene evidence to known samples of different species of trees. These markers follow Mendelian genetics and have the other desired qualities of markers chosen for DNA typing methodologies due to variability, short length, prevalence, and reproducibility. Amplified fragment length polymorphism (AFLP) is a rapid method that can be used in cases, where a particular plant species has not been sequenced in the past and no known STRs have been identified. After extraction and purification, samples can be PCR-amplified similar to methods used for human and other nonhuman DNA in order to obtain the necessary quantity of DNA for separation and detection by capillary electrophoresis, gel electrophoresis methods, or sequencing technologies.

Insect DNA Typing

Forensic entomologists study insects found on decomposing bodies to help determine the time of death and other aspects of an investigation. The insects commonly found on decomposing bodies can vary by species, but the morphologies can be similar between them, and therefore, DNA typing can be helpful to distinguish between insect species. A number of insect species found on bodies in death investigations have been studied for the potential to individualize through DNA analysis. In addition, different methods of DNA analysis have been studied and utilized in these types of forensic investigations, mostly involving regions of mitochondrial DNA. A number of DNA extraction methods are also available that can be used to obtain insect DNA for further analysis. Fast technology for analysis cards have been successfully used for the extraction and storage of insect DNA samples. There are also DNA extraction kits available from a variety of companies. Among these are the Genomic DNA Extraction Kit for Arthropod Samples by Cartagen Molecular, Inc. (San Carlos, CA) and the E.Z.N.A Insect DNA Kit (Omega Bio-Tek, Norcross, GA).

Diptera larvae have forensic entomological significance and are often difficult to distinguish by morphology and therefore have been studied to see if DNA analysis is a more precise method for identification between species. PCR–restriction fragment length polymorphism (RFLP) has been used to differentiate between most Diptera families, such as calliphoridae, muscidae, and sarcophagidae, by amplifying and detecting sequences within the internal transcribed spacer (ITS) regions of the ribosomal DNA gene repeat. Both sequence and length variation within the mitochondrial DNA control region of Diptera calliphoridae species and the subunits of the cytochrome oxidase (COI or COII) gene in Diptera calliphoridae, sarcophagidae, and phoridae have been researched for forensic entomological applications. Regions of ribosomal RNA (rRNA) have been studied and used to differentiate between different insect species, including the 16S rRNA region within Diptera muscidae, the 28S rRNA gene within Diptera calliphoridae, and the 18S–28S rRNA genes within the various Diptera species. Often empty puparial cases and other fragments left behind by the flies are found on decomposing bodies and could potentially be used for DNA analysis to identify the fly species if degradation is not an issue. Although studies have been conducted on insect species commonly found on human remains and certain species have been identified through DNA analysis, more research and validation studies need to be conducted for insect DNA analysis to be more widely utilized in the forensic community.

Microbial DNA Typing from Soil Samples

Just as in situations involving animals, insects, or plants, microbes can be DNA typed in a variety of soil samples for use in forensic investigations. Soil is sometimes an important piece of evidence in a case, and it can be used to help link people or evidence to specific scenes using a variety of different methods. Other than looking at the physical characteristic differences between soils in different locales, there are also microbes within the soil that can be characterized for forensic analyses. The similarities between samples coming from the same location, differences in bacterial composition existing between various locations, and changes in bacterial communities within soil samples have all been studied to see if bacterial DNA typing of soil samples can be effective in forensic investigations.

Extraction of Microbial DNA in Soil Samples

In order to be able to further distinguish these samples, the DNA needs to first be extracted from the soil, which requires breaking open cells to recover DNA. As with human DNA typing methods, PCR inhibitors can sometimes be recovered along with the DNA with the use of certain extraction methods. This is one of the problems that analysts encounter with soil DNA typing because soil samples frequently contain chemical contaminants. A study on the potential of bacterial DNA typing for forensic use discussed that humic acids are a typical component within some soil samples and that this chemical is a known PCR inhibitor.

Although there is no universal standard for the method of DNA extraction for soil samples due to differences in soil origins, commercial kits are now available for forensic purposes. As with human applications, samples may sometimes need to be diluted, further purified, or chemically modified to diminish the presence of PCR inhibitors in an attempt to prevent problems during DNA typing. These kits contain the proper elements to assist the analyst with these potential problems and allow the analyst to obtain DNA that is ready for PCR. A kit that is available for forensic use is the UltraClean Soil DNA Isolation Kit (MO BIO Laboratories, Inc., Carlsbad, CA), which contains reagents for extraction and purification aimed at lessening the presence of PCR inhibitors in soil samples (http://www.mobio.com). The use of a bead solution, along with heat, detergent, and vortex action, allows this kit to concentrate DNA onto a silica filter, which can then be recovered by a wash step for further processing. The same company also makes a PowerSoil DNA Isolation Kit that can be used with more difficult and complex soil samples. The Soil-Master DNA Extraction Kit (Epicentre Biotechnologies, Madison, WI) utilizes spin column technology, cell lysis conditions, and chromatography in order to recover DNA that can then be amplified by the polymerase chain reaction (http://www.epibio.com). Each of the kits provides detailed protocols, alternative troubleshooting options, and reagents favoring the removal of chemical inhibitors, as well as a goal of maximizing DNA quality. These kits are easy to use and do not require an overabundance of time. Other kits made by different companies are also available to forensic analysts for soil DNA extraction, including the Soil DNA Isolation Kit (Norgen Biotech Corp., Ontario, Canada) and the E.Z.N.A Soil DNA Kit (Omega Bio-Tek, Norcross, GA).

Amplification and Typing of Microbial DNA in Soil Samples

Since forensic science laboratories routinely use PCR amplification and automated DNA sequencing instrumentation to amplify and process samples, a variety of DNA analysis methods can be used. AFLP uses restriction enzymes to digest sequences of DNA-containing adaptors that are recognized by primers, resulting in amplified product that can be detected on a polyacrylamide gel or by capillary electrophoresis. Automated-ribosomal intergenic spacer analysis (A-RISA) can also be used to amplify sequences of interest located between genes for the small and large ribosomal subunits, and the amplification product can be detected on a silver-stained gel. Amplicon length heterogeneity-PCR (LH-PCR) has been studied as a way of detecting changes in bacterial composition of soils associated with decomposing cadavers. Terminal restriction fragment length polymorphism (T-RFLP) is another method that has been studied for DNA typing of soil samples. The terminal fragments of 16S ribosomal gene, as well as other genes, have been amplified, digested, and fluorescently tagged for detection during electrophoresis. This method has detected differences between soil samples from nearby differing locations (sampling comparisons), but further studies need to be done on the differences in microbial communities within stratified regions of the same soil (depth comparisons). The resulting T-RFLP data is less difficult to interpret and the sensitivity is sufficient for forensic applications.

Implications for the Future of Microbial DNA Typing of Soil Samples in Forensic Casework

In order to perform any of these methods, certain equipment and instrumentation are needed that are all readily available in a forensic DNA laboratory, and therefore, soil DNA typing can be easily adapted within laboratories with proper training. Since sufficient variation can exist in soil samples, DNA typing of these types of samples is a potentially useful application in forensic DNA laboratories. Although bacterial DNA typing of soil samples can be a useful application in the field of forensic science, processing this evidence can be very challenging for forensic scientists. The challenges associated with this method include variability of bacteria within soil samples due to environmental differences and changes and soil stratification and the necessary conditions required to process these types of evidentiary samples, and additional validation studies are essential for the overall success of this method.

See also: **Biology/DNA/Botany:** Cannabis DNA Typing Methods; **Biology/DNA/Entomology:** Overview; **Biology/DNA/Wildlife:** DNA and Endangered Species.

Further Reading

Baute, D.T., Satkoski, J.A., Spear, T.F., et al., 2008. Analysis of forensic SNPs in the canine mtDNA HV1 mutational hotspot region. Journal of Forensic Science 53 (6), 1325–1333.

Bellis, C., Ashton, K.J., Freney, L., Blair, B., Griffiths, L.R., 2003. A molecular genetic approach for forensic animal species identification. Forensic Science International 134 (2–3), 99–108.

Coyle, H.M. (Ed.), 2008. Nonhuman DNA Typing: Theory and Casework Applications. CRC Press, Boca Raton, FL.

Ferri, G., Alù, M., Corradini, B., Beduschi, G., 2009. Forensic botany: species identification of botanical trace evidence using a multigene barcoding approach. International Journal of Legal Medicine 123 (5), 395–401.

Fridez, F., Rochat, S., Coquoz, R., 1999. Individual identification of cats and dogs using mitochondrial DNA tandem repeats? Science and Justice 39 (3), 167–171.

Halverson, J.L., Basten, C., 2005. Forensic DNA identification of animal-derived trace evidence: tools for linking victims and suspects. Croatian Medical Journal 46 (4), 598–605.

Heath, L.E., Saunders, V.A., 2006. Assessing the potential of bacterial DNA profiling for forensic soil comparisons. Journal of Forensic Sciences 51, 1062–1068. http://dx.doi.org/10.1111/j.1556-4029.2006.00208.x.

Kanthaswamy, S., 2009. The Development and Validation of a Standardized Canine STR Panel for Use in Forensic Casework (NIJ Grant No. 2004-DN-BX-K007 Final Report). National Institute of Justice (NIJ) National Criminal Justice Reference Service. http://www.ncjrs.gov/pdffiles1/nij/grants/226639.pdf.

Macdonald, C.A., Ang, R., Cordiner, S.J., Horswell, J., 2011. Discrimination of soils at regional and local levels using bacterial and fungal T-RFLP profiling. Journal of Forensic Sciences 56, 61–69. http://dx.doi.org/10.1111/j.1556-4029.2010.01542.x.

Menotti-Raymond, M., David, V.A., Stephens, J.C., Lyons, L.A., O'Brien, S.J., 1997. Genetic individualization of domestic cats using feline STR loci for forensic applications. Journal of Forensic Sciences 42 (6), 1039–1051.

Meyers, M.S., Foran, D.R., 2008. Spatial and temporal influences on bacterial profiling of forensic soil samples. Journal of Forensic Sciences 53, 652–660. http://dx.doi.org/10.1111/j.1556-4029.2008.00728.x.

Miller Coyle, H., Lee, C.L., Lin, W.Y., Lee, H.C., Palmbach, T.M., 2005. Forensic botany: using plant evidence to aid in forensic death investigation. Croatian Medical Journal 46 (4), 606–612.

Preativatanyou, K., Sirisup, N., Payungporn, S., 2010. Mitochondrial DNA-based identification of some forensically important blowflies in Thailand. Forensic Science International 202, 97–101.

Tarditi, C.R., Grahn, R.A., Evans, J.J., Kurushima, J.D., chondrial DNA sequencing of cat hair: an informative Forensic Sciences 56, 36–46. http://dx.doi.org/10.1 01592.x.

Wells, J.D., Williams, D.W., 2007. Validation of a DNA-base Chrysomyinae (Diptera: Calliphoridae) used in a death in Journal of Legal Medicine 121 (1), 1–8.

Next-Generation Sequencing Technologies

B Sobrino, Grupo de Medicina Xenomica-USC, Instituto de Investigación Sanitaria de Santiago, Spain
M Brión, Xenética de enfermidades cardiovasculares e oftalmolóxicas, Instituto de Investigación Sanitaria de Santiago-CHUS, Spain

Glossary

Next-generation sequencing technologies High-throughput sequencing technologies that parallelize the sequencing process, producing millions of sequences at once at a much lower per-base cost than conventional Sanger sequencing.

Targeted enrichment Methods to enrich a sequence library for specific regions of a genome.

Introduction

In the last few years, massively parallel DNA-sequencing platforms, known as next-generation sequencing (NGS) technologies, have been developed to make it feasible to directly sequence the whole genome of an individual in a few days. Thus, it would provide a powerful tool to study DNA and RNA samples. These technological advances open up new opportunities for many applications such as whole genome and targeted resequencing, sequencing de novo, expression analysis, and epigenetic studies.

In some cases, instead of using the general term of NGS, these technologies are referred to as second- and third-generation sequencing. Second-generation sequencing technologies require a clonal amplification step previous to the sequence reaction, whereas third-generation sequencing technologies are based on single-molecule sequencing (Sanger sequencing is the first generation).

There are currently several commercially available NGS platforms and still a few more in development. The goal of these technologies is to sequence a whole human genome for $1000; it seems that this could be accomplished by the end of 2012. According to the press release of two different companies, Life Technologies, with the new platform Ion Proton and Illumina with HiSeq2500, both will be able to sequence the whole human genome in several hours.

In addition to the technological characteristics of the platforms, it is very important to consider the amount of data produced by these platforms, making bioinformatics support extremely crucial.

In the forensic field, some disciplines could immediately benefit from its application, while others would require additional studies before deciding whether they could be incorporated.

NGS Technologies

NGS workflow can be divided into template preparation, sequencing, and data analysis.

Template preparation for genomic applications on NGS platforms involves several steps, as follows: random shearing of DNA into smaller sizes, library preparation, capture of the regions of interest in the case of targeted resequencing application, and clonal amplification, with the exception of those technologies based on single-molecule sequencing. During the process of capturing and library preparation, it is possible to barcode samples, which enables one to pool multiple samples per sequencing run, taking advantage of the high throughput of the NGS platforms.

The amount of DNA required is determined by the type of library, the capture method, and the sequencing technology altogether. As each method has advantages and drawbacks, all these factors need to be considered in order to select the best approach for each application.

As mentioned earlier, the difference between what is called second- and third-generation platforms is the existence of an amplification step prior to sequencing reaction. The technologies that required a previous amplification step perform clonal amplification of the templates either on the surface of beds in emulsion polymerase chain reaction (PCR) or on a glass support. The first one is used by 454 Roche, SOLiD, and Ion Torrent. Illumina relies on a bridge PCR on a glass slide to amplify small fragments of DNA. In this approach, forward and reverse PCR primers are attached to a solid surface, and, as a consequence of this, amplification products originating from any single template molecule remain immobilized and clustered to a physical position on the slide.

 http://dx.doi.org/10.1016/B978-0-12-800647-4.00046-1

Nowadays, there are different sequencing strategies that can be generally grouped in sequencing by synthesis that comprises nucleotide incorporation by a polymerase or in sequencing by ligation, which is based on the use of DNA ligases (**Table 1**). In addition to this, new methods are being developed, such as the ones based on nanopores; even so, they are not yet commercially available.

Although NGS platforms such as 454 Roche, Illumina, Ion Torrent, Helicos, and Pacific BS rely on sequencing by synthesis, there are important differences among them.

The 454 Roche was the first NGS platform available as a commercial product. Sequencing is performed by pyrosequencing. In this method, the incorporation of a nucleotide by DNA polymerase results in the release of pyrophosphate, which initiates a series of downstream reactions that ultimately produce light by a luciferase. The light can be correlated with specific nucleotide incorporation because they are added following a sequential order. This is one of the sequencing technologies with longer reads, up to 1000 bp.

The Illumina system is based on sequencing by synthesis in which all four nucleotides are added simultaneously to the flow cell channels, along with the polymerase, for incorporation into the oligo-primed cluster fragments obtained after bridge PCR. Unlike 454, fluorescently labeled nucleotide terminators are used on this platform. The maximum read length is 150 bp.

In the case of the Ion phosphoglycerate mutase (PGM) Sequencer (Life Technologies), sequence data are obtained by directly sensing the ions produced by template-directed DNA polymerase synthesis using all natural nucleotides on the ion chip. The ion chip contains ion-sensitive, field-effect transistor-based sensors in millions of wells, which allow parallel and simultaneous detection of independent sequencing reactions. Unlike the other technologies in which the throughput is determined by the equipment, the Ion PGM throughput is determined by the chip used for sequencing. There are currently three chips available with a capacity of 10 MB to 1 GB. The read length achieved with this platform is 200 bp. Life Technologies released a new platform in 2012 called Ion Proton Sequencer based on the same technology as Ion PGM, but with a higher capacity. With the Ion Proton Chip I, it would be possible to sequence two exomes, whereas, with the Ion Proton Chip II, the whole human genome would be sequenced for $1000 in several hours.

NGS platforms that are based on single-molecule sequencing such as Helicos Biosciences and Pacific Biosciences, in which sequencing is performed directly on the DNA, seem to be very promising as they would avoid any amplification step.

The Helicos system was the first commercial release of a single-molecule sequencing instrument. The DNA fragments are hybridized to primers covalently anchored in random positions on a glass coverslip in a flow cell. The primer, polymerase, and labeled nucleotides are added to the glass support. The base incorporated into the synthesis strand is determined by analysis of the emitted fluorescence signal. As in other platforms, many millions of fragments are sequenced at the same time.

Table 1 Comparison of commercially available next-generation sequencing platforms

Technology	*Amplification method*	*Sequencing method*	*Instrument*	*Read length (bp)*	*Throughput (MB/run)*	*Run time*	*Web site*
454	Emulsion polymerase chain reaction (PCR)	Synthesis (pyrosequencing)	454-GS Junior	400	50 MB	10 h	http://www.roche.com
			454-FLX+	700	900 MB	23 h	
Illumina	Bridge PCR	Synthesis	Illumina-MiSeq	150 + 150	>1 GB	27 h	http://www.illumina.com/
			Illumina-GAII	150 + 150	95 GB	14 days	
			Illumina-HiScanSQ	100 + 100	150 GB	11 days	
			Illumina-HiSeq1000	100 + 100	300 GB	11 days	
			Illumina-HiSeq2000	100 + 100	600 GB	11 days	
SOLiD	Emulsion PCR	Ligation	SOLiD-5500	75 + 35	90 GB	7 days	http://www.lifetechnologies.com
			SOLiD-5500xl	75 + 35	180 GB	7 days	
Ion torrent	Emulsion PCR	Synthesis (H^+ detection)	Ion PGM – 314 chip	200	>10 MB	2 h	
			Ion PGM – 316 chip	200	>100 MB	2 h	http://www.iontorrent.com/
			Ion PGM – 318 chip	200	>1 GB	2 h	

The PacBio BS is a single-molecule and real-time sequencing system. The main differences compared with any other technology are that single polymerase molecules are attached to the solid support and it provides an extra-long read.

The SOLiD system is based on sequencing by ligation and the use of two-base encoded probes. A universal sequencing primer is hybridized to templates and a pool of fluorescently labeled octamer probes, containing all possible combinations of A, C, G, and T at positions 1–5, interrogates the sequence of the unknown template on each bead. Only the probe homologous to the first five bases of the template will be ligated to the universal sequencing primer. Up to 15 cycles of ligation, detection, and cleavage record the color at every fifth position, given a maximum length read of 75 bp.

Targeted Enrichment

Methods for capturing regions of interest when a particular portion of the genome need to be analyzed have been developed, allowing to reduce costs and efforts significantly compared with whole-genome sequencing.

Considering even the different capture strategies, the workflow for targeted resequencing for candidate regions, genes, or exome sequencing is very similar. Depending on the method used for capturing the regions of interest, the capture occurs before or after creating the library. Once the capture library is created, it is clonally amplified followed by massive parallel sequencing.

Capture strategies can be broadly grouped into three main groups (**Table 2**).

PCR Amplification

A PCR is used to amplify the region of interest. The main advantage of this technique is the small amount of starting material required. Considering that the amount of DNA is a major limitation in forensic samples, the strategies based on the PCR approach seem to be the most suitable for forensic analyses.

If the region of interest is a large kilobase-sized, contiguous region, long PCR using high-fidelity polymerases could be used.

On the other hand, different strategies have been developed over the last few years to amplify simultaneously hundreds of fragments of DNA when required. Access Array System (Fluidigm) uses a microfluidic chip with nanoliter-scale chambers, where the simultaneous amplification of 48 different fragments in 48 samples is performed. By incorporating the adaptor sequences into the primer design, the amplicon products are ready to go directly into clonal amplification.

Microdroplet-PCR technology developed by RainDance Technologies involves the use of emulsion PCR in a microfluidic device, creating droplets of primers in oil solution. The primer droplets that are targeted to different regions of the genome merge with separate droplets that contain fragmented genomic DNA and PCR reagents. These mixed droplets are thermal cycled in a single tube. The encapsulation of microdroplet PCR reactions prevents possible primer–pair interactions, allowing an efficient simultaneous amplification of up to 20,000 targeted sequences.

Illumina and Life Technologies have followed similar strategies to capture regions for MiSeq and Ion PGM Sequencer, respectively. Illumina has launched the TrueSeq Custom Amplicon Kit for multiplex amplification of up to 384 amplicons per sample. Life Technologies has recently developed a multiplex PCR to amplify, in a single tube, up to 480 amplicons known as Ion AmpliSeq Cancer Panel. Only the cancer panel is currently available; however, it has been announced by the company that custom panels for up to 1536 amplicons would be soon available.

Circularization

Enrichment by DNA fragment circularization is based on the use of probes comprising a single-stranded DNA oligonucleotide that contains two sequences at its ends that are complementary to noncontiguous stretches of a target genomic fragment, but in a reversed linear order. Specific hybridization among probes and complementary genomic DNA generates

Table 2 Most common targeted enrichment methods

Approach	*Method*	*Kit*[a]	*NGS compatibility*[b]
Polymerase chain reaction (PCR)	Long-PCR	1	1, 2, 3, 4
	Access Array System (Fluidigm)	1	1, 2, 3, 4
	Microdroplet PCR (RainDance)	1, 2	1, 2, 3, 4
	AmpliSeq technology (Life Technologies)	1, 2	4
	TrueSeq Amplicon Kit (Illumina)	1	2
Circularization	HaloPlex (Halo Genomics)	1	2
	Selector (Halo Genomics)	1, 2	1, 2, 3, 4
In-solution hybridization	SureSelect (Agilent)	1, 3	2, 3
	SeqCap EZ (NimbleGen)	1, 3	1, 2, 3
	TrueSeq Enrichment Kit (Illumina)	1, 3	2
	TargetSeq (Life Technologies)	1, 3	3, 4

[a]Custom (1), specific gene panel (ej. cancer panel) (2), exome panel (3).
[b]454 (1), Illumina (2), SOLiD (3), Ion PGM Sequencer (4).

circular DNA, which is amplified through rolling circle amplification.

Halo Genomics has developed two different strategies based on the circularization method, Selector and HaloPlex. The first one, Selector Target Enrichment system, is based on multiple displacement amplification. This strategy produces circular DNA that is amplified in a whole-genome amplification reaction. The resulting high-molecular DNA product is compatible with all NGS library preparation protocols. To achieve this, the DNA sample is first fragmented using restriction enzymes. After that, the probe library is added so as to hybridize the targeted fragments. Each probe is an oligonucleotide designed to hybridize both ends of a targeted DNA restriction fragment, thereby guiding the targeted fragments to form circular DNA molecules. The circular molecules are closed by ligation and then amplified. The next step is library preparation.

In the case of HaloPlex technology, PCR products are ready for pooling and direct sequencing. It is not necessary to create the library after the capturing since the probes also contain a specific sequencing motif that is incorporated during the circularization. This motif allows the incorporation of specific library adaptors and barcodes during the amplification. At present, this product is optimized only for Illumina.

Hybridization

Enrichment by hybridization is based on the hybridization of specific probes complementary to the regions of interest with the input sample, either in solution or on a solid support. The first hybridization approaches were based on array capture, but it is currently more the use of in-solution hybridization. Fragment libraries are hybridized to biotinylated probes in solution and subsequently recovered with streptavidin-magnetic beads, amplified and sequenced in the platform of choice.

All vendors (Agilent, NimbleGen, Illumina, and Life Technologies) offer either kits predesigned for specific applications such as exome sequencing, cancer, etc., or custom panels to be designed by the user. There are diverse kits for different sizes of the region of interest from a range less than 100 KB up to 60 MB.

Applications in Forensic Sciences

Nowadays, it is not certain whether the use of NGS technologies will be extended in forensics in the near future or whether they will replace current technologies, as very few forensic laboratories have started to test them. Needless to say, in some forensic disciplines, NGS would provide additional and powerful tools to solve problems not yet resolved. Importantly, before its use in real casework, it would be necessary to assess the sensitivity, specificity, and accuracy of each approach.

In forensic genetics, short tandem repeats (STRs) are routinely used for human identification. Current methods are PCR-based fragment analysis and capillary electrophoresis, estimating the number of repeat units of each marker. The use of NGS allows detecting not only the number of repeats but also single base pair substitutions or repeating structure variation. As the STRs used in forensic casework are usually between 100 and 500 bp, only the NGS technologies with long reads are compatible with this application.

NGS could provide a rapid, high-throughput and cost-effective tool for mitochondrial DNA sequencing, while its use in forensics would require optimization of the protocols altogether with the algorithm analysis in order to get quality data to meet forensic criteria. It is very common that forensic samples are easily degraded, therefore, in these cases, NGS technologies with short reads would be more appropriate.

Sudden cardiac death is a challenging problem in forensic pathology because the cause of the death is in many cases not detectable during autopsy. Several genetic cardiac disorders such as arrhythmogenic abnormalities and structural cardiomyopathies are associated with sudden death. The analysis of genes involved in these pathologies would help in the diagnosis, not only improving the search for the cause of death but also allowing genetic counseling of relatives at risk. Genetic diagnosis of these diseases is not easy as they are genetically heterogeneous. However, using NGS it is possible to perform a targeted resequencing of all the genes associated with genetic cardiac disorders or even the whole exome.

In the field of microbial forensics, whole-genome sequencing is a powerful tool for microbial genome characterization. The identification of the pathogen and its origin is crucial in criminal investigation of bioterrorism attacks and epidemiological investigation. Its usefulness in this field has been demonstrated by the sequencing of the German enterohemorrhagic *Escherichia coli* O104:H4 outbreak in May 2011. Previously, other microbial pathogens such as *Bacillus anthracis* and *Yersinia pestis* have been already characterized using NGS. Previous methods were limited to Sanger sequencing of a small number of strains or isolates to identify potentially informative markers, followed by genotyping of selected markers in additional strands, whereas NGS makes feasible the sequencing in parallel of multiple bacterial genomes in a short period of time and at a relatively low cost.

See also: **Anthropology/Odontology:** Personal Identification in Forensic Anthropology; **Biology/DNA:** Forensic DNA Phenotyping: DNA Testing for Externally Visible Characteristics; Microbiology and Bioterrorism; Mitochondrial DNA; Short Tandem Repeats; Single-Nucleotide Polymorphisms; **Forensic Medicine/Causes of Death:** Sudden Infant Death Syndrome (SIDS); Sudden Natural Death; **Methods:** Capillary Electrophoresis: Basic Principles.

Further Reading

Berglund, E.C., Kiialainen, A., Syvänen, A.C., 2011. Next-generation sequencing technologies and applications for human genetic history and forensics. Investigative Genetics 2, 23.

Brion, M., Quintela, I., Sobrino, B., et al., 2010. New technologies in the genetic approach to sudden cardiac death in the young. Forensic Science International 203 (1–3), 15–24.

Cummings, C.A., Bormann Chung, C.A., Fang, R., et al., 2010. Accurate, rapid and high-throughput detection of strain-specific polymorphisms in *Bacillus anthracis* and *Yersinia pestis* by next-generation sequencing. Investigative Genetics 1 (1), 5.

Fordyce, S.L., Avila-Arcos, M.C., Rockenbauer, E., et al., 2011. High-throughput sequencing of core STR loci for forensic genetic investigations using the Roche Genome Sequencer FLX platform. BioTechniques 51 (2), 127–133.

Glenn, T.C., 2011. Field guide to next-generation DNA sequencers. Molecular Ecology Resources 11 (5), 759–769.

Mellmann, A., Harmsen, D., Cummings, C.A., et al., 2011. Prospective genomic characterization of the German enterohemorrhagic *Escherichia coli* O104:H4 outbreak by rapid next generation sequencing technology. PLoS One 6 (7), e22751.

Mertes, F., Elsharawy, A., Sauer, S., et al., 2011. Targeted enrichment of genomic DNA regions for next-generation sequencing. Briefings in Functional Genomics 10 (6), 374–386.

Metzker, M.L., 2010. Sequencing technologies – the next generation. Nature Reviews Genetics 11 (1), 31–46.

Shendure, J., Ji, H., 2008. Next-generation DNA sequencing. Nature Biotechnology 26 (10), 1135–1145.

Laboratory Automation and LIMS in Forensics

M Stangegaard, AJ Hansen, and N Morling, University of Copenhagen, Copenhagen, Denmark

Glossary

Accuracy In the current document, accuracy is used to define the degree of closeness of the measured value to the actual or true value. An accurate process will show results close to the actual or true value.

Automated liquid handler (ALH) An automated pipetting robot that utilizes preprogrammed scripts to perform laboratory processes.

Calibration curve An ALH may employ a calibration curve to compensate for differences between the physical pumps and liquid handling systems. By measuring the actual volumes delivered by each pipette, a calibration curve can be generated enabling an ALH to attain accurate pipetting over a defined volume range.

Carrier Holder for labware that is designed to fit onto the worktable of an ALH. A carrier may hold several pieces of labware. Usually, different carriers are required to hold different types of labware.

Firmware A small piece of software that is stored directly in the electronic circuits of, for example, an instrument. Typically, this software is not accessible to the user. In ALHs, firmware may be used to control the individual mechanical parts.

Instrument software Dedicated software used to program scripts for an ALH. Instrument software is usually supplied with the ALH. The software and the possibilities and options as well as terminology vary greatly between vendors.

Labware Items that may be placed on the ALH worktable such as microtiter plates, tubes, tips, troughs, etc., are generally denoted as "labware."

Liquid class In the current document, the word liquid class is used. A liquid class is a subpart of a script that contains a collection of detailed parameters controlling the pipetting operation. A liquid class typically contains instructions to the ALH regarding pipetting speeds, size of air gaps and, in some instrument software, also calibration curves. An ALH may use many different liquid classes in a single script enabling precise liquid handling. In some instrument software, liquid classes are denoted as "liquid types" or "liquid handling parameters."

Pipetting technique Pipetting techniques resemble liquid classes, but contain more adjustment options. The term "pipetting technique" is used in the instrument software from Beckman Coulter in combination with underlying pipetting templates that are used to control the tip movement inside the well/tube for each aspiration–dispense operation.

Precision In the current document, precision is used to define the degree of reproducibility or repeatability. A precise process will show the same results with unchanged conditions. A precise process does not infer that the process is accurate.

Script In the current document, the word script is used. A script is a series of software instructions that directs the ALH to perform the desired functions such as aspirating–dispensing liquids, recording of bar codes, transfer of labware, and so on. In some instrument software, scripts are denoted as "methods" or "routines."

Worktable In the current document, the word "worktable" is used. The worktable is a graphical representation of the area used by the ALH to process samples. In some instrument software, worktable is denoted as "instrument deck" or "deck layout."

Introduction

Automation of manual pipetting devices commenced in the 1970s with the introduction of the digital diluter by the Hamilton Company. The first automated liquid handler (ALH) was presented in 1983. The term laboratory automation or simply automation usually refers to the use of these ALHs. Presently, ALHs are commercially available from

 http://dx.doi.org/10.1016/B978-0-12-800647-4.00047-3

many vendors. Some are sold as stand-alone (open platform) systems, while others are designed and constructed according to detailed specifications set forth by the customer. Many options exist for integration of equipment such as centrifuges, scales, heater/shakers, magnetic purification units, conveyer belts, sealers, PCR cyclers, and more. Hence, this combination allows complete laboratory processes to be performed without manual intervention. Applying automated systems in the laboratory is not per definition the most economical solution. It depends on the capacity of the automated system and the sample throughput of the laboratory. However, implementation of automated solutions has several other important advantages for a forensic laboratory. ALHs run or execute scripts containing detailed instructions that enable liquid-dependent pipetting to compensate for variations in the physical characteristics of the liquid such as viscosity, volatility, and so on, similar to manual pipetting by a laboratory technician. An ALH will perform the same set of pipetting operations during each run, reducing intra- and interoperator-induced variations. ALHs are incapable of performing actions that they are not programmed to perform, and the risk of sample misplacement or unintended pipetting is close to zero, given that the ALH is designed and programmed with this in mind and samples and reagents are loaded correctly. Finally, automation of more complex laboratory processes will often reduce process time and increase process capacity. In this chapter, the choice of liquid handler, validation and implementation of liquid handlers in a forensic and accredited environment, and operation and maintenance of liquid handlers are discussed.

What is a Laboratory Information Management System

A laboratory information management system (LIMS) is a computer system that manages sample-related information, results of analyses, manual and automated laboratory workflows, user profiles, user access, and so on. Some LIMSs also include options for managing case report information. The level of sample management and options for addition of laboratory result in the LIMS differ between system and vendor. Many different "commercial off-the-shelf (COTS) systems" exist. However, forensic laboratories may choose to either modify a COTS system to fit specific local requirements or develop their own LIMS. Usage of a LIMS requires that the information entered is trustworthy. Hence, much effort must be put into ensuring the validity of sample data and results upon registration in the LIMS, and whenever possible, electronic data and automated result entry should be applied. If manual data entry is the only option, the data should be entered independently twice or at least approved by a second operator.

General Benefits of Laboratory Automation and LIMS

Implementation of laboratory automation and LIMS in forensic environments is about prioritizing and managing resources. Implementation and validation of laboratory automation systems and LIMS are neither simple nor cheap. Furthermore, dedicated staff should be assigned to perform routine maintenance and support of both automated instruments as well as the LIMS to ensure that the systems are up-to-date and deliver the expected performance. Automation reduces the amount of manual processing of samples and a LIMS eliminates manual sample tracking. Combined, laboratory automation and LIMS reduce the sample-to-sample processing variation and, when used correctly, reduce the risk of sample misplacement. Implementation of laboratory automation and LIMS may enable a laboratory to better handle the daily fluctuation and reduce the throughput time. Most importantly, implementation of laboratory automation with LIMS integration enables laboratories to increase the throughput far beyond what is attainable using manual processing. Furthermore, implementation of additional identical ALHs is relatively simple and provides the laboratory with a scalable solution, should throughput requirement increase.

Selection of an ALH

Multiple ALHs are now commercially available. In general, they are all capable of performing the task their name suggests, namely automated handling of liquids. The general differences between the liquid handlers are mainly caused by (1) the way the ALHs aspirate and dispense the liquids, (2) the software used to program and control the instrument, and (3) the degree of integration of additional equipment with the instrument and the software.

General Differences between ALHs

Most ALHs function by positive displacement of either air or a "system liquid." ALHs using air displacement function, in principle, as conventional hand-held pipettes. ALHs relying on system liquid generally utilize distilled water as system liquid. As the compressibility of water is less dependent upon changes in temperature and pressure than air, some regard liquid-driven ALHs to be better in situations involving large temperature/pressure fluctuations. Some ALHs are capable of monitoring the processing of the pipetting, for example, by following the liquid by conductive tips or comparing the pressure difference encountered during pipetting with a predefined liquid-specific reference. This reduces the effect of bubbles and clots and improves overall confidence to the results.

The instrument software used to generate the scripts varies greatly between vendors. Some programs enable scripts to be programmed by dragging function boxes into a vertical or horizontal row resembling the principle of Lego. Others rely on line-to-line programming. The level of control of the function of ALHs also varies greatly between different types of software. Details such as direct control of the tip movement inside the well/tube during pipetting may be possible in one type of software while being impossible in another. Functionalities such as locking of scripts to prevent undesired modifications, user control, etc., also vary between the various instrument software solutions. For larger ALHs with integrated equipment, the instrument software may assist the programmer by scheduling the resources of the ALH enabling faster completion of the script. The instrument software may also include tools for locking or validating a script once it has been completed and sufficiently tested. In general, the different vendors have different tools for safeguarding a validated method. Some are more efficient than others.

ALHs may be divided into three main groups based on their size and flexibility. Small liquid handlers may be closed systems with dedicated functionalities such as small DNA extractors or small ALHs with limited flexibility and integration options. Medium-sized ALHs are typically more open and flexible, enabling a higher degree of customization and integration of various components and equipment. Large ALHs typically contain multiple components such as handling arms, sealers, capper/decappers, centrifuges, cameras, and so on, and are capable of performing complex processes without manual intervention, enabling large ALHs to function as a production line. A rule of thumb is, the more complex the solution, the more complex and extensive the validation. Hence, the choice of solution should fit a laboratory's needs—a big, complex, and expensive ALH is not always better than a simple solution.

Automation of Laboratory Processes

Crucial to the selection of the optimal ALH for a specific laboratory process is a careful evaluation of the laboratory process that the ALH is planned to perform. The evaluation is best prepared by listing each individual operation of the process, that is, all transfers of sample/reagents, movements of samples, etc. The evaluation should result in a list of requirements specifying in detail the demands. The list of requirements should specify the requirements to accuracy and precision of the individual liquid transfer steps in the process. The requirements should also state requirements for which type of tips to be used. As disposable conductive filter-tips are expensive, ALHs equipped with reusable washable tips may be advantageous should filter-tips should not be required. The list of requirements should also include relevant evaluation requirements of all potentially integrated equipment such as magnetic units, heater/shakers, etc. The requirements should be as stringent as the intended processes require them to be. If a LIMS is to be used in connection with the instrument, requirements to the input/output file formats should also be specified. On the basis of the list of requirements, the best ALH for that laboratory process may be identified. For laboratories with limited automation experience, vendors with available local/regional support should be prioritized.

Before the implementation and validation of an ALH, a backup solution should be considered. As with all technical equipment, ALHs may malfunction due to a collision or a failure on one of the components. The more equipment that has been integrated on the ALH, the greater the risk of one of the components to malfunction or break down rendering the entire automated system out of service. A situation where a group of samples are required to be processed on a single instrument—a key instrument—should be avoided. One solution, following validation of one ALH is to purchase and validate a second identical ALH. The sample flow through the laboratory may then be directed to either of the two liquid handlers. In any case, key instruments should not be used at more than around 70% capacity to reduce the sample backlog from growing too fast in case of the ALH being out of service. Laboratories operating with a key instrument should have an alternative sample processing solution as backup.

An important consideration regarding integration of various components into one ALH is a cost-benefit evaluation. Typically, integration of equipment from the same vendor is straightforward and the instrument software is prepared for the equipment. Integration of third-party equipment must be considered more thoroughly. Generally, it is cumbersome and time-consuming and the integration must be weighed against manual intervention for completion of the process on stand-alone equipment. Depending upon technical competences of the laboratory staff, integration of third-party equipment may not be economically justifiable. Hence, a solution requiring manual intervention during the laboratory process may be the best, economically feasible solution.

LIMS Support/Integration

LIMS integration requires exchange of information either by a shared database or transfer of files. The level of available LIMS support may have a significant impact on the selection of the optimal ALH. Laboratories with no or very limited LIMS support may benefit from choosing simple stand-alone ALHs. The simplest ALH may be controlled by a simple control panel rather than a PC. This reduces the cost of the instrument and the validation as well as the requirements to the operators in terms of computer skills. LIMS integration may not be possible with these instruments. The flexibility and the integration options of the smaller ALHs may be significantly lower than those of the medium-sized ALHs or simply not existing.

However, being simple with limited flexibility ensures that fewer options must be tested and validated enabling faster validation and implementation.

Medium-sized ALHs generally offer greater flexibility, and options for integration as well as communication with a LIMS. The pipetting arm may be automatic adjustable (span) enabling the ALHs to efficiently transfer samples from tubes to plates or vice versa. The deck size allows for multiple tubes in carriers as well as microtiter plates and hence allows more complex processes. This enables the medium-sized ALHs to be used for more complex laboratory processes utilizing various labware. The instrument software controlling most medium-sized ALHs enables processing of samples according to information contained in simple input files, for example, generated by a LIMS. Medium-sized ALHs may be used without LIMS integration, but they generally benefit from LIMS integration.

Integration of multiple components or equipment may enable larger ALHs to perform several usually separate laboratory processes without requirements for manual intervention. Such ALHs may be referred to as production lines. These systems may have a sample processing capacity hardly attainable using manual processing. Such systems seem of little relevance unless they are supported and integrated with an efficient LIMS guiding the flow of samples.

Bar Codes

Bar codes are available in many forms and as commercially available fonts. The information contained in a bar code is dependent upon the type of bar code used. Some bar codes are one-dimensional and do not hold as much information per unit area when compared to two-dimensional bar codes. While some one-dimensional bar codes also contain the humanly readable text held in the bar code, two-dimensional bar codes are not humanly readable. Many commercially available tubes and microtiter plates can be prebarcoded with a unique number. Usage of prebarcoded tubes generally requires LIMS integration to link the sample identification with the number of the bar-coded tube.

Custom bar codes may be manually applied to tubes and microtiter plates during sample registration or job creation. Labeling of sample tubes and plates with bar codes enables ALHs equipped with bar code scanners to control the position of the samples as well as the orientation of the microtiter plates, record the labels on the tubes and plates and report the processed samples and plates to either a LIMS or a report file. Sample tracking by bar codes is most efficiently performed with LIMS integration. The LIMS may be programmed to update the status of the processed samples with batch number, instrument details, etc. upon completion of a job. This requires that the ALH automatically generates an output file containing this information and transfers the file to the LIMS.

Recent interest in radiofrequency identification technologies (RFID) for tagging and tracking evidence may indicate a new direction for LIMS, chains of custody, and warehousing.

Tubes versus Microtiter Plates

One important decision before selecting an ALH is whether the laboratory processes require samples to be processed in tubes or in microtiter plates. Processing of samples in tubes increases the risk of sample misplacement if not a proper control method such as bar codes is efficiently used. However, having samples in individual tubes eases processing of reruns.

Processing of samples in microtiter plates reduces the risk of sample misplacement as well as the number of manual number controls per sample. However, reruns of individual samples in microtiter plates are difficult to perform manually and, in general, require an ALH capable of processing a few preselected samples (cherry picking). Carriers for both conventional flip-cap tubes such as the conventional Eppendorf tubes and support bases for microtiter plates are commercially available from several vendors.

Validation of Automated Systems and Laboratory Processes

When an ALH is installed, the vendor should perform an "instrument qualification" test to verify that all the components are present and functioning according to the user requirement or "design qualification" set forth by the laboratory. The result of the instrument qualification test should be documented and stored by the laboratory. The laboratory may perform an additional "operational qualification" test to ensure that the ALH functions according to the intended use, before commencing actual validation of the ALH.

What Is Validation

According to the ISO 17025 standard, validation is defined as "… the confirmation by examination and the provision of objective evidence that the particular requirements for a specific intended use are fulfilled." In other words, validation is the process that demonstrates that a process or method is robust, reliable, and reproducible in the hands of the technical staff in the laboratory.

Validation Process

Implementation and validation of ALHs are most efficiently handled using project management tools. Hence, a project group containing dedicated staff should be formed and the project prioritized by the laboratory management. In practice, this ensures faster and more robust implementation and validation of the ALHs. Following validation of the ALH, the project group should assist the receiving laboratory in training and maintaining the ALH.

Before commencing a validation project, the instrument should be tested to ensure that it meets the demands of the intended process. This testing may be referred to as "instrument qualification" or "user acceptance test." Instrument qualification should provide documented evidence that the intended process may be satisfactorily executed on the specific instrument.

Script Design

For computerized systems such as ALHs and LIMS, the definition of validation may be interpreted in such a way that every possible relevant outcome of the script should be tested. This should be taken into account prior to script development for ALHs. Most scripts will at some point in time require changes that invalidate the initial validation, hence requiring a revalidation before use. If the process flow in the script is designed as in **Figure 1(a)**, validation and revalidation may be extremely costly and time-consuming. However, by using a process flow as depicted in **Figure 1(b)**, validation and revalidation may be a simple operation, requiring only a single execution of the full script and treatment of four plates. In comparison, the script design in **Figure 1(a)** would require four runs and a total of 10 plates.

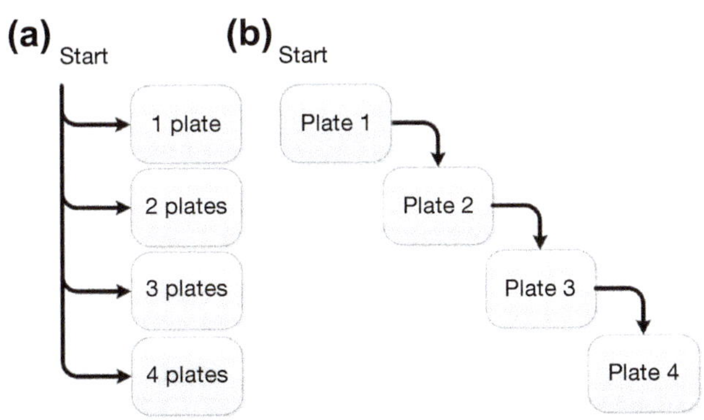

Figure 1 Script design. A script designed to treat from one to four plates may be differently programmed structurally. (a) The script is designed to treat either one plate, two plates, three plates, or four plates based on initial user input. (b) The script is designed to start with plate one and continue through plate two, three, and four until all the plates are treated.

Following completion of the initial script version, testing should commence before the actual validation experiments. Replacing reagents with water may be used to verify the script performance as well as LIMS integration in terms of acceptance of input from the LIMS and generation of output acceptable to the LIMS. Differentially colored water may be used to verify sample positioning, reagent additions, etc. For validation, a representative number of samples should be tested to ensure that the system delivers reproducible and reliable results. Defining the required number of samples to be used for this is a trade-off. For some processes, a magic number of 50 is often mentioned. With automated processes potentially working in 96, 384, or even 1536 well microtiter plates, this number seems irrelevant. Running 50 samples may seem too little as this is less than one full plate. Running 50 plates will be too expensive in terms of reagents and time-consuming in terms of data analysis. Hence, determining the relevant number of samples to be tested very much depends upon process-specific conditions. The relevant number of samples and other relevant acceptance test criteria should be defined before the validation process by or in agreement with the laboratory management.

Worktable Layout

Using small modifications to the carriers may prevent the operators from orienting or placing the labware incorrectly. For microtiter plates bar coded on one of the sides, the position, orientation, and identity may be controlled and verified by ALH in combination with the LIMS initially in the script before sample processing. For simple ALHs, the positioning may be assisted by the use of different types of microtiter plates for source and destinations. Plate orientation may be controlled by addition of elements on the worktable such as small stainless steel spikes located at positions where the microtiter plate has defined characteristics (**Figure 2**).

Volume Verification

Verification of the volumes delivered by the ALH must be performed. Verification of the volumes dispensed by the ALH should be performed using the same or alternative representative volumes and aspirate–dispense cycles as used in the script(s) to be validated. The aspirate–dispense cycles should employ the same liquid classes as well as other pipetting parameters such as pipetting techniques and/or pipetting templates as the actual script(s). It may be most practical to write dedicated volume verification scripts for each ALH. Volume verification may be used to optimize liquid classes or pipetting techniques to meet the demands posed to pipetting accuracy and precision.

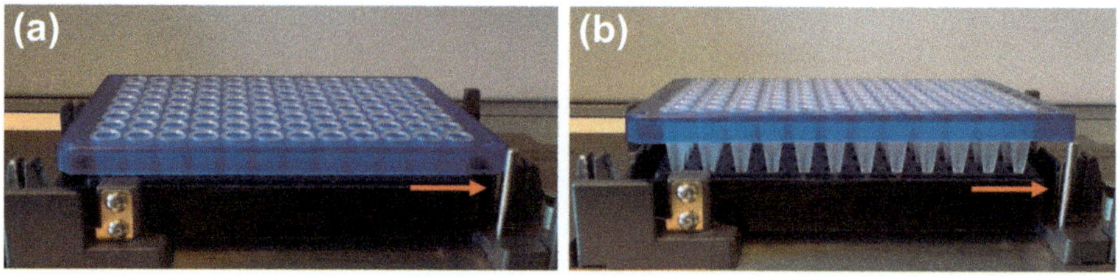

Figure 2 Microtiter plate orientation. A stainless steel spike located in the lower right corner indicated with a red arrow is used to secure the orientation of a microtiter plate on a Beckman Coulter Biomek 3000 robot. The microtiter plate (Eppendorf twin.tec) lacks all corners but the corner closest to position A1. Correct orientation of the microtiter plate is with well A1 in the upper left corner. (a) Correct orientation of the microtiter plate. Position A1 is in the upper left corner. (b) Incorrect orientation of the microtiter plate. Position A1 is in the lower right corner. The spike prevents the plate from being placed incorrectly in the support base.

Volume verification may be performed using gravimetry, fluorescence, absorbance, or radioisotopic techniques. Radioisotopic techniques are impractical due to the biohazard and the many restrictions on radioactive materials and will not be discussed.

Fluorescence

Volume verification by fluorescence requires that a liquid mixed with a fluorescent dye is aspirated and dispensed using the same volumes and aspirate–dispense cycles as the actual script(s). The destination plate should be compatible with a fluorescent-based reader and have flat-bottom wells to ensure maximal signal recording. Repetition of the aspirate–dispense cycles will provide the statistics required. Following dispensing, and signal recording, the signal strengths recorded in each well can be used to calculate the dispensed volume of liquid. This requires use of a standard curve spanning the volumes used. This standard curve should be contained in the same plate as the volume measurement to eliminate potential plate effects. A large number of fluorescent dyes are commercially available. However, fluorescent dyes are known to photo bleach reducing the measurement precision. Furthermore, the signal strength of fluorescent dyes is strongly influenced by factors such as pH and ionic strength.

Absorbance

Volume verification using absorbance is, in principle, similar to fluorescence-based techniques. Unlike fluorescence, volume verification by absorbance takes advantage of the physical properties of some dyes to block the passage of light. Dyes used for absorbance are hence not as sensitive to photodecomposition, influence by the pH, and ionic strengths as fluorescent dyes. Furthermore, plate readers capable of recording fluorescence are significantly more complex and expensive than the simpler absorbance plate readers. Using a standard curve and repeated aspirate–dispense cycles of the volume to be tested, an accurate measurement of the pipetting operation may be obtained.

Gravimetric

The gravimetric technique is based on the same principle as conventional weighing of dispensed liquid by a manual plunger-operated pipette. The technique generally requires a high precision scale to be integrated in the ALH. The gravimetric techniques may be tailored to use the same liquids such as anticoagulated blood, blood from deceased, other body fluids, PCR master mix, volatile reagents, etc., enabling accurate testing of the complete aspirate–dispense cycles as well as the liquid parameters. Knowledge of the density of the liquid is required to calculate the dispensed volume. However, integration of the scale may be time-consuming and limited to the possibility offered in the ALH software. Furthermore, the scale may not easily be moved between ALHs and hence the same solution may not be employed on all ALHs in the laboratory. The gravimetric method may be performed without integrating the scale on the ALH. The process would then be performed by manual weighing of tubes/plates before and after each pipetting operation. This procedure is laborious and time-consuming.

For handling of samples in plates, the gravimetric techniques only provide the weight of the entire plate unless the change in weight is recorded following each individual dispense operation. Hence, the result obtained is an average over the entire plate and individual variations within the pipetting may be difficult to record. It may be possible to integrate the scale in the ALH script enabling recording of individual pipetting operation, but this may be limited by the options available within the software.

Input/Output Files

Most medium-sized or larger ALHs have the option of accepting and generating files. Typically, these files are simple text files with a predefined structure and formatting. If the ALH is integrated with a LIMS, this may ensure that only samples in queue for the process being performed on the ALH are treated. The ALH may also be directed to use an input file to ensure correct positioning of the samples on the worktable before sample treatment by controlling the bar codes on the sample tubes or plates, preventing sample misplacement. The output file from the ALH may be generated following sample treatment. The LIMS may be programmed to accept this file and update the status of the treated samples and optionally include any obtained results. Validation of the usage of these files should focus on ensuring that acceptable files are generated, that they contain the expected information, they are located as expected, and they are capable of inducing the required response in the ALH/LIMS.

Validation Strategy

Validation of the automated process on the ALH should be as thorough as necessary. One frequent problem is not having an agreement with the laboratory management regarding the extent of the validation and what results are acceptable. Hence, before commencing the actual validation experiments, an agreement between the laboratory management and the project manager should be made. The agreement should depict the extent of experiments including type and number of samples as well as test acceptance criteria. The test acceptance criteria should be the laboratory management minimum requirements to the system.

Modular Testing

Validation of individual components of an integrated system or individual subscripts within a larger script or specific LIMS interactions may be performed on a modular basis. Examples of modular testing include volume verification of the pipettes on an ALH, regent distribution from a trough to preselected wells in a microtiter plate, generation of output file, or import and processing of a file. Relevant results from the modular testing could be included in the final validation report as confirmation of the function of the individual components and interactions. However, a validation should never be based solely on multiple modular tests of the involved components.

Holistic Testing

In holistic testing, the entire system is viewed as a black box and the final output is recorded and evaluated. The individual substeps during processing of the samples are ignored. Holistic testing should be performed only when the individual components or substeps have been sufficiently tested using modular testing. The final validation of an automated system should imply holistic testing to demonstrate that the system functions as a whole and the interaction between substeps is as expected.

Contamination Testing

The worktables of ALHs are often limited in space. During execution of the script, tips filled with samples or reagents may pass over open wells or tubes. If the liquid classes are not properly optimized, dripping may occur. Cross-contamination may be identified by running a series of known samples, for example, in a checkerboard format in which the sample in every other well/tube is replaced with water.

Accuracy and Precision

To ensure that the system is robust and yields accurate and precise results, the same set of known samples should be processed using the same set of downstream instruments several times over several days. Comparison of the results and potential log or report files should provide evidence to support that the system provides accurate and precise results. Using samples with known concentrations of either DNA or inhibitors, or other effectors provides information on the accuracy of the results.

Sensitivity and Stochastic Studies

Identification of the lower operation range of the system is best found using dilution series of known samples. Samples with known concentrations may be purchased for this purpose. The dilution series should extend beyond the expected upper and lower detection threshold of the system. Repeating the sensitivity run enables detection of potential stochastic effects from exponential enzymatic reactions such as the PCR. The operating concentration thresholds should be defined on the basis of both the sensitivity of the system and the absence of stochastic effects.

Operation and Maintenance of Automated Instruments in Forensic Environments

Operation of automated instruments in forensic and accredited environments infers that the systems must be safeguarded from modifications or adjustments that will invalidate the validation. Though this may seem obvious, it may easily be overlooked due to lack of detailed knowledge of the instrument software and related equipment. Different vendors have developed different solutions for safeguarding their systems. Some solutions appear more practical than others. In addition, the instrument must be tested with predefined intervals in order to verify that the performance remains within the specifications.

Shared Components of Validated Scripts

The instrument software used to control the ALH or a COTS LIMS often provides various levels of user rights. The typical operator has rights only to execute validated scripts or perform simple routine steps in a LIMS. Hence, the danger rarely lies in the daily users, but in the persons with super user rights. Only details regarding ALH are discussed in the following section.

Instrument software may utilize several shared components. Examples of this include liquid classes, pipetting techniques, labware information, worktable layout, etc. As the components are shared, it infers that they are shared across different scripts. Hence, if a liquid class is modified in one script, the changes are transferred to all other scripts using that liquid class. As the liquid class contains the pipetting parameters, and for some software also calibration curves, changes in a liquid class should at the very least be accompanied by volume verification of all relevant volumes. In some instrument software, this also includes validated and locked scripts. Others may have various ways of safeguarding the validated scripts.

Development of new scripts for testing on an instrument also used for routine work should be performed with utmost care with shared components. A modification of, for example, a liquid class in a script under development that is also used in a script used for routine work may result in modification of the way a liquid is aspirated or dispensed. To prevent this, liquid classes and other customizable components should be script specific, for example, by using the script name as a part of the component name.

Instrument Software and Script Updates

As with other software solutions, new versions of the ALH software are occasionally released. Often, the new version adds extended functionalities in addition to fixing reported bugs. Implementation of new software versions should be performed only when required and accompanied by revalidation of the system and scripts.

Change Strategy

Before making changes to instruments and software used for routine or accredited use, a change strategy should be established. A change strategy is an evaluation of the planned changes and a risk assessment of the consequences. Following completion of the change strategy, it should be documented and included in the revalidation.

Software Updates

The simplest solution for updating the ALH software while allowing for continuous use of the ALH during revalidation is to install the updated software on a new PC and only use this new PC during validation. The PCs should be properly labeled to ensure that samples are not processed with the unvalidated software update. Some ALHs (Tecan, etc.) may require firmware (Section "Firmware Upgrade") upgrading in combination with the software upgrade. Switching between the new and old PC should here also be accompanied by a firmware upgrade or downgrade, respectively.

Script Updates

Substitution of one type of labware, for example, plate type, for another may require modifications in the scripts. Calibration of the instrument by modifying the liquid classes by the addition of a calibration curve is another way of modifying a script. Integration of additional equipment on the ALH or integration with the LIMS system may also require the script to be updated.

All script updates should be performed in a structured and planned manner ensuring that only the desired changes are made. The change strategy may also be used here. Revalidation of the script should focus on verifying the consequences of the introduced changes. The number of samples or runs required to document this should depend on both the system and the changes.

Firmware Upgrade

The firmware of various components of the ALH may be updated by a service engineer during regular preventative maintenance (PM) of the ALH. Rarely, the laboratory is informed about this unless the laboratory has made arrangement with the service companies. Updating the firmware of the parts of the instruments that control, for example, liquid handling or temperature, potentially alters the function of the ALH and hence, in principle, invalidates the instrument. To prevent the service engineer from performing the update, a procedure or signed agreement for how this should be performed should be available prior to PMs. Firmware updates should be handled like other instrument updates. The effect of the update should be estimated and suitable experiments that can verify that the instrument performs as well or better following the update should be conducted and evaluated before the instrument is used for routine work again.

Maintenance

ALHs must be checked at regular intervals ensuring the performance continues to meet the demands posed to all parts of the ALH. These demands may be specified in the user requirement or a modification of these requirements. Most vendors offer a service agreement with planned and detailed PM inspections. The service agreement may include a defined maximum company response time in case of instrument breakdown as well as different levels of PMs. The laboratory should choose the service agreement containing the required balance of service and support options for each instrument. During a PM, a trained and certified service engineer inspects and verifies that the instrument performs according to a check list. Worn parts such as drive belts, system liquid tubings, and so on, are replaced with new ones. The specific details of the PM are contained in the service agreement. Following a PM, the service engineer should complete a service document specifying the performance of the instrument. This document should be filed as documentation for the performance status of the instrument. Following a PM, the laboratory should perform a performance check of the instrument with known samples to ensure that the instrument performs according to the user requirements before any samples are processed on the instrument. The pipetting performance should be verified ensuring that the expected volume is also the delivered volume. It is crucial that the aspiration–dispense cycles used in the actual validated scripts are controlled with the relevant volumes. If it is not possible to have this performed during a PM by the service engineer, the laboratory should implement their own volume verification strategy. For integrated equipment such as magnetic separation units, heater/shakers, etc., tests should be defined and designed ensuring that the equipment performs as inspected under those conditions as required in the validated scripts.

Summary

Laboratory automation including ALHs and LIMS is undergoing a major development. The current options for automation, integration, transfer of data as well as data management seem endless and nothing seems impossible to automate and integrate in the production flow. Even simple laboratory equipment may provide an option for data transfer to a LIMS. For a forensic environment, the challenges are to ensure that the quality of the automated processes is comparable to or better than that of manual processing. Preferably, implementation of laboratory automation should not only increase sample throughput, the quality of the obtained results of the laboratory processes should also be increased. Furthermore, the automated solutions should have a quality so that they can be validated and accredited according to ISO 17025 or a similar internationally recognized standard. To ensure that the quality of the data management of laboratory results meets the quality of the automated laboratory processes, an efficient LIMS is required. The LIMS should be capable of ensuring efficient processing of the samples through all laboratory steps as well as of storing not only the obtained results but also sufficient information of each process step, enabling traceability and chain of custody.

See also: **Biology/DNA:** Accreditation in Forensic DNA Analysis; DNA Extraction and Quantification; Short Tandem Repeats; Single-Nucleotide Polymorphisms; **Biology/DNA/Methods/Analytical Techniques:** Capillary Electrophoresis in Forensic Genetics.

Further Reading

Bartels, H., Walser, P., 1983. Automation of wet chemical analysis with AMICA. Fresenius' Journal of Analytical Chemistry 315, 6–11.

Bradshaw, J.T., Knaide, T., Rogers, A., Curtis, R., 2005. Multichannel verification system (MVS): a dual-dye ratiometric photometry system for performance verification of multichannel liquid delivery devices. Journal of the Association for Laboratory Automation 10, 35–42.

Brevnov, M., Mundt, J., Benfield, J., et al., 2009. Automated extraction of DNA from forensic sample types using the PrepFiler automated forensic DNA extraction kit. Journal of the Association for Laboratory Automation 14, 294–302.

Butler, J.M., Tomsey, C.S., Kline, M.C., 2004. Can the Validation Process in Forensic DNA Typing Be Standardized? 15th International Symposium on Human Identification. Promega Corporation, Phoenix, AZ.

Fregeau, C.J., Lett, C.M., Elliott, J., Yensen, C., Fourney, R.M., 2008. Automated processing of forensic casework samples using robotic workstations equipped with nondisposable tips: contamination prevention. Journal of Forensic Sciences 53, 632–651.

Fregeau, C.J., Lett, C.M., Fourney, R.M., 2010. Validation of a DNA IQ-based extraction method for TECAN robotic liquid handling workstations for processing casework. Forensic Science International. Genetics 4, 292–304.

Gurevitch, D., 2004. Economic justification of laboratory automation. Journal of the Association for Laboratory Automation 9, 33–43.

Hansson, O., Albinsson, L., 2008. Automatic data processing of reference DNA-profiles from FTA and non-FTA samples. Forensic Science International: Genetics Supplement Series 1, 29–31.

Houck, M.M., Daugherty, E., 2009. Radio frequency identification devices (RFID) as a means of evidence tracking. Forensic Science Policy and Management 1, 135–143.

Olsen, A.N., Christiansen, L.C., Nielsen, S.J., et al., 2009. Customizing a commercial laboratory information management system for a forensic genetic laboratory. Forensic Science International: Genetics Supplement Series 2, 77–79.

Stangegaard, M., Frøslev, T.G., Frank-Hansen, R., Hansen, A.J., Morling, N., 2011. Automated extraction of DNA from blood and PCR setup using a Tecan freedom EVOW liquid handler for forensic genetic STR typing of reference sample. Journal of Laboratory Automation 16, 134.

Stangegaard, M., Hansen, A.J., Frøslev, T.G., Morling, N., 2011. A simple method for validation and verification of pipettes mounted on automated liquid handlers. Journal of Laboratory Automation 16 (5), 381–386.

Stangegaard, M., Jørgensen, M., Hansen, A.J., Morling, N., 2009. Automated extraction of DNA from reference samples from various types of biological materials on the Qiagen BioRobot EZ1 Workstation. Forensic Science International: Genetics Supplement Series 2, 69–70.

Stangegaard, M., Tomas, C., Hansen, A.J., Frank-Hansen, R., Børsting, C., Morling, N., 2008. Biomek-3000 and GenPlex SNP genotyping in forensic genetics. Journal of the Association for Laboratory Automation 13, 297–303.

Tack, L.C., Thomas, M., Reich, K., 2005. Automated forensic DNA purification optimized for FTA card punches and identifiler STR-based PCR analysis. Journal of the Association for Laboratory Automation 10, 231–236.
Xie, I.H., Wang, M.H., Carpenter, R., Wu, H.Y., 2004. Automated calibration of TECAN genesis liquid handling workstation utilizing an online balance and density meter. Assay and Drug Development Technologies 2, 71–80.

Relevant Websites

http://www.ecaconsortium.net – European Consortium for Accreditation.
http://www.labautopedia.com – LabAutopedia: The Society for Laboratory Automation and Screening (SLAS) Network.
http://limsource.com – LIMS and ELNS: The Online Scientific Community.

DNA and Endangered Species

JC-I Lee, National Taiwan University, Taipei, Taiwan ROC; Institute of Forensic Medicine, New Taipei, Taiwan ROC
H-M Hsieh and L-C Tsai, Central Police University, Taoyuan, Taiwan ROC

Glossary

AFLP Amplified fragment length polymorphism. AFLP method is developed by combining the techniques of RFLP and PCR for DNA fingerprinting. Genomic DNA is digested by restriction enzymes and the restricted fragments are preselectively and selectively amplified by different combination of primers.
Microsatellite DNA Also named short tandem repeat (STR). It usually ranges from 2 to 7 bp for per repeat unit, and the blocks often extend less than 150 bp. STR markers are used for human individualization and paternity test.
Minisatellite DNA Also named VNTR previously. It usually ranges from 10 to 100 bp for per repeat unit, and the block often extends between 100 bp and 20 kb.
PCR Polymerase chain reaction. PCR is a DNA amplification technique. Exponential amplification of DNA is performed through multiple cycles of denaturation, annealing, and extension by thermal stable polymerase.
RAPD Random amplification of polymorphic DNA. RAPD is one of the methods to examine the whole genome. A random oligonucleotide of approximately 10 bases is usually used to amplify DNA.
RFLP Restriction fragment length polymorphism. RFLP is a method by combining the restriction enzyme digestion of the whole genome and southern hybridization with specific probes.

Introduction

Considerable quantities of endangered animals are poached or killed for use in traditional medicine, food products, and decoration. For commercial benefits, the trade of endangered species and those requiring conservation is a serious problem in many regions of the world. In 1973, the Convention on International Trade in Endangered Species of Wild Fauna and Flora (CITES) was signed for international cooperation to protect the species against overexploitation through international trade. Presently, there are more than 5000 species of fauna and 28 000 species of flora listed on the three CITES appendices. Appendix I lists the most endangered species threatened with extinction and prohibited from commercial international trade. Appendix II lists the species that may become threatened with extinction if their trade is not strictly regulated and only authorized with an export permit for international trade. Appendix III comprises the species that are already regulated in trade by the member countries, and it is necessary for other members to help control their trade. More than 650, 4300, and 150 animal species (including subspecies and populations) are listed in Appendices I, II, and III, respectively. The endangered species listed in Appendix I comprises mammals, birds, reptiles, amphibians, fishes, and invertebrates, in which mammals are major and comprise almost half of these species, and birds are the second major.

For investigating the illegal trade and protecting the endangered species, unambiguous identification of the animal species is absolutely important. Usually, species identification of animals can be performed by using morphological and chemical approaches. The morphological methods based on osteology, microscopy, and necropsy are developed. However, samples seized by law executors are frequently processed or pulverized so that visual identification is no longer possible. For example, processed meat, such as the products of sausage, jerky, and canned foods, cannot be identified by bare eyes. The chemical methods through toxicology, stable isotopes, and peptide markers are used. Some of them were well established and adopted in forensic applications. However, the others are not routinely used and only tested in a laboratory, but with the potential to be used in the future. Species identification by molecular DNA tool is one of the alternative and most effective methods presently available. Each species will have its specific pattern. Other than species identification, DNA identification is also used in individualization, paternity testing, and phylogenetic analysis for tracing the sources of endangered animals.

 http://dx.doi.org/10.1016/B978-0-12-800647-4.00048-5

For conservation, restoration, or evaluation of the distribution of the endangered species, the genetic structure and variance of wildlife population are as well analyzed by DNA methods. The methods established for DNA testing to investigate the animals are restriction fragment length polymorphism (RFLP) or PCR–RFLP, random amplification of polymorphic DNA (RAPD) fingerprinting, amplified fragment length polymorphism (AFLP), and PCR (or nested PCR)-sequencing of the specific loci. In this article, the genetic methods for DNA identification and their applications on endangered species are described.

DNA Analysis Methods

Restriction Fragment Length Polymorphism

RFLP is a method by combining the restriction enzyme digestion of the whole genome and southern hybridization with specific probes. It was first used in a criminal case by Dr Alec Jeffreys with minisatellite marker of human as the probe. The repeat unit of minisatellite DNA (also named VNTR previously) usually ranges from 10 to 100 bp and the block often extends between 100 bp and 20 kb. For animals, five minisatellite probes were used in analysis of the DNA variability and parentage testing in captive bird *Waldrapp ibises* (*Geronticus eremita*). For the wildlife, it is one of the most endangered birds. The VNTR markers for the animal species, such as pigeons (*Columba livia*), sheep (*Ovis aries*), Japanese sika deer (*Cervus nippon*), and sturgeon (*Acipenser*, *Huso*, and *Scaphirhynchus*), were reported to have also existed in mitochondrial control region other than nuclear chromosome. Its polymorphism is suitable for genetic analysis. Other than VNTR, RFLP has been used in the analysis of the genetic divergence on NADH subunits 5 and 6 for the Portuguese endangered fish species (*Chondrostoma lusitanicum*). However, this method requires at least 1 μg of high-molecular weight DNA, and is also time-consuming.

Polymerase Chain Reaction–Restriction Fragment Length Polymorphism

PCR–RFLP is developed by combining the methods of PCR and RFLP for improving the efficiency of RFLP. By this method, the specific DNA fragment is amplified and then the PCR products are digested with restriction enzyme. The specific DNA usually targeted includes cytochrome b, 12S rRNA, and 16S rRNA genes. The species-specific profiles will be observed. PCR–RFLP analysis of cytochrome b gene was used for forensic authentication of three Indian snake species, *Python molurus*, *Naja naja*, and *Xenochrophis piscator*, and used in species identification of Korean long-tailed goral (*Nemorhaedus caudatus*), which is one of the most endangered species in South Korea. PCR–RFLP for cytochrome b gene was also adopted in the identification of fecal samples for tamaraw (*Bubalus mindorensis*). This species of buffalo is endemic to the Philippine island of Mindoro. Analysis of 12S rRNA by this method was used in the identification of endangered Indian deer species. The species identified by this method include chital (*Cervus axis*), spotted deer (*Axis axis*), hog deer (*Axis porcinus*), barking deer (*Muntiacus muntjak*), sika deer (*C. nippon*), musk deer (*Moschus chrysogaster*), and sambar (*Cervus unicolor*). For 16S rRNA gene analysis, PCR–RFLP pattern was used in the determination of Egyptian buffalo (*Bubalus bubalis*), which is the domestic species.

RAPD Fingerprinting

RAPD fingerprinting is one of the methods to examine the whole genome. It is unnecessary to obtain prior information of sequences to perform the test. A random oligonucleotide of approximately 10 bases is usually used to amplify DNA, and the products are analyzed by agarose or polyacrylamide gel with slab or capillary electrophoresis. The RAPD profile is interpreted by comparing the fingerprint with the standards of the known species. RAPD is the method first used in linking the botanic evidence of a *Palo verde* tree to the defendant in forensic science. Analysis of population genetic structure and variability using RAPD markers in the endemic and endangered plant species of *Limonium dufourii* (Plumbaginaceae) was reported. For endangered animals, RAPD was used in the analysis of the genetic diversity and the population structure of the endangered Blanca Cacereña bovine breed. RAPD markers were also used to determine the genetic diversity of the endangered worm *Peripatus acacioi* by silver-stained polyacrylamide gel analysis. However, the reproducibility of this method is frequently affected by the quality of samples and condition of DNA amplification (e.g., sensitive to the changes of annealing temperature). Therefore, this method is not suitable for highly degraded forensic samples.

Amplified Fragment Length Polymorphism

AFLP method is developed by combining the techniques of RFLP and PCR for DNA fingerprinting. Genomic DNA is digested by restriction enzymes and the restricted fragments are preselectively and selectively amplified by different combination of primers. The PCR products are detected on denaturing polyacrylamide gels by slab or capillary electrophoresis. This method was used to determine the species-specific marker of endangered black muntjac (*Muntiacus crinifrons*) for authentication. The fluorescent-AFLP markers were used to assess the genetic diversity for four species of threatened Chinese eared pheasant (*Crossoptilon crossoptilon*, *Crossoptilon harmani*, *Crossoptilon auritum*, and *Crossoptilon mantchuricum*). AFLP is a method with high specificity; however, it is time-consuming to obtain the idoneous primer pairs to distinguish different species (or subspecies) or populations.

PCR (or Nested PCR) Sequencing of the Specific Loci

The specific loci include the mitochondrial cytochrome b gene (cyt b), cytochrome *c* oxidase subunit I (COI) gene, 12S rRNA gene, 16S rRNA gene, and D-loop. Mitochondrial DNA is of maternal inheritance and multiple copies per cell. The complete mitochondrial genome of human was first reported by Anderson and coworkers in 1981, and revised later by Andrews in 1999. In forensic science, analysis of control region (D-loop) of mitochondrial DNA has been used in genealogy determination (e.g., the child and the grandmother), especially for highly degraded evidences (e.g., bones and hair shafts). Animal specimens seized by law executors are frequently processed and with highly degraded nature. Therefore, most of the targeted loci for analysis are on the mitochondria. The universal primers or specific primers for the specific species are used in PCR amplification and DNA sequencing. For highly degraded samples, the nested PCR was usually adopted to amplify DNA. PCR products of the first amplification are used as the template in the second amplification. However, this method is time-consuming and probably with a contamination problem. The PCR products were sequenced by the dideoxy chain termination method. Sequence analysis could be performed with computer packages, such as BioEdit for sequence alignment and Phylip for phylogenetic analysis. For similarity search, sequences are compared with those registered in the databank GenBank or EMBL. For interpretation of the results, for example, the report of Hsieh et al. showed that there was 3% less variation for the analyzed 402 bp of cytochrome b within any one species examined. It is important to realize the sequence variations for the analyzed gene of intraspecies and interspecies to obtain the confidence in species determination.

Analysis of the sequence of cytochrome b gene has been used in species identification of the endangered rhinoceros (*Rhinoceros unicornis, Rhinoceros sondaicus, Dicerorhinus sumatrensis, Ceratotherium simum,* and *Diceros bicornis*), Tibetan antelope (*Pantholops hodgsonii*), Indian sawback turtles (*Kachuga tecta*), elephants (*Elephas maximus,* Loxodonta sp.), tigers (*Panthera tigris*), avian species petrel (*Calonectris diomedea*), and snakes (*P. molurus*). It was also used in evaluating the genetic diversity and phylogenetic relationships of an endangered Coachella Valley fringe-toed lizard (*Uma inornata*). For the endangered species of red panda (*Ailurus fulgens*), cytochrome b was sequenced to assess the phylogeography and subspecific variation for conservation. Furthermore, analysis for single-nucleotide polymorphisms (SNPs) in the cytochrome b gene through a multiplex reaction with single-base primer extension was used to identify animal species using forensic hairs as the materials in a case of pet animal abuse.

DNA sequences for 648 bp of the avian COI gene are included in the Barcode of Life Data System (BOLD) and proved to be valuable for species identification. It was used to identify the species of three unknown samples in forensic wildlife cases in South Africa.

PCR amplification and sequence analysis of 12S rRNA was used in the analysis of the phylogenetic relationships of cottontails (*Sylvilagus,* Lagomorpha). The genus of *Sylvilagus* includes several endangered or commercially important species.

Sequences of the 16S rRNA were used to examine the genomic variations for the identification of eight endangered Pecoran species. The species included are blackbuck (*Antilope cervicapra*), goral (*Naemorhedus goral*), nilgai (*Boselaphus tragocamelus*), chital (*C. axis*), thamin (*Cervus eldi*), sambar (*C. unicolor*), hog deer (*A. porcinus*), and musk deer (*M. chrysogaster*).

Variations of mitochondrial control region for the endangered Okinawa rail (*Gallirallus okinawae*) were evaluated in phylogenetic analysis. The full sequence (1159 bp) of the control region for endemic Formosan pangolin (*Manis pentadactyla pentadactyla*) was established for application on identification of the confiscated scales from endangered pangolin. Analysis of the control region (292 bp) and 13 nuclear markers were used in the determination of the taxonomic status and relationships for three highly endangered and closely related right whale species (*Eubalaena glacialis, Eubalaena australis,* and *Eubalaena japonica*).

Furthermore, complete mitochondrial genome sequences were analyzed to increase the phylogenetic resolution of bears (Ursidae) and an endangered Japanese frog *Odorrana ishikawae*. All the bear genera have been classified as the endangered animals. Six mitochondrial genes (cytochrome *b*, ND2, COI, ATPase 8/6, and CRI, totally 3571 bp) were used in the phylogenetic analysis of an endangered Mexican sparrow (*Spizella wortheni*). Mitochondrial cytochrome b, control region, and tRNA were sequenced to investigate the phylogeography among the Asian elephants (*E. maximus*). Sequences of the mitochondrial genes, including 12S rRNA, 16S rRNA, cytochrome b, and control region, were applied for measuring the genetic diversity of the potentially endangered antelope *Arabian oryx*. Sequences of 12S rRNA, 16S rRNA, and cytochrome b gene were used to identify a small dried skin evidence in a case study of a small Indian civet (*Viverricula indica*). The partial fragment of another mitochondrial gene, ND4, for endangered group of the Pacific cutthroat trout (*Oncorhynchus clarki* ssp.: Salmonidae) was sequenced to examine the phylogeny.

Cytochrome b and COI are the most commonly analyzed genes in forensic science. A detailed comparison of these two loci is performed by Shanan S. Tobe et al. They reported that cytochrome b could be better than COI for mammalian species identification and phylogeny though the results were similar.

STR Typing

For tracing the sources or genealogy of the seized samples suspected to be from endangered species, the microsatellite

DNA is usually used. The microsatellite DNA, also named short tandem repeat (STR), ranges from 2 to 7 bp per repeat unit, and the blocks often extend less than 150 bp. It is routinely used in human identification and paternity tests. Microsatellites with repeat unit of 4 or 5 bp are adopted most frequently under considerations of the amplification artifacts (such as stutters) and resolution of the following analysis system. Microsatellites have been used in genetic identification for domestic species, such as cats, cattle, dogs, horses, and pigeons. For endangered animals, certain systems are also developed. A set of microsatellite markers was used for individual identification, parentage test, and population monitoring in an endangered Eastern imperial eagle (*Aquila heliaca*) population. Another system by DNA fingerprinting with nonradioactive-labeled oligonucleotide probes (e.g., $GGAT_4$ and $GACA_4$) for hybridization was developed for paternity testing of endangered species of birds (e.g., prey or parrots). Twelve unlinked autosomal microsatellites were used with three Y-STRs, a male-specific ZFX/ZFY, and mtDNA control region to identify a serial wolf (*Canis lupus*) killing in Italy.

Validation of the DNA Identification Methods

Validation of the DNA identification methods is absolutely important to ensure the efficacy and accuracy, and it must be performed before the methods applied on real case identification. Validation usually includes evaluation of the reproducibility, cross-reactivity (or species specificity), DNA template concentration, precision, environmental factors, PCR conditions, heteroplasmy, mixture, and consistency for different sources from the same individual. For example, validation of the COI gene was performed by Dawnay et al. to access its utility in forensic species identification. Experiments investigating reproducibility, environmental conditions, DNA template concentration, thermocycling parameters, heteroplasmy, mixed DNA, chemical treatments, and substrate variation were conducted. They reported that analysis of the COI sequence could provide accurate results for species identification when the adequate database was available.

There are multiple copies of mitochondrial DNA per cell, and contamination is the critical issue. Therefore, quality assurance/quality control must be performed when mitochondrial DNA is typing. DNA Commission of the International Society for Forensic Genetics (ISFG) provides the guidelines for mitochondrial DNA typing. In the guidelines, it is indicated that controlling and monitoring contamination was the major concern for quality assurance/quality control. For example, performing the DNA extraction and PCR amplification with blank or negative control is requested for detecting the contamination. The cleanliness of laboratory room and materials used is also demanded. The work surface must be cleaned completely to avoid the cross-contamination between samples. Furthermore, in some reports it was suggested to determine the species by more than one DNA marker to ensure the accuracy, especially when the DNA databank is insufficient. Recommendations for using nonhuman (animal) DNA in forensic genetic investigations are also provided by ISFG at the International Society for Forensic Genetics 23rd Congress.

Conclusions

DNA analysis of the endangered species is widely used in forensic science to identify its real species or genealogy, and in population genetics for conservation or restoration. In these methods, RFLP has been used in genetic analysis of endangered fishes and birds; PCR–RFLP in species identification of endangered Korean long-tailed goral and Indian deer species; RAPD in analysis of the genetic diversity of endangered bovine and worm; AFLP in determination of the species-specific marker of endangered black muntjac for authentication. The method of PCR (or nested PCR) sequencing of the specific loci on mitochondrial DNA is one of the most popular methods. It has been used in species identification of the endangered rhinoceros, Tibetan antelope, Indian sawback turtles, elephants, tigers, petrels, and snakes; and in evaluating the genetic diversity and phylogenetic relationships of the endangered lizard and red panda. STR typing has been used in individual identification, parentage test, and population monitoring in the endangered eagle population. Validation of these DNA analysis methods usually includes the evaluation of the reproducibility, cross-reactivity, DNA template concentration, precision, environmental factors, PCR conditions, heteroplasmy, mixture, and consistency for different sources from the same individual. The methods proven to be efficient and accurate are then used in the identification of forensic specimens by following the established SOP.

See also: **Biology/DNA:** DNA Databases; DNA Extraction and Quantification.

Further Reading

Balitzki-Korte, B., Anslinger, K., Bartsch, C., Rolf, B., 2005. Species identification by means of pyrosequencing the mitochondrial 12S rRNA gene. International Journal of Legal Medicine 119, 291–294.

Bell, L.S., 2011. Forensic science in support of wildlife conservation efforts-morphological and chemical approaches (global trends). Forensic Science Review 23, 29–35.

Hebert, P.D., Cywinska, A., Ball, S.L., deWaard, J.R., 2003. Biological identifications through DNA barcodes. Proceedings. Biological Sciences/The Royal Society 270, 313–321.

Hsieh, H.M., Chiang, H.L., Tsai, L.C., et al., 2001. Cytochrome b gene for species identification of the conservation animals. Forensic Science International 122, 7–18.

Hsieh, H.M., Huang, L.H., Tsai, L.C., et al., 2003. Species identification of rhinoceros horns using the cytochrome b gene. Forensic Science International 136, 1–11.
Hsieh, H.M., Huang, L.H., Tsai, L.C., et al., 2006. Species identification of Kachuga tecta using the cytochrome b gene. Journal of Forensic Science 51, 52–56.
Hsieh, H.M., Lee, J.C.I., Wu, J.H., et al., 2011. Establishing the pangolin mitochondrial D-loop sequences from the confiscated scales. Forensic Science International: Genetics 5, 303–307.
Hsieh, H.M., Tsai, L.C., Lee, J.C.I., 2011. Forensic science in support of wildlife conservation efforts-developments in genetic approaches in Taiwan. Forensic Science Review 23, 19–27.
Irwin, D.M., Kocher, T.D., Wilson, A.C., 1991. Evolution of the cytochrome b gene of mammals. Journal of Molecular Evolution 32, 128–144.
Lee, J.C.I., Hsieh, H.M., Huang, L.H., et al., 2009. Ivory identification by DNA profiling of cytochrome b gene. International Journal of Legal Medicine 123, 117–121.
Lee, J.C.I., Tsai, L.C., Huang, M.T., et al., 2008. A novel strategy for avian species identification by cytochrome b gene. Electrophoresis 29, 2413–2418.
Lee, J.C.I., Tsai, L.C., Liao, S.P., Linacre, A., Hsieh, H.M., 2009. Species identification using the cytochrome b gene of commercial turtle shells. Forensic Science International: Genetics 3, 67–73.
Lee, J.C.I., Tsai, L.C., Yang, C.Y., et al., 2006. DNA profiling of shahtoosh. Electrophoresis 27, 3359–3362.
Linacre, A., 2011. Forensic science in support of wildlife conservation efforts-genetic approaches (global trends). Forensic Science Reviews 23, 9–18.
Wijnstekers, W., 2011. The Convention on International Trade in Endangered Species of Wild Fauna and Flora (CITES)-35 years of global efforts to ensure that international trade in wild animals and plants is legal and sustainable. Forensic Science Review 23, 1–8.

Key Terms

Animal DNA, Automated liquid handling, Automation, DNA, DNA extraction methods, Electrospray ionization, Feline and canine genotyping methods, Forensic genetics, Forensics, Insect DNA, Laboratory automation, LIMS, Mass spectrometry, Massive parallel sequencing, Microbial profiling, Mitochondrial DNA, Next-generation sequencing, Project management, Short tandem repeats, Soil DNA analysis, Species identification, STR, T-RFLP, Targeted enrichment, Time of flight, Validation.

Review Questions

1. How does analyzing DNA by mass spectrometry differ from conventional methods?
2. What would be the advantages of using mass spectrometry for forensic DNA analysis? What would the disadvantages be?
3. Does mass spectrometry offer more detailed information than conventional DNA analysis? Why or why not?
4. Does mass spectrometry work with mitochondrial DNA?
5. How does mass spectrometry improve the analysis of heteroplasmy?
6. Is it feasible that mass spectrometry would become the dominate method in forensic DNA analysis? Why or why not?
7. With what kinds of cases can nonhuman DNA analysis assist?
8. How is nonhuman DNA analysis different from human DNA analysis (other than the obvious)? How do the application and methods differ?
9. How can animals be witnesses?
10. What are the limitations of nonhuman mitochondrial DNA? What is its real strength?
11. Of what use would plant DNA be in a criminal case? Why?
12. How does next-generation sequencing (NGS) work? How is it different from conventional forensic DNA methods?
13. How is PCR different in NGS?
14. What is circularization? What does it do for NGS?
15. What are the potential applications for nonhuman DNA analysis by NGS? Beyond forensic science, how could NGS be applied to other investigations?

Discussion Questions

1. What would the value of nonhuman DNA be in an investigation? How could identifying someone's pet matter to a criminal case?
2. Few forensic laboratories are equipped to analyze nonhuman DNA. Why is this? What are the challenges to an operational laboratory to do nonhuman DNA cases?
3. Imagine that a body is found in a location, wrapped in a plastic bag. Animal hairs, plant material, insect larvae, and soil are associated with the body in the bag. What answers could nonhuman DNA analysis provide to investigators? How could this help the investigation beyond the identity of the victim?

4. Next-generation sequencing (NGS) is a reality and entire genomes can be analyzed for $1000. So-called "rapid DNA" systems provide conventional analysis of a forensic sample in 75 min for a few hundred dollars. Which is better? Why? What are the potential problems with each approach?
5. What are the limitations—scientific, legal, operational—to adopting new methods in forensic DNA analysis? Why do they exist? How can they be overcome?

Additional Readings

Debeljak, M., Freed, D.N., Welch, J.A., Haley, L., Beierl, K., Iglehart, B.S., Pallavajjala, P., Gocke, D., Leffell, M., Lin, M.-T., Pevsner, J., Wheelan, S., Eshleman, J.R., 2014. Haplotype counting by next-generation sequencing for ultrasensitive human DNA detection. The Journal of Molecular Diagnostics 16 (5), 495–503.

Iyengar, A., 2013. Forensic DNA analysis for animal protection and biodiversity conservation: a review. Journal for Nature Conservation 22 (3), 95–205. http://dx.doi.org/10.1016/j.jnc.2013.12.001.

Kidd, K.K., Pakstis, A.J., Speed, W.C., Lagacé, R., Chang, J., Wootton, S., Haigh, E., Kidd, J.R., 2014. Current sequencing technology makes microhaplotypes a powerful new type of genetic marker for forensics. Forensic Science International: Genetics 12, 215–224. http://dx.doi.org/10.1016/j.fsigen.2014.06.014.

Kiesler, K.M., Coble, M.D., Hall, T.A., Vallone, P.M., 2014. Comparison of base composition analysis and Sanger sequencing of mitochondrial DNA for four US population groups. Forensic Science International: Genetics 8 (1), 226–232.

Kitpipit, T., Chotigeat, W., Linacre, A., Thanakiatkrai, P., 2014. Forensic animal DNA analysis using economical two-step direct PCR. Forensic Science, Medicine, and Pathology 10 (1), 29–38.

Mucci, N., Mengoni, C., Randi, E., 2014. Wildlife DNA forensics against crime: resolution of a case of tortoise theft. Forensic Science International: Genetics 8 (1), 200–202.

INDEX

Note: Page numbers followed by "b," "f," and "t" indicate boxes, figures, and tables respectively.

A

D

E

F

G

H

Q

R

S

V

W

X

Y

Z

CPI Antony Rowe
Chippenham, UK
2017-11-10 18:24